SO-BIN-851

JUSTICE LEAGUE
ENDLESS WINTER

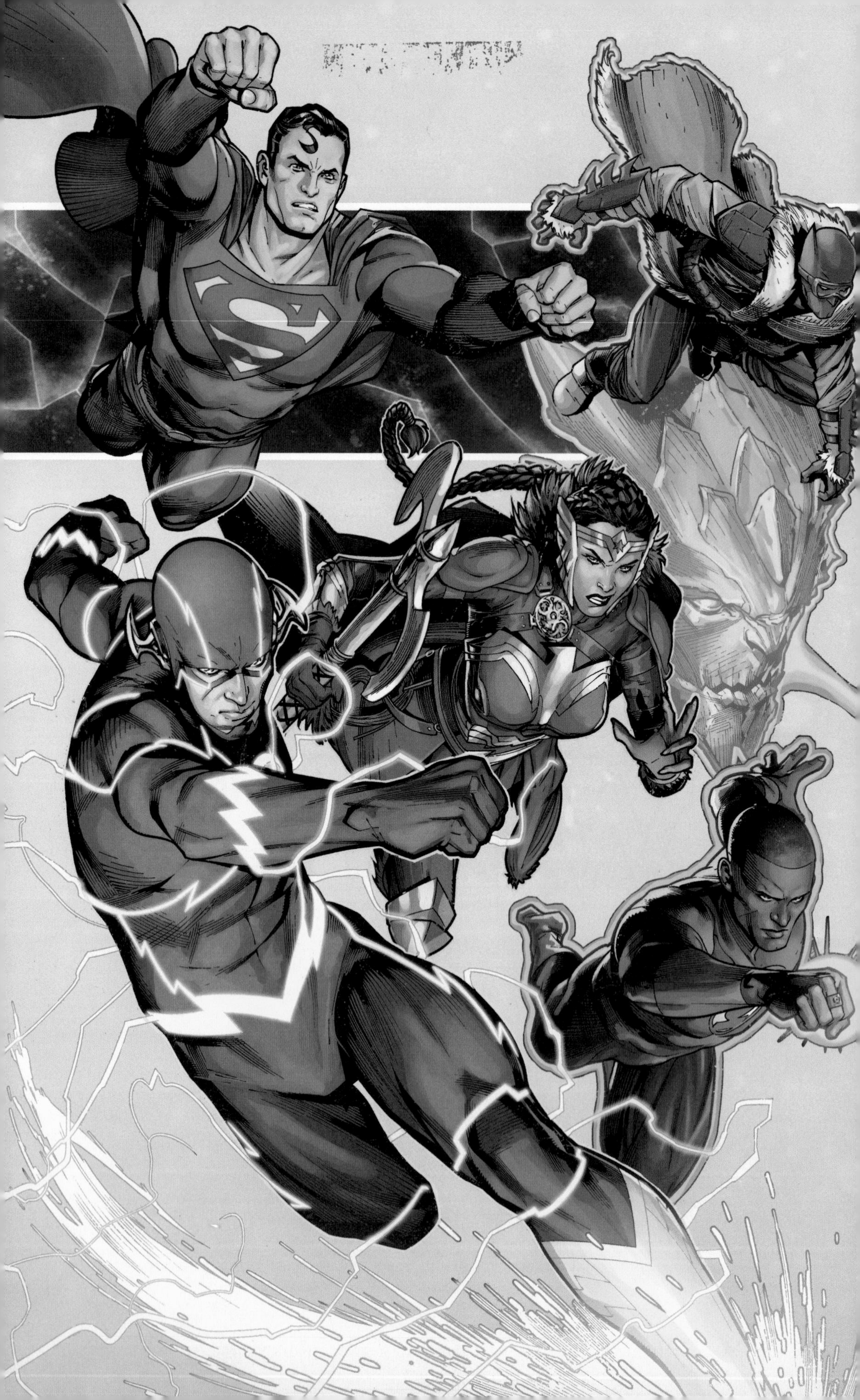

WITHDRAWN
CHARLESTON COUNTY LIBRARY

★ JUSTICE LEAGUE
ENDLESS WINTER

ANDY LANNING AND **RON MARZ**
writers

HOWARD PORTER · MARCO SANTUCCI · CLAYTON HENRY · PHIL HESTER
ANDE PARKS · MIGUEL MENDONCA · XERMANICO · JESUS MERINO
CAM SMITH · AMANCAY NAHUELPAN · BRANDON PETERSON
CARMINE DI GIANDOMENICO
artists

HI-FI · ARIF PRIANTO · MARCELO MAIOLO · IVAN PLASCENCIA
ALEX SINCLAIR · JUNE CHUNG · MIKE ATIYEH
colorists

ANDWORLD DESIGN · A LARGER WORLD STUDIOS' TROY PETERI
STEVE WANDS · DAVE SHARPE · CLAYTON COWLES
TOM NAPOLITANO · ROB LEIGH · WES ABBOTT
letterers

MIKEL JANÍN
collection cover artist

SUPERMAN CREATED BY JERRY SIEGEL AND JOE SHUSTER.
BY SPECIAL ARRANGEMENT WITH THE JERRY SIEGEL FAMILY.

ALEX R. CARR, JAMIE S. RICH, MIKE COTTON
Editors – Original Series

ANDREA SHEA, BRITTANY HOLZHERR
Associate Editors – Original Series

MARQUIS DRAPER, BIXIE MATHIEU
Assistant Editor – Original Series

ANDREA SHEA
Editor – Collected Edition

MARQUIS DRAPER
Assistant Editor – Collected Edition

STEVE COOK
Design Director – Books

MEGEN BELLERSEN
Publication Design

CHRISTY SAWYER
Publication Production

MARIE JAVINS
Editor-in-Chief, DC Comics

DANIEL CHERRY III
Senior VP – General Manager

JIM LEE
Publisher & Chief Creative Officer

JOEN CHOE
VP – Global Brand & Creative Services

DON FALLETTI
VP – Manufacturing Operations & Workflow Management

LAWRENCE GANEM
VP – Talent Services

ALISON GILL
Senior VP – Manufacturing & Operations

NICK J. NAPOLITANO
VP – Manufacturing Administration & Design

NANCY SPEARS
VP – Revenue

JUSTICE LEAGUE: ENDLESS WINTER

Published by DC Comics. Compilation and all new material Copyright © 2021 DC Comics. All
Rights Reserved. Originally published in single magazine form in *Justice League: Endless Winter*
1-2, *The Flash* 767, *Superman: Endless Winter Special* 1, *Aquaman* 66, *Justice League* 58, *Teen Titans:
Endless Winter Special* 1, *Justice League Dark* 29, *Black Adam: Endless Winter Special* 1. Copyright ©
2020 DC Comics. All Rights Reserved. All characters, their distinctive likenesses, and related
elements featured in this publication are trademarks of DC Comics. The stories, characters,
and incidents featured in this publication are entirely fictional. DC Comics does not read or
accept unsolicited submissions of ideas, stories, or artwork.
DC – a WarnerMedia Company.

DC Comics, 2900 West Alameda Ave., Burbank, CA 91505
Printed by Transcontinental Interglobe, Beauceville, QC, Canada.
10/1/2021. First Printing.
ISBN: 978-1-77951-153-9

Library of Congress Cataloging-in-Publication Data is available.

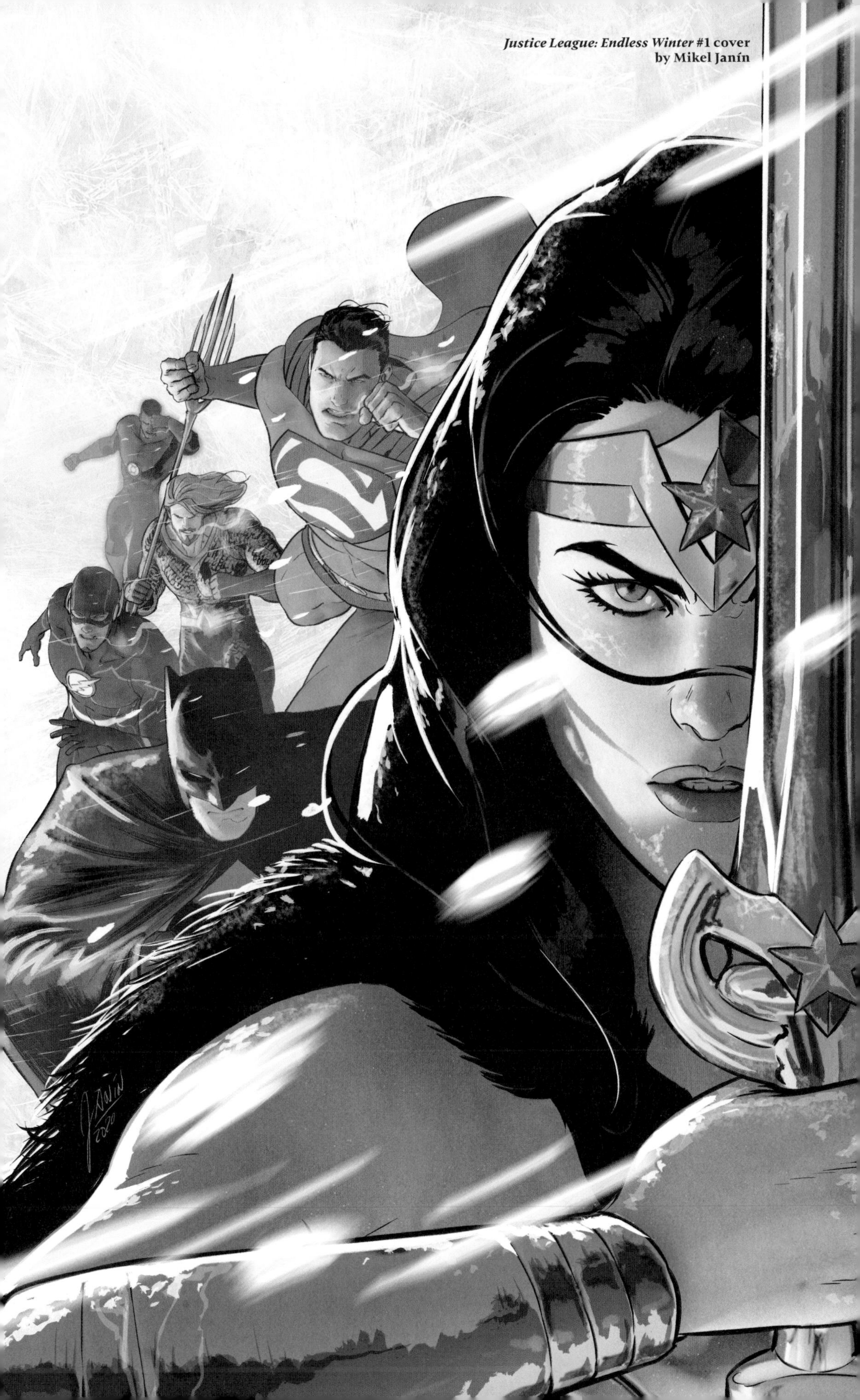

Justice League: Endless Winter #1 cover
by Mikel Janín

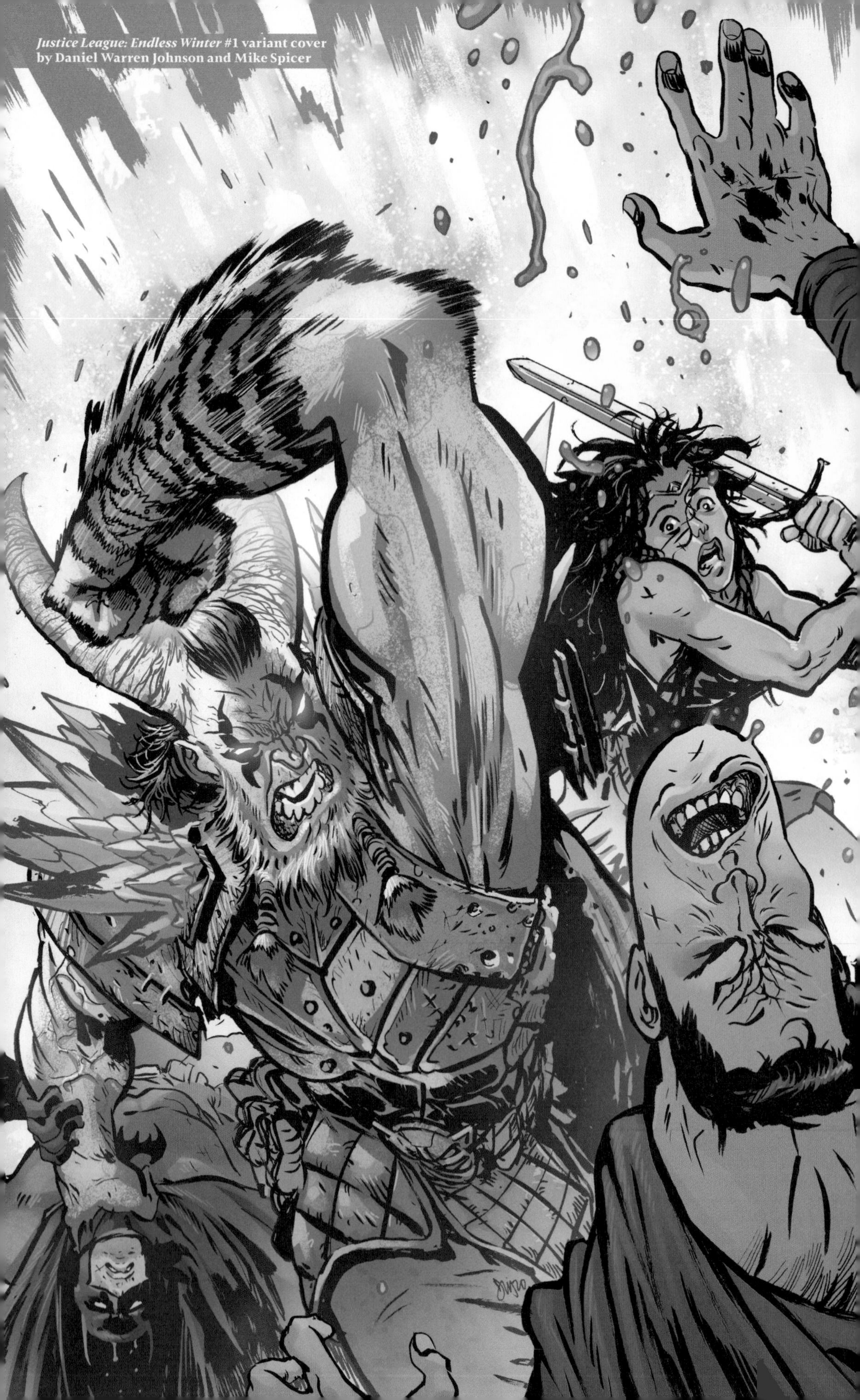

Justice League: Endless Winter #1 variant cover
by Daniel Warren Johnson and Mike Spicer

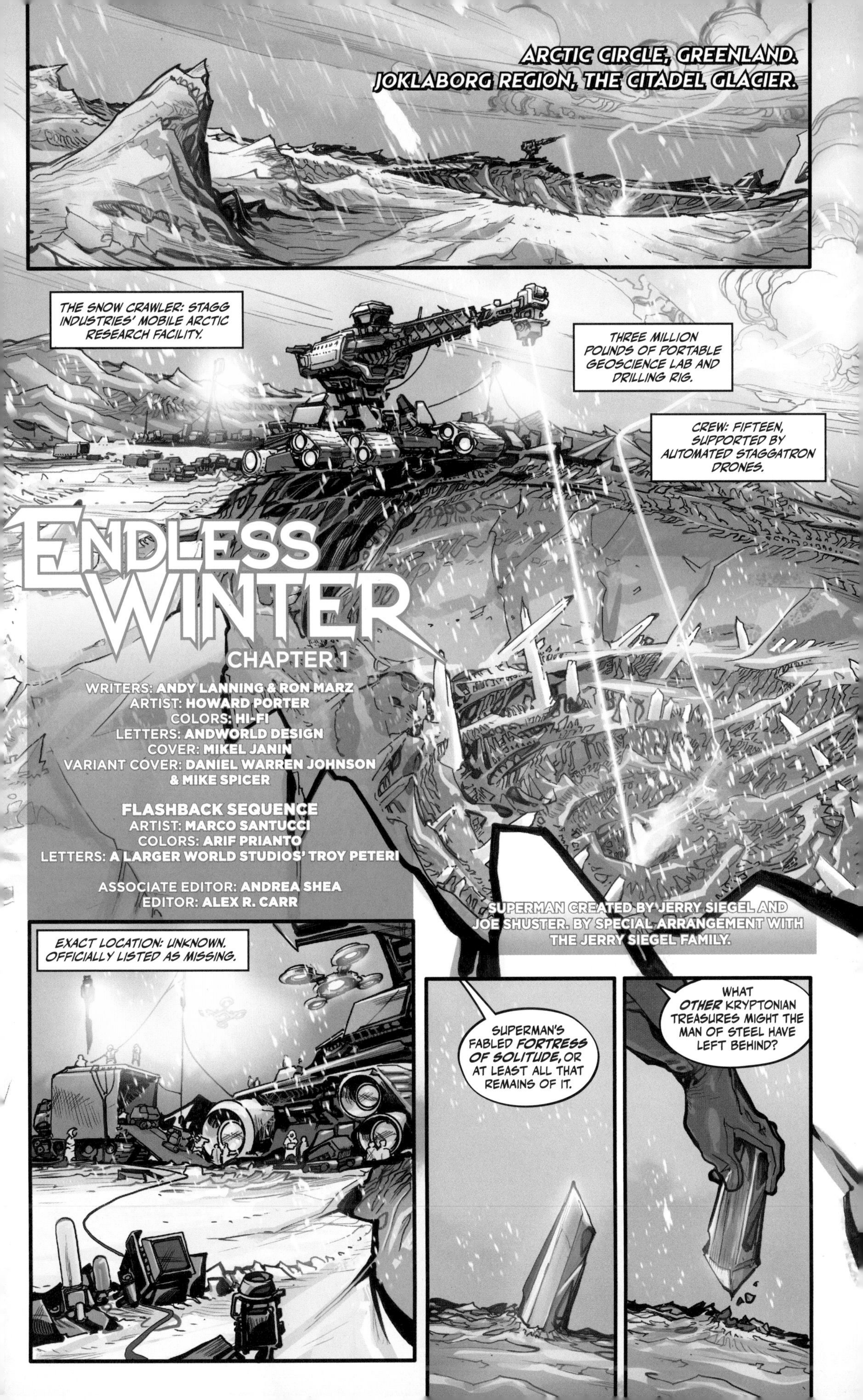
ARCTIC CIRCLE, GREENLAND.
JOKLABORG REGION, THE CITADEL GLACIER.
THE SNOW CRAWLER: STAGG INDUSTRIES' MOBILE ARCTIC RESEARCH FACILITY.
THREE MILLION POUNDS OF PORTABLE GEOSCIENCE LAB AND DRILLING RIG.
CREW: FIFTEEN, SUPPORTED BY AUTOMATED STAGGATRON DRONES.
ENDLESS WINTER
CHAPTER 1
WRITERS: ANDY LANNING & RON MARZ
ARTIST: HOWARD PORTER
COLORS: HI-FI
LETTERS: ANDWORLD DESIGN
COVER: MIKEL JANIN
VARIANT COVER: DANIEL WARREN JOHNSON & MIKE SPICER
FLASHBACK SEQUENCE
ARTIST: MARCO SANTUCCI
COLORS: ARIF PRIANTO
LETTERS: A LARGER WORLD STUDIOS' TROY PETERI
ASSOCIATE EDITOR: ANDREA SHEA
EDITOR: ALEX R. CARR
SUPERMAN CREATED BY JERRY SIEGEL AND JOE SHUSTER. BY SPECIAL ARRANGEMENT WITH THE JERRY SIEGEL FAMILY.
EXACT LOCATION: UNKNOWN. OFFICIALLY LISTED AS MISSING.
SUPERMAN'S FABLED FORTRESS OF SOLITUDE, OR AT LEAST ALL THAT REMAINS OF IT.
WHAT OTHER KRYPTONIAN TREASURES MIGHT THE MAN OF STEEL HAVE LEFT BEHIND?

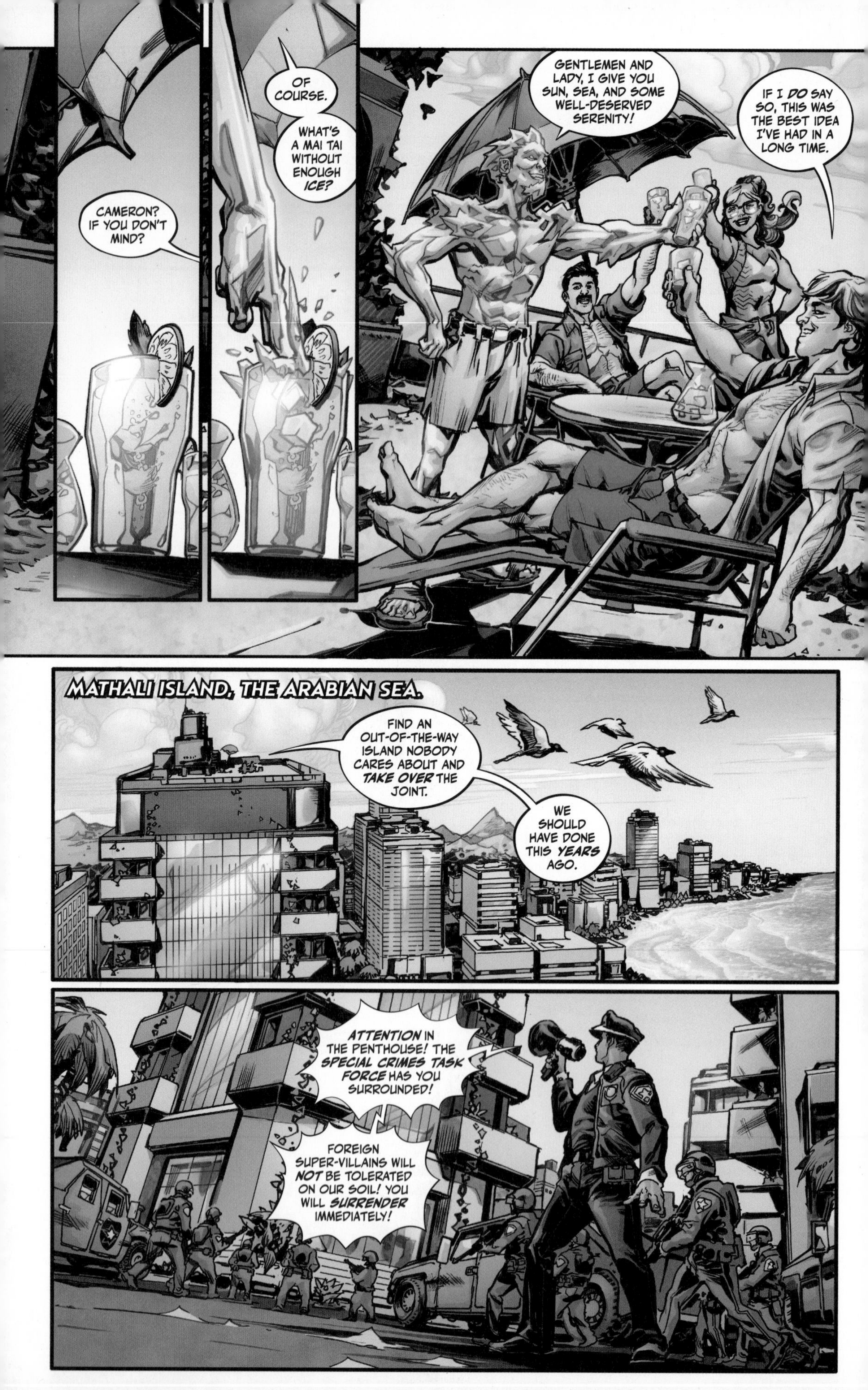
CAMERON? IF YOU DON'T MIND?
OF COURSE.
WHAT'S A MAI TAI WITHOUT ENOUGH *ICE?*
GENTLEMEN AND LADY, I GIVE YOU SUN, SEA, AND SOME WELL-DESERVED SERENITY!
IF I *DO* SAY SO, THIS WAS THE BEST IDEA I'VE HAD IN A LONG TIME.
MATHALI ISLAND, THE ARABIAN SEA.
FIND AN OUT-OF-THE-WAY ISLAND NOBODY CARES ABOUT AND *TAKE OVER* THE JOINT.
WE SHOULD HAVE DONE THIS *YEARS* AGO.
ATTENTION IN THE PENTHOUSE! THE *SPECIAL CRIMES TASK FORCE* HAS YOU SURROUNDED!
FOREIGN SUPER-VILLAINS WILL *NOT* BE TOLERATED ON OUR SOIL! YOU WILL *SURRENDER* IMMEDIATELY!

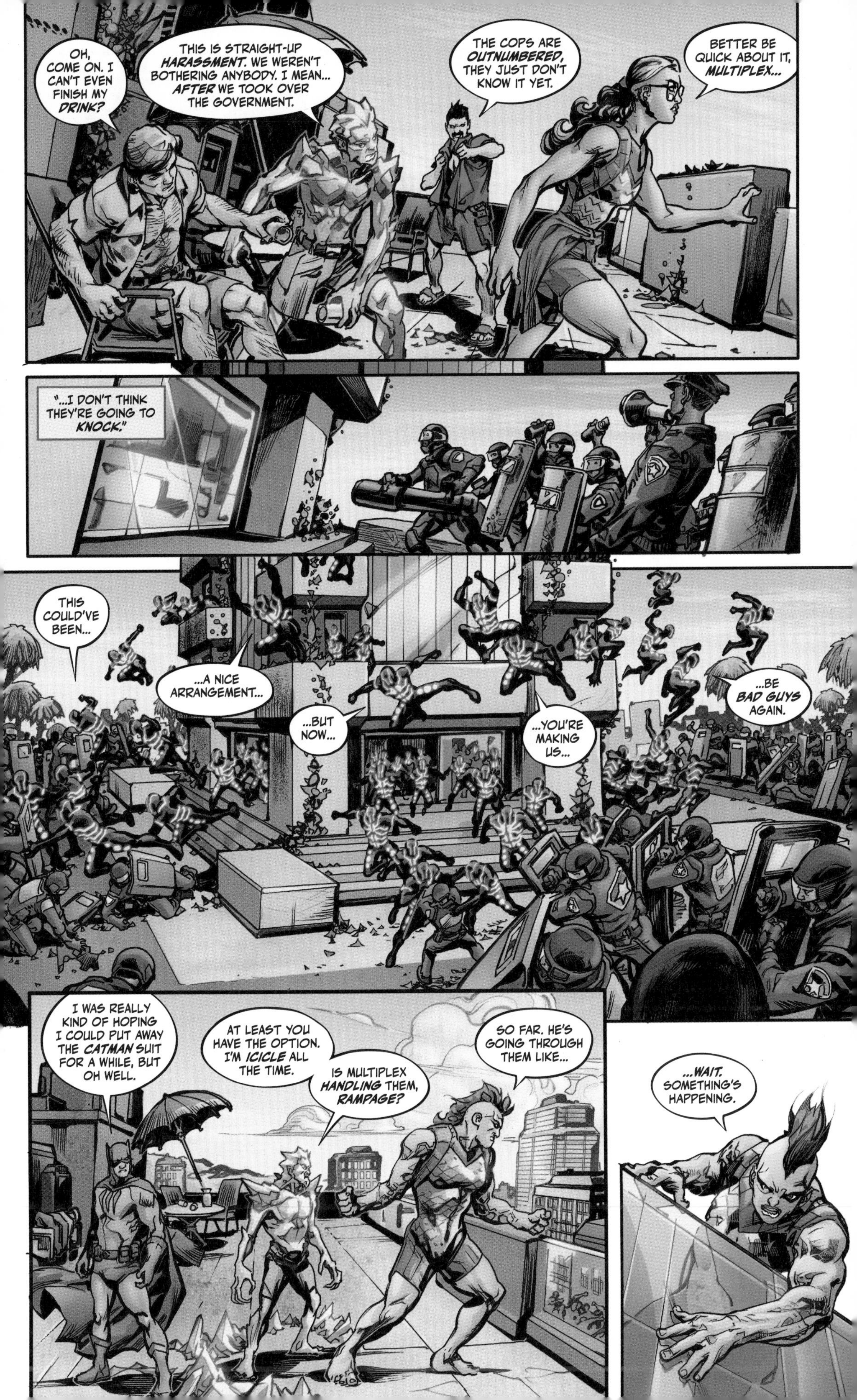
OH, COME ON. I CAN'T EVEN FINISH MY DRINK?
THIS IS STRAIGHT-UP HARASSMENT. WE WEREN'T BOTHERING ANYBODY. I MEAN... AFTER WE TOOK OVER THE GOVERNMENT.
THE COPS ARE OUTNUMBERED, THEY JUST DON'T KNOW IT YET.
BETTER BE QUICK ABOUT IT, MULTIPLEX...
"...I DON'T THINK THEY'RE GOING TO KNOCK."
THIS COULD'VE BEEN...
...A NICE ARRANGEMENT...
...BUT NOW...
...YOU'RE MAKING US...
...BE BAD GUYS AGAIN.
I WAS REALLY KIND OF HOPING I COULD PUT AWAY THE CATMAN SUIT FOR A WHILE, BUT OH WELL.
AT LEAST YOU HAVE THE OPTION. I'M ICICLE ALL THE TIME.
IS MULTIPLEX HANDLING THEM, RAMPAGE?
SO FAR. HE'S GOING THROUGH THEM LIKE...
...WAIT. SOMETHING'S HAPPENING.

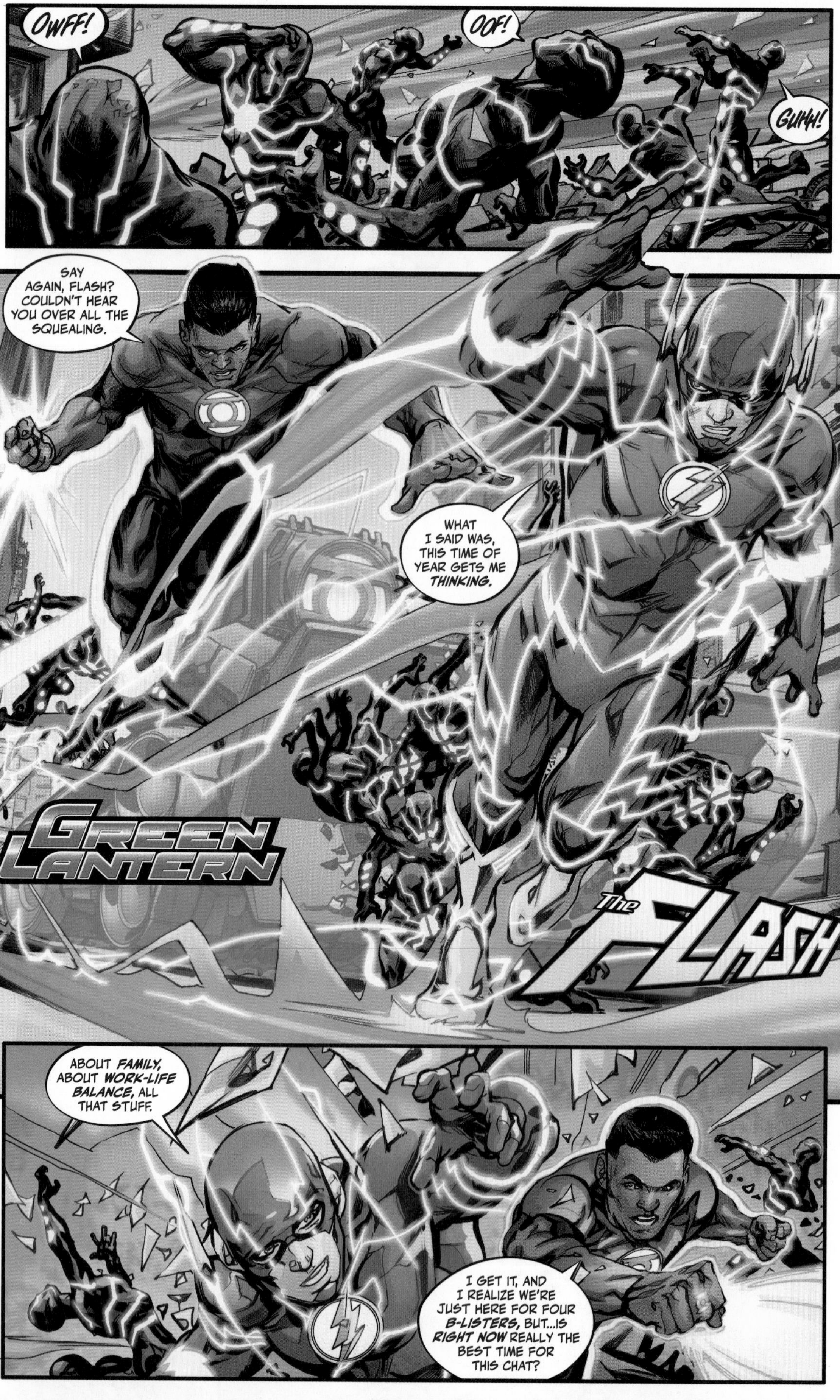
OWFF!
OOF!
GUHH!
SAY AGAIN, FLASH? COULDN'T HEAR YOU OVER ALL THE SQUEALING.
WHAT I SAID WAS, THIS TIME OF YEAR GETS ME *THINKING*.
GREEN LANTERN
The FLASH
ABOUT *FAMILY*, ABOUT *WORK-LIFE BALANCE*, ALL THAT STUFF.
I GET IT, AND I REALIZE WE'RE JUST HERE FOR FOUR *B-LISTERS*, BUT...IS *RIGHT NOW* REALLY THE BEST TIME FOR THIS CHAT?

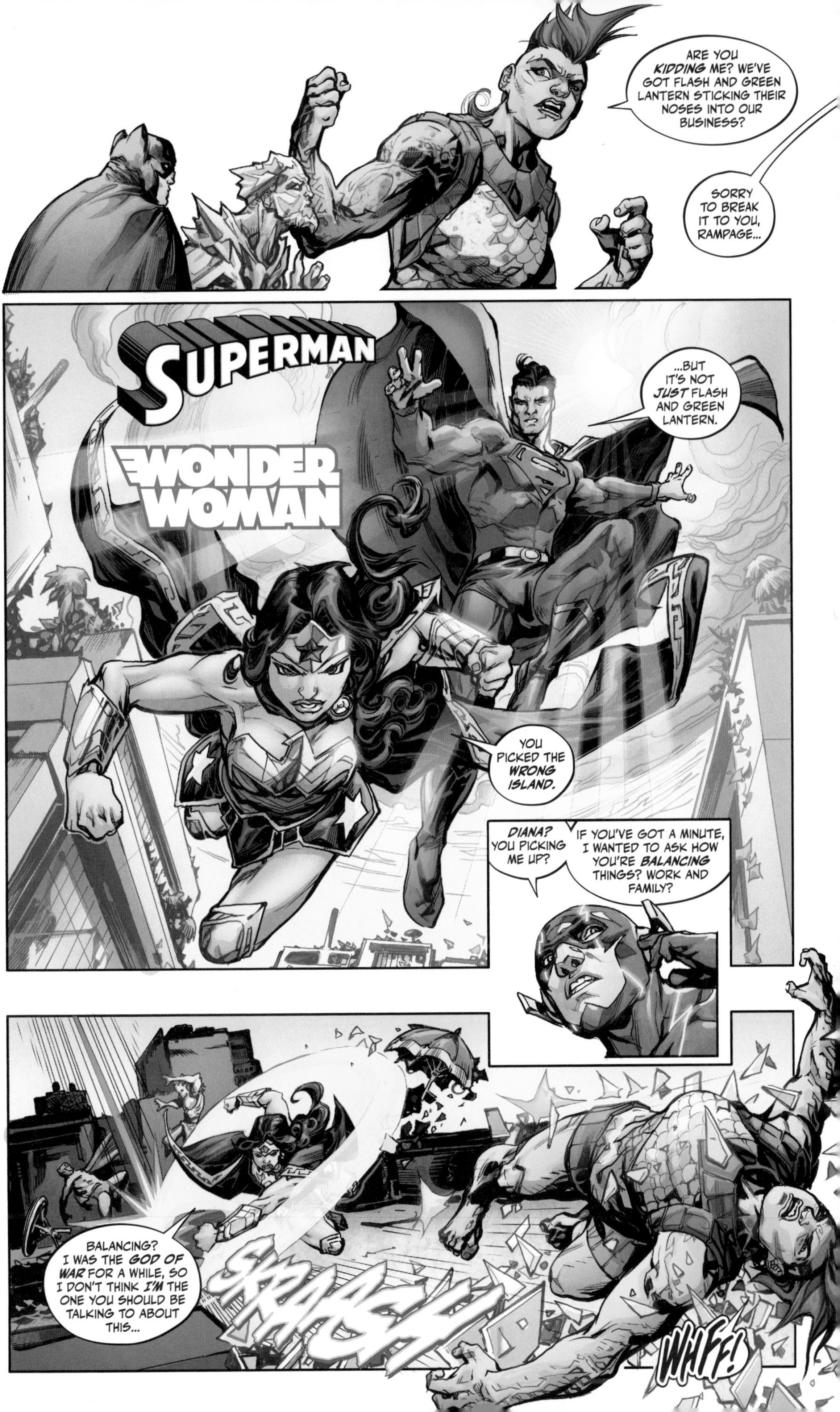
ARE YOU KIDDING ME? WE'VE GOT FLASH AND GREEN LANTERN STICKING THEIR NOSES INTO OUR BUSINESS?
SORRY TO BREAK IT TO YOU, RAMPAGE...
SUPERMAN
WONDER WOMAN
...BUT IT'S NOT JUST FLASH AND GREEN LANTERN.
YOU PICKED THE WRONG ISLAND.
DIANA? YOU PICKING ME UP?
IF YOU'VE GOT A MINUTE, I WANTED TO ASK HOW YOU'RE BALANCING THINGS? WORK AND FAMILY?
BALANCING? I WAS THE GOD OF WAR FOR A WHILE, SO I DON'T THINK I'M THE ONE YOU SHOULD BE TALKING TO ABOUT THIS...
SKRASH
WHFF!

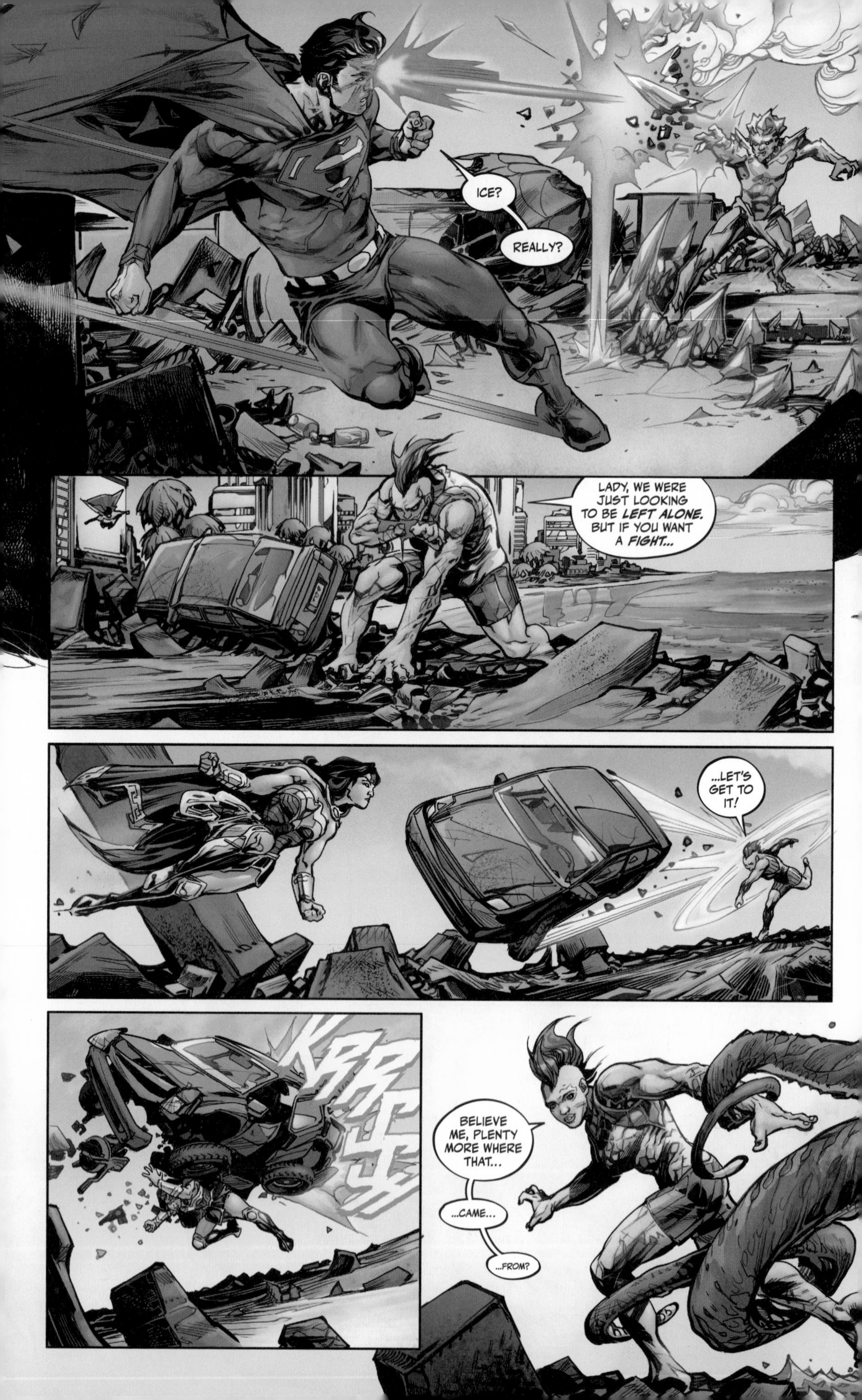
ICE?
REALLY?
LADY, WE WERE JUST LOOKING TO BE LEFT ALONE. BUT IF YOU WANT A FIGHT...
...LET'S GET TO IT!
BELIEVE ME, PLENTY MORE WHERE THAT...
...CAME...
...FROM?

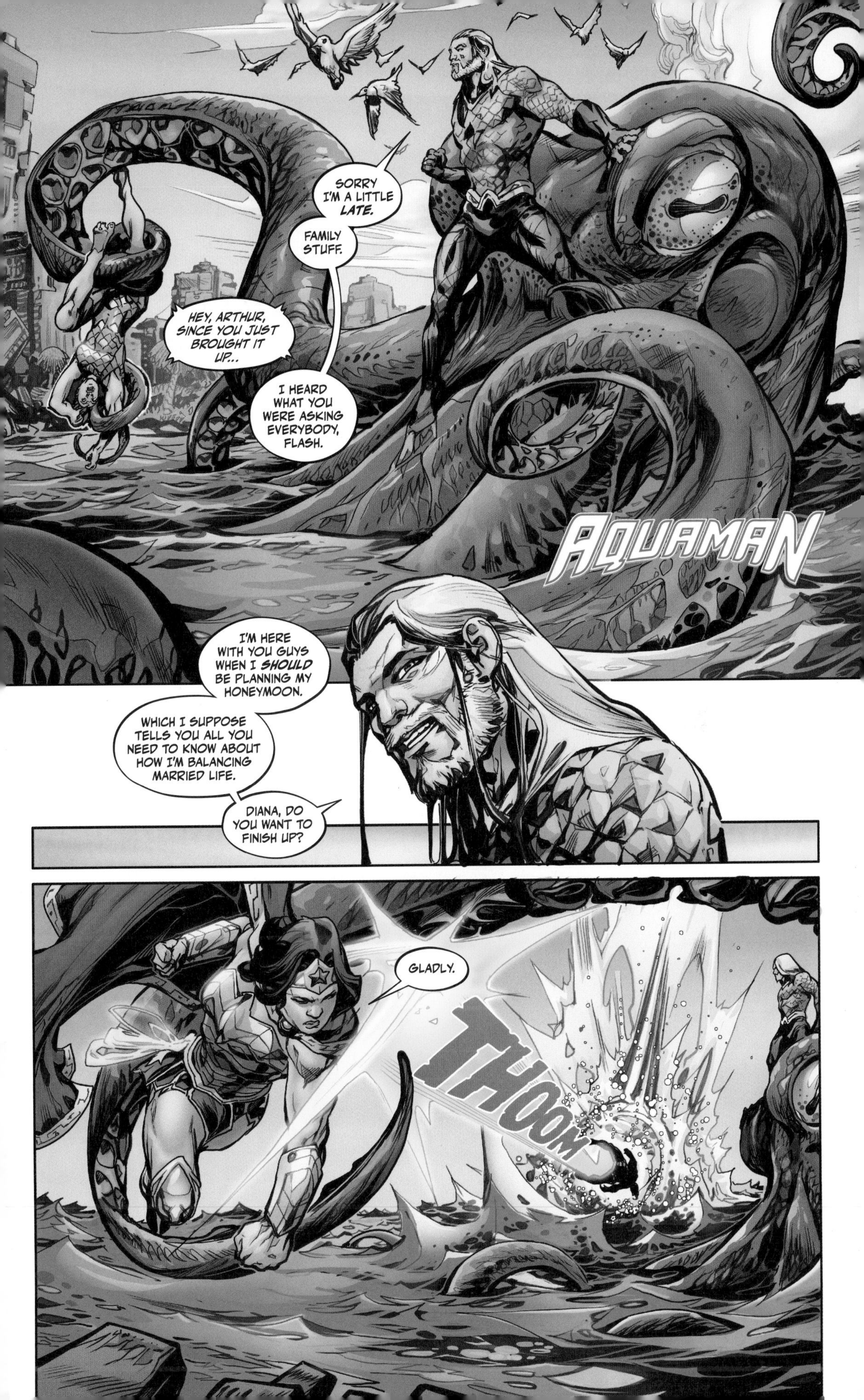

SORRY I'M A LITTLE *LATE.*
FAMILY STUFF.
HEY, ARTHUR, SINCE YOU JUST BROUGHT IT UP...
I HEARD WHAT YOU WERE ASKING EVERYBODY, FLASH.
AQUAMAN
I'M HERE WITH YOU GUYS WHEN I *SHOULD* BE PLANNING MY HONEYMOON.
WHICH I SUPPOSE TELLS YOU ALL YOU NEED TO KNOW ABOUT HOW I'M BALANCING MARRIED LIFE.
DIANA, DO YOU WANT TO FINISH UP?
GLADLY.
THOOM

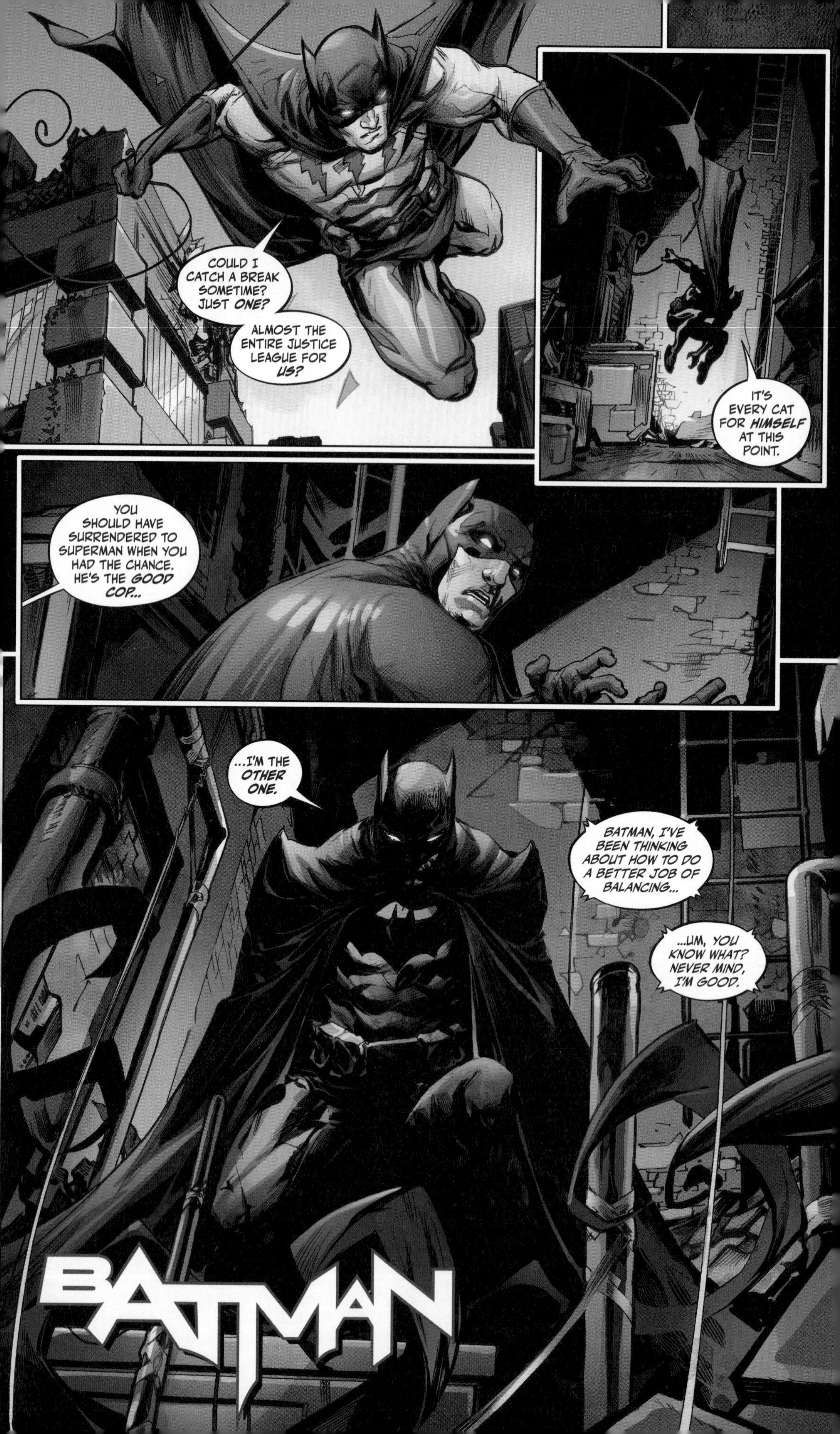
COULD I CATCH A BREAK SOMETIME? JUST ONE?
ALMOST THE ENTIRE JUSTICE LEAGUE FOR US?
IT'S EVERY CAT FOR HIMSELF AT THIS POINT.
YOU SHOULD HAVE SURRENDERED TO SUPERMAN WHEN YOU HAD THE CHANCE. HE'S THE GOOD COP...
...I'M THE OTHER ONE.
BATMAN, I'VE BEEN THINKING ABOUT HOW TO DO A BETTER JOB OF BALANCING...
...UM, YOU KNOW WHAT? NEVER MIND, I'M GOOD.
BATMAN

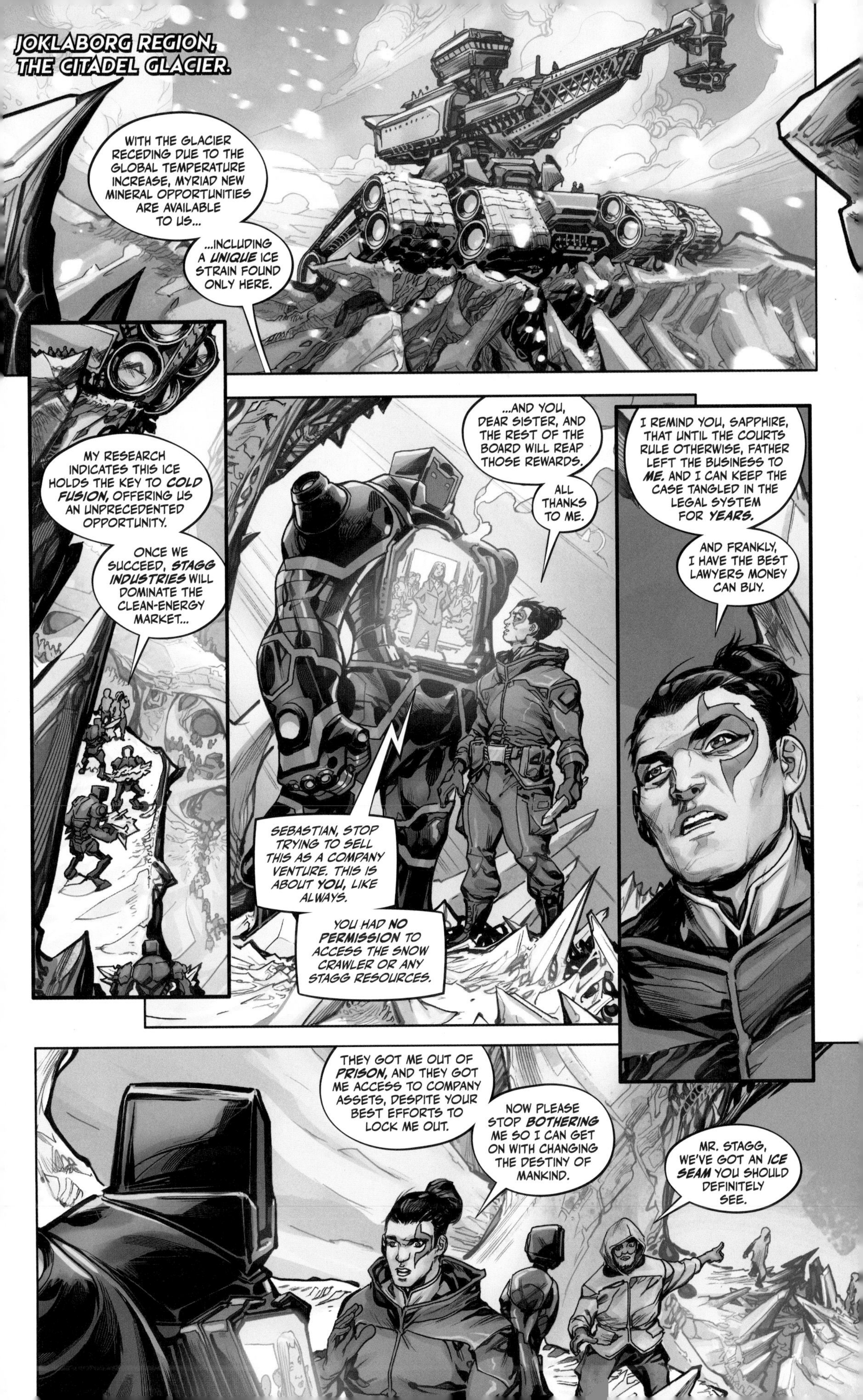
JOKLABORG REGION, THE CITADEL GLACIER.
WITH THE GLACIER RECEDING DUE TO THE GLOBAL TEMPERATURE INCREASE, MYRIAD NEW MINERAL OPPORTUNITIES ARE AVAILABLE TO US...
...INCLUDING A UNIQUE ICE STRAIN FOUND ONLY HERE.
MY RESEARCH INDICATES THIS ICE HOLDS THE KEY TO COLD FUSION, OFFERING US AN UNPRECEDENTED OPPORTUNITY.
ONCE WE SUCCEED, STAGG INDUSTRIES WILL DOMINATE THE CLEAN-ENERGY MARKET...
...AND YOU, DEAR SISTER, AND THE REST OF THE BOARD WILL REAP THOSE REWARDS.
ALL THANKS TO ME.
SEBASTIAN, STOP TRYING TO SELL THIS AS A COMPANY VENTURE. THIS IS ABOUT YOU, LIKE ALWAYS.
YOU HAD NO PERMISSION TO ACCESS THE SNOW CRAWLER OR ANY STAGG RESOURCES.
I REMIND YOU, SAPPHIRE, THAT UNTIL THE COURTS RULE OTHERWISE, FATHER LEFT THE BUSINESS TO ME. AND I CAN KEEP THE CASE TANGLED IN THE LEGAL SYSTEM FOR YEARS.
AND FRANKLY, I HAVE THE BEST LAWYERS MONEY CAN BUY.
THEY GOT ME OUT OF PRISON, AND THEY GOT ME ACCESS TO COMPANY ASSETS, DESPITE YOUR BEST EFFORTS TO LOCK ME OUT.
NOW PLEASE STOP BOTHERING ME SO I CAN GET ON WITH CHANGING THE DESTINY OF MANKIND.
MR. STAGG, WE'VE GOT AN ICE SEAM YOU SHOULD DEFINITELY SEE.

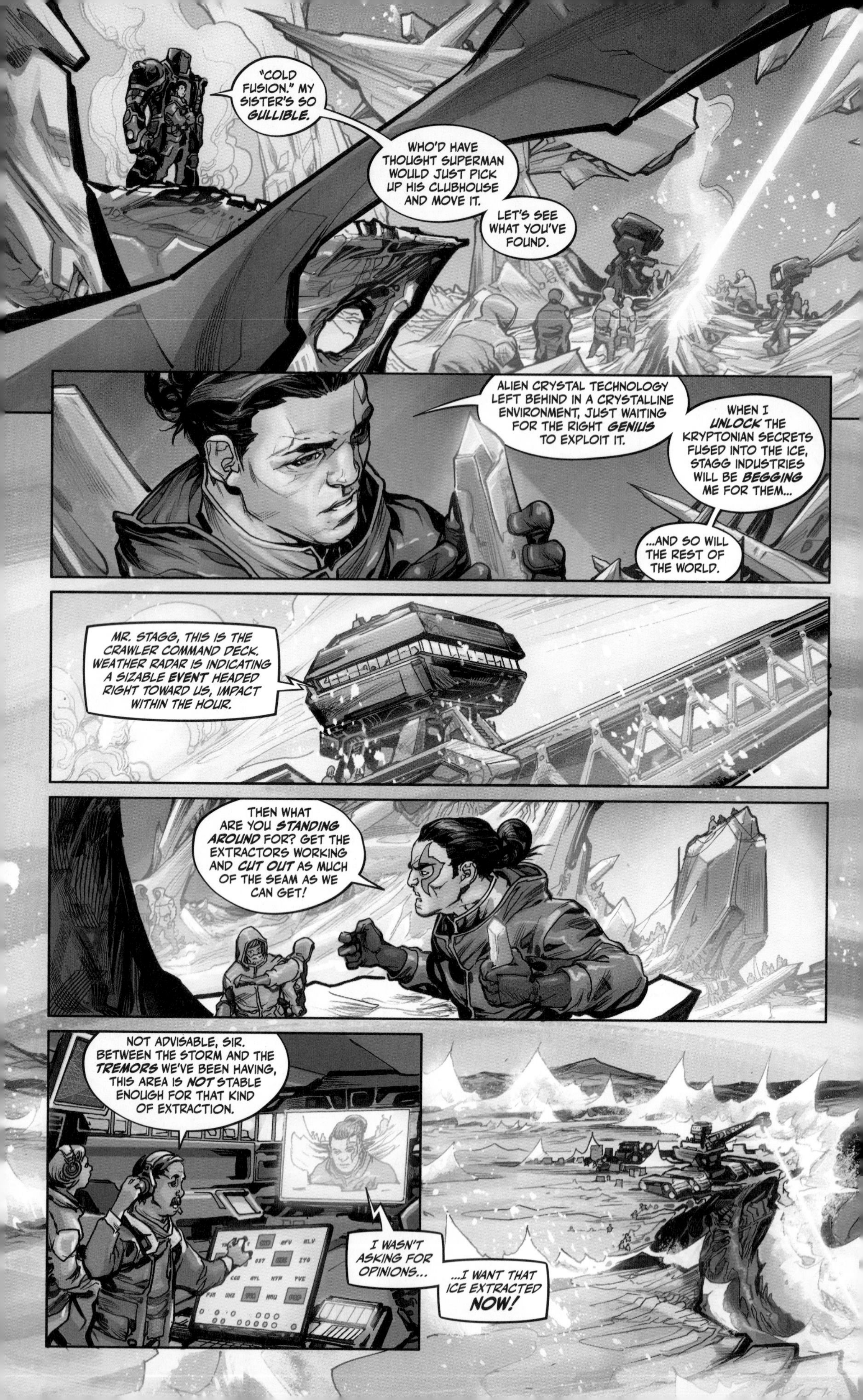
"COLD FUSION." MY SISTER'S SO GULLIBLE.
WHO'D HAVE THOUGHT SUPERMAN WOULD JUST PICK UP HIS CLUBHOUSE AND MOVE IT.
LET'S SEE WHAT YOU'VE FOUND.
ALIEN CRYSTAL TECHNOLOGY LEFT BEHIND IN A CRYSTALLINE ENVIRONMENT, JUST WAITING FOR THE RIGHT GENIUS TO EXPLOIT IT.
WHEN I UNLOCK THE KRYPTONIAN SECRETS FUSED INTO THE ICE, STAGG INDUSTRIES WILL BE BEGGING ME FOR THEM...
...AND SO WILL THE REST OF THE WORLD.
MR. STAGG, THIS IS THE CRAWLER COMMAND DECK. WEATHER RADAR IS INDICATING A SIZABLE EVENT HEADED RIGHT TOWARD US, IMPACT WITHIN THE HOUR.
THEN WHAT ARE YOU STANDING AROUND FOR? GET THE EXTRACTORS WORKING AND CUT OUT AS MUCH OF THE SEAM AS WE CAN GET!
NOT ADVISABLE, SIR. BETWEEN THE STORM AND THE TREMORS WE'VE BEEN HAVING, THIS AREA IS NOT STABLE ENOUGH FOR THAT KIND OF EXTRACTION.
I WASN'T ASKING FOR OPINIONS...
...I WANT THAT ICE EXTRACTED NOW!

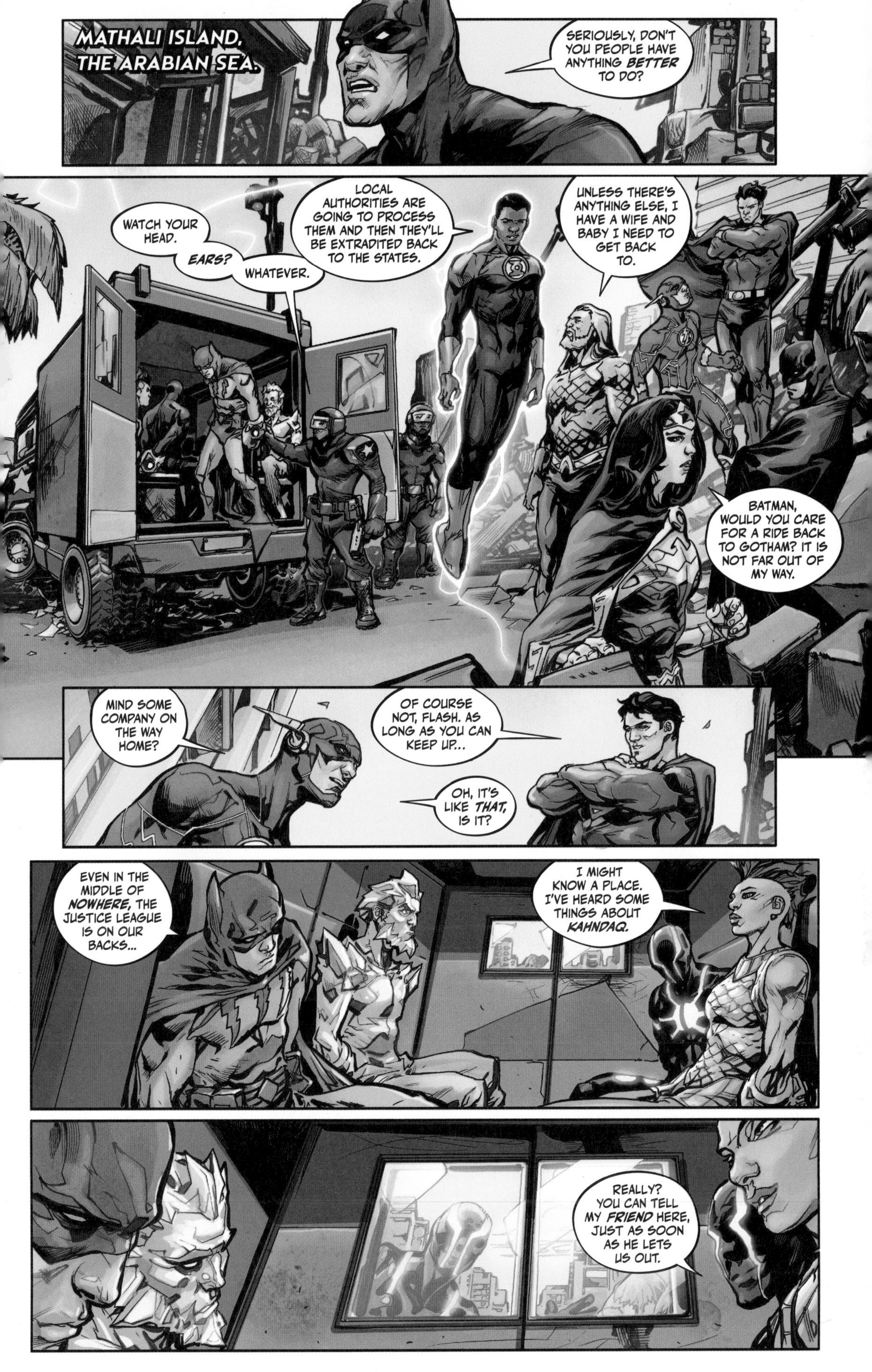
MATHALI ISLAND, THE ARABIAN SEA.
SERIOUSLY, DON'T YOU PEOPLE HAVE ANYTHING BETTER TO DO?
WATCH YOUR HEAD.
EARS?
WHATEVER.
LOCAL AUTHORITIES ARE GOING TO PROCESS THEM AND THEN THEY'LL BE EXTRADITED BACK TO THE STATES.
UNLESS THERE'S ANYTHING ELSE, I HAVE A WIFE AND BABY I NEED TO GET BACK TO.
BATMAN, WOULD YOU CARE FOR A RIDE BACK TO GOTHAM? IT IS NOT FAR OUT OF MY WAY.
MIND SOME COMPANY ON THE WAY HOME?
OF COURSE NOT, FLASH. AS LONG AS YOU CAN KEEP UP...
OH, IT'S LIKE THAT, IS IT?
EVEN IN THE MIDDLE OF NOWHERE, THE JUSTICE LEAGUE IS ON OUR BACKS...
I MIGHT KNOW A PLACE. I'VE HEARD SOME THINGS ABOUT KAHNDAQ.
REALLY? YOU CAN TELL MY FRIEND HERE, JUST AS SOON AS HE LETS US OUT.

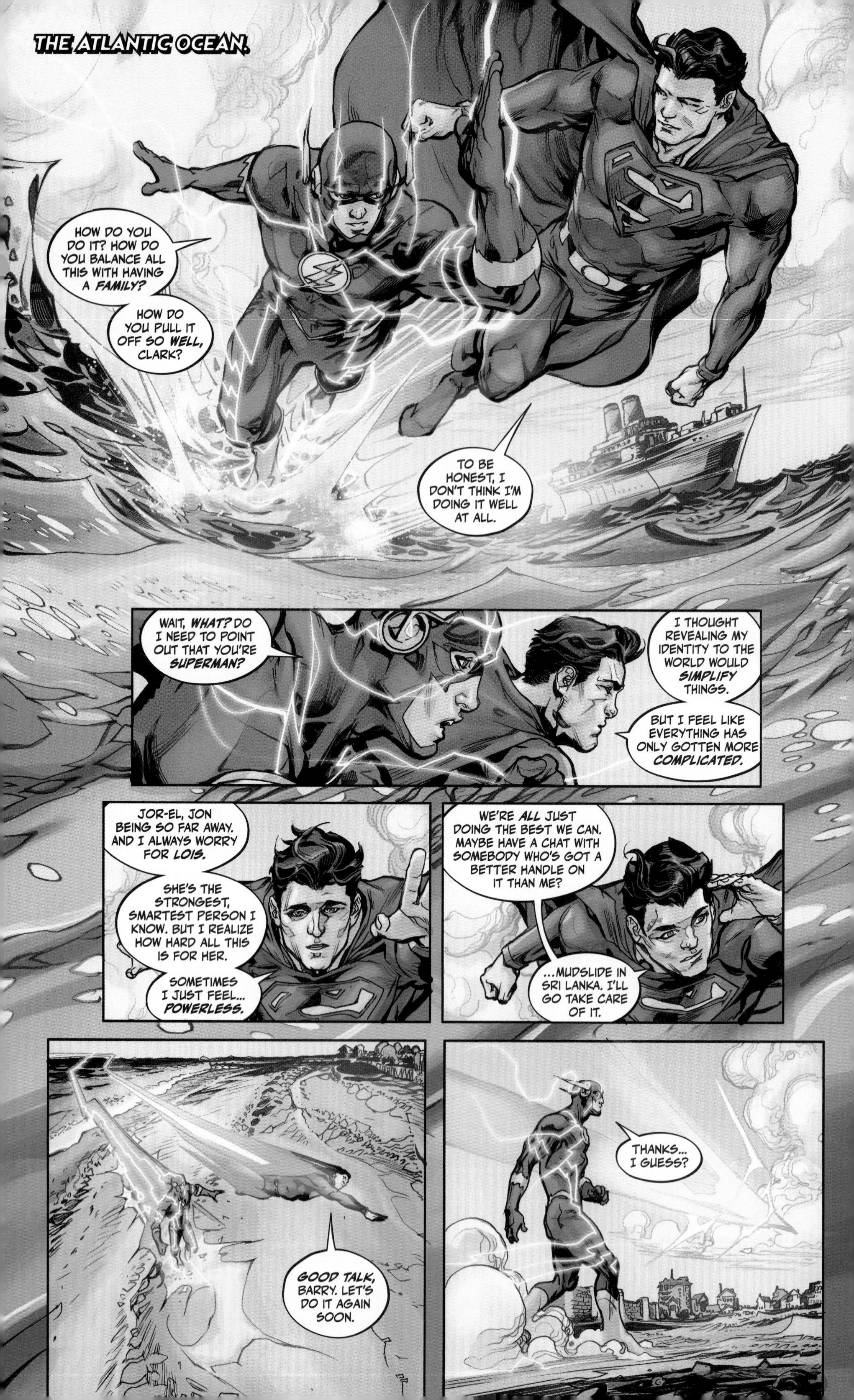

THE ATLANTIC OCEAN.
HOW DO YOU DO IT? HOW DO YOU BALANCE ALL THIS WITH HAVING A FAMILY?
HOW DO YOU PULL IT OFF SO WELL, CLARK?
TO BE HONEST, I DON'T THINK I'M DOING IT WELL AT ALL.
WAIT, WHAT? DO I NEED TO POINT OUT THAT YOU'RE SUPERMAN?
I THOUGHT REVEALING MY IDENTITY TO THE WORLD WOULD SIMPLIFY THINGS.
BUT I FEEL LIKE EVERYTHING HAS ONLY GOTTEN MORE COMPLICATED.
JOR-EL, JON BEING SO FAR AWAY. AND I ALWAYS WORRY FOR LOIS.
SHE'S THE STRONGEST, SMARTEST PERSON I KNOW. BUT I REALIZE HOW HARD ALL THIS IS FOR HER.
SOMETIMES I JUST FEEL... POWERLESS.
WE'RE ALL JUST DOING THE BEST WE CAN. MAYBE HAVE A CHAT WITH SOMEBODY WHO'S GOT A BETTER HANDLE ON IT THAN ME?
...MUDSLIDE IN SRI LANKA. I'LL GO TAKE CARE OF IT.
GOOD TALK, BARRY. LET'S DO IT AGAIN SOON.
THANKS... I GUESS?

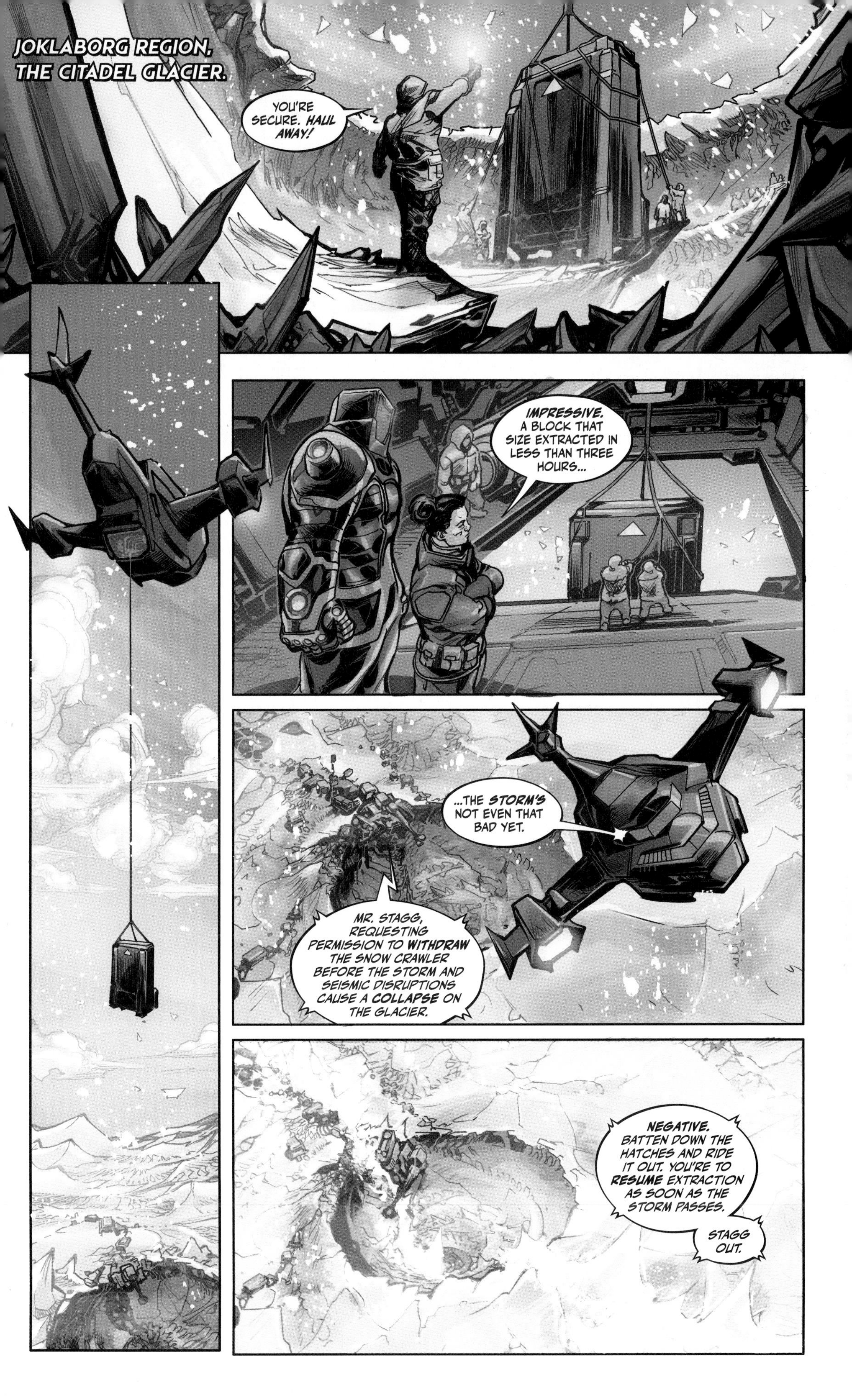
JOKLABORG REGION, THE CITADEL GLACIER.
YOU'RE SECURE. HAUL AWAY!
IMPRESSIVE. A BLOCK THAT SIZE EXTRACTED IN LESS THAN THREE HOURS...
...THE STORM'S NOT EVEN THAT BAD YET.
MR. STAGG, REQUESTING PERMISSION TO WITHDRAW THE SNOW CRAWLER BEFORE THE STORM AND SEISMIC DISRUPTIONS CAUSE A COLLAPSE ON THE GLACIER.
NEGATIVE. BATTEN DOWN THE HATCHES AND RIDE IT OUT. YOU'RE TO RESUME EXTRACTION AS SOON AS THE STORM PASSES.
STAGG OUT.

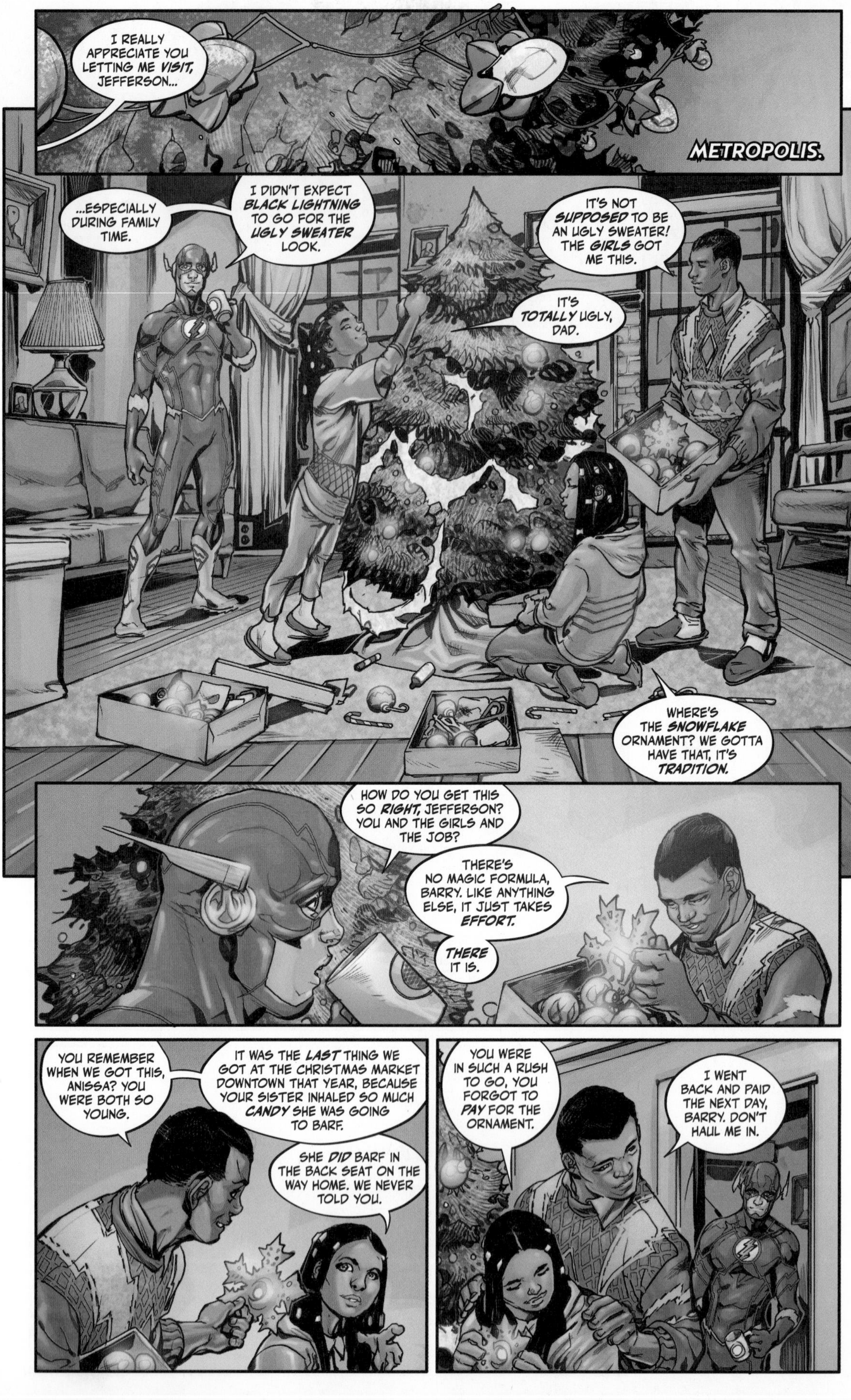

I REALLY APPRECIATE YOU LETTING ME VISIT, JEFFERSON...
METROPOLIS.
...ESPECIALLY DURING FAMILY TIME.
I DIDN'T EXPECT BLACK LIGHTNING TO GO FOR THE UGLY SWEATER LOOK.
IT'S NOT SUPPOSED TO BE AN UGLY SWEATER! THE GIRLS GOT ME THIS.
IT'S TOTALLY UGLY, DAD.
WHERE'S THE SNOWFLAKE ORNAMENT? WE GOTTA HAVE THAT, IT'S TRADITION.
HOW DO YOU GET THIS SO RIGHT, JEFFERSON? YOU AND THE GIRLS AND THE JOB?
THERE'S NO MAGIC FORMULA, BARRY. LIKE ANYTHING ELSE, IT JUST TAKES EFFORT.
THERE IT IS.
YOU REMEMBER WHEN WE GOT THIS, ANISSA? YOU WERE BOTH SO YOUNG.
IT WAS THE LAST THING WE GOT AT THE CHRISTMAS MARKET DOWNTOWN THAT YEAR, BECAUSE YOUR SISTER INHALED SO MUCH CANDY SHE WAS GOING TO BARF.
SHE DID BARF IN THE BACK SEAT ON THE WAY HOME. WE NEVER TOLD YOU.
YOU WERE IN SUCH A RUSH TO GO, YOU FORGOT TO PAY FOR THE ORNAMENT.
I WENT BACK AND PAID THE NEXT DAY, BARRY. DON'T HAUL ME IN.

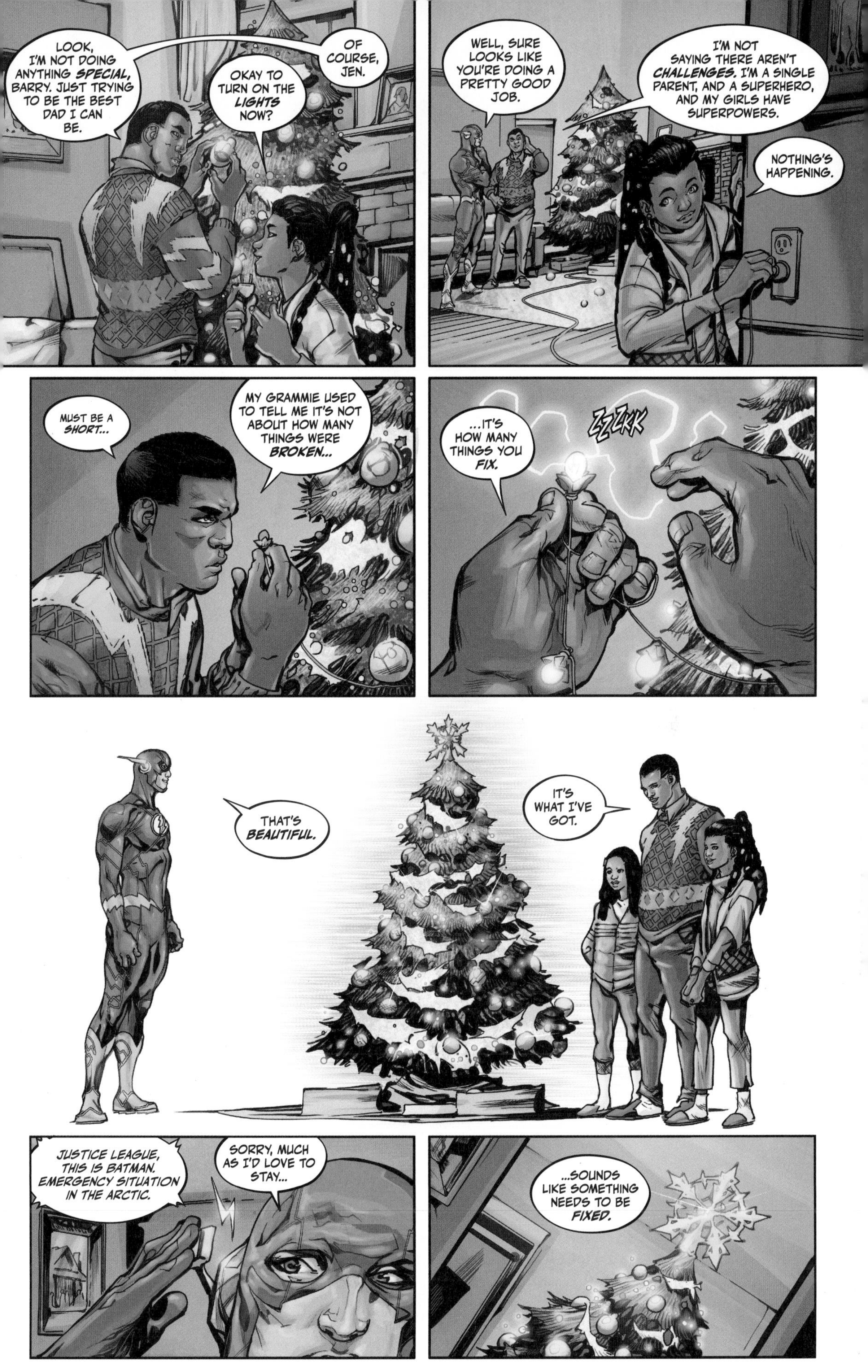
LOOK, I'M NOT DOING ANYTHING SPECIAL, BARRY. JUST TRYING TO BE THE BEST DAD I CAN BE.
OF COURSE, JEN.
OKAY TO TURN ON THE LIGHTS NOW?
WELL, SURE LOOKS LIKE YOU'RE DOING A PRETTY GOOD JOB.
I'M NOT SAYING THERE AREN'T CHALLENGES. I'M A SINGLE PARENT, AND A SUPERHERO, AND MY GIRLS HAVE SUPERPOWERS.
NOTHING'S HAPPENING.
MUST BE A SHORT...
MY GRAMMIE USED TO TELL ME IT'S NOT ABOUT HOW MANY THINGS WERE BROKEN...
...IT'S HOW MANY THINGS YOU FIX.
ZZZKK
THAT'S BEAUTIFUL.
IT'S WHAT I'VE GOT.
JUSTICE LEAGUE, THIS IS BATMAN. EMERGENCY SITUATION IN THE ARCTIC.
SORRY, MUCH AS I'D LOVE TO STAY...
...SOUNDS LIKE SOMETHING NEEDS TO BE FIXED.

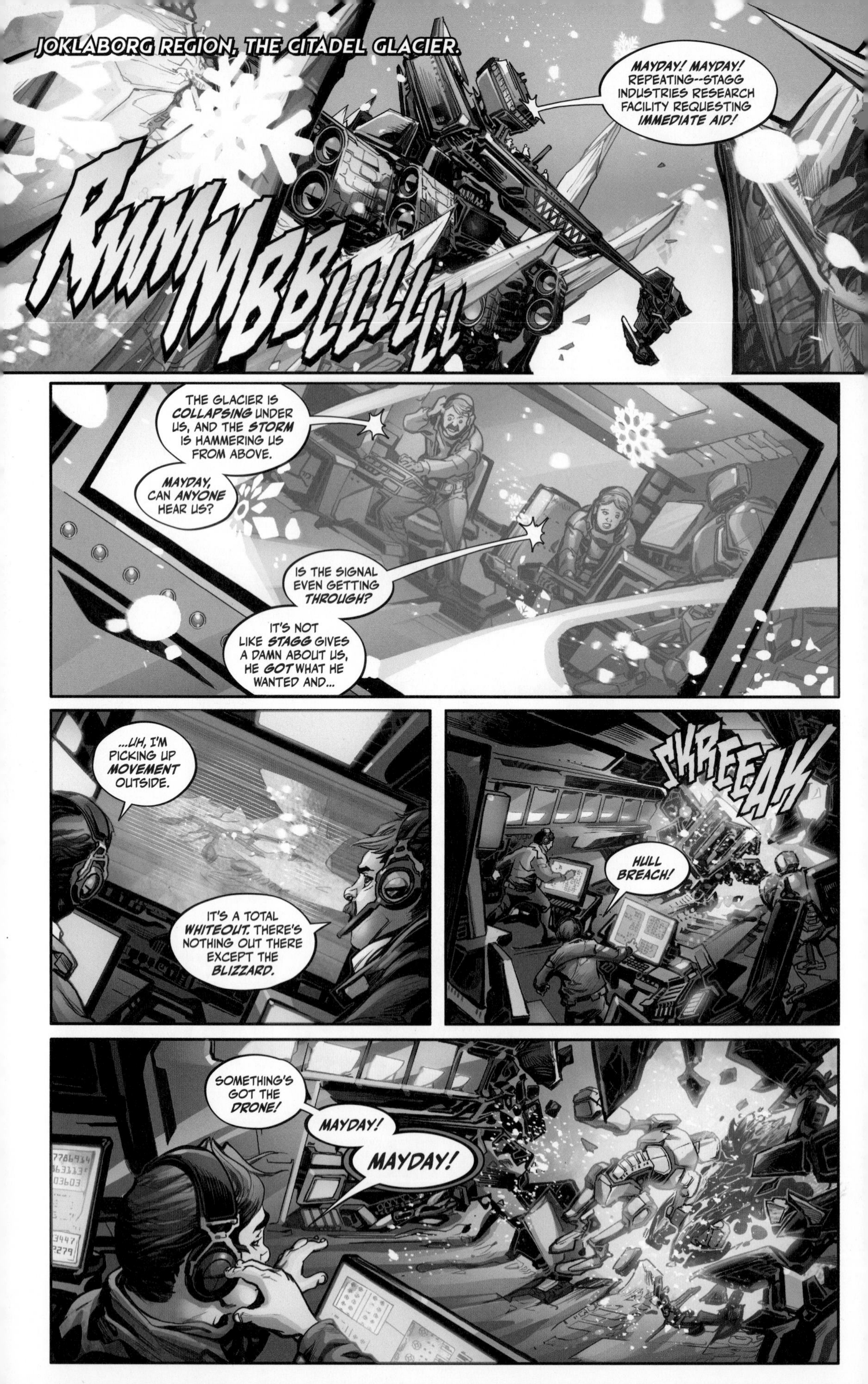
JOKLABORG REGION, THE CITADEL GLACIER.
MAYDAY! MAYDAY! REPEATING--STAGG INDUSTRIES RESEARCH FACILITY REQUESTING IMMEDIATE AID!
RMMMBBLLLLLL
THE GLACIER IS COLLAPSING UNDER US, AND THE STORM IS HAMMERING US FROM ABOVE.
MAYDAY, CAN ANYONE HEAR US?
IS THE SIGNAL EVEN GETTING THROUGH?
IT'S NOT LIKE STAGG GIVES A DAMN ABOUT US, HE GOT WHAT HE WANTED AND...
...UH, I'M PICKING UP MOVEMENT OUTSIDE.
IT'S A TOTAL WHITEOUT. THERE'S NOTHING OUT THERE EXCEPT THE BLIZZARD.
SKREEAK
HULL BREACH!
SOMETHING'S GOT THE DRONE!
MAYDAY!
MAYDAY!

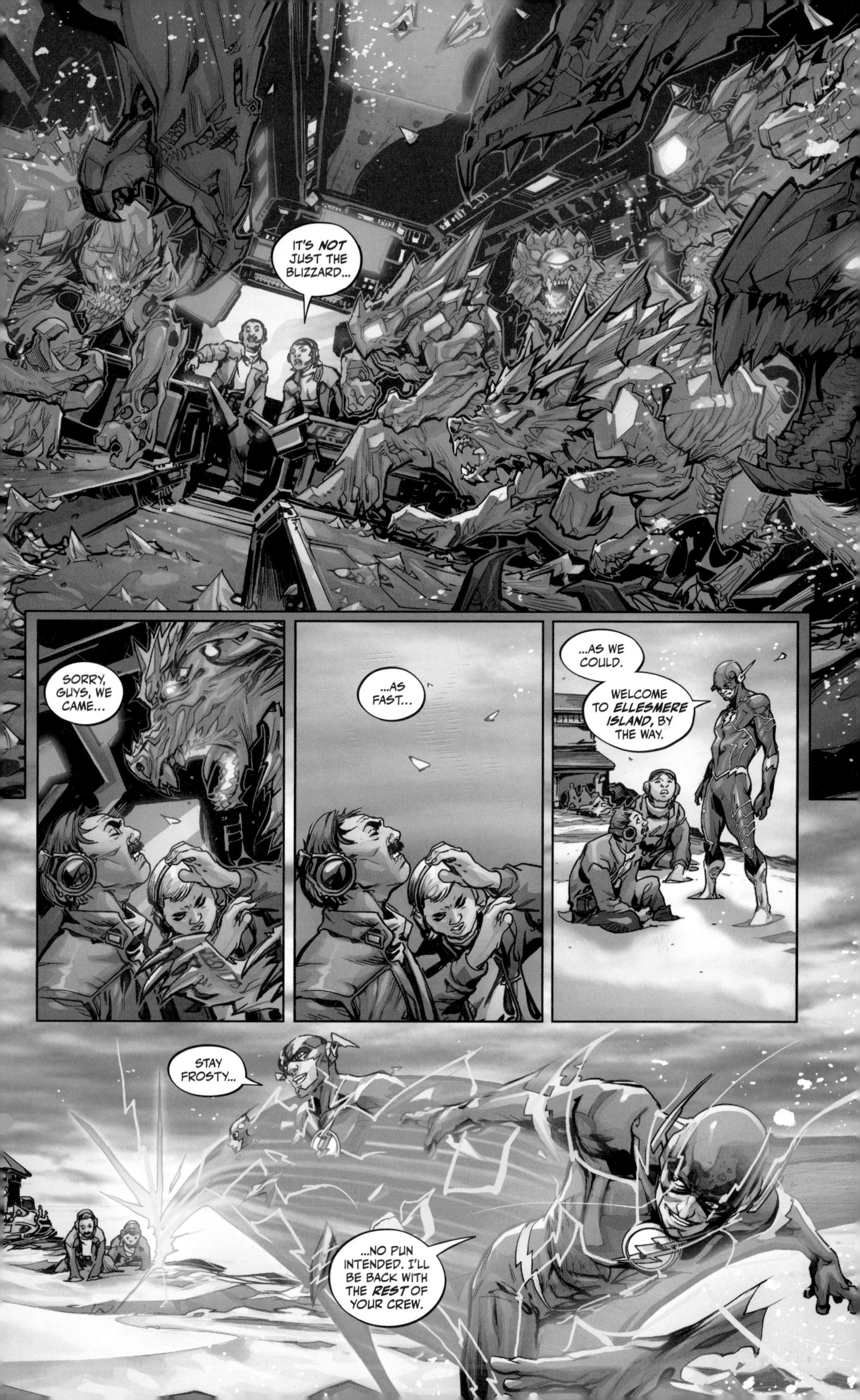
IT'S NOT JUST THE BLIZZARD...
SORRY, GUYS, WE CAME...
...AS FAST...
...AS WE COULD.
WELCOME TO ELLESMERE ISLAND, BY THE WAY.
STAY FROSTY...
...NO PUN INTENDED. I'LL BE BACK WITH THE REST OF YOUR CREW.

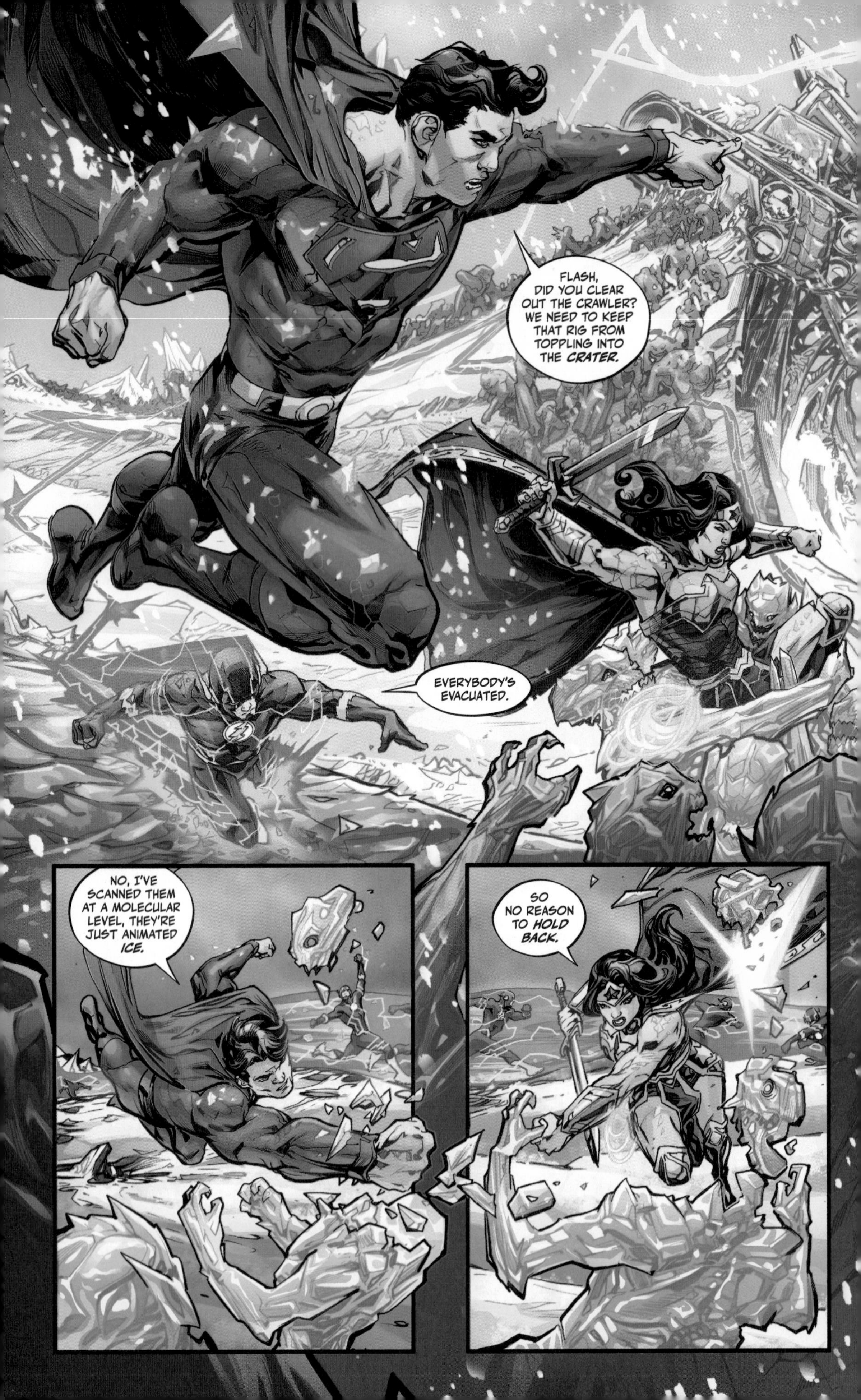
FLASH, DID YOU CLEAR OUT THE CRAWLER? WE NEED TO KEEP THAT RIG FROM TOPPLING INTO THE *CRATER.*
EVERYBODY'S EVACUATED.
NO, I'VE SCANNED THEM AT A MOLECULAR LEVEL, THEY'RE JUST ANIMATED *ICE.*
SO NO REASON TO *HOLD BACK.*

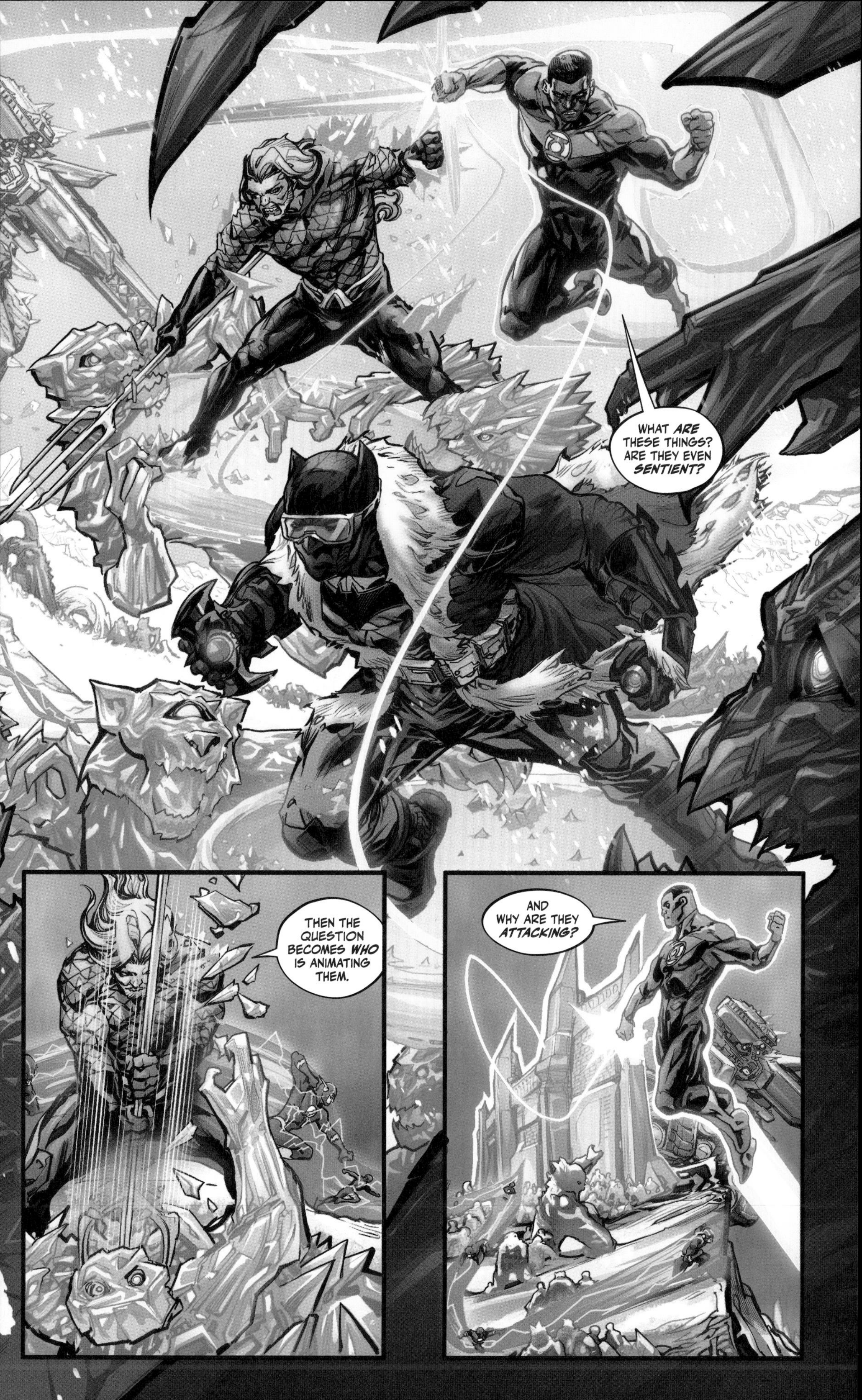
WHAT *ARE* THESE THINGS? ARE THEY EVEN *SENTIENT?*
THEN THE QUESTION BECOMES *WHO* IS ANIMATING THEM.
AND WHY ARE THEY *ATTACKING?*

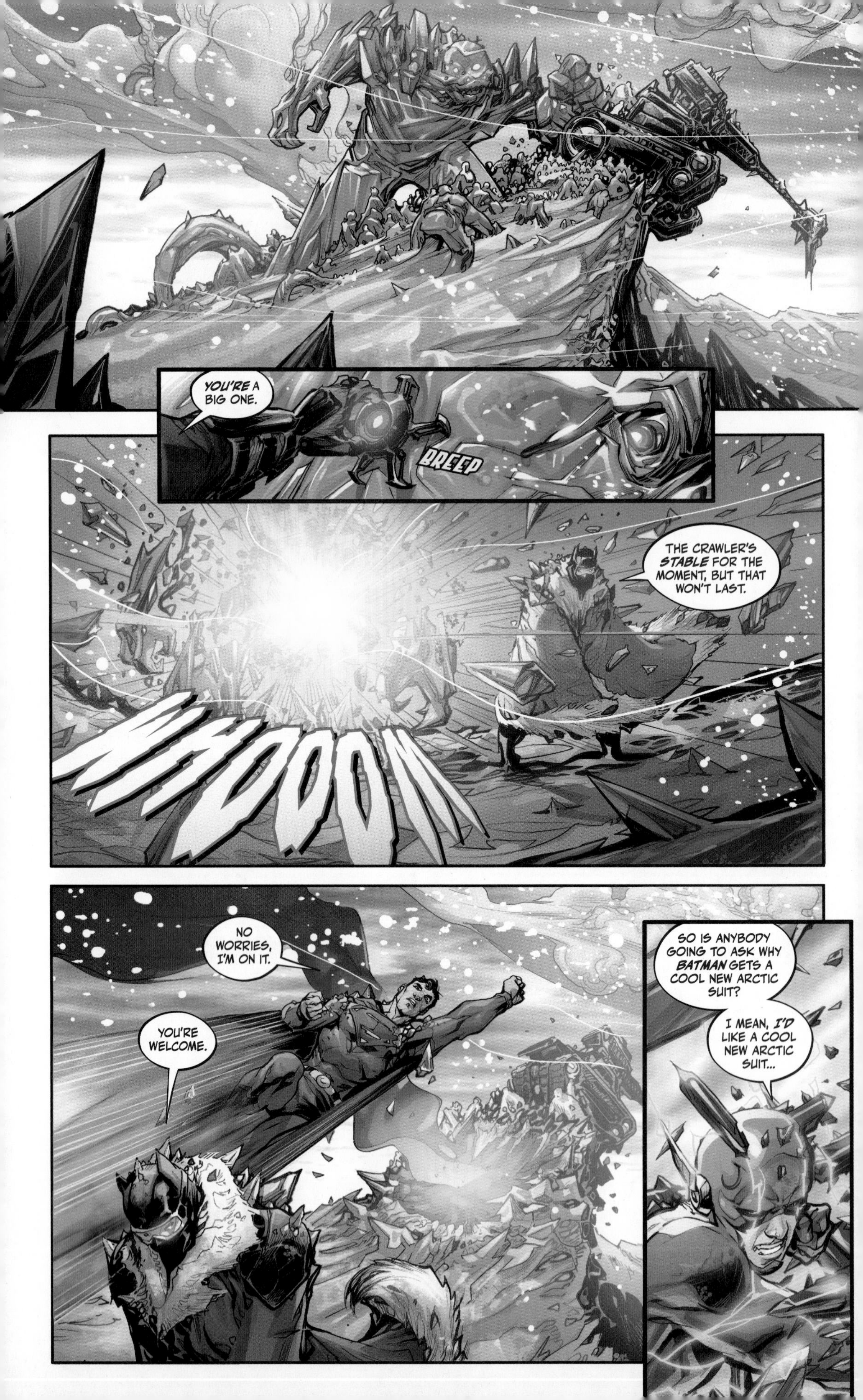
YOU'RE A BIG ONE.
BREEP
THE CRAWLER'S STABLE FOR THE MOMENT, BUT THAT WON'T LAST.
WHOOOM
NO WORRIES, I'M ON IT.
YOU'RE WELCOME.
SO IS ANYBODY GOING TO ASK WHY BATMAN GETS A COOL NEW ARCTIC SUIT?
I MEAN, I'D LIKE A COOL NEW ARCTIC SUIT...

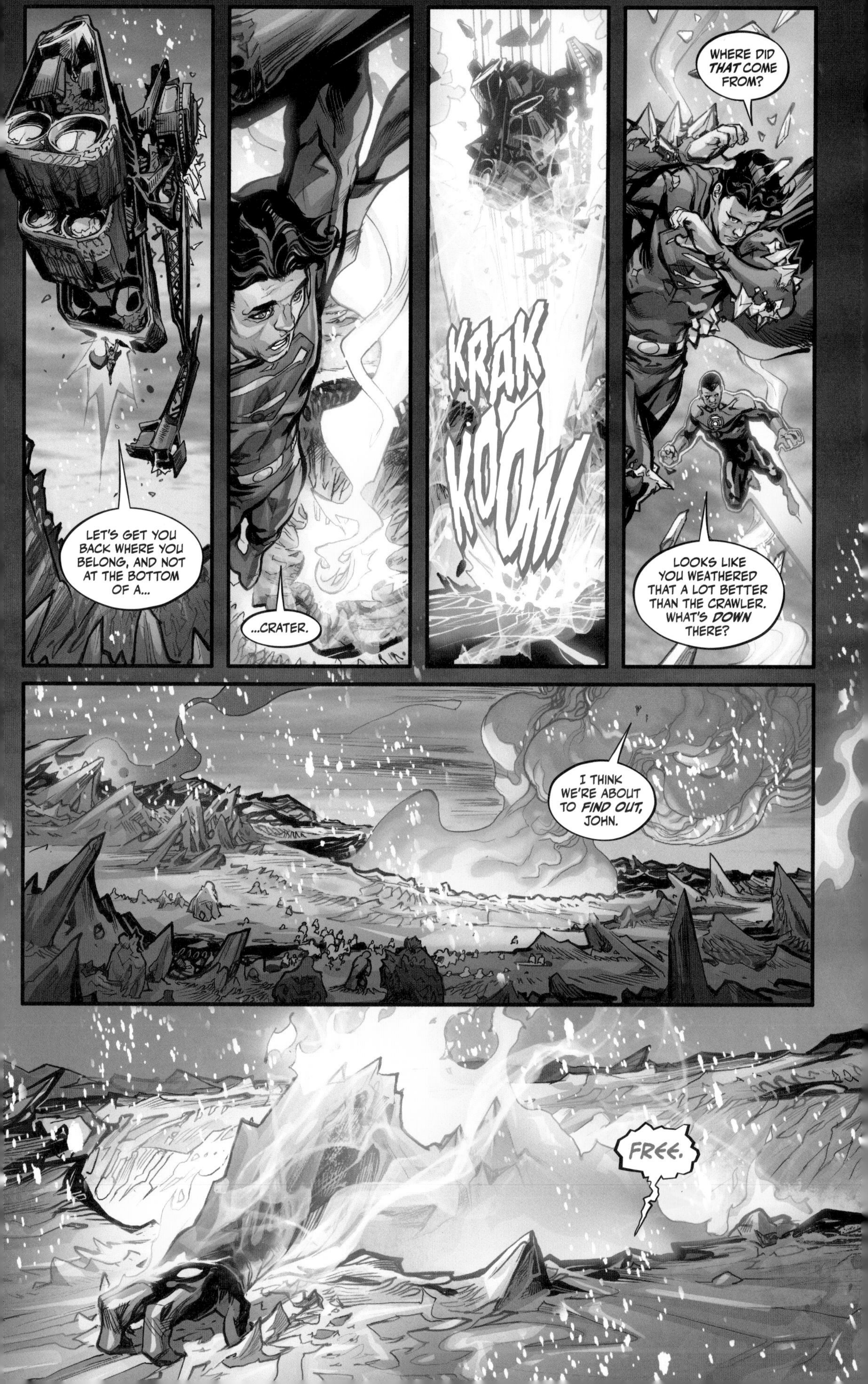
LET'S GET YOU BACK WHERE YOU BELONG, AND NOT AT THE BOTTOM OF A...
...CRATER.
KRAK KOOM
WHERE DID *THAT* COME FROM?
LOOKS LIKE YOU WEATHERED THAT A LOT BETTER THAN THE CRAWLER. WHAT'S *DOWN* THERE?
I THINK WE'RE ABOUT TO *FIND OUT*, JOHN.
FREE.

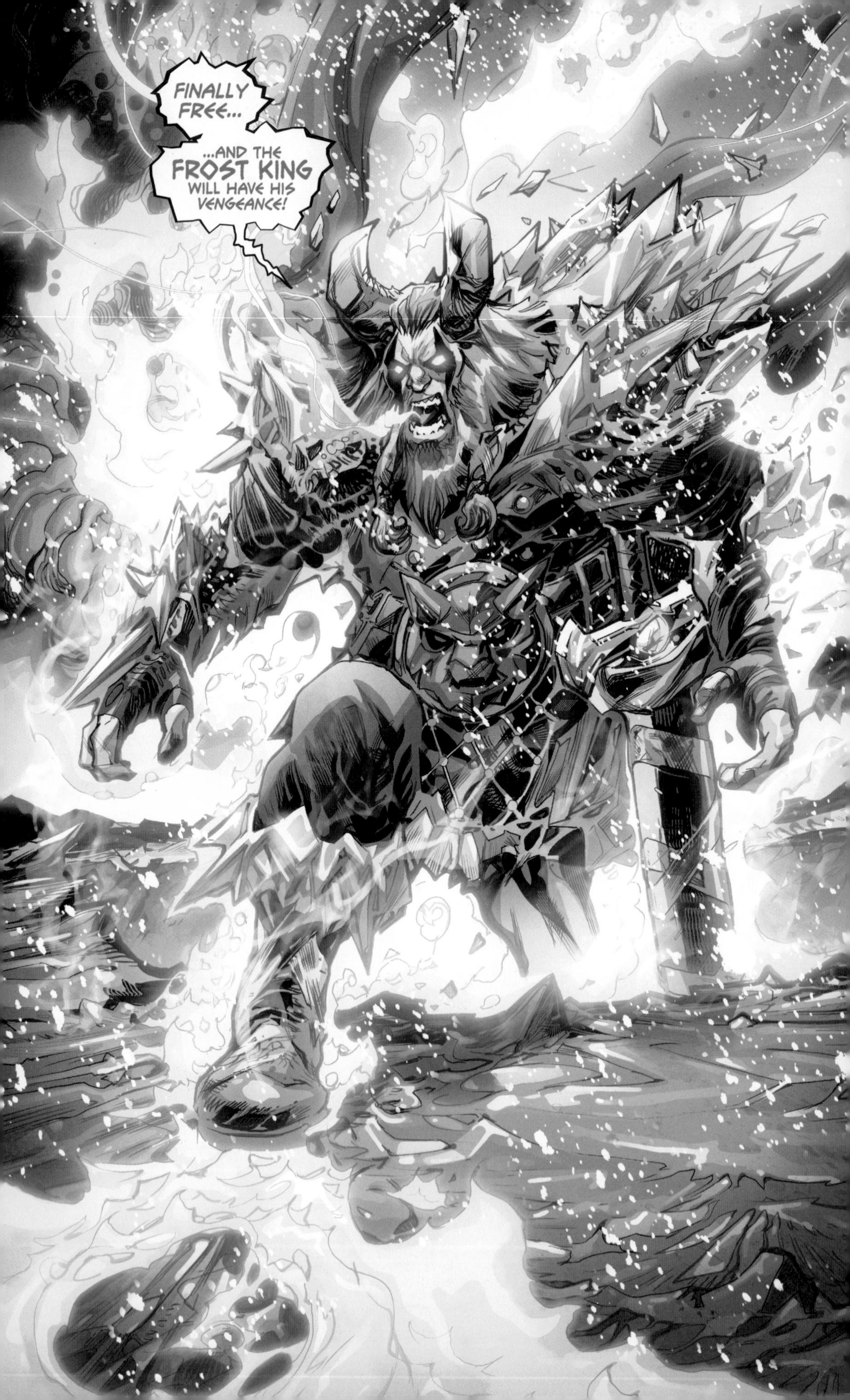
FINALLY FREE...
...AND THE FROST KING WILL HAVE HIS VENGEANCE!

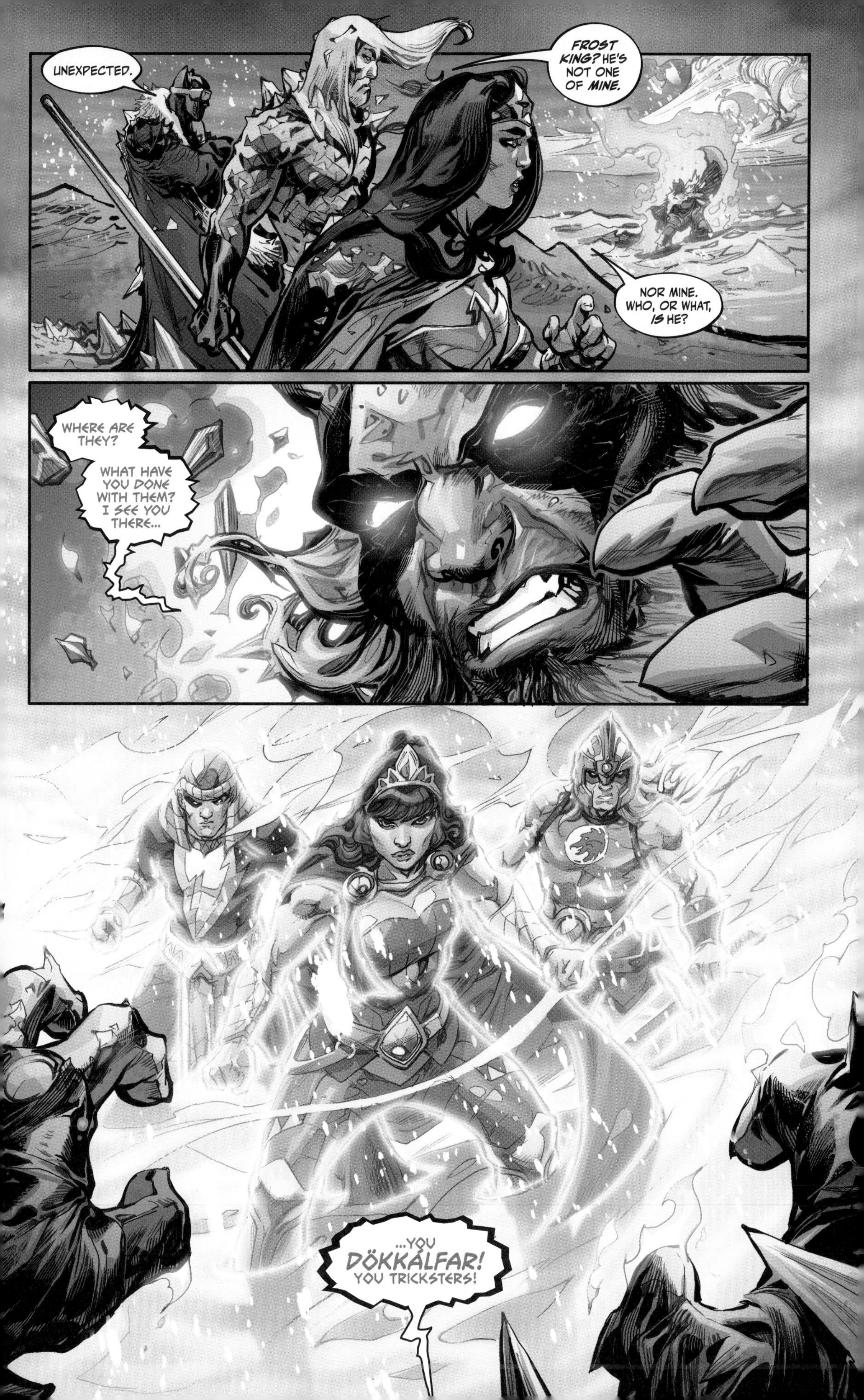
UNEXPECTED.
FROST KING? HE'S NOT ONE OF MINE.
NOR MINE. WHO, OR WHAT, IS HE?
WHERE ARE THEY?
WHAT HAVE YOU DONE WITH THEM? I SEE YOU THERE...
...YOU DÖKKÁLFAR! YOU TRICKSTERS!

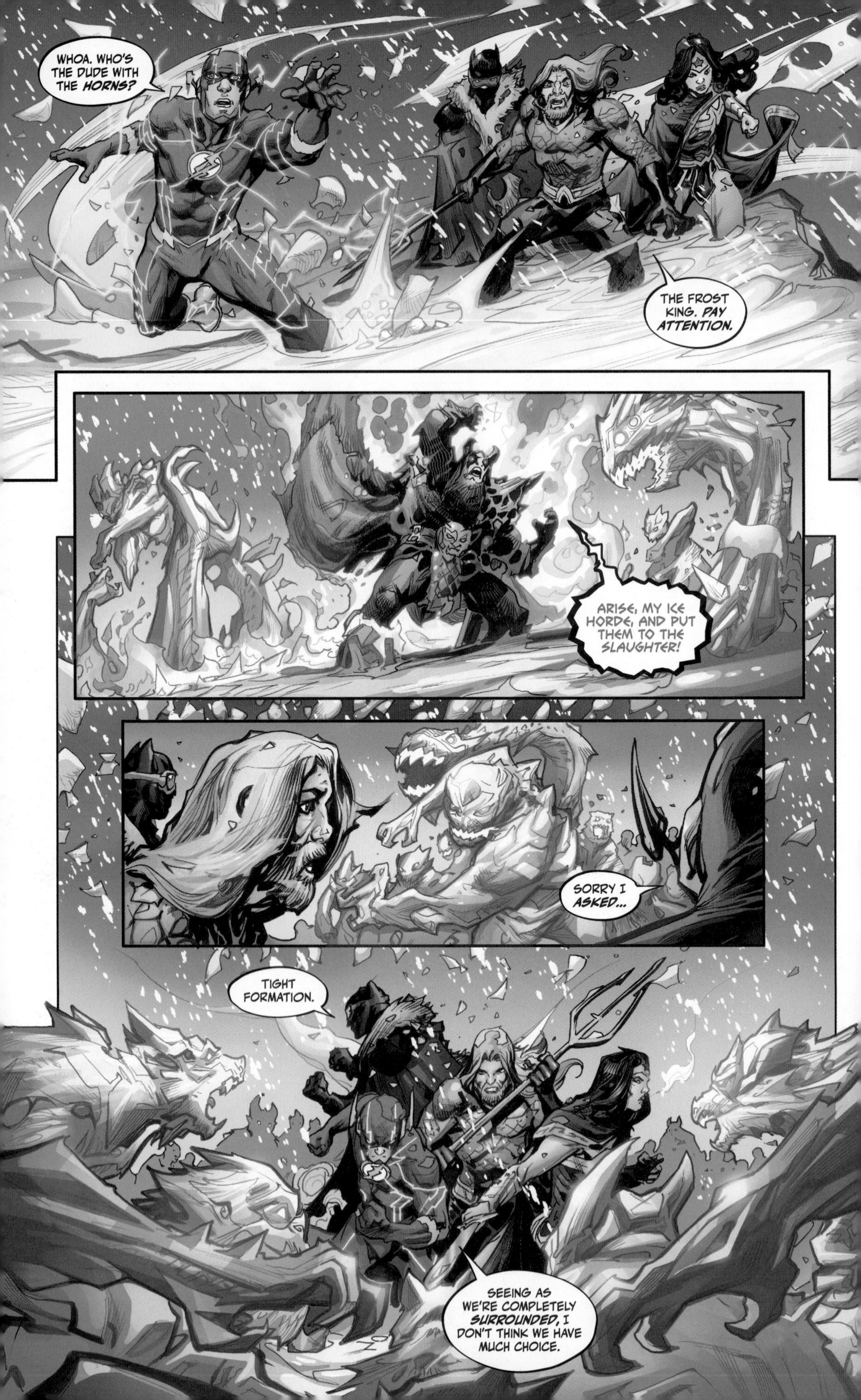
WHOA. WHO'S THE DUDE WITH THE HORNS?
THE FROST KING. PAY ATTENTION.
ARISE, MY ICE HORDE, AND PUT THEM TO THE SLAUGHTER!
SORRY I ASKED...
TIGHT FORMATION.
SEEING AS WE'RE COMPLETELY SURROUNDED, I DON'T THINK WE HAVE MUCH CHOICE.

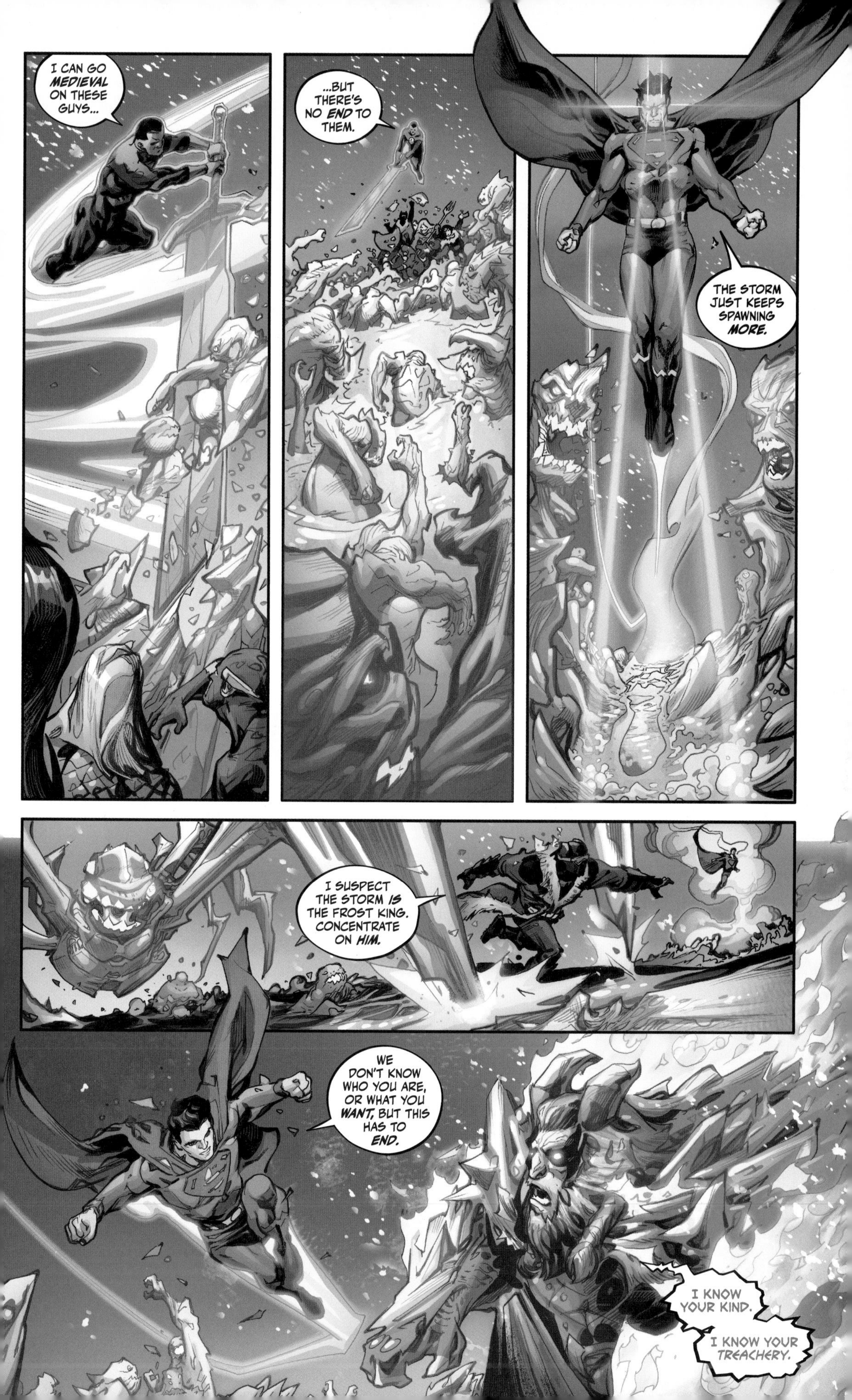
I CAN GO MEDIEVAL ON THESE GUYS...
...BUT THERE'S NO END TO THEM.
THE STORM JUST KEEPS SPAWNING MORE.
I SUSPECT THE STORM IS THE FROST KING. CONCENTRATE ON HIM.
WE DON'T KNOW WHO YOU ARE, OR WHAT YOU WANT, BUT THIS HAS TO END.
I KNOW YOUR KIND.
I KNOW YOUR TREACHERY.

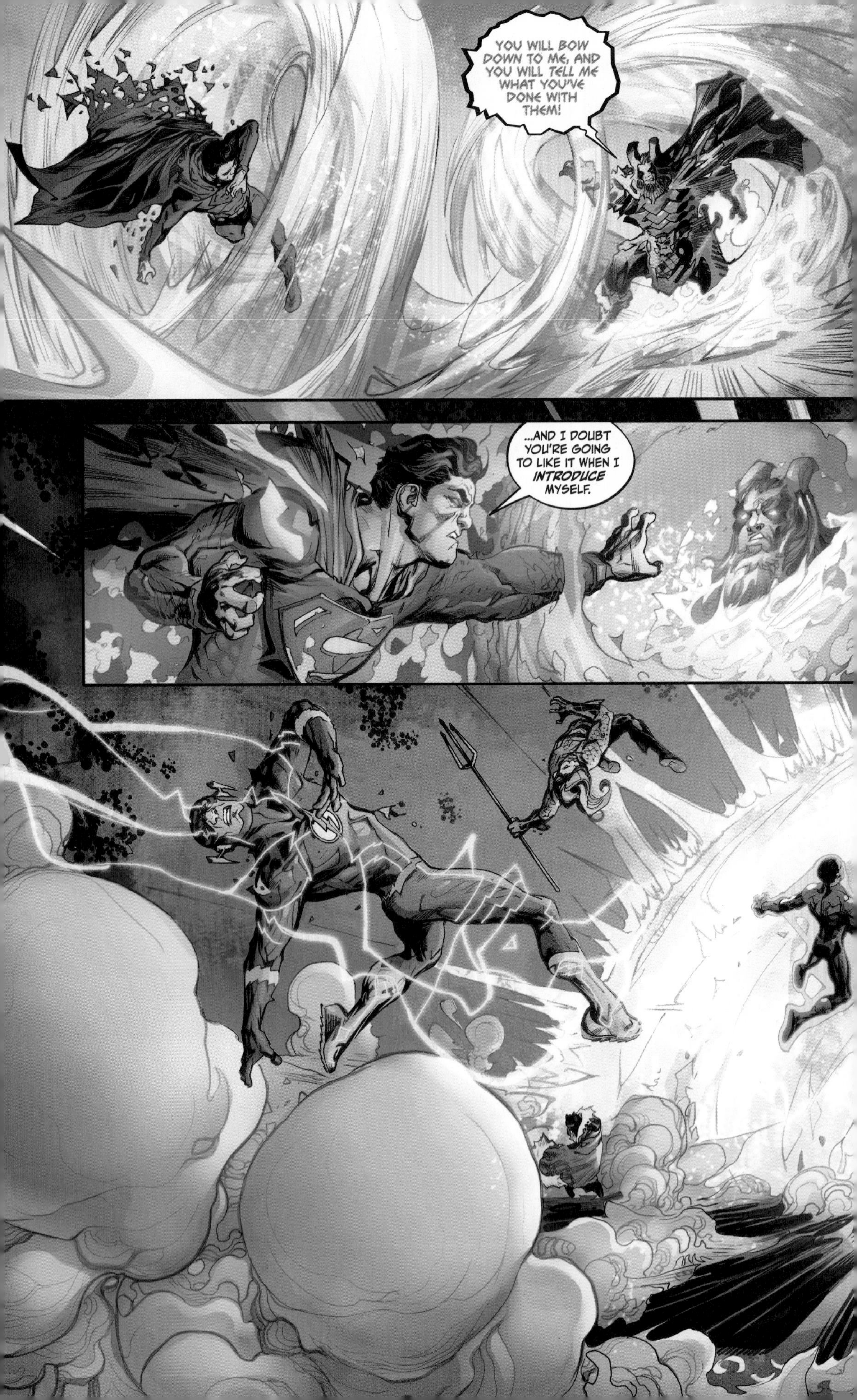
YOU WILL BOW DOWN TO ME, AND YOU WILL TELL ME WHAT YOU'VE DONE WITH THEM!
...AND I DOUBT YOU'RE GOING TO LIKE IT WHEN I INTRODUCE MYSELF.

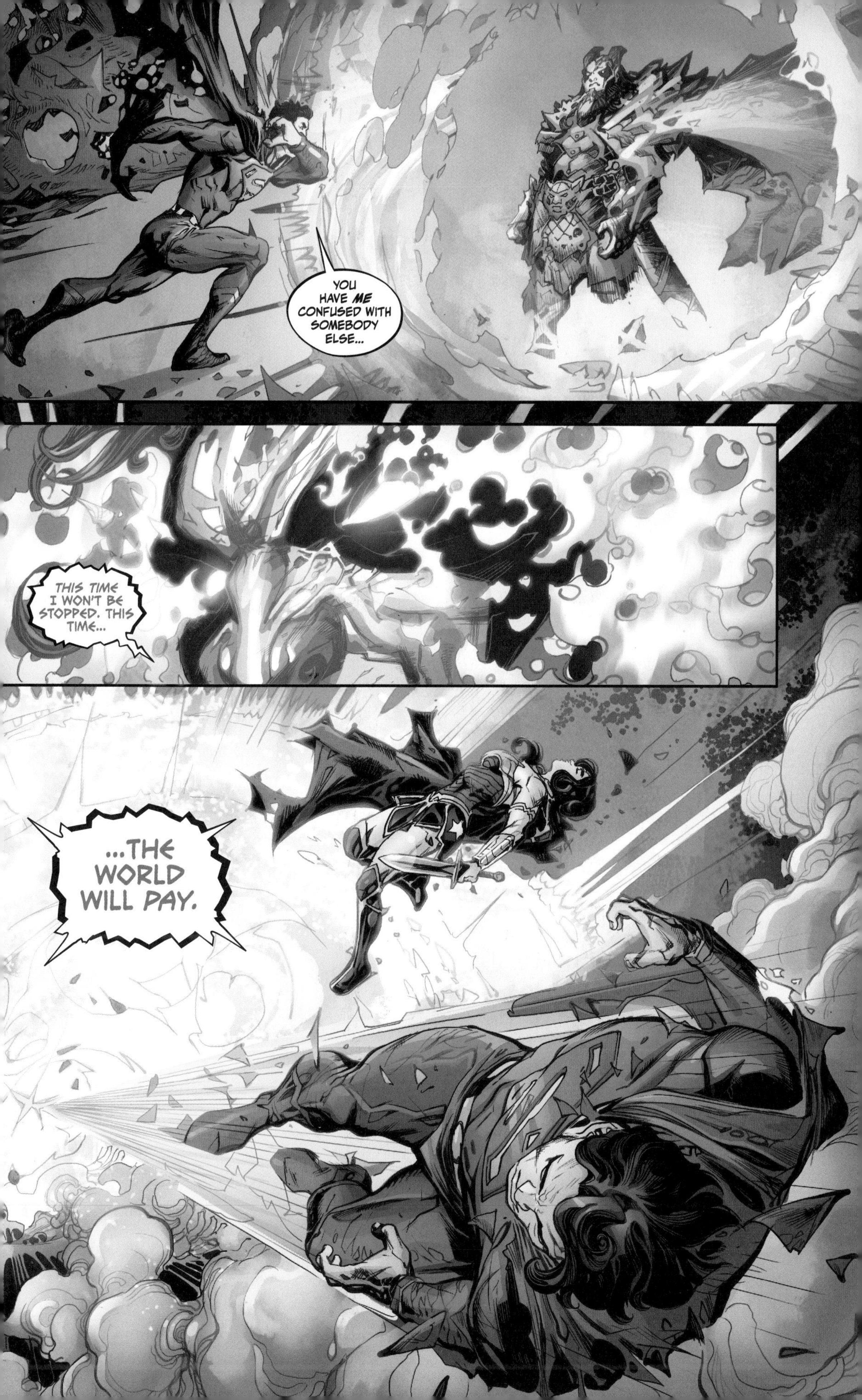
YOU HAVE *ME* CONFUSED WITH SOMEBODY ELSE...
THIS TIME I WON'T BE STOPPED. THIS TIME...
...THE WORLD WILL PAY.

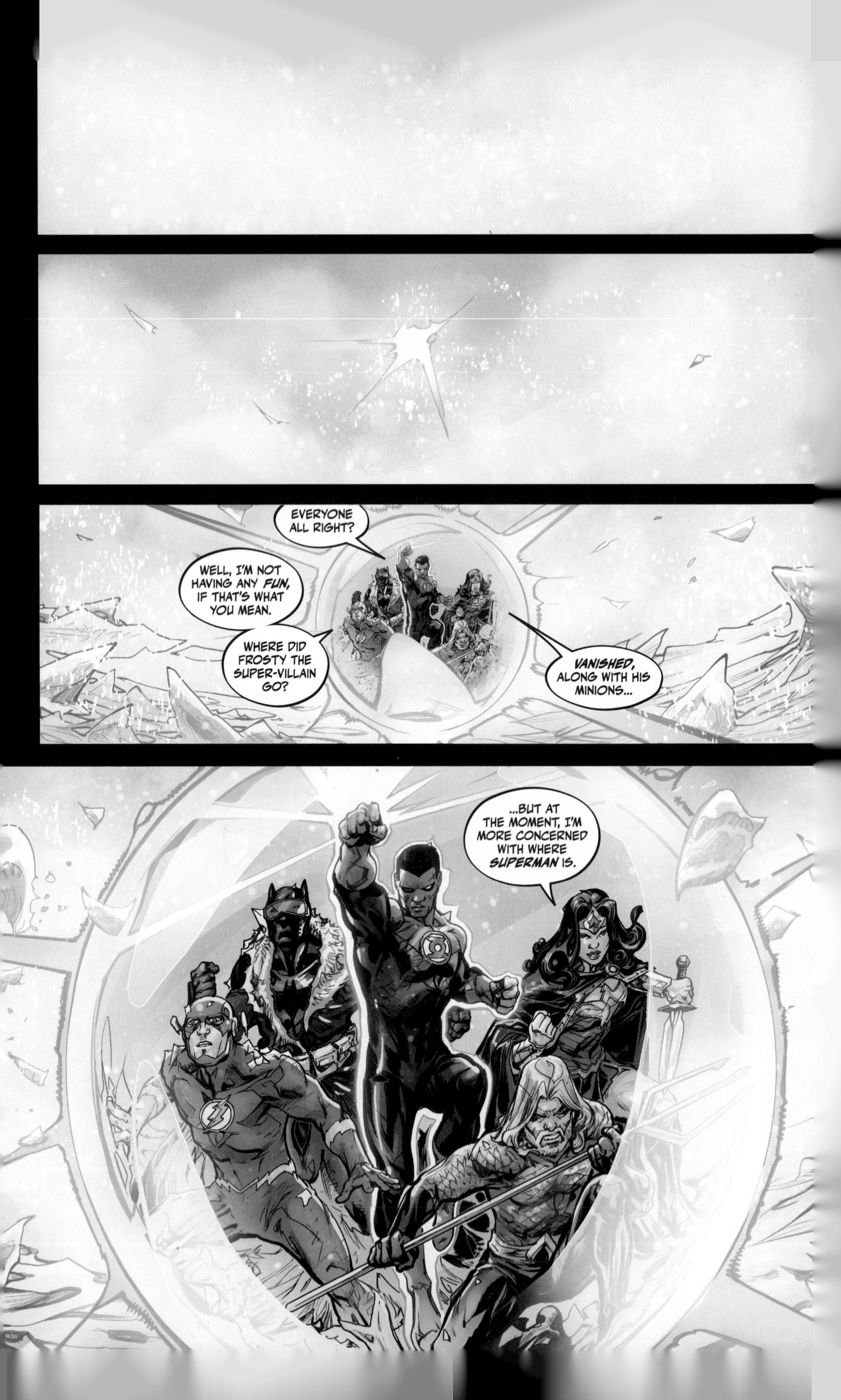
EVERYONE ALL RIGHT?
WELL, I'M NOT HAVING ANY *FUN*, IF THAT'S WHAT YOU MEAN.
WHERE DID FROSTY THE SUPER-VILLAIN GO?
VANISHED, ALONG WITH HIS MINIONS...
...BUT AT THE MOMENT, I'M MORE CONCERNED WITH WHERE *SUPERMAN* IS.

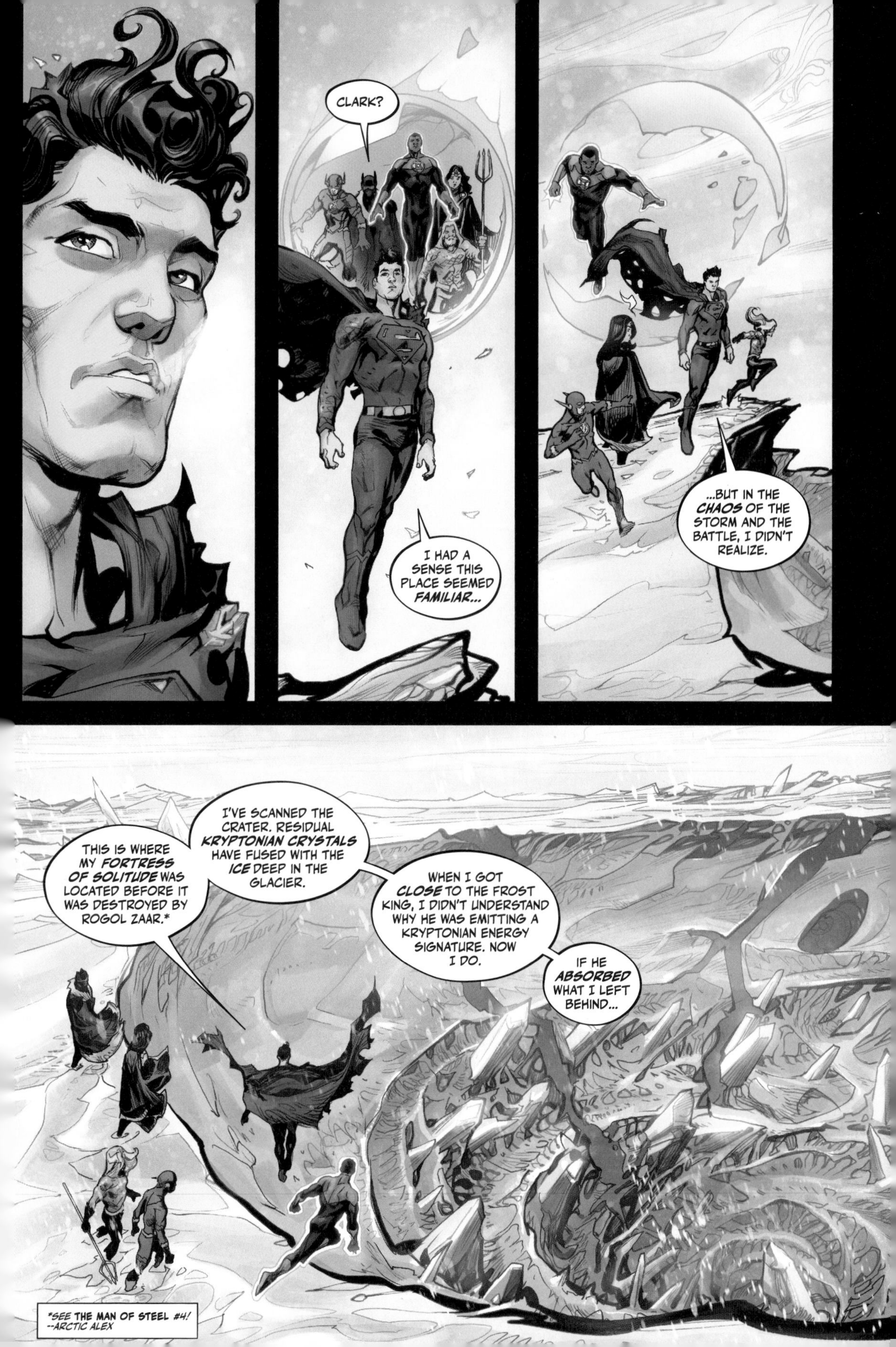
CLARK?
I HAD A SENSE THIS PLACE SEEMED FAMILIAR...
...BUT IN THE CHAOS OF THE STORM AND THE BATTLE, I DIDN'T REALIZE.
THIS IS WHERE MY FORTRESS OF SOLITUDE WAS LOCATED BEFORE IT WAS DESTROYED BY ROGOL ZAAR.*
I'VE SCANNED THE CRATER. RESIDUAL KRYPTONIAN CRYSTALS HAVE FUSED WITH THE ICE DEEP IN THE GLACIER.
WHEN I GOT CLOSE TO THE FROST KING, I DIDN'T UNDERSTAND WHY HE WAS EMITTING A KRYPTONIAN ENERGY SIGNATURE. NOW I DO.
IF HE ABSORBED WHAT I LEFT BEHIND...
*SEE THE MAN OF STEEL #4! --ARCTIC ALEX

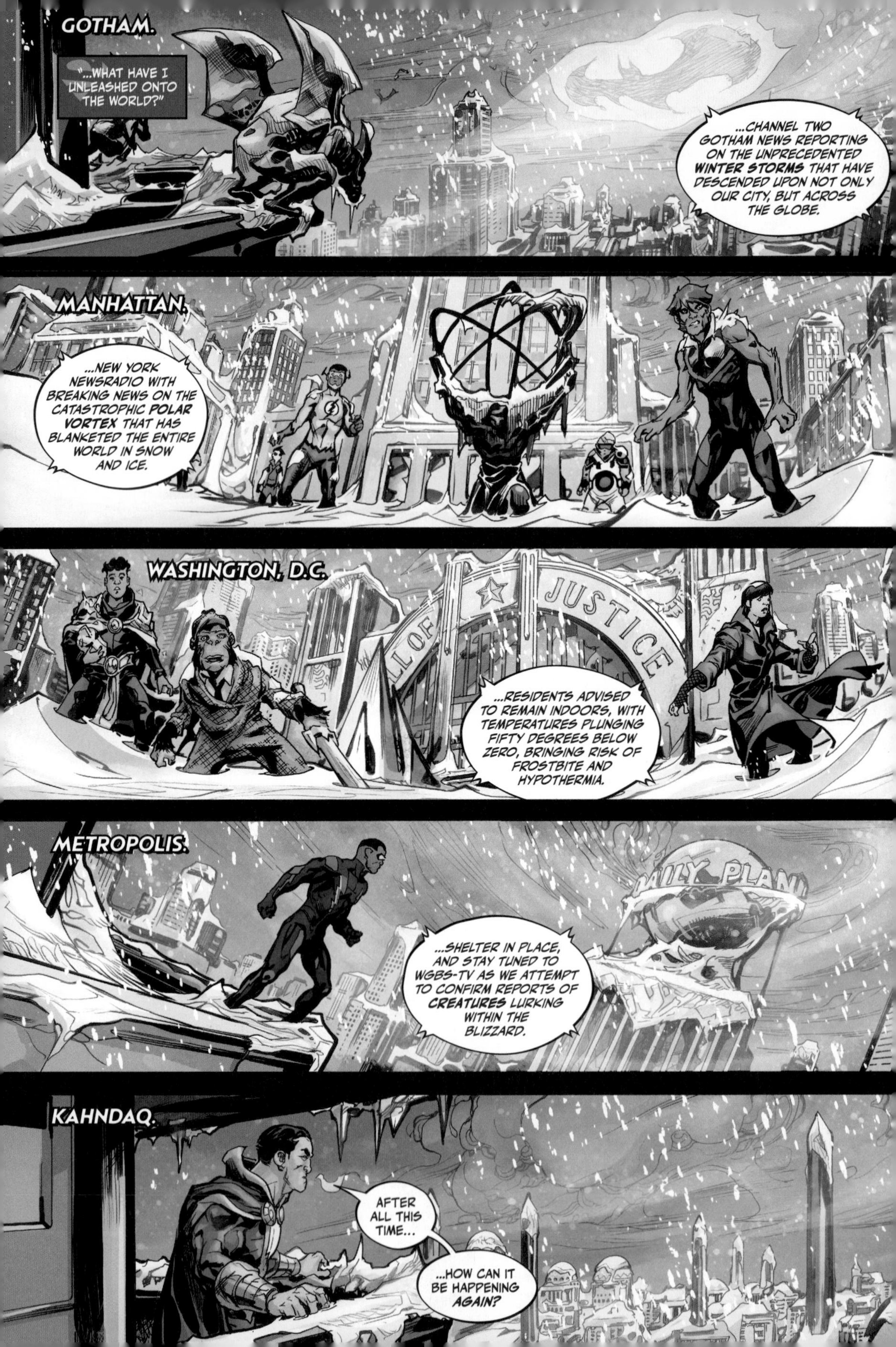

GOTHAM.
"...WHAT HAVE I UNLEASHED ONTO THE WORLD?"
...CHANNEL TWO GOTHAM NEWS REPORTING ON THE UNPRECEDENTED WINTER STORMS THAT HAVE DESCENDED UPON NOT ONLY OUR CITY, BUT ACROSS THE GLOBE.
MANHATTAN.
...NEW YORK NEWSRADIO WITH BREAKING NEWS ON THE CATASTROPHIC POLAR VORTEX THAT HAS BLANKETED THE ENTIRE WORLD IN SNOW AND ICE.
WASHINGTON, D.C.
...RESIDENTS ADVISED TO REMAIN INDOORS, WITH TEMPERATURES PLUNGING FIFTY DEGREES BELOW ZERO, BRINGING RISK OF FROSTBITE AND HYPOTHERMIA.
METROPOLIS.
...SHELTER IN PLACE, AND STAY TUNED TO WGBS-TV AS WE ATTEMPT TO CONFIRM REPORTS OF CREATURES LURKING WITHIN THE BLIZZARD.
KAHNDAQ.
AFTER ALL THIS TIME...
...HOW CAN IT BE HAPPENING AGAIN?

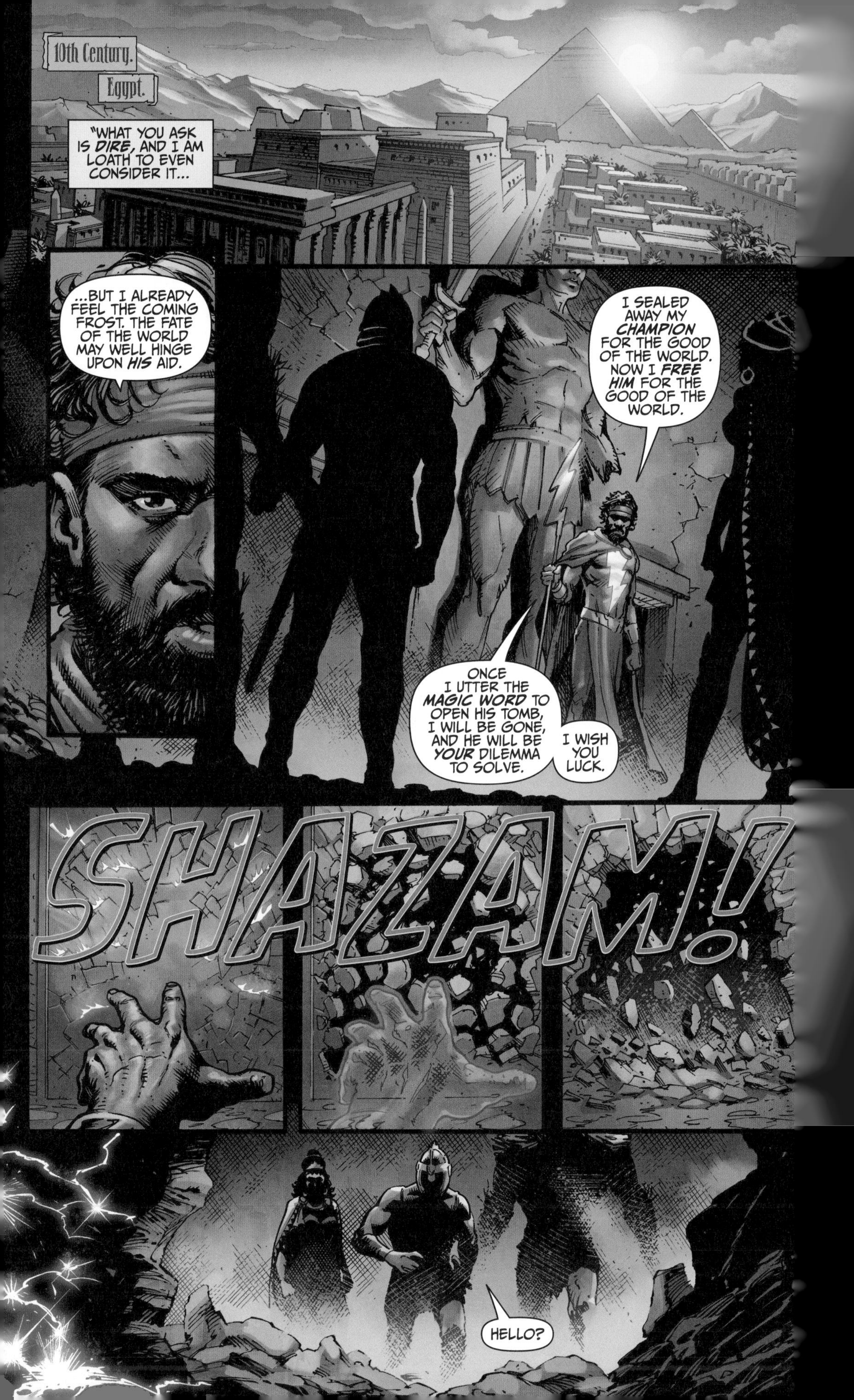
10th Century.
Egypt.
"WHAT YOU ASK IS DIRE, AND I AM LOATH TO EVEN CONSIDER IT...
...BUT I ALREADY FEEL THE COMING FROST. THE FATE OF THE WORLD MAY WELL HINGE UPON HIS AID.
I SEALED AWAY MY CHAMPION FOR THE GOOD OF THE WORLD. NOW I FREE HIM FOR THE GOOD OF THE WORLD.
ONCE I UTTER THE MAGIC WORD TO OPEN HIS TOMB, I WILL BE GONE, AND HE WILL BE YOUR DILEMMA TO SOLVE.
I WISH YOU LUCK.
SHAZAM!
HELLO?

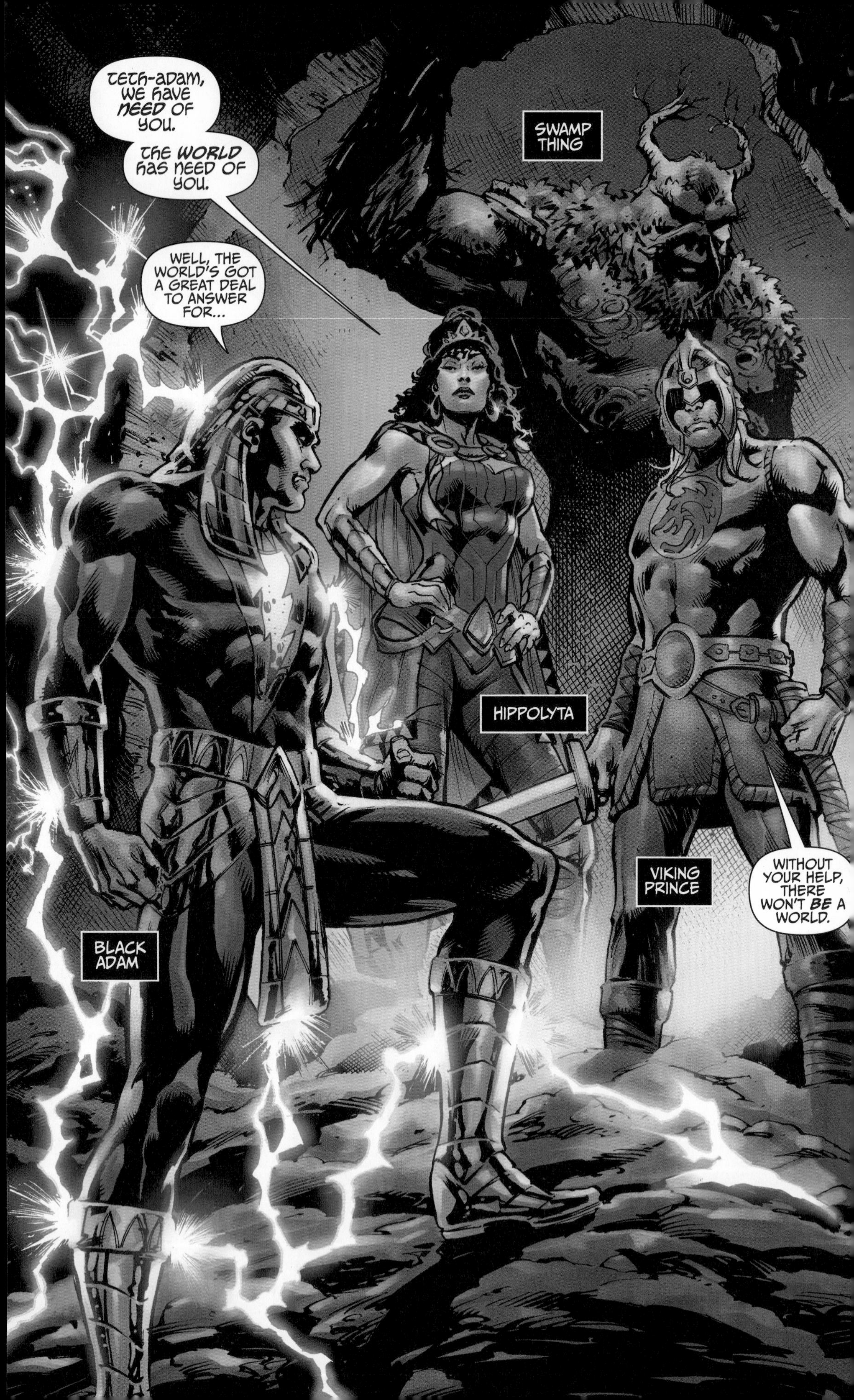
TETH-ADAM, WE HAVE NEED OF YOU.
THE WORLD HAS NEED OF YOU.
SWAMP THING
WELL, THE WORLD'S GOT A GREAT DEAL TO ANSWER FOR...
HIPPOLYTA
VIKING PRINCE
WITHOUT YOUR HELP, THERE WON'T BE A WORLD.
BLACK ADAM

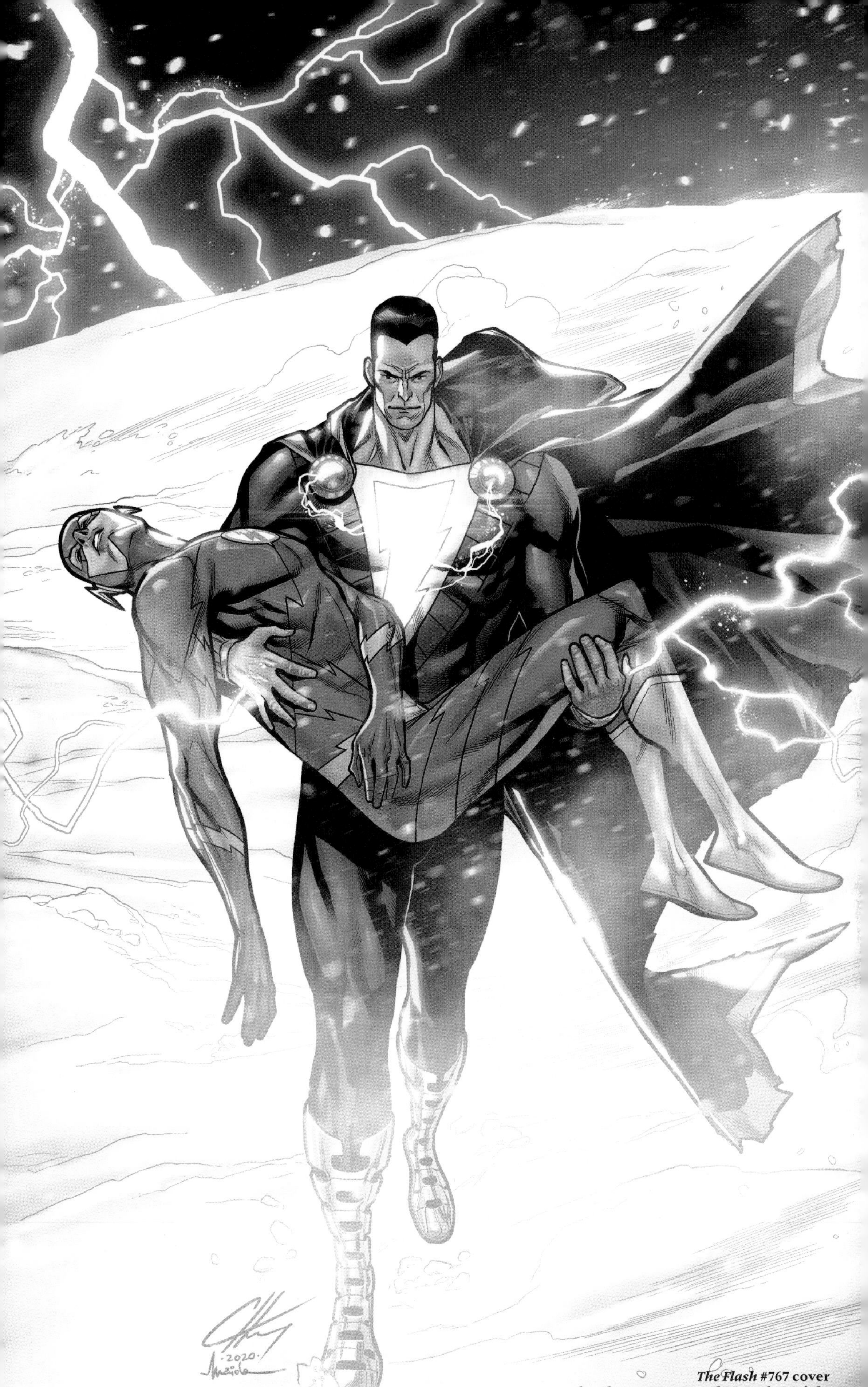
2020

The Flash #767 cover
by Clayton Henry and Marcelo Maiolo

The Flash #767 variant cover
by Hicham Habchi

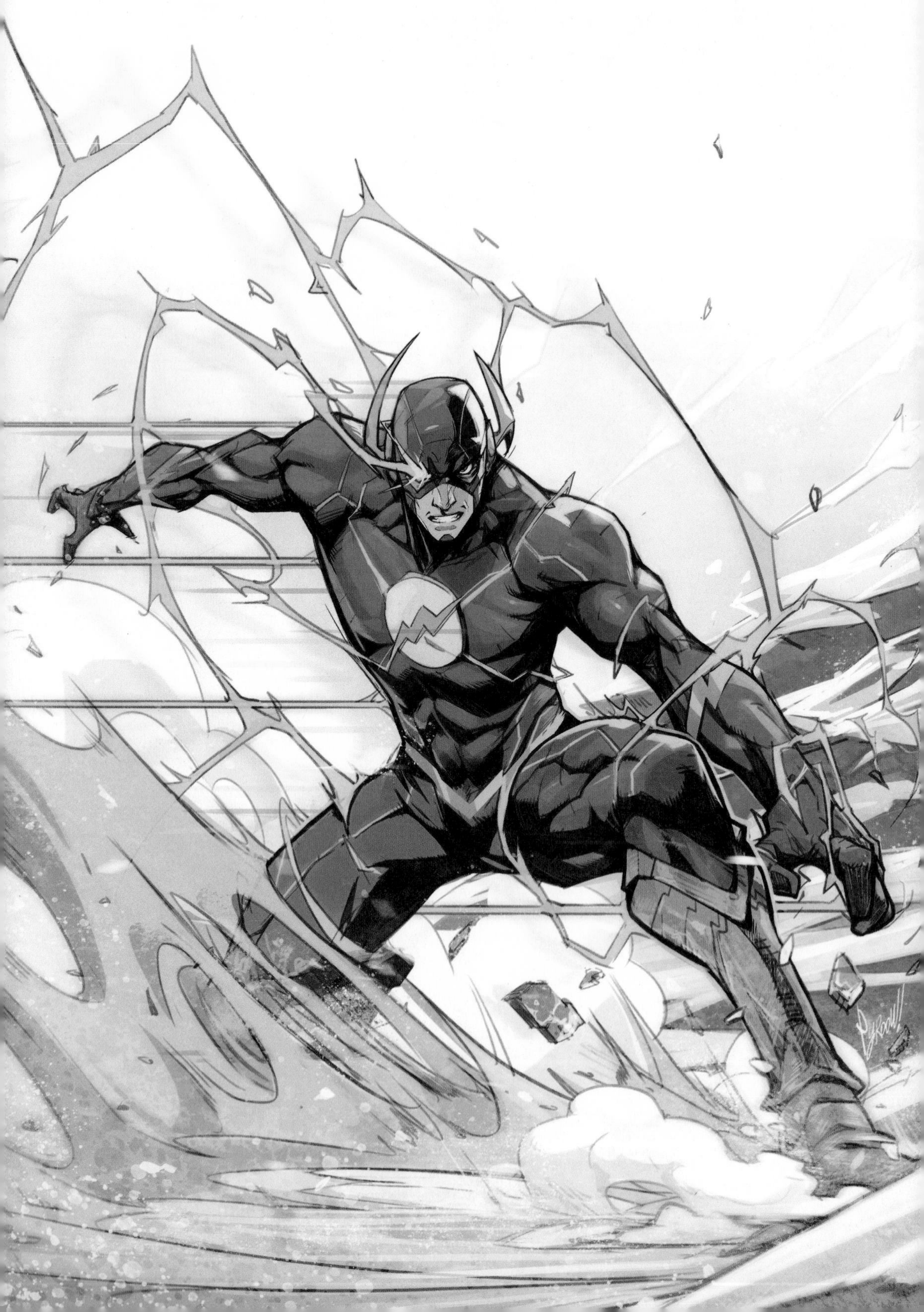

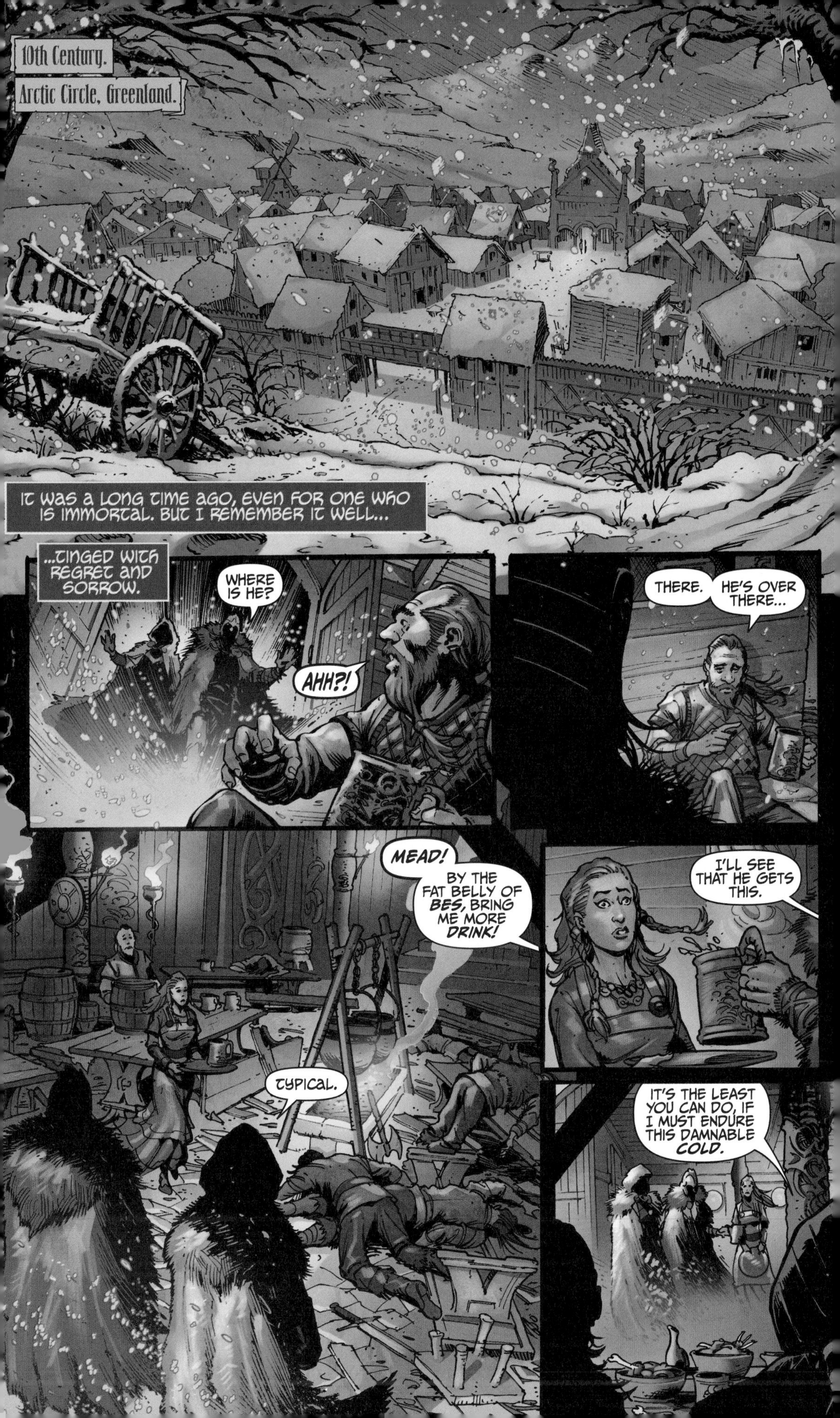
10th Century.
Arctic Circle, Greenland.
IT WAS A LONG TIME AGO, EVEN FOR ONE WHO IS IMMORTAL. BUT I REMEMBER IT WELL...
...TINGED WITH REGRET AND SORROW.
WHERE IS HE?
AHH?!
THERE.
HE'S OVER THERE...
MEAD!
BY THE FAT BELLY OF BES, BRING ME MORE DRINK!
I'LL SEE THAT HE GETS THIS.
TYPICAL.
IT'S THE LEAST YOU CAN DO, IF I MUST ENDURE THIS DAMNABLE COLD.

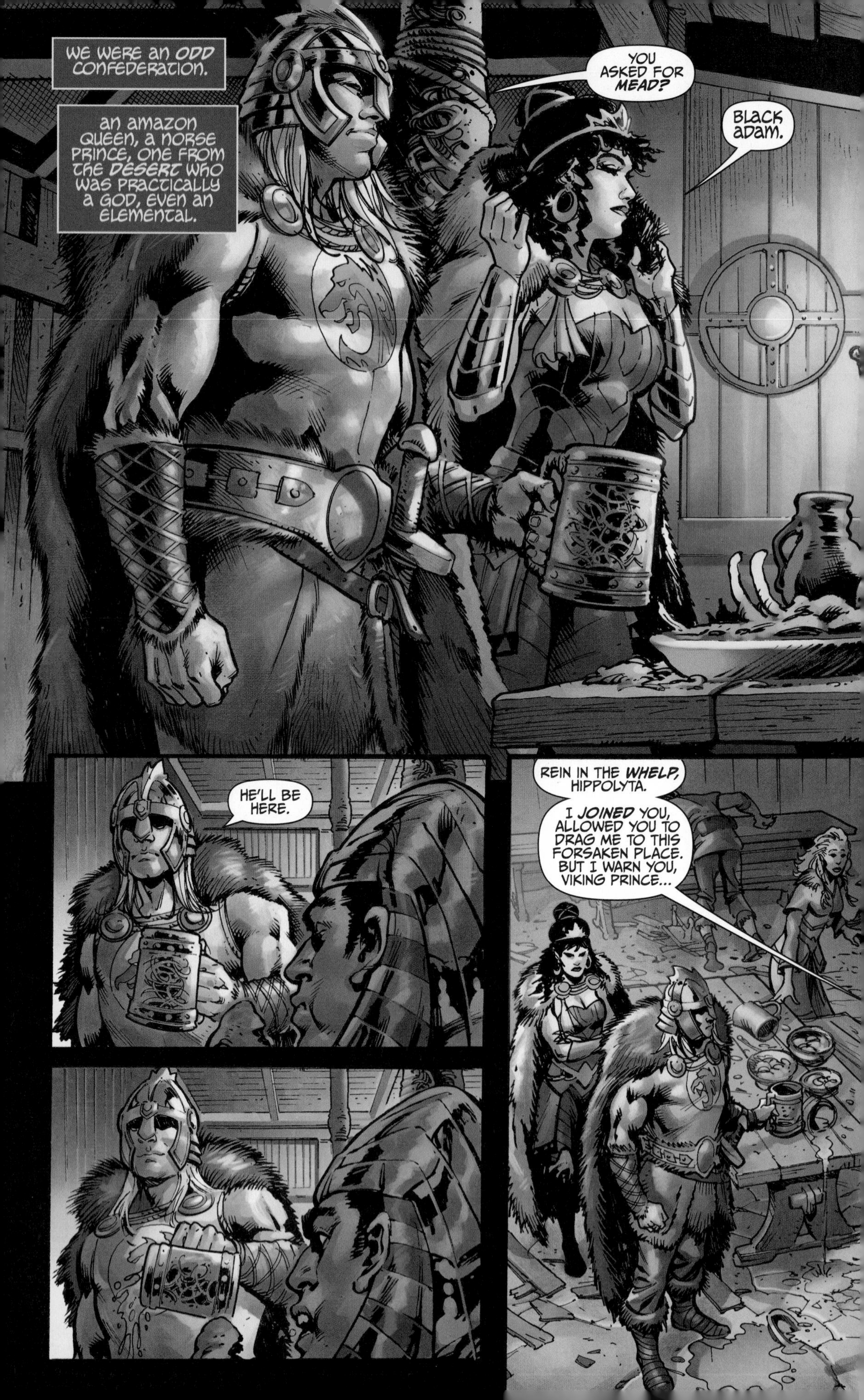
WE WERE AN ODD CONFEDERATION.
AN AMAZON QUEEN, A NORSE PRINCE, ONE FROM THE DESERT WHO WAS PRACTICALLY A GOD, EVEN AN ELEMENTAL.
YOU ASKED FOR MEAD?
BLACK ADAM.
HE'LL BE HERE.
REIN IN THE WHELP, HIPPOLYTA.
I JOINED YOU, ALLOWED YOU TO DRAG ME TO THIS FORSAKEN PLACE. BUT I WARN YOU, VIKING PRINCE...

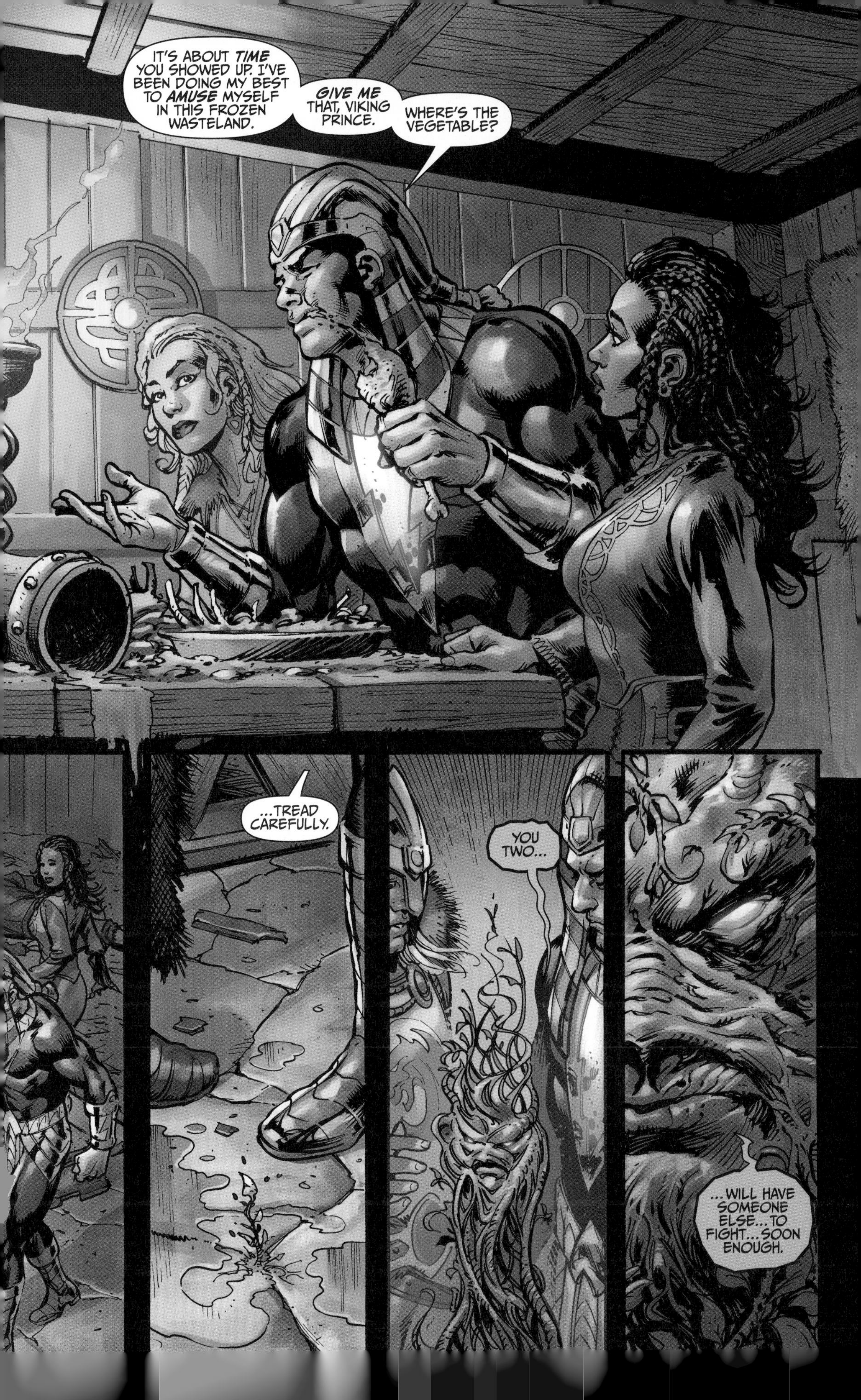
IT'S ABOUT *TIME* YOU SHOWED UP. I'VE BEEN DOING MY BEST TO *AMUSE* MYSELF IN THIS FROZEN WASTELAND.
GIVE ME THAT, VIKING PRINCE.
WHERE'S THE VEGETABLE?
...TREAD CAREFULLY.
YOU TWO...
...WILL HAVE SOMEONE ELSE...TO FIGHT...SOON ENOUGH.

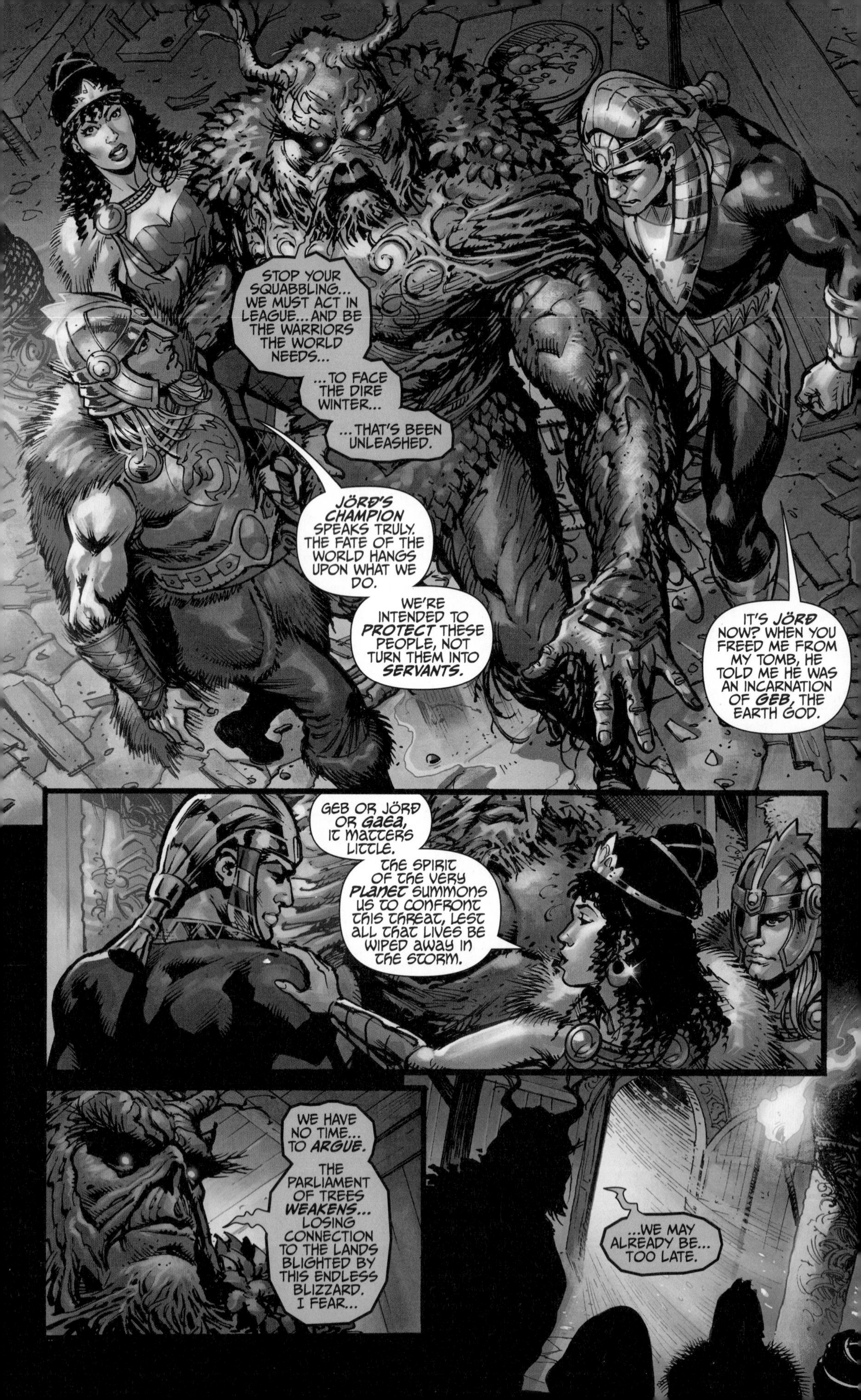
STOP YOUR SQUABBLING... WE MUST ACT IN LEAGUE...AND BE THE WARRIORS THE WORLD NEEDS...
...TO FACE THE DIRE WINTER...
...THAT'S BEEN UNLEASHED.
JÖRÐ'S CHAMPION SPEAKS TRULY. THE FATE OF THE WORLD HANGS UPON WHAT WE DO.
WE'RE INTENDED TO PROTECT THESE PEOPLE, NOT TURN THEM INTO SERVANTS.
IT'S JÖRÐ NOW? WHEN YOU FREED ME FROM MY TOMB, HE TOLD ME HE WAS AN INCARNATION OF GEB, THE EARTH GOD.
GEB OR JÖRÐ OR GAEA, IT MATTERS LITTLE.
THE SPIRIT OF THE VERY PLANET SUMMONS US TO CONFRONT THIS THREAT, LEST ALL THAT LIVES BE WIPED AWAY IN THE STORM.
WE HAVE NO TIME... TO ARGUE.
THE PARLIAMENT OF TREES WEAKENS... LOSING CONNECTION TO THE LANDS BLIGHTED BY THIS ENDLESS BLIZZARD. I FEAR...
...WE MAY ALREADY BE... TOO LATE.

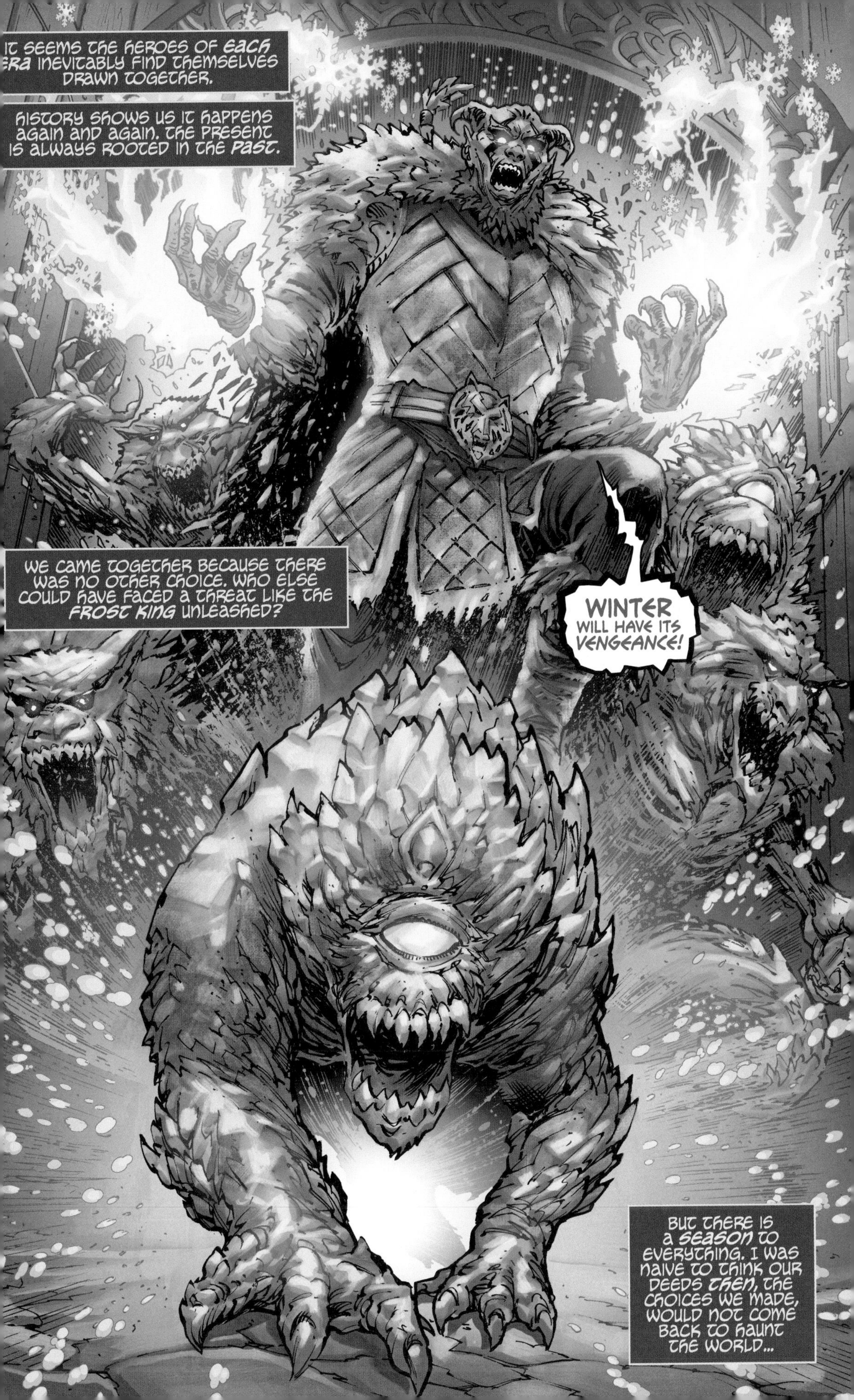
IT SEEMS THE HEROES OF EACH ERA INEVITABLY FIND THEMSELVES DRAWN TOGETHER.
HISTORY SHOWS US IT HAPPENS AGAIN AND AGAIN. THE PRESENT IS ALWAYS ROOTED IN THE PAST.
WE CAME TOGETHER BECAUSE THERE WAS NO OTHER CHOICE. WHO ELSE COULD HAVE FACED A THREAT LIKE THE FROST KING UNLEASHED?
WINTER WILL HAVE ITS VENGEANCE!
BUT THERE IS A SEASON TO EVERYTHING. I WAS NAIVE TO THINK OUR DEEDS THEN, THE CHOICES WE MADE, WOULD NOT COME BACK TO HAUNT THE WORLD...

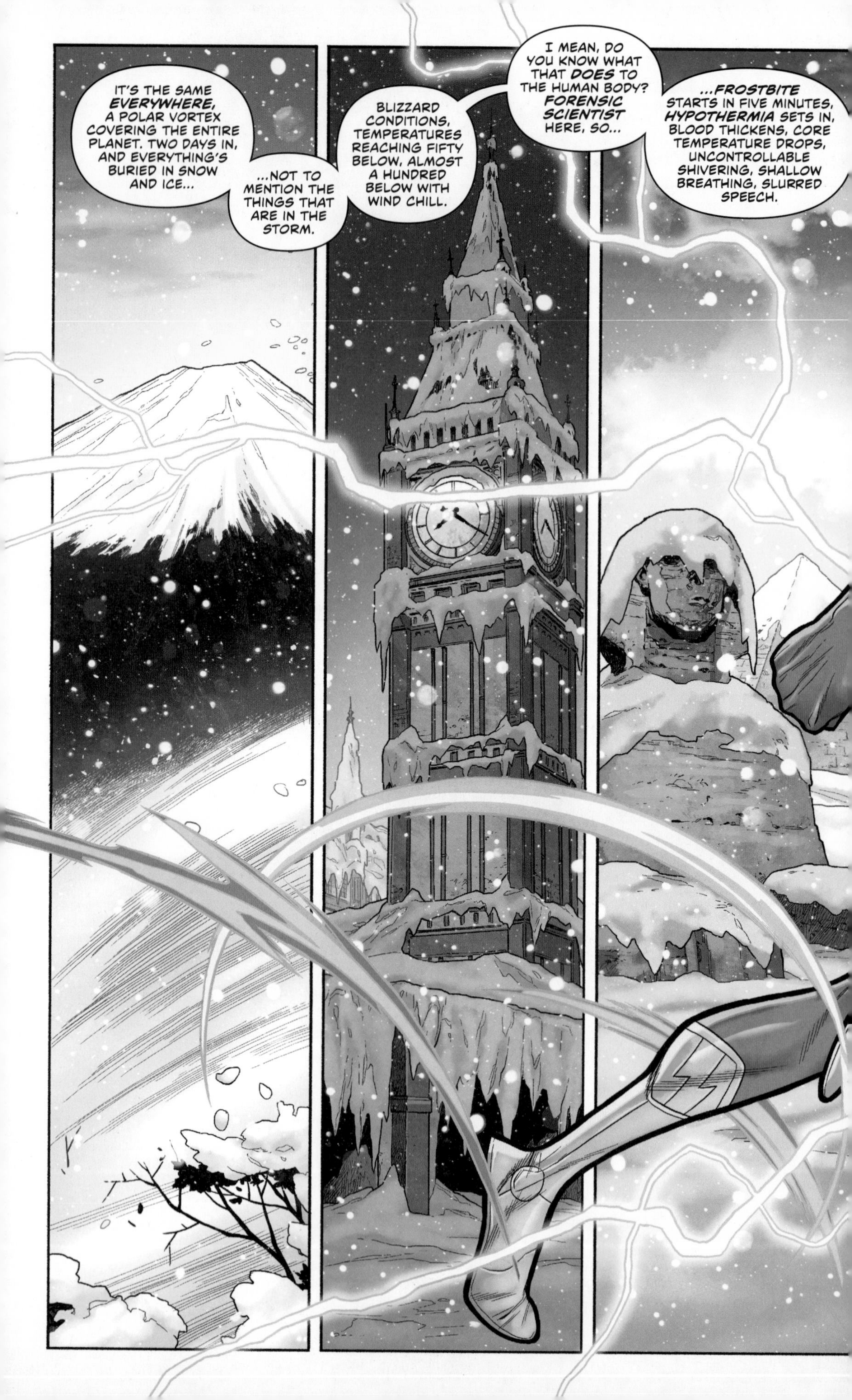
IT'S THE SAME EVERYWHERE, A POLAR VORTEX COVERING THE ENTIRE PLANET. TWO DAYS IN, AND EVERYTHING'S BURIED IN SNOW AND ICE...
...NOT TO MENTION THE THINGS THAT ARE IN THE STORM.
BLIZZARD CONDITIONS, TEMPERATURES REACHING FIFTY BELOW, ALMOST A HUNDRED BELOW WITH WIND CHILL.
I MEAN, DO YOU KNOW WHAT THAT DOES TO THE HUMAN BODY? FORENSIC SCIENTIST HERE, SO...
...FROSTBITE STARTS IN FIVE MINUTES, HYPOTHERMIA SETS IN, BLOOD THICKENS, CORE TEMPERATURE DROPS, UNCONTROLLABLE SHIVERING, SHALLOW BREATHING, SLURRED SPEECH.

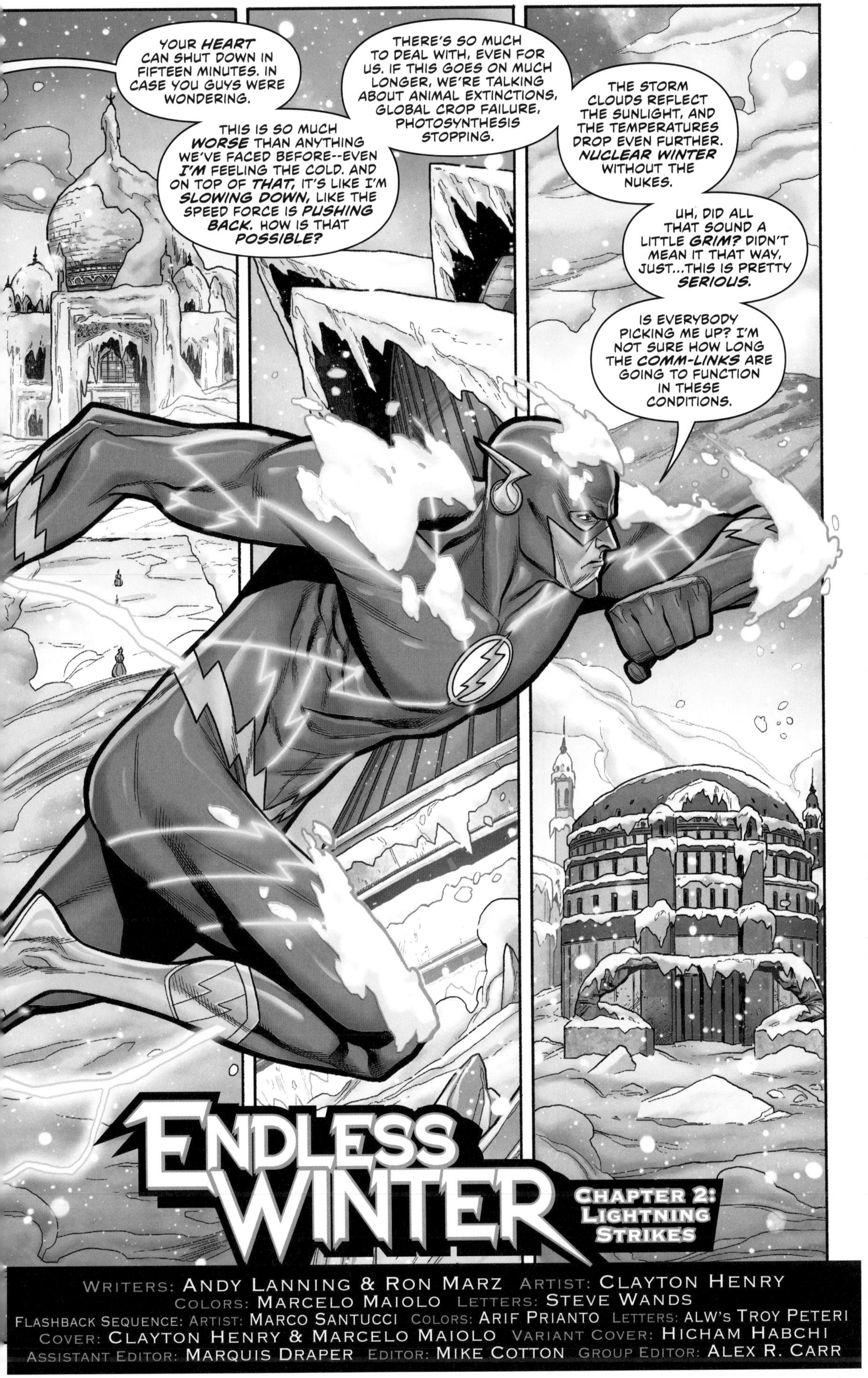
YOUR HEART CAN SHUT DOWN IN FIFTEEN MINUTES. IN CASE YOU GUYS WERE WONDERING.
THIS IS SO MUCH WORSE THAN ANYTHING WE'VE FACED BEFORE--EVEN I'M FEELING THE COLD. AND ON TOP OF THAT, IT'S LIKE I'M SLOWING DOWN, LIKE THE SPEED FORCE IS PUSHING BACK. HOW IS THAT POSSIBLE?
THERE'S SO MUCH TO DEAL WITH, EVEN FOR US. IF THIS GOES ON MUCH LONGER, WE'RE TALKING ABOUT ANIMAL EXTINCTIONS, GLOBAL CROP FAILURE, PHOTOSYNTHESIS STOPPING.
THE STORM CLOUDS REFLECT THE SUNLIGHT, AND THE TEMPERATURES DROP EVEN FURTHER. NUCLEAR WINTER WITHOUT THE NUKES.
UH, DID ALL THAT SOUND A LITTLE GRIM? DIDN'T MEAN IT THAT WAY, JUST...THIS IS PRETTY SERIOUS.
IS EVERYBODY PICKING ME UP? I'M NOT SURE HOW LONG THE COMM-LINKS ARE GOING TO FUNCTION IN THESE CONDITIONS.
ENDLESS WINTER
CHAPTER 2: LIGHTNING STRIKES

WRITERS: ANDY LANNING & RON MARZ ARTIST: CLAYTON HENRY
COLORS: MARCELO MAIOLO LETTERS: STEVE WANDS
FLASHBACK SEQUENCE: ARTIST: MARCO SANTUCCI COLORS: ARIF PRIANTO LETTERS: ALW's TROY PETERI
COVER: CLAYTON HENRY & MARCELO MAIOLO VARIANT COVER: HICHAM HABCHI
ASSISTANT EDITOR: MARQUIS DRAPER EDITOR: MIKE COTTON GROUP EDITOR: ALEX R. CARR

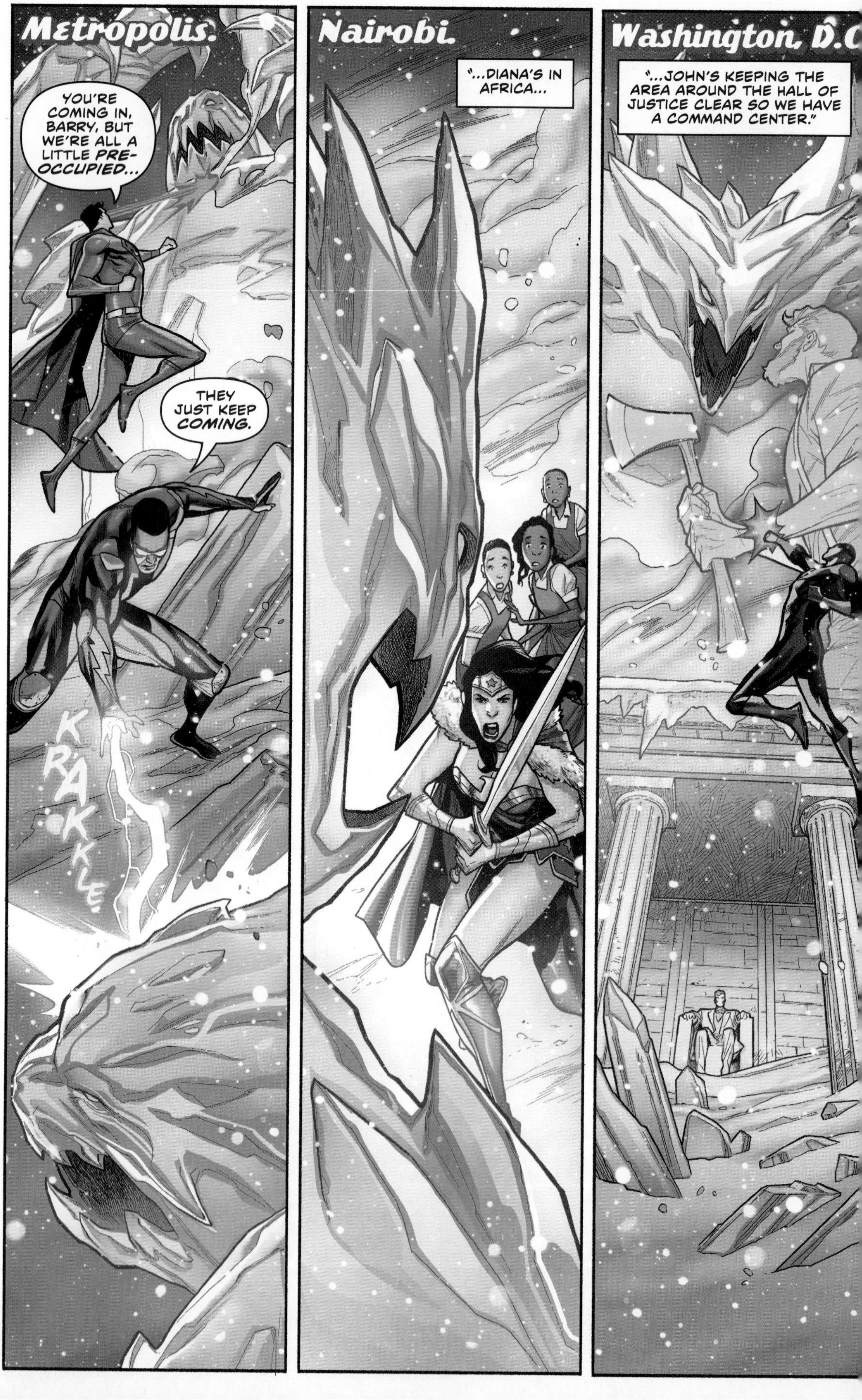
Metropolis.
YOU'RE COMING IN, BARRY, BUT WE'RE ALL A LITTLE PRE-OCCUPIED...
THEY JUST KEEP COMING.
KRAKKLE
Nairobi.
"...DIANA'S IN AFRICA...
Washington, D.C.
"...JOHN'S KEEPING THE AREA AROUND THE HALL OF JUSTICE CLEAR SO WE HAVE A COMMAND CENTER."

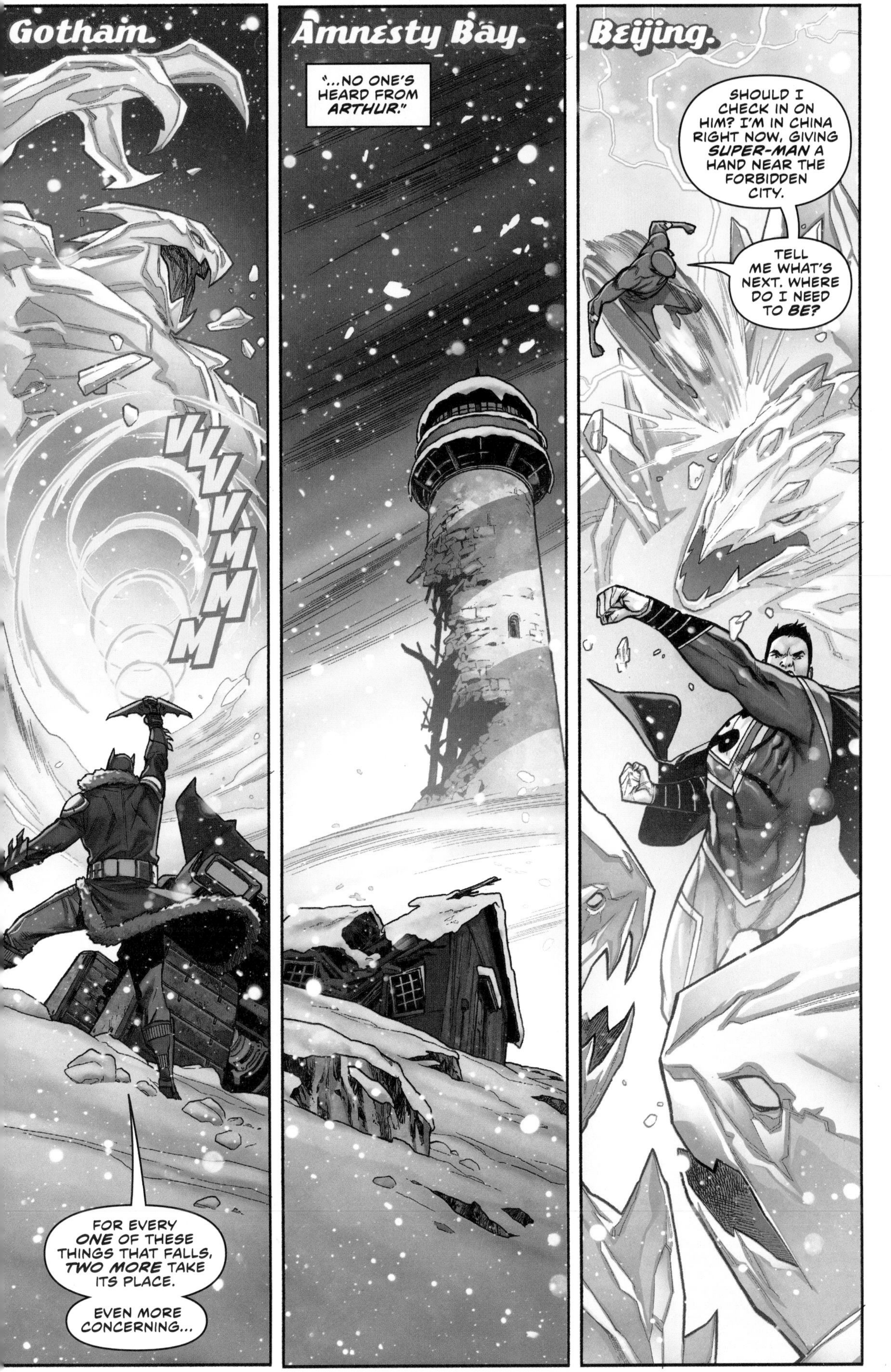

Gotham.
VVVVMMMM
FOR EVERY ONE OF THESE THINGS THAT FALLS, TWO MORE TAKE ITS PLACE.
EVEN MORE CONCERNING...
Amnesty Bay.
"...NO ONE'S HEARD FROM ARTHUR."
Beijing.
SHOULD I CHECK IN ON HIM? I'M IN CHINA RIGHT NOW, GIVING SUPER-MAN A HAND NEAR THE FORBIDDEN CITY.
TELL ME WHAT'S NEXT. WHERE DO I NEED TO BE?

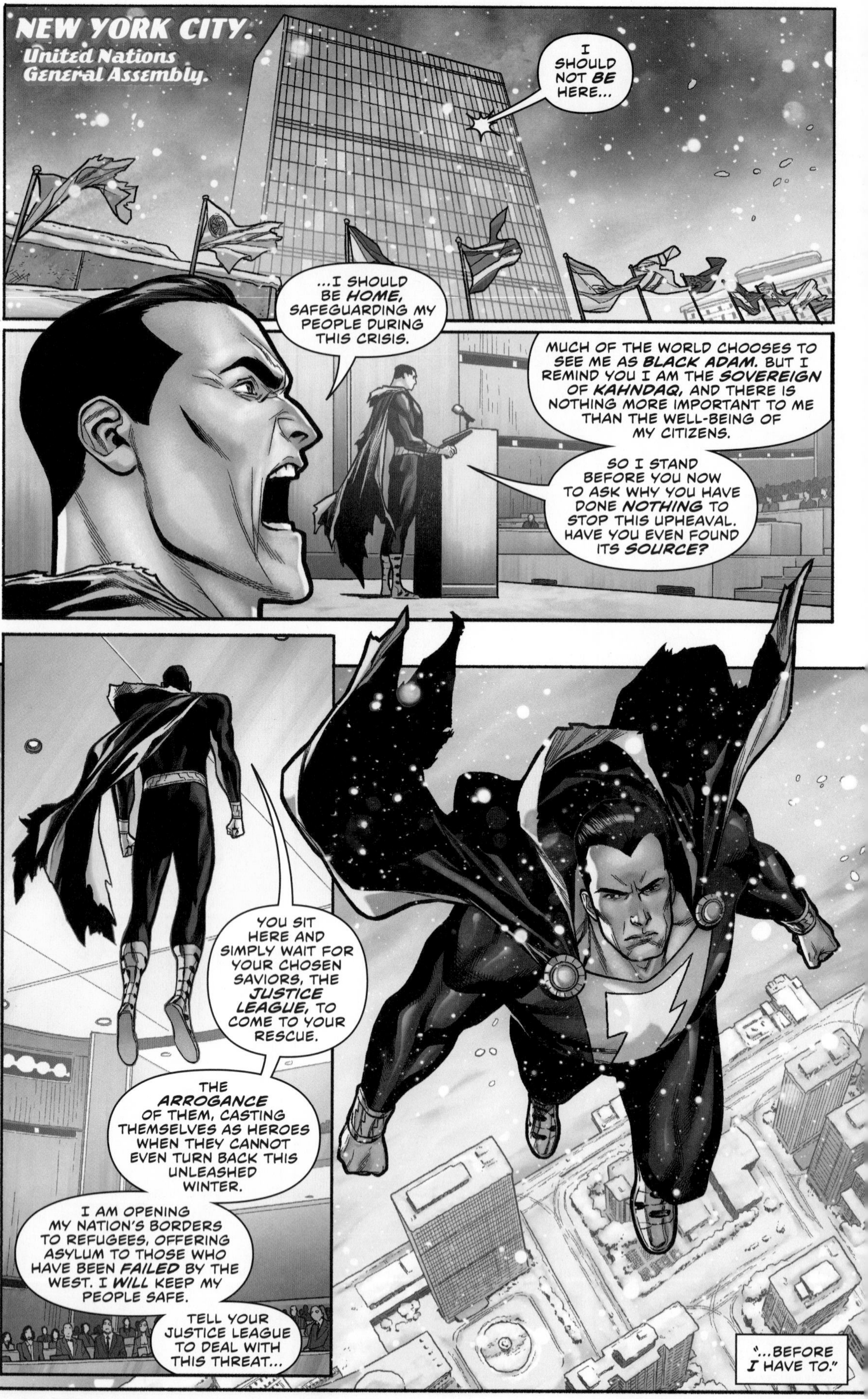
NEW YORK CITY.
United Nations General Assembly.
I SHOULD NOT BE HERE...
...I SHOULD BE HOME, SAFEGUARDING MY PEOPLE DURING THIS CRISIS.
MUCH OF THE WORLD CHOOSES TO SEE ME AS BLACK ADAM. BUT I REMIND YOU I AM THE SOVEREIGN OF KAHNDAQ, AND THERE IS NOTHING MORE IMPORTANT TO ME THAN THE WELL-BEING OF MY CITIZENS.
SO I STAND BEFORE YOU NOW TO ASK WHY YOU HAVE DONE NOTHING TO STOP THIS UPHEAVAL. HAVE YOU EVEN FOUND ITS SOURCE?
YOU SIT HERE AND SIMPLY WAIT FOR YOUR CHOSEN SAVIORS, THE JUSTICE LEAGUE, TO COME TO YOUR RESCUE.
THE ARROGANCE OF THEM, CASTING THEMSELVES AS HEROES WHEN THEY CANNOT EVEN TURN BACK THIS UNLEASHED WINTER.
I AM OPENING MY NATION'S BORDERS TO REFUGEES, OFFERING ASYLUM TO THOSE WHO HAVE BEEN FAILED BY THE WEST. I WILL KEEP MY PEOPLE SAFE.
TELL YOUR JUSTICE LEAGUE TO DEAL WITH THIS THREAT...
"...BEFORE I HAVE TO."

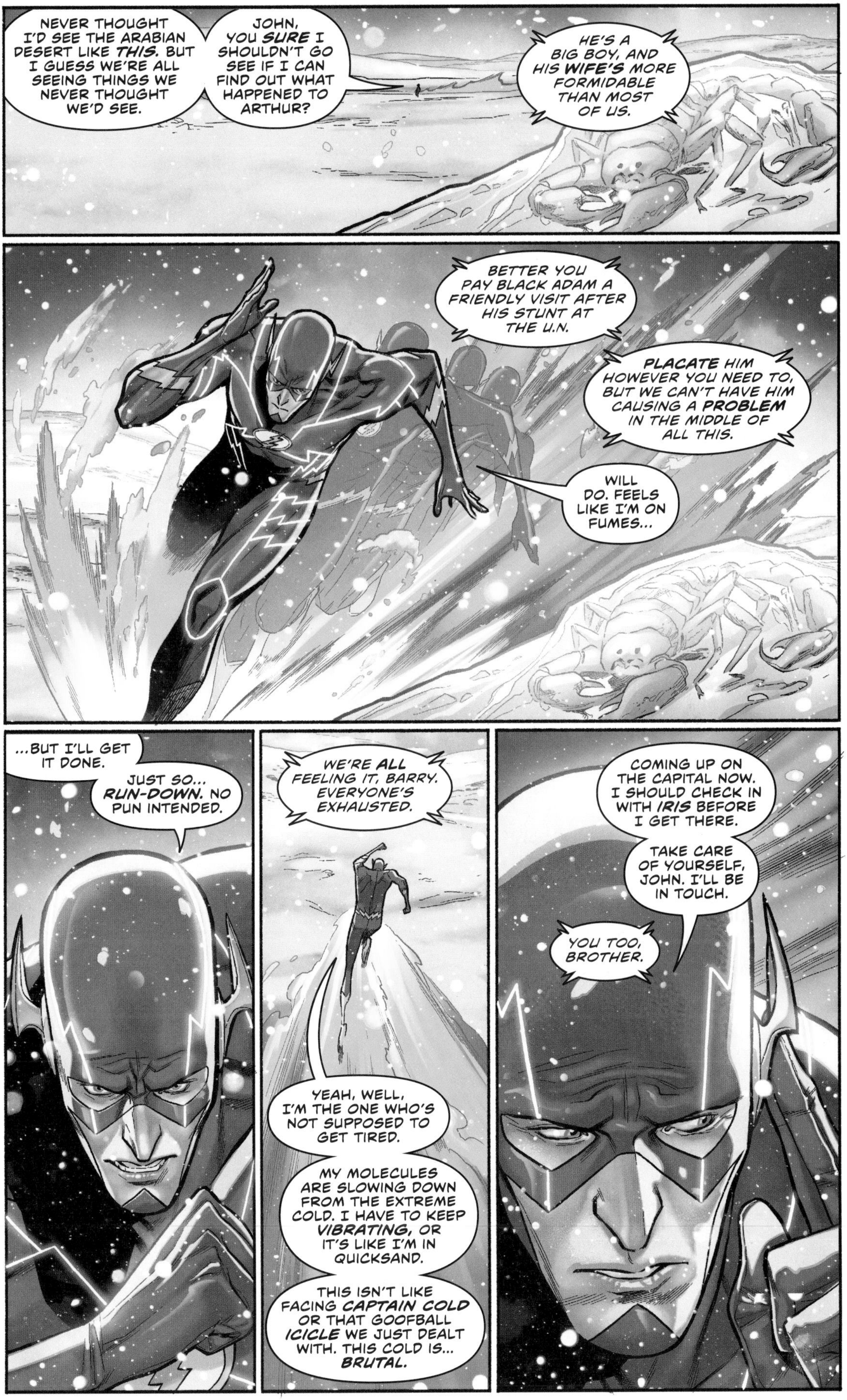
NEVER THOUGHT I'D SEE THE ARABIAN DESERT LIKE THIS. BUT I GUESS WE'RE ALL SEEING THINGS WE NEVER THOUGHT WE'D SEE.
JOHN, YOU SURE I SHOULDN'T GO SEE IF I CAN FIND OUT WHAT HAPPENED TO ARTHUR?
HE'S A BIG BOY, AND HIS WIFE'S MORE FORMIDABLE THAN MOST OF US.
BETTER YOU PAY BLACK ADAM A FRIENDLY VISIT AFTER HIS STUNT AT THE U.N.
PLACATE HIM HOWEVER YOU NEED TO, BUT WE CAN'T HAVE HIM CAUSING A PROBLEM IN THE MIDDLE OF ALL THIS.
WILL DO. FEELS LIKE I'M ON FUMES...
...BUT I'LL GET IT DONE.
JUST SO... RUN-DOWN. NO PUN INTENDED.
WE'RE ALL FEELING IT, BARRY. EVERYONE'S EXHAUSTED.
YEAH, WELL, I'M THE ONE WHO'S NOT SUPPOSED TO GET TIRED.
MY MOLECULES ARE SLOWING DOWN FROM THE EXTREME COLD. I HAVE TO KEEP VIBRATING, OR IT'S LIKE I'M IN QUICKSAND.
THIS ISN'T LIKE FACING CAPTAIN COLD OR THAT GOOFBALL ICICLE WE JUST DEALT WITH. THIS COLD IS... BRUTAL.
COMING UP ON THE CAPITAL NOW. I SHOULD CHECK IN WITH IRIS BEFORE I GET THERE.
TAKE CARE OF YOURSELF, JOHN. I'LL BE IN TOUCH.
YOU TOO, BROTHER.

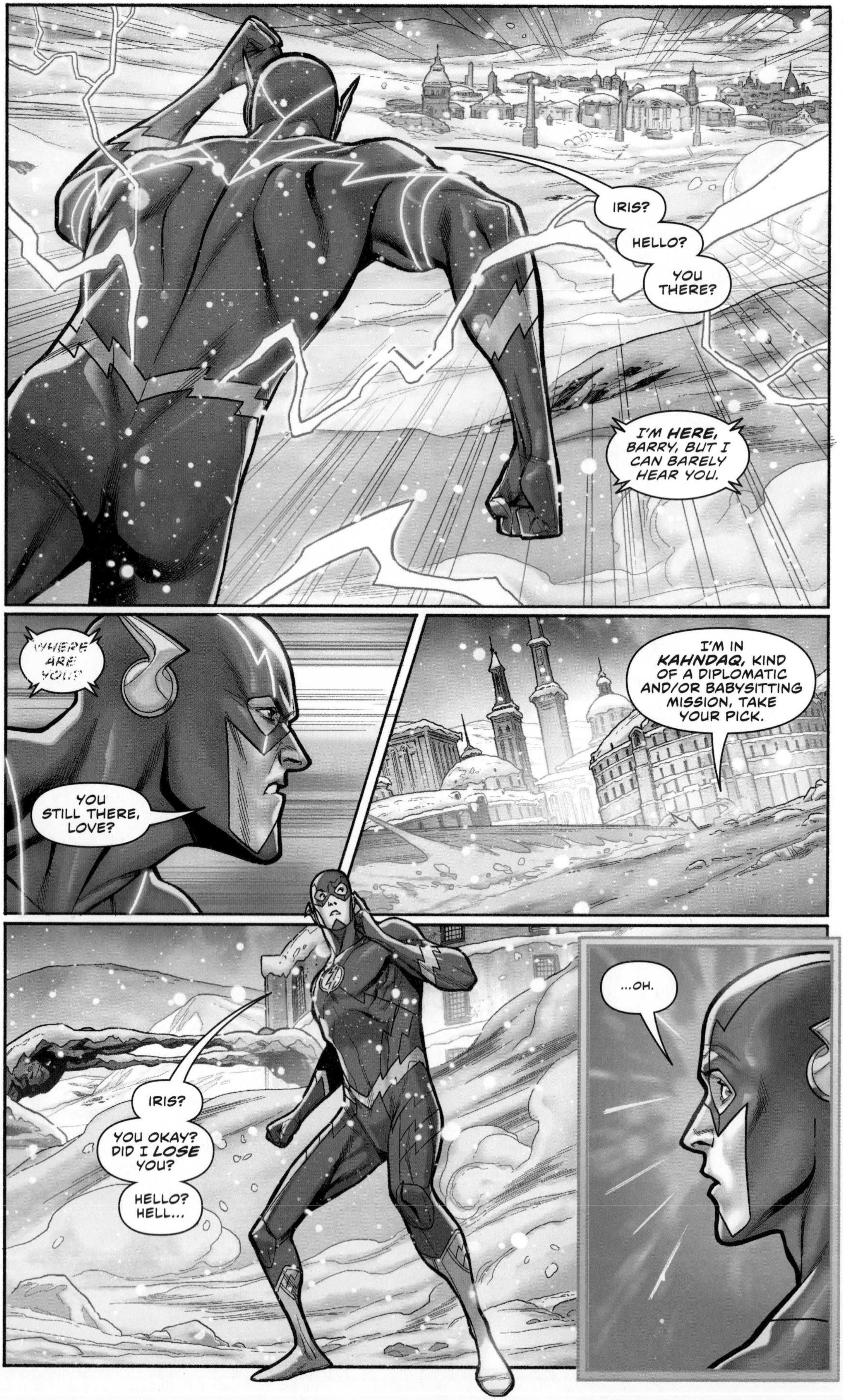
IRIS?
HELLO?
YOU THERE?
I'M *HERE,* BARRY, BUT I CAN BARELY HEAR YOU.
WHERE ARE YOU?
YOU STILL THERE, LOVE?
I'M IN *KAHNDAQ,* KIND OF A DIPLOMATIC AND/OR BABYSITTING MISSION, TAKE YOUR PICK.
IRIS?
YOU OKAY? DID I *LOSE* YOU?
HELLO? HELL...
...OH.

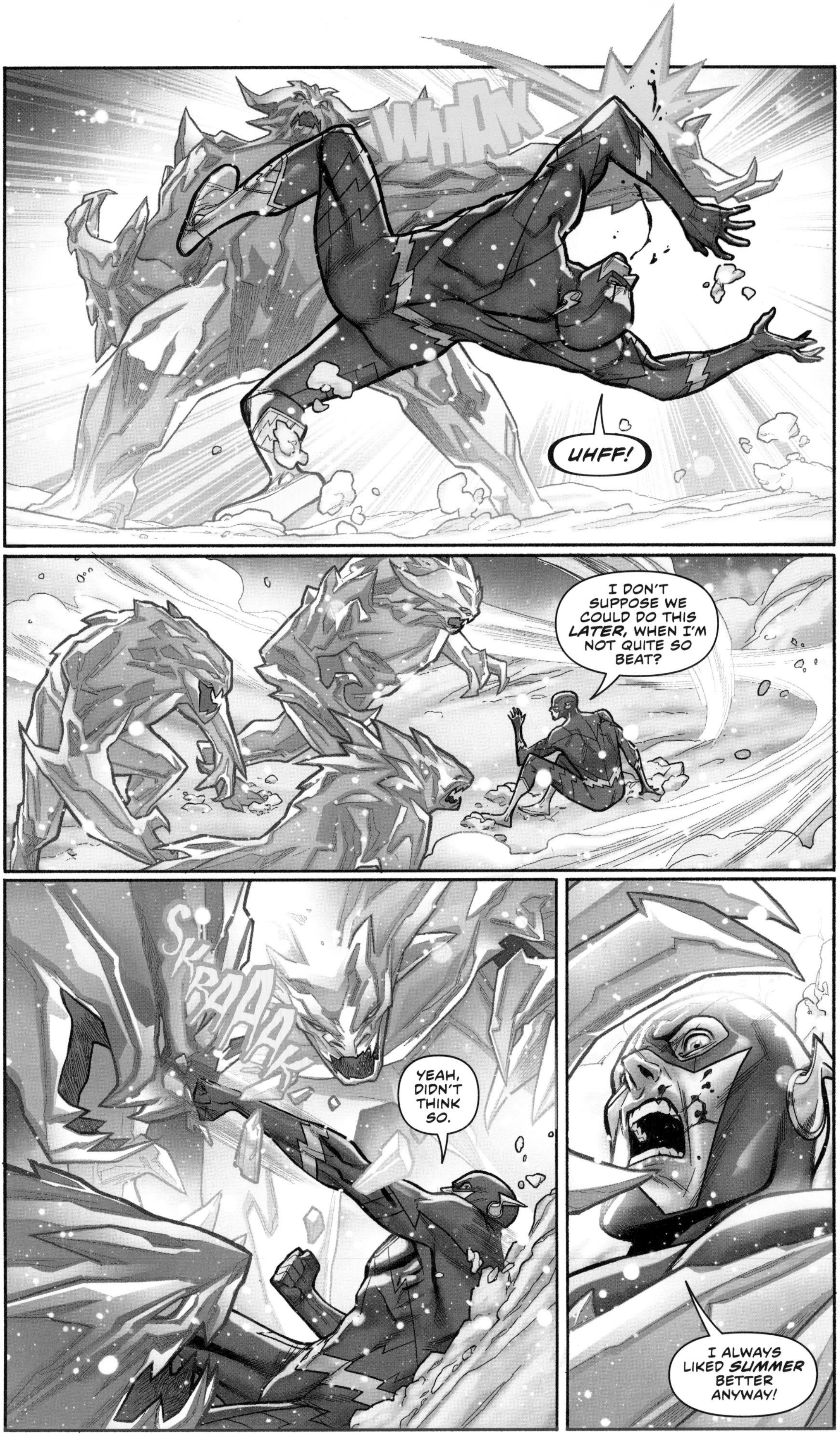
WHAK
UHFF!
I DON'T SUPPOSE WE COULD DO THIS LATER, WHEN I'M NOT QUITE SO BEAT?
SKRAAAK
YEAH, DIDN'T THINK SO.
I ALWAYS LIKED SUMMER BETTER ANYWAY!

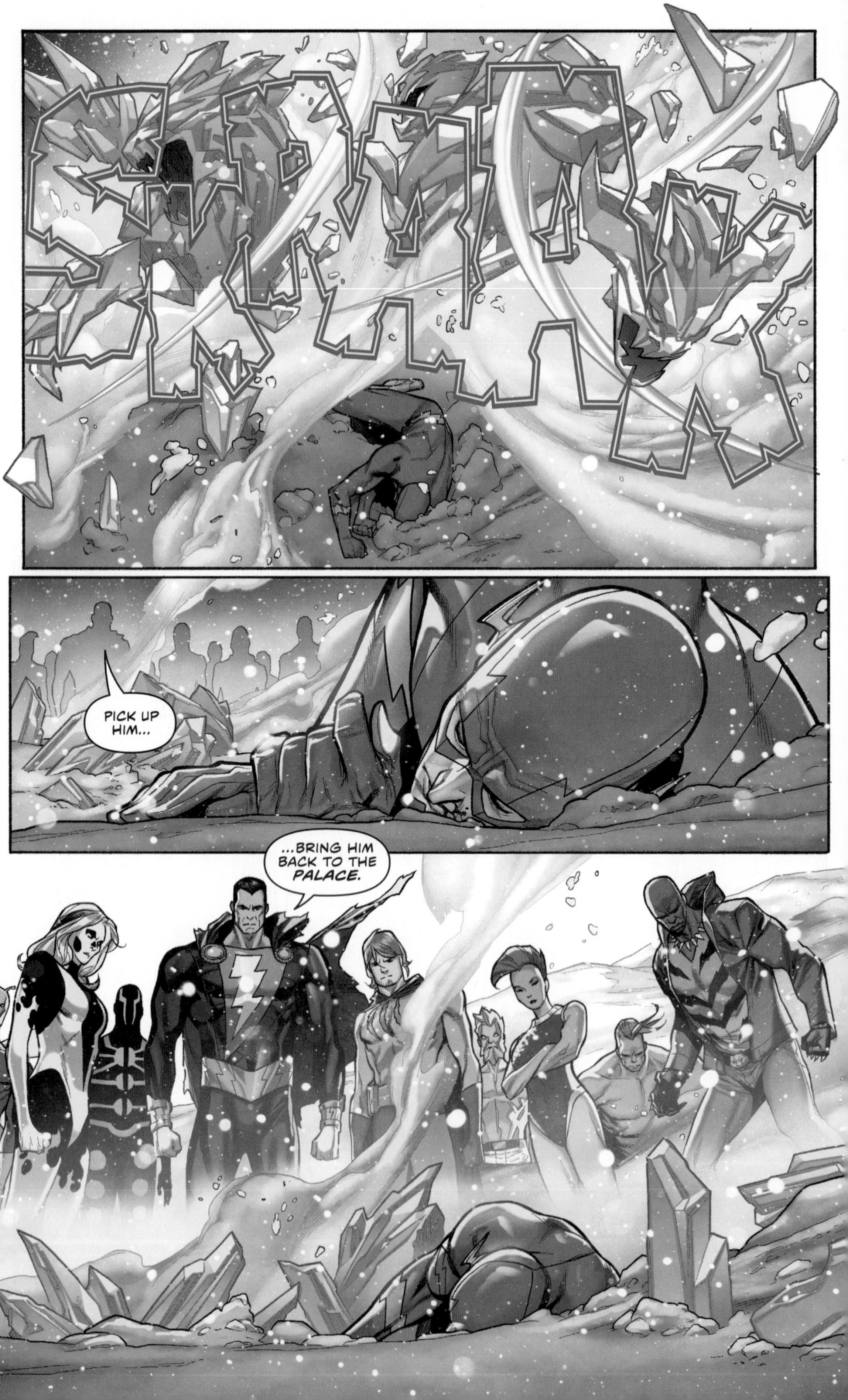
PICK UP HIM...
...BRING HIM BACK TO THE PALACE.

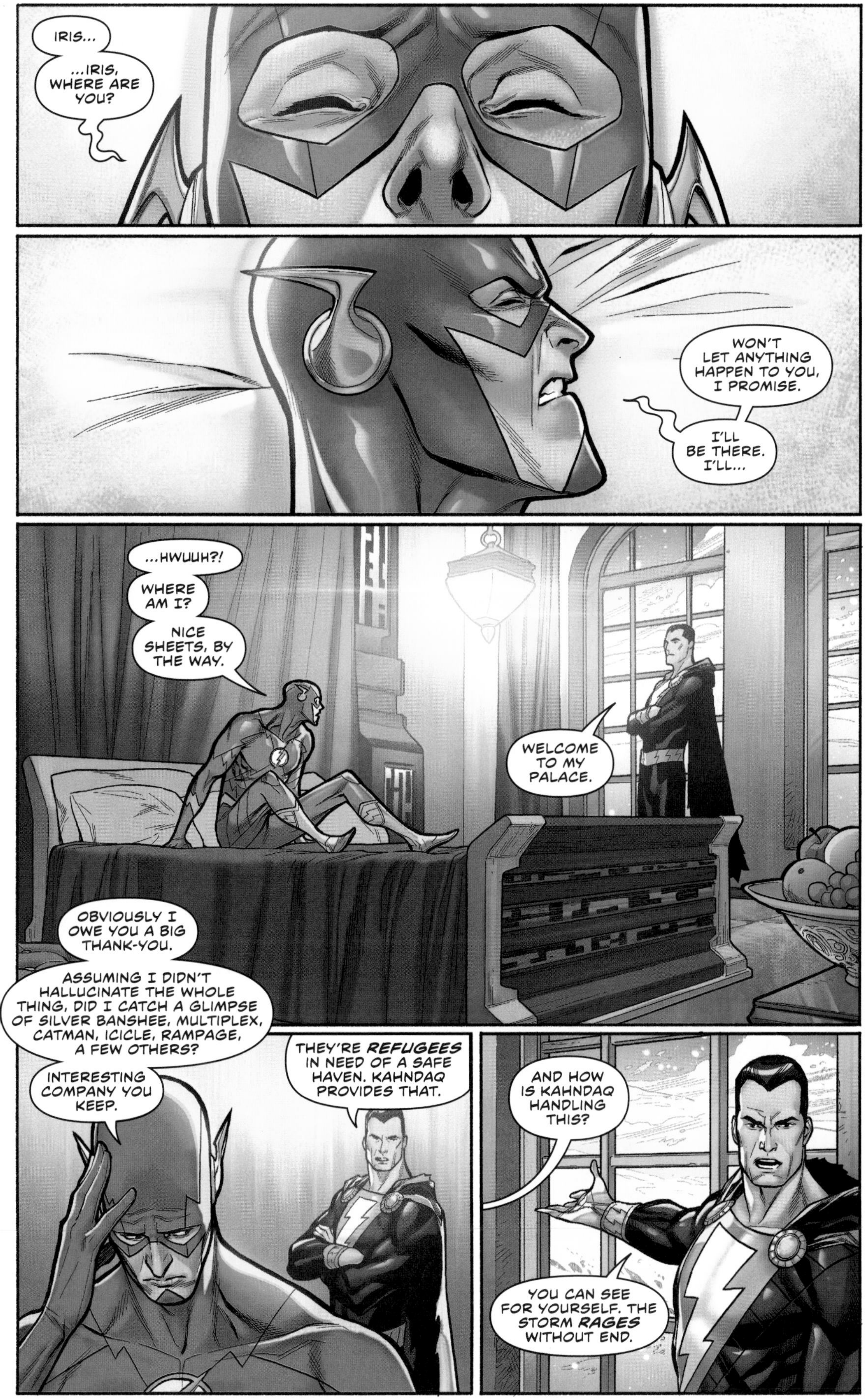
IRIS...
...IRIS, WHERE ARE YOU?
WON'T LET ANYTHING HAPPEN TO YOU, I PROMISE.
I'LL BE THERE. I'LL...
...HWUUH?!
WHERE AM I?
NICE SHEETS, BY THE WAY.
WELCOME TO MY PALACE.
OBVIOUSLY I OWE YOU A BIG THANK-YOU.
ASSUMING I DIDN'T HALLUCINATE THE WHOLE THING, DID I CATCH A GLIMPSE OF SILVER BANSHEE, MULTIPLEX, CATMAN, ICICLE, RAMPAGE, A FEW OTHERS?
INTERESTING COMPANY YOU KEEP.
THEY'RE *REFUGEES* IN NEED OF A SAFE HAVEN. KAHNDAQ PROVIDES THAT.
AND HOW IS KAHNDAQ HANDLING THIS?
YOU CAN SEE FOR YOURSELF. THE STORM *RAGES* WITHOUT END.

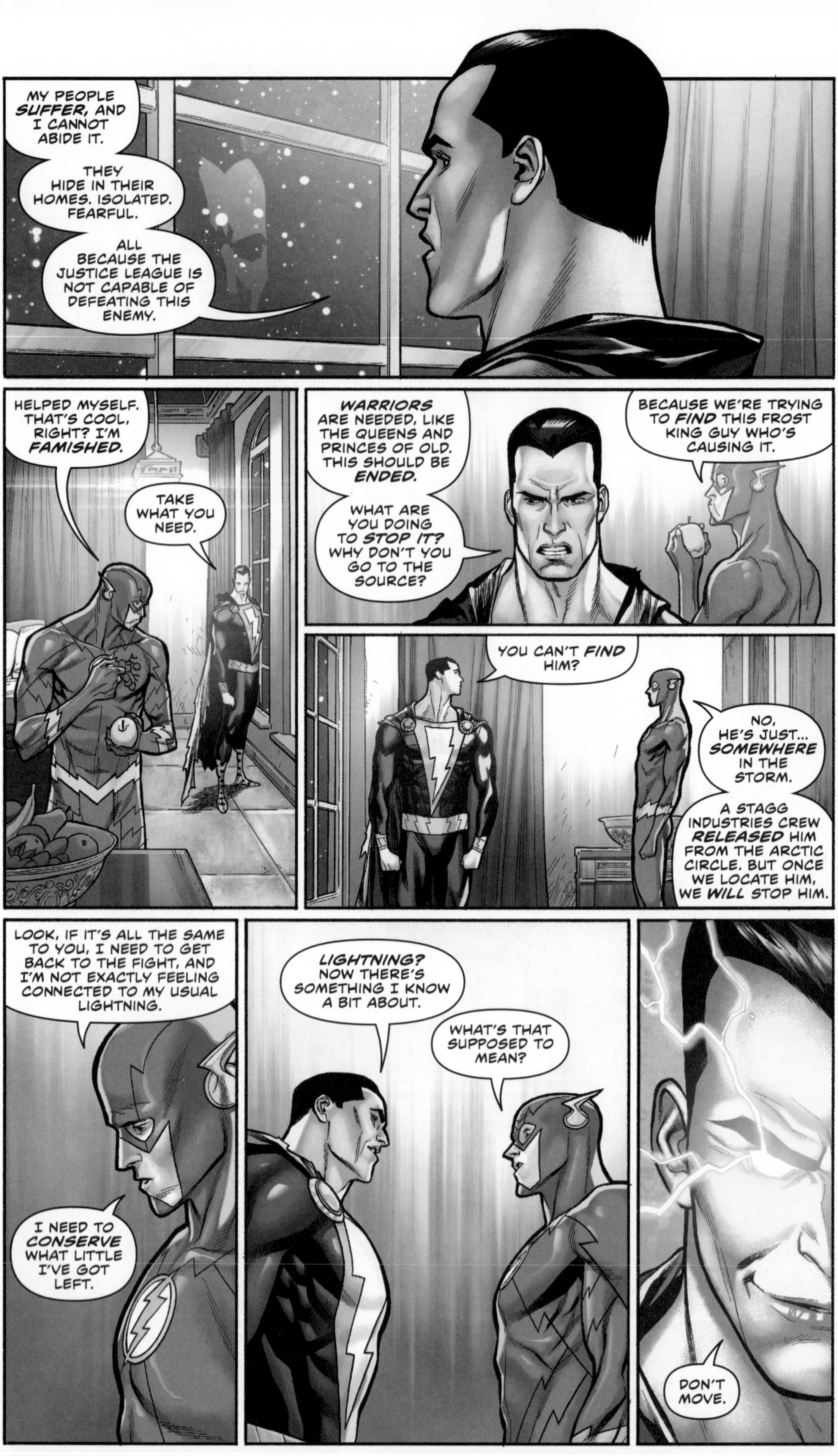
MY PEOPLE SUFFER, AND I CANNOT ABIDE IT.
THEY HIDE IN THEIR HOMES. ISOLATED. FEARFUL.
ALL BECAUSE THE JUSTICE LEAGUE IS NOT CAPABLE OF DEFEATING THIS ENEMY.
HELPED MYSELF. THAT'S COOL, RIGHT? I'M FAMISHED.
TAKE WHAT YOU NEED.
WARRIORS ARE NEEDED, LIKE THE QUEENS AND PRINCES OF OLD. THIS SHOULD BE ENDED.
WHAT ARE YOU DOING TO STOP IT? WHY DON'T YOU GO TO THE SOURCE?
BECAUSE WE'RE TRYING TO FIND THIS FROST KING GUY WHO'S CAUSING IT.
YOU CAN'T FIND HIM?
NO, HE'S JUST... SOMEWHERE IN THE STORM.
A STAGG INDUSTRIES CREW RELEASED HIM FROM THE ARCTIC CIRCLE. BUT ONCE WE LOCATE HIM, WE WILL STOP HIM.
LOOK, IF IT'S ALL THE SAME TO YOU, I NEED TO GET BACK TO THE FIGHT, AND I'M NOT EXACTLY FEELING CONNECTED TO MY USUAL LIGHTNING.
I NEED TO CONSERVE WHAT LITTLE I'VE GOT LEFT.
LIGHTNING? NOW THERE'S SOMETHING I KNOW A BIT ABOUT.
WHAT'S THAT SUPPOSED TO MEAN?
DON'T MOVE.

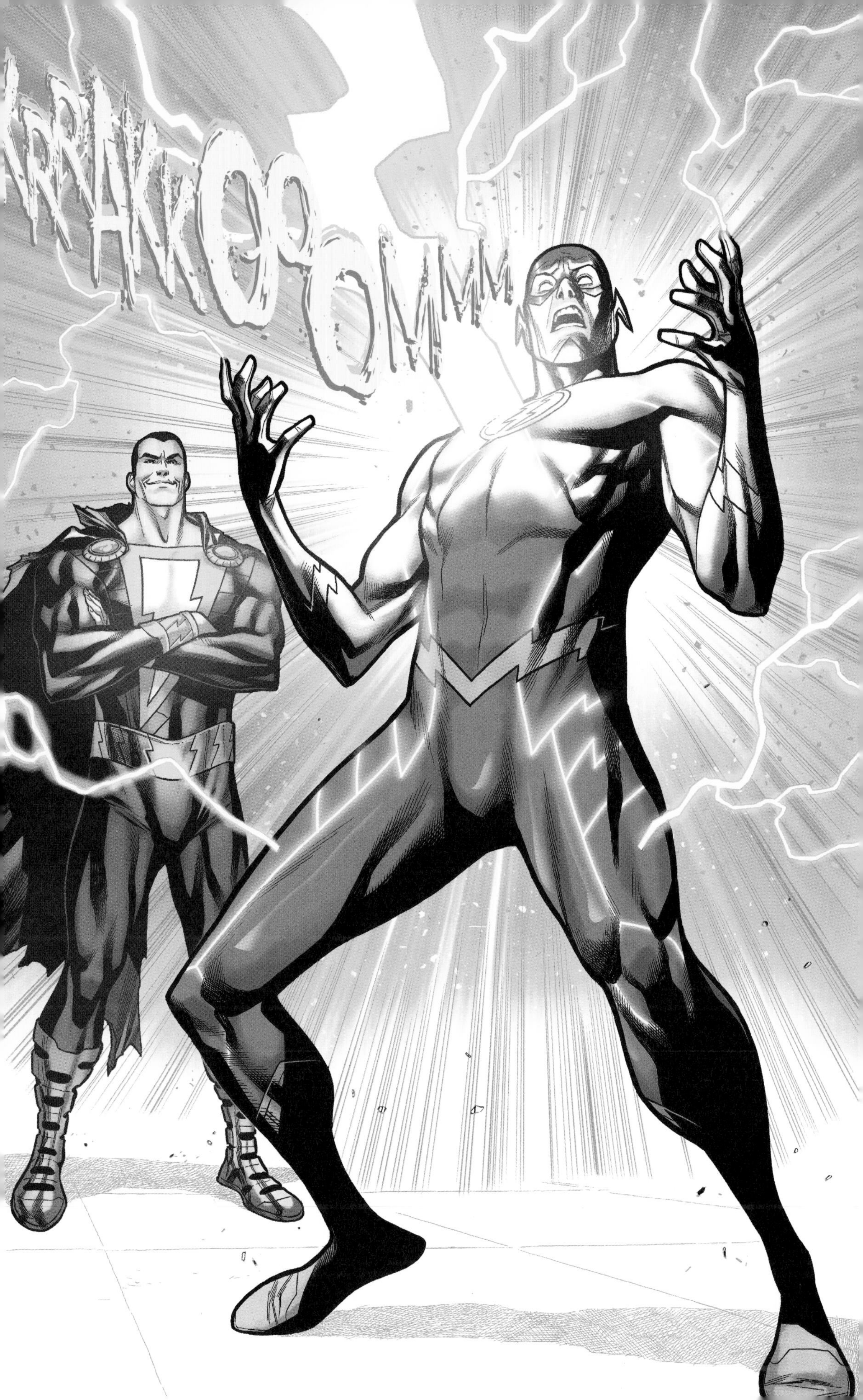
RRAKKOOOMMM

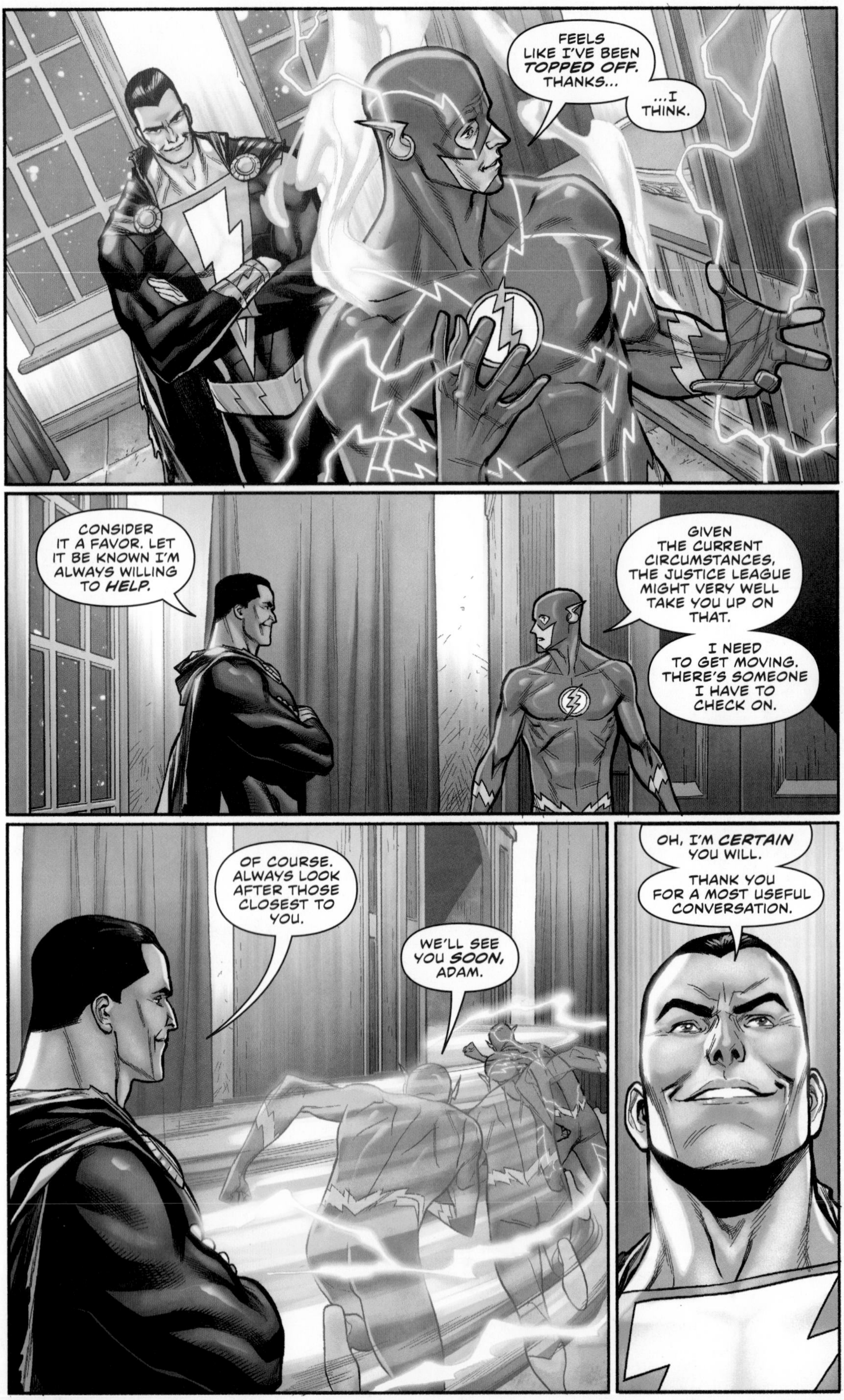
FEELS LIKE I'VE BEEN TOPPED OFF. THANKS...
...I THINK.
CONSIDER IT A FAVOR. LET IT BE KNOWN I'M ALWAYS WILLING TO HELP.
GIVEN THE CURRENT CIRCUMSTANCES, THE JUSTICE LEAGUE MIGHT VERY WELL TAKE YOU UP ON THAT.
I NEED TO GET MOVING. THERE'S SOMEONE I HAVE TO CHECK ON.
OF COURSE. ALWAYS LOOK AFTER THOSE CLOSEST TO YOU.
WE'LL SEE YOU SOON, ADAM.
OH, I'M CERTAIN YOU WILL.
THANK YOU FOR A MOST USEFUL CONVERSATION.

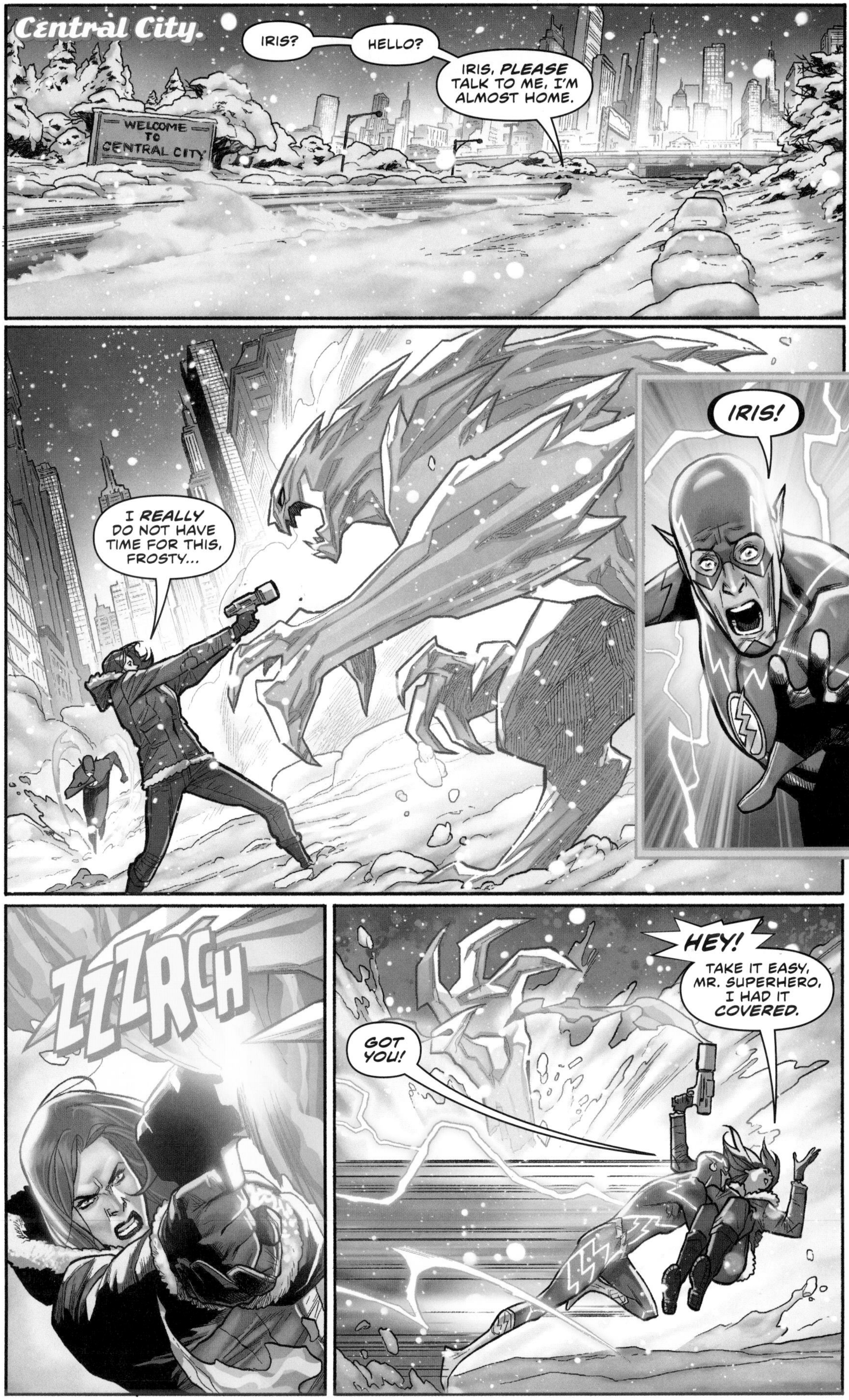
Central City.
IRIS?
HELLO?
IRIS, PLEASE TALK TO ME, I'M ALMOST HOME.
WELCOME TO CENTRAL CITY
I REALLY DO NOT HAVE TIME FOR THIS, FROSTY...
IRIS!
ZZZRCH
GOT YOU!
HEY!
TAKE IT EASY, MR. SUPERHERO, I HAD IT COVERED.

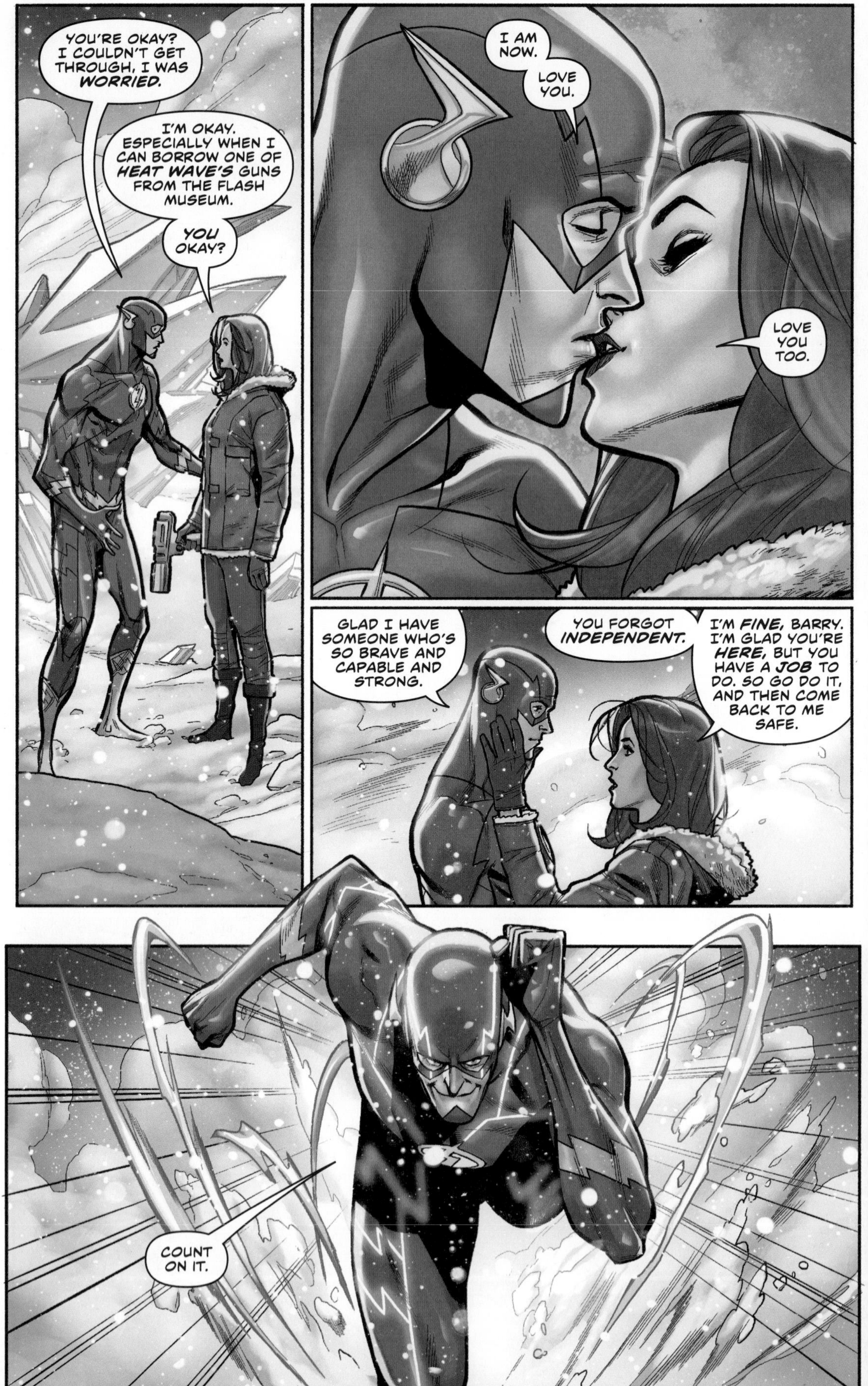
YOU'RE OKAY? I COULDN'T GET THROUGH, I WAS WORRIED.
I'M OKAY. ESPECIALLY WHEN I CAN BORROW ONE OF HEAT WAVE'S GUNS FROM THE FLASH MUSEUM.
YOU OKAY?
I AM NOW.
LOVE YOU.
LOVE YOU TOO.
GLAD I HAVE SOMEONE WHO'S SO BRAVE AND CAPABLE AND STRONG.
YOU FORGOT INDEPENDENT.
I'M FINE, BARRY. I'M GLAD YOU'RE HERE, BUT YOU HAVE A JOB TO DO. SO GO DO IT, AND THEN COME BACK TO ME SAFE.
COUNT ON IT.

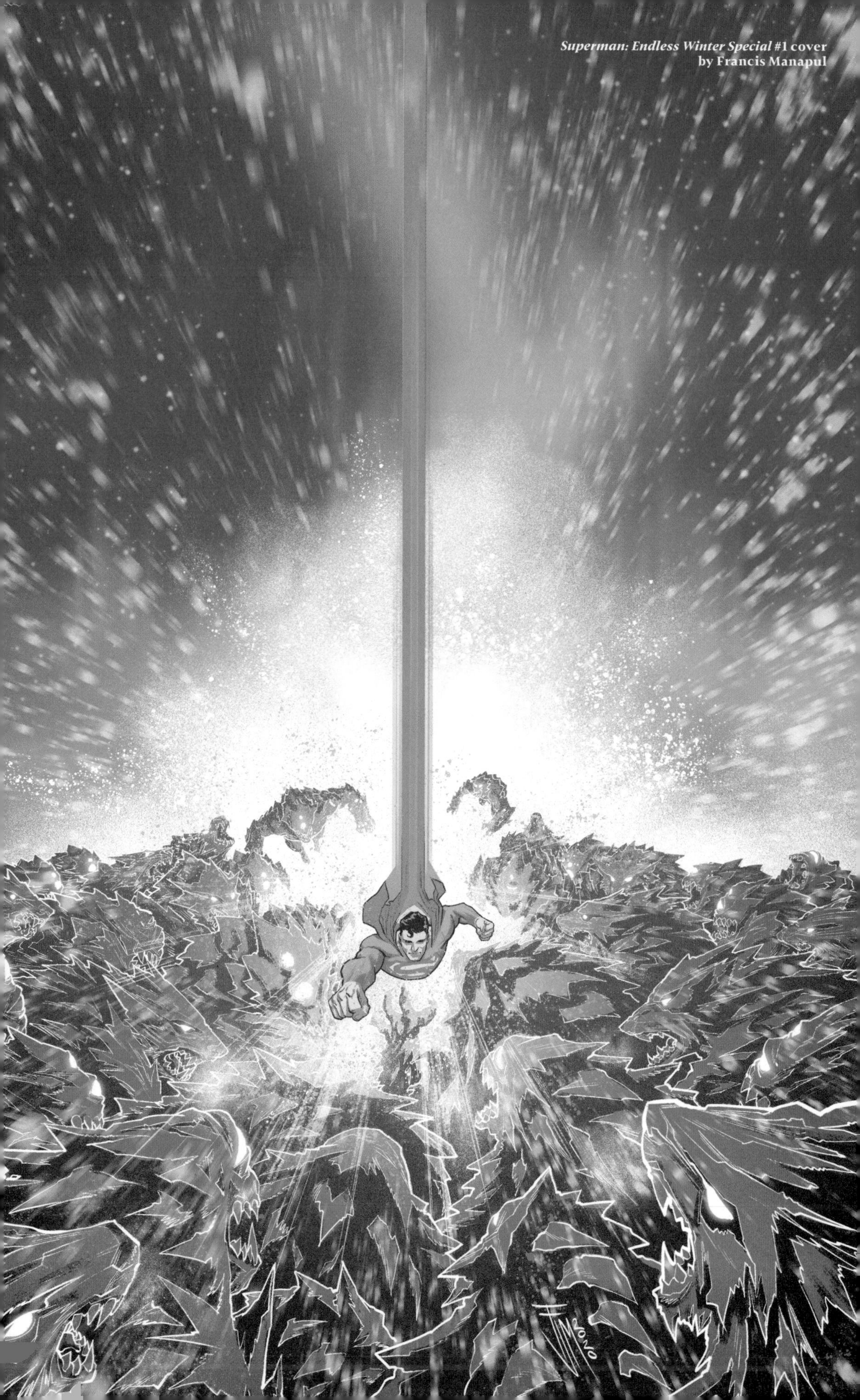

Superman: Endless Winter Special #1 cover
by Francis Manapul

***Superman: Endless Winter Special* #1 variant cover**
by Rafael Grassetti

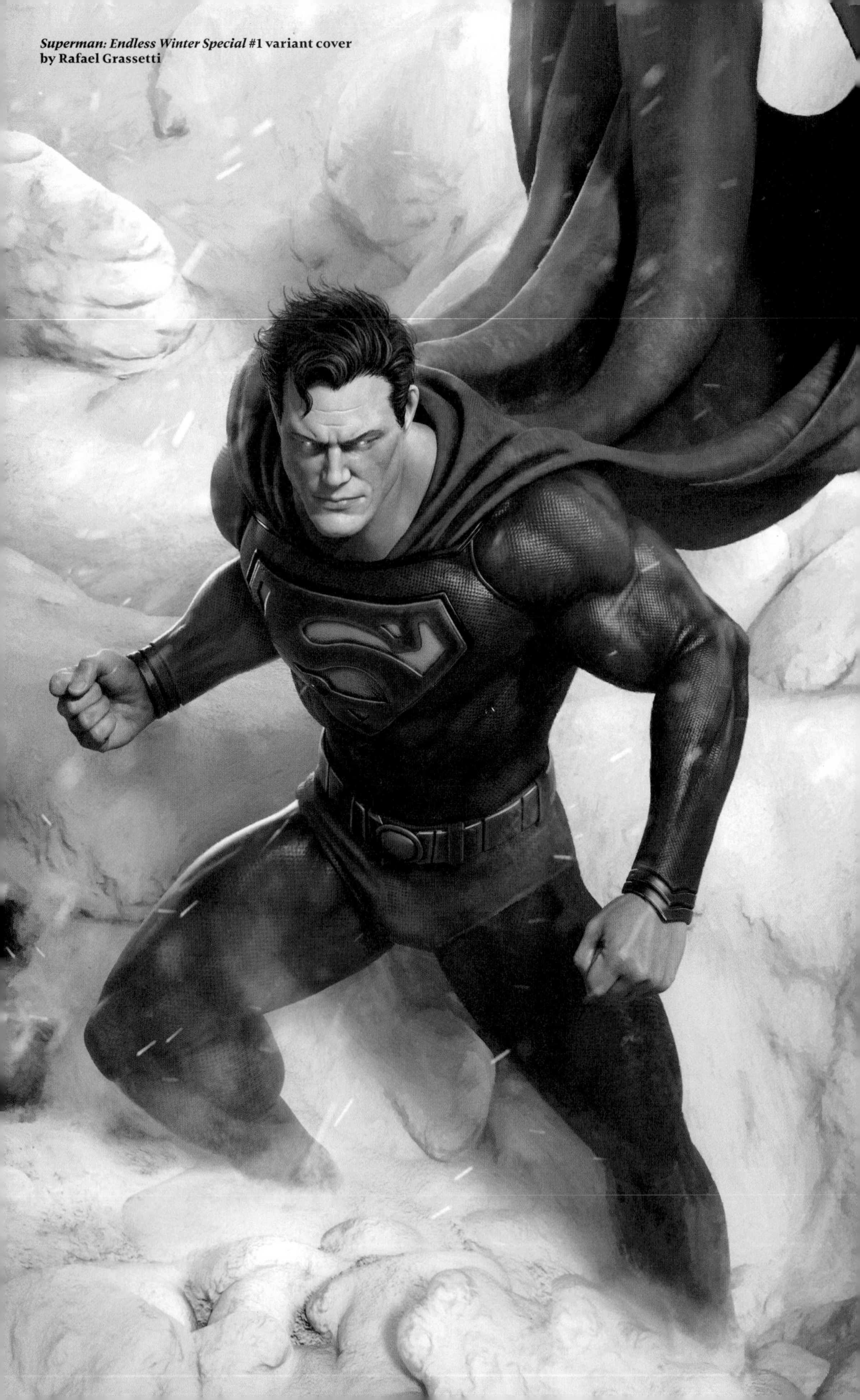

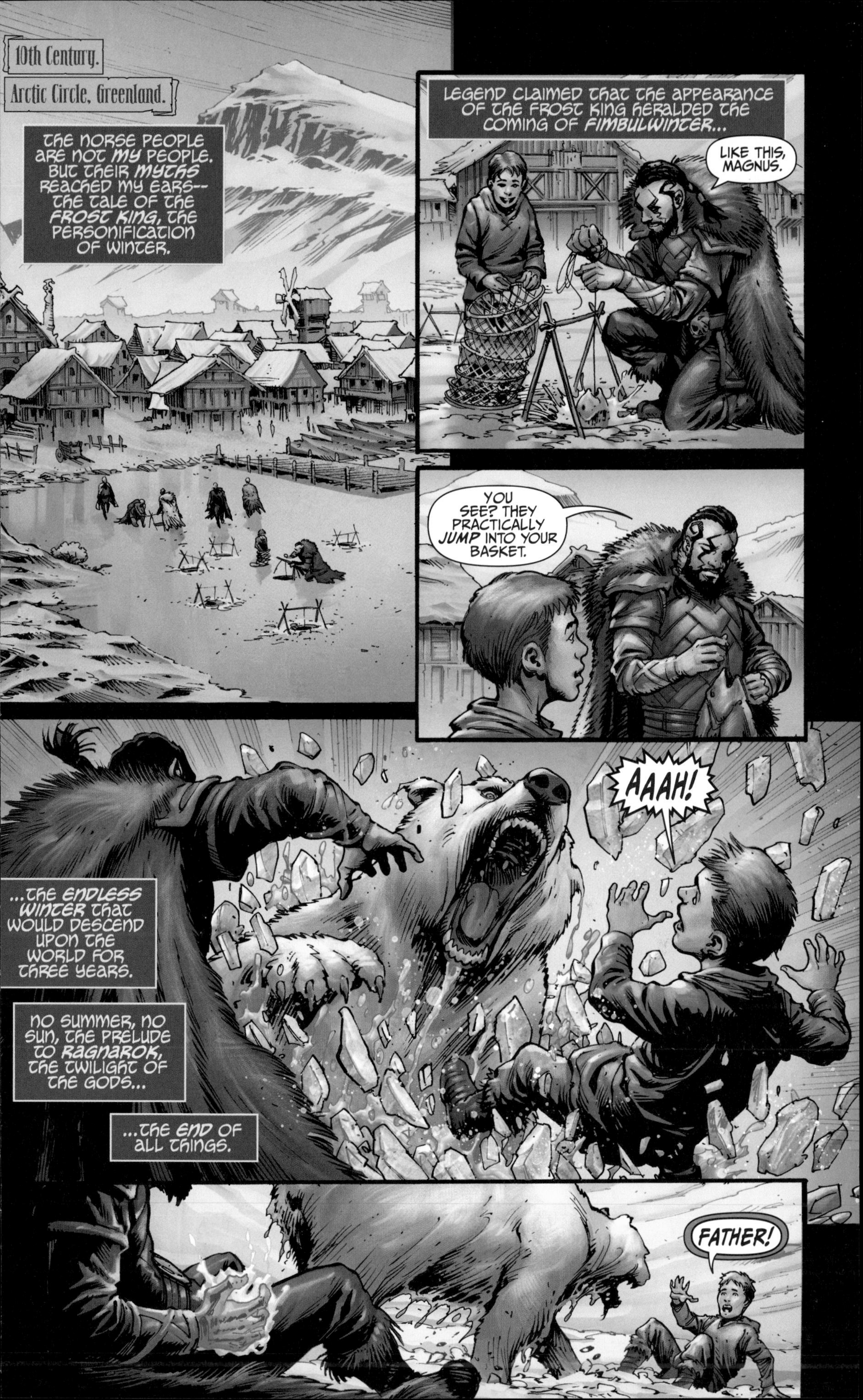

10th Century.
Arctic Circle, Greenland.
THE NORSE PEOPLE ARE NOT MY PEOPLE. BUT THEIR MYTHS REACHED MY EARS-- THE TALE OF THE FROST KING, THE PERSONIFICATION OF WINTER.
LEGEND CLAIMED THAT THE APPEARANCE OF THE FROST KING HERALDED THE COMING OF FIMBULWINTER...
LIKE THIS, MAGNUS.
YOU SEE? THEY PRACTICALLY JUMP INTO YOUR BASKET.
AAAH!
...THE ENDLESS WINTER THAT WOULD DESCEND UPON THE WORLD FOR THREE YEARS.
NO SUMMER, NO SUN, THE PRELUDE TO RAGNAROK, THE TWILIGHT OF THE GODS...
...THE END OF ALL THINGS.
FATHER!

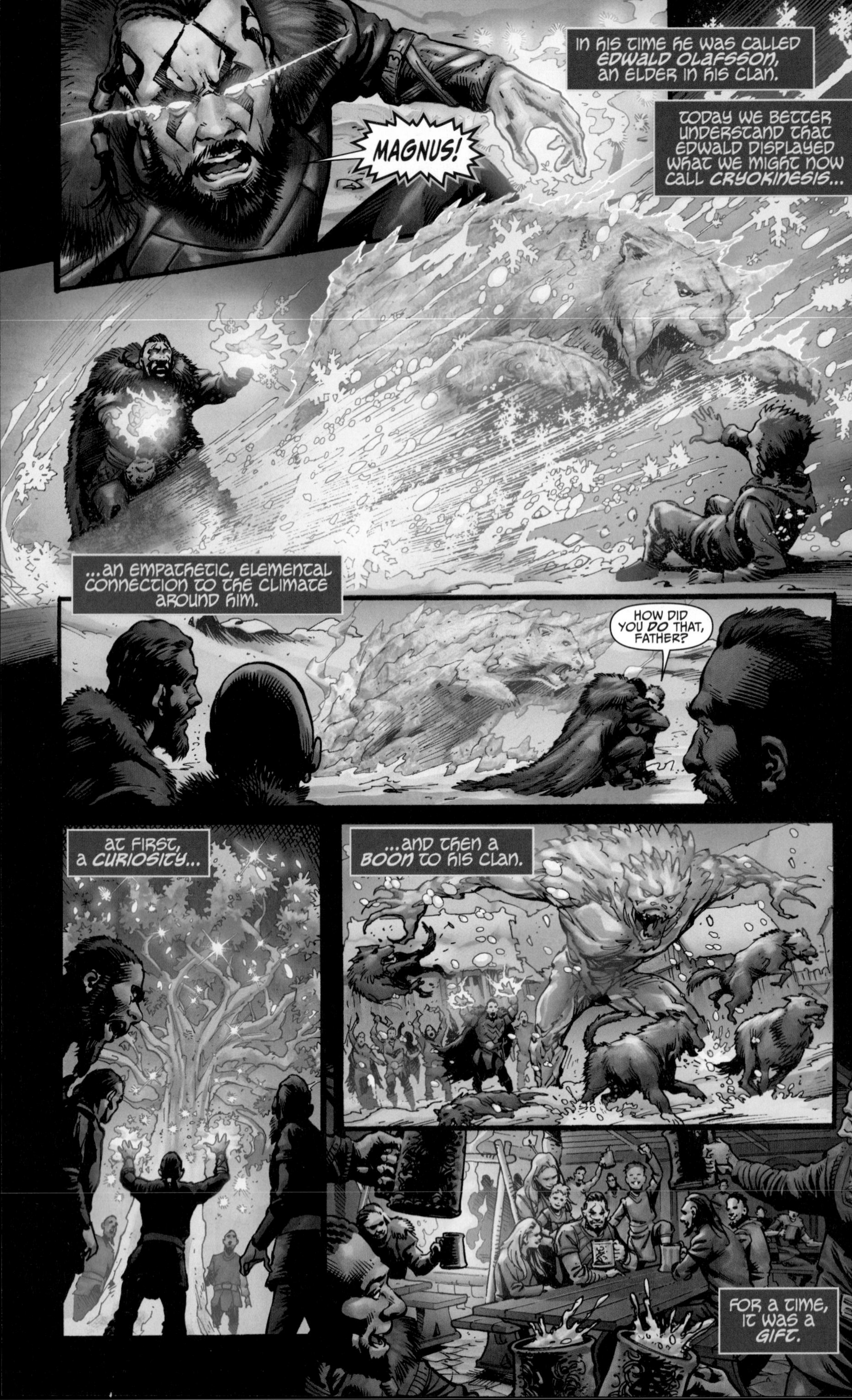

IN HIS TIME HE WAS CALLED EDWALD OLAFSSON, AN ELDER IN HIS CLAN.
MAGNUS!
TODAY WE BETTER UNDERSTAND THAT EDWALD DISPLAYED WHAT WE MIGHT NOW CALL CRYOKINESIS...
...AN EMPATHETIC, ELEMENTAL CONNECTION TO THE CLIMATE AROUND HIM.
HOW DID YOU DO THAT, FATHER?
AT FIRST, A CURIOSITY...
...AND THEN A BOON TO HIS CLAN.
FOR A TIME, IT WAS A GIFT.

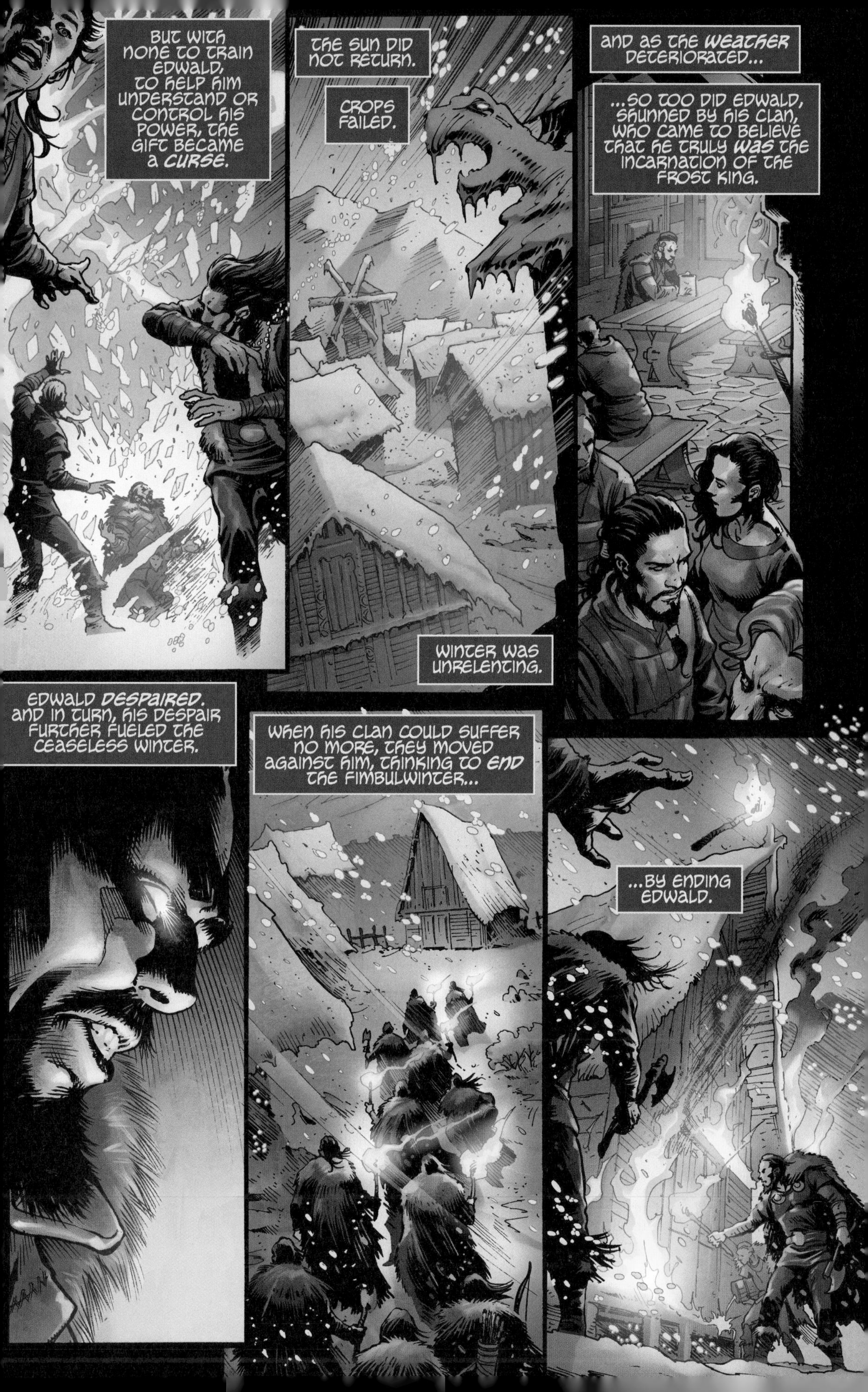
BUT WITH NONE TO TRAIN EDWALD, TO HELP HIM UNDERSTAND OR CONTROL HIS POWER, THE GIFT BECAME A *CURSE*.
THE SUN DID NOT RETURN.
CROPS FAILED.
WINTER WAS UNRELENTING.
AND AS THE *WEATHER* DETERIORATED...
...SO TOO DID EDWALD, SHUNNED BY HIS CLAN, WHO CAME TO BELIEVE THAT HE TRULY *WAS* THE INCARNATION OF THE FROST KING.
EDWALD *DESPAIRED*. AND IN TURN, HIS DESPAIR FURTHER FUELED THE CEASELESS WINTER.
WHEN HIS CLAN COULD SUFFER NO MORE, THEY MOVED AGAINST HIM, THINKING TO *END* THE FIMBULWINTER...
...BY ENDING EDWALD.

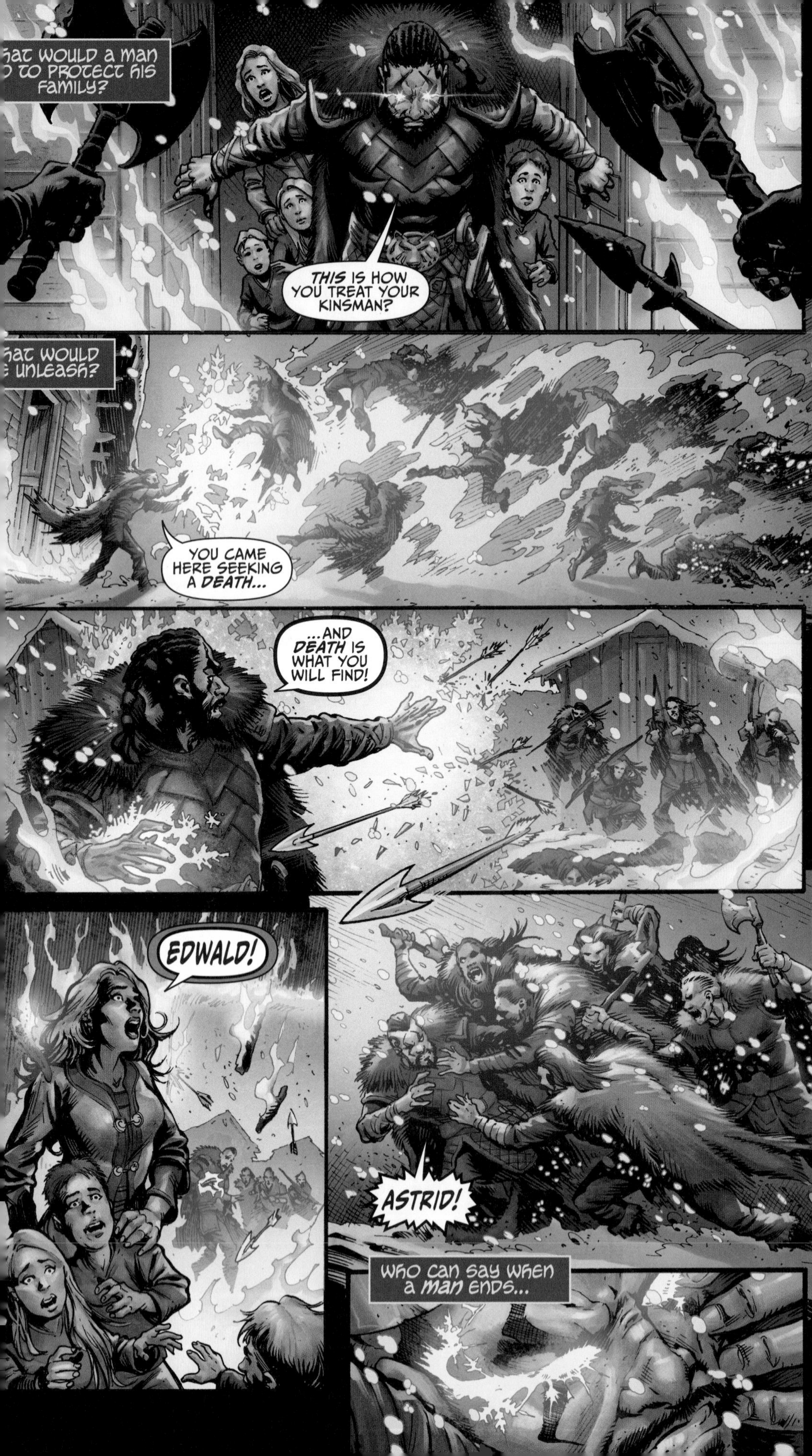
hat would a man
o to protect his
family?
THIS IS HOW YOU TREAT YOUR KINSMAN?
hat would
e unleash?
YOU CAME HERE SEEKING A DEATH...
...AND DEATH IS WHAT YOU WILL FIND!
EDWALD!
ASTRID!
Who can say when a man ends...

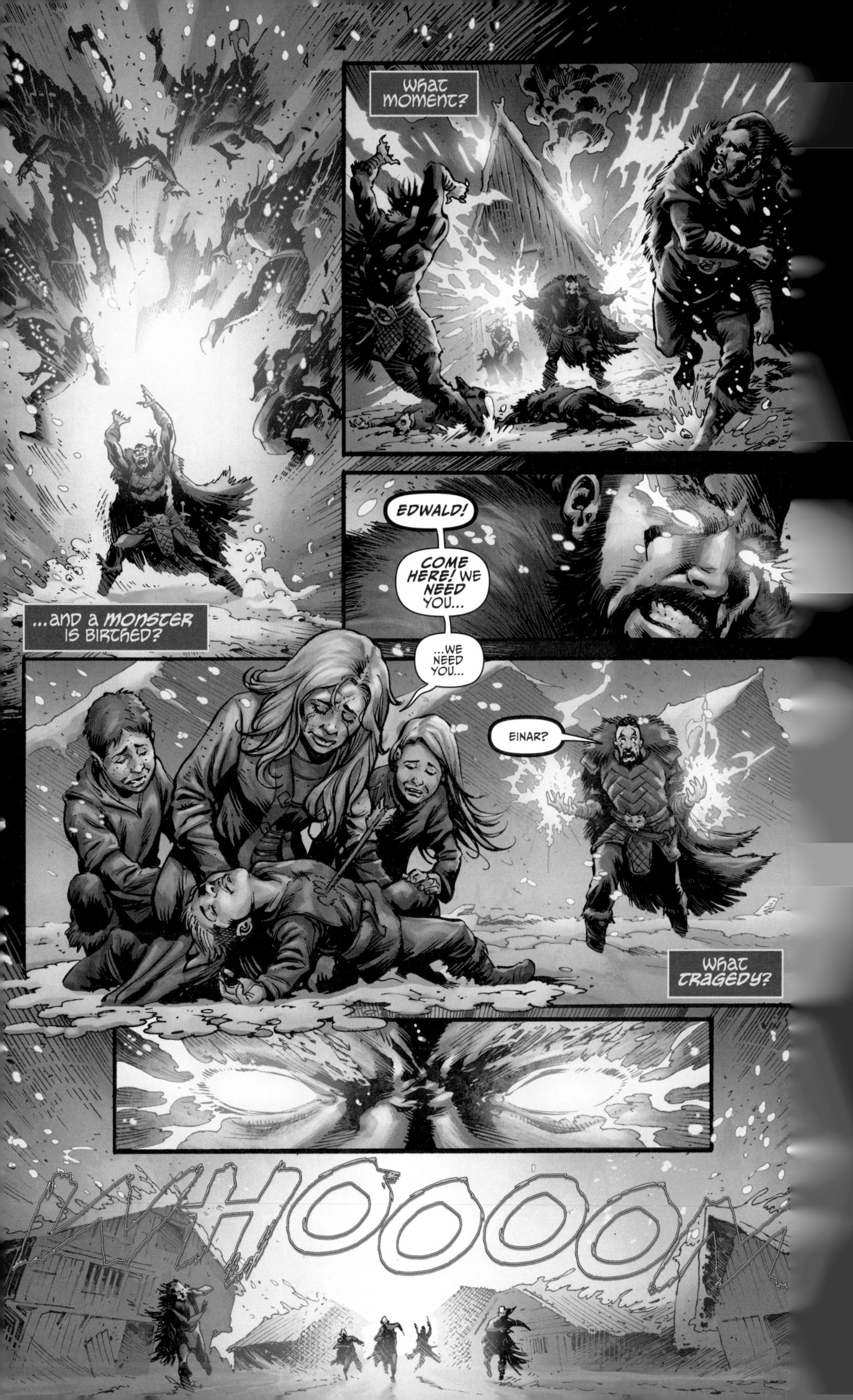

WHAT MOMENT?
...AND A MONSTER IS BIRTHED?
EDWALD!
COME HERE! WE NEED YOU...
...WE NEED YOU...
EINAR?
WHAT TRAGEDY?
WHOOOOM

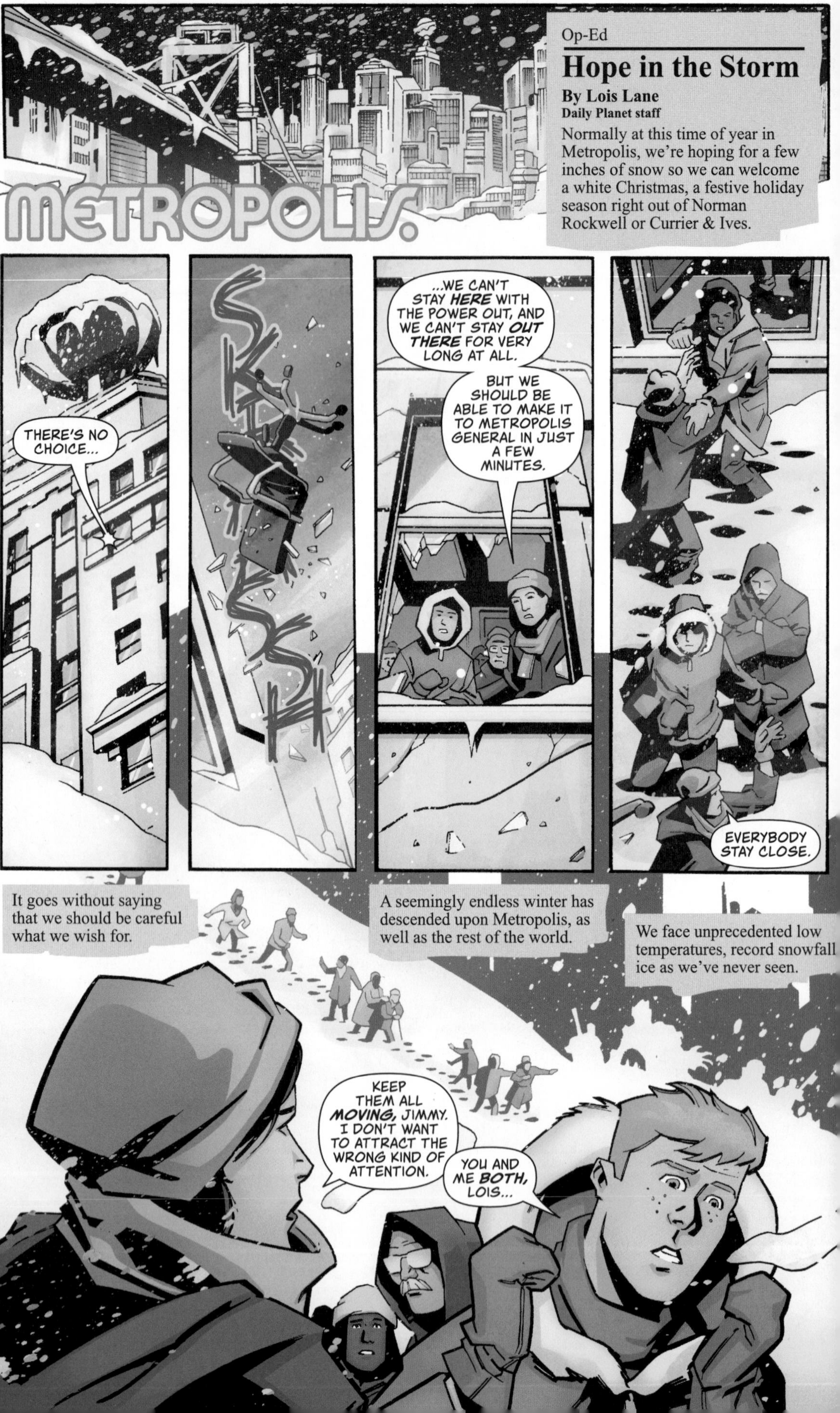

Op-Ed
Hope in the Storm
By Lois Lane
Daily Planet staff
Normally at this time of year in Metropolis, we're hoping for a few inches of snow so we can welcome a white Christmas, a festive holiday season right out of Norman Rockwell or Currier & Ives.
METROPOLIS.
THERE'S NO CHOICE...
...WE CAN'T STAY HERE WITH THE POWER OUT, AND WE CAN'T STAY OUT THERE FOR VERY LONG AT ALL.
BUT WE SHOULD BE ABLE TO MAKE IT TO METROPOLIS GENERAL IN JUST A FEW MINUTES.
EVERYBODY STAY CLOSE.
It goes without saying that we should be careful what we wish for.
A seemingly endless winter has descended upon Metropolis, as well as the rest of the world.
We face unprecedented low temperatures, record snowfall ice as we've never seen.
KEEP THEM ALL MOVING, JIMMY. I DON'T WANT TO ATTRACT THE WRONG KIND OF ATTENTION.
YOU AND ME BOTH, LOIS...

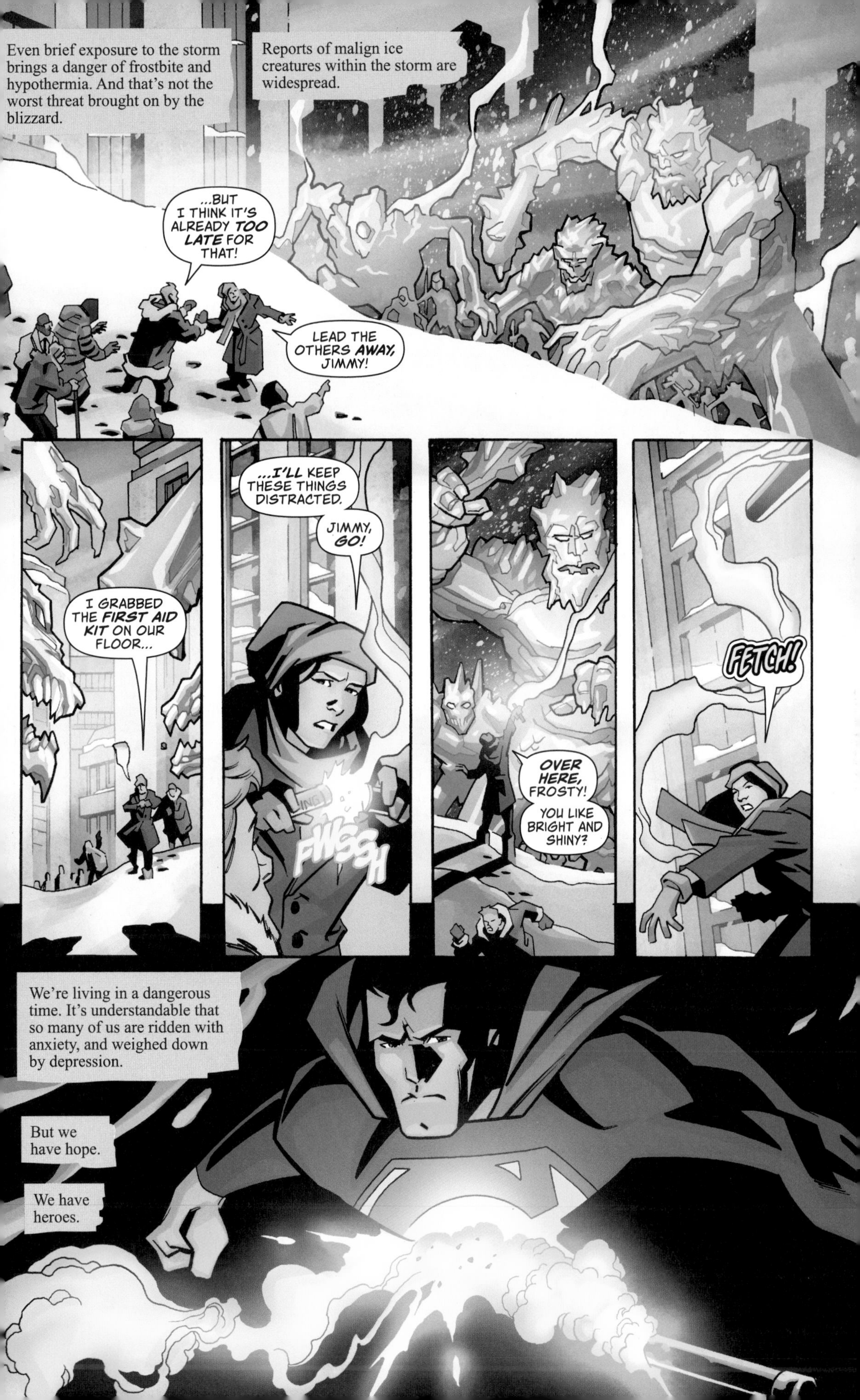

Even brief exposure to the storm brings a danger of frostbite and hypothermia. And that's not the worst threat brought on by the blizzard.
Reports of malign ice creatures within the storm are widespread.
...BUT I THINK IT'S ALREADY TOO LATE FOR THAT!
LEAD THE OTHERS AWAY, JIMMY!
I GRABBED THE FIRST AID KIT ON OUR FLOOR...
...I'LL KEEP THESE THINGS DISTRACTED.
JIMMY, GO!
FWSSH
OVER HERE, FROSTY!
YOU LIKE BRIGHT AND SHINY?
FETCH!
We're living in a dangerous time. It's understandable that so many of us are ridden with anxiety, and weighed down by depression.
But we have hope.
We have heroes.

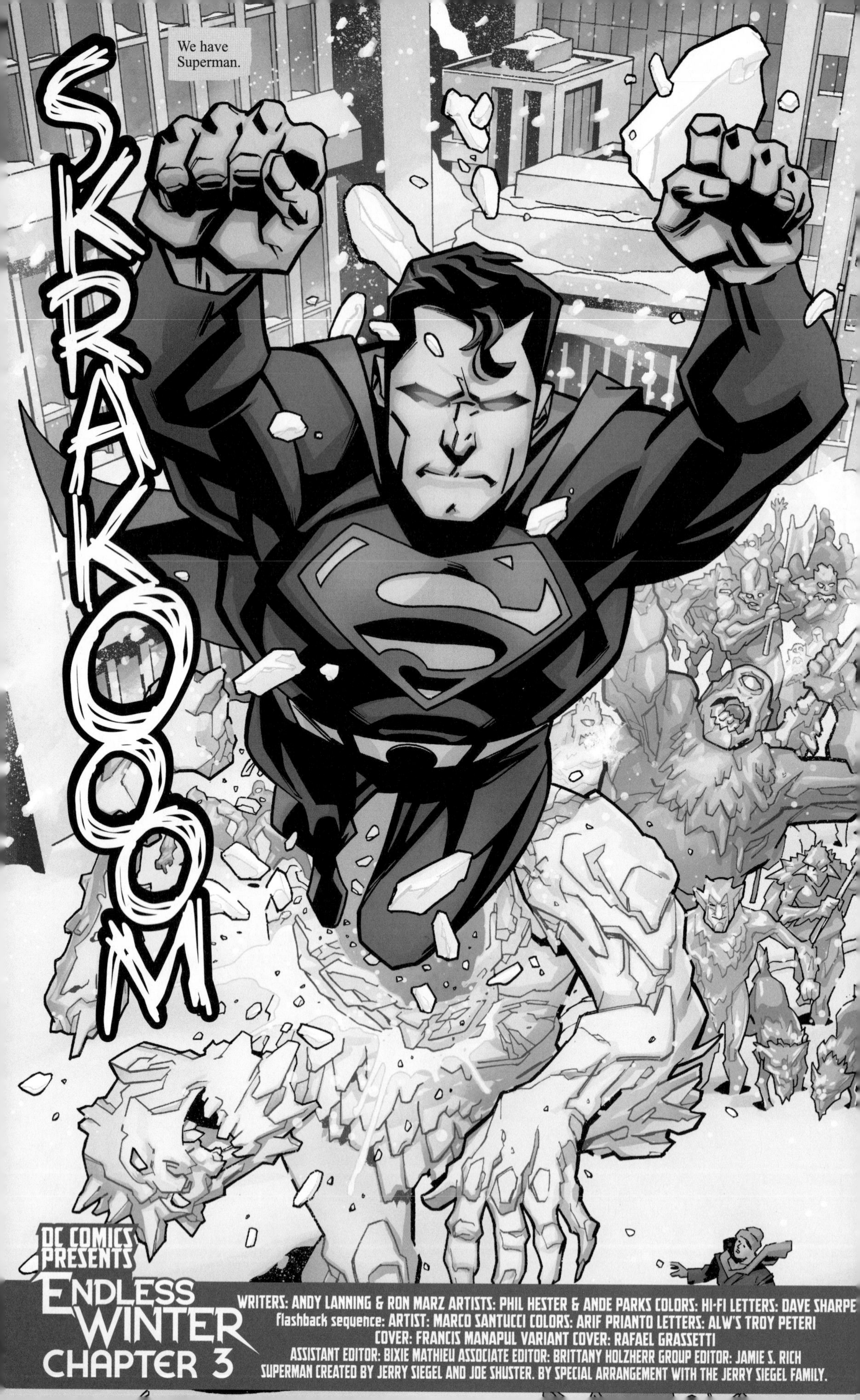
We have Superman.
SKRAKOOOM
DC COMICS PRESENTS
ENDLESS WINTER CHAPTER 3
WRITERS: ANDY LANNING & RON MARZ ARTISTS: PHIL HESTER & ANDE PARKS COLORS: HI-FI LETTERS: DAVE SHARPE
flashback sequence: ARTIST: MARCO SANTUCCI COLORS: ARIF PRIANTO LETTERS: ALW'S TROY PETERI
COVER: FRANCIS MANAPUL VARIANT COVER: RAFAEL GRASSETTI
ASSISTANT EDITOR: BIXIE MATHIEU ASSOCIATE EDITOR: BRITTANY HOLZHERR GROUP EDITOR: JAMIE S. RICH
SUPERMAN CREATED BY JERRY SIEGEL AND JOE SHUSTER. BY SPECIAL ARRANGEMENT WITH THE JERRY SIEGEL FAMILY.

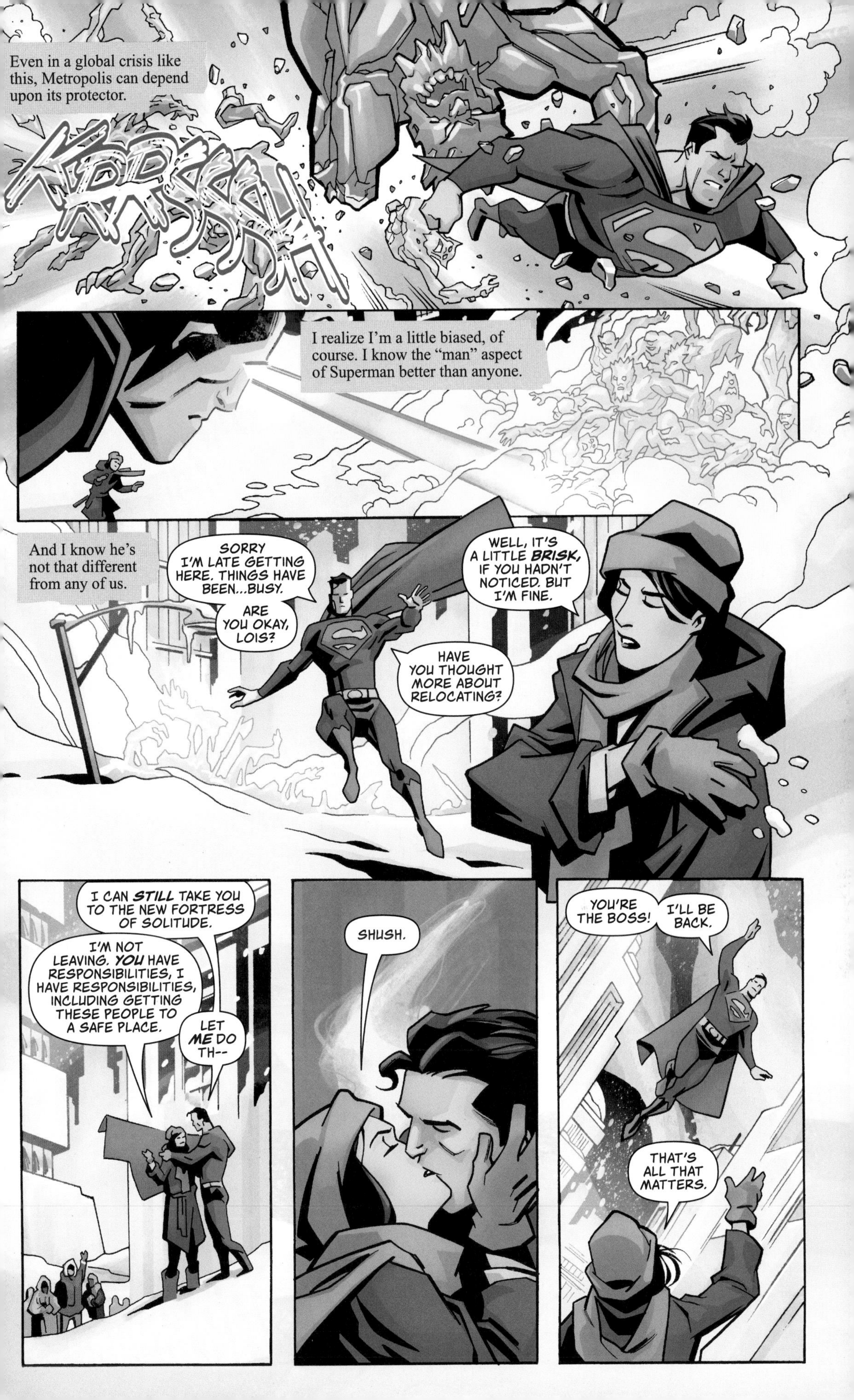
Even in a global crisis like this, Metropolis can depend upon its protector.
I realize I'm a little biased, of course. I know the "man" aspect of Superman better than anyone.
And I know he's not that different from any of us.
SORRY I'M LATE GETTING HERE. THINGS HAVE BEEN...BUSY.
ARE YOU OKAY, LOIS?
WELL, IT'S A LITTLE BRISK, IF YOU HADN'T NOTICED. BUT I'M FINE.
HAVE YOU THOUGHT MORE ABOUT RELOCATING?
I CAN STILL TAKE YOU TO THE NEW FORTRESS OF SOLITUDE.
I'M NOT LEAVING. YOU HAVE RESPONSIBILITIES, I HAVE RESPONSIBILITIES, INCLUDING GETTING THESE PEOPLE TO A SAFE PLACE.
LET ME DO TH--
SHUSH.
YOU'RE THE BOSS!
I'LL BE BACK.
THAT'S ALL THAT MATTERS.

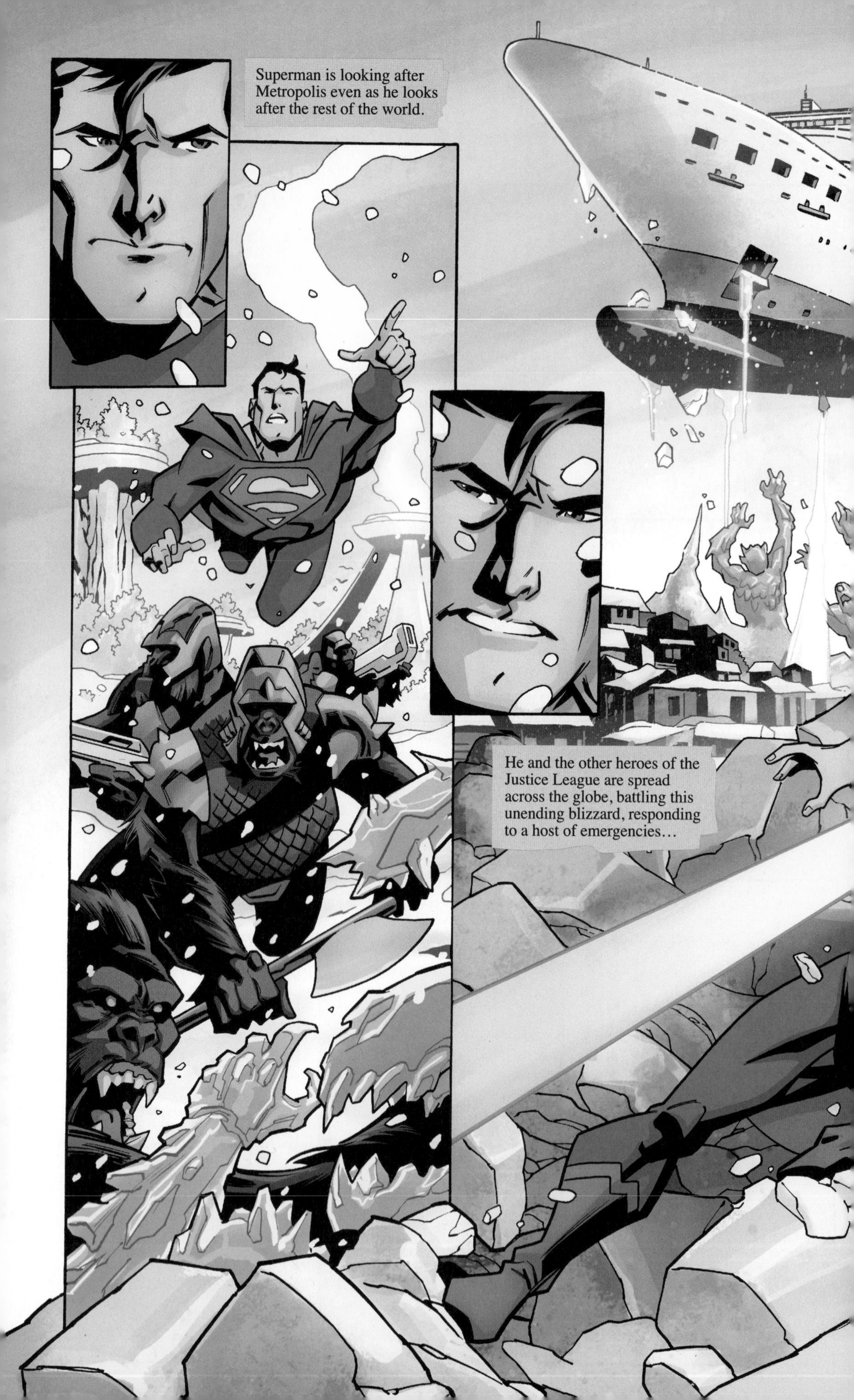
Superman is looking after Metropolis even as he looks after the rest of the world.
He and the other heroes of the Justice League are spread across the globe, battling this unending blizzard, responding to a host of emergencies…

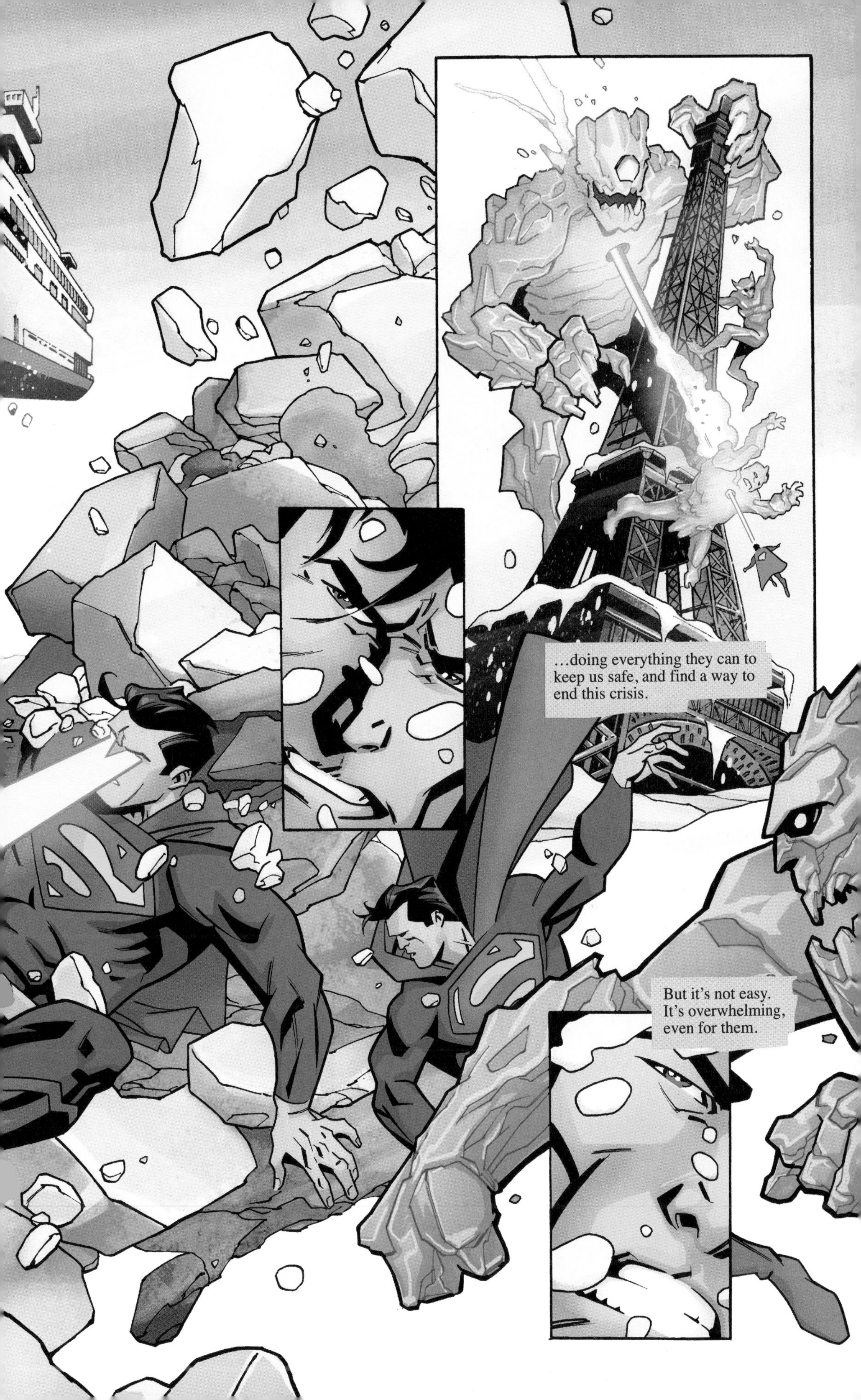
…doing everything they can to keep us safe, and find a way to end this crisis.
But it's not easy. It's overwhelming, even for them.

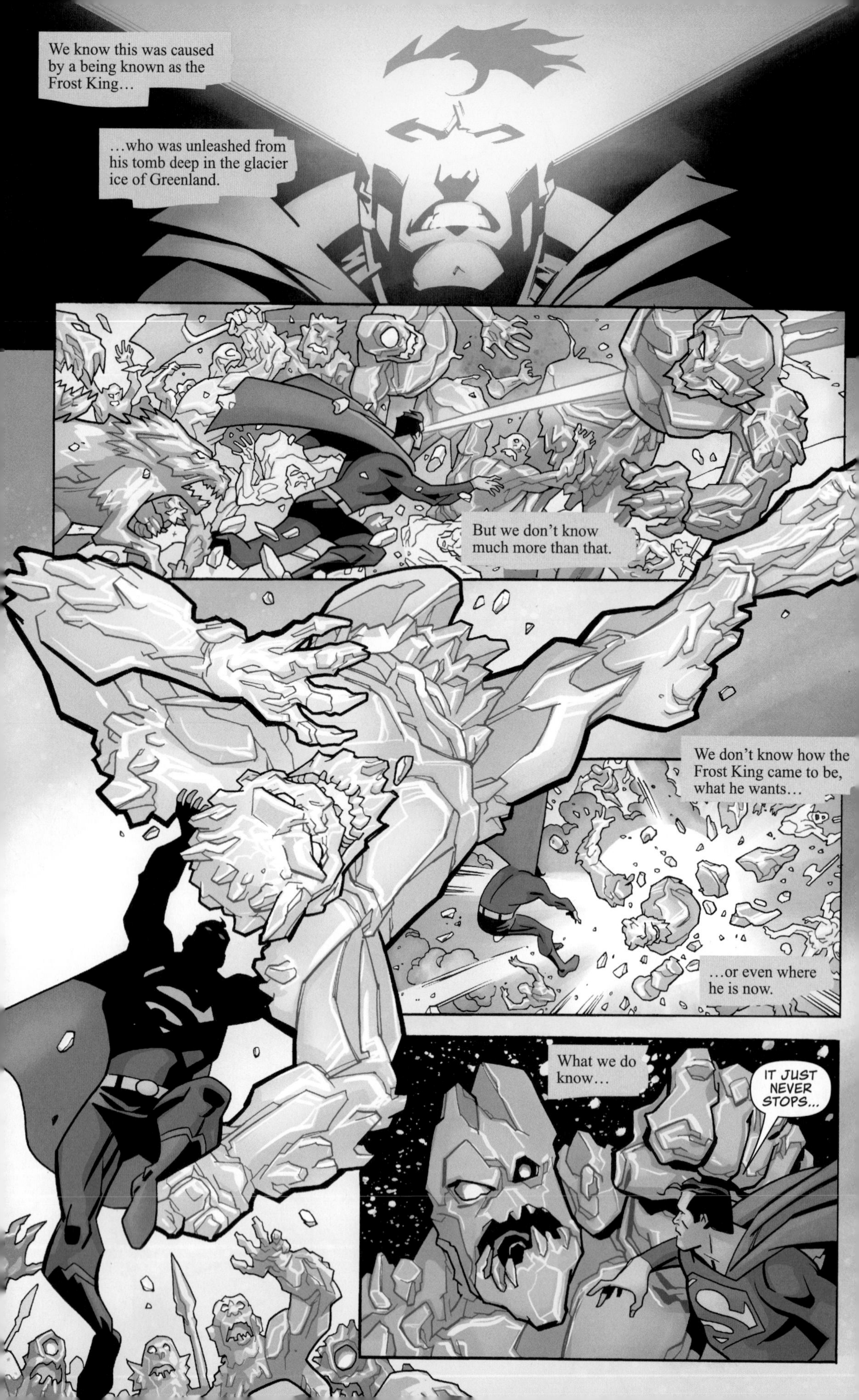
We know this was caused by a being known as the Frost King…
…who was unleashed from his tomb deep in the glacier ice of Greenland.
But we don't know much more than that.
We don't know how the Frost King came to be, what he wants…
…or even where he is now.
What we do know…
IT JUST NEVER STOPS...

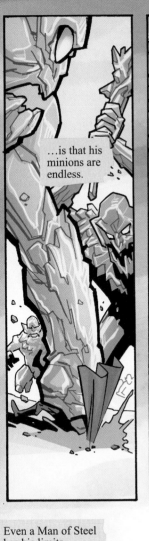

...is that his minions are endless.

For each that falls, another rises to take its place.

And another.

And another.

And another.

Mindless hordes spawned by the blizzard, not truly alive.

Even a Man of Steel has his limits.

I CAN'T **DO** THIS.

Right now we all feel like we're fighting a battle that never ends. We can't see a way out.

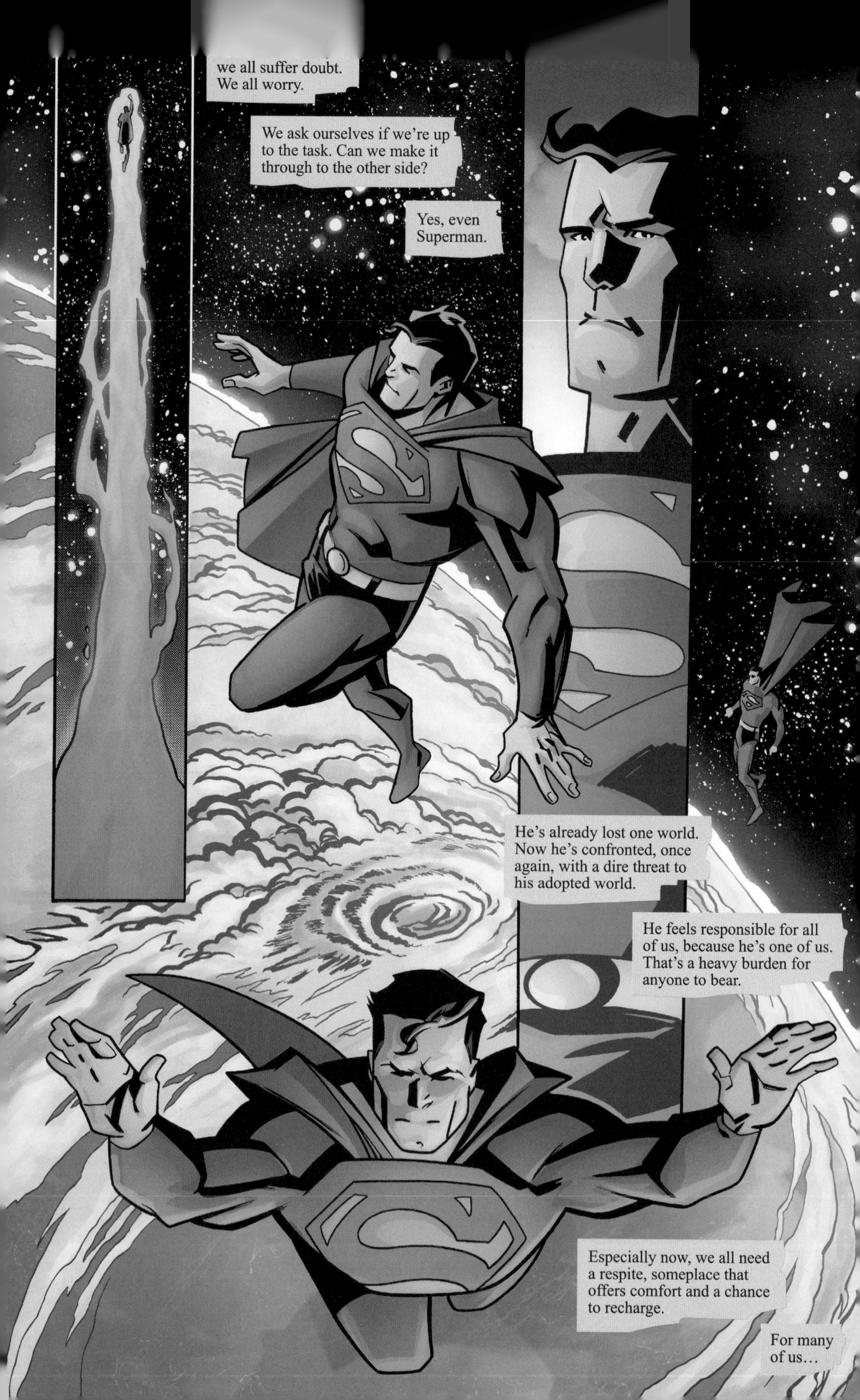
we all suffer doubt. We all worry.
We ask ourselves if we're up to the task. Can we make it through to the other side?
Yes, even Superman.
He's already lost one world. Now he's confronted, once again, with a dire threat to his adopted world.
He feels responsible for all of us, because he's one of us. That's a heavy burden for anyone to bear.
Especially now, we all need a respite, someplace that offers comfort and a chance to recharge.
For many of us…

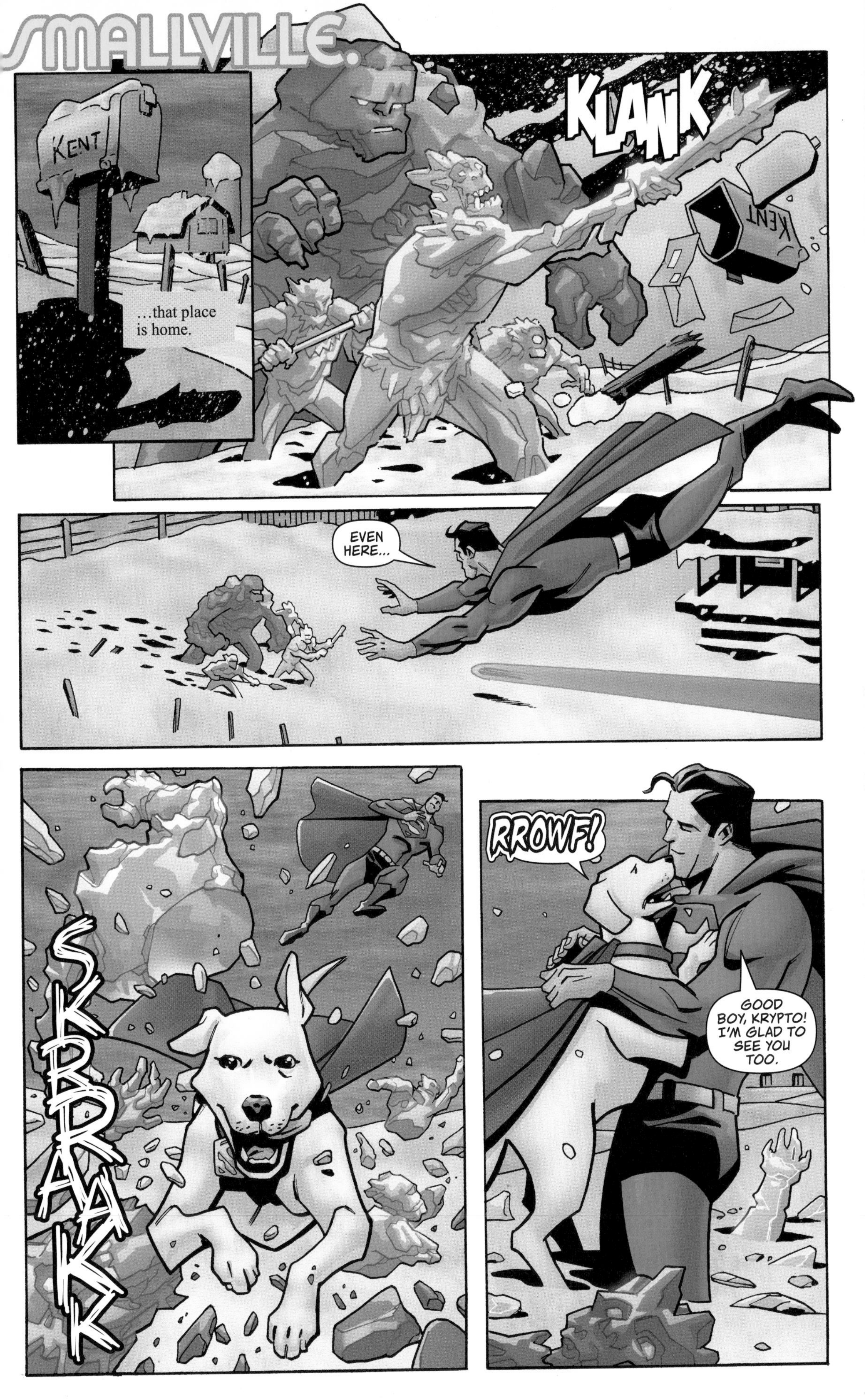
SMALLVILLE.
KENT
…that place is home.
KLANK
KENT
EVEN HERE…
SKBRAAKK
RROWF!
GOOD BOY, KRYPTO! I'M GLAD TO SEE YOU TOO.

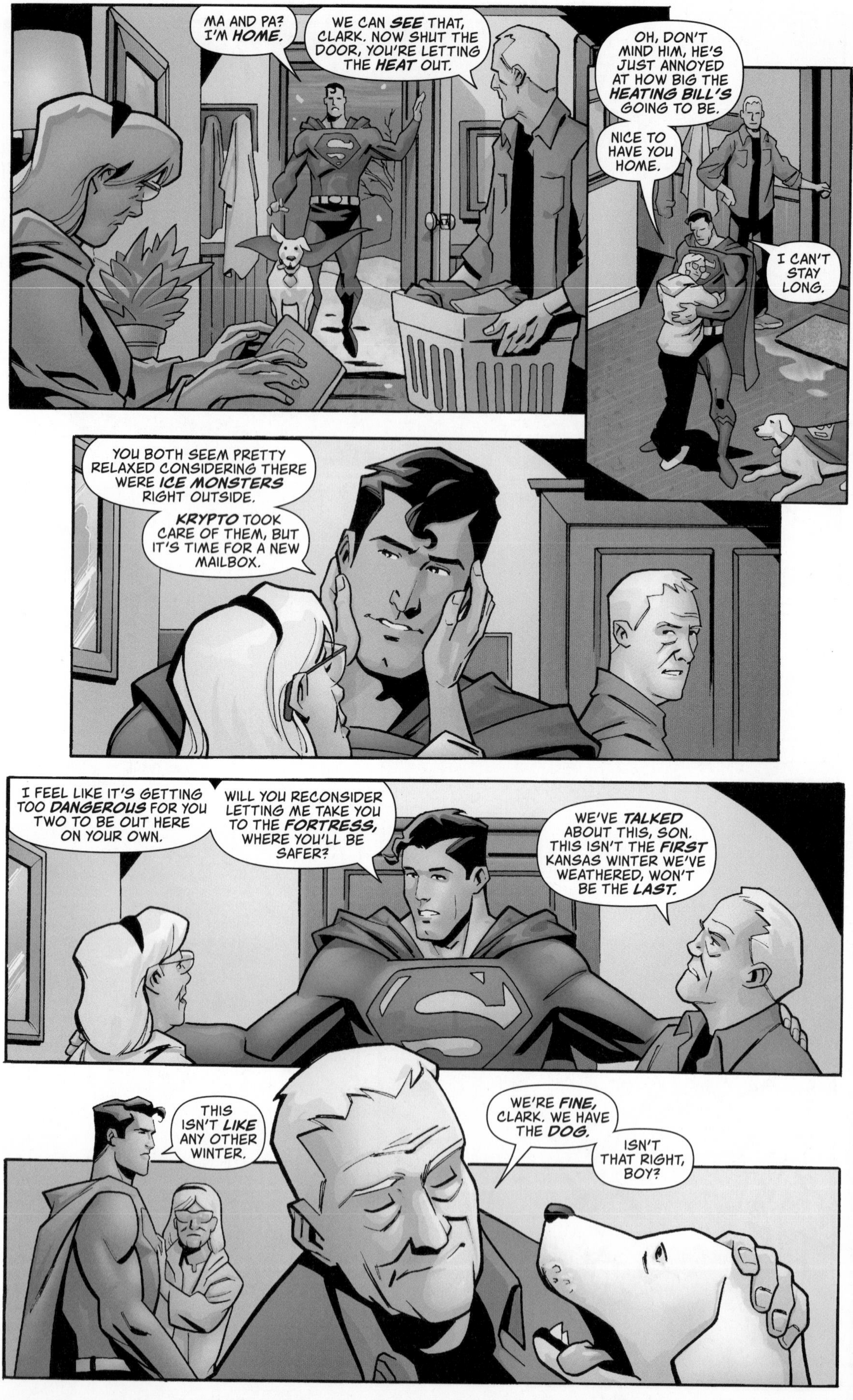
MA AND PA? I'M HOME.
WE CAN SEE THAT, CLARK. NOW SHUT THE DOOR, YOU'RE LETTING THE HEAT OUT.
OH, DON'T MIND HIM, HE'S JUST ANNOYED AT HOW BIG THE HEATING BILL'S GOING TO BE.
NICE TO HAVE YOU HOME.
I CAN'T STAY LONG.
YOU BOTH SEEM PRETTY RELAXED CONSIDERING THERE WERE ICE MONSTERS RIGHT OUTSIDE.
KRYPTO TOOK CARE OF THEM, BUT IT'S TIME FOR A NEW MAILBOX.
I FEEL LIKE IT'S GETTING TOO DANGEROUS FOR YOU TWO TO BE OUT HERE ON YOUR OWN.
WILL YOU RECONSIDER LETTING ME TAKE YOU TO THE FORTRESS, WHERE YOU'LL BE SAFER?
WE'VE TALKED ABOUT THIS, SON. THIS ISN'T THE FIRST KANSAS WINTER WE'VE WEATHERED, WON'T BE THE LAST.
THIS ISN'T LIKE ANY OTHER WINTER.
WE'RE FINE, CLARK. WE HAVE THE DOG.
ISN'T THAT RIGHT, BOY?

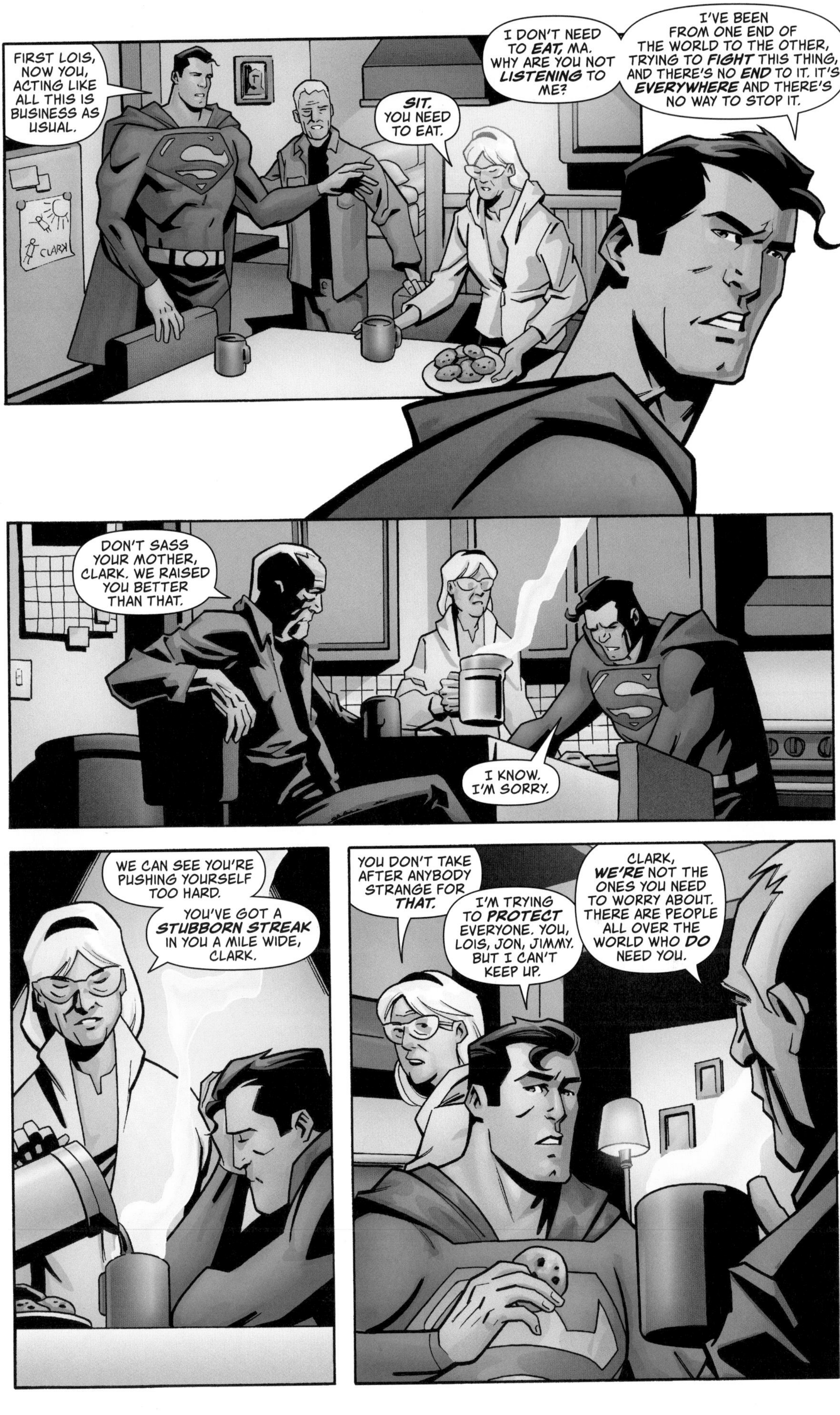
FIRST LOIS, NOW YOU, ACTING LIKE ALL THIS IS BUSINESS AS USUAL.
SIT. YOU NEED TO EAT.
I DON'T NEED TO EAT, MA. WHY ARE YOU NOT LISTENING TO ME?
I'VE BEEN FROM ONE END OF THE WORLD TO THE OTHER, TRYING TO FIGHT THIS THING, AND THERE'S NO END TO IT. IT'S EVERYWHERE AND THERE'S NO WAY TO STOP IT.
DON'T SASS YOUR MOTHER, CLARK. WE RAISED YOU BETTER THAN THAT.
I KNOW. I'M SORRY.
WE CAN SEE YOU'RE PUSHING YOURSELF TOO HARD.
YOU'VE GOT A STUBBORN STREAK IN YOU A MILE WIDE, CLARK.
YOU DON'T TAKE AFTER ANYBODY STRANGE FOR THAT.
I'M TRYING TO PROTECT EVERYONE. YOU, LOIS, JON, JIMMY. BUT I CAN'T KEEP UP.
CLARK, WE'RE NOT THE ONES YOU NEED TO WORRY ABOUT. THERE ARE PEOPLE ALL OVER THE WORLD WHO DO NEED YOU.
CLARK

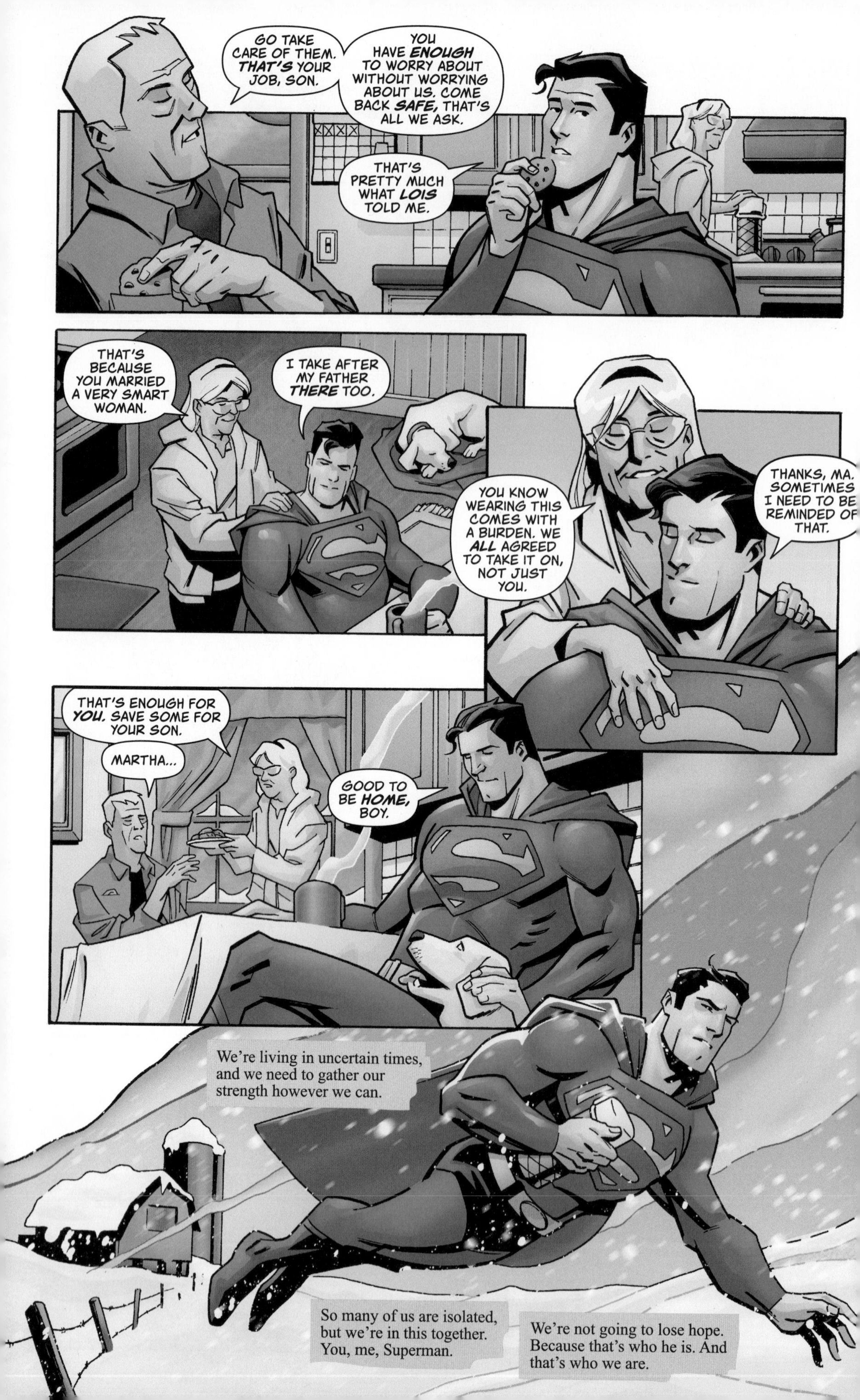
GO TAKE CARE OF THEM. THAT'S YOUR JOB, SON.
YOU HAVE ENOUGH TO WORRY ABOUT WITHOUT WORRYING ABOUT US. COME BACK SAFE, THAT'S ALL WE ASK.
THAT'S PRETTY MUCH WHAT LOIS TOLD ME.
THAT'S BECAUSE YOU MARRIED A VERY SMART WOMAN.
I TAKE AFTER MY FATHER THERE TOO.
YOU KNOW WEARING THIS COMES WITH A BURDEN. WE ALL AGREED TO TAKE IT ON, NOT JUST YOU.
THANKS, MA. SOMETIMES I NEED TO BE REMINDED OF THAT.
THAT'S ENOUGH FOR YOU. SAVE SOME FOR YOUR SON.
MARTHA...
GOOD TO BE HOME, BOY.
We're living in uncertain times, and we need to gather our strength however we can.
So many of us are isolated, but we're in this together. You, me, Superman.
We're not going to lose hope. Because that's who he is. And that's who we are.

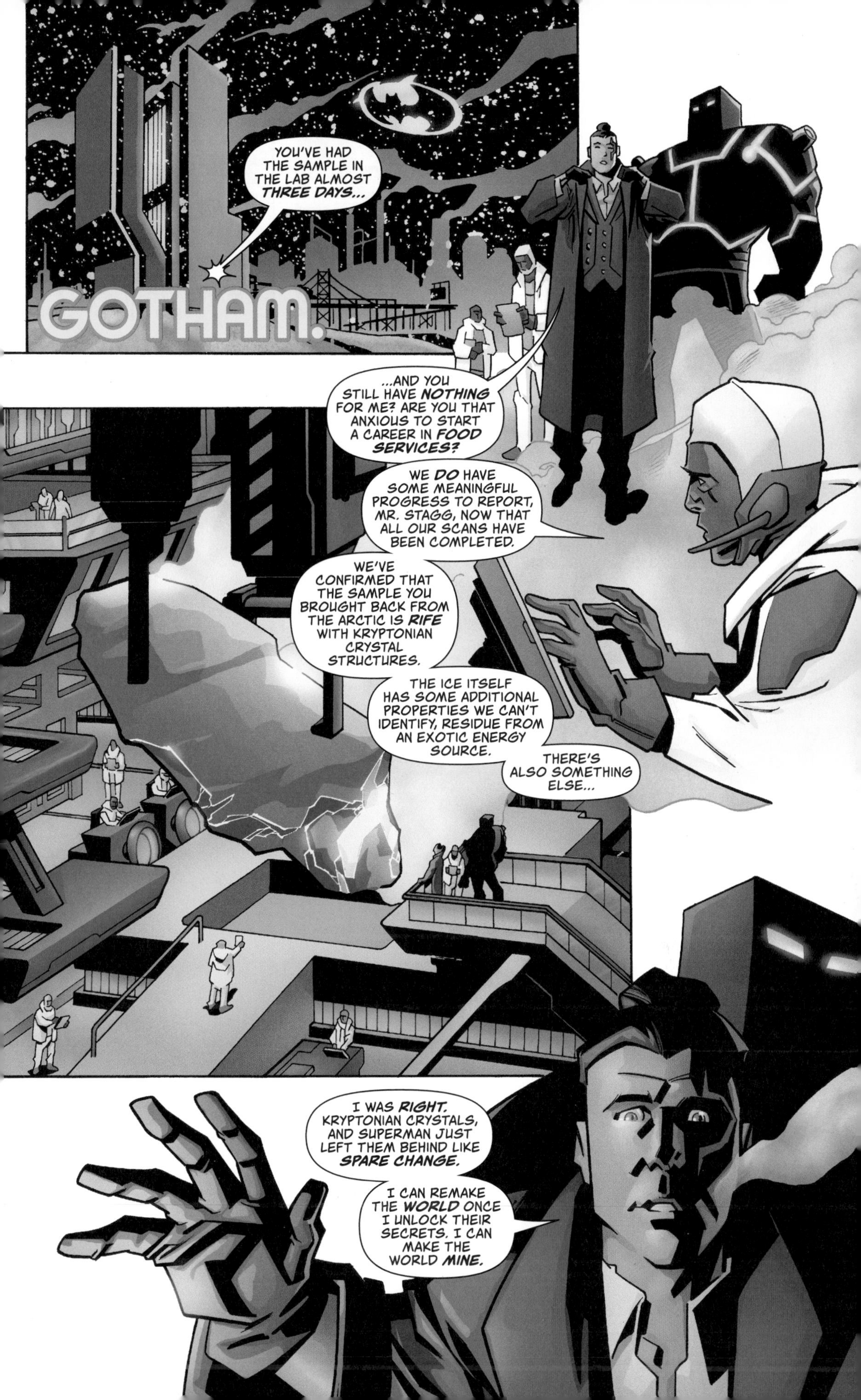
GOTHAM.
YOU'VE HAD THE SAMPLE IN THE LAB ALMOST THREE DAYS...
...AND YOU STILL HAVE NOTHING FOR ME? ARE YOU THAT ANXIOUS TO START A CAREER IN FOOD SERVICES?
WE DO HAVE SOME MEANINGFUL PROGRESS TO REPORT, MR. STAGG, NOW THAT ALL OUR SCANS HAVE BEEN COMPLETED.
WE'VE CONFIRMED THAT THE SAMPLE YOU BROUGHT BACK FROM THE ARCTIC IS RIFE WITH KRYPTONIAN CRYSTAL STRUCTURES.
THE ICE ITSELF HAS SOME ADDITIONAL PROPERTIES WE CAN'T IDENTIFY, RESIDUE FROM AN EXOTIC ENERGY SOURCE.
THERE'S ALSO SOMETHING ELSE...
I WAS RIGHT. KRYPTONIAN CRYSTALS, AND SUPERMAN JUST LEFT THEM BEHIND LIKE SPARE CHANGE.
I CAN REMAKE THE WORLD ONCE I UNLOCK THEIR SECRETS. I CAN MAKE THE WORLD MINE.

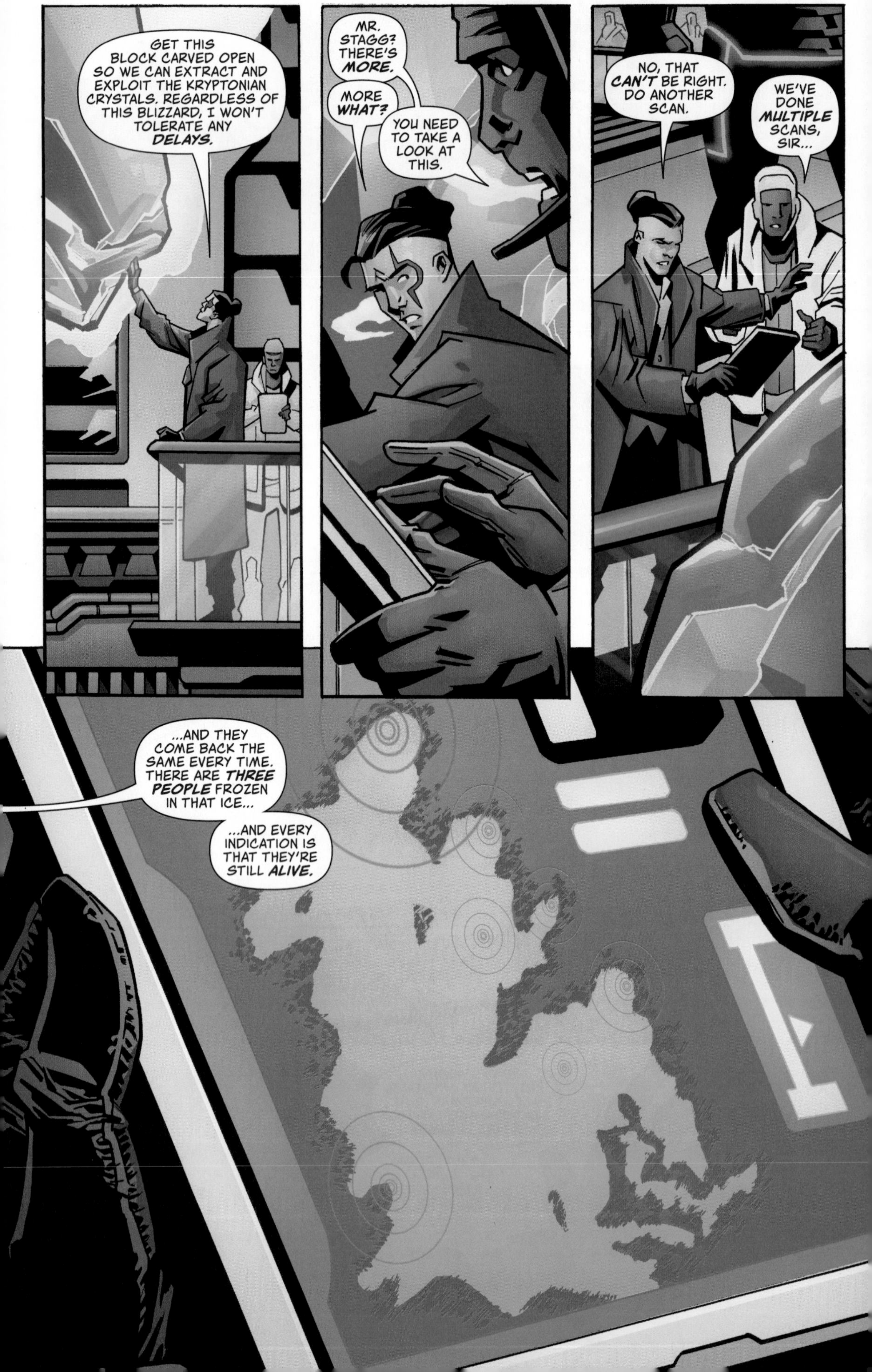
GET THIS BLOCK CARVED OPEN SO WE CAN EXTRACT AND EXPLOIT THE KRYPTONIAN CRYSTALS. REGARDLESS OF THIS BLIZZARD, I WON'T TOLERATE ANY DELAYS.
MR. STAGG? THERE'S MORE.
MORE WHAT?
YOU NEED TO TAKE A LOOK AT THIS.
NO, THAT CAN'T BE RIGHT. DO ANOTHER SCAN.
WE'VE DONE MULTIPLE SCANS, SIR...
...AND THEY COME BACK THE SAME EVERY TIME. THERE ARE THREE PEOPLE FROZEN IN THAT ICE...
...AND EVERY INDICATION IS THAT THEY'RE STILL ALIVE.

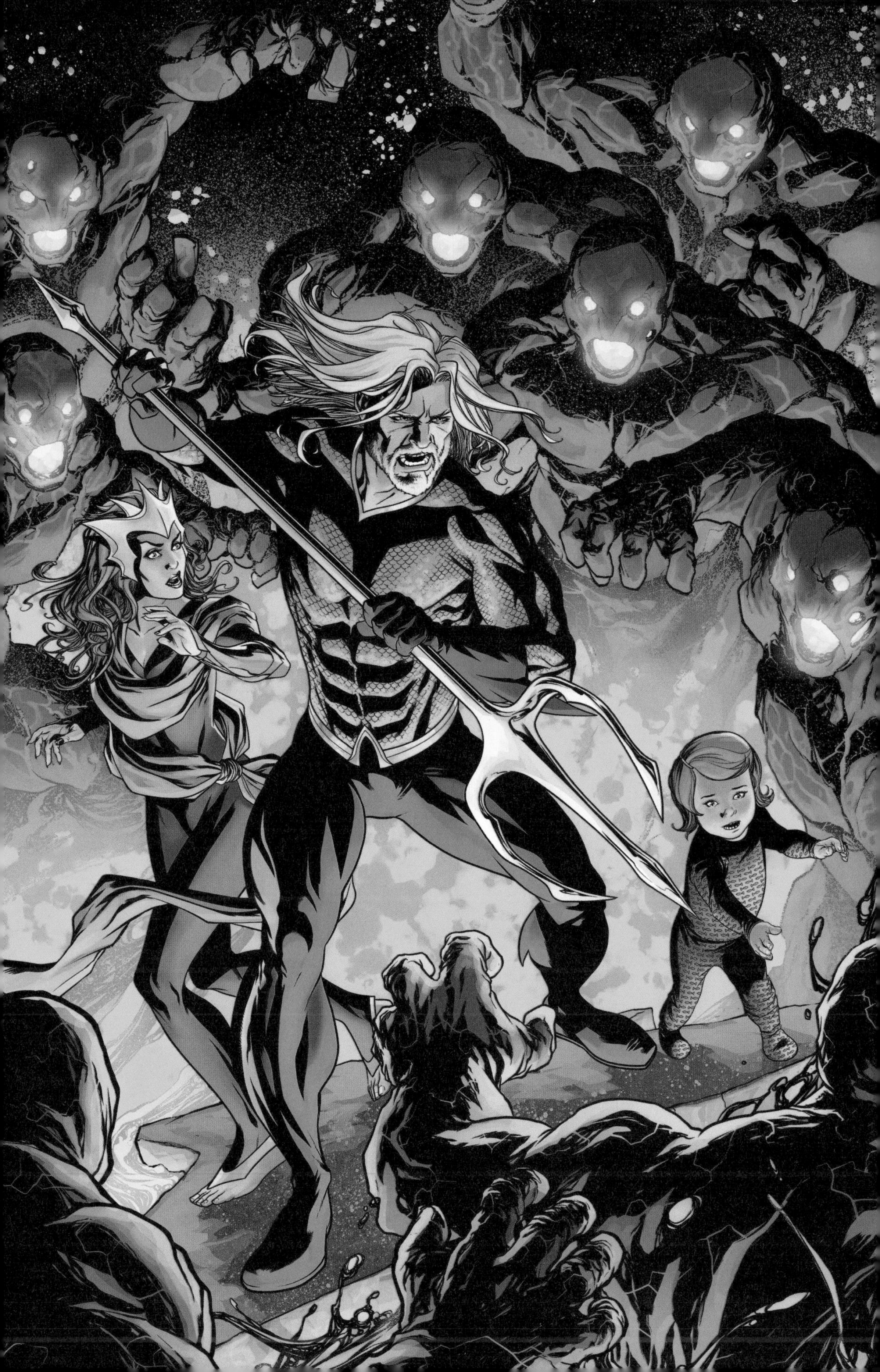

Aquaman #66 cover
by Mike McKone and Peter Steigerwald

Aquaman #66 variant cover
by Dima Ivanov

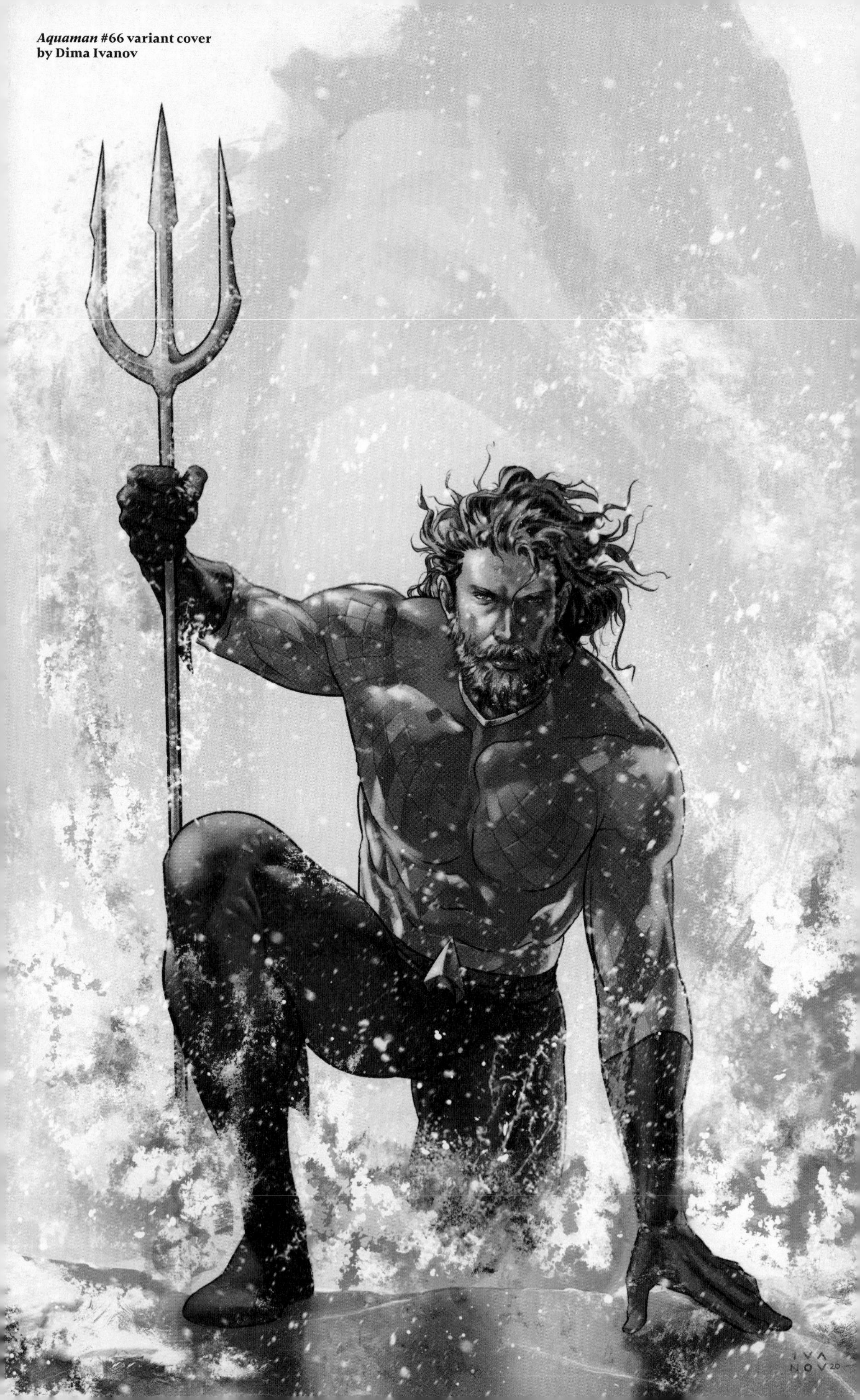

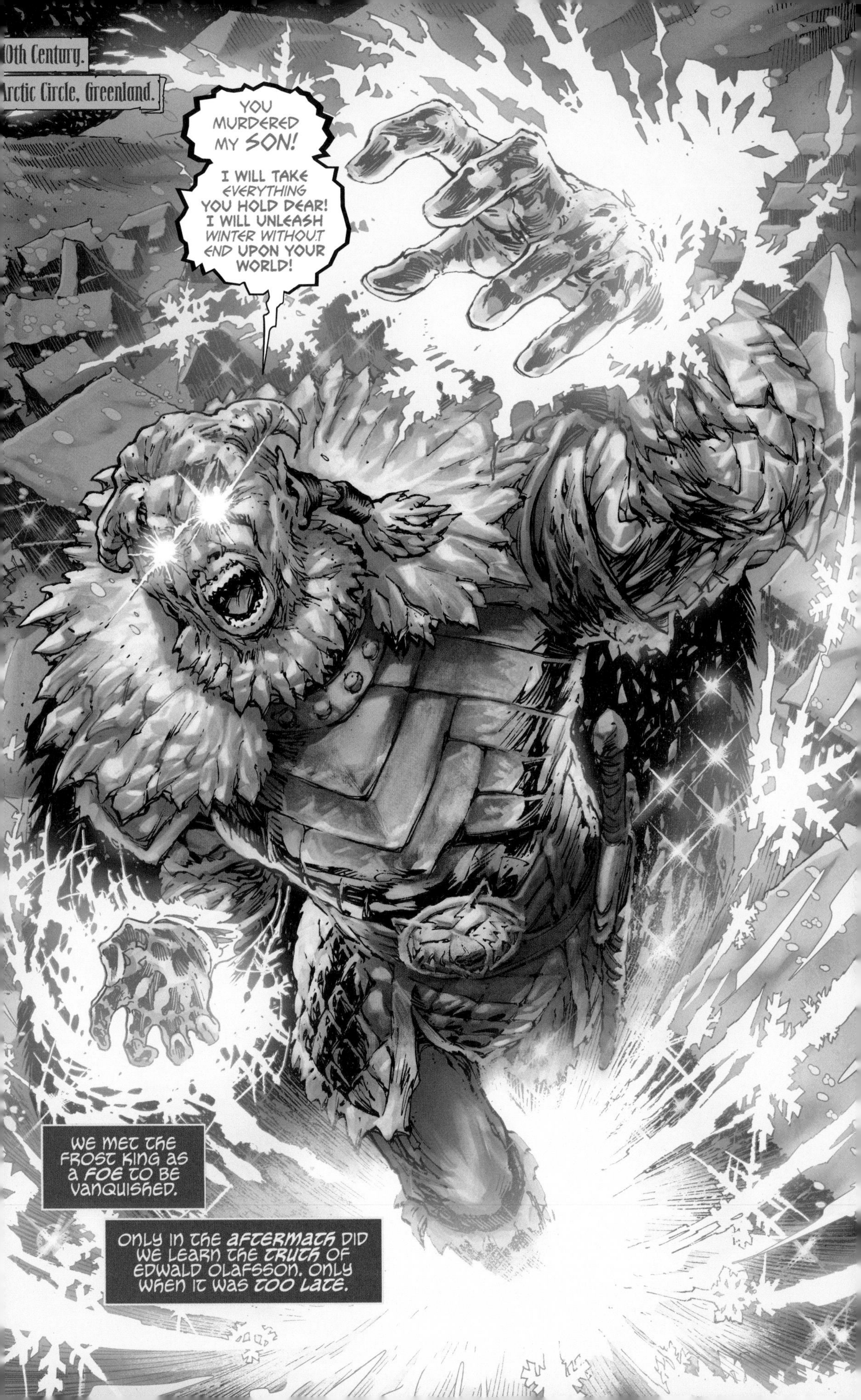
0th Century.
Arctic Circle, Greenland.
YOU MURDERED MY SON!
I WILL TAKE EVERYTHING YOU HOLD DEAR! I WILL UNLEASH WINTER WITHOUT END UPON YOUR WORLD!
WE MET THE FROST KING AS A FOE TO BE VANQUISHED.
ONLY IN THE AFTERMATH DID WE LEARN THE TRUTH OF EDWALD OLAFSSON. ONLY WHEN IT WAS TOO LATE.

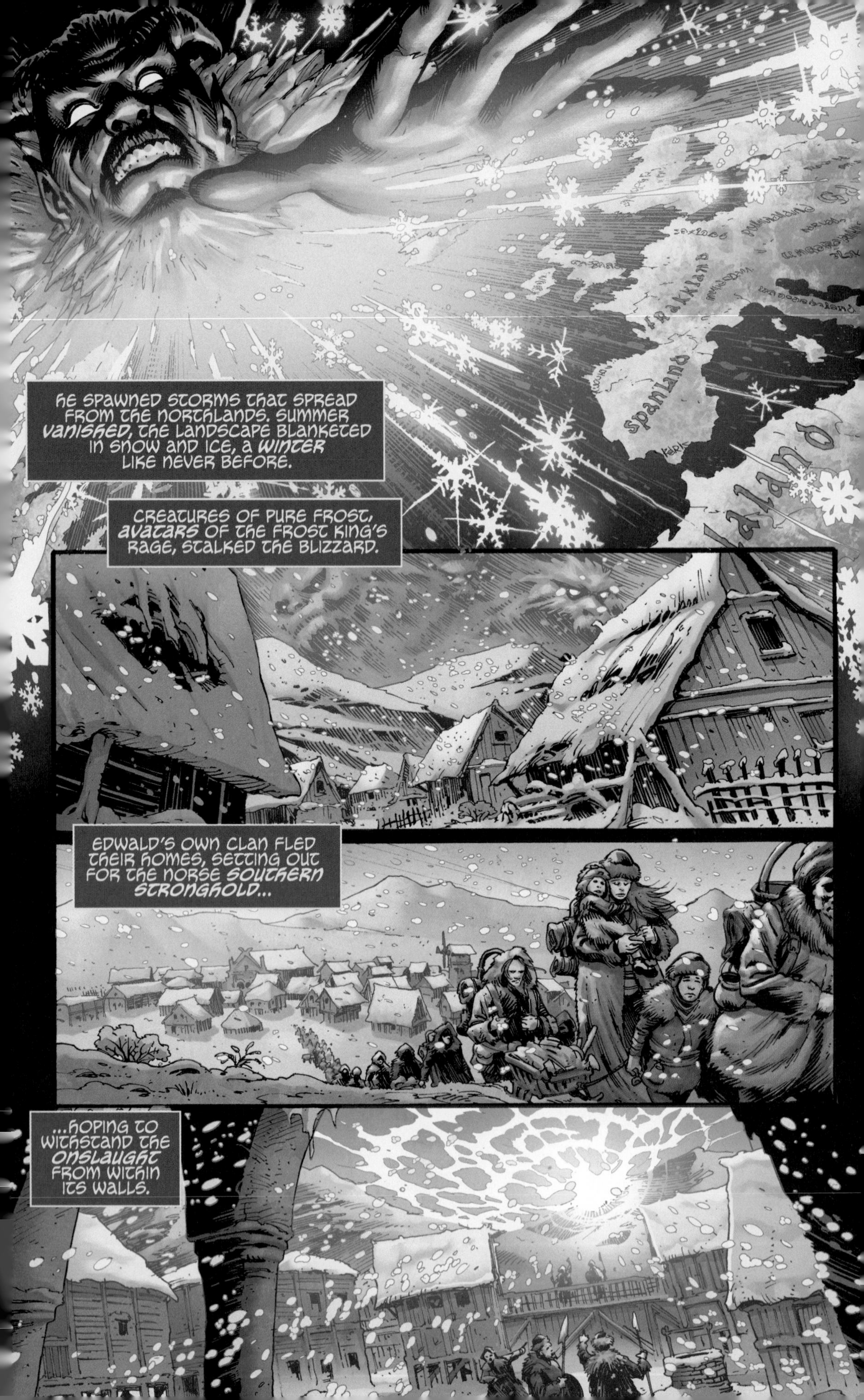

HE SPAWNED STORMS THAT SPREAD FROM THE NORTHLANDS. SUMMER VANISHED, THE LANDSCAPE BLANKETED IN SNOW AND ICE, A WINTER LIKE NEVER BEFORE.
spanLand
CREATURES OF PURE FROST, AVATARS OF THE FROST KING'S RAGE, STALKED THE BLIZZARD.
EDWALD'S OWN CLAN FLED THEIR HOMES, SETTING OUT FOR THE NORSE SOUTHERN STRONGHOLD...
...HOPING TO WITHSTAND THE ONSLAUGHT FROM WITHIN ITS WALLS.

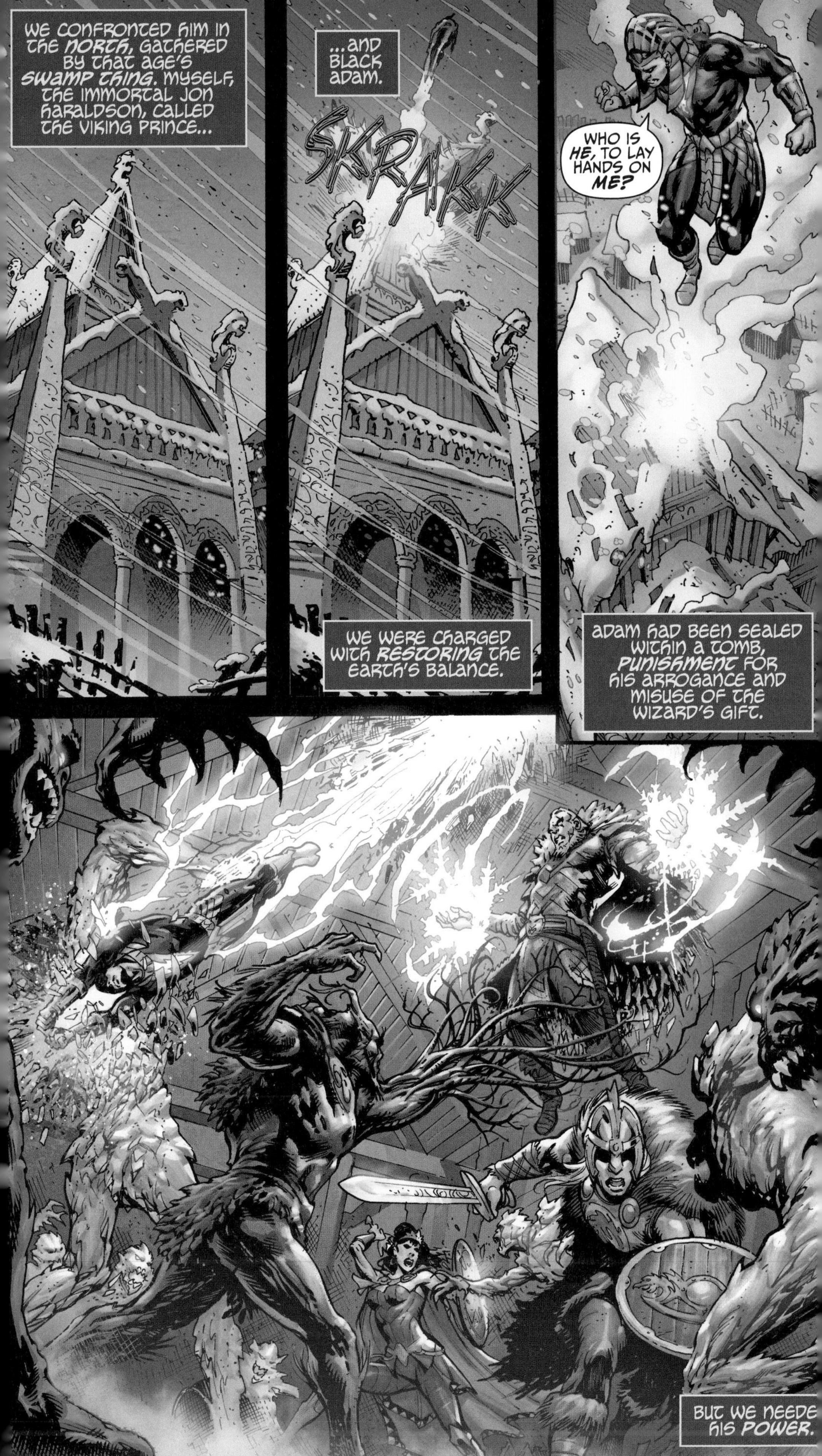
WE CONFRONTED HIM IN THE NORTH, GATHERED BY THAT AGE'S SWAMP THING. MYSELF, THE IMMORTAL JON HARALDSON, CALLED THE VIKING PRINCE...
...AND BLACK ADAM.
SKRAKK
WE WERE CHARGED WITH RESTORING THE EARTH'S BALANCE.
WHO IS HE, TO LAY HANDS ON ME?
ADAM HAD BEEN SEALED WITHIN A TOMB, PUNISHMENT FOR HIS ARROGANCE AND MISUSE OF THE WIZARD'S GIFT.
BUT WE NEEDE
HIS POWER.

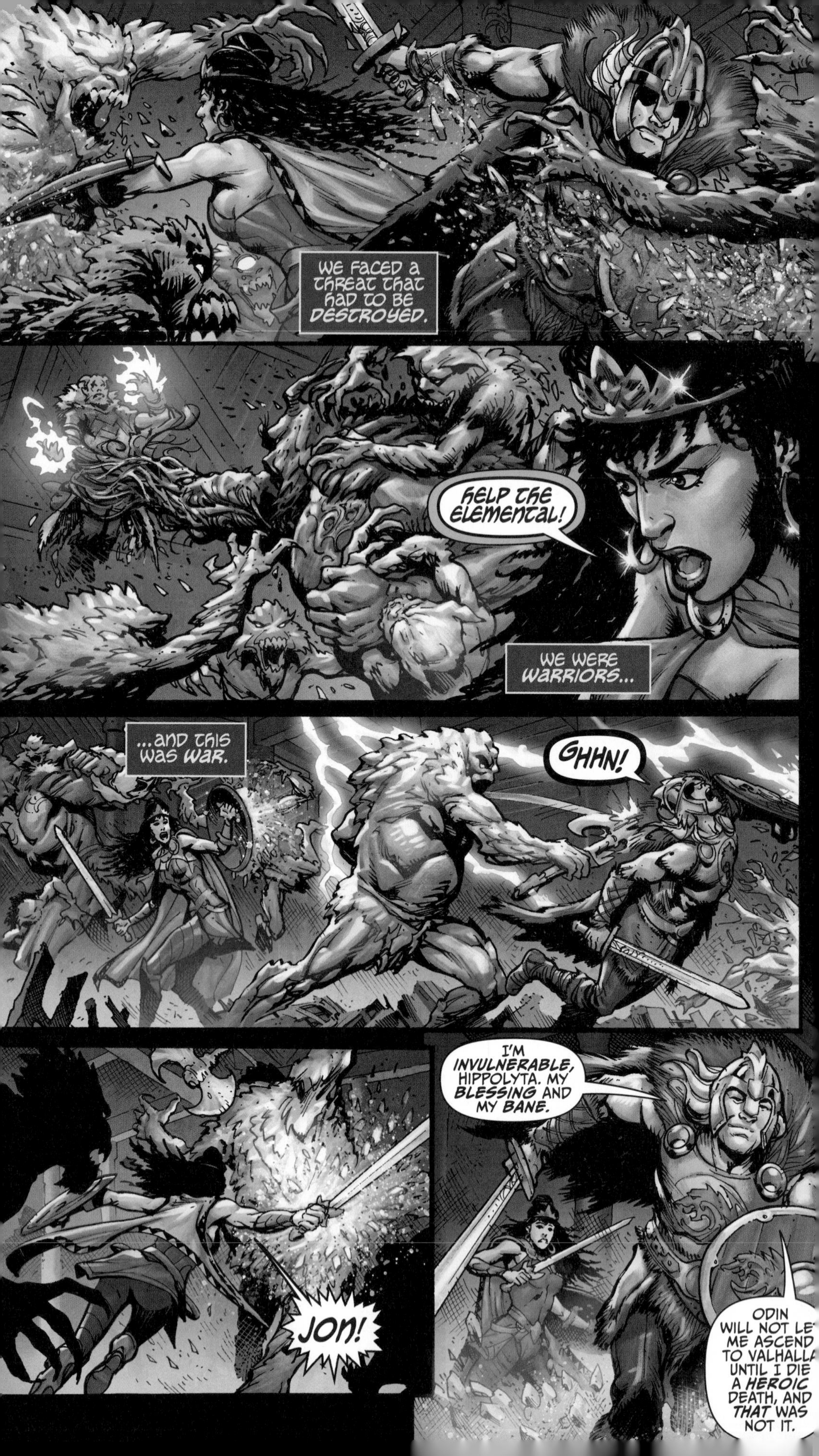
WE FACED A THREAT THAT HAD TO BE DESTROYED.
HELP THE ELEMENTAL!
WE WERE WARRIORS...
...AND THIS WAS WAR.
GHHN!
JON!
I'M INVULNERABLE, HIPPOLYTA. MY BLESSING AND MY BANE.
ODIN WILL NOT LET ME ASCEND TO VALHALLA UNTIL I DIE A HEROIC DEATH, AND THAT WAS NOT IT.

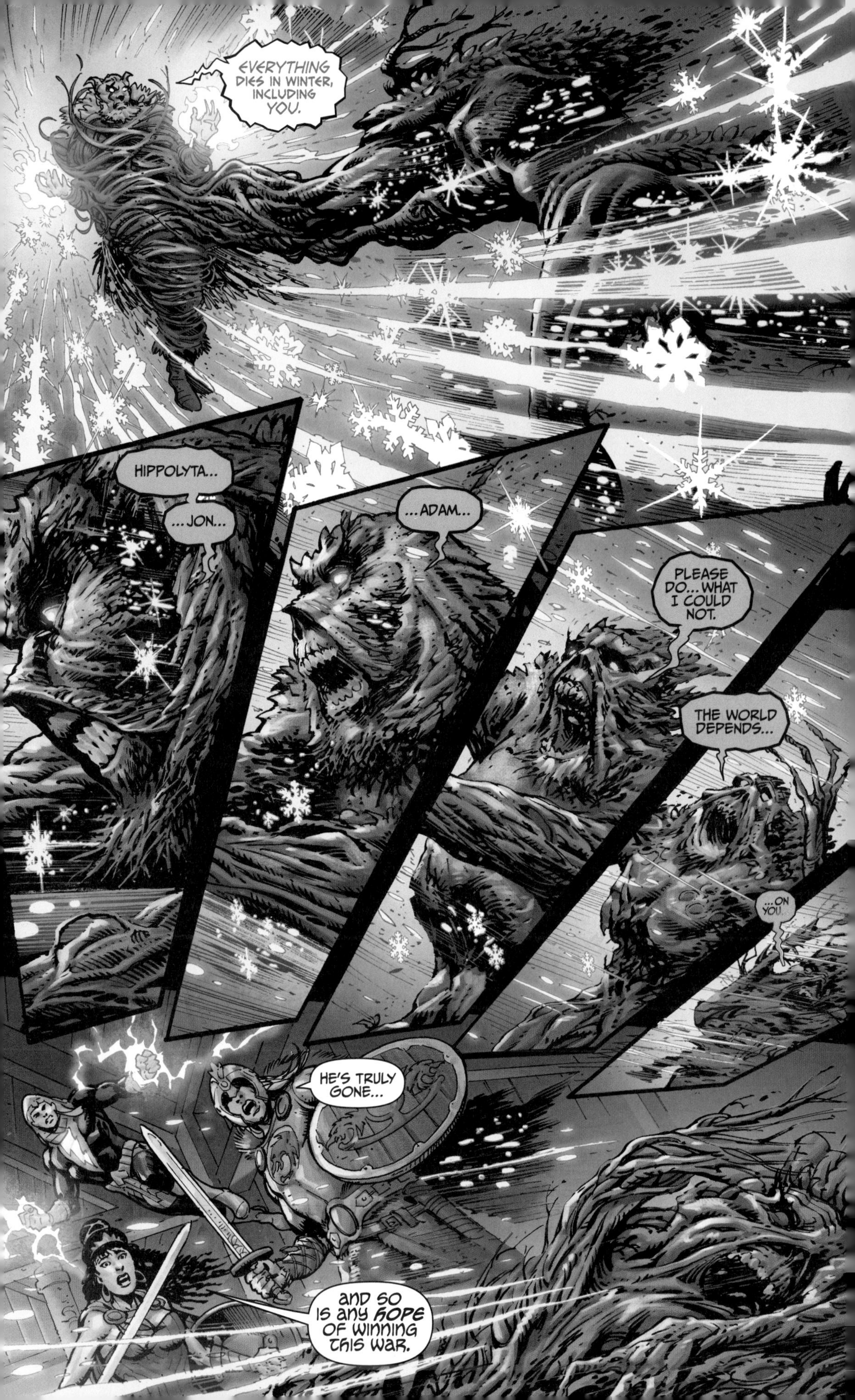
EVERYTHING DIES IN WINTER, INCLUDING YOU.
HIPPOLYTA...
...JON...
...ADAM...
PLEASE DO... WHAT I COULD NOT.
THE WORLD DEPENDS...
...ON YOU.
HE'S TRULY GONE...
AND SO IS ANY HOPE OF WINNING THIS WAR.

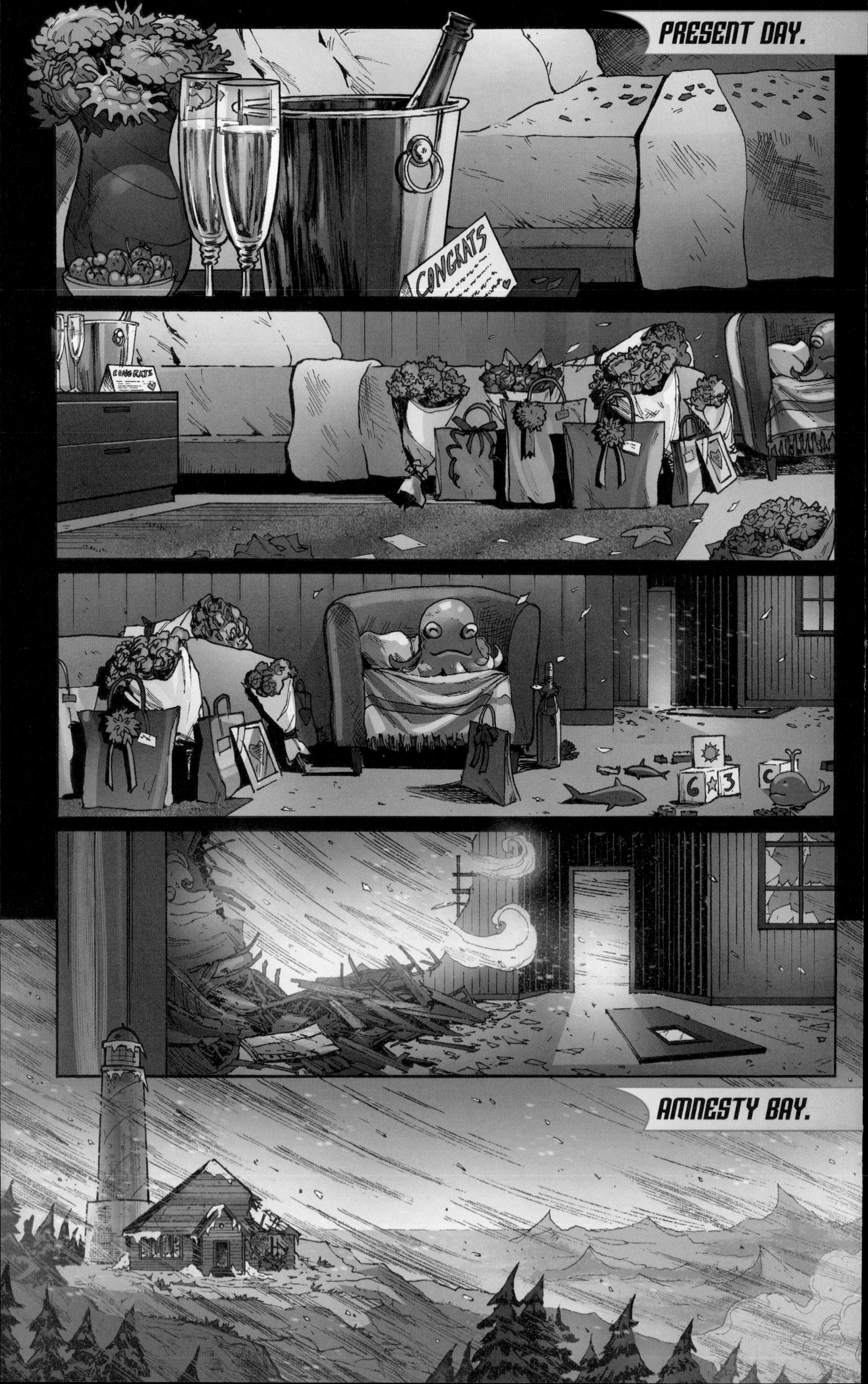
PRESENT DAY.
CONGRATS
CONGRATS
AMNESTY BAY.

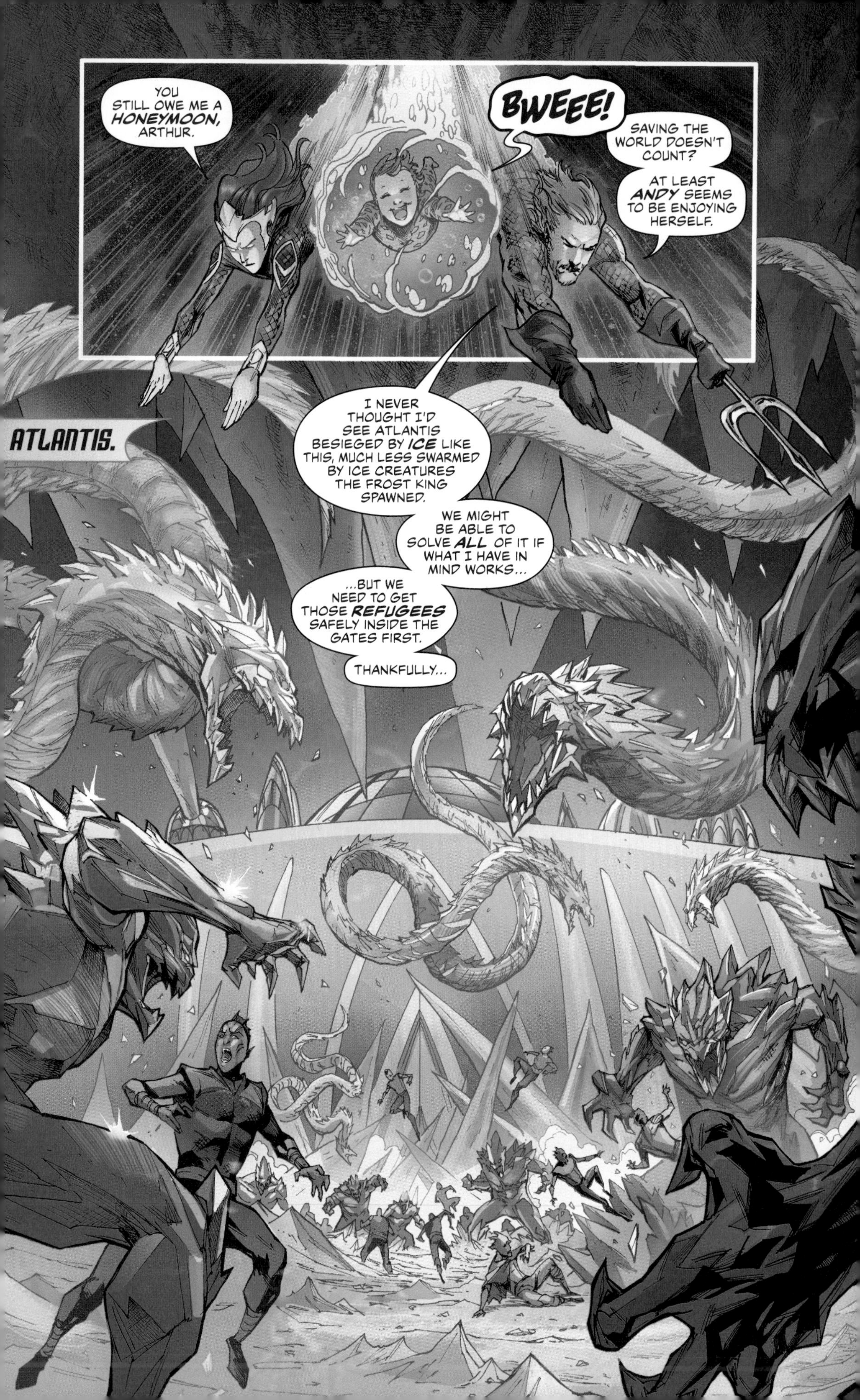
YOU STILL OWE ME A HONEYMOON, ARTHUR.
BWEEE!
SAVING THE WORLD DOESN'T COUNT?
AT LEAST ANDY SEEMS TO BE ENJOYING HERSELF.
ATLANTIS.
I NEVER THOUGHT I'D SEE ATLANTIS BESIEGED BY ICE LIKE THIS, MUCH LESS SWARMED BY ICE CREATURES THE FROST KING SPAWNED.
WE MIGHT BE ABLE TO SOLVE ALL OF IT IF WHAT I HAVE IN MIND WORKS...
...BUT WE NEED TO GET THOSE REFUGEES SAFELY INSIDE THE GATES FIRST.
THANKFULLY...

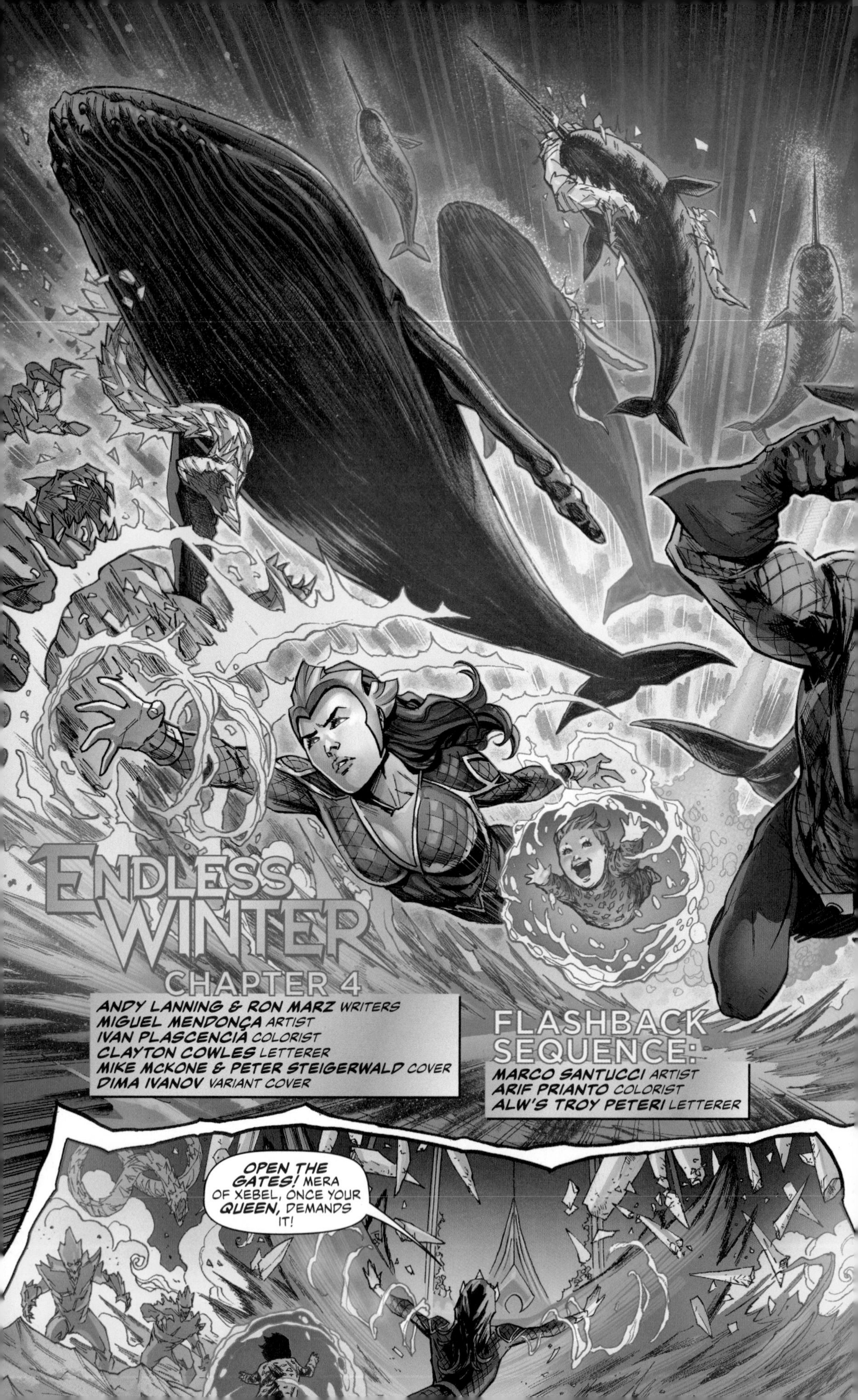
ENDLESS WINTER
CHAPTER 4
ANDY LANNING & RON MARZ WRITERS
MIGUEL MENDONÇA ARTIST
IVAN PLASCENCIA COLORIST
CLAYTON COWLES LETTERER
MIKE MCKONE & PETER STEIGERWALD COVER
DIMA IVANOV VARIANT COVER
FLASHBACK SEQUENCE:
MARCO SANTUCCI ARTIST
ARIF PRIANTO COLORIST
ALW'S TROY PETERI LETTERER
OPEN THE GATES! MERA OF XEBEL, ONCE YOUR QUEEN, DEMANDS IT!

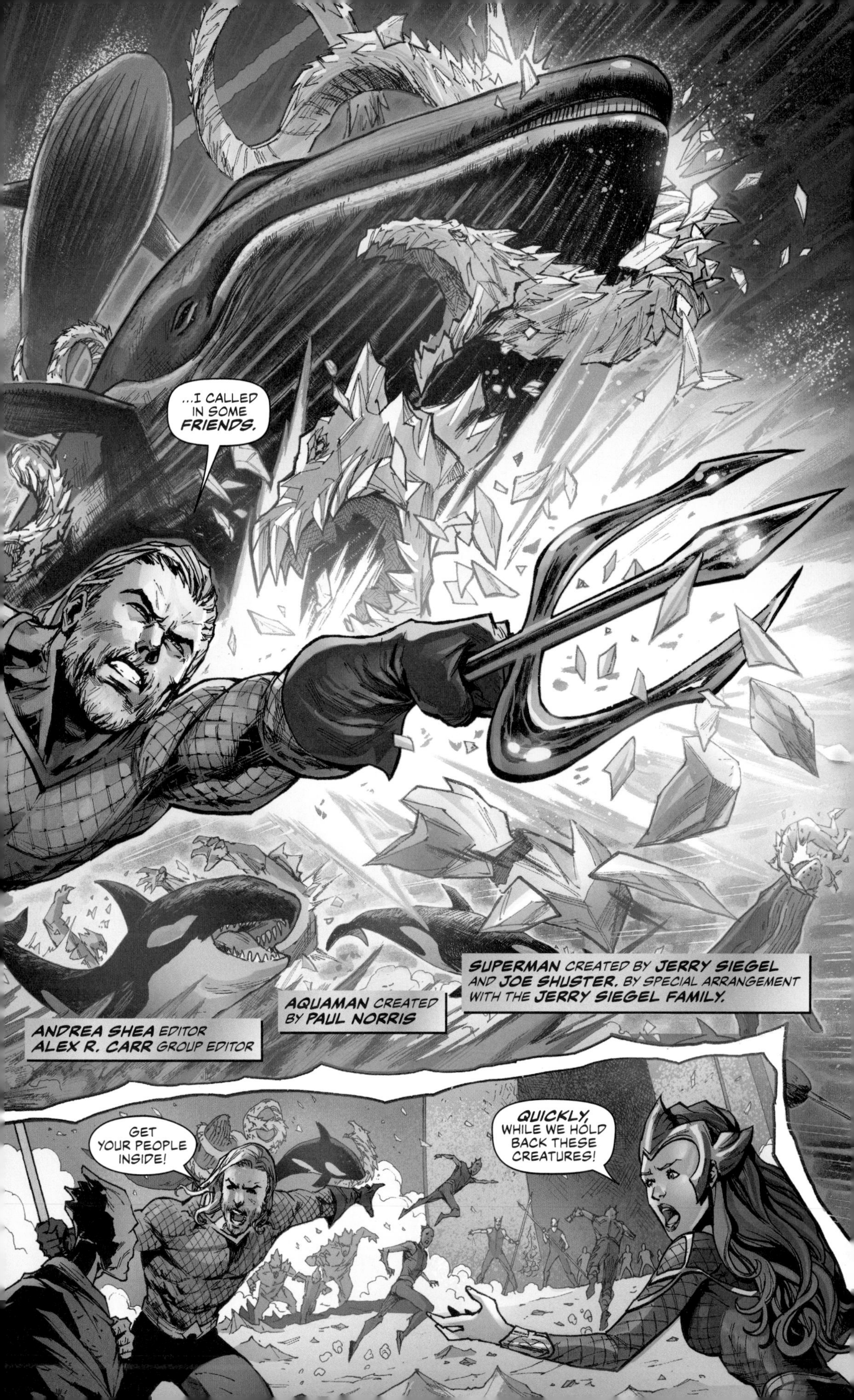
...I CALLED IN SOME FRIENDS.
ANDREA SHEA EDITOR
ALEX R. CARR GROUP EDITOR
AQUAMAN CREATED BY PAUL NORRIS
SUPERMAN CREATED BY JERRY SIEGEL AND JOE SHUSTER. BY SPECIAL ARRANGEMENT WITH THE JERRY SIEGEL FAMILY.
GET YOUR PEOPLE INSIDE!
QUICKLY, WHILE WE HOLD BACK THESE CREATURES!

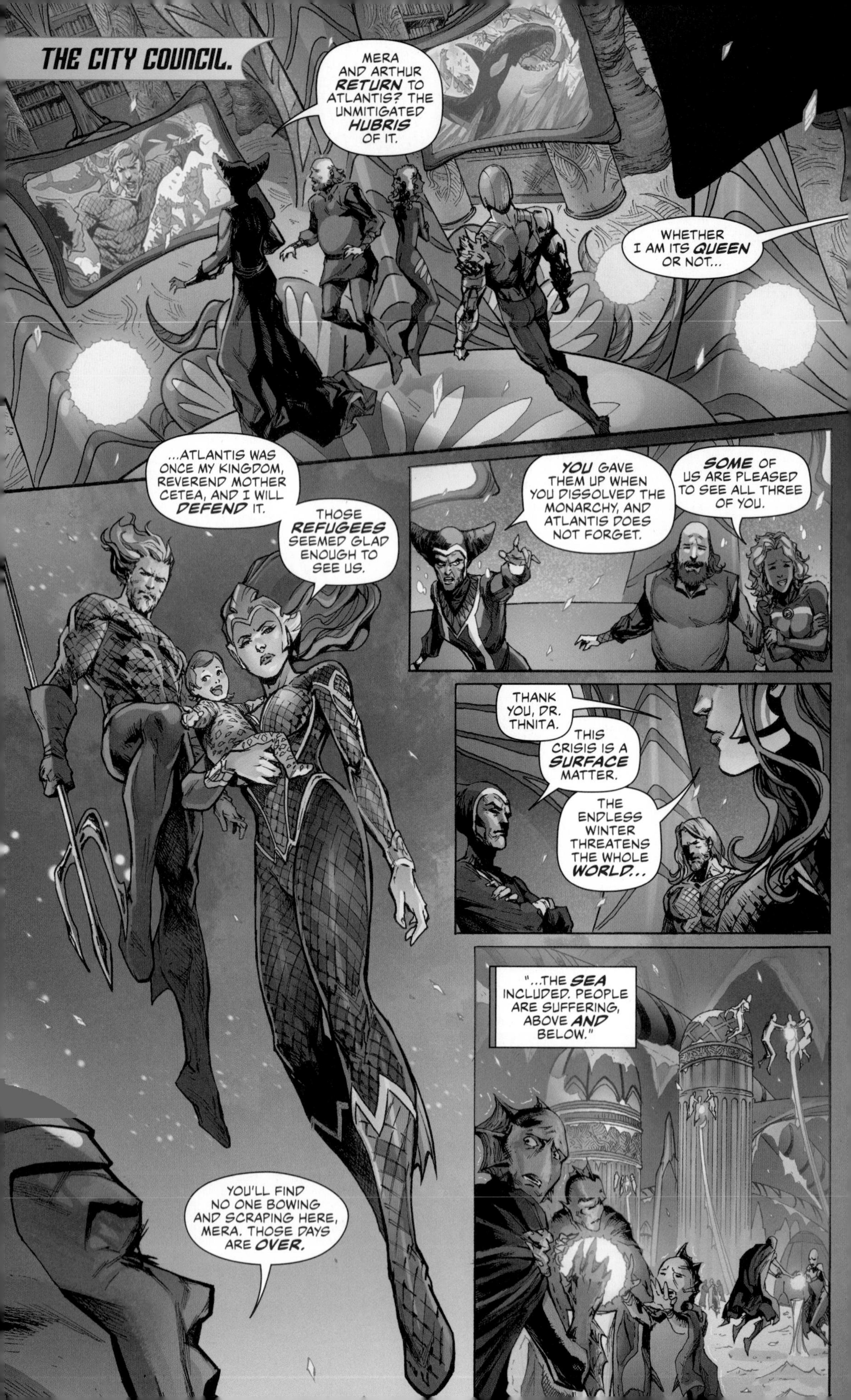
THE CITY COUNCIL.
MERA AND ARTHUR RETURN TO ATLANTIS? THE UNMITIGATED HUBRIS OF IT.
WHETHER I AM ITS QUEEN OR NOT...
...ATLANTIS WAS ONCE MY KINGDOM, REVEREND MOTHER CETEA, AND I WILL DEFEND IT.
THOSE REFUGEES SEEMED GLAD ENOUGH TO SEE US.
YOU'LL FIND NO ONE BOWING AND SCRAPING HERE, MERA. THOSE DAYS ARE OVER.
YOU GAVE THEM UP WHEN YOU DISSOLVED THE MONARCHY, AND ATLANTIS DOES NOT FORGET.
SOME OF US ARE PLEASED TO SEE ALL THREE OF YOU.
THANK YOU, DR. THNITA.
THIS CRISIS IS A SURFACE MATTER.
THE ENDLESS WINTER THREATENS THE WHOLE WORLD...
"...THE SEA INCLUDED. PEOPLE ARE SUFFERING, ABOVE AND BELOW."

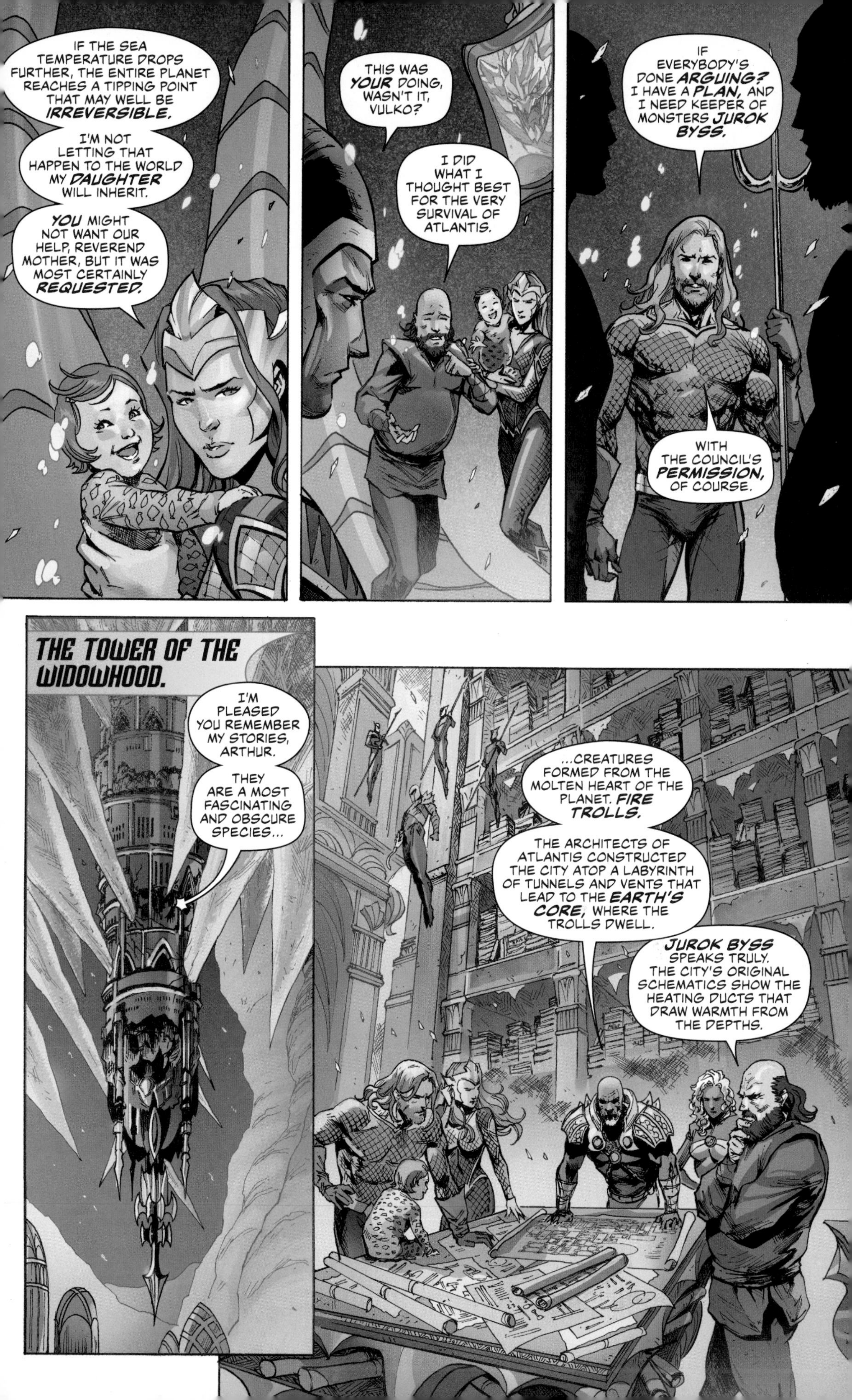
IF THE SEA TEMPERATURE DROPS FURTHER, THE ENTIRE PLANET REACHES A TIPPING POINT THAT MAY WELL BE IRREVERSIBLE.
I'M NOT LETTING THAT HAPPEN TO THE WORLD MY DAUGHTER WILL INHERIT.
YOU MIGHT NOT WANT OUR HELP, REVEREND MOTHER, BUT IT WAS MOST CERTAINLY REQUESTED.
THIS WAS YOUR DOING, WASN'T IT, VULKO?
I DID WHAT I THOUGHT BEST FOR THE VERY SURVIVAL OF ATLANTIS.
IF EVERYBODY'S DONE ARGUING? I HAVE A PLAN, AND I NEED KEEPER OF MONSTERS JUROK BYSS.
WITH THE COUNCIL'S PERMISSION, OF COURSE.
THE TOWER OF THE WIDOWHOOD.
I'M PLEASED YOU REMEMBER MY STORIES, ARTHUR.
THEY ARE A MOST FASCINATING AND OBSCURE SPECIES...
...CREATURES FORMED FROM THE MOLTEN HEART OF THE PLANET. FIRE TROLLS.
THE ARCHITECTS OF ATLANTIS CONSTRUCTED THE CITY ATOP A LABYRINTH OF TUNNELS AND VENTS THAT LEAD TO THE EARTH'S CORE, WHERE THE TROLLS DWELL.
JUROK BYSS SPEAKS TRULY. THE CITY'S ORIGINAL SCHEMATICS SHOW THE HEATING DUCTS THAT DRAW WARMTH FROM THE DEPTHS.

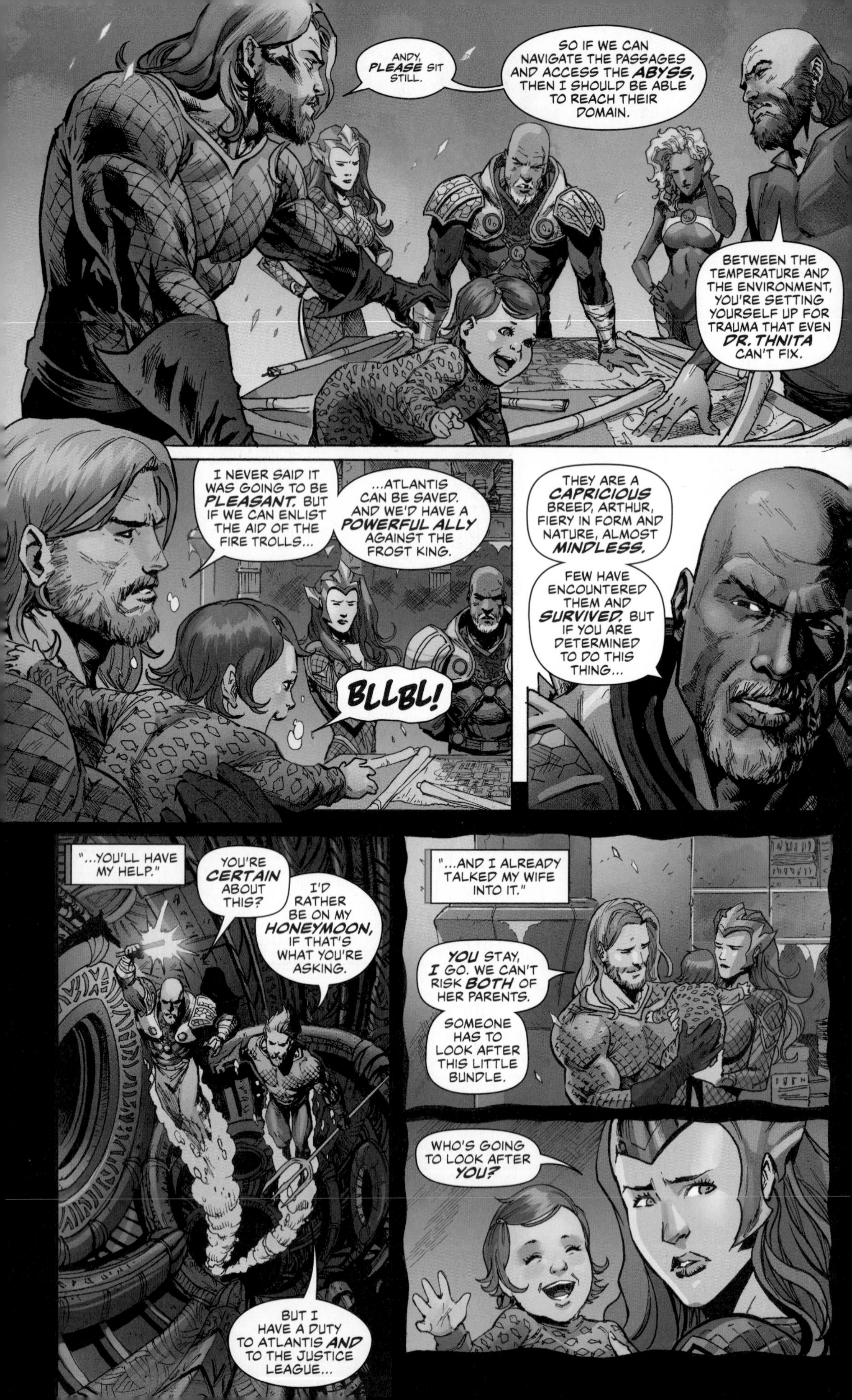
ANDY, PLEASE SIT STILL.
SO IF WE CAN NAVIGATE THE PASSAGES AND ACCESS THE ABYSS, THEN I SHOULD BE ABLE TO REACH THEIR DOMAIN.
BETWEEN THE TEMPERATURE AND THE ENVIRONMENT, YOU'RE SETTING YOURSELF UP FOR TRAUMA THAT EVEN DR. THNITA CAN'T FIX.
I NEVER SAID IT WAS GOING TO BE PLEASANT. BUT IF WE CAN ENLIST THE AID OF THE FIRE TROLLS...
...ATLANTIS CAN BE SAVED. AND WE'D HAVE A POWERFUL ALLY AGAINST THE FROST KING.
BLLBL!
THEY ARE A CAPRICIOUS BREED, ARTHUR, FIERY IN FORM AND NATURE, ALMOST MINDLESS.
FEW HAVE ENCOUNTERED THEM AND SURVIVED. BUT IF YOU ARE DETERMINED TO DO THIS THING...
"...YOU'LL HAVE MY HELP."
YOU'RE CERTAIN ABOUT THIS?
I'D RATHER BE ON MY HONEYMOON, IF THAT'S WHAT YOU'RE ASKING.
BUT I HAVE A DUTY TO ATLANTIS AND TO THE JUSTICE LEAGUE...
"...AND I ALREADY TALKED MY WIFE INTO IT."
YOU STAY, I GO. WE CAN'T RISK BOTH OF HER PARENTS.
SOMEONE HAS TO LOOK AFTER THIS LITTLE BUNDLE.
WHO'S GOING TO LOOK AFTER YOU?

I EXPECT MERA WAS NOT PLEASED.

DUTY CALLS TO BOTH OF US.

MY MOTHER'S SENSE OF DUTY SPLIT MY FAMILY APART.

AND I KNOW MERA'S SENSE OF DUTY IS JUST AS STRONG.

SOMETIMES I WONDER IF I'M JUST FATED TO REPEAT THE MISTAKES MY PARENTS MADE.

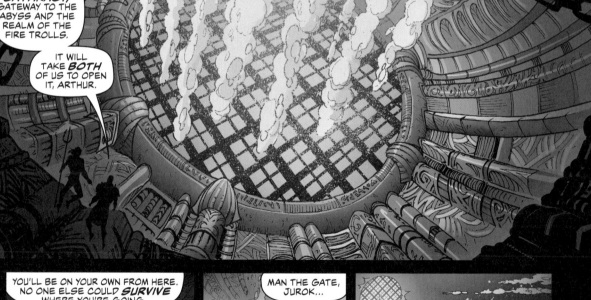

WELCOME TO THE GREAT CATARACT, GATEWAY TO THE ABYSS AND THE REALM OF THE FIRE TROLLS.

IT WILL TAKE BOTH OF US TO OPEN IT, ARTHUR.

YOU'LL BE ON YOUR OWN FROM HERE. NO ONE ELSE COULD SURVIVE WHERE YOU'RE GOING.

MAN THE GATE, JUROK...

...I'LL BE BACK.

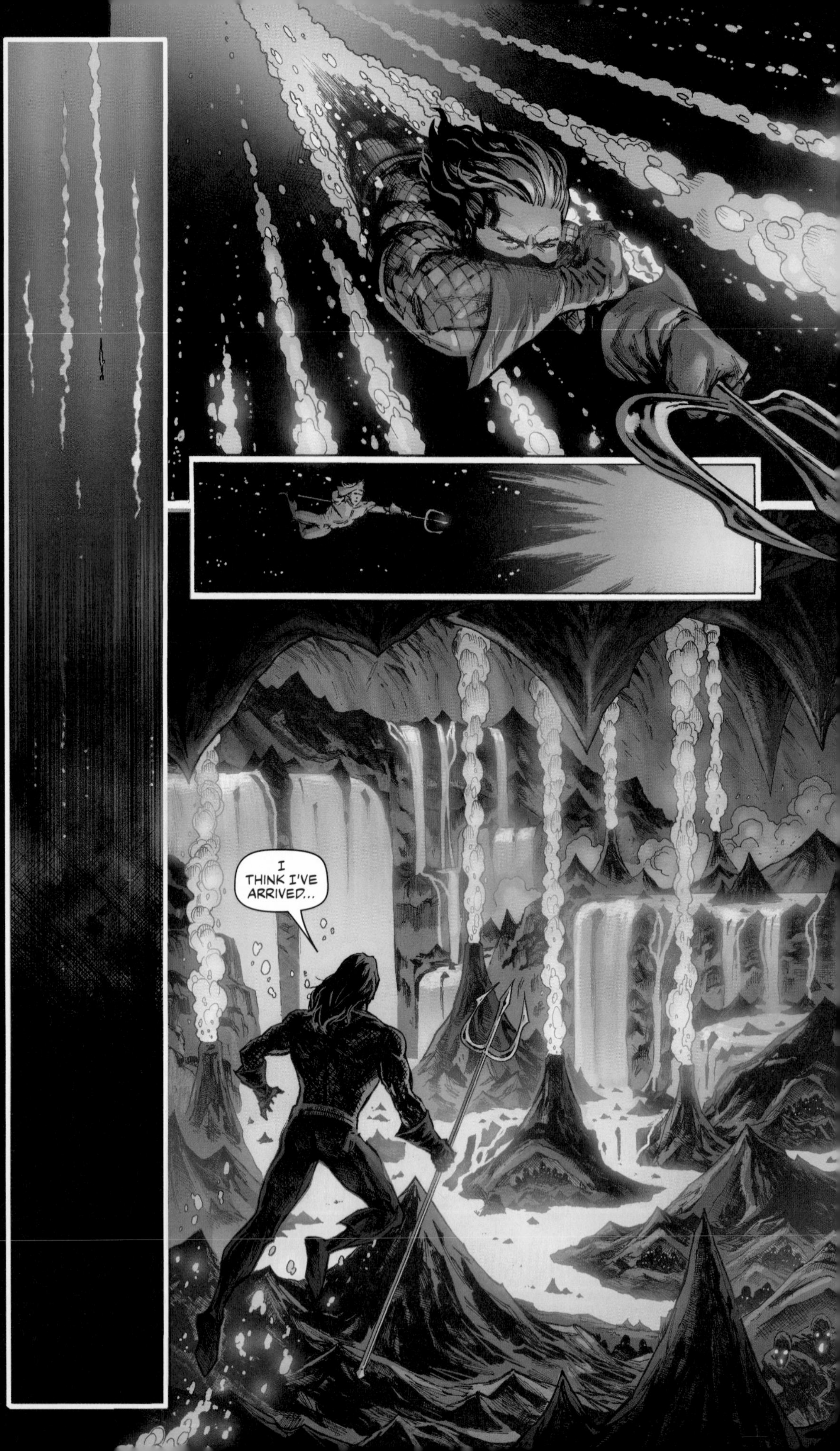
I THINK I'VE ARRIVED...

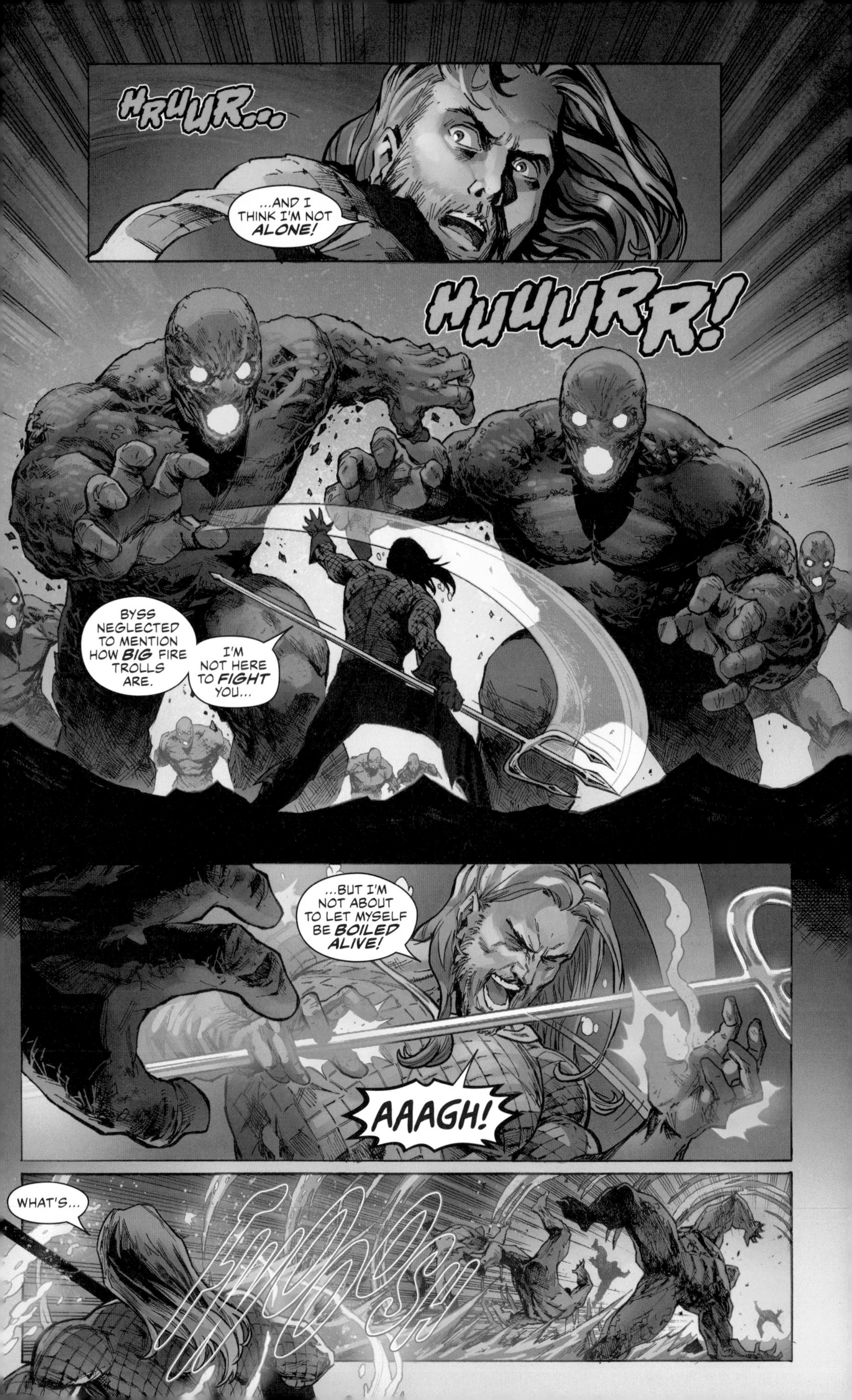
HRUUR...
...AND I THINK I'M NOT ALONE!
HUUURRR!
BYSS NEGLECTED TO MENTION HOW BIG FIRE TROLLS ARE.
I'M NOT HERE TO FIGHT YOU...
...BUT I'M NOT ABOUT TO LET MYSELF BE BOILED ALIVE!
AAAGH!
WHAT'S...

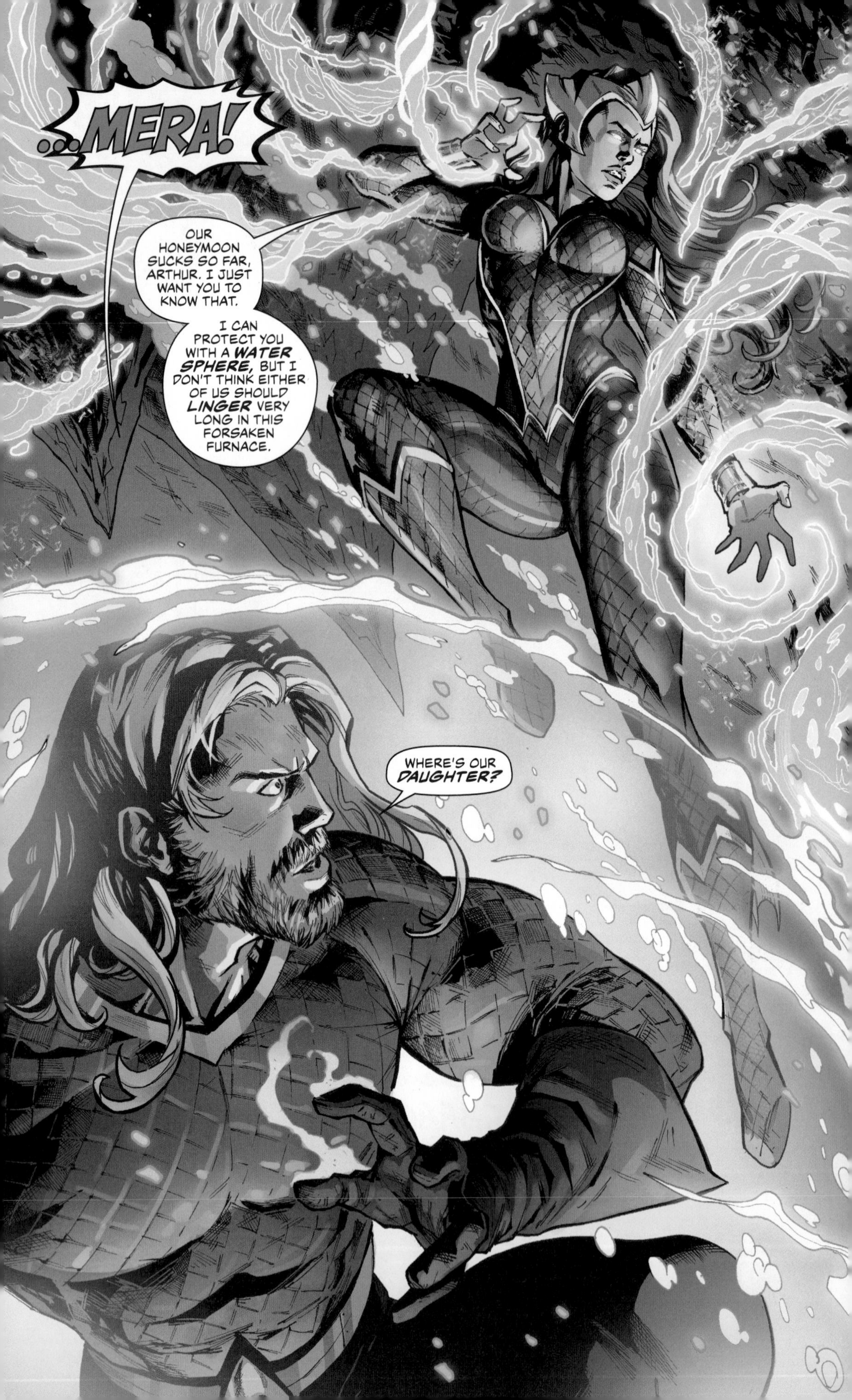

...MERA!
OUR HONEYMOON SUCKS SO FAR, ARTHUR. I JUST WANT YOU TO KNOW THAT.
I CAN PROTECT YOU WITH A WATER SPHERE, BUT I DON'T THINK EITHER OF US SHOULD LINGER VERY LONG IN THIS FORSAKEN FURNACE.
WHERE'S OUR DAUGHTER?

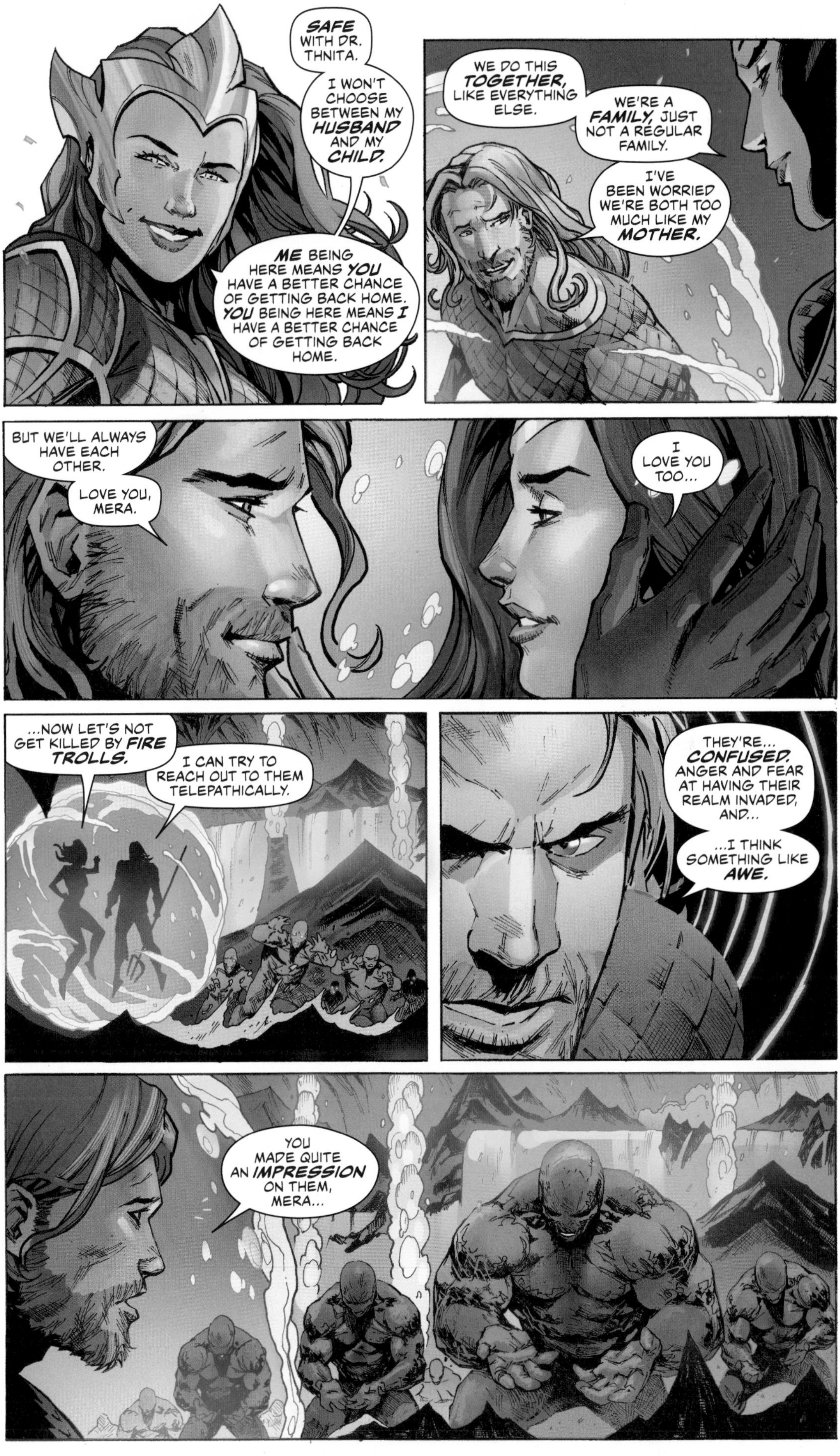

SAFE WITH DR. THNITA.
I WON'T CHOOSE BETWEEN MY HUSBAND AND MY CHILD.
ME BEING HERE MEANS YOU HAVE A BETTER CHANCE OF GETTING BACK HOME. YOU BEING HERE MEANS I HAVE A BETTER CHANCE OF GETTING BACK HOME.
WE DO THIS TOGETHER, LIKE EVERYTHING ELSE.
WE'RE A FAMILY, JUST NOT A REGULAR FAMILY.
I'VE BEEN WORRIED WE'RE BOTH TOO MUCH LIKE MY MOTHER.
BUT WE'LL ALWAYS HAVE EACH OTHER.
LOVE YOU, MERA.
I LOVE YOU TOO...
...NOW LET'S NOT GET KILLED BY FIRE TROLLS.
I CAN TRY TO REACH OUT TO THEM TELEPATHICALLY.
THEY'RE... CONFUSED. ANGER AND FEAR AT HAVING THEIR REALM INVADED, AND...
...I THINK SOMETHING LIKE AWE.
YOU MADE QUITE AN IMPRESSION ON THEM, MERA...

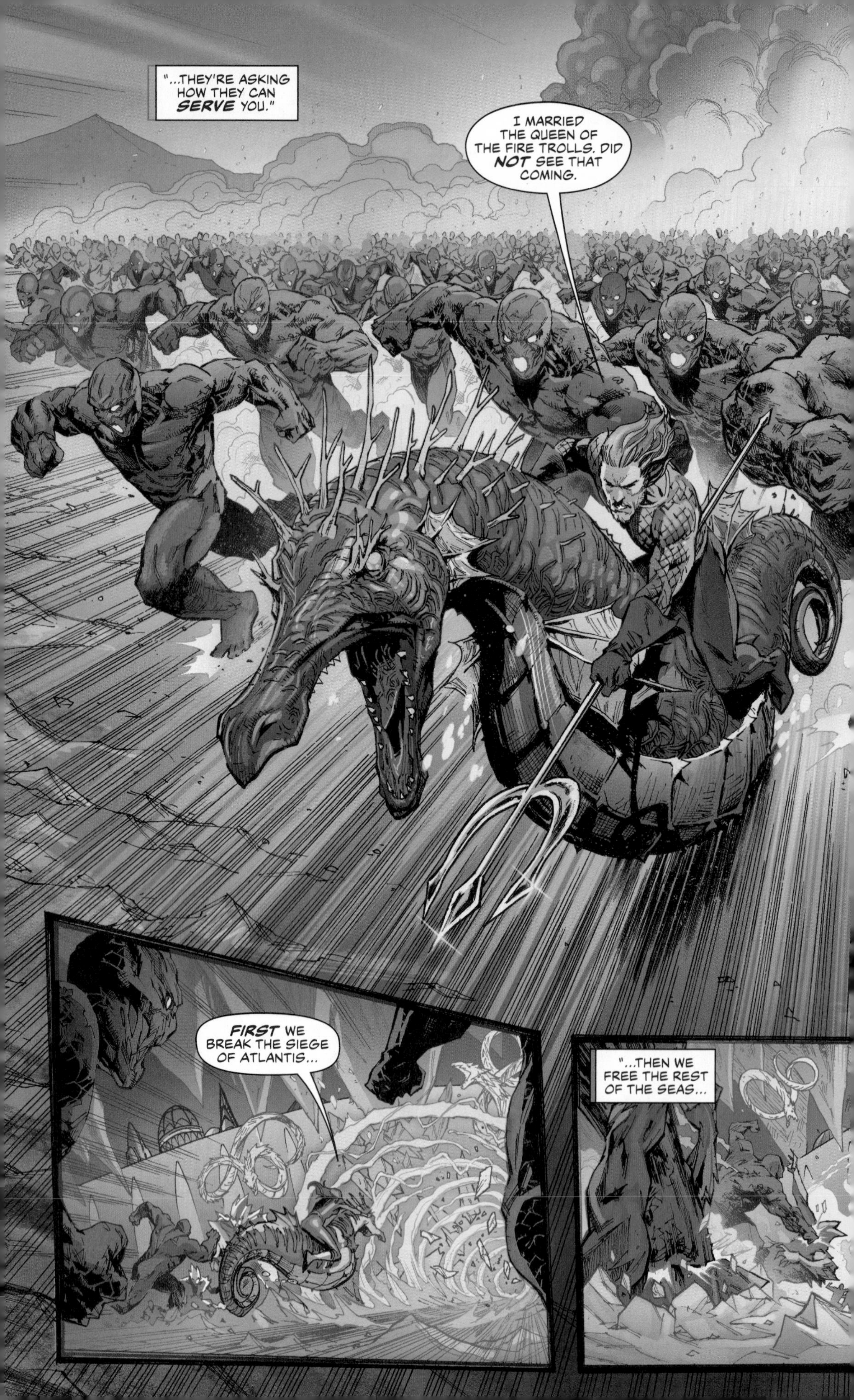
"...THEY'RE ASKING HOW THEY CAN SERVE YOU."
I MARRIED THE QUEEN OF THE FIRE TROLLS. DID NOT SEE THAT COMING.
FIRST WE BREAK THE SIEGE OF ATLANTIS...
"...THEN WE FREE THE REST OF THE SEAS...

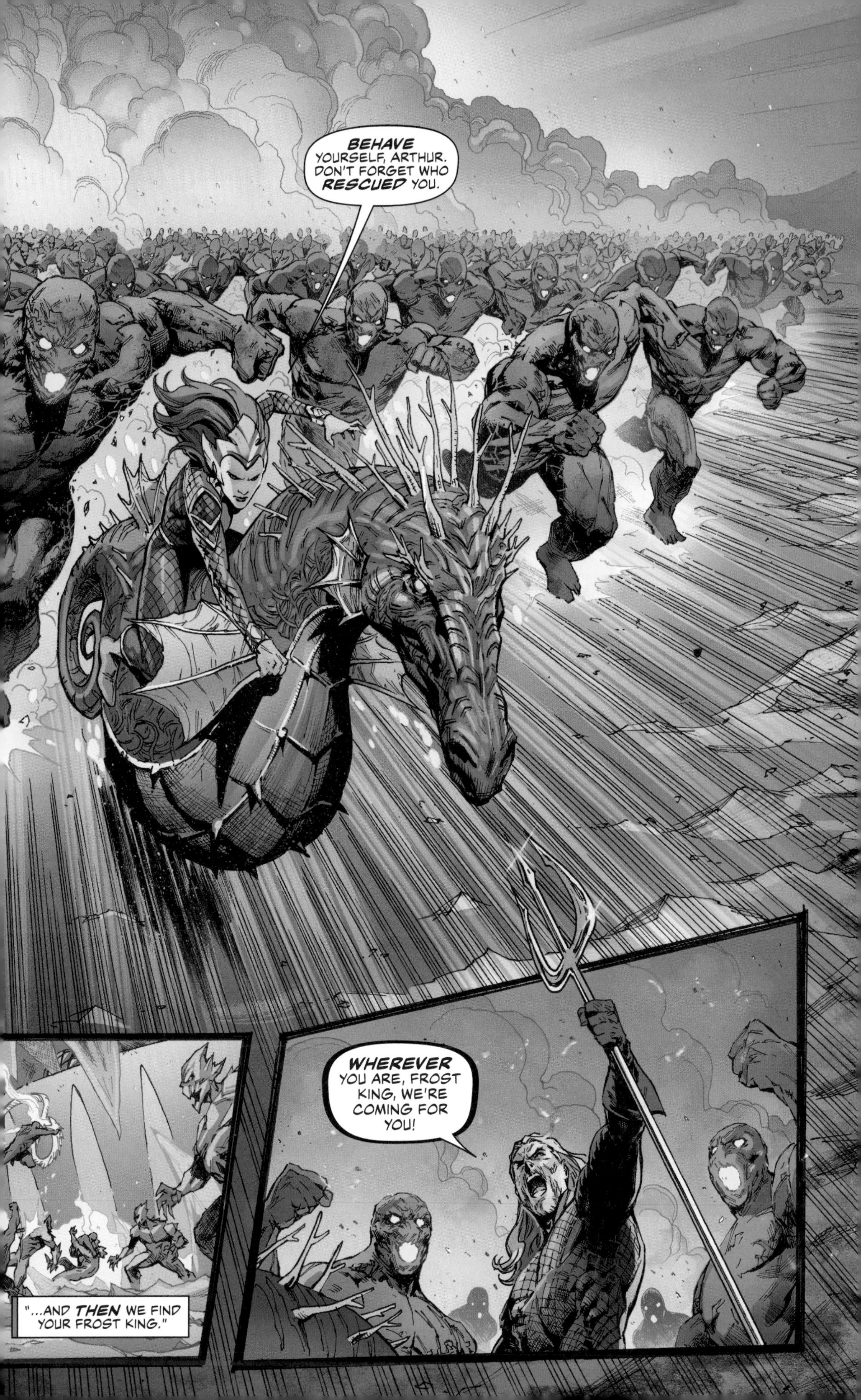
BEHAVE YOURSELF, ARTHUR. DON'T FORGET WHO RESCUED YOU.
"...AND THEN WE FIND YOUR FROST KING."
WHEREVER YOU ARE, FROST KING, WE'RE COMING FOR YOU!

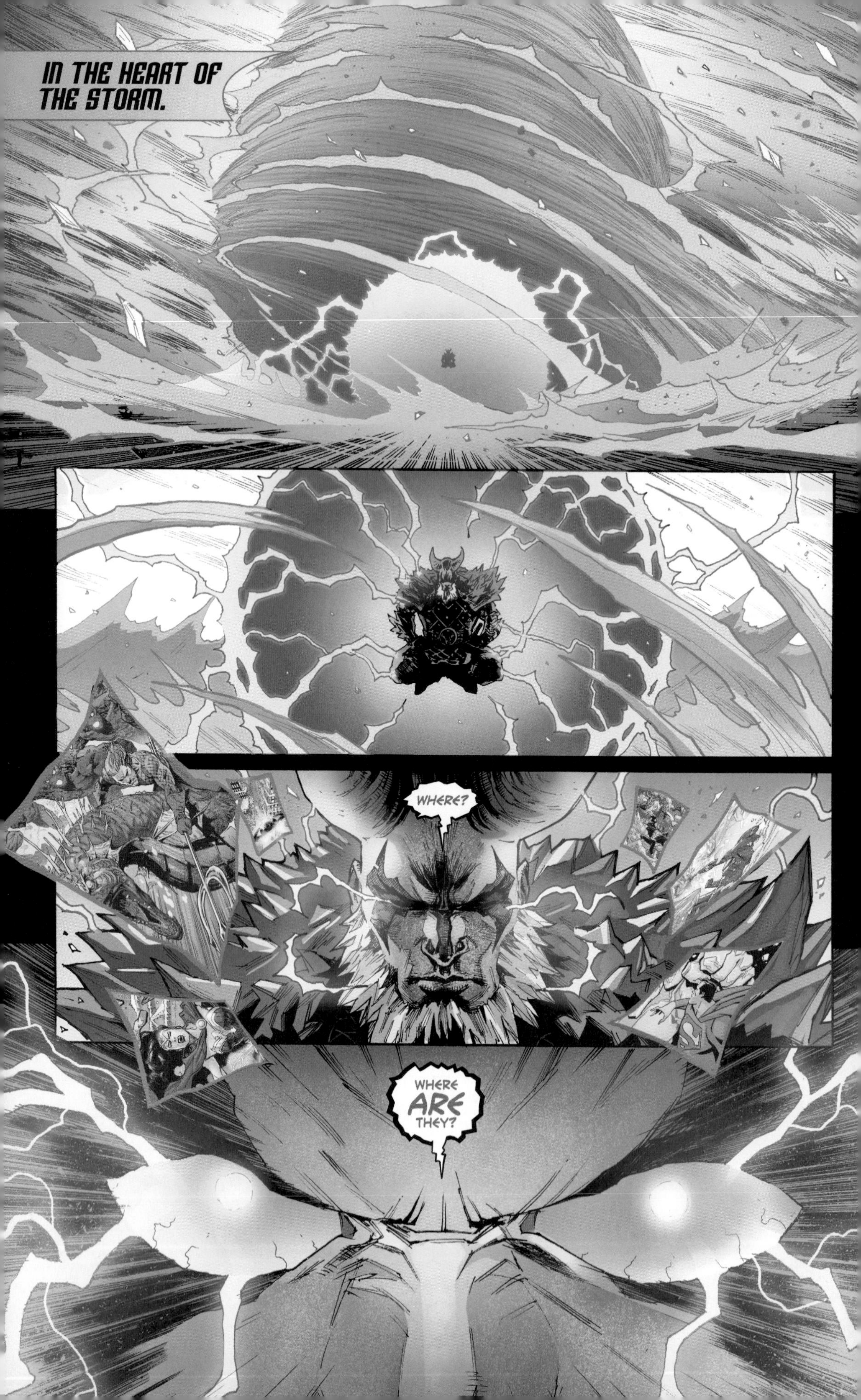
IN THE HEART OF THE STORM.
WHERE?
WHERE ARE THEY?

Justice League #58 cover
by Francis Manapul

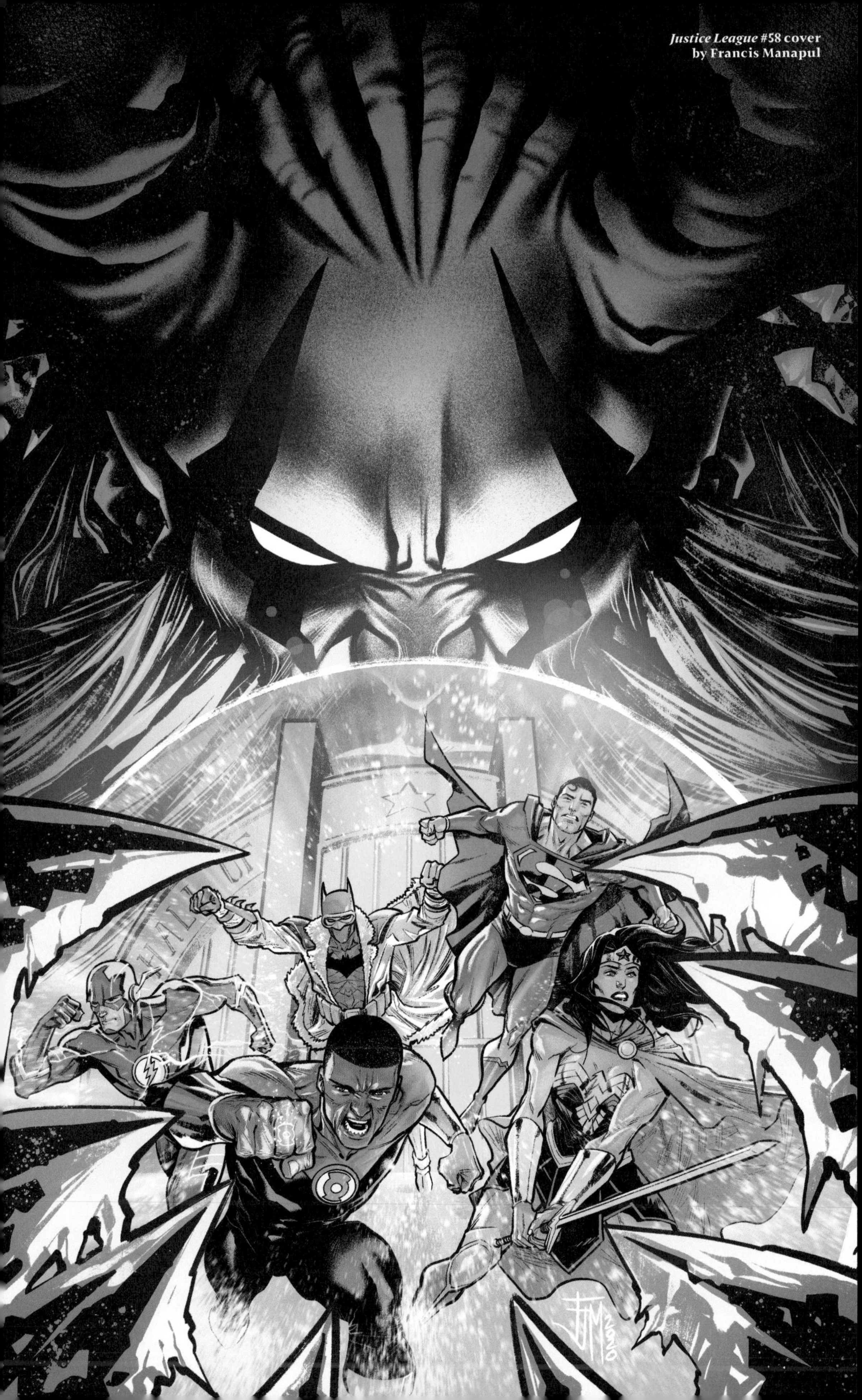

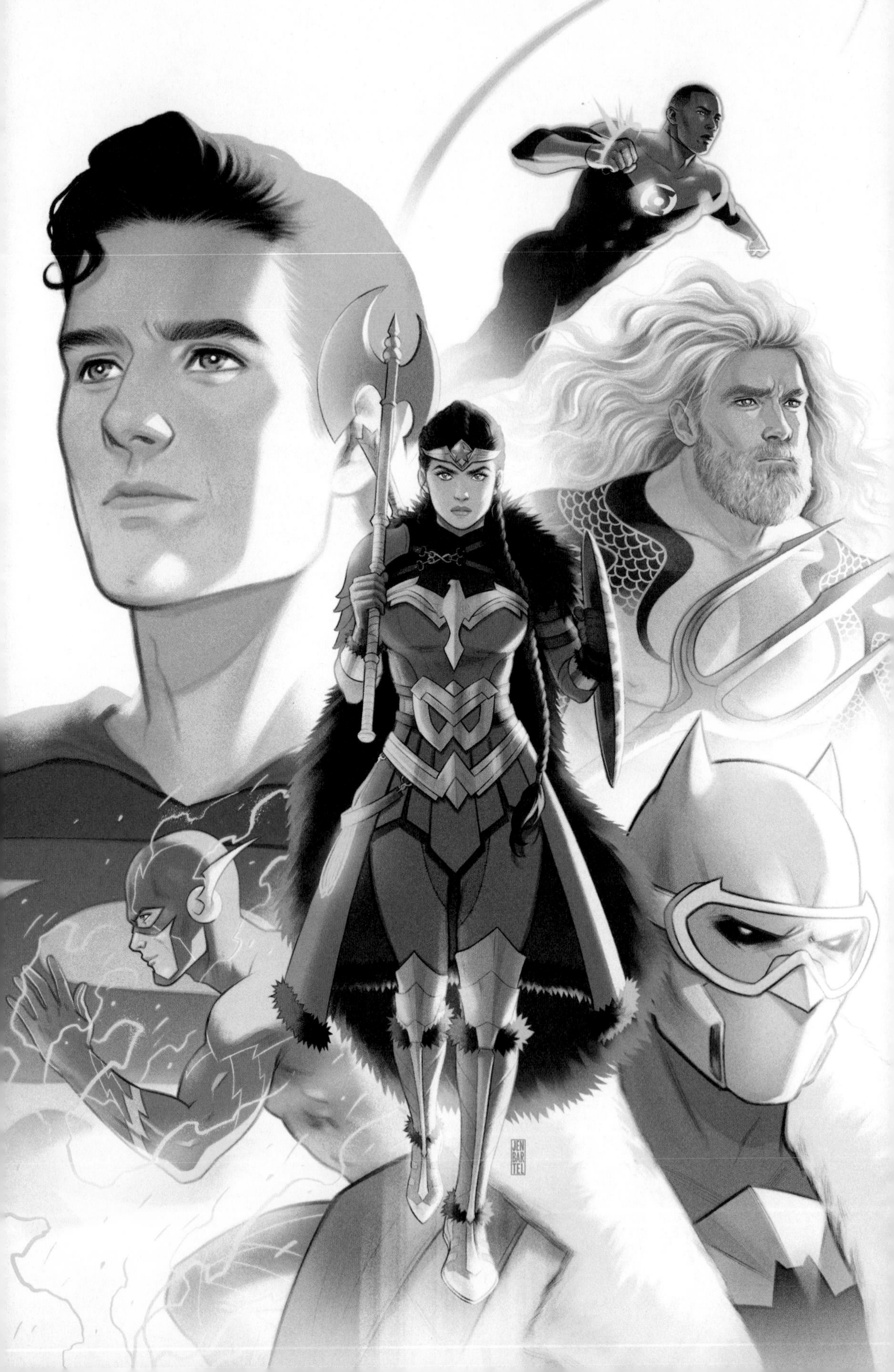
JEN BARTEL

***Justice League* #58 variant cover**
by Jen Bartel

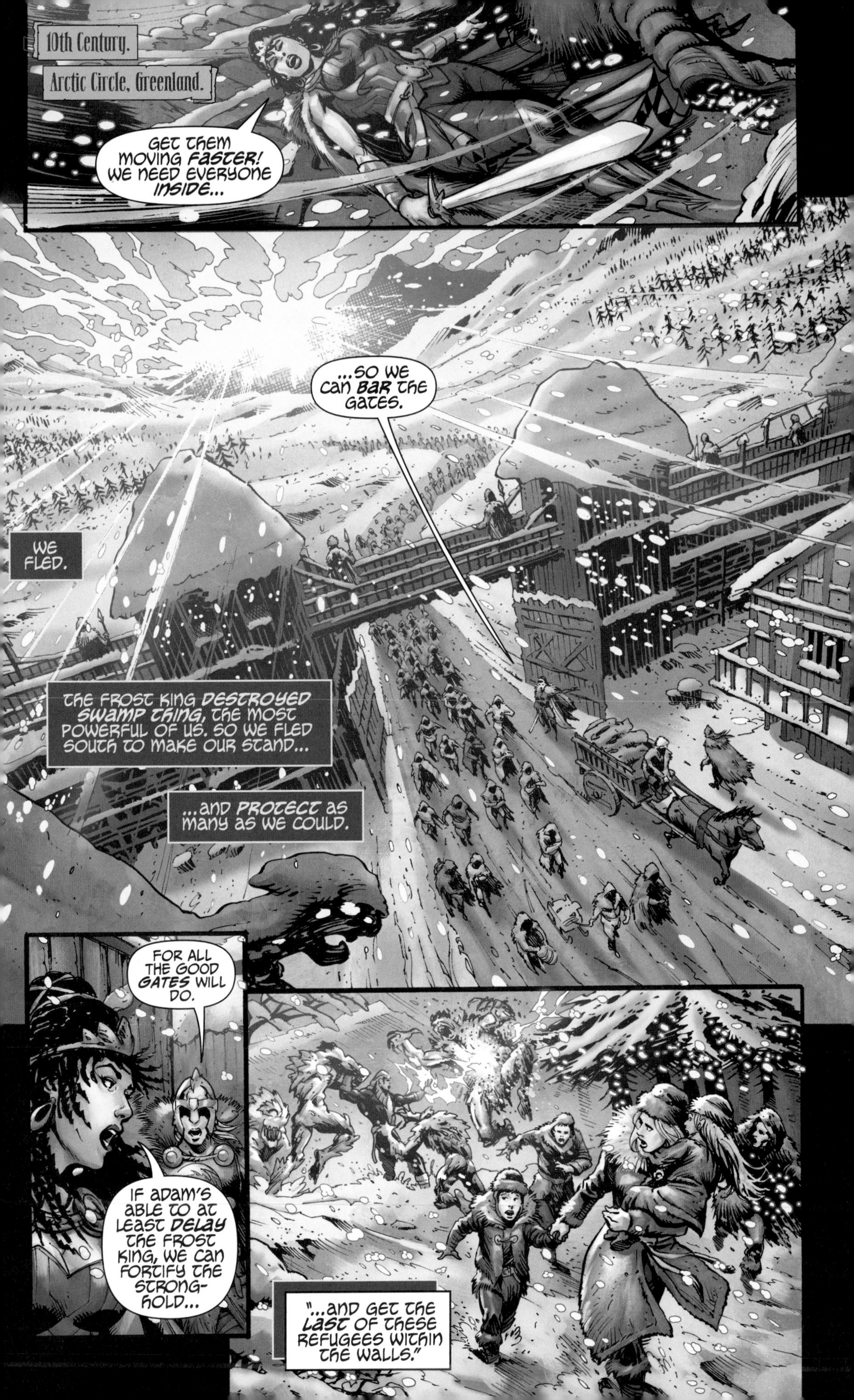
10th Century.
Arctic Circle, Greenland.
GET THEM MOVING FASTER! WE NEED EVERYONE INSIDE...
...SO WE CAN BAR THE GATES.
WE FLED.
THE FROST KING DESTROYED SWAMP THING, THE MOST POWERFUL OF US. SO WE FLED SOUTH TO MAKE OUR STAND...
...AND PROTECT AS MANY AS WE COULD.
FOR ALL THE GOOD GATES WILL DO.
IF ADAM'S ABLE TO AT LEAST DELAY THE FROST KING, WE CAN FORTIFY THE STRONG-HOLD...
"...AND GET THE LAST OF THESE REFUGEES WITHIN THE WALLS."

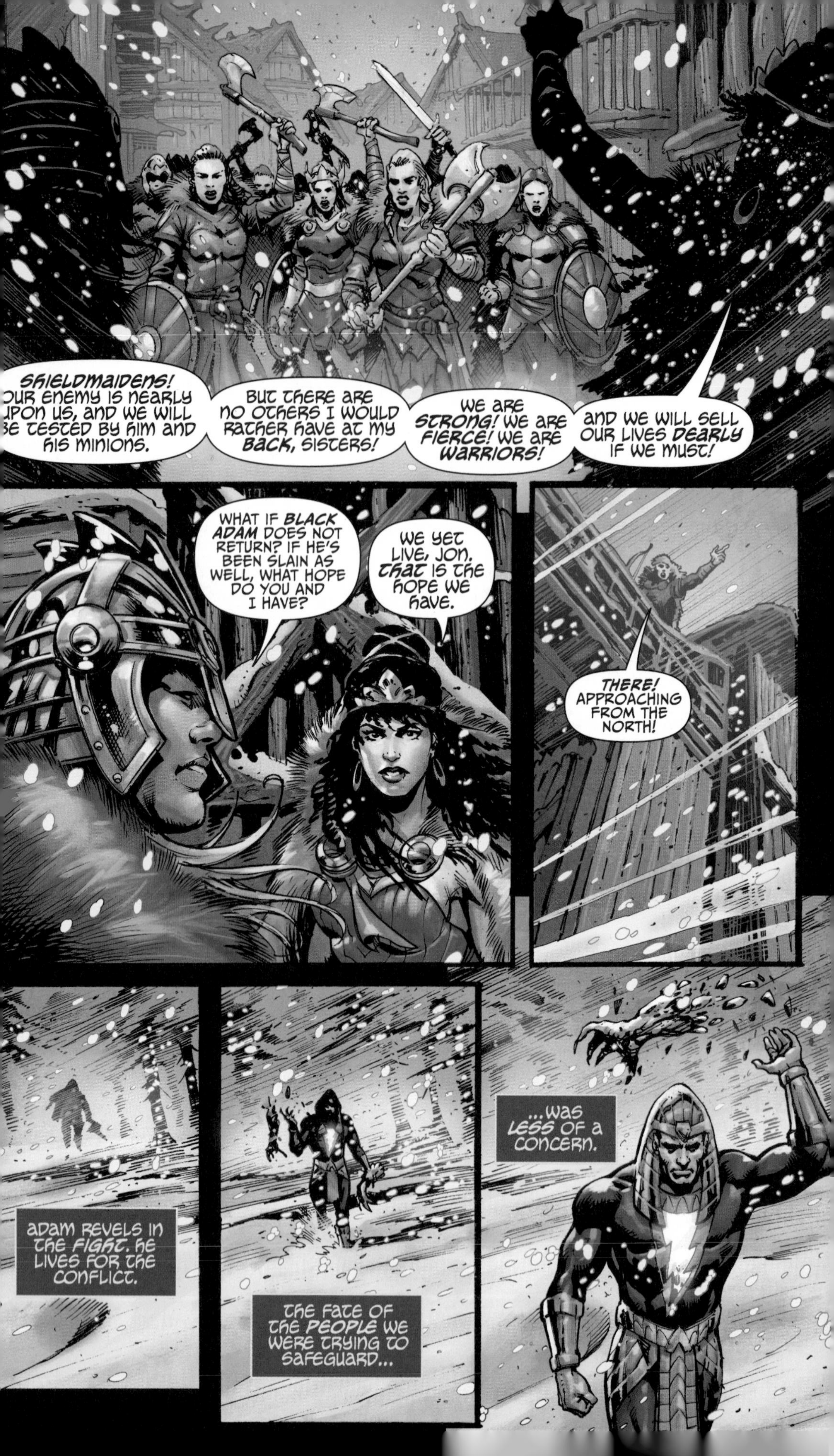
SHIELDMAIDENS! OUR ENEMY IS NEARLY UPON US, AND WE WILL BE TESTED BY HIM AND HIS MINIONS.
BUT THERE ARE NO OTHERS I WOULD RATHER HAVE AT MY BACK, SISTERS!
WE ARE STRONG! WE ARE FIERCE! WE ARE WARRIORS!
AND WE WILL SELL OUR LIVES DEARLY IF WE MUST!
WHAT IF BLACK ADAM DOES NOT RETURN? IF HE'S BEEN SLAIN AS WELL, WHAT HOPE DO YOU AND I HAVE?
WE YET LIVE, JON. THAT IS THE HOPE WE HAVE.
THERE! APPROACHING FROM THE NORTH!
ADAM REVELS IN THE FIGHT. HE LIVES FOR THE CONFLICT.
THE FATE OF THE PEOPLE WE WERE TRYING TO SAFEGUARD...
...WAS LESS OF A CONCERN.

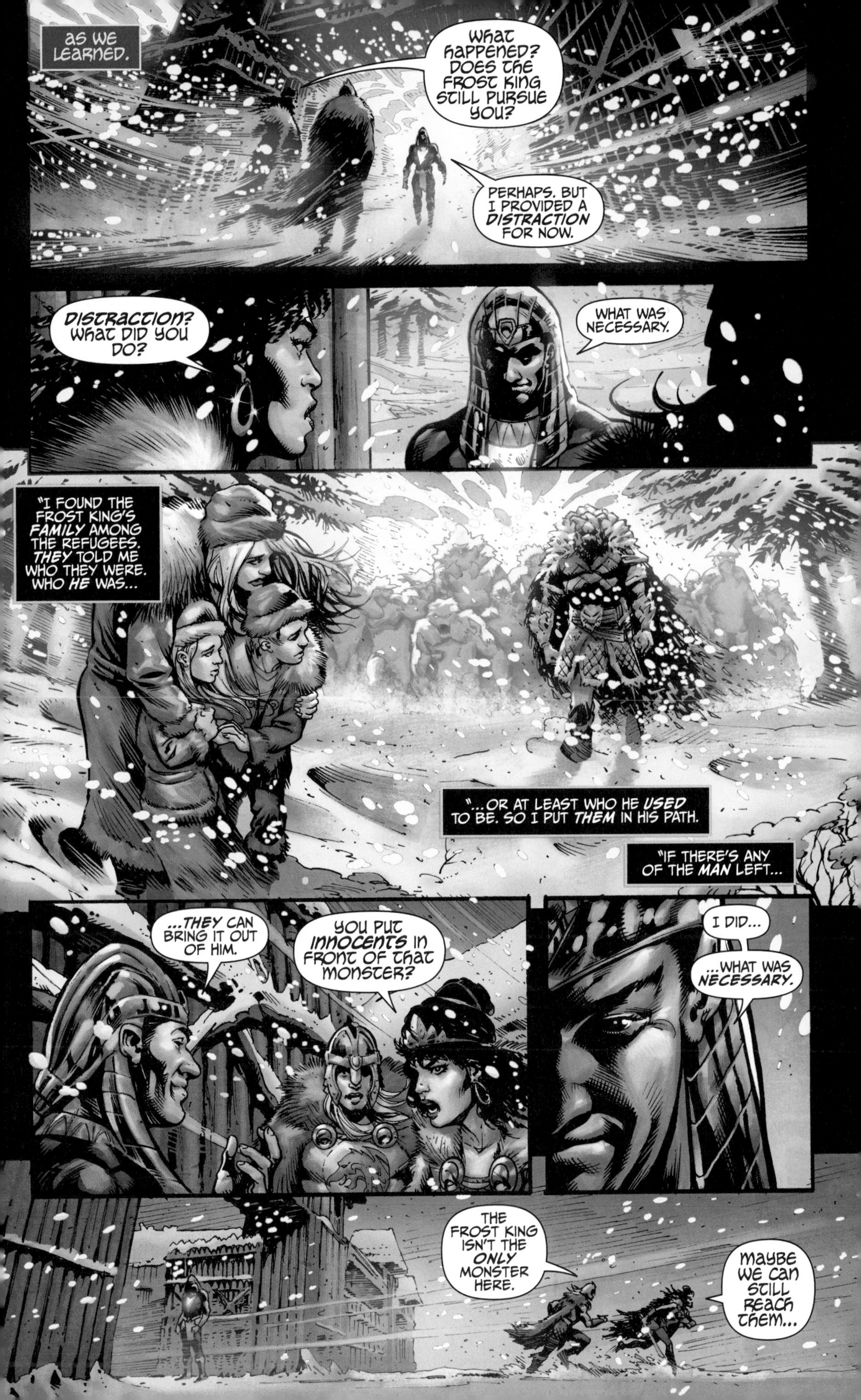

AS WE LEARNED.
WHAT HAPPENED? DOES THE FROST KING STILL PURSUE YOU?
PERHAPS. BUT I PROVIDED A DISTRACTION FOR NOW.
DISTRACTION? WHAT DID YOU DO?
WHAT WAS NECESSARY.
"I FOUND THE FROST KING'S FAMILY AMONG THE REFUGEES. THEY TOLD ME WHO THEY WERE. WHO HE WAS...
"...OR AT LEAST WHO HE USED TO BE. SO I PUT THEM IN HIS PATH.
"IF THERE'S ANY OF THE MAN LEFT...
...THEY CAN BRING IT OUT OF HIM.
YOU PUT INNOCENTS IN FRONT OF THAT MONSTER?
I DID...
...WHAT WAS NECESSARY.
THE FROST KING ISN'T THE ONLY MONSTER HERE.
MAYBE WE CAN STILL REACH THEM...

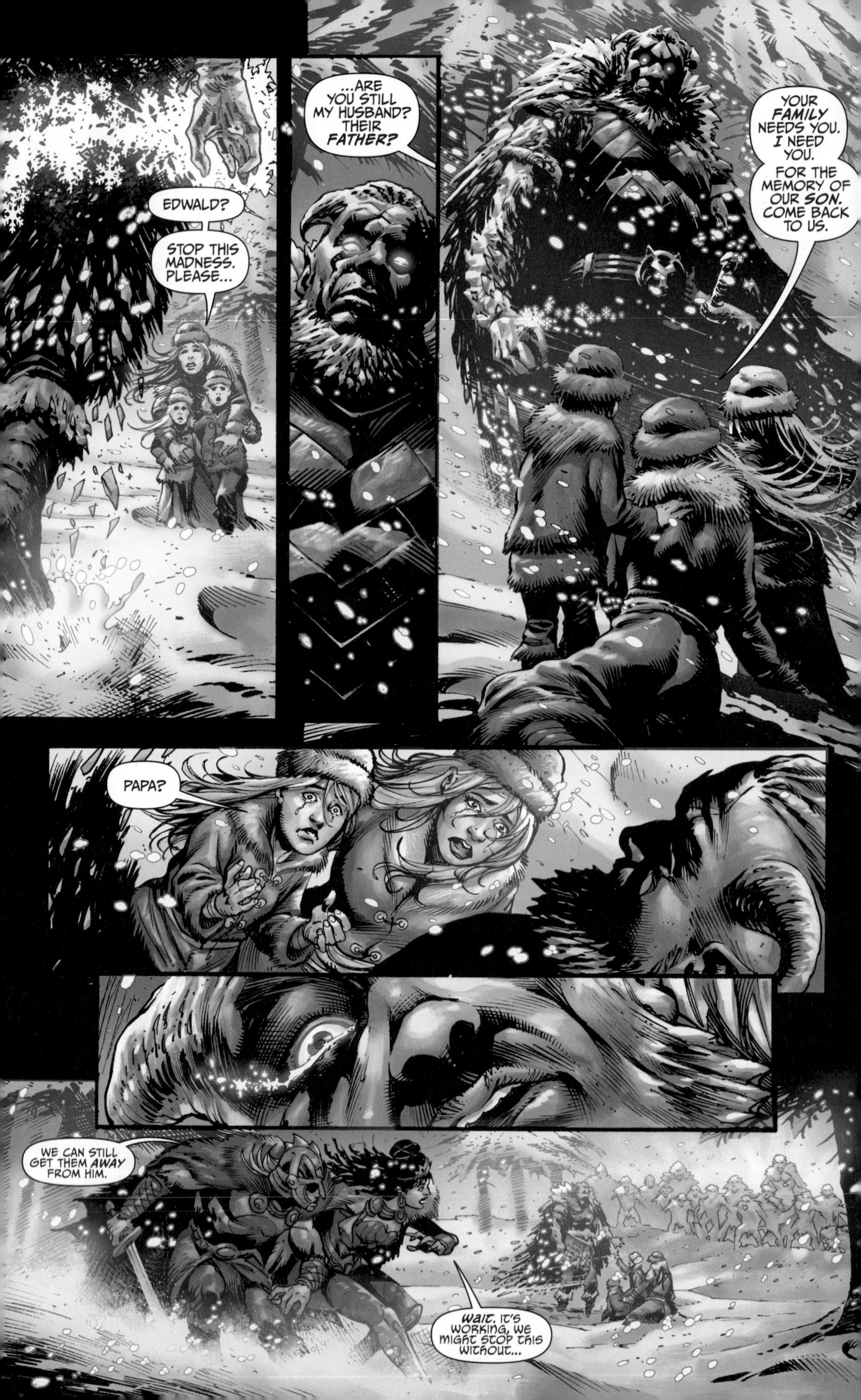
EDWALD?
STOP THIS MADNESS. PLEASE...
...ARE YOU STILL MY HUSBAND? THEIR FATHER?
YOUR FAMILY NEEDS YOU. I NEED YOU.
FOR THE MEMORY OF OUR SON. COME BACK TO US.
PAPA?
WE CAN STILL GET THEM AWAY FROM HIM.
WAIT. IT'S WORKING, WE MIGHT STOP THIS WITHOUT...

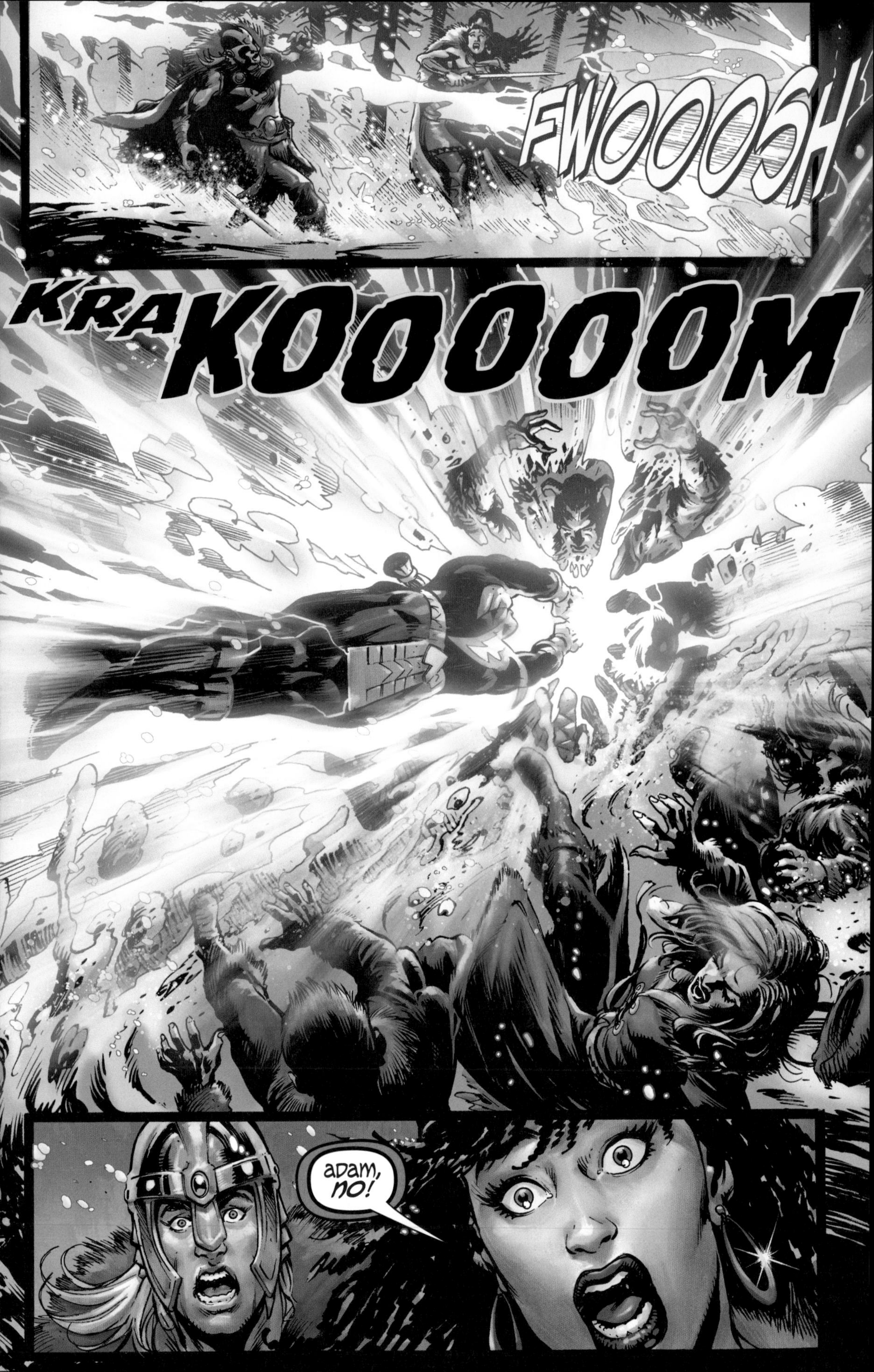
FWOOOSH
KRAKOOOOOM
ADAM, NO!

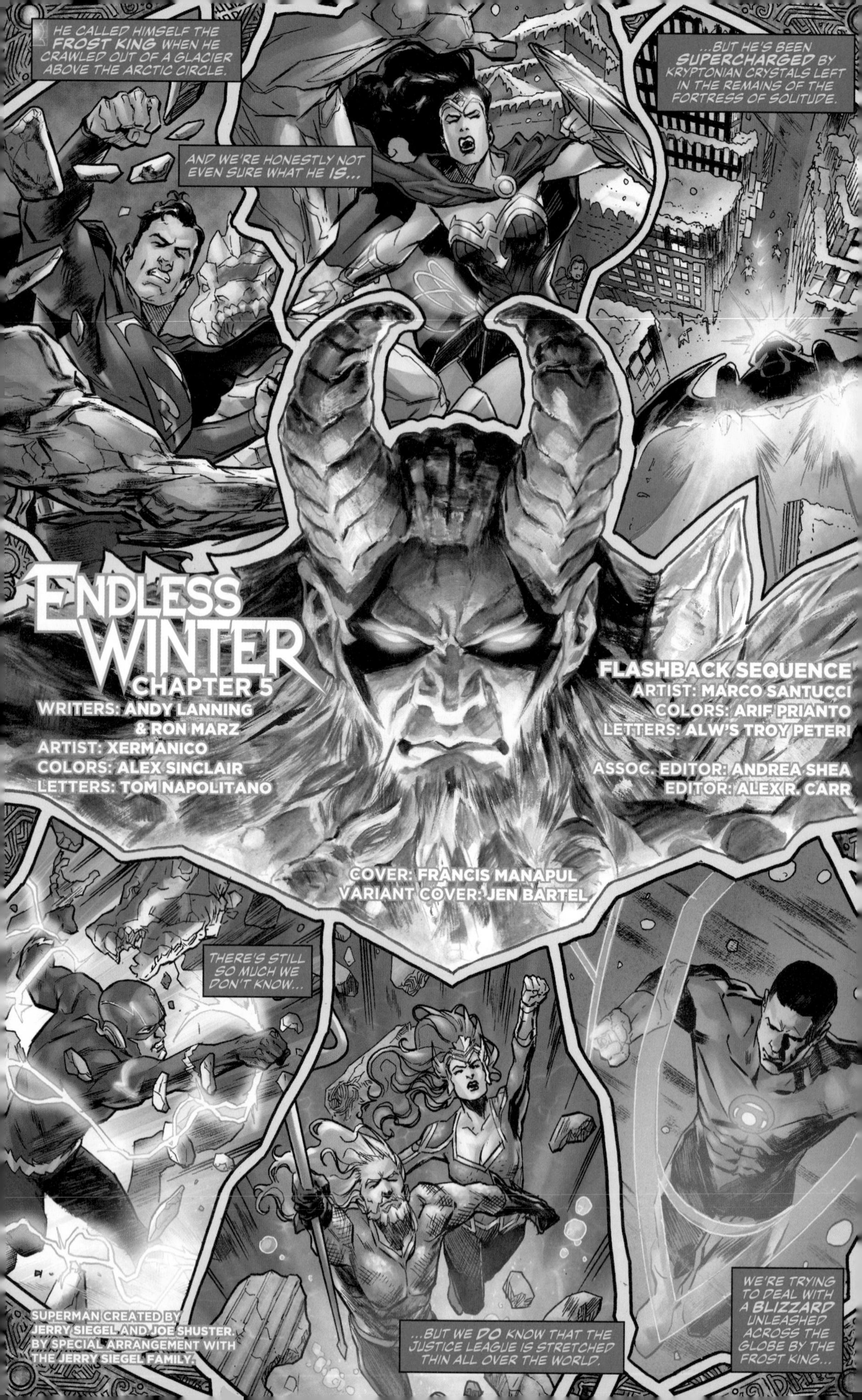
HE CALLED HIMSELF THE FROST KING WHEN HE CRAWLED OUT OF A GLACIER ABOVE THE ARCTIC CIRCLE.
...BUT HE'S BEEN SUPERCHARGED BY KRYPTONIAN CRYSTALS LEFT IN THE REMAINS OF THE FORTRESS OF SOLITUDE.
AND WE'RE HONESTLY NOT EVEN SURE WHAT HE IS...
ENDLESS WINTER
CHAPTER 5
WRITERS: ANDY LANNING & RON MARZ
ARTIST: XERMANICO
COLORS: ALEX SINCLAIR
LETTERS: TOM NAPOLITANO
FLASHBACK SEQUENCE
ARTIST: MARCO SANTUCCI
COLORS: ARIF PRIANTO
LETTERS: ALW'S TROY PETERI
ASSOC. EDITOR: ANDREA SHEA
EDITOR: ALEX R. CARR
COVER: FRANCIS MANAPUL
VARIANT COVER: JEN BARTEL
THERE'S STILL SO MUCH WE DON'T KNOW...
SUPERMAN CREATED BY JERRY SIEGEL AND JOE SHUSTER. BY SPECIAL ARRANGEMENT WITH THE JERRY SIEGEL FAMILY.
...BUT WE DO KNOW THAT THE JUSTICE LEAGUE IS STRETCHED THIN ALL OVER THE WORLD.
WE'RE TRYING TO DEAL WITH A BLIZZARD UNLEASHED ACROSS THE GLOBE BY THE FROST KING...

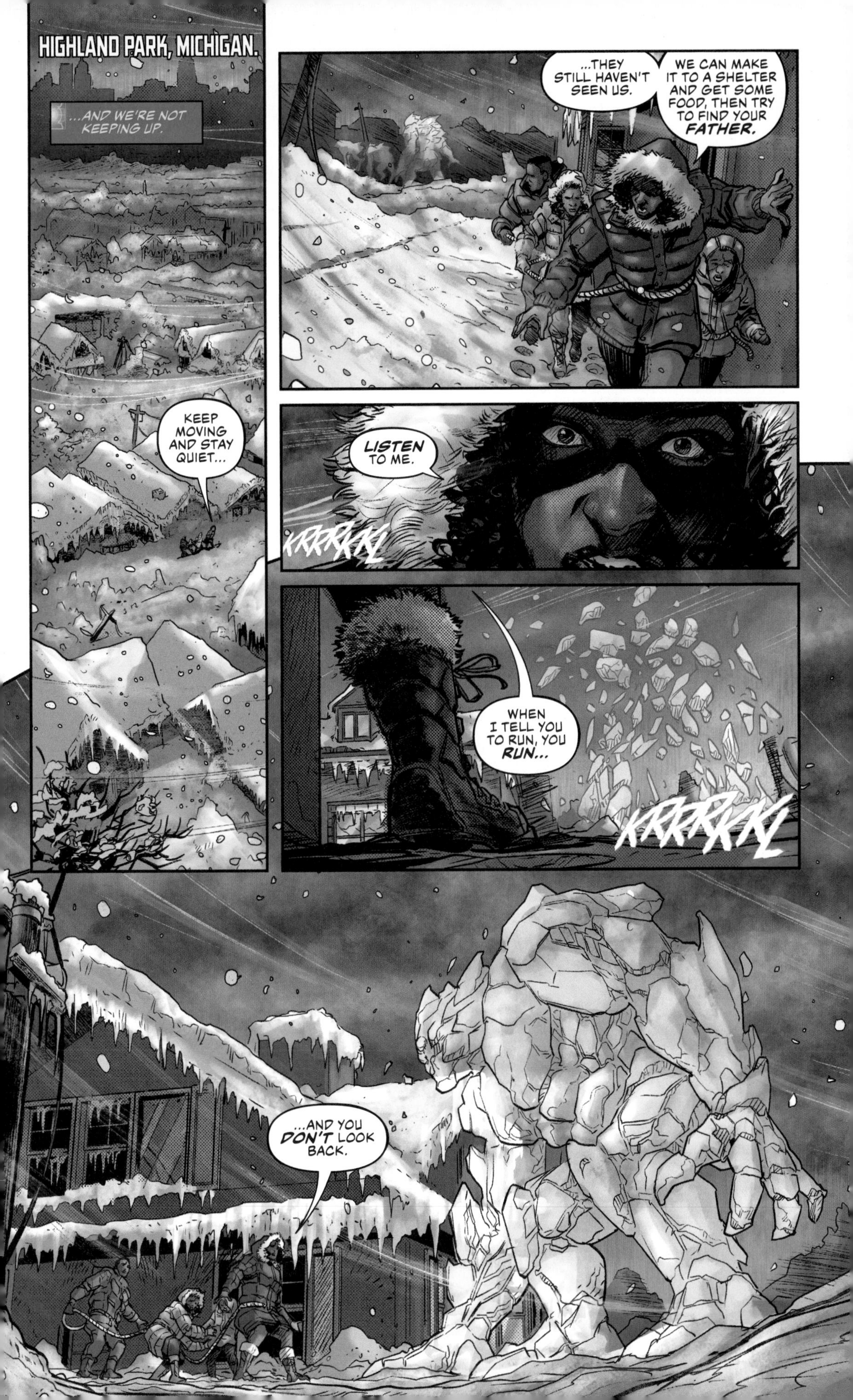
HIGHLAND PARK, MICHIGAN.
...AND WE'RE NOT KEEPING UP.
...THEY STILL HAVEN'T SEEN US.
WE CAN MAKE IT TO A SHELTER AND GET SOME FOOD, THEN TRY TO FIND YOUR FATHER.
KEEP MOVING AND STAY QUIET...
LISTEN TO ME.
KRRRKKL
WHEN I TELL YOU TO RUN, YOU RUN...
KRRRKKL
...AND YOU DON'T LOOK BACK.

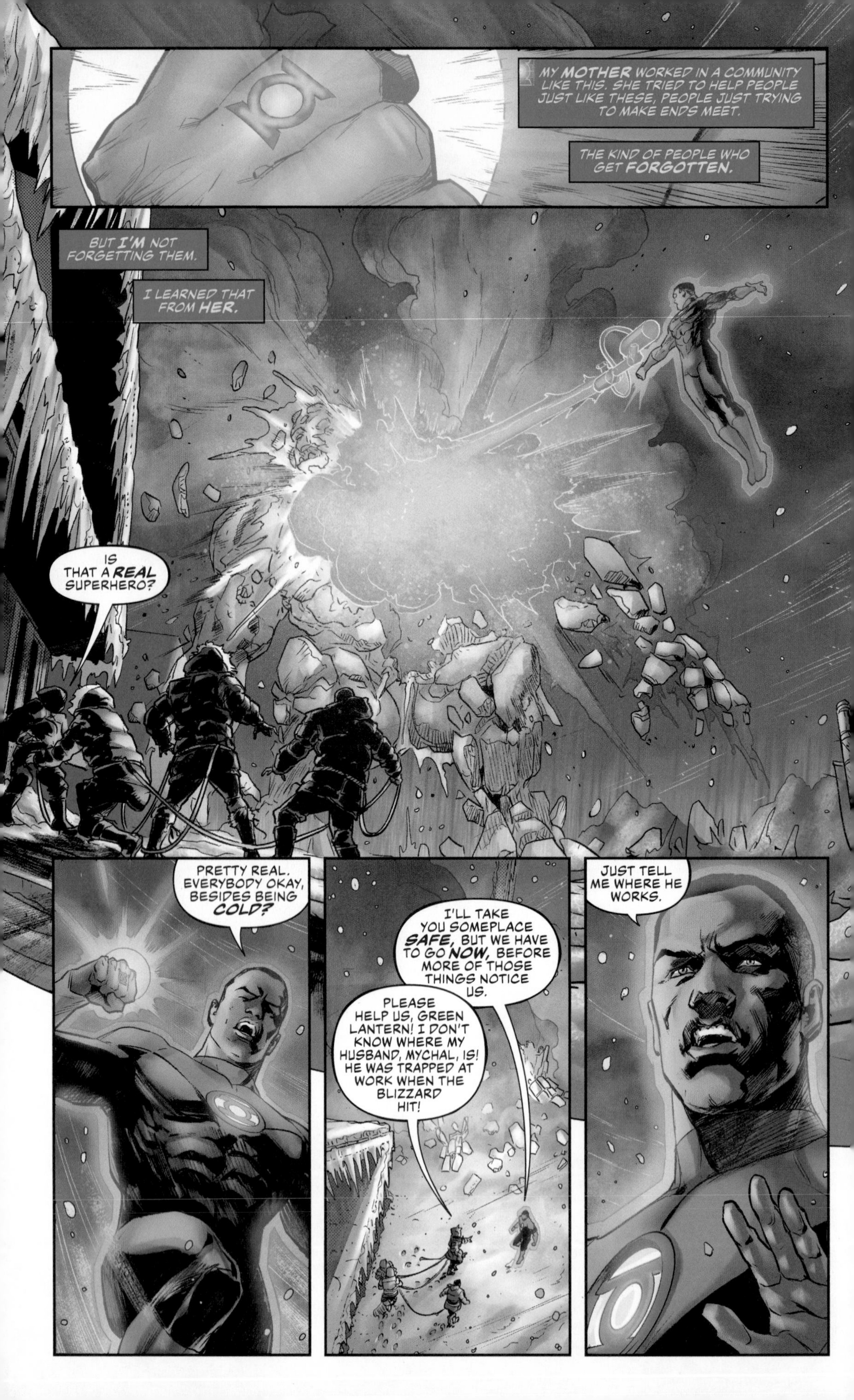

MY MOTHER WORKED IN A COMMUNITY LIKE THIS. SHE TRIED TO HELP PEOPLE JUST LIKE THESE, PEOPLE JUST TRYING TO MAKE ENDS MEET.
THE KIND OF PEOPLE WHO GET FORGOTTEN.
BUT I'M NOT FORGETTING THEM.
I LEARNED THAT FROM HER.
IS THAT A REAL SUPERHERO?
PRETTY REAL. EVERYBODY OKAY, BESIDES BEING COLD?
I'LL TAKE YOU SOMEPLACE SAFE, BUT WE HAVE TO GO NOW, BEFORE MORE OF THOSE THINGS NOTICE US.
PLEASE HELP US, GREEN LANTERN! I DON'T KNOW WHERE MY HUSBAND, MYCHAL, IS! HE WAS TRAPPED AT WORK WHEN THE BLIZZARD HIT!
JUST TELL ME WHERE HE WORKS.

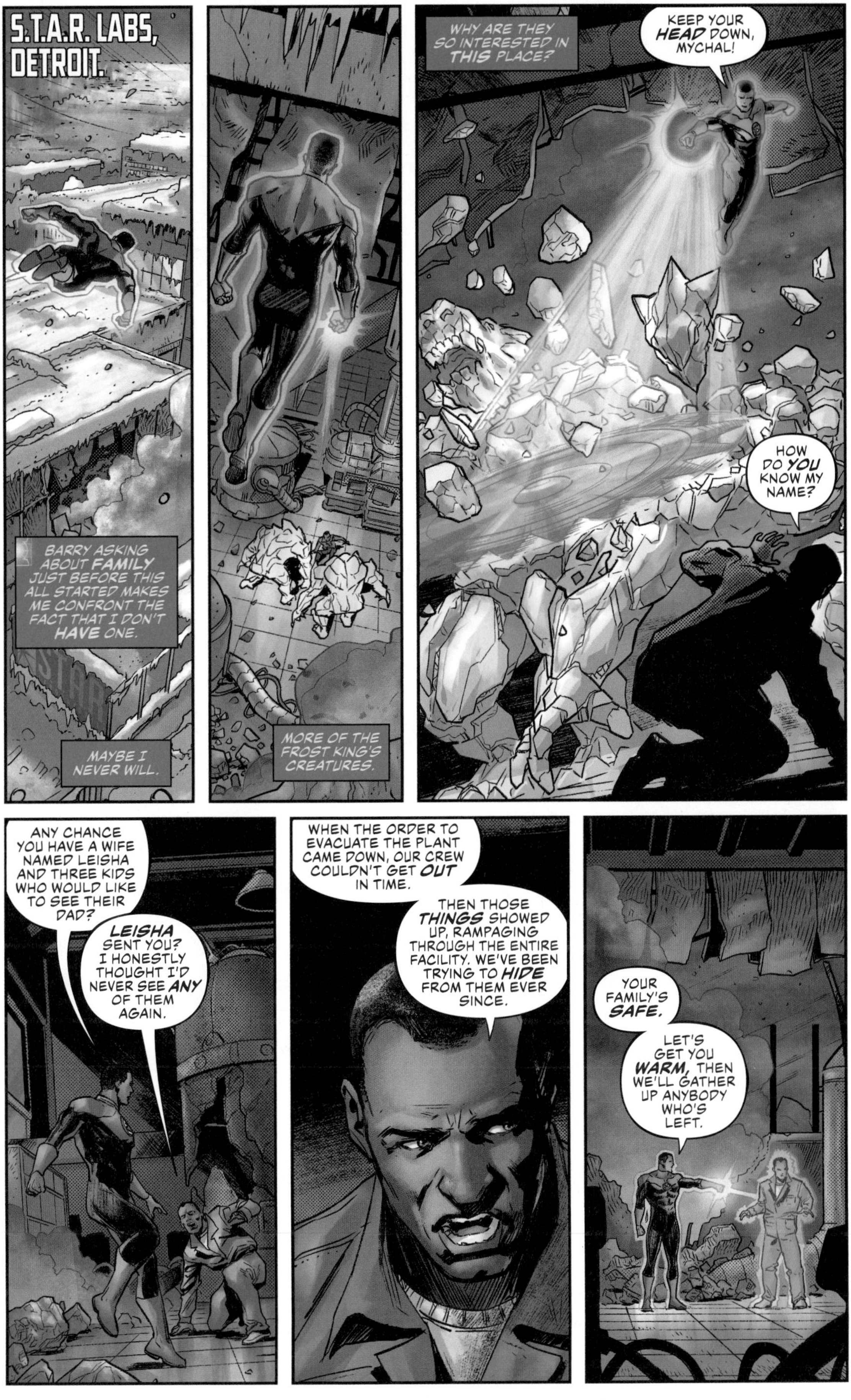
S.T.A.R. LABS, DETROIT.
BARRY ASKING ABOUT FAMILY JUST BEFORE THIS ALL STARTED MAKES ME CONFRONT THE FACT THAT I DON'T HAVE ONE.
MAYBE I NEVER WILL.
MORE OF THE FROST KING'S CREATURES.
WHY ARE THEY SO INTERESTED IN THIS PLACE?
KEEP YOUR HEAD DOWN, MYCHAL!
HOW DO YOU KNOW MY NAME?
ANY CHANCE YOU HAVE A WIFE NAMED LEISHA AND THREE KIDS WHO WOULD LIKE TO SEE THEIR DAD?
LEISHA SENT YOU? I HONESTLY THOUGHT I'D NEVER SEE ANY OF THEM AGAIN.
WHEN THE ORDER TO EVACUATE THE PLANT CAME DOWN, OUR CREW COULDN'T GET OUT IN TIME.
THEN THOSE THINGS SHOWED UP, RAMPAGING THROUGH THE ENTIRE FACILITY. WE'VE BEEN TRYING TO HIDE FROM THEM EVER SINCE.
YOUR FAMILY'S SAFE.
LET'S GET YOU WARM, THEN WE'LL GATHER UP ANYBODY WHO'S LEFT.

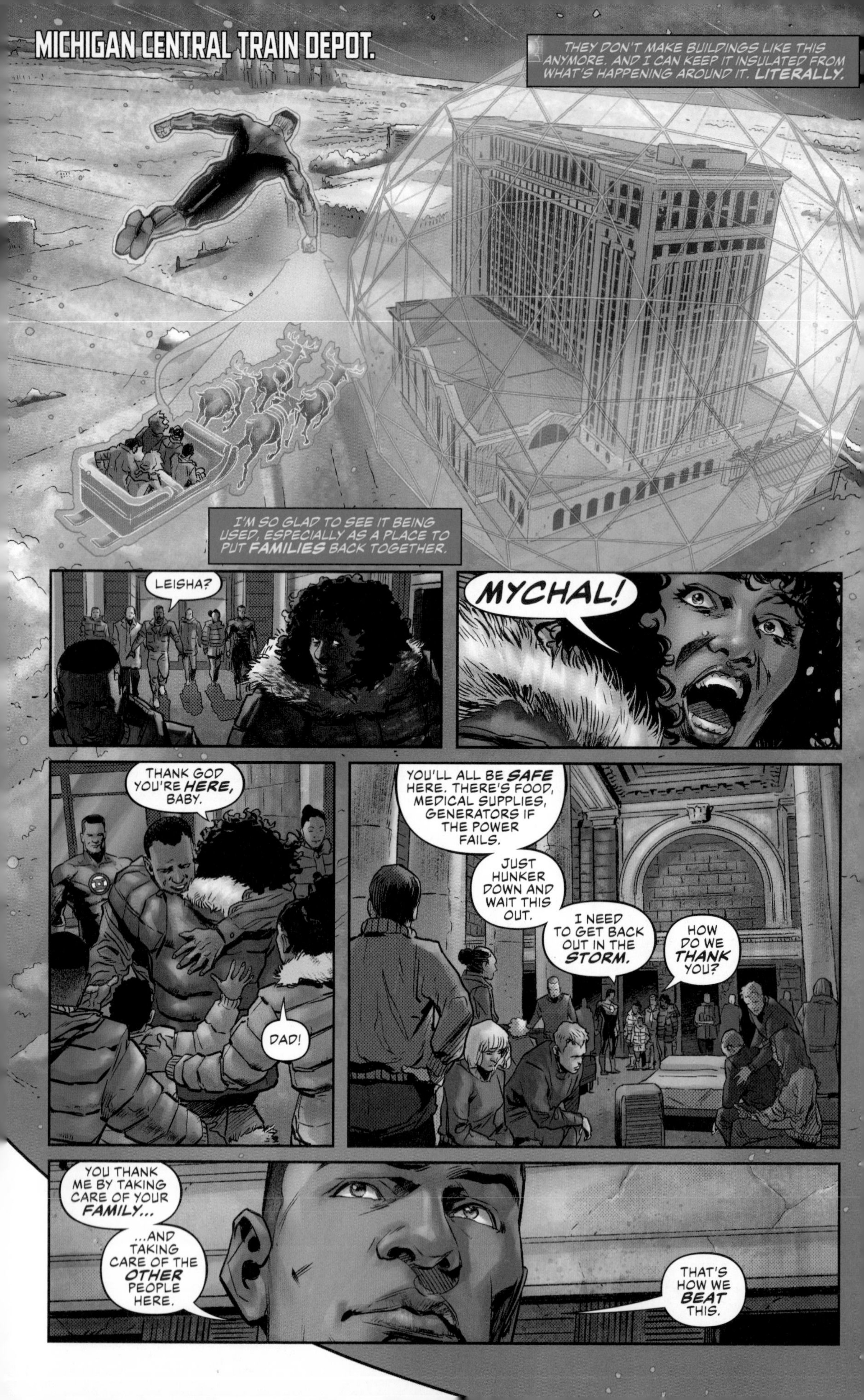
MICHIGAN CENTRAL TRAIN DEPOT.
THEY DON'T MAKE BUILDINGS LIKE THIS ANYMORE. AND I CAN KEEP IT INSULATED FROM WHAT'S HAPPENING AROUND IT. LITERALLY.
I'M SO GLAD TO SEE IT BEING USED, ESPECIALLY AS A PLACE TO PUT FAMILIES BACK TOGETHER.
LEISHA?
MYCHAL!
THANK GOD YOU'RE HERE, BABY.
DAD!
YOU'LL ALL BE SAFE HERE. THERE'S FOOD, MEDICAL SUPPLIES, GENERATORS IF THE POWER FAILS.
JUST HUNKER DOWN AND WAIT THIS OUT.
I NEED TO GET BACK OUT IN THE STORM.
HOW DO WE THANK YOU?
YOU THANK ME BY TAKING CARE OF YOUR FAMILY...
...AND TAKING CARE OF THE OTHER PEOPLE HERE.
THAT'S HOW WE BEAT THIS.

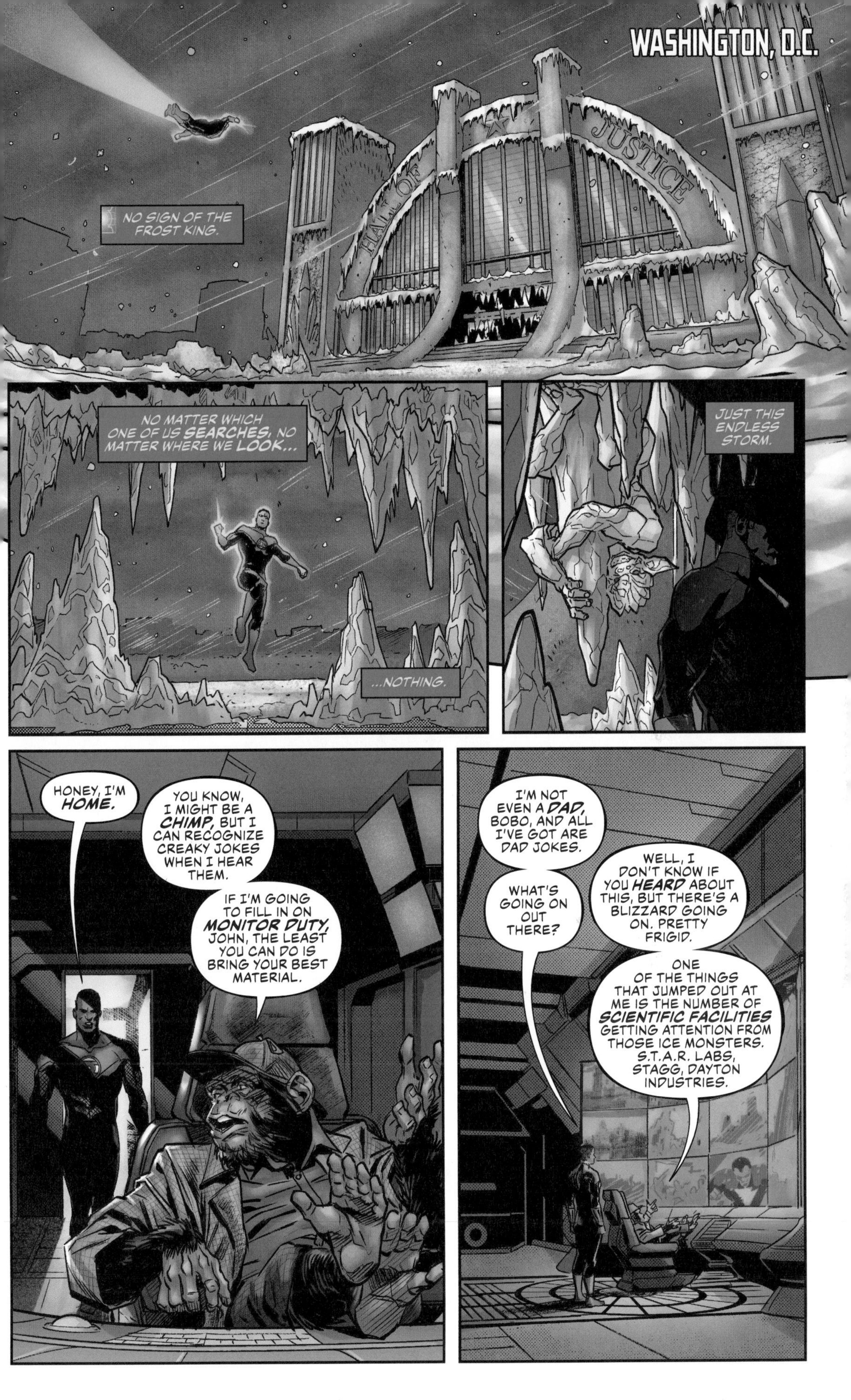

WASHINGTON, D.C.
HALL OF JUSTICE
NO SIGN OF THE FROST KING.
NO MATTER WHICH ONE OF US SEARCHES, NO MATTER WHERE WE LOOK...
...NOTHING.
JUST THIS ENDLESS STORM.
HONEY, I'M HOME.
YOU KNOW, I MIGHT BE A CHIMP, BUT I CAN RECOGNIZE CREAKY JOKES WHEN I HEAR THEM.
IF I'M GOING TO FILL IN ON MONITOR DUTY, JOHN, THE LEAST YOU CAN DO IS BRING YOUR BEST MATERIAL.
I'M NOT EVEN A DAD, BOBO, AND ALL I'VE GOT ARE DAD JOKES.
WHAT'S GOING ON OUT THERE?
WELL, I DON'T KNOW IF YOU HEARD ABOUT THIS, BUT THERE'S A BLIZZARD GOING ON. PRETTY FRIGID.
ONE OF THE THINGS THAT JUMPED OUT AT ME IS THE NUMBER OF SCIENTIFIC FACILITIES GETTING ATTENTION FROM THOSE ICE MONSTERS. S.T.A.R. LABS, STAGG, DAYTON INDUSTRIES.

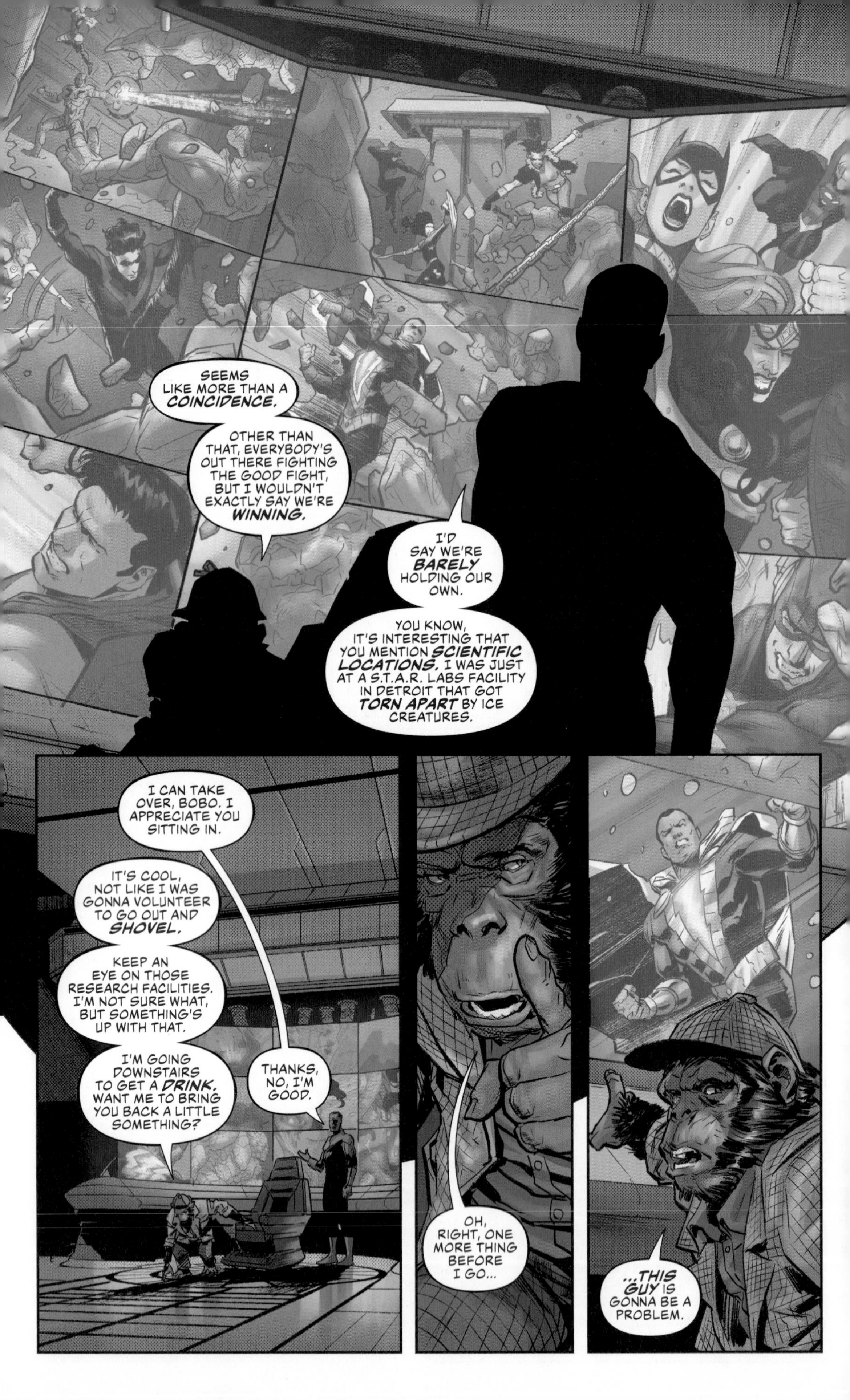
SEEMS LIKE MORE THAN A *COINCIDENCE.*
OTHER THAN THAT, EVERYBODY'S OUT THERE FIGHTING THE GOOD FIGHT, BUT I WOULDN'T EXACTLY SAY WE'RE *WINNING.*
I'D SAY WE'RE *BARELY* HOLDING OUR OWN.
YOU KNOW, IT'S INTERESTING THAT YOU MENTION *SCIENTIFIC LOCATIONS.* I WAS JUST AT A S.T.A.R. LABS FACILITY IN DETROIT THAT GOT *TORN APART* BY ICE CREATURES.
I CAN TAKE OVER, BOBO. I APPRECIATE YOU SITTING IN.
IT'S COOL, NOT LIKE I WAS GONNA VOLUNTEER TO GO OUT AND *SHOVEL.*
KEEP AN EYE ON THOSE RESEARCH FACILITIES. I'M NOT SURE WHAT, BUT SOMETHING'S UP WITH THAT.
I'M GOING DOWNSTAIRS TO GET A *DRINK.* WANT ME TO BRING YOU BACK A LITTLE SOMETHING?
THANKS, NO, I'M GOOD.
OH, RIGHT, ONE MORE THING BEFORE I GO...
...THIS GUY IS GONNA BE A PROBLEM.

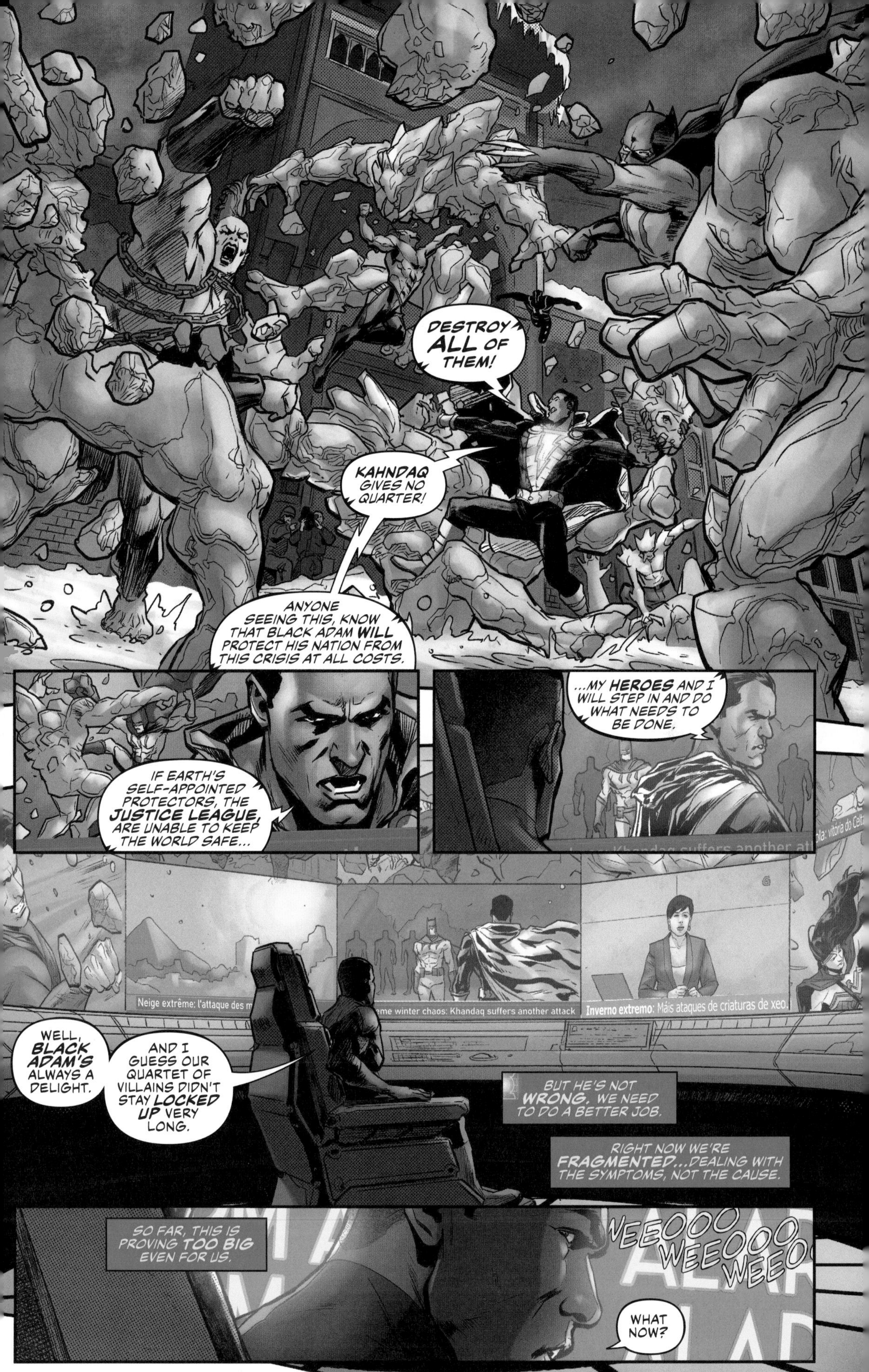
DESTROY ALL OF THEM!
KAHNDAQ GIVES NO QUARTER!
ANYONE SEEING THIS, KNOW THAT BLACK ADAM WILL PROTECT HIS NATION FROM THIS CRISIS AT ALL COSTS.
IF EARTH'S SELF-APPOINTED PROTECTORS, THE JUSTICE LEAGUE, ARE UNABLE TO KEEP THE WORLD SAFE...
...MY HEROES AND I WILL STEP IN AND DO WHAT NEEDS TO BE DONE.
Khandaq suffers another att
Neige extrême: l'attaque des m
eme winter chaos: Khandaq suffers another attack
Inverno extremo: Máis ataques de criaturas de xeo.
WELL, BLACK ADAM'S ALWAYS A DELIGHT.
AND I GUESS OUR QUARTET OF VILLAINS DIDN'T STAY LOCKED UP VERY LONG.
BUT HE'S NOT WRONG. WE NEED TO DO A BETTER JOB.
RIGHT NOW WE'RE FRAGMENTED...DEALING WITH THE SYMPTOMS, NOT THE CAUSE.
SO FAR, THIS IS PROVING TOO BIG EVEN FOR US.
WEEOOO WEEOOO WEEO
WHAT NOW?

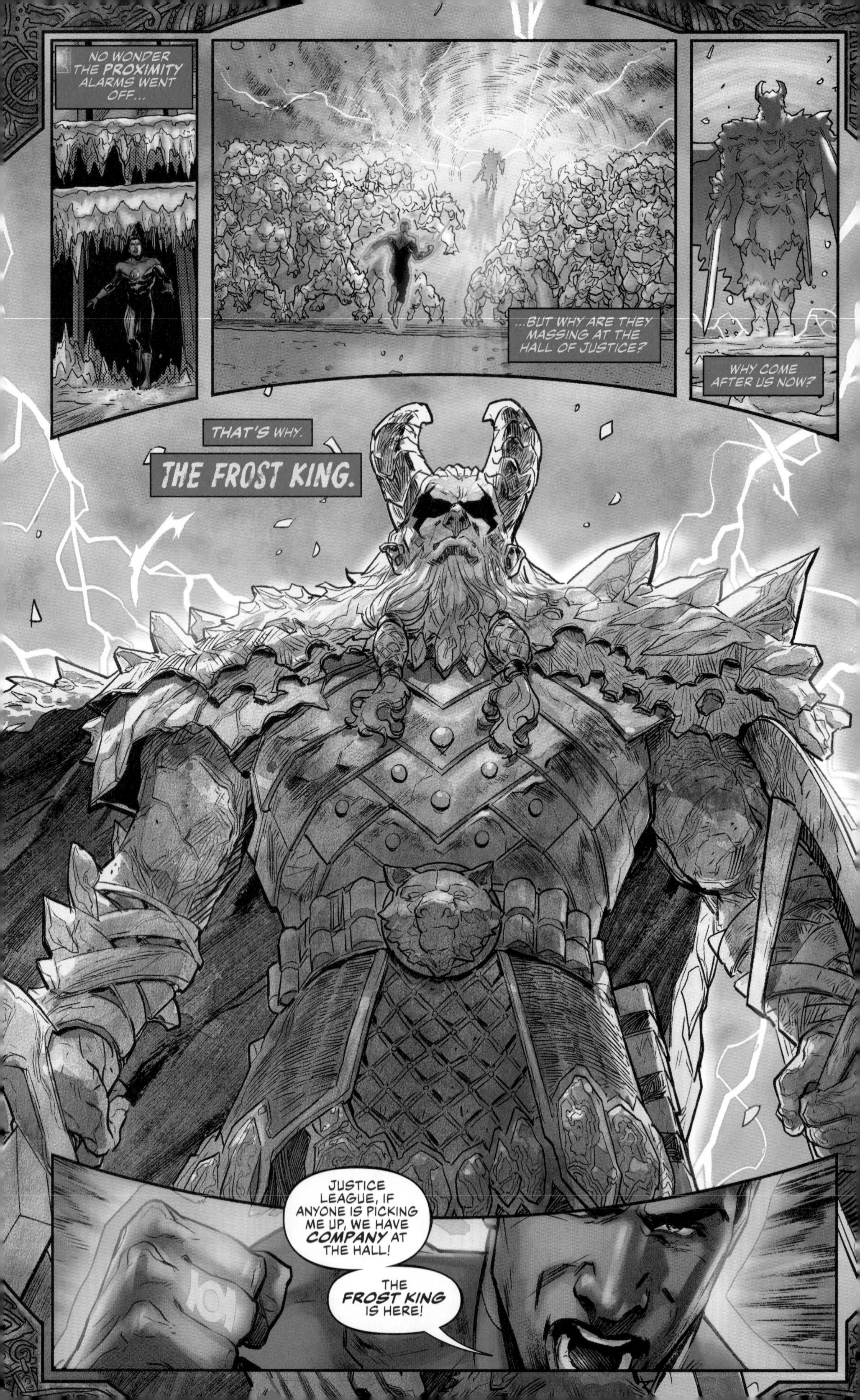

NO WONDER THE PROXIMITY ALARMS WENT OFF...
...BUT WHY ARE THEY MASSING AT THE HALL OF JUSTICE?
WHY COME AFTER US NOW?
THAT'S WHY.
THE FROST KING.
JUSTICE LEAGUE, IF ANYONE IS PICKING ME UP, WE HAVE COMPANY AT THE HALL!
THE FROST KING IS HERE!

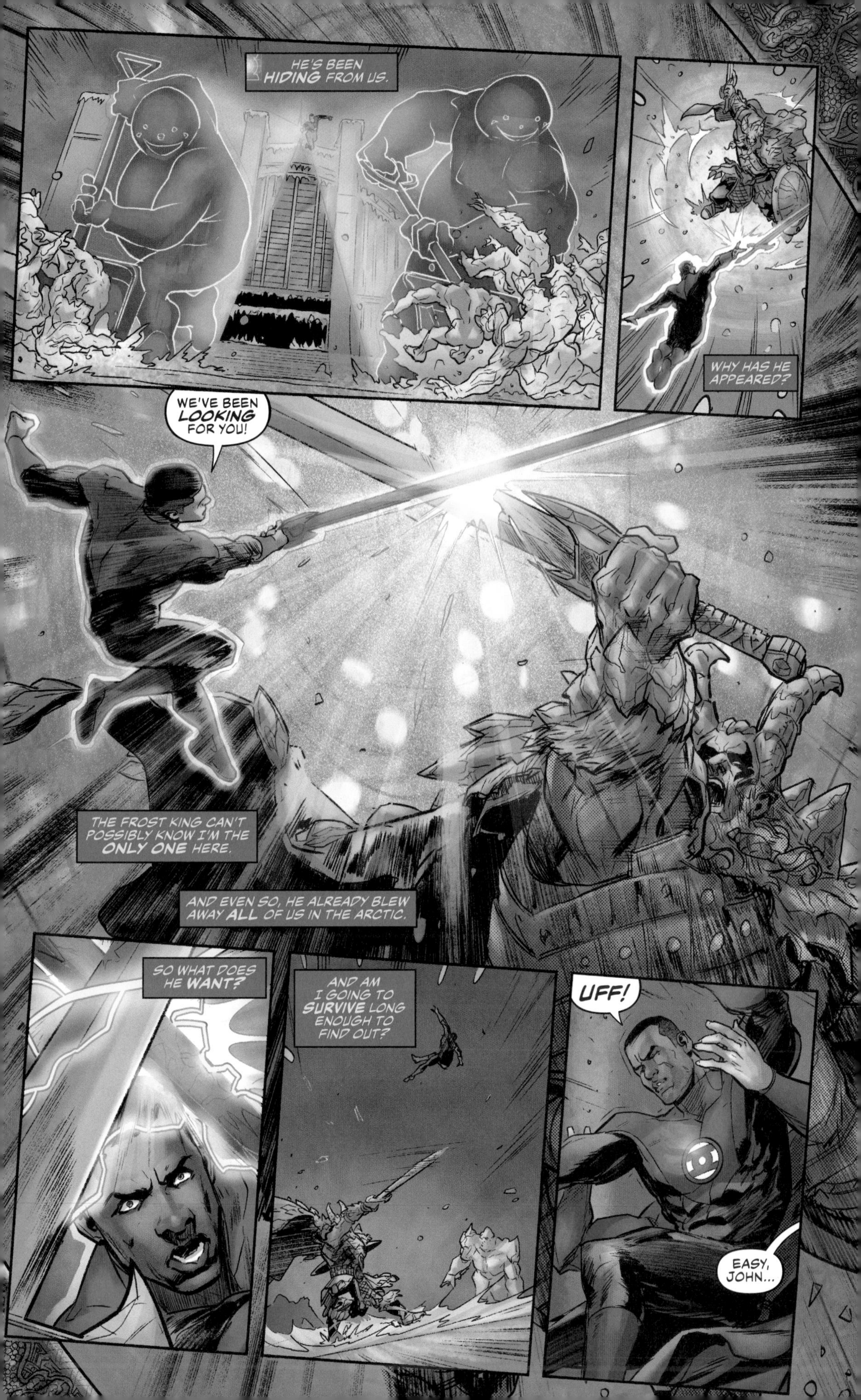
HE'S BEEN HIDING FROM US.
WHY HAS HE APPEARED?
WE'VE BEEN LOOKING FOR YOU!
THE FROST KING CAN'T POSSIBLY KNOW I'M THE ONLY ONE HERE.
AND EVEN SO, HE ALREADY BLEW AWAY ALL OF US IN THE ARCTIC.
SO WHAT DOES HE WANT?
AND AM I GOING TO SURVIVE LONG ENOUGH TO FIND OUT?
UFF!
EASY, JOHN...

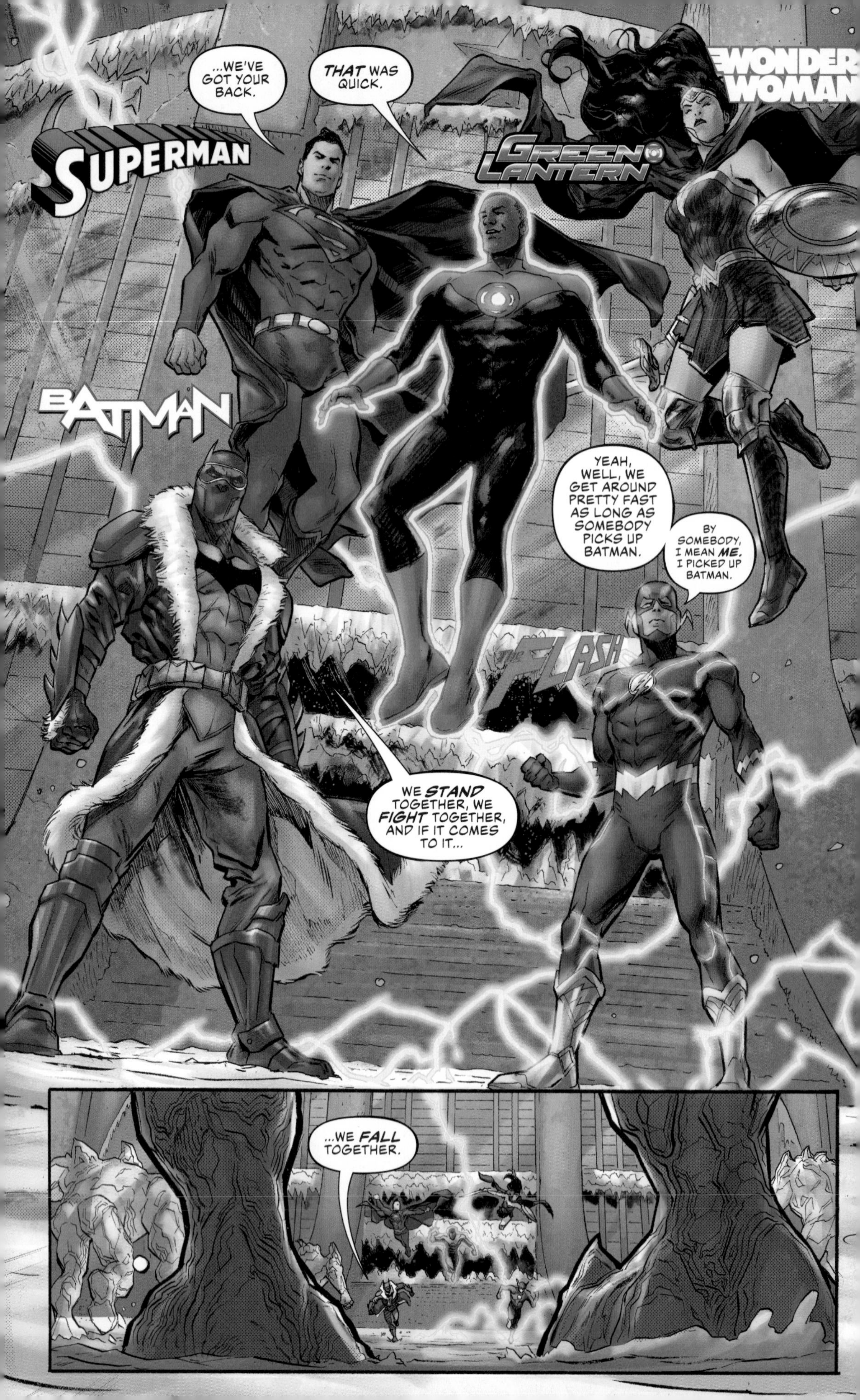
...WE'VE GOT YOUR BACK.
THAT WAS QUICK.
SUPERMAN
GREEN LANTERN
WONDER WOMAN
BATMAN
YEAH, WELL, WE GET AROUND PRETTY FAST AS LONG AS SOMEBODY PICKS UP BATMAN.
BY SOMEBODY, I MEAN ME. I PICKED UP BATMAN.
THE FLASH
WE STAND TOGETHER, WE FIGHT TOGETHER, AND IF IT COMES TO IT...
...WE FALL TOGETHER.

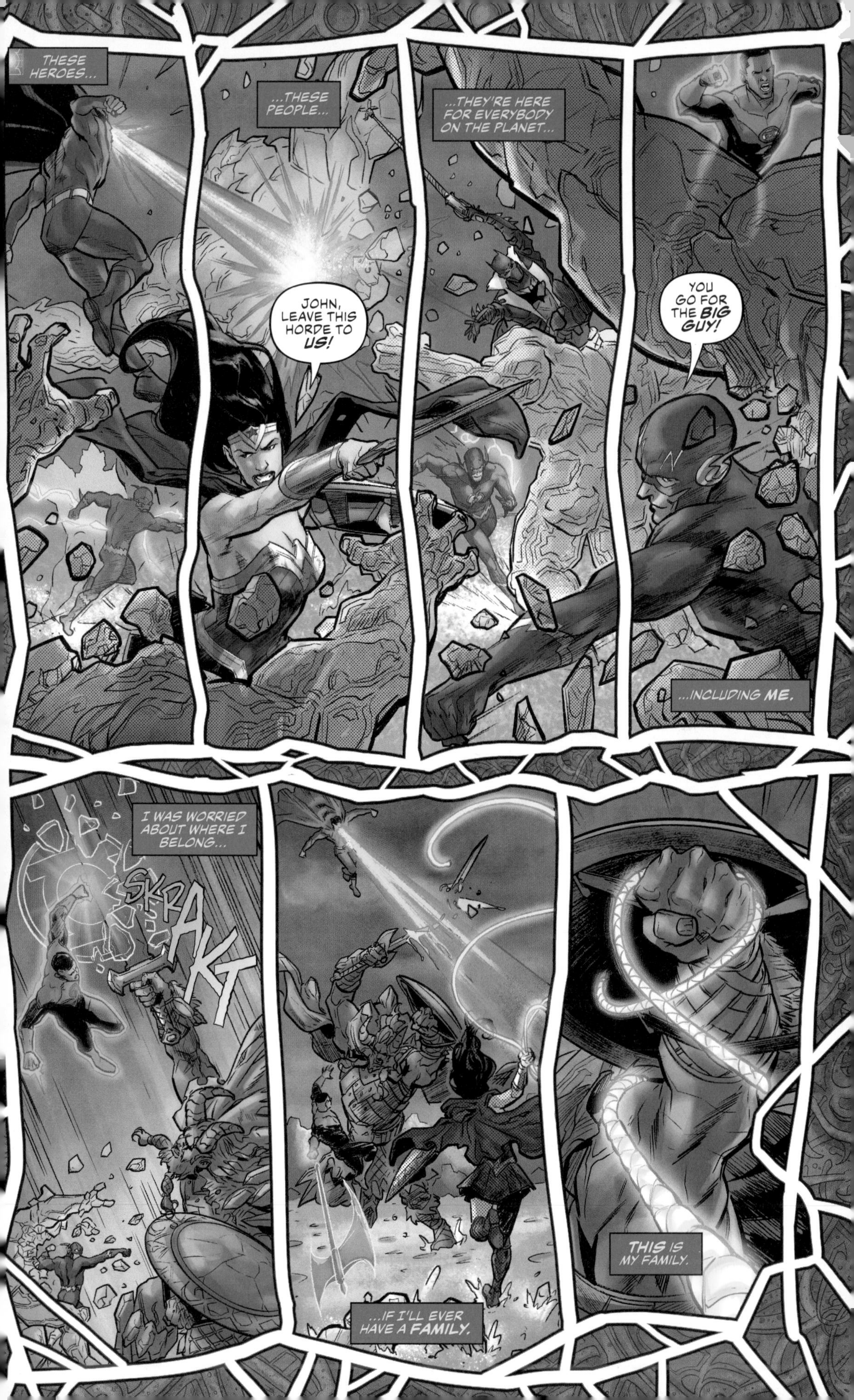
THESE HEROES...
...THESE PEOPLE...
JOHN, LEAVE THIS HORDE TO US!
...THEY'RE HERE FOR EVERYBODY ON THE PLANET...
YOU GO FOR THE BIG GUY!
...INCLUDING ME.
I WAS WORRIED ABOUT WHERE I BELONG...
SKRAKT
...IF I'LL EVER HAVE A FAMILY.
THIS IS MY FAMILY.

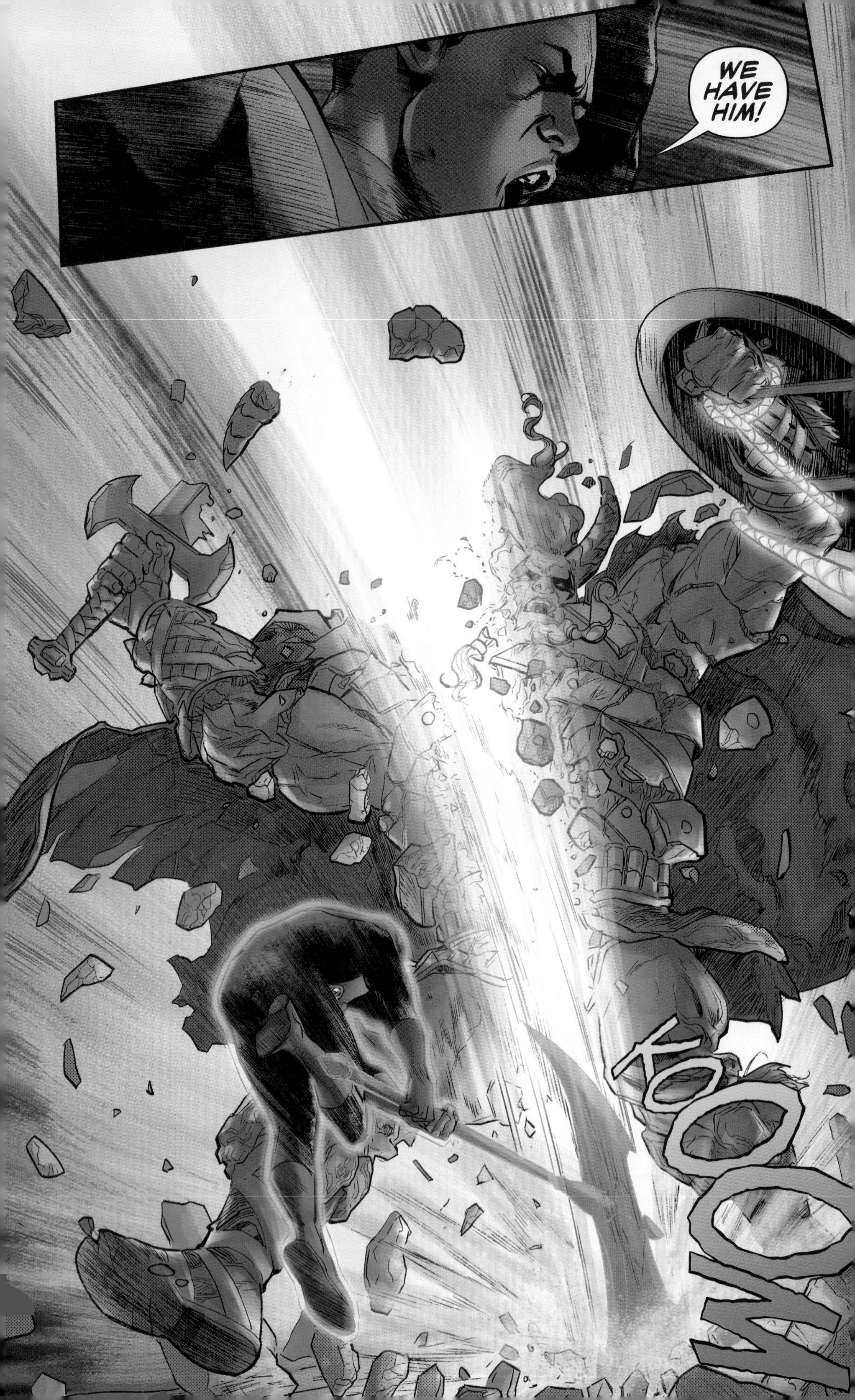
WE HAVE HIM!
KOOOM

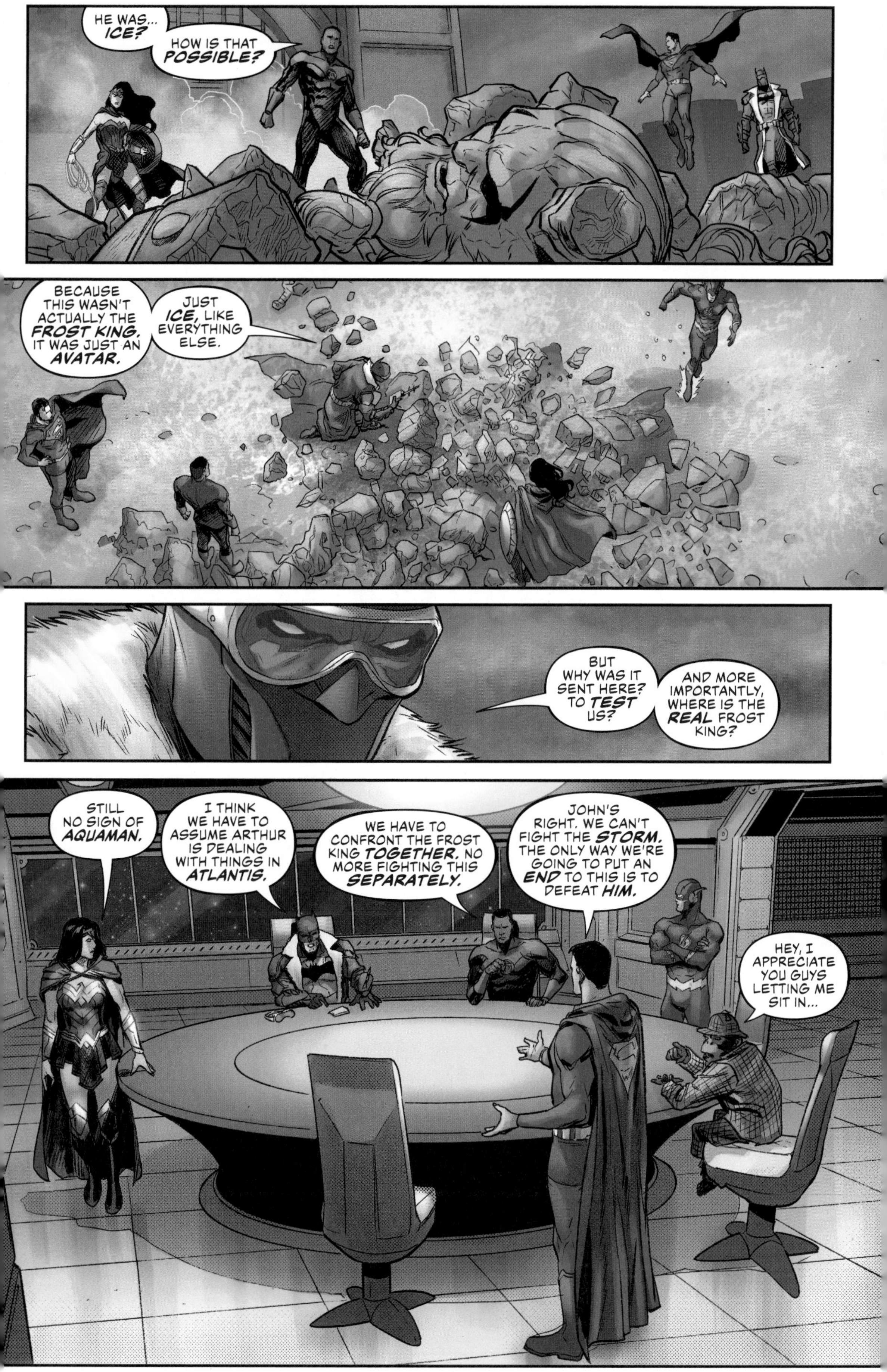
HE WAS... ICE?
HOW IS THAT POSSIBLE?
BECAUSE THIS WASN'T ACTUALLY THE FROST KING. IT WAS JUST AN AVATAR.
JUST ICE, LIKE EVERYTHING ELSE.
BUT WHY WAS IT SENT HERE? TO TEST US?
AND MORE IMPORTANTLY, WHERE IS THE REAL FROST KING?
STILL NO SIGN OF AQUAMAN.
I THINK WE HAVE TO ASSUME ARTHUR IS DEALING WITH THINGS IN ATLANTIS.
WE HAVE TO CONFRONT THE FROST KING TOGETHER. NO MORE FIGHTING THIS SEPARATELY.
JOHN'S RIGHT. WE CAN'T FIGHT THE STORM. THE ONLY WAY WE'RE GOING TO PUT AN END TO THIS IS TO DEFEAT HIM.
HEY, I APPRECIATE YOU GUYS LETTING ME SIT IN...

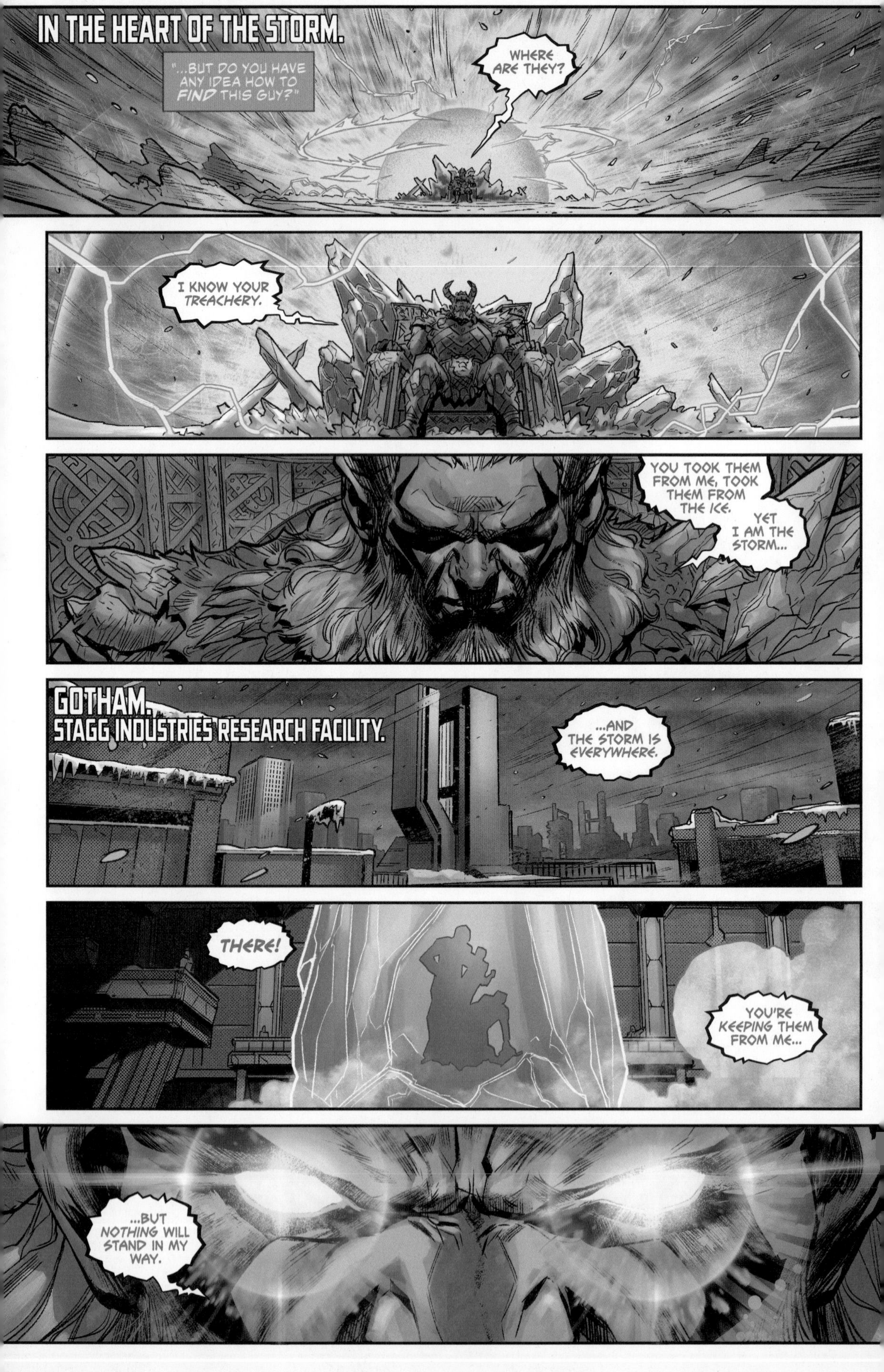
IN THE HEART OF THE STORM.
"...BUT DO YOU HAVE ANY IDEA HOW TO FIND THIS GUY?"
WHERE ARE THEY?
I KNOW YOUR TREACHERY.
YOU TOOK THEM FROM ME, TOOK THEM FROM THE ICE.
YET I AM THE STORM...
GOTHAM. STAGG INDUSTRIES RESEARCH FACILITY.
...AND THE STORM IS EVERYWHERE.
THERE!
YOU'RE KEEPING THEM FROM ME...
...BUT NOTHING WILL STAND IN MY WAY.

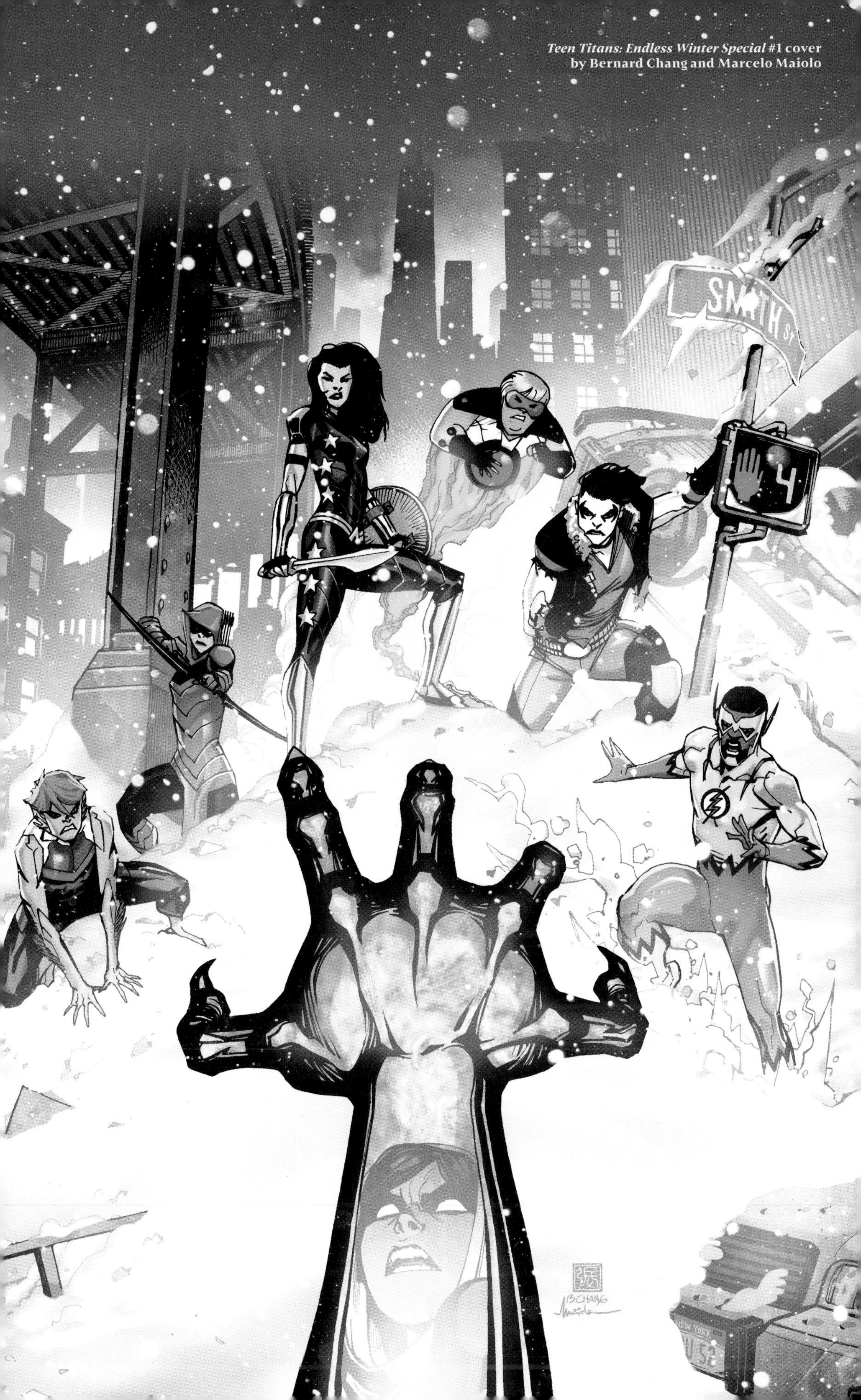
SMITH ST
NEW YORK
B.CHANG

Teen Titans: Endless Winter Special #1 cover
by Bernard Chang and Marcelo Maiolo

Teen Titans: Endless Winter Special #1 variant cover
by Simone Di Meo

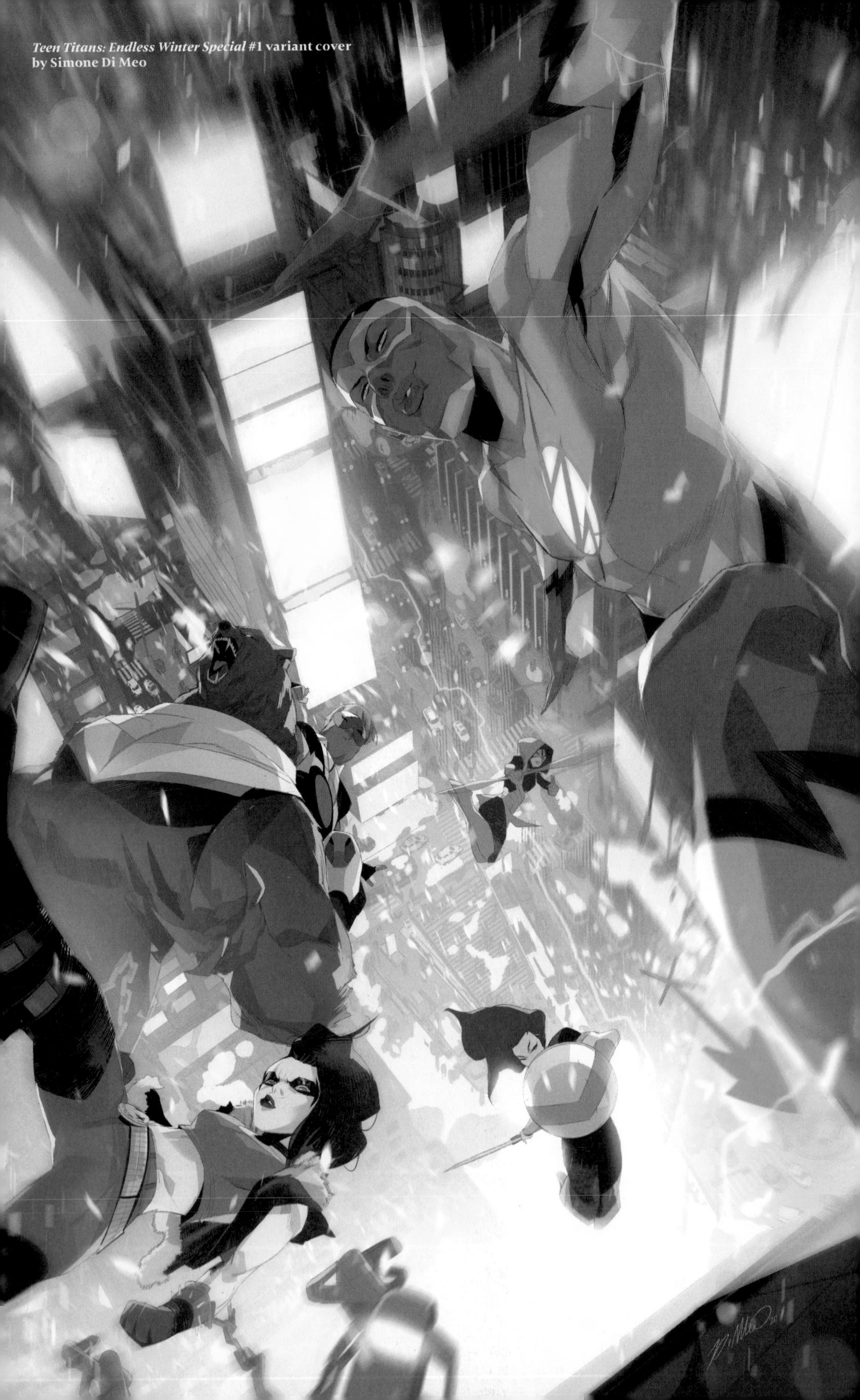

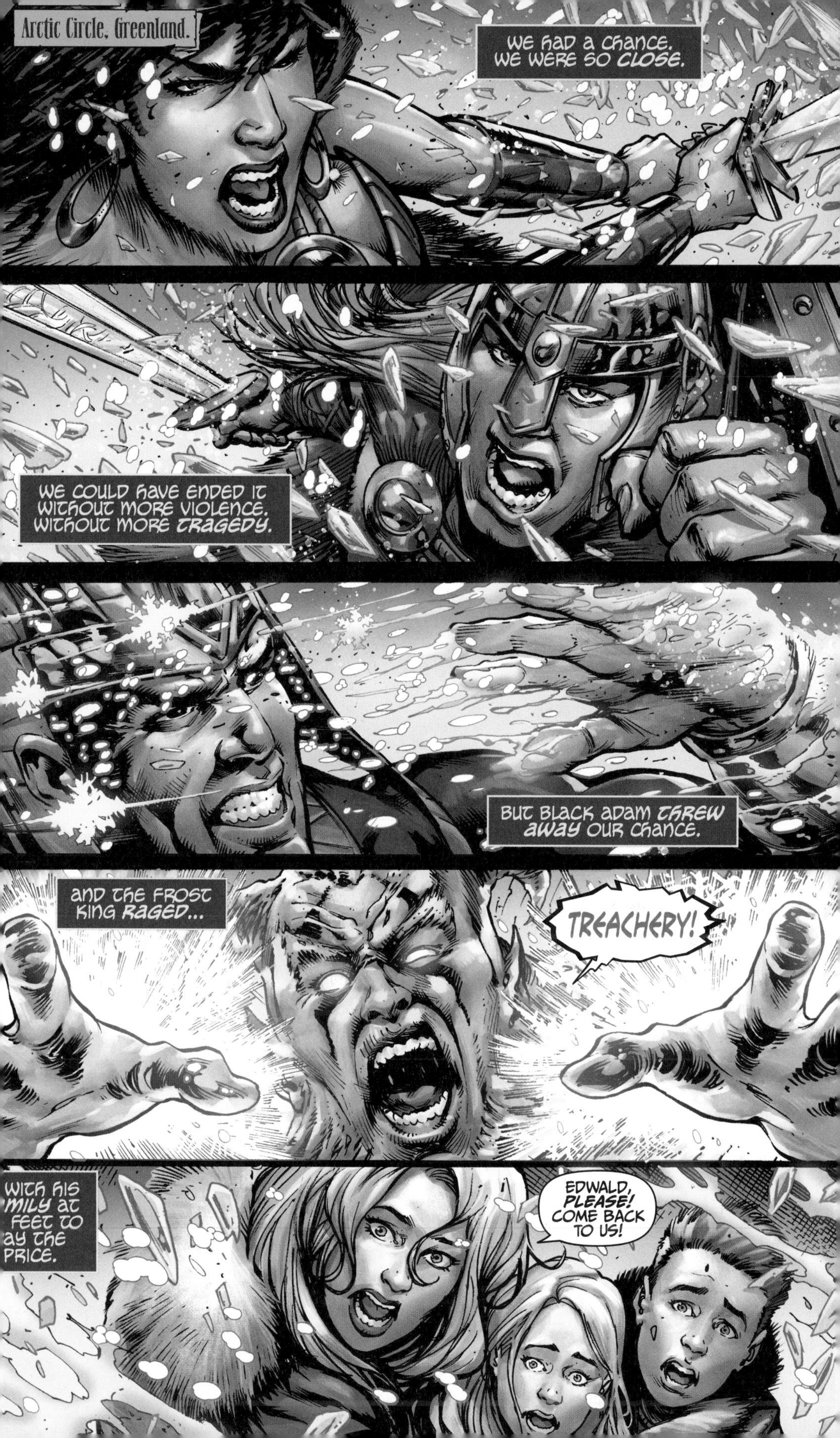
Arctic Circle, Greenland.
WE HAD A CHANCE. WE WERE SO CLOSE.
WE COULD HAVE ENDED IT WITHOUT MORE VIOLENCE. WITHOUT MORE TRAGEDY.
BUT BLACK ADAM THREW AWAY OUR CHANCE.
AND THE FROST KING RAGED...
TREACHERY!
EDWALD, PLEASE! COME BACK TO US!

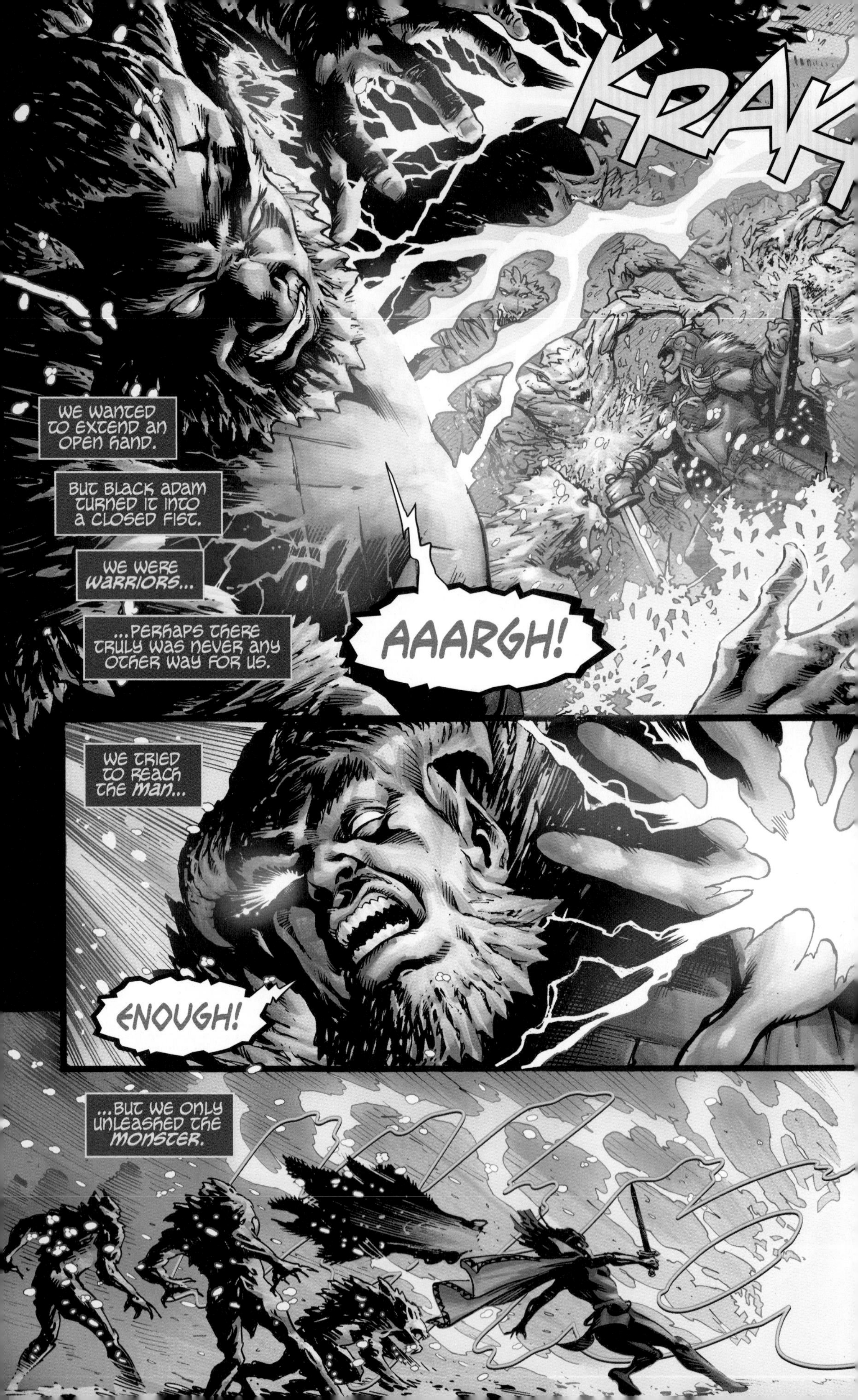
KRAK
WE WANTED TO EXTEND AN OPEN HAND.
BUT BLACK ADAM TURNED IT INTO A CLOSED FIST.
WE WERE *WARRIORS*...
...PERHAPS THERE TRULY WAS NEVER ANY OTHER WAY FOR US.
AAARGH!
WE TRIED TO REACH THE *MAN*...
ENOUGH!
...BUT WE ONLY UNLEASHED THE *MONSTER*.

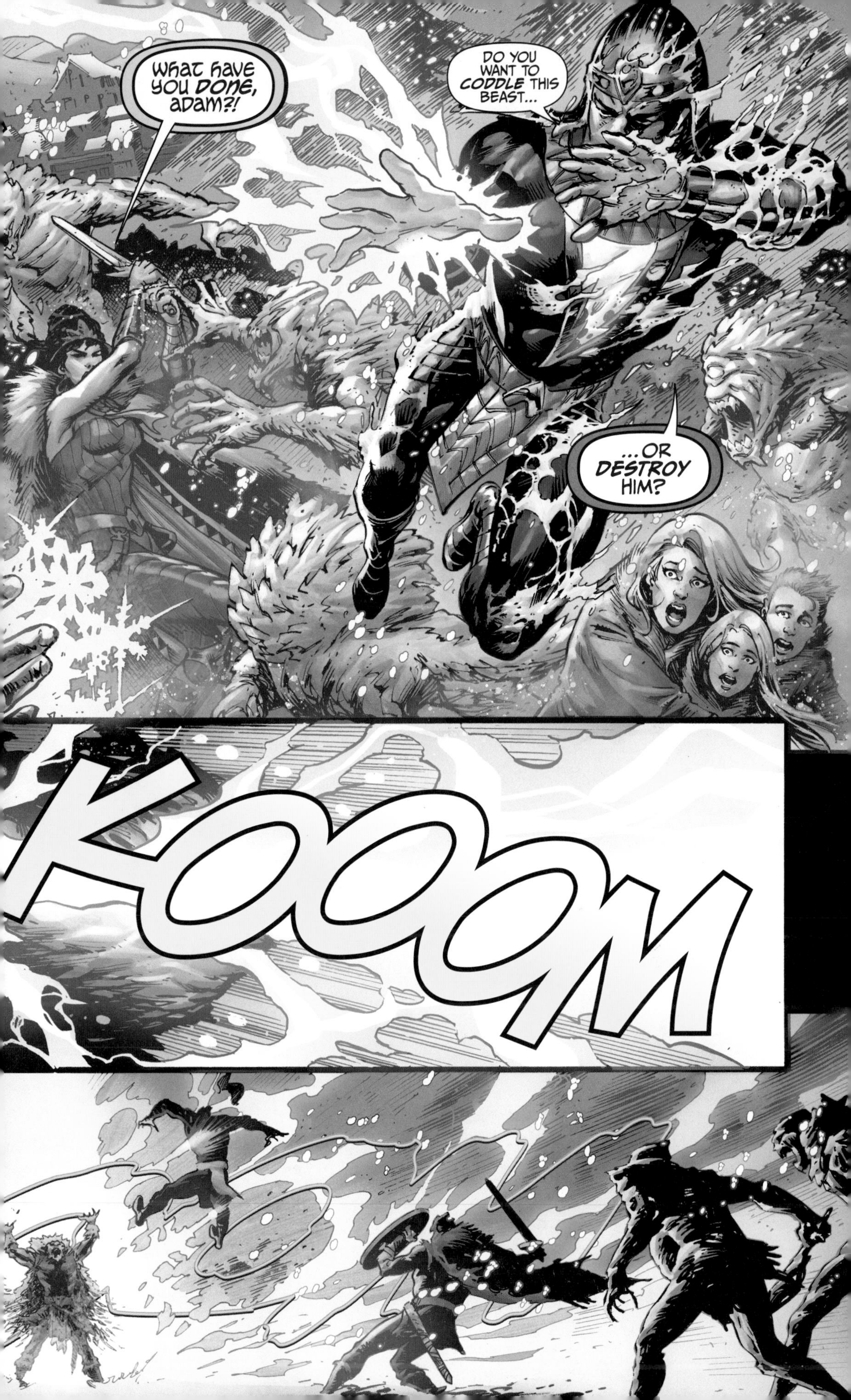
WHAT HAVE YOU DONE, ADAM?!
DO YOU WANT TO CODDLE THIS BEAST...
...OR DESTROY HIM?
KOOOM

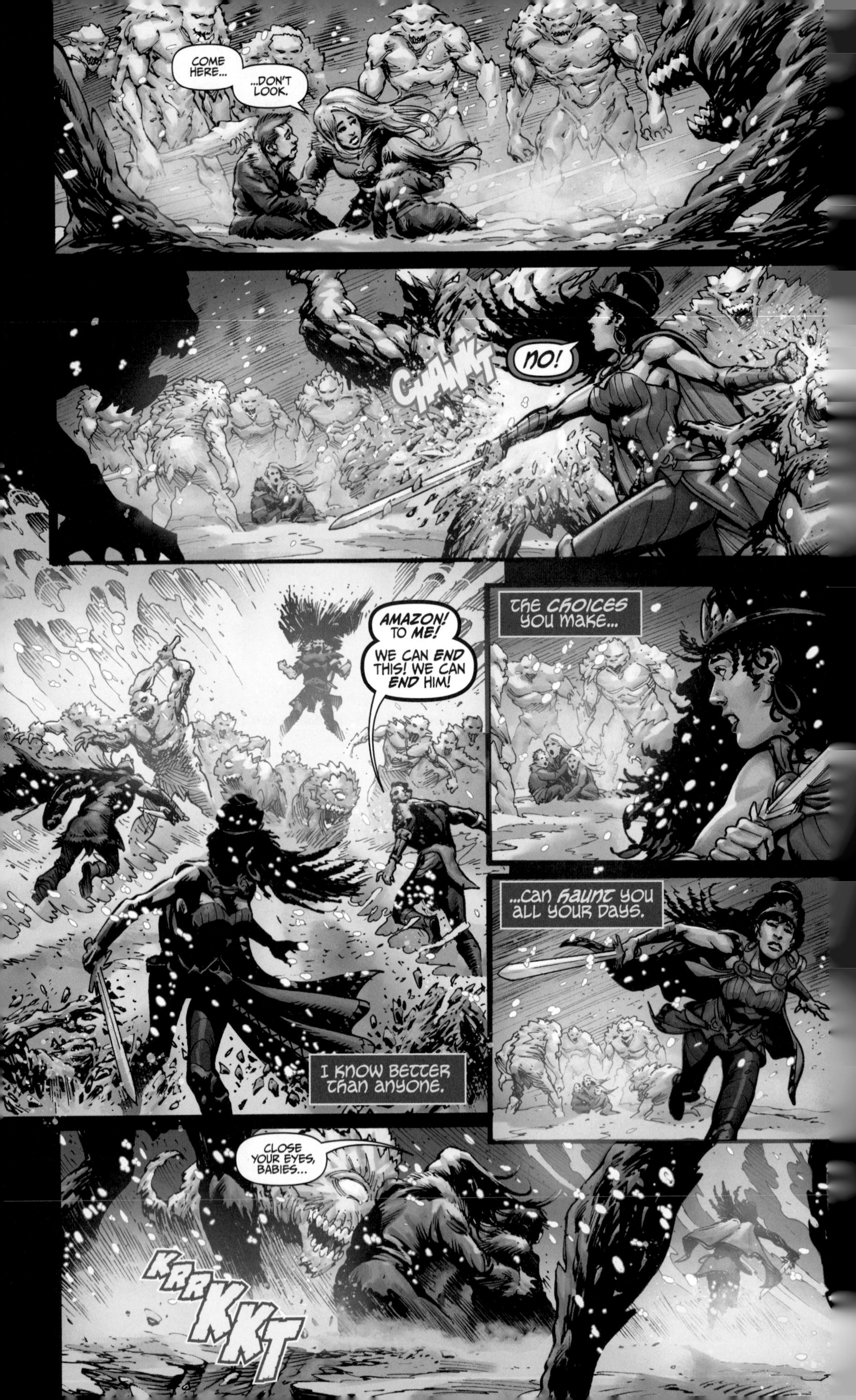

COME HERE...
...DON'T LOOK.
CHANKT
NO!
AMAZON! TO ME!
WE CAN END THIS! WE CAN END HIM!
I KNOW BETTER THAN ANYONE.
THE CHOICES YOU MAKE...
...CAN HAUNT YOU ALL YOUR DAYS.
CLOSE YOUR EYES, BABIES...
KRRRKKT

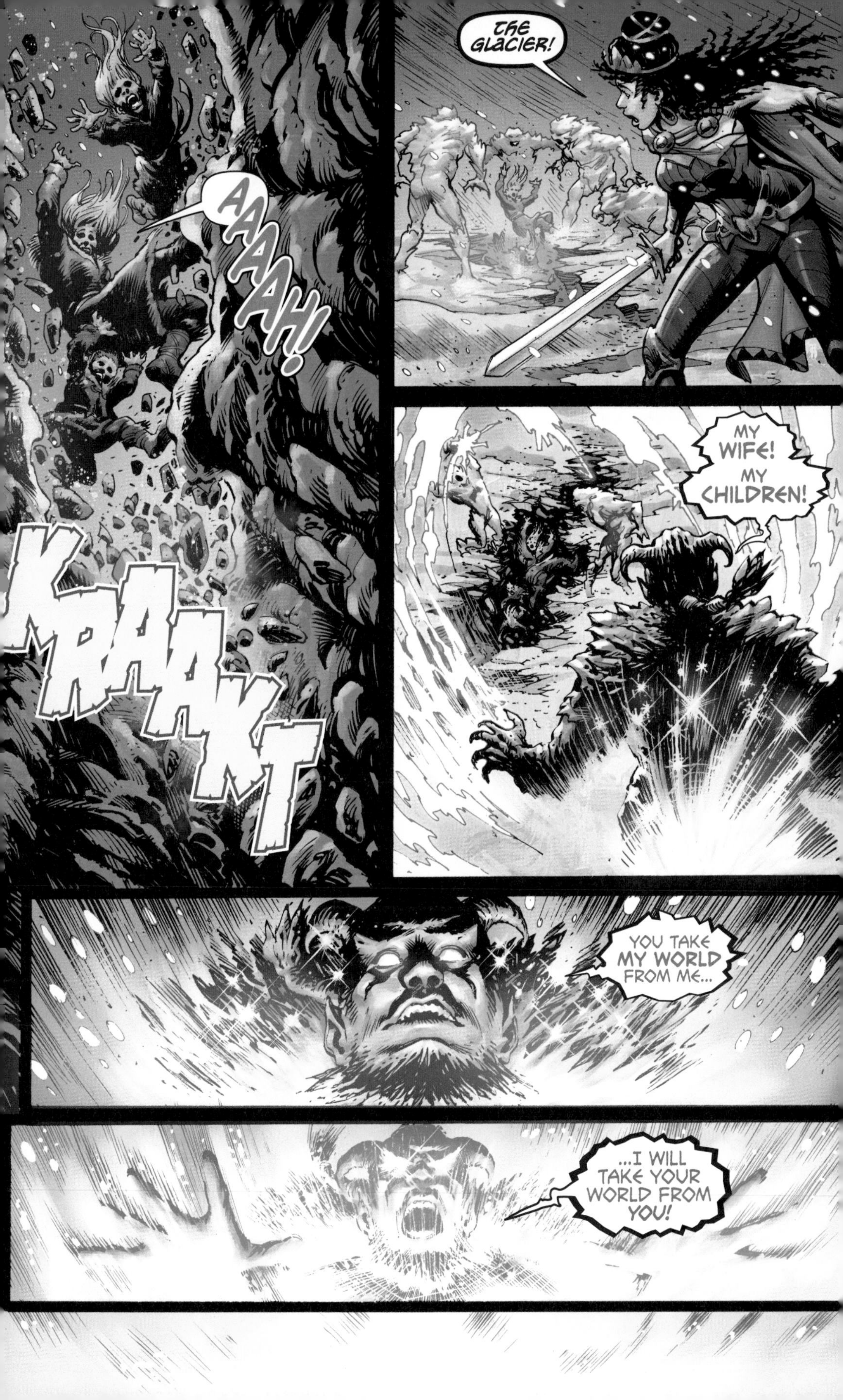
AAAAAH!
KRAAKT
THE GLACIER!
MY WIFE! MY CHILDREN!
YOU TAKE MY WORLD FROM ME...
...I WILL TAKE YOUR WORLD FROM YOU!

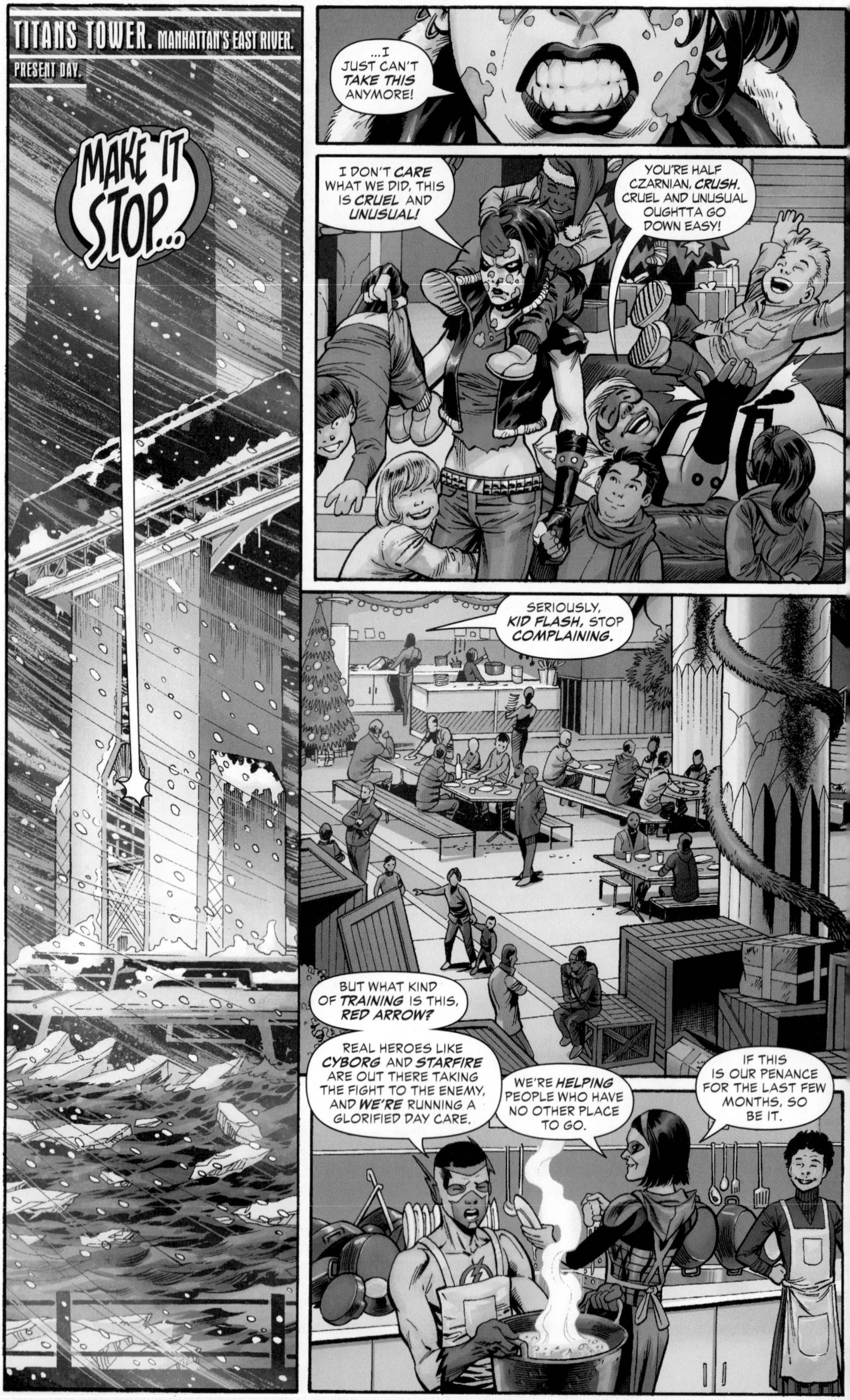
TITANS TOWER. MANHATTAN'S EAST RIVER.
PRESENT DAY.
MAKE IT STOP...
...I JUST CAN'T TAKE THIS ANYMORE!
I DON'T CARE WHAT WE DID, THIS IS CRUEL AND UNUSUAL!
YOU'RE HALF CZARNIAN, CRUSH. CRUEL AND UNUSUAL OUGHTTA GO DOWN EASY!
SERIOUSLY, KID FLASH, STOP COMPLAINING.
BUT WHAT KIND OF TRAINING IS THIS, RED ARROW?
REAL HEROES LIKE CYBORG AND STARFIRE ARE OUT THERE TAKING THE FIGHT TO THE ENEMY, AND WE'RE RUNNING A GLORIFIED DAY CARE.
WE'RE HELPING PEOPLE WHO HAVE NO OTHER PLACE TO GO.
IF THIS IS OUR PENANCE FOR THE LAST FEW MONTHS, SO BE IT.

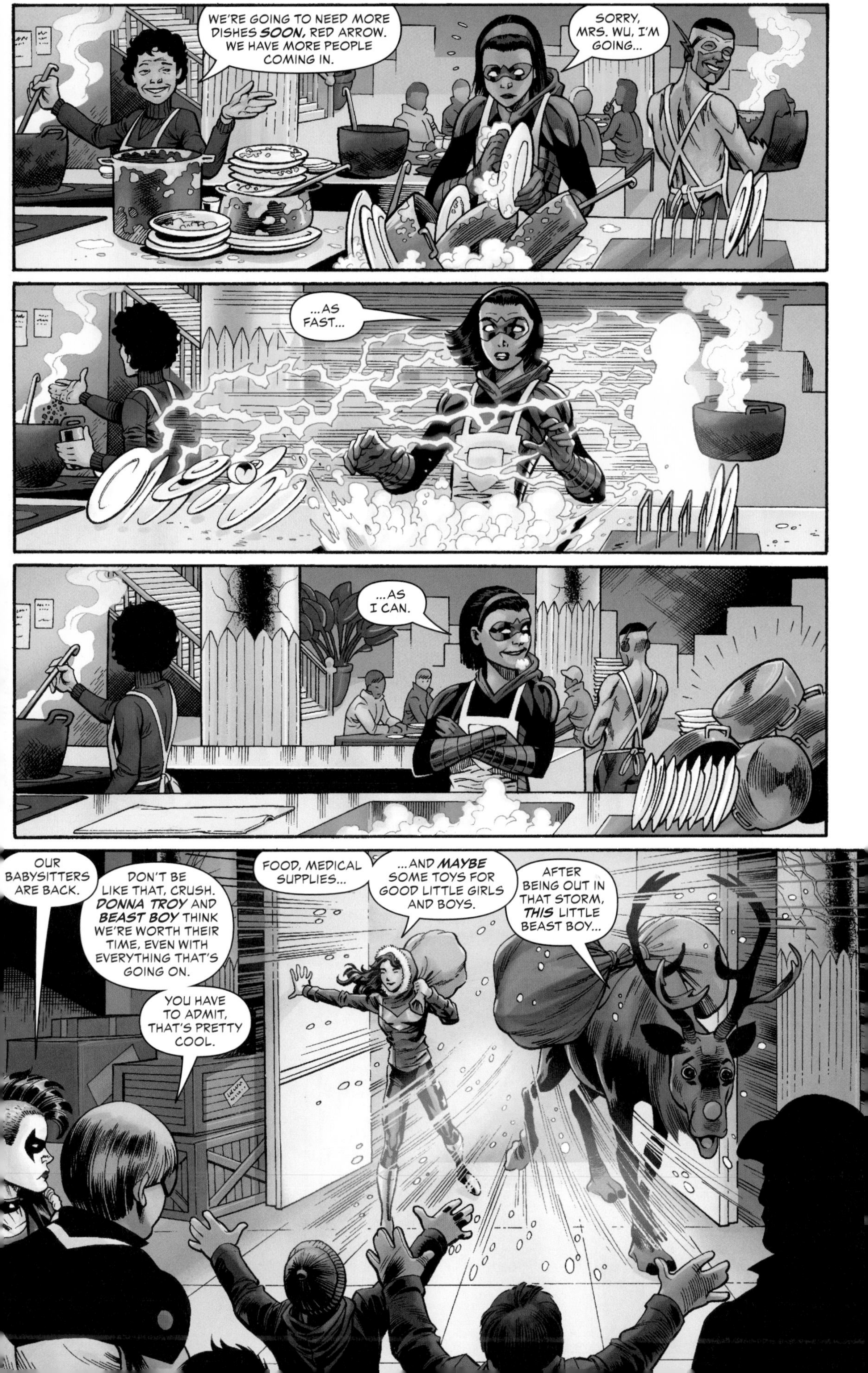
WE'RE GOING TO NEED MORE DISHES SOON, RED ARROW. WE HAVE MORE PEOPLE COMING IN.
SORRY, MRS. WU, I'M GOING...
...AS FAST...
...AS I CAN.
OUR BABYSITTERS ARE BACK.
DON'T BE LIKE THAT, CRUSH. DONNA TROY AND BEAST BOY THINK WE'RE WORTH THEIR TIME, EVEN WITH EVERYTHING THAT'S GOING ON.
YOU HAVE TO ADMIT, THAT'S PRETTY COOL.
FOOD, MEDICAL SUPPLIES...
...AND MAYBE SOME TOYS FOR GOOD LITTLE GIRLS AND BOYS.
AFTER BEING OUT IN THAT STORM, THIS LITTLE BEAST BOY...

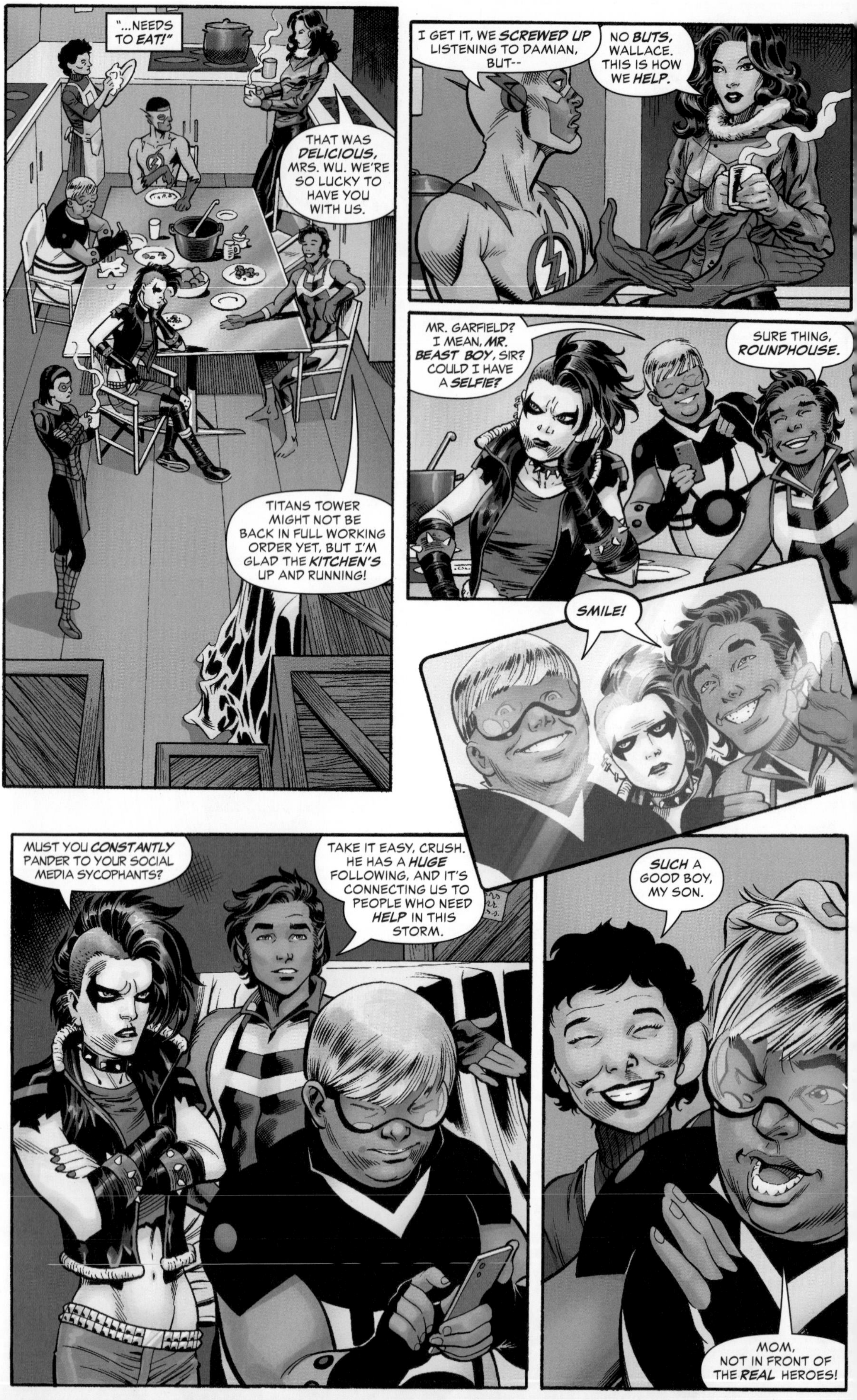
"...NEEDS TO EAT!"
THAT WAS DELICIOUS, MRS. WU. WE'RE SO LUCKY TO HAVE YOU WITH US.
TITANS TOWER MIGHT NOT BE BACK IN FULL WORKING ORDER YET, BUT I'M GLAD THE KITCHEN'S UP AND RUNNING!
I GET IT, WE SCREWED UP LISTENING TO DAMIAN, BUT--
NO BUTS, WALLACE. THIS IS HOW WE HELP.
MR. GARFIELD? I MEAN, MR. BEAST BOY, SIR? COULD I HAVE A SELFIE?
SURE THING, ROUNDHOUSE.
SMILE!
MUST YOU CONSTANTLY PANDER TO YOUR SOCIAL MEDIA SYCOPHANTS?
TAKE IT EASY, CRUSH. HE HAS A HUGE FOLLOWING, AND IT'S CONNECTING US TO PEOPLE WHO NEED HELP IN THIS STORM.
SUCH A GOOD BOY, MY SON.
MOM, NOT IN FRONT OF THE REAL HEROES!

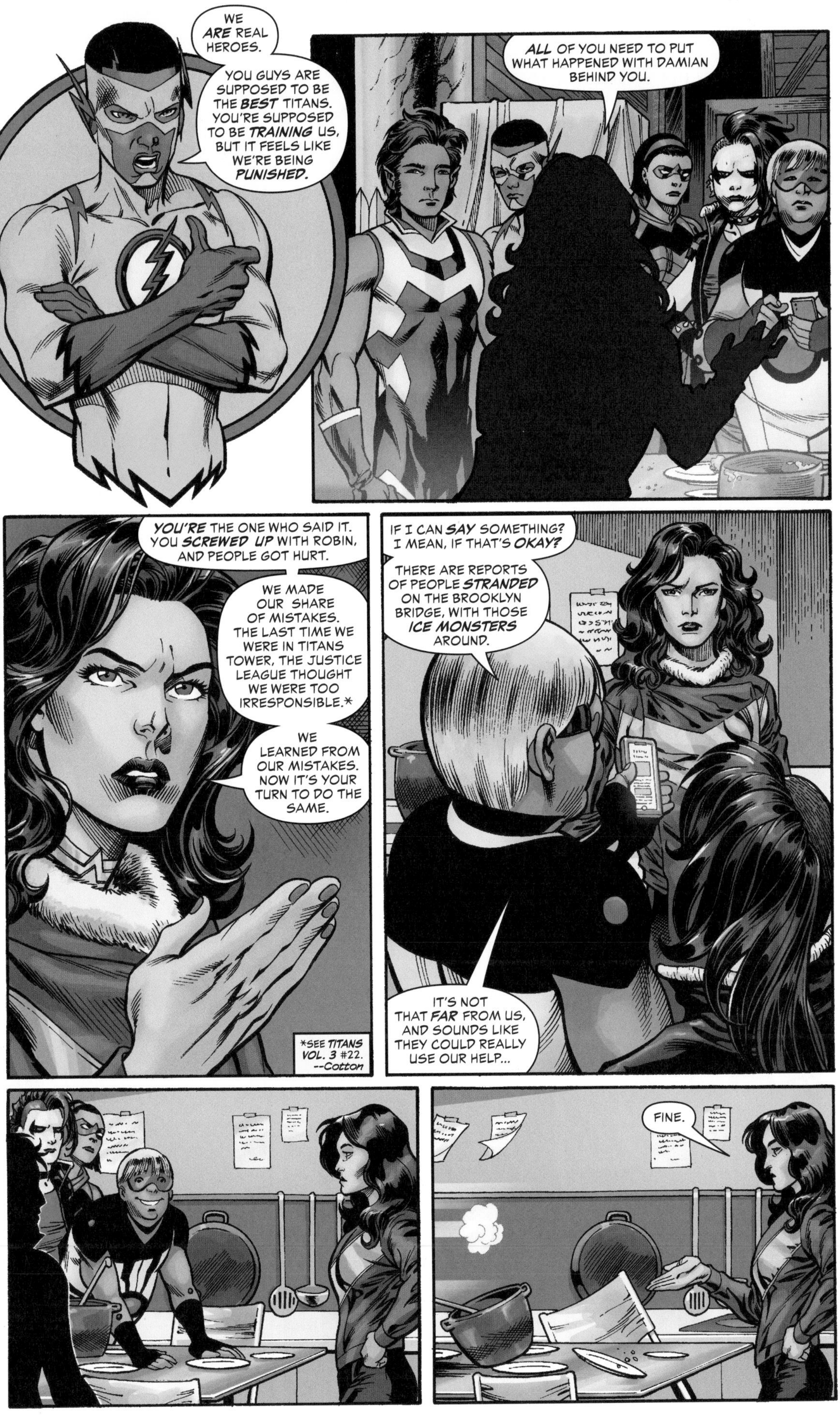
WE ARE REAL HEROES.
YOU GUYS ARE SUPPOSED TO BE THE BEST TITANS. YOU'RE SUPPOSED TO BE TRAINING US, BUT IT FEELS LIKE WE'RE BEING PUNISHED.
ALL OF YOU NEED TO PUT WHAT HAPPENED WITH DAMIAN BEHIND YOU.
YOU'RE THE ONE WHO SAID IT. YOU SCREWED UP WITH ROBIN, AND PEOPLE GOT HURT.
WE MADE OUR SHARE OF MISTAKES. THE LAST TIME WE WERE IN TITANS TOWER, THE JUSTICE LEAGUE THOUGHT WE WERE TOO IRRESPONSIBLE.*
WE LEARNED FROM OUR MISTAKES. NOW IT'S YOUR TURN TO DO THE SAME.
*SEE TITANS VOL. 3 #22. --Cotton
IF I CAN SAY SOMETHING? I MEAN, IF THAT'S OKAY?
THERE ARE REPORTS OF PEOPLE STRANDED ON THE BROOKLYN BRIDGE, WITH THOSE ICE MONSTERS AROUND.
IT'S NOT THAT FAR FROM US, AND SOUNDS LIKE THEY COULD REALLY USE OUR HELP...
FINE.

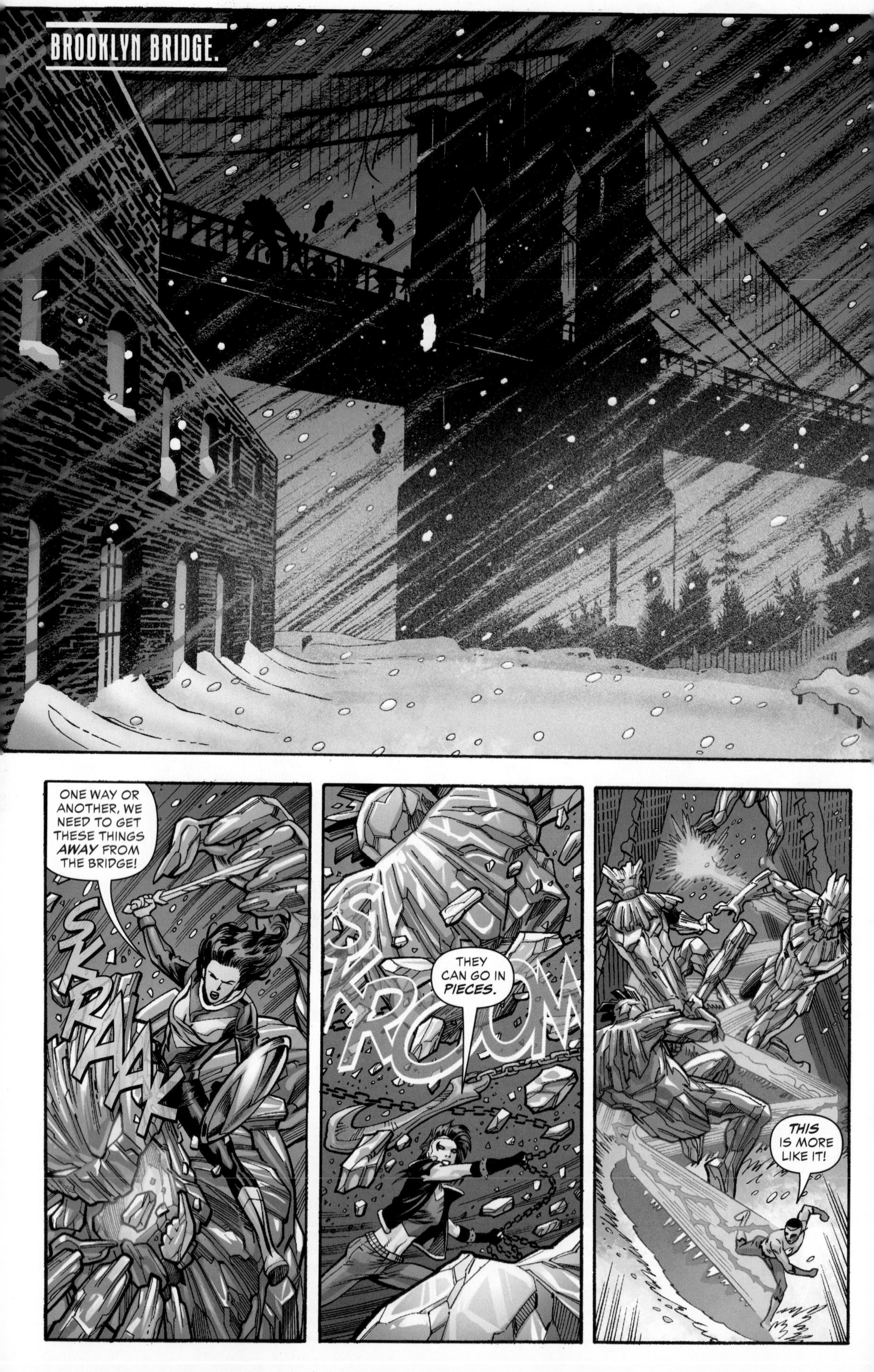

BROOKLYN BRIDGE.
ONE WAY OR ANOTHER, WE NEED TO GET THESE THINGS AWAY FROM THE BRIDGE!
SKRAAAK
SKROOM
THEY CAN GO IN PIECES.
THIS IS MORE LIKE IT!

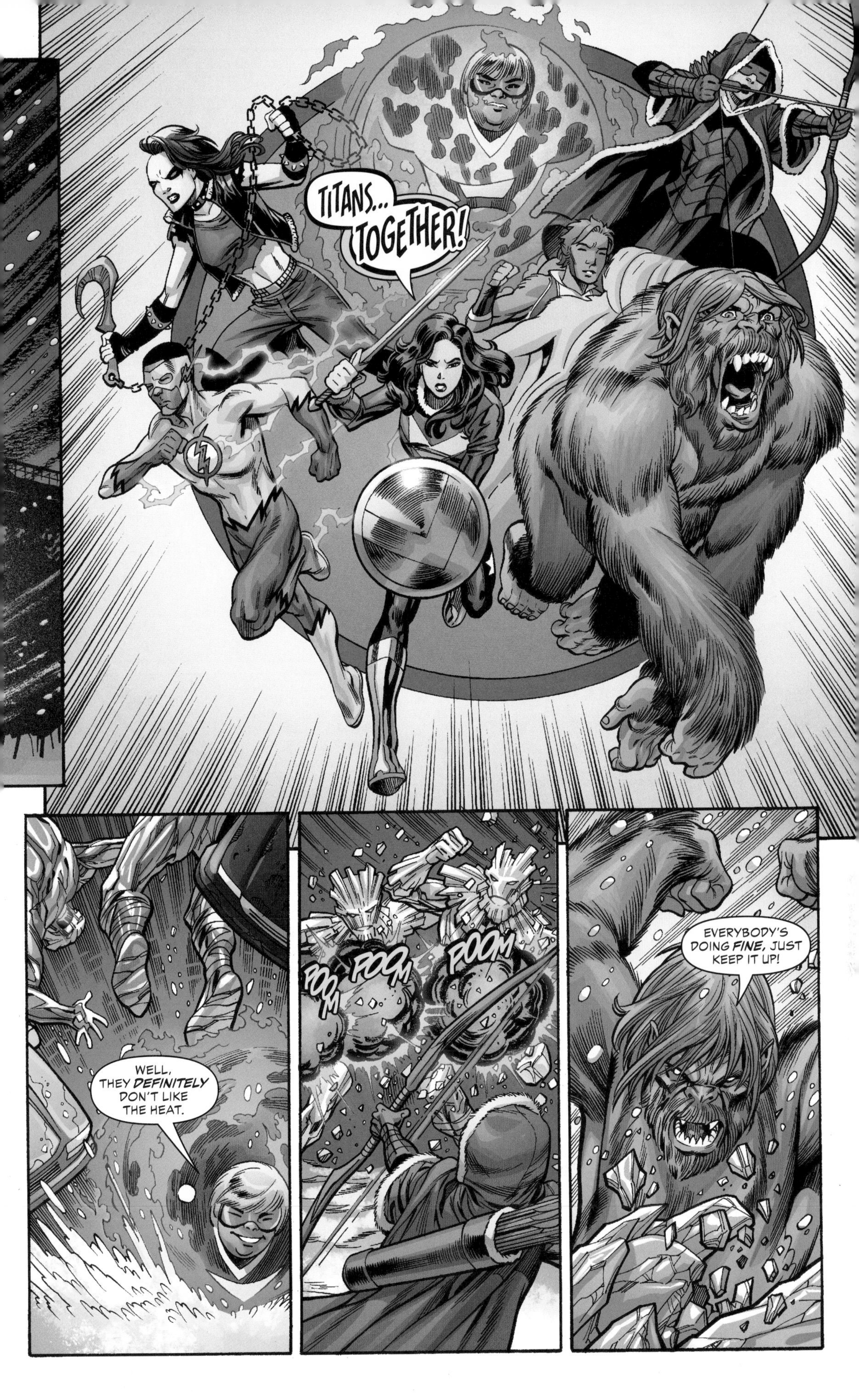
TITANS... TOGETHER!
WELL, THEY DEFINITELY DON'T LIKE THE HEAT.
POOM
POOM
POOM
EVERYBODY'S DOING FINE, JUST KEEP IT UP!

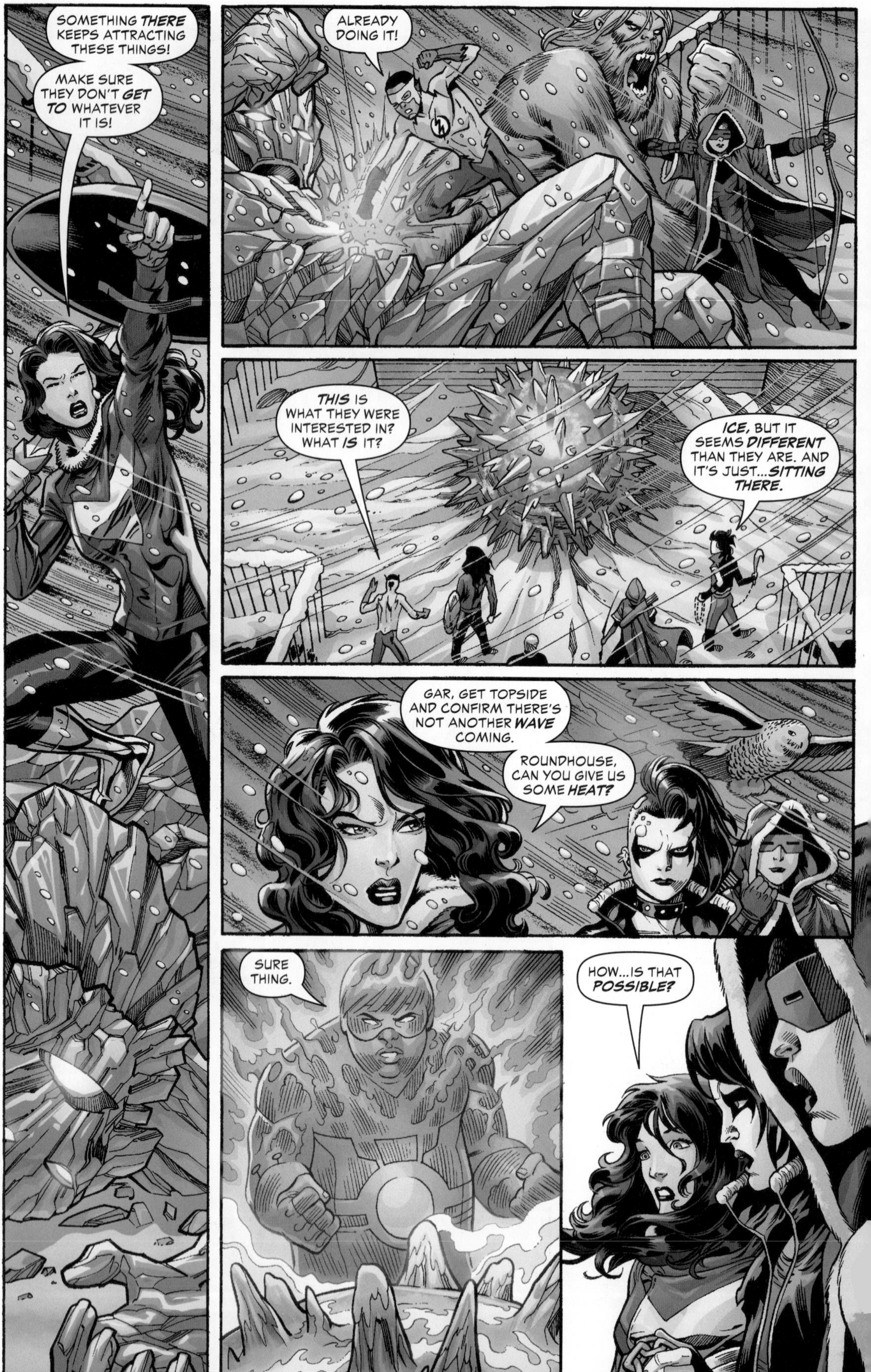

SOMETHING THERE KEEPS ATTRACTING THESE THINGS!
MAKE SURE THEY DON'T GET TO WHATEVER IT IS!
ALREADY DOING IT!
THIS IS WHAT THEY WERE INTERESTED IN? WHAT IS IT?
ICE, BUT IT SEEMS DIFFERENT THAN THEY ARE. AND IT'S JUST...SITTING THERE.
GAR, GET TOPSIDE AND CONFIRM THERE'S NOT ANOTHER WAVE COMING.
ROUNDHOUSE, CAN YOU GIVE US SOME HEAT?
SURE THING.
HOW...IS THAT POSSIBLE?

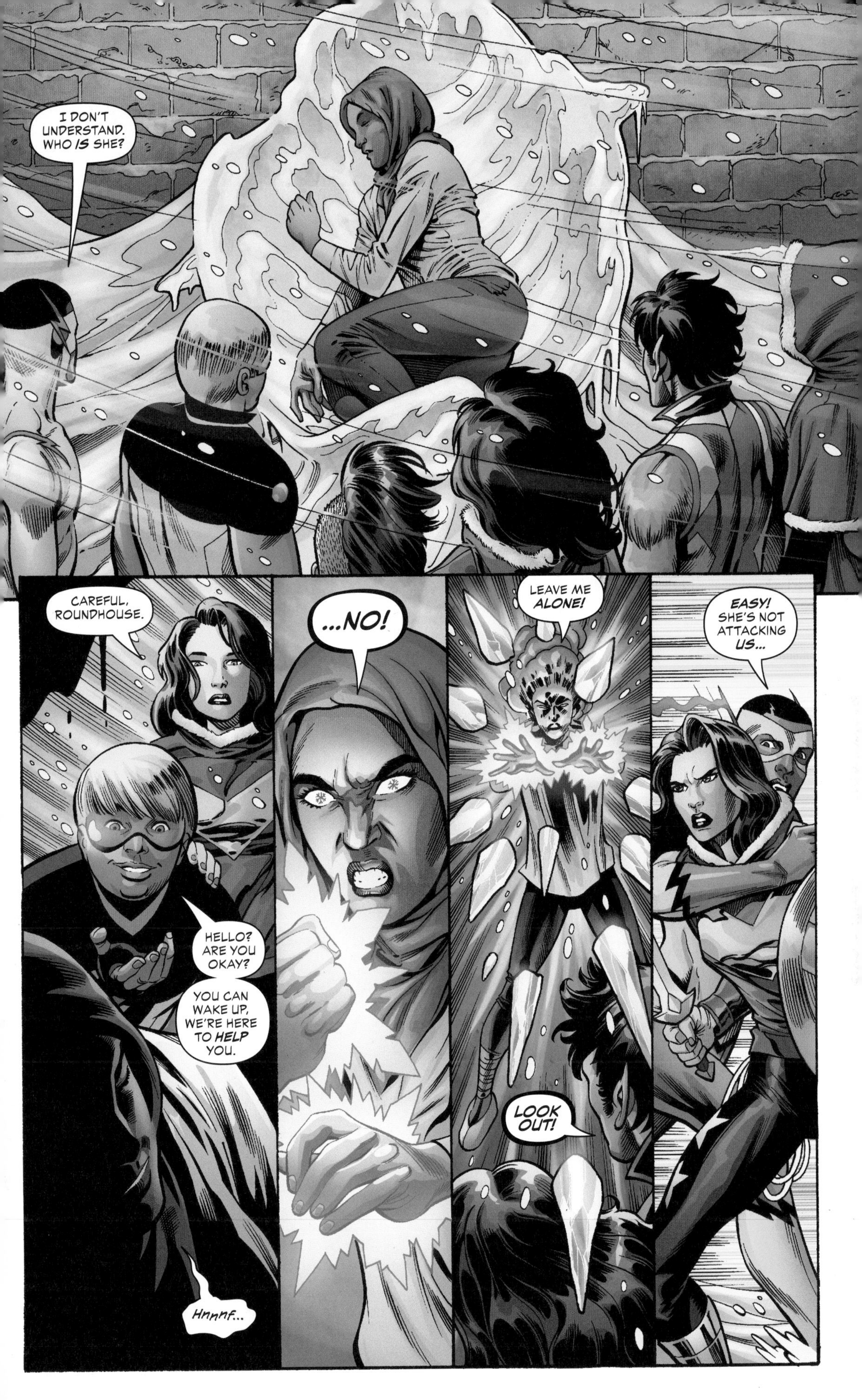
I DON'T UNDERSTAND. WHO IS SHE?
CAREFUL, ROUNDHOUSE.
HELLO? ARE YOU OKAY?
YOU CAN WAKE UP, WE'RE HERE TO HELP YOU.
Hnnnf...
...NO!
LEAVE ME ALONE!
LOOK OUT!
EASY! SHE'S NOT ATTACKING US...

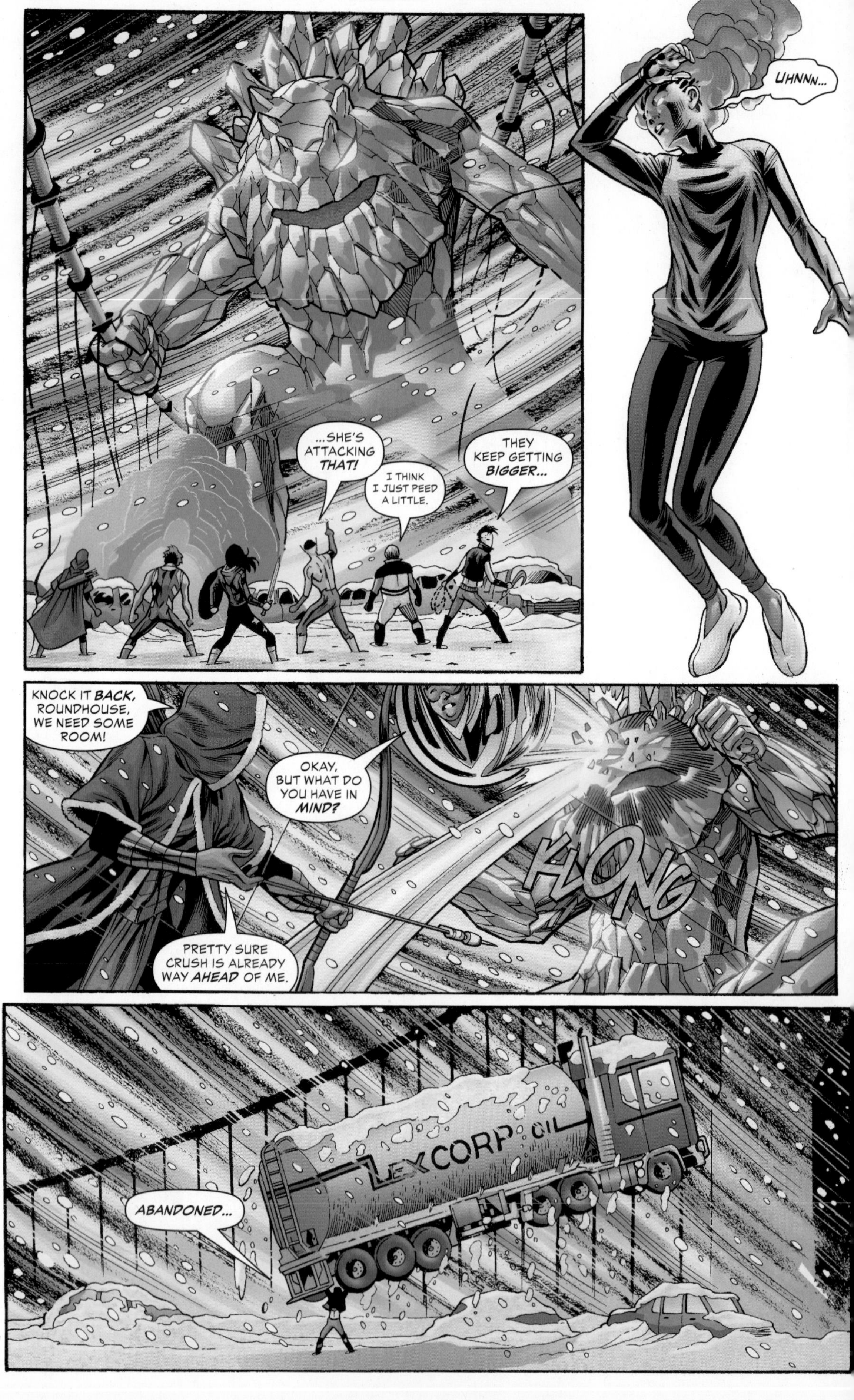
UHNNN...
...SHE'S ATTACKING THAT!
I THINK I JUST PEED A LITTLE.
THEY KEEP GETTING BIGGER...
KNOCK IT BACK, ROUNDHOUSE, WE NEED SOME ROOM!
OKAY, BUT WHAT DO YOU HAVE IN MIND?
KLONG
PRETTY SURE CRUSH IS ALREADY WAY AHEAD OF ME.
LEXCORP OIL
ABANDONED...

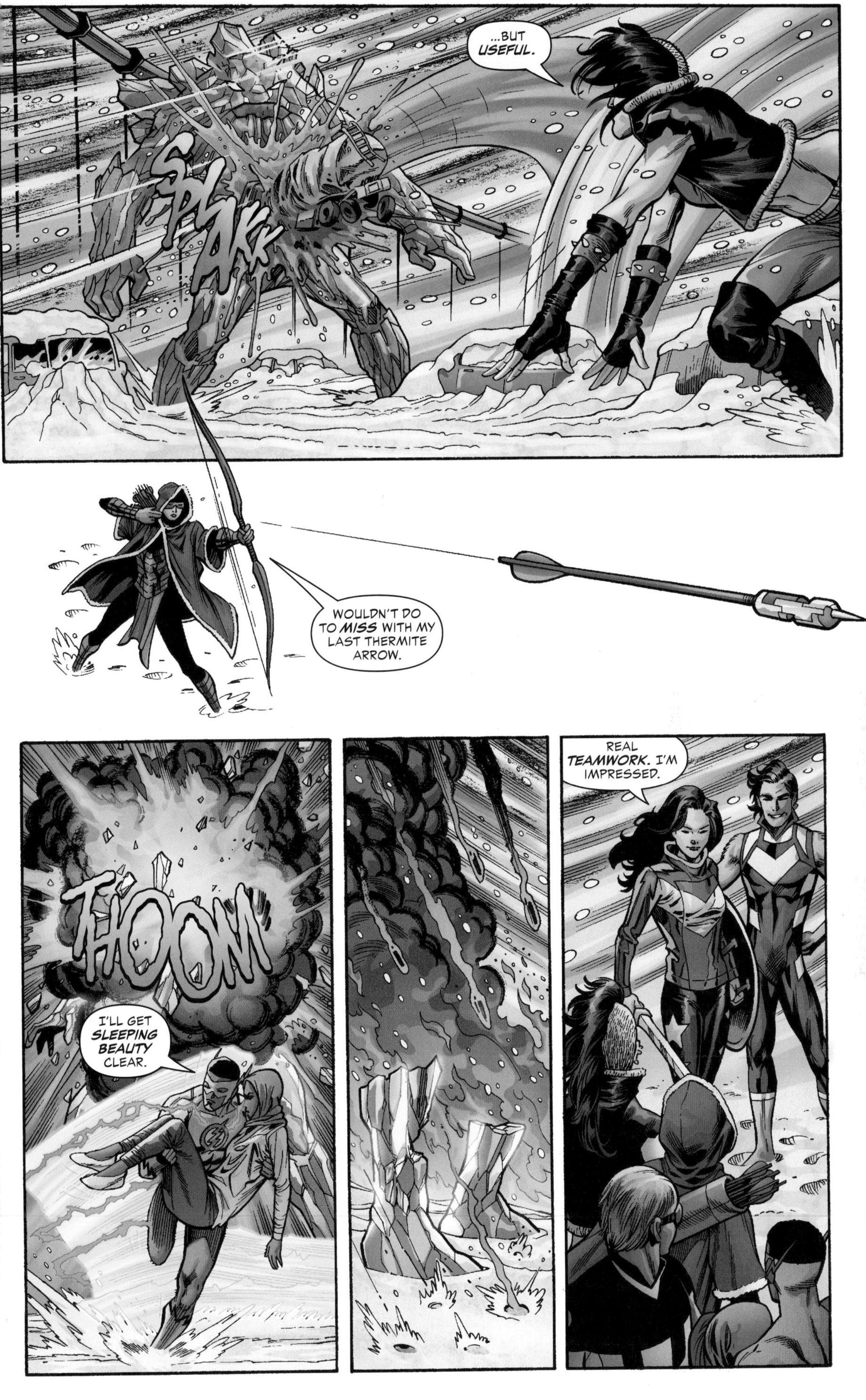

SPLAKK
...BUT USEFUL.
WOULDN'T DO TO MISS WITH MY LAST THERMITE ARROW.
THOOM
I'LL GET SLEEPING BEAUTY CLEAR.
REAL TEAMWORK. I'M IMPRESSED.

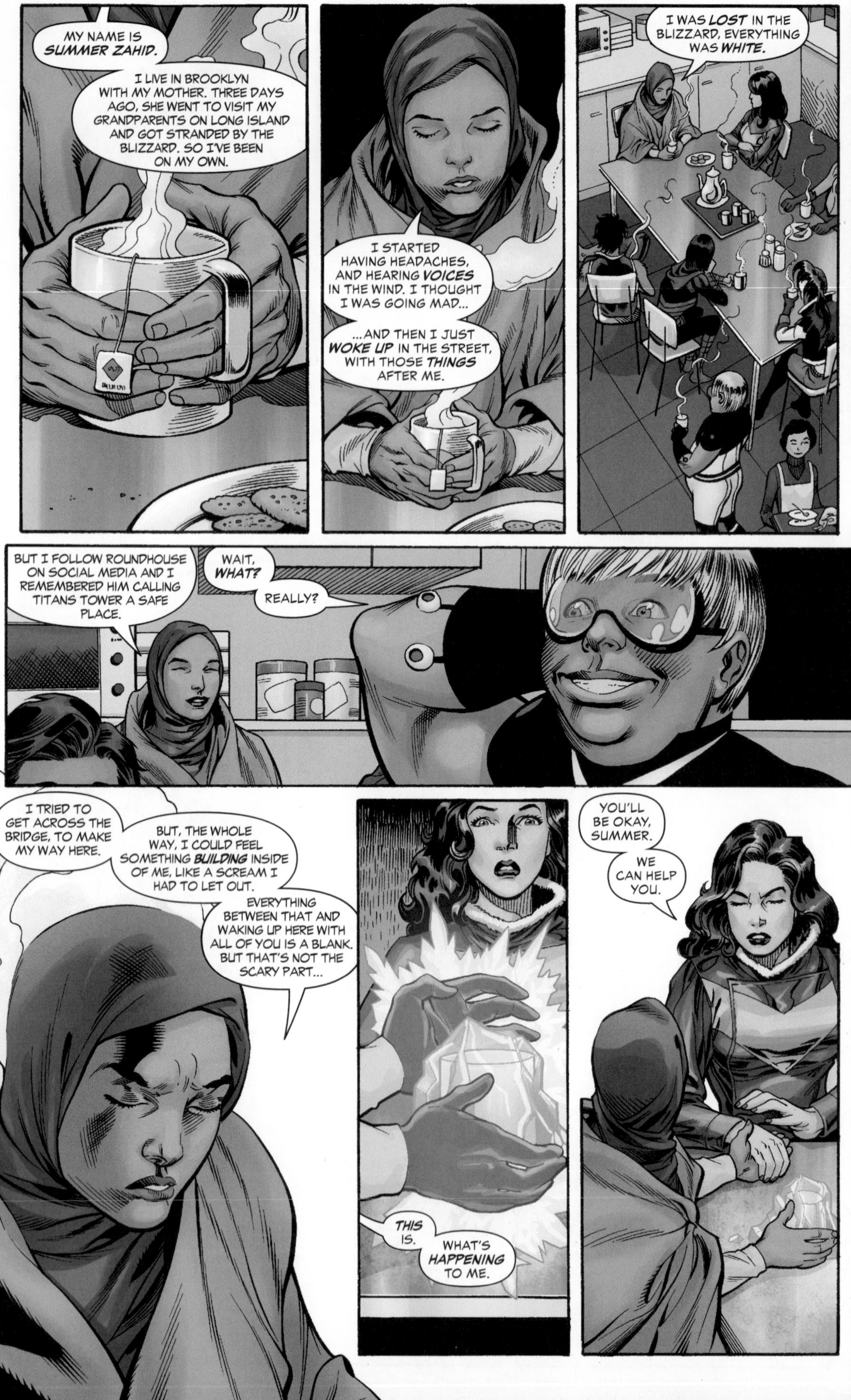

MY NAME IS SUMMER ZAHID.
I LIVE IN BROOKLYN WITH MY MOTHER. THREE DAYS AGO, SHE WENT TO VISIT MY GRANDPARENTS ON LONG ISLAND AND GOT STRANDED BY THE BLIZZARD. SO I'VE BEEN ON MY OWN.
I STARTED HAVING HEADACHES, AND HEARING VOICES IN THE WIND. I THOUGHT I WAS GOING MAD...
...AND THEN I JUST WOKE UP IN THE STREET, WITH THOSE THINGS AFTER ME.
I WAS LOST IN THE BLIZZARD, EVERYTHING WAS WHITE.
BUT I FOLLOW ROUNDHOUSE ON SOCIAL MEDIA AND I REMEMBERED HIM CALLING TITANS TOWER A SAFE PLACE.
WAIT, WHAT?
REALLY?
I TRIED TO GET ACROSS THE BRIDGE, TO MAKE MY WAY HERE.
BUT, THE WHOLE WAY, I COULD FEEL SOMETHING BUILDING INSIDE OF ME, LIKE A SCREAM I HAD TO LET OUT.
EVERYTHING BETWEEN THAT AND WAKING UP HERE WITH ALL OF YOU IS A BLANK. BUT THAT'S NOT THE SCARY PART...
THIS IS.
WHAT'S HAPPENING TO ME.
YOU'LL BE OKAY, SUMMER.
WE CAN HELP YOU.

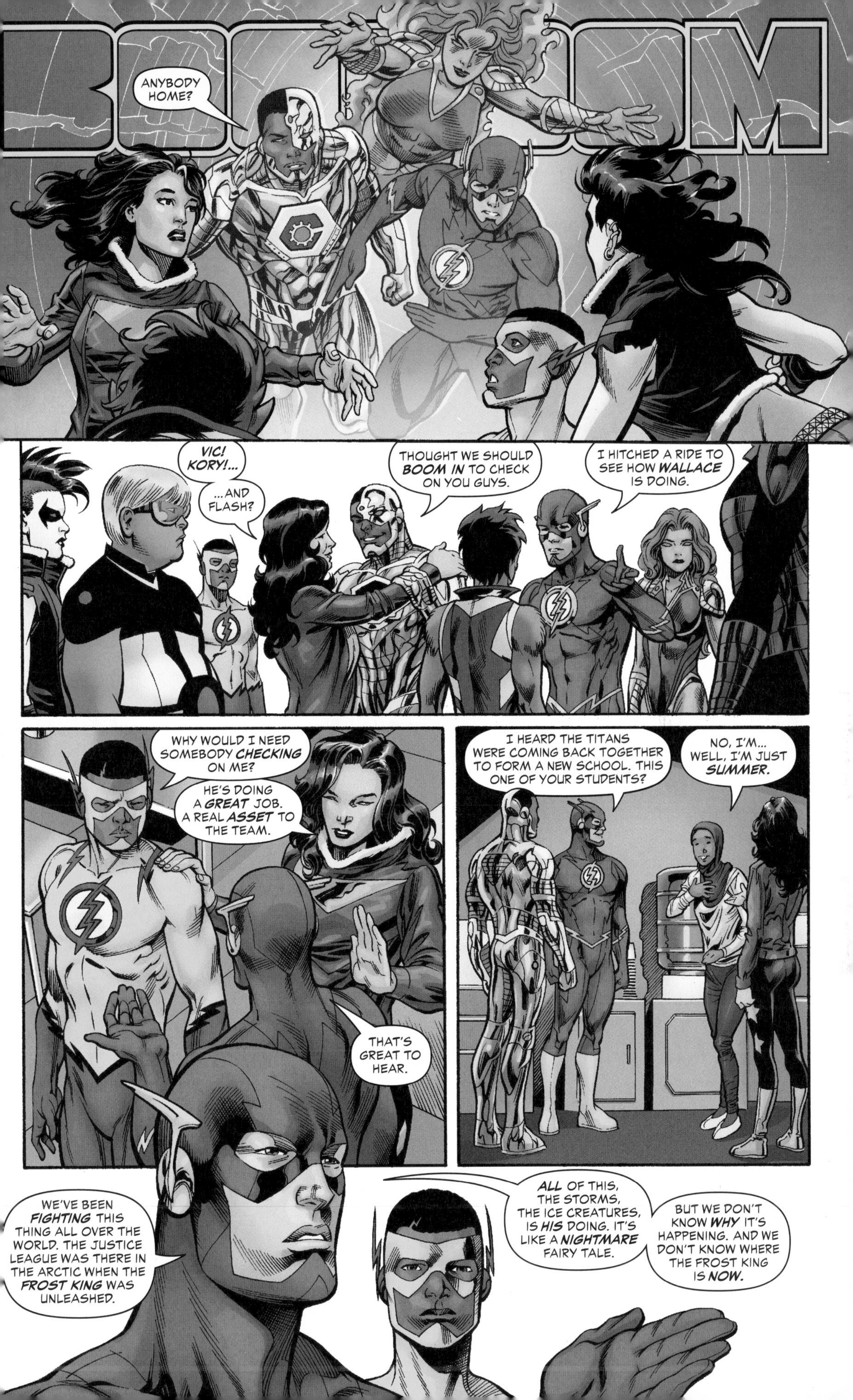

BOOOOM
ANYBODY HOME?
VIC! KORY!...
...AND FLASH?
THOUGHT WE SHOULD BOOM IN TO CHECK ON YOU GUYS.
I HITCHED A RIDE TO SEE HOW WALLACE IS DOING.
WHY WOULD I NEED SOMEBODY CHECKING ON ME?
HE'S DOING A GREAT JOB. A REAL ASSET TO THE TEAM.
THAT'S GREAT TO HEAR.
I HEARD THE TITANS WERE COMING BACK TOGETHER TO FORM A NEW SCHOOL. THIS ONE OF YOUR STUDENTS?
NO, I'M... WELL, I'M JUST SUMMER.
WE'VE BEEN FIGHTING THIS THING ALL OVER THE WORLD. THE JUSTICE LEAGUE WAS THERE IN THE ARCTIC WHEN THE FROST KING WAS UNLEASHED.
ALL OF THIS, THE STORMS, THE ICE CREATURES, IS HIS DOING. IT'S LIKE A NIGHTMARE FAIRY TALE.
BUT WE DON'T KNOW WHY IT'S HAPPENING. AND WE DON'T KNOW WHERE THE FROST KING IS NOW.

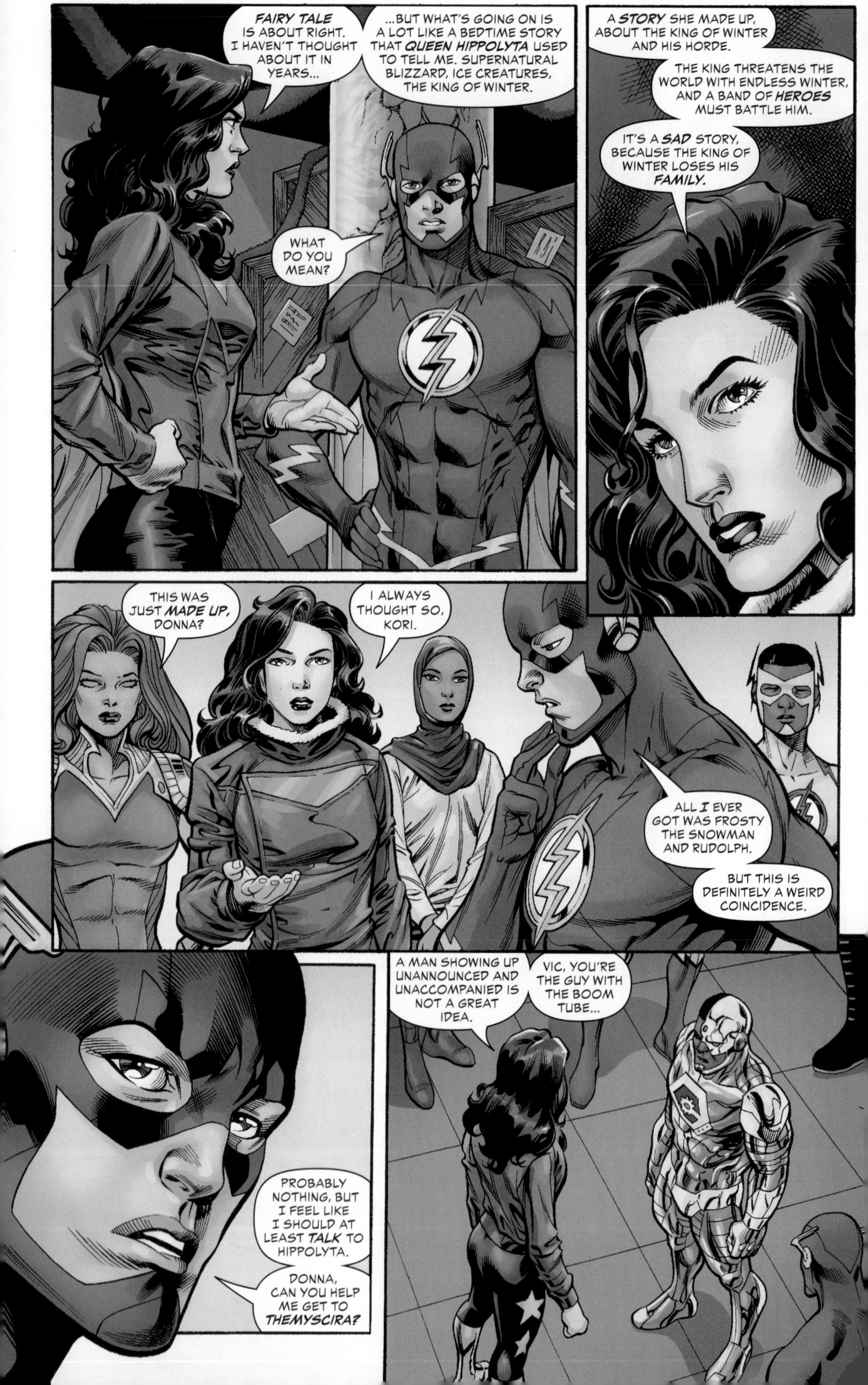
FAIRY TALE IS ABOUT RIGHT. I HAVEN'T THOUGHT ABOUT IT IN YEARS...
...BUT WHAT'S GOING ON IS A LOT LIKE A BEDTIME STORY THAT QUEEN HIPPOLYTA USED TO TELL ME. SUPERNATURAL BLIZZARD, ICE CREATURES, THE KING OF WINTER.
WHAT DO YOU MEAN?
A STORY SHE MADE UP, ABOUT THE KING OF WINTER AND HIS HORDE.
THE KING THREATENS THE WORLD WITH ENDLESS WINTER, AND A BAND OF HEROES MUST BATTLE HIM.
IT'S A SAD STORY, BECAUSE THE KING OF WINTER LOSES HIS FAMILY.
THIS WAS JUST MADE UP, DONNA?
I ALWAYS THOUGHT SO, KORI.
ALL I EVER GOT WAS FROSTY THE SNOWMAN AND RUDOLPH.
BUT THIS IS DEFINITELY A WEIRD COINCIDENCE.
PROBABLY NOTHING, BUT I FEEL LIKE I SHOULD AT LEAST TALK TO HIPPOLYTA.
DONNA, CAN YOU HELP ME GET TO THEMYSCIRA?
A MAN SHOWING UP UNANNOUNCED AND UNACCOMPANIED IS NOT A GREAT IDEA.
VIC, YOU'RE THE GUY WITH THE BOOM TUBE...

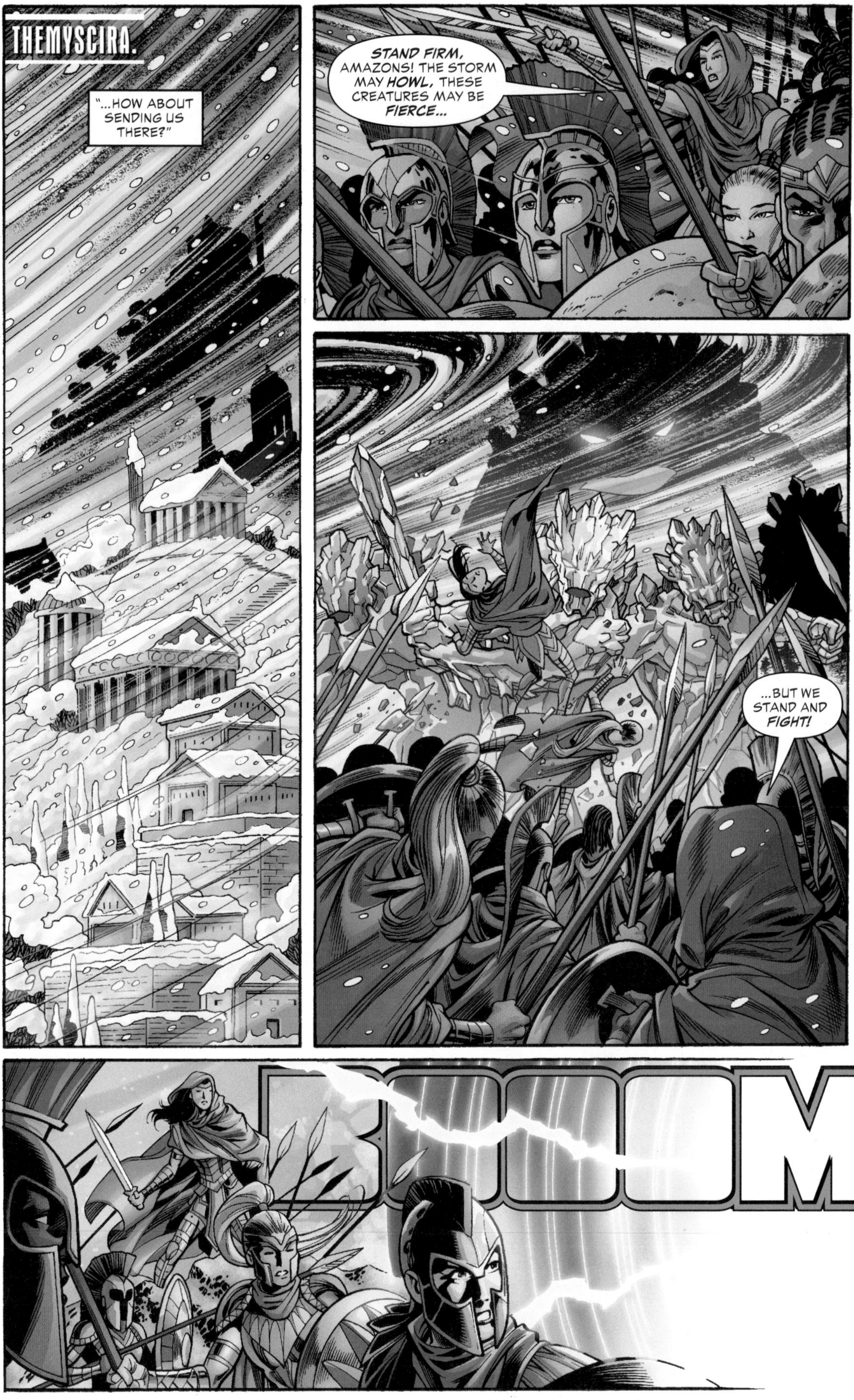
THEMYSCIRA.
"...HOW ABOUT SENDING US THERE?"
STAND FIRM, AMAZONS! THE STORM MAY HOWL, THESE CREATURES MAY BE FIERCE...
...BUT WE STAND AND FIGHT!
BOOOOM

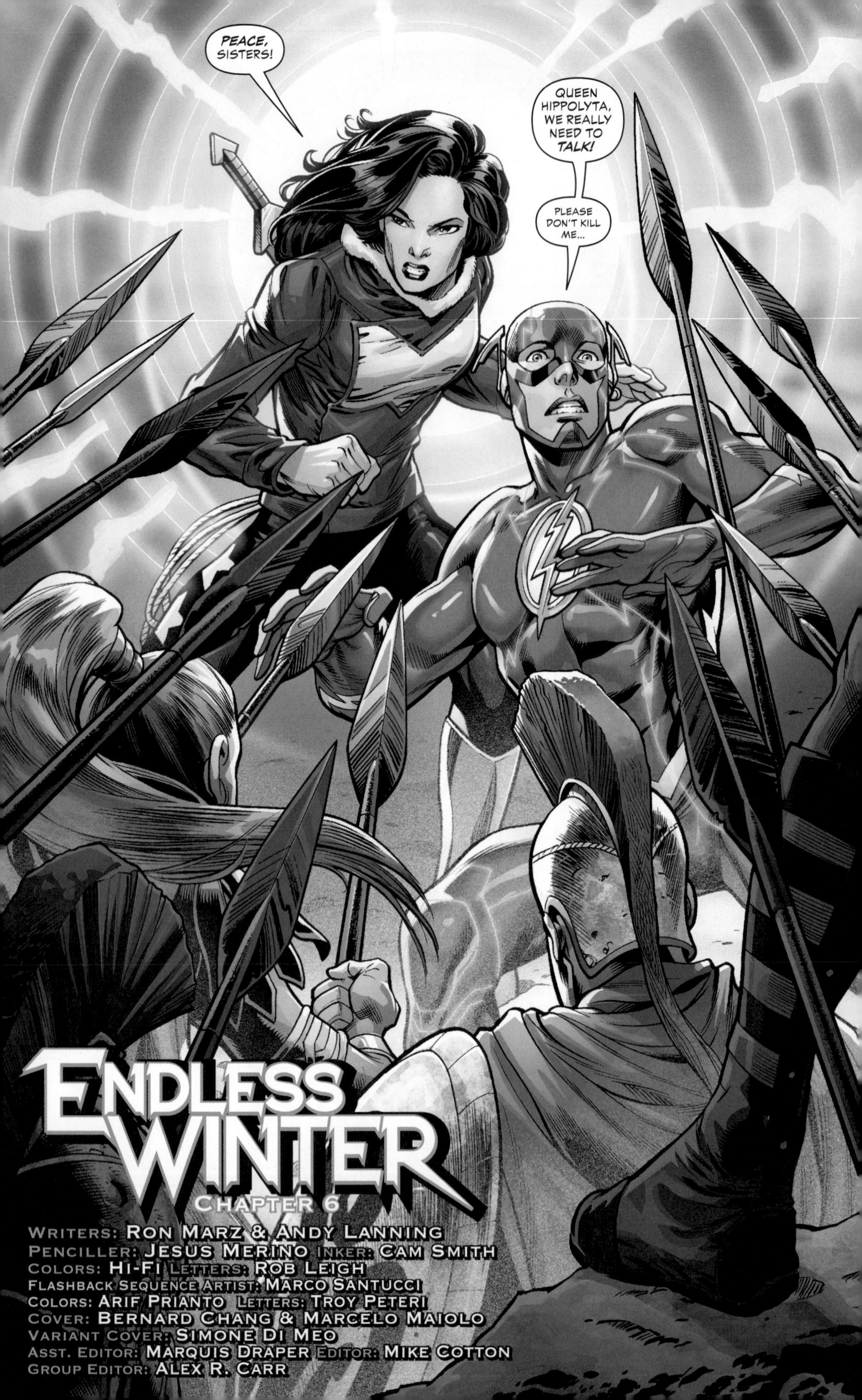

PEACE, SISTERS!
QUEEN HIPPOLYTA, WE REALLY NEED TO TALK!
PLEASE DON'T KILL ME...
ENDLESS WINTER
CHAPTER 6
WRITERS: RON MARZ & ANDY LANNING
PENCILLER: JESUS MERINO INKER: CAM SMITH
COLORS: HI-FI LETTERS: ROB LEIGH
FLASHBACK SEQUENCE ARTIST: MARCO SANTUCCI
COLORS: ARIF PRIANTO LETTERS: TROY PETERI
COVER: BERNARD CHANG & MARCELO MAIOLO
VARIANT COVER: SIMONE DI MEO
ASST. EDITOR: MARQUIS DRAPER EDITOR: MIKE COTTON
GROUP EDITOR: ALEX R. CARR

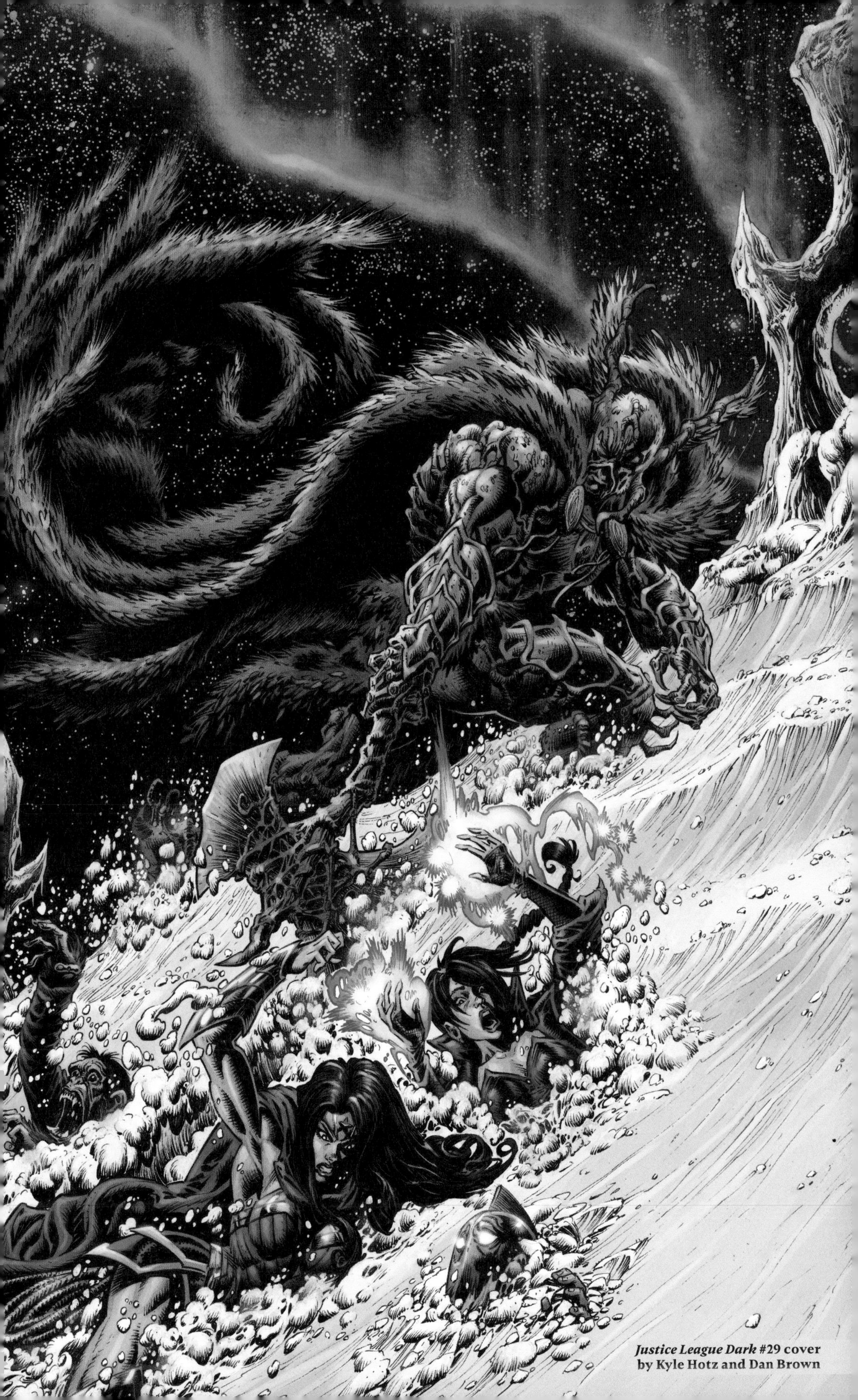

Justice League Dark #29 cover
by Kyle Hotz and Dan Brown

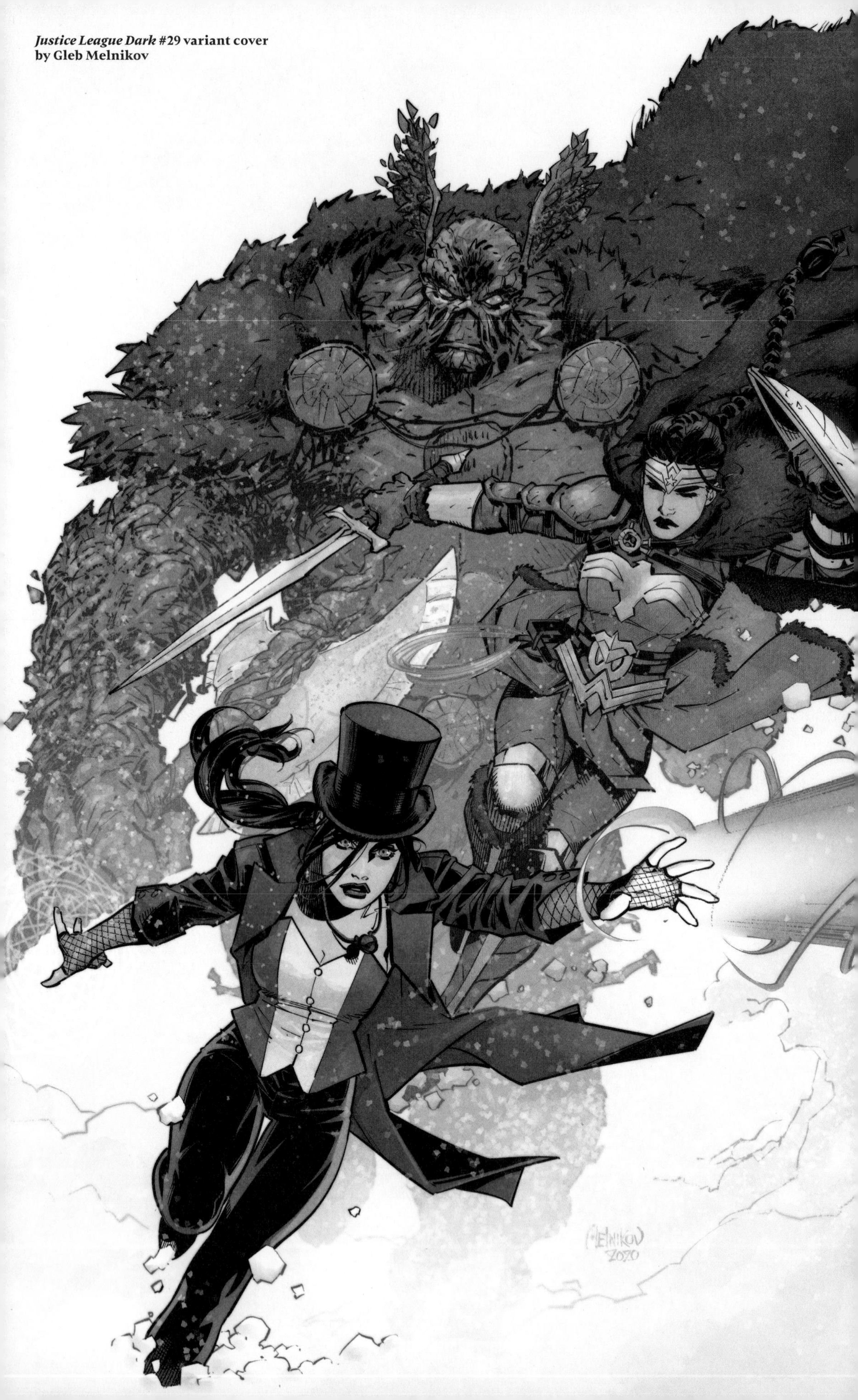
MELNIKOV
2020
Justice League Dark #29 variant cover
by Gleb Melnikov

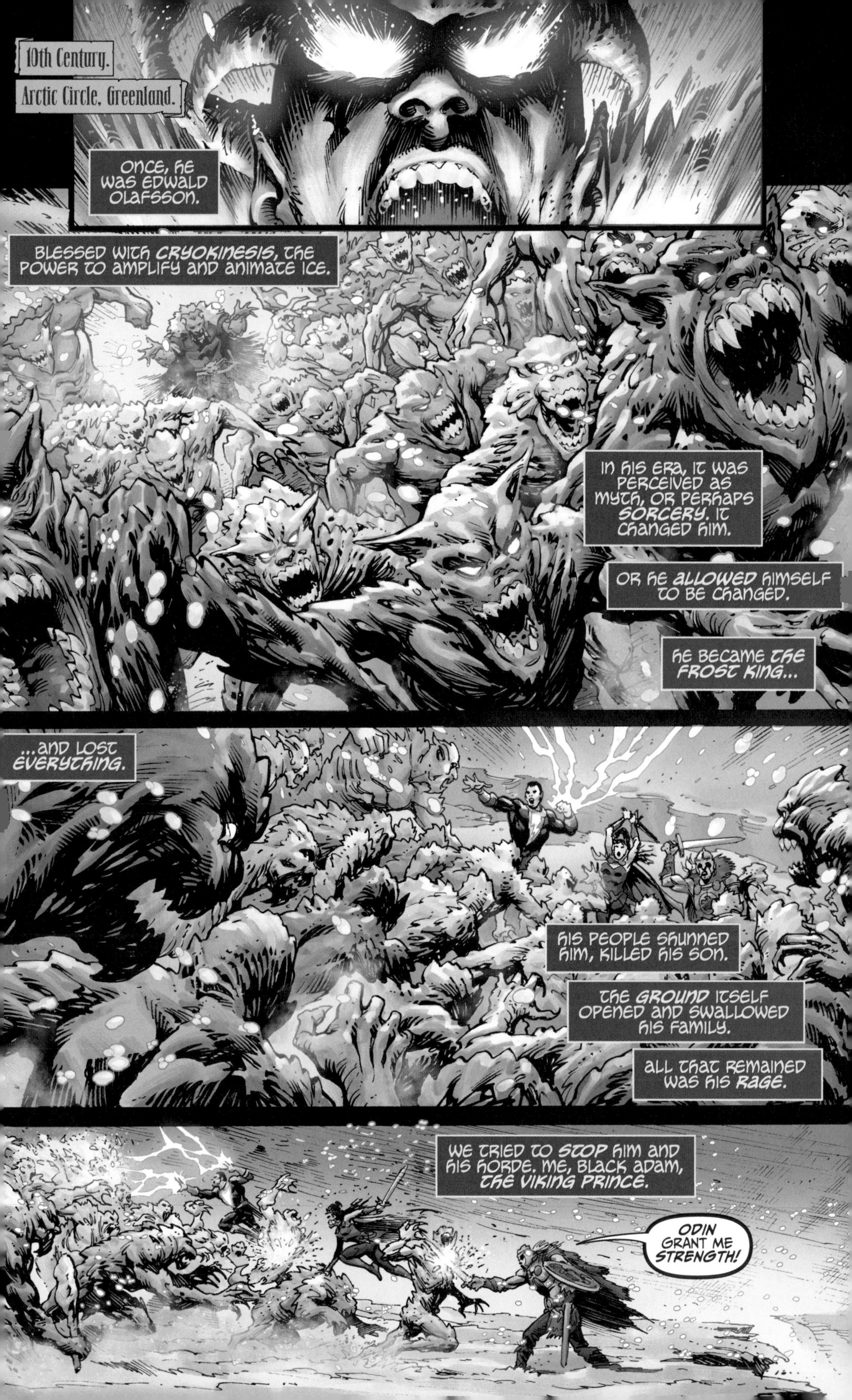
10th Century.
Arctic Circle, Greenland.
ONCE, HE WAS EDWALD OLAFSSON.
BLESSED WITH CRYOKINESIS, THE POWER TO AMPLIFY AND ANIMATE ICE.
IN HIS ERA, IT WAS PERCEIVED AS MYTH, OR PERHAPS SORCERY. IT CHANGED HIM.
OR HE ALLOWED HIMSELF TO BE CHANGED.
HE BECAME THE FROST KING...
...AND LOST EVERYTHING.
HIS PEOPLE SHUNNED HIM, KILLED HIS SON.
THE GROUND ITSELF OPENED AND SWALLOWED HIS FAMILY.
ALL THAT REMAINED WAS HIS RAGE.
WE TRIED TO STOP HIM AND HIS HORDE. ME, BLACK ADAM, THE VIKING PRINCE.
ODIN GRANT ME STRENGTH!

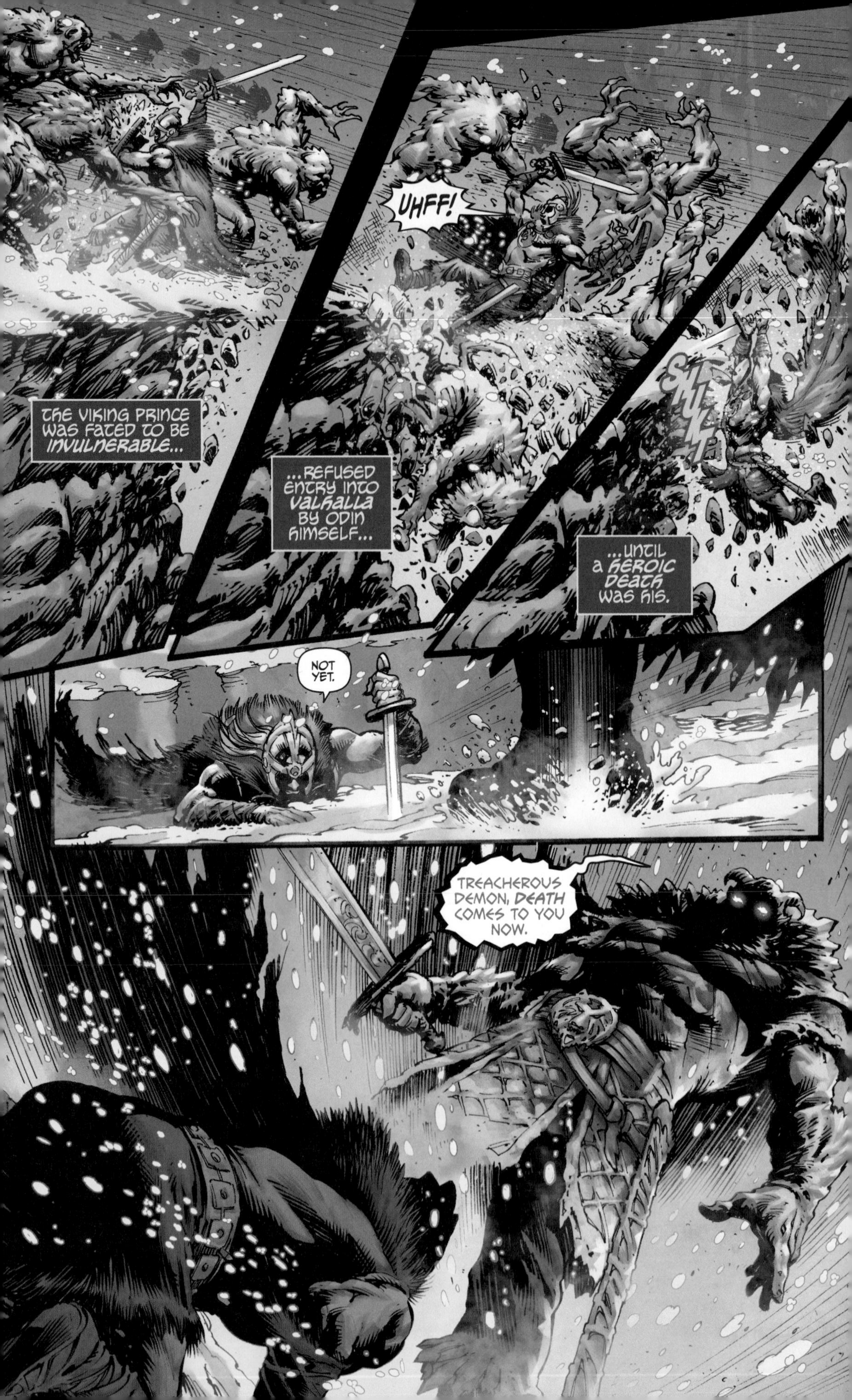
UHFF!
THE VIKING PRINCE WAS FATED TO BE INVULNERABLE...
...REFUSED ENTRY INTO VALHALLA BY ODIN HIMSELF...
...UNTIL A HEROIC DEATH WAS HIS.
NOT YET.
TREACHEROUS DEMON, DEATH COMES TO YOU NOW.

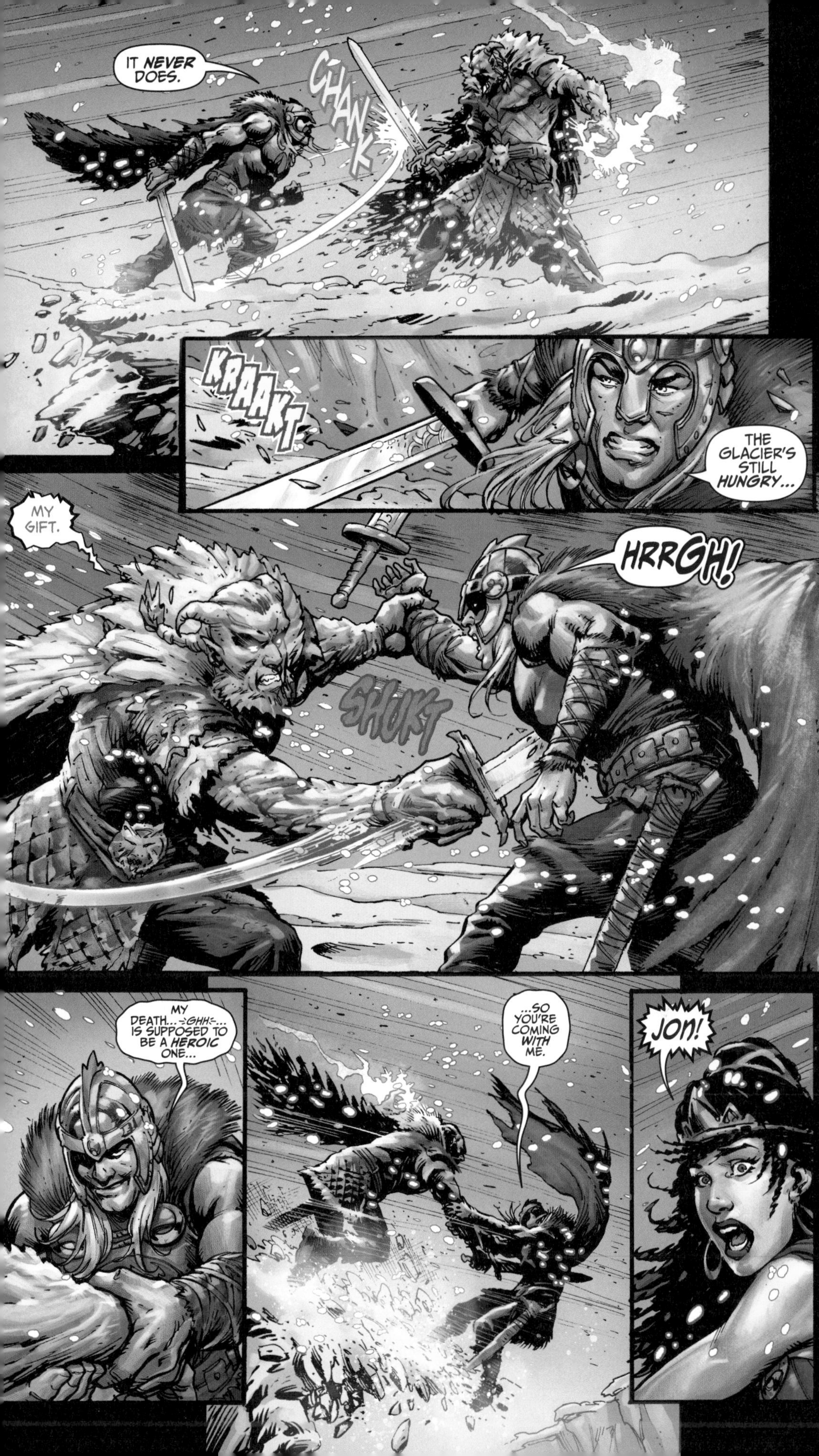
IT NEVER DOES.
CHANK
KRAAKT
THE GLACIER'S STILL HUNGRY...
MY GIFT.
HRRGH!
SHUKT
MY DEATH... GHH... IS SUPPOSED TO BE A HEROIC ONE...
...SO YOU'RE COMING WITH ME.
JON!

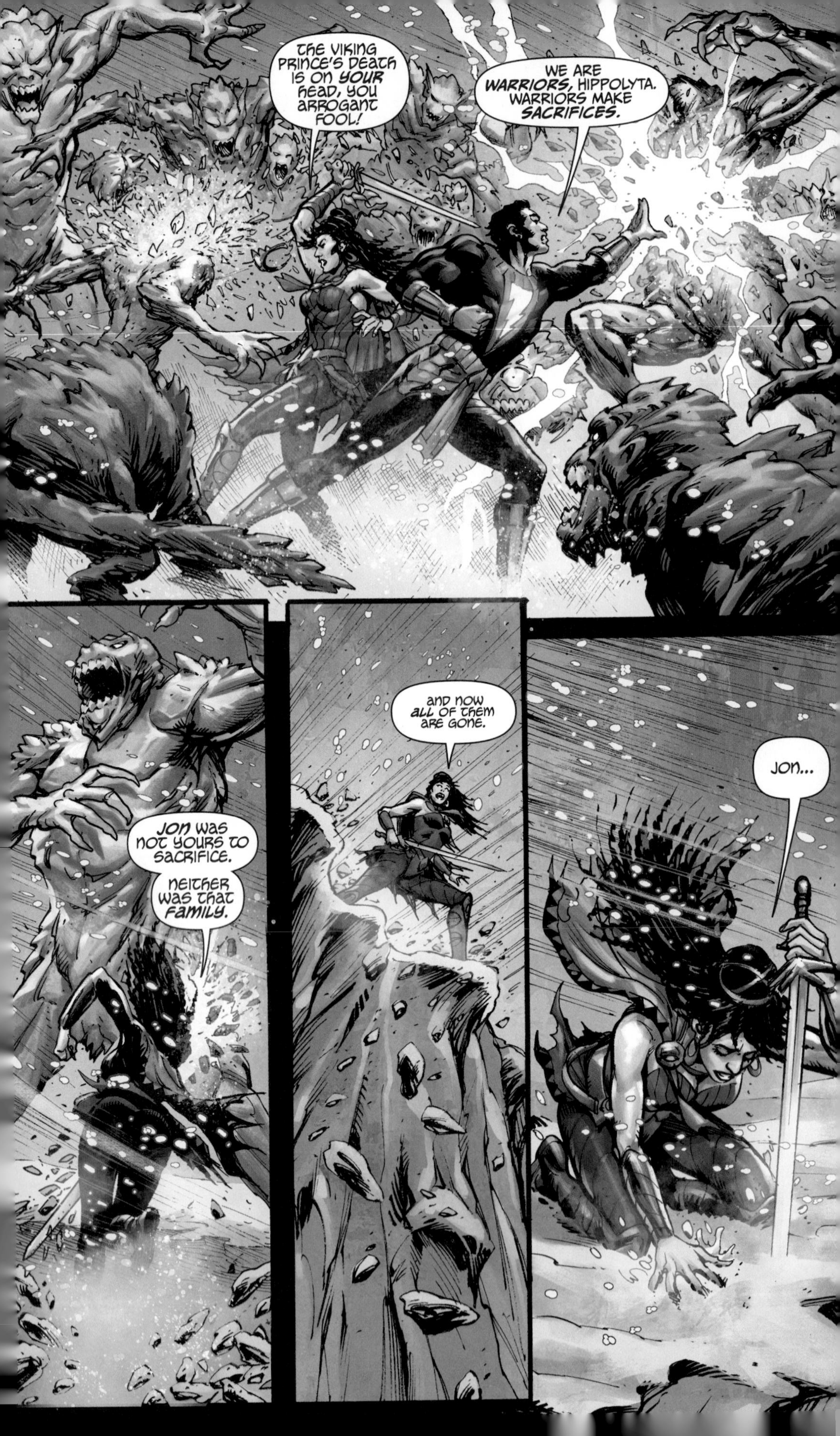
THE VIKING PRINCE'S DEATH IS ON YOUR HEAD, YOU ARROGANT FOOL!
WE ARE WARRIORS, HIPPOLYTA. WARRIORS MAKE SACRIFICES.
JON WAS NOT YOURS TO SACRIFICE.
NEITHER WAS THAT FAMILY.
AND NOW ALL OF THEM ARE GONE.
JON...

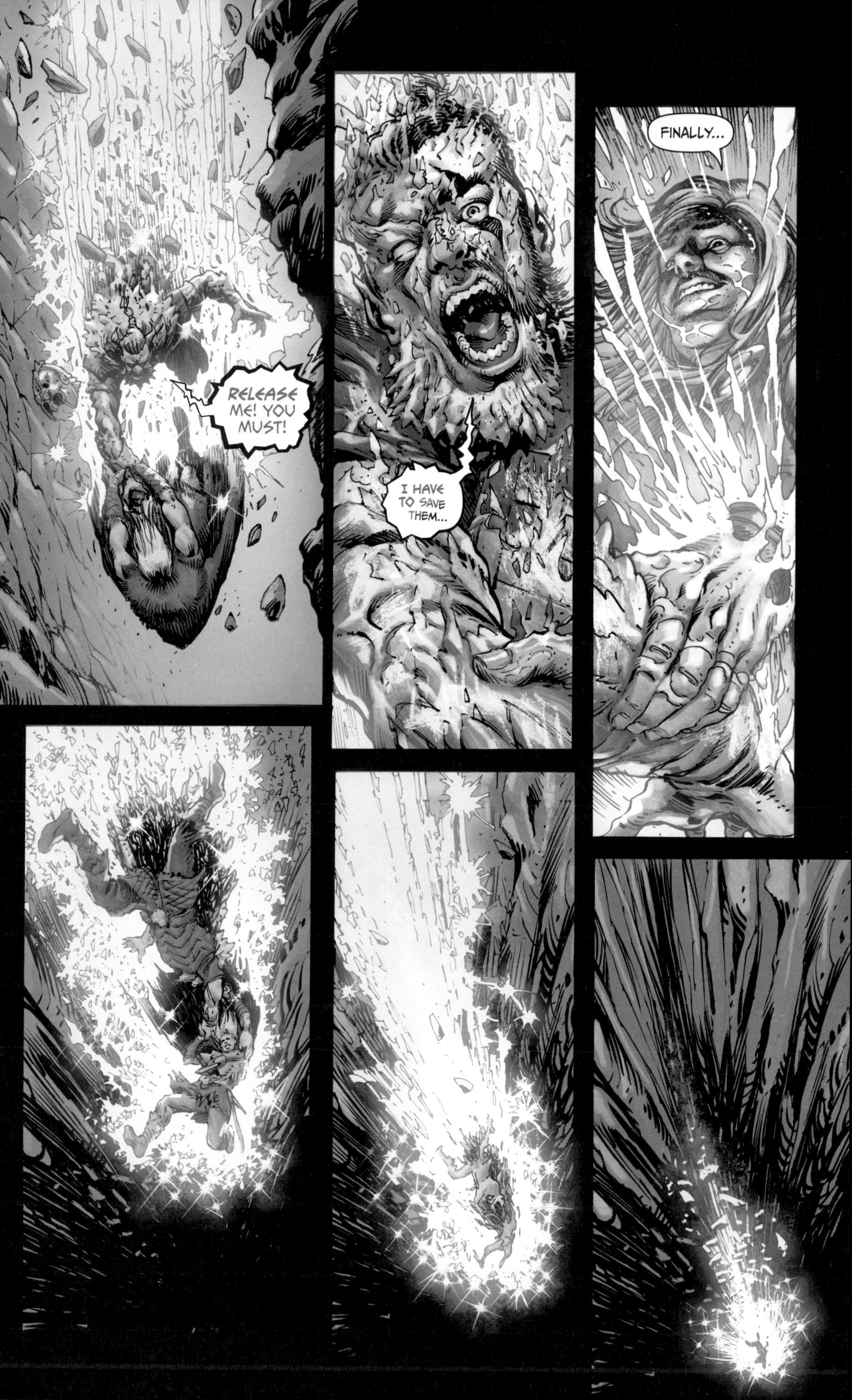
RELEASE ME! YOU MUST!
I HAVE TO SAVE THEM...
FINALLY...

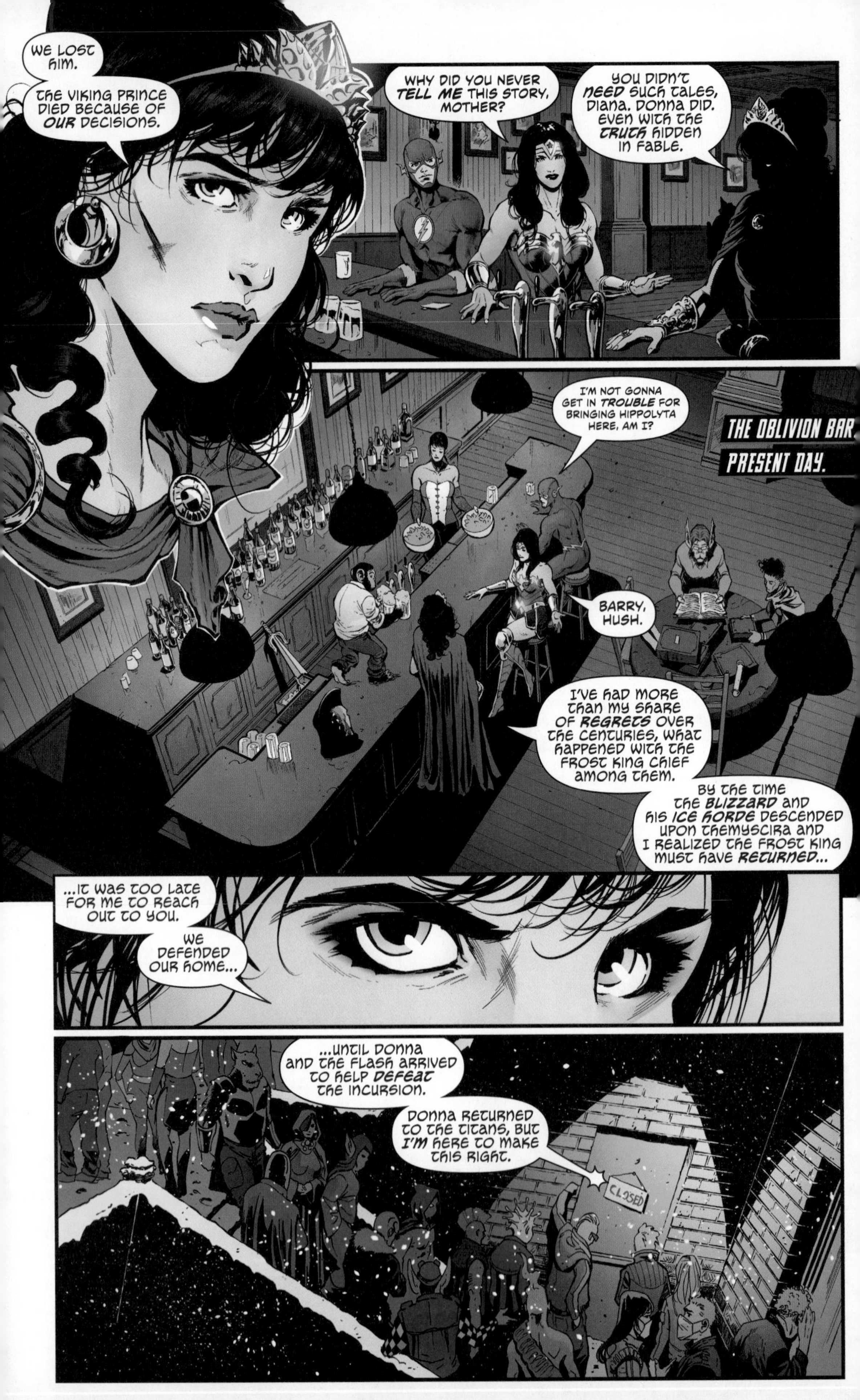

WE LOST HIM.
THE VIKING PRINCE DIED BECAUSE OF OUR DECISIONS.
WHY DID YOU NEVER TELL ME THIS STORY, MOTHER?
YOU DIDN'T NEED SUCH TALES, DIANA. DONNA DID. EVEN WITH THE TRUTH HIDDEN IN FABLE.
THE OBLIVION BAR
PRESENT DAY.
I'M NOT GONNA GET IN TROUBLE FOR BRINGING HIPPOLYTA HERE, AM I?
BARRY, HUSH.
I'VE HAD MORE THAN MY SHARE OF REGRETS OVER THE CENTURIES, WHAT HAPPENED WITH THE FROST KING CHIEF AMONG THEM.
BY THE TIME THE BLIZZARD AND HIS ICE HORDE DESCENDED UPON THEMYSCIRA AND I REALIZED THE FROST KING MUST HAVE RETURNED...
...IT WAS TOO LATE FOR ME TO REACH OUT TO YOU.
WE DEFENDED OUR HOME...
...UNTIL DONNA AND THE FLASH ARRIVED TO HELP DEFEAT THE INCURSION.
DONNA RETURNED TO THE TITANS, BUT I'M HERE TO MAKE THIS RIGHT.
CLOSED

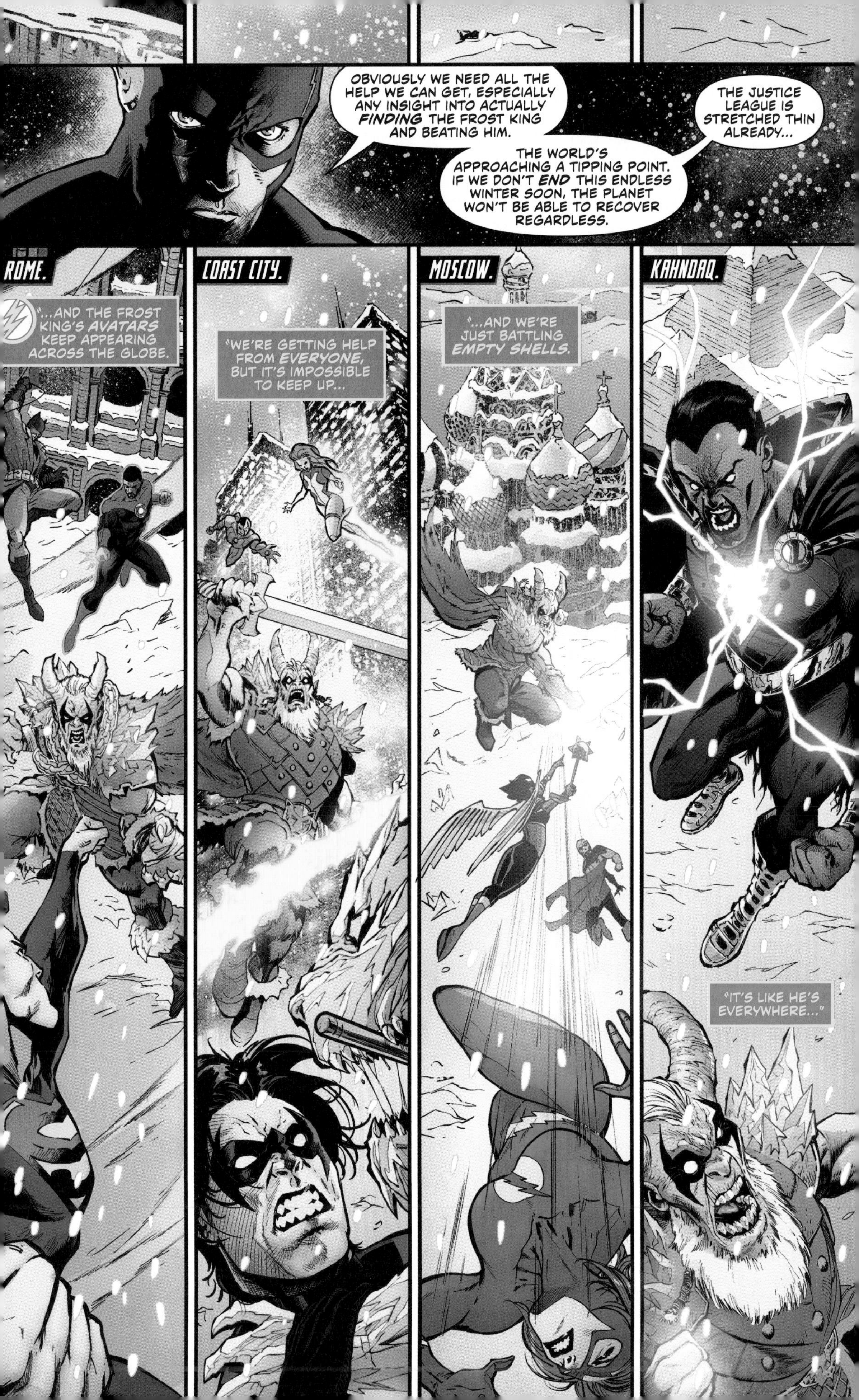
OBVIOUSLY WE NEED ALL THE HELP WE CAN GET, ESPECIALLY ANY INSIGHT INTO ACTUALLY FINDING THE FROST KING AND BEATING HIM.
THE WORLD'S APPROACHING A TIPPING POINT. IF WE DON'T END THIS ENDLESS WINTER SOON, THE PLANET WON'T BE ABLE TO RECOVER REGARDLESS.
THE JUSTICE LEAGUE IS STRETCHED THIN ALREADY...
ROME.
"...AND THE FROST KING'S AVATARS KEEP APPEARING ACROSS THE GLOBE.
COAST CITY.
"WE'RE GETTING HELP FROM EVERYONE, BUT IT'S IMPOSSIBLE TO KEEP UP...
MOSCOW.
"...AND WE'RE JUST BATTLING EMPTY SHELLS.
KAHNDAQ.
"IT'S LIKE HE'S EVERYWHERE..."

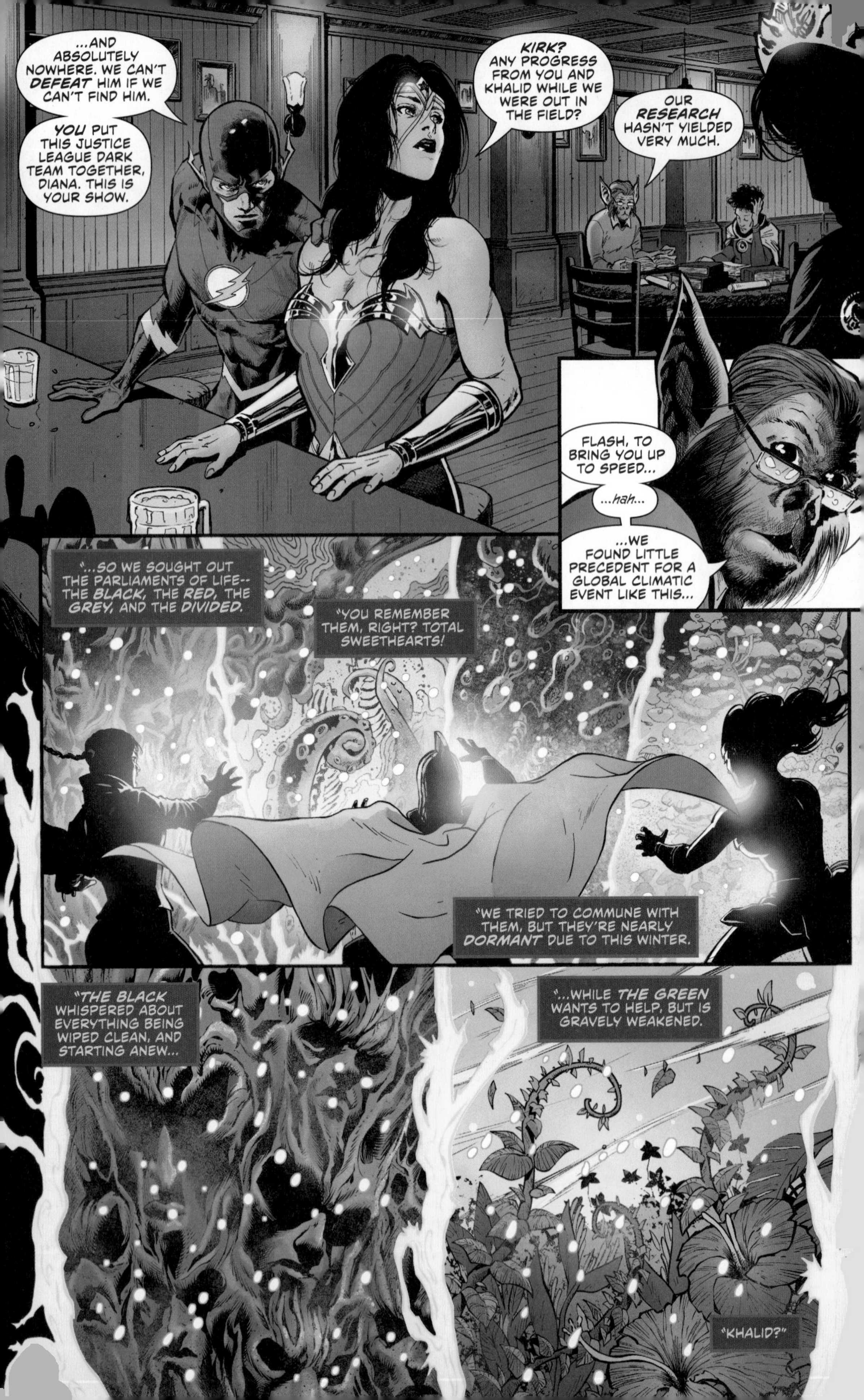

...AND ABSOLUTELY NOWHERE. WE CAN'T DEFEAT HIM IF WE CAN'T FIND HIM.
YOU PUT THIS JUSTICE LEAGUE DARK TEAM TOGETHER, DIANA. THIS IS YOUR SHOW.
KIRK? ANY PROGRESS FROM YOU AND KHALID WHILE WE WERE OUT IN THE FIELD?
OUR RESEARCH HASN'T YIELDED VERY MUCH.
FLASH, TO BRING YOU UP TO SPEED...
...hah...
...WE FOUND LITTLE PRECEDENT FOR A GLOBAL CLIMATIC EVENT LIKE THIS...
"...SO WE SOUGHT OUT THE PARLIAMENTS OF LIFE--THE BLACK, THE RED, THE GREY, AND THE DIVIDED.
"YOU REMEMBER THEM, RIGHT? TOTAL SWEETHEARTS!
"WE TRIED TO COMMUNE WITH THEM, BUT THEY'RE NEARLY DORMANT DUE TO THIS WINTER.
"THE BLACK WHISPERED ABOUT EVERYTHING BEING WIPED CLEAN, AND STARTING ANEW...
"...WHILE THE GREEN WANTS TO HELP, BUT IS GRAVELY WEAKENED.
"KHALID?"

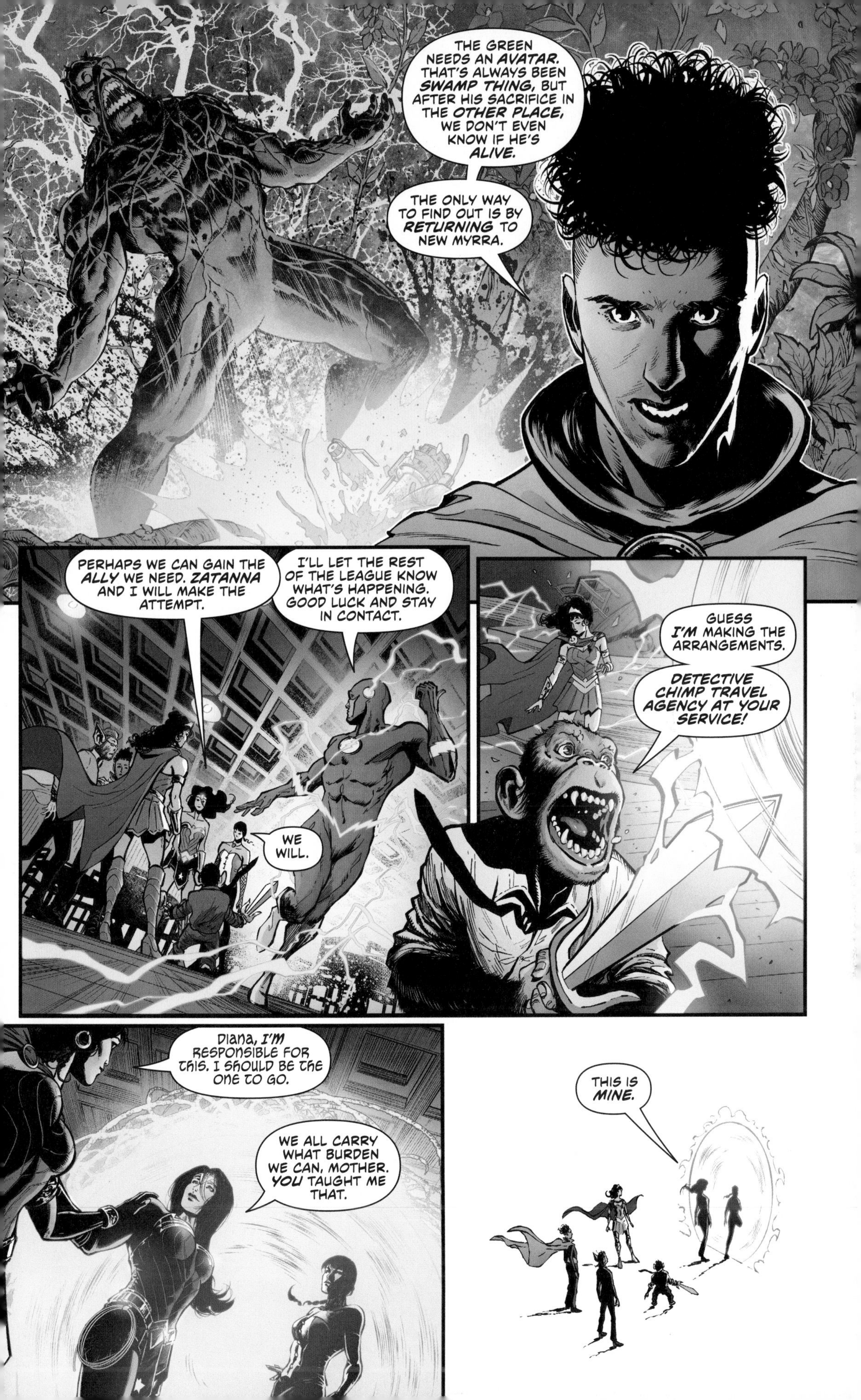
THE GREEN NEEDS AN AVATAR. THAT'S ALWAYS BEEN SWAMP THING, BUT AFTER HIS SACRIFICE IN THE OTHER PLACE, WE DON'T EVEN KNOW IF HE'S ALIVE.
THE ONLY WAY TO FIND OUT IS BY RETURNING TO NEW MYRRA.
PERHAPS WE CAN GAIN THE ALLY WE NEED. ZATANNA AND I WILL MAKE THE ATTEMPT.
I'LL LET THE REST OF THE LEAGUE KNOW WHAT'S HAPPENING. GOOD LUCK AND STAY IN CONTACT.
WE WILL.
GUESS I'M MAKING THE ARRANGEMENTS.
DETECTIVE CHIMP TRAVEL AGENCY AT YOUR SERVICE!
Diana, I'M RESPONSIBLE FOR THIS. I SHOULD BE THE ONE TO GO.
WE ALL CARRY WHAT BURDEN WE CAN, MOTHER. YOU TAUGHT ME THAT.
THIS IS MINE.

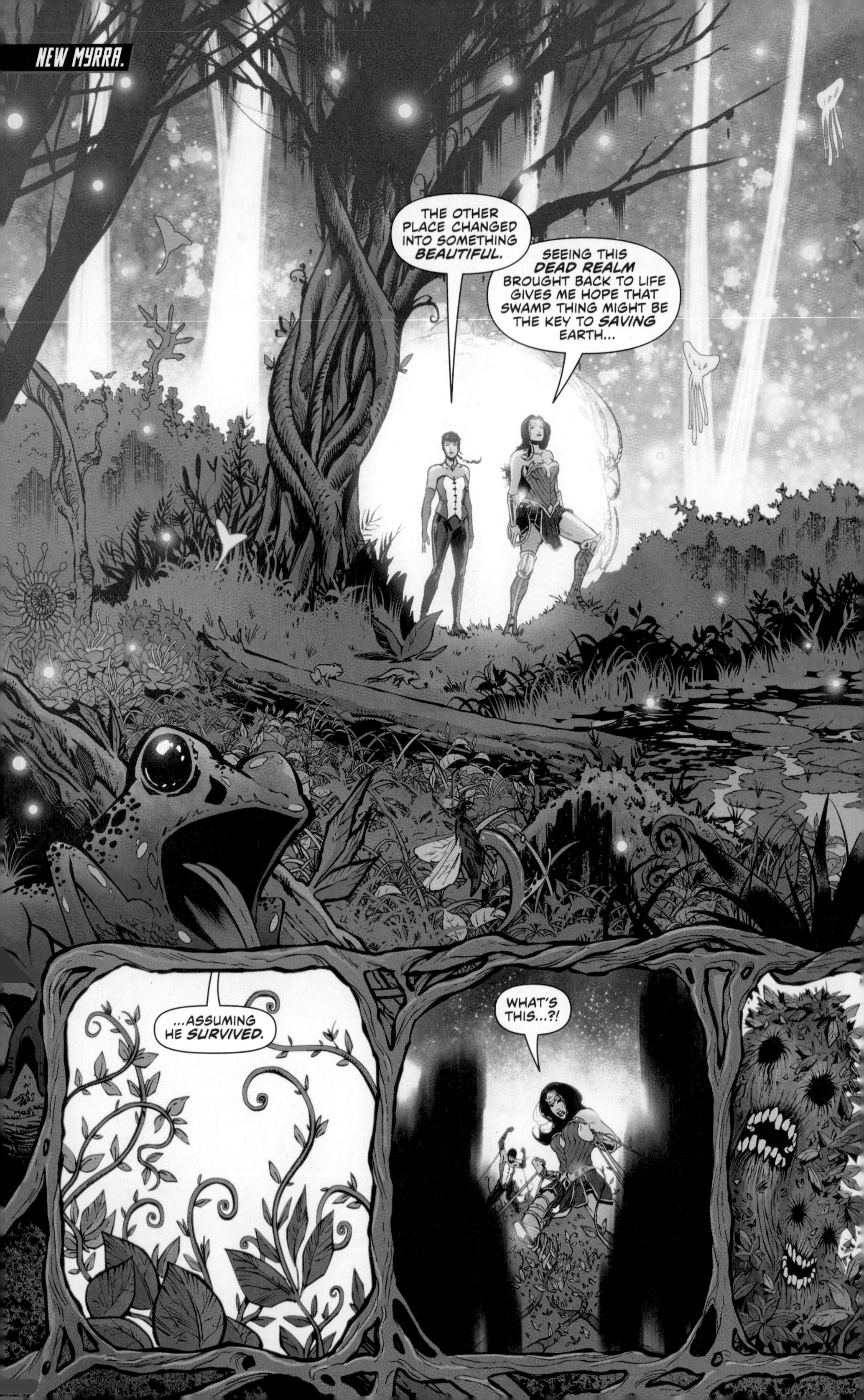
NEW MYRRA.
THE OTHER PLACE CHANGED INTO SOMETHING *BEAUTIFUL.*
SEEING THIS *DEAD REALM* BROUGHT BACK TO LIFE GIVES ME HOPE THAT SWAMP THING MIGHT BE THE KEY TO *SAVING* EARTH...
...ASSUMING HE *SURVIVED.*
WHAT'S THIS...?!

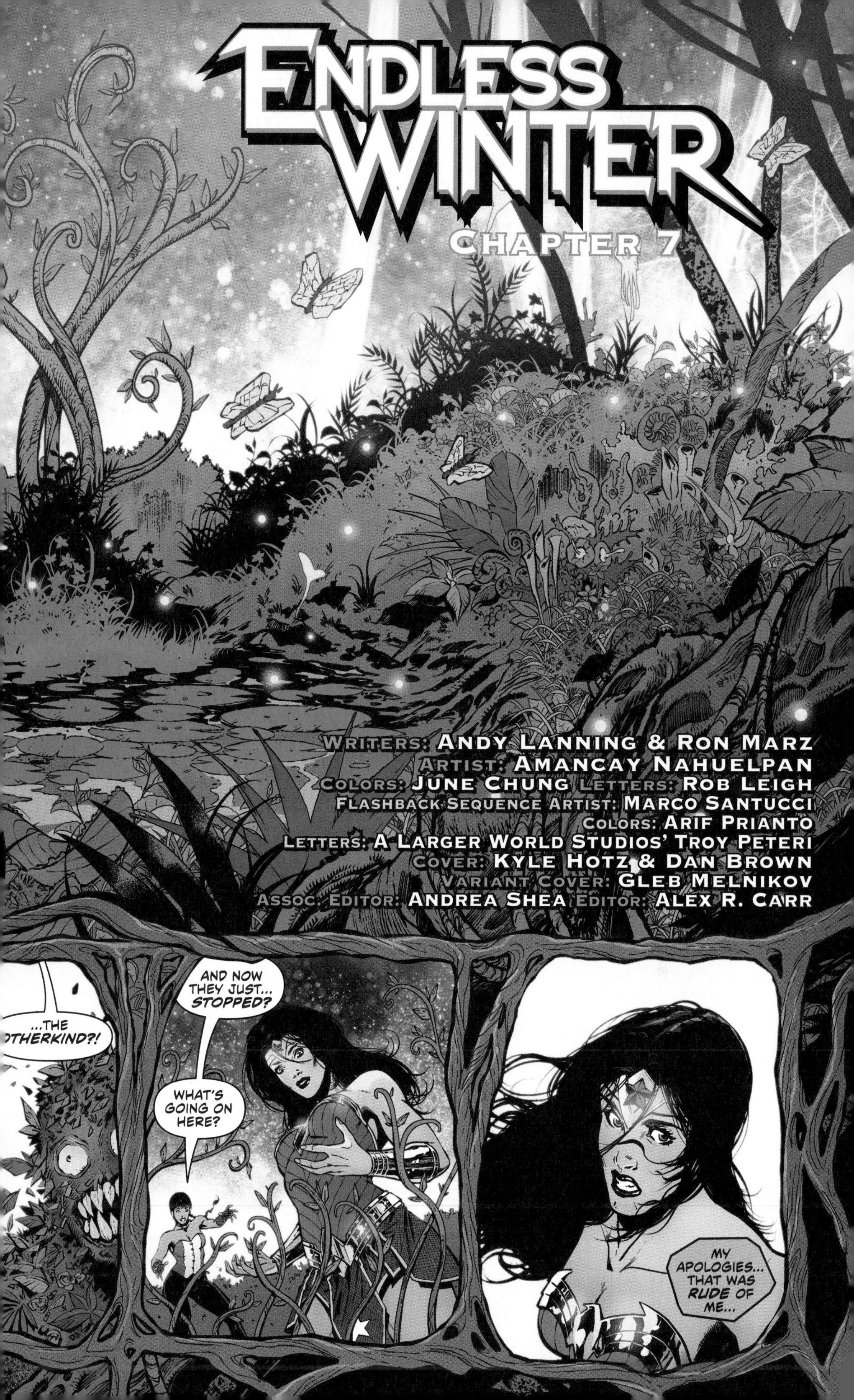

ENDLESS WINTER
CHAPTER 7
WRITERS: ANDY LANNING & RON MARZ
ARTIST: AMANCAY NAHUELPAN
COLORS: JUNE CHUNG LETTERS: ROB LEIGH
FLASHBACK SEQUENCE ARTIST: MARCO SANTUCCI
COLORS: ARIF PRIANTO
LETTERS: A LARGER WORLD STUDIOS' TROY PETERI
COVER: KYLE HOTZ & DAN BROWN
VARIANT COVER: GLEB MELNIKOV
ASSOC. EDITOR: ANDREA SHEA EDITOR: ALEX R. CARR
...THE OTHERKIND?!
AND NOW THEY JUST... STOPPED?
WHAT'S GOING ON HERE?
MY APOLOGIES... THAT WAS RUDE OF ME...

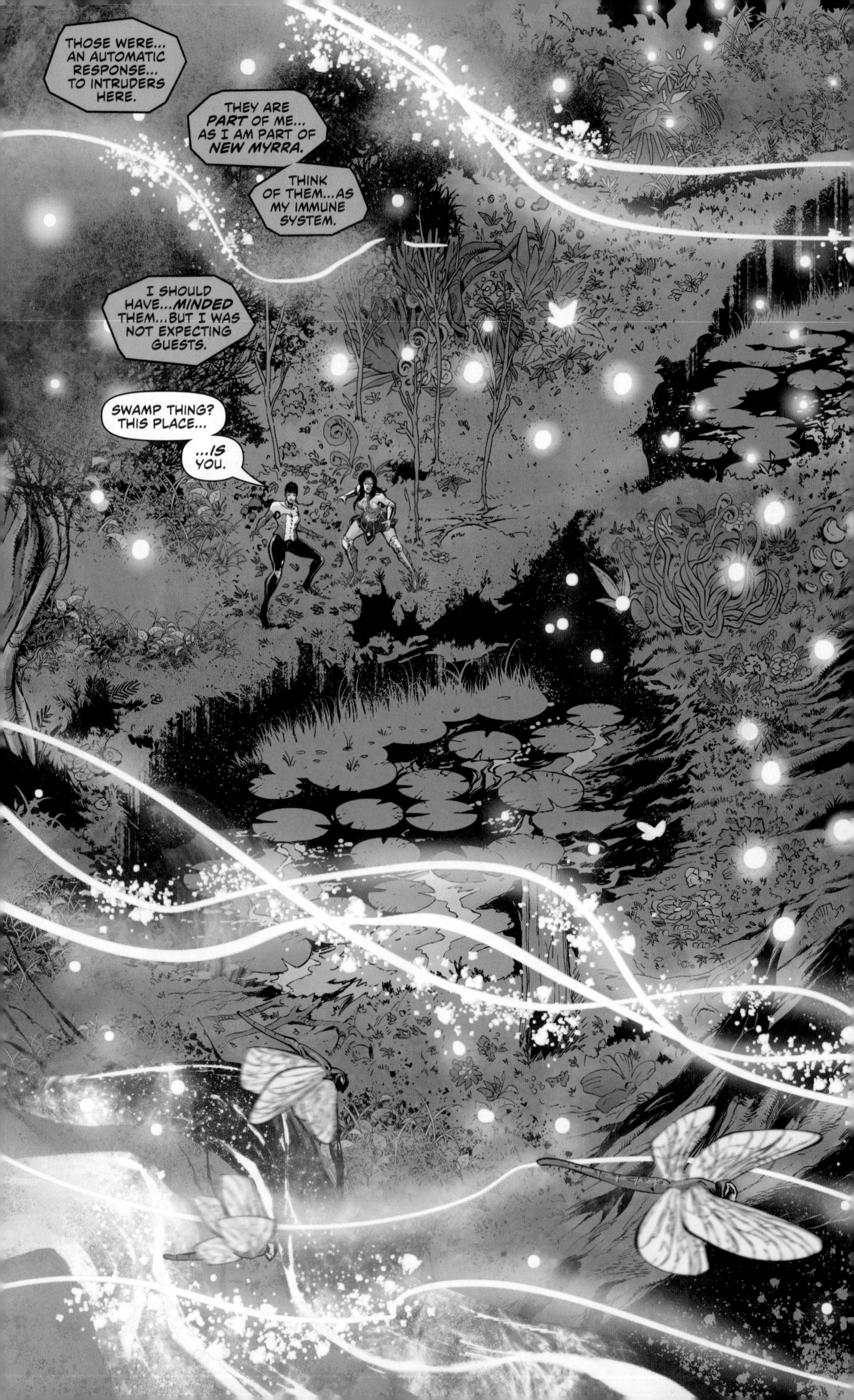
THOSE WERE... AN AUTOMATIC RESPONSE... TO INTRUDERS HERE.
THEY ARE *PART* OF ME... AS I AM PART OF *NEW MYRRA*.
THINK OF THEM...AS MY IMMUNE SYSTEM.
I SHOULD HAVE...*MINDED* THEM...BUT I WAS NOT EXPECTING GUESTS.
SWAMP THING? THIS PLACE...
...*IS* YOU.

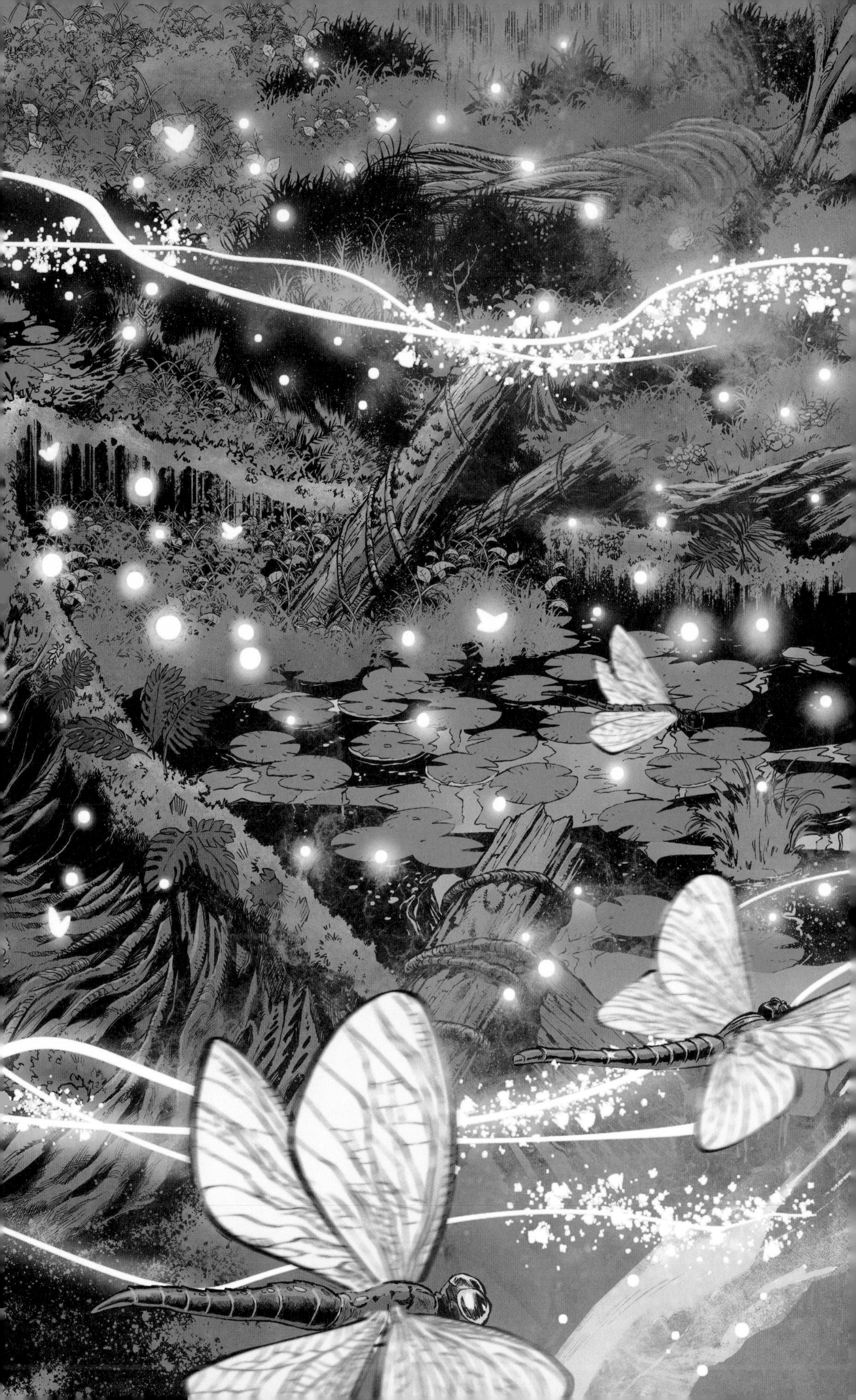

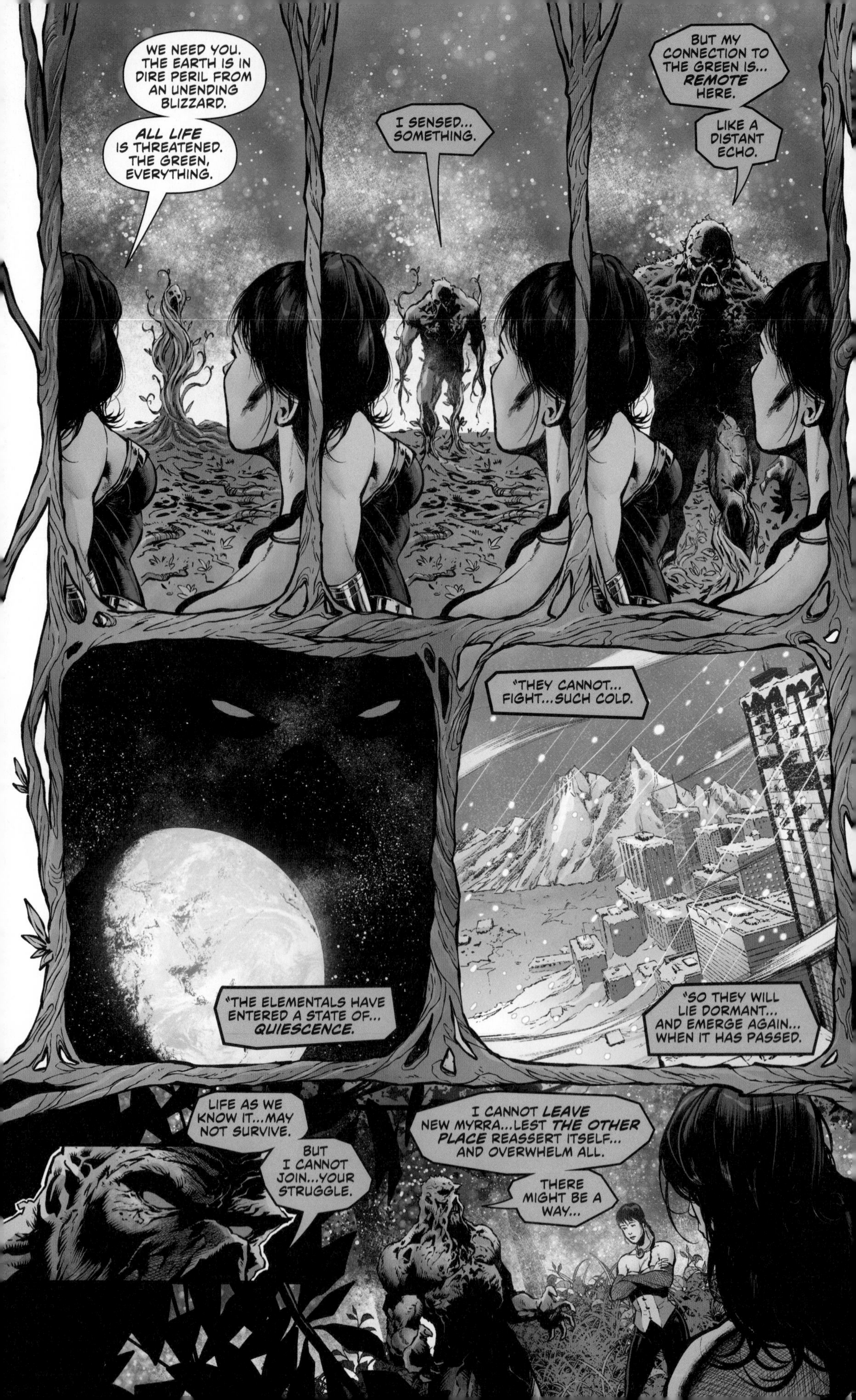

WE NEED YOU. THE EARTH IS IN DIRE PERIL FROM AN UNENDING BLIZZARD.
ALL LIFE IS THREATENED. THE GREEN, EVERYTHING.
I SENSED... SOMETHING.
BUT MY CONNECTION TO THE GREEN IS... REMOTE HERE.
LIKE A DISTANT ECHO.
"THE ELEMENTALS HAVE ENTERED A STATE OF... QUIESCENCE.
"THEY CANNOT... FIGHT...SUCH COLD.
"SO THEY WILL LIE DORMANT... AND EMERGE AGAIN... WHEN IT HAS PASSED.
LIFE AS WE KNOW IT...MAY NOT SURVIVE.
BUT I CANNOT JOIN...YOUR STRUGGLE.
I CANNOT LEAVE NEW MYRRA...LEST THE OTHER PLACE REASSERT ITSELF... AND OVERWHELM ALL.
THERE MIGHT BE A WAY...

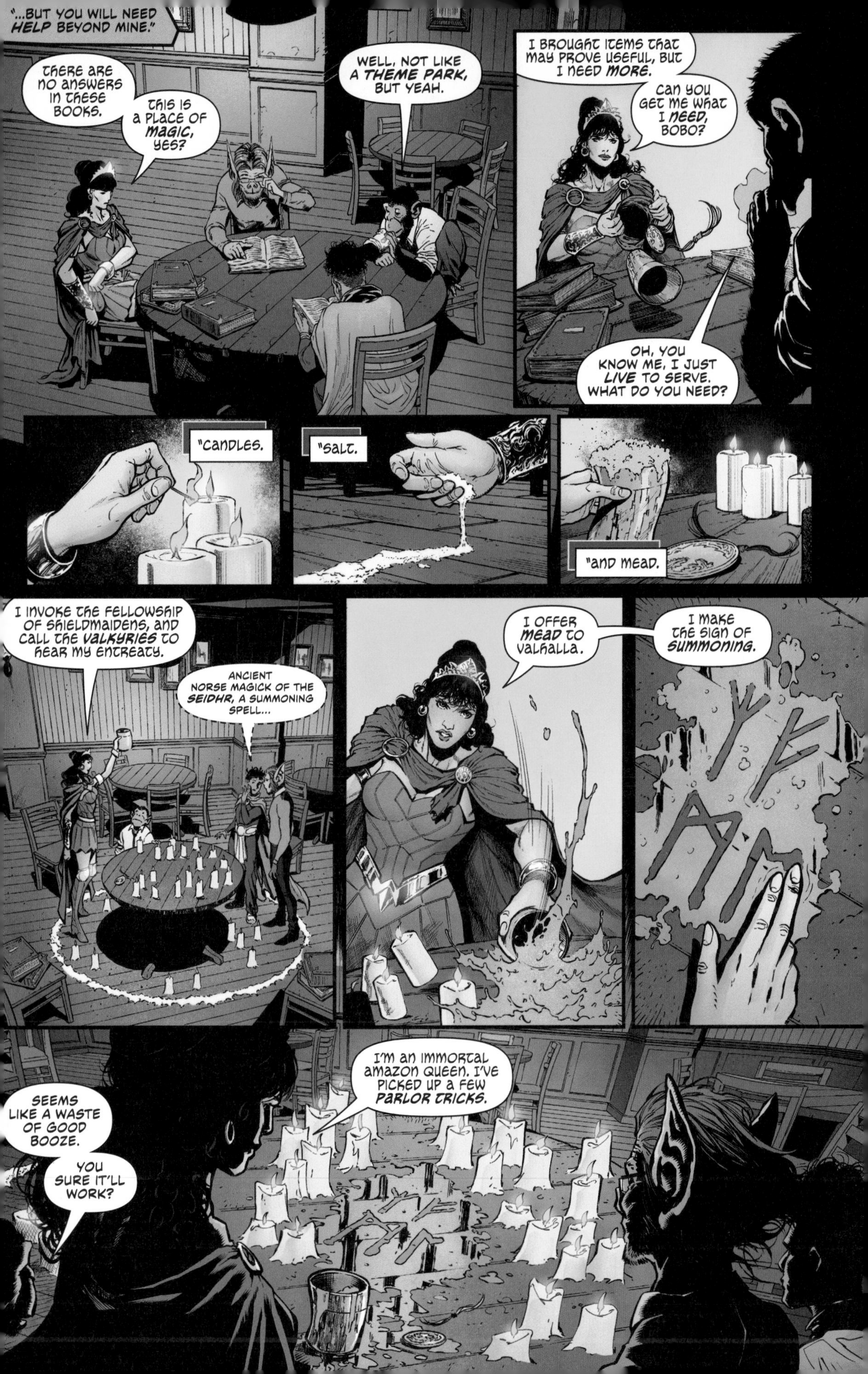
"...BUT YOU WILL NEED HELP BEYOND MINE."
THERE ARE NO ANSWERS IN THESE BOOKS.
THIS IS A PLACE OF MAGIC, YES?
WELL, NOT LIKE A THEME PARK, BUT YEAH.
I BROUGHT ITEMS THAT MAY PROVE USEFUL, BUT I NEED MORE.
CAN YOU GET ME WHAT I NEED, BOBO?
OH, YOU KNOW ME, I JUST LIVE TO SERVE. WHAT DO YOU NEED?
"CANDLES.
"SALT.
"AND MEAD.
I INVOKE THE FELLOWSHIP OF SHIELDMAIDENS, AND CALL THE VALKYRIES TO HEAR MY ENTREATY.
ANCIENT NORSE MAGICK OF THE SEIDHR, A SUMMONING SPELL...
I OFFER MEAD TO VALHALLA.
I MAKE THE SIGN OF SUMMONING.
SEEMS LIKE A WASTE OF GOOD BOOZE.
YOU SURE IT'LL WORK?
I'M AN IMMORTAL AMAZON QUEEN. I'VE PICKED UP A FEW PARLOR TRICKS.

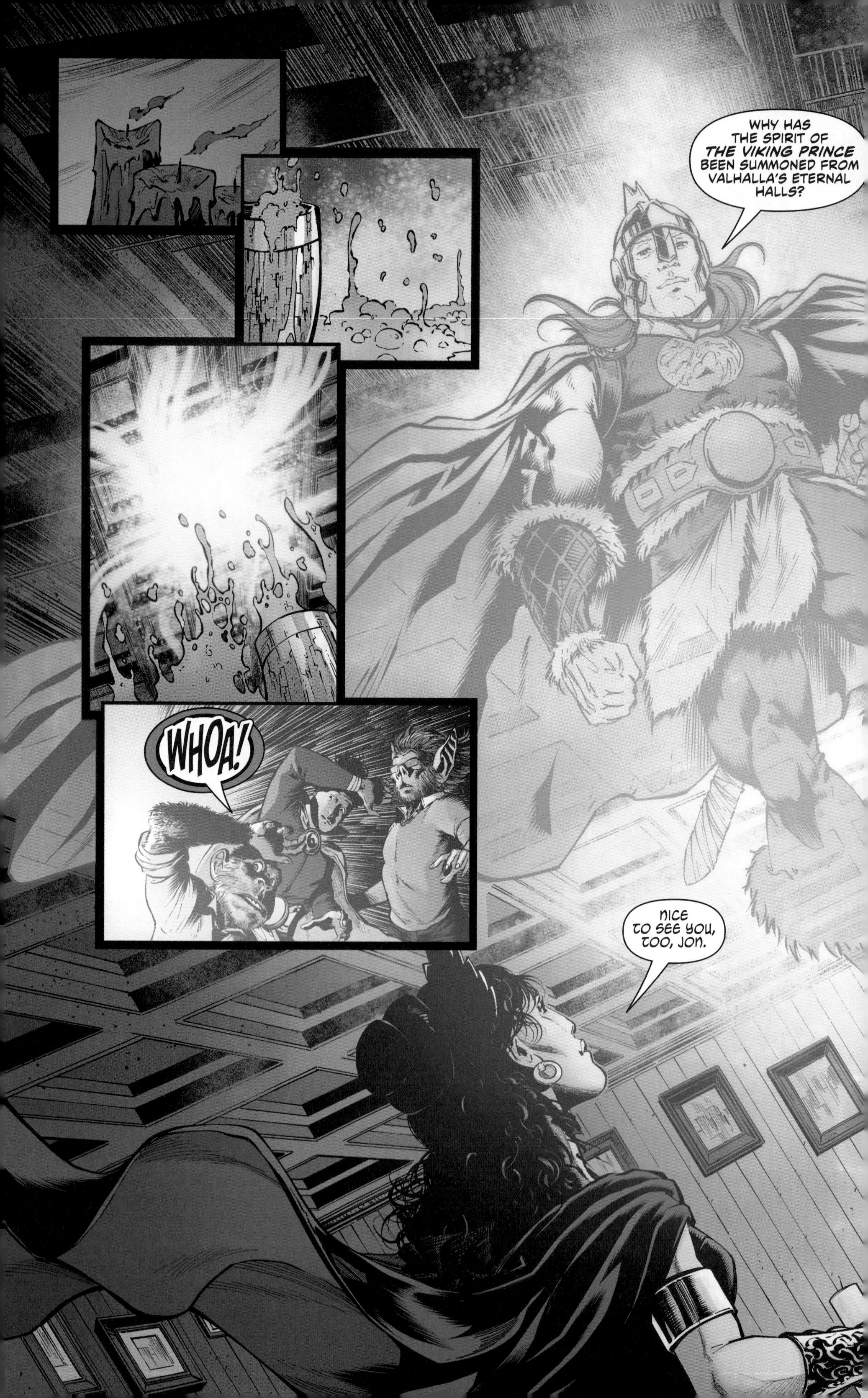
WHY HAS THE SPIRIT OF *THE VIKING PRINCE* BEEN SUMMONED FROM VALHALLA'S ETERNAL HALLS?
WHOA!
NICE TO SEE YOU, TOO, JON.

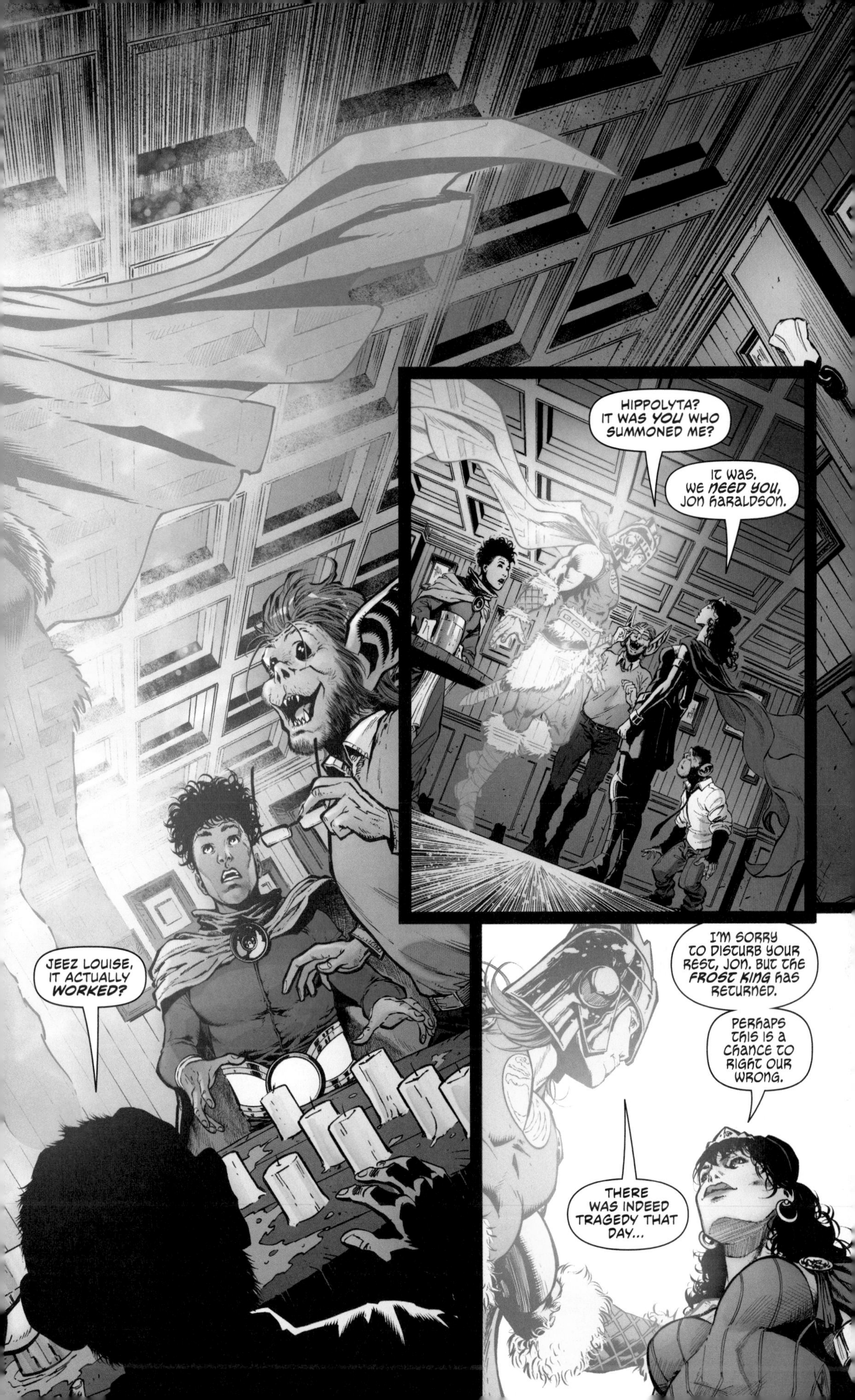
HIPPOLYTA? IT WAS YOU WHO SUMMONED ME?
IT WAS. WE NEED YOU, JON HARALDSON.
JEEZ LOUISE, IT ACTUALLY WORKED?
I'M SORRY TO DISTURB YOUR REST, JON. BUT THE FROST KING HAS RETURNED.
PERHAPS THIS IS A CHANCE TO RIGHT OUR WRONG.
THERE WAS INDEED TRAGEDY THAT DAY...

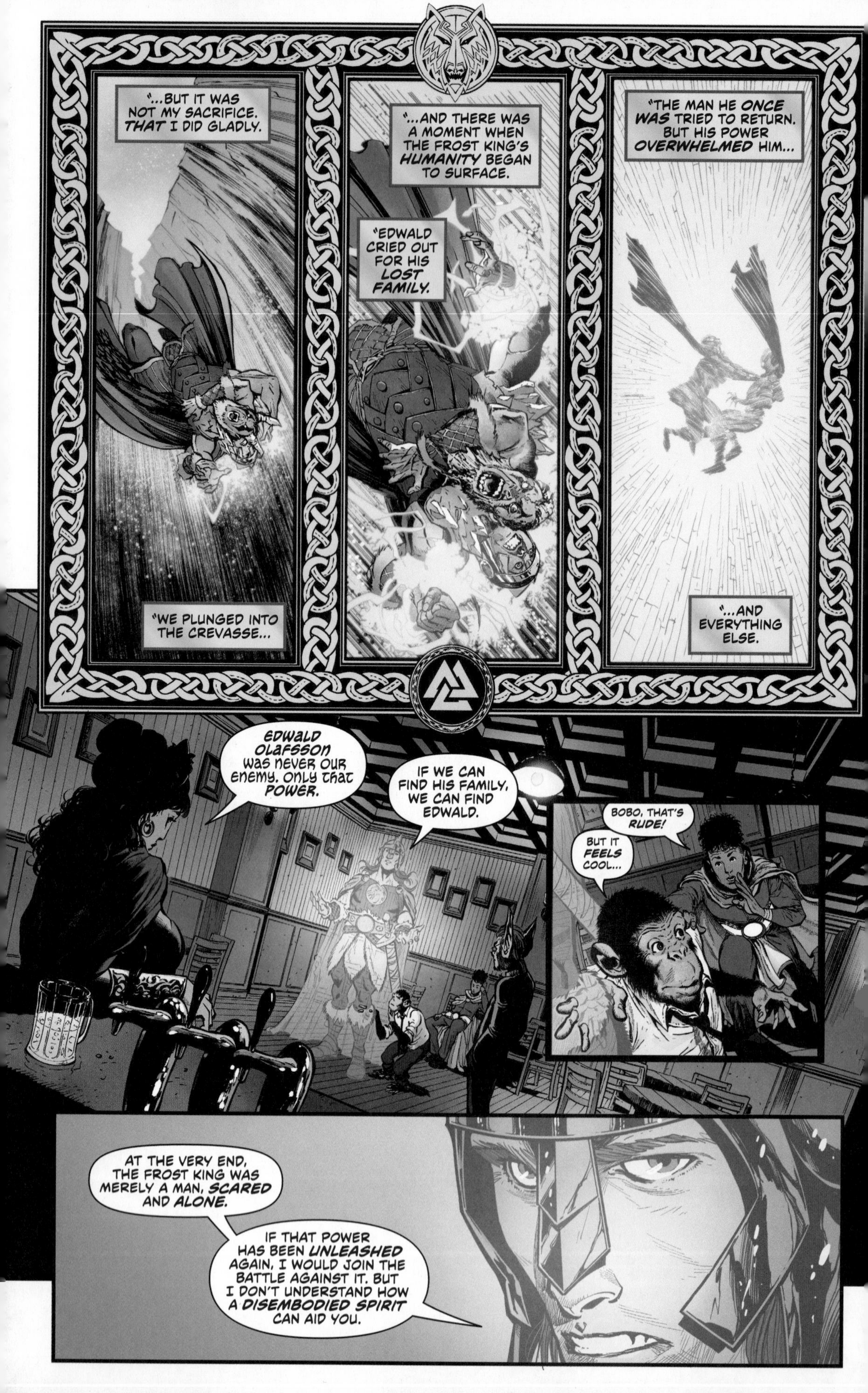
"...BUT IT WAS NOT MY SACRIFICE. THAT I DID GLADLY.
"WE PLUNGED INTO THE CREVASSE...
"...AND THERE WAS A MOMENT WHEN THE FROST KING'S HUMANITY BEGAN TO SURFACE.
"EDWALD CRIED OUT FOR HIS LOST FAMILY.
"THE MAN HE ONCE WAS TRIED TO RETURN. BUT HIS POWER OVERWHELMED HIM...
"...AND EVERYTHING ELSE.
EDWALD OLAFSSON WAS NEVER OUR ENEMY. ONLY THAT POWER.
IF WE CAN FIND HIS FAMILY, WE CAN FIND EDWALD.
BOBO, THAT'S RUDE!
BUT IT FEELS COOL...
AT THE VERY END, THE FROST KING WAS MERELY A MAN, SCARED AND ALONE.
IF THAT POWER HAS BEEN UNLEASHED AGAIN, I WOULD JOIN THE BATTLE AGAINST IT. BUT I DON'T UNDERSTAND HOW A DISEMBODIED SPIRIT CAN AID YOU.

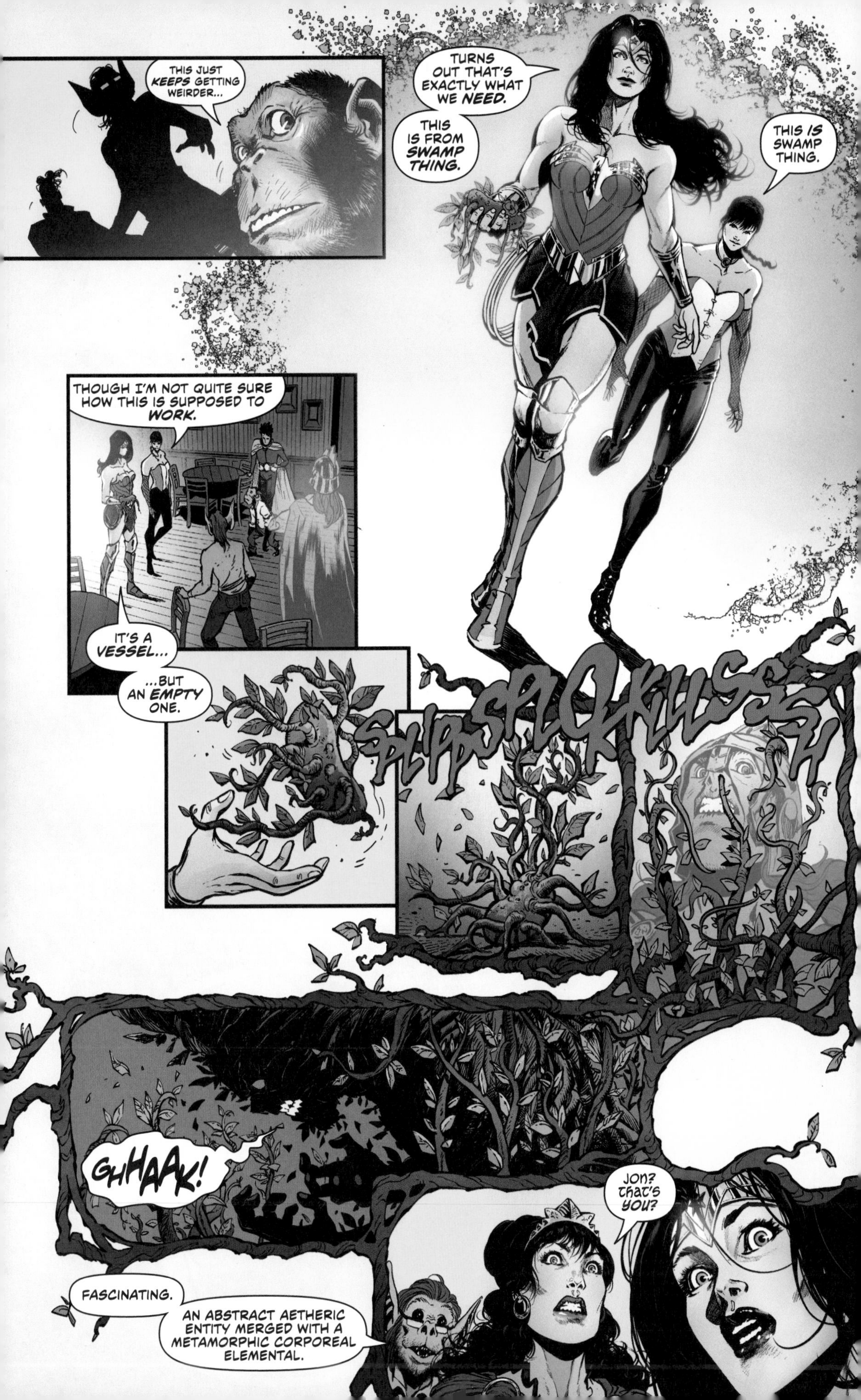
THIS JUST KEEPS GETTING WEIRDER...
TURNS OUT THAT'S EXACTLY WHAT WE NEED.
THIS IS FROM SWAMP THING.
THIS IS SWAMP THING.
THOUGH I'M NOT QUITE SURE HOW THIS IS SUPPOSED TO WORK.
IT'S A VESSEL...
...BUT AN EMPTY ONE.
SPLIPSPLOKKLLSSSH
GHHAAK!
JON? THAT'S YOU?
FASCINATING.
AN ABSTRACT AETHERIC ENTITY MERGED WITH A METAMORPHIC CORPOREAL ELEMENTAL.

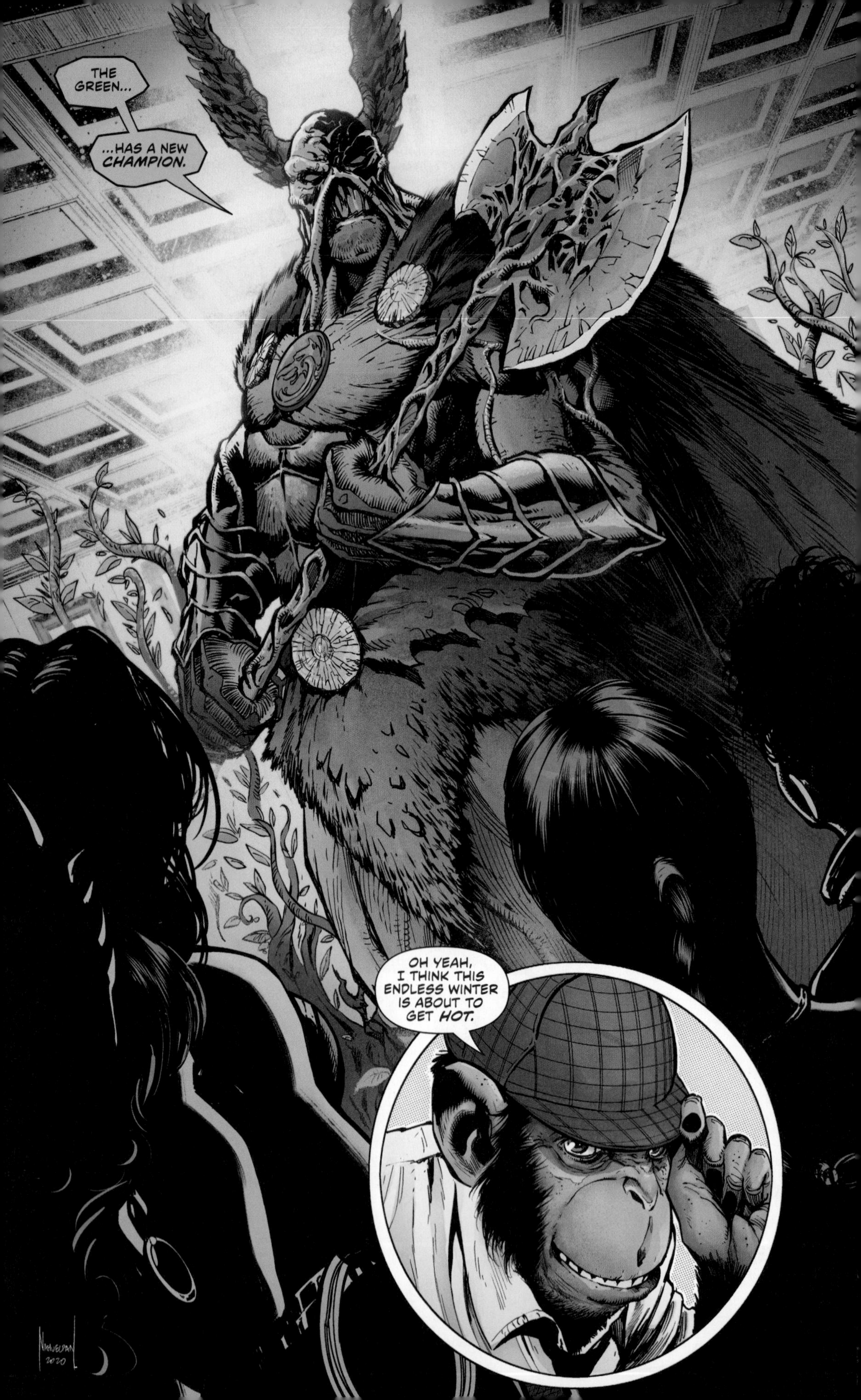
THE GREEN...
...HAS A NEW CHAMPION.
OH YEAH, I THINK THIS ENDLESS WINTER IS ABOUT TO GET HOT.

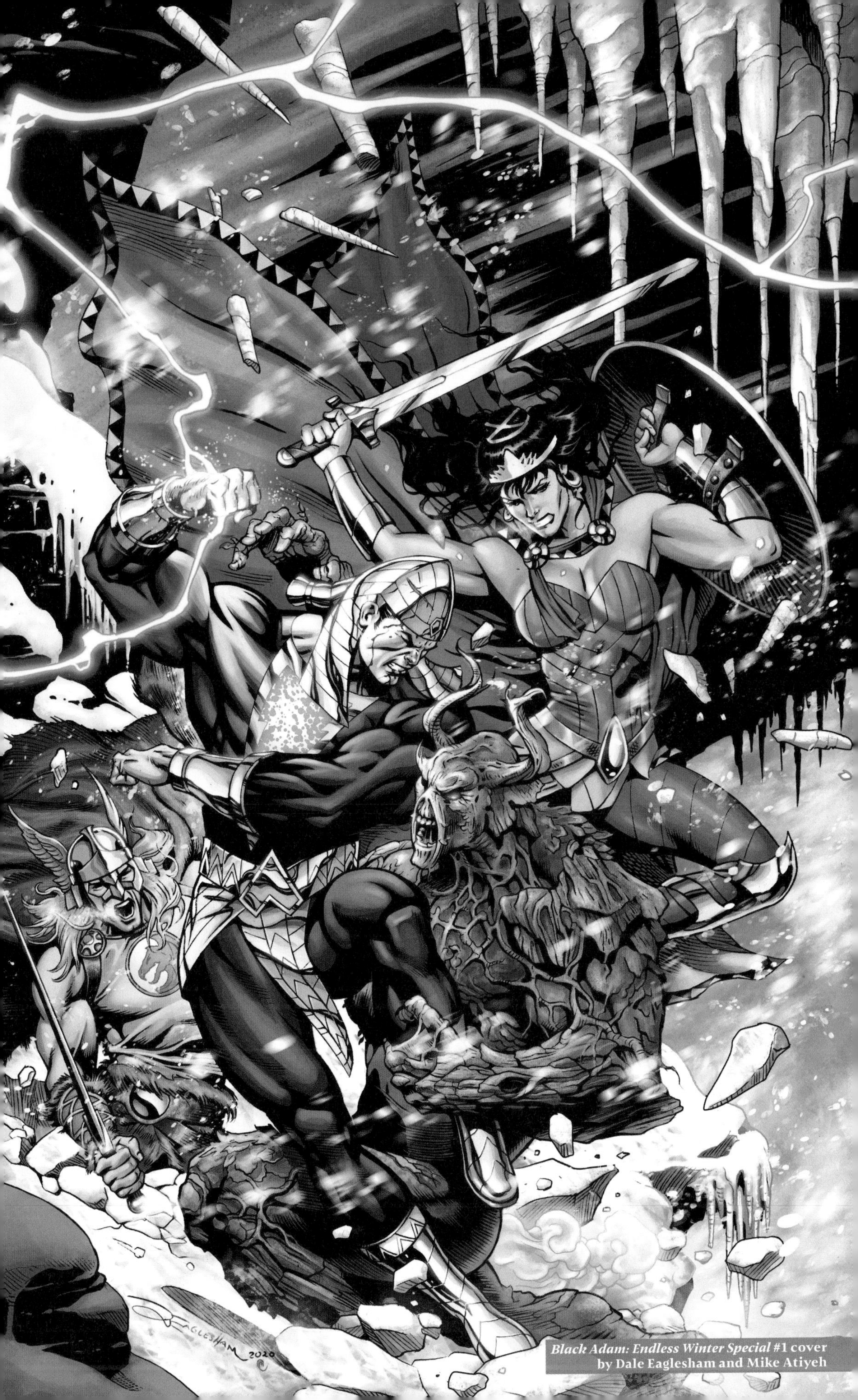
EAGLESHAM 2020

Black Adam: Endless Winter Special #1 cover
by Dale Eaglesham and Mike Atiyeh

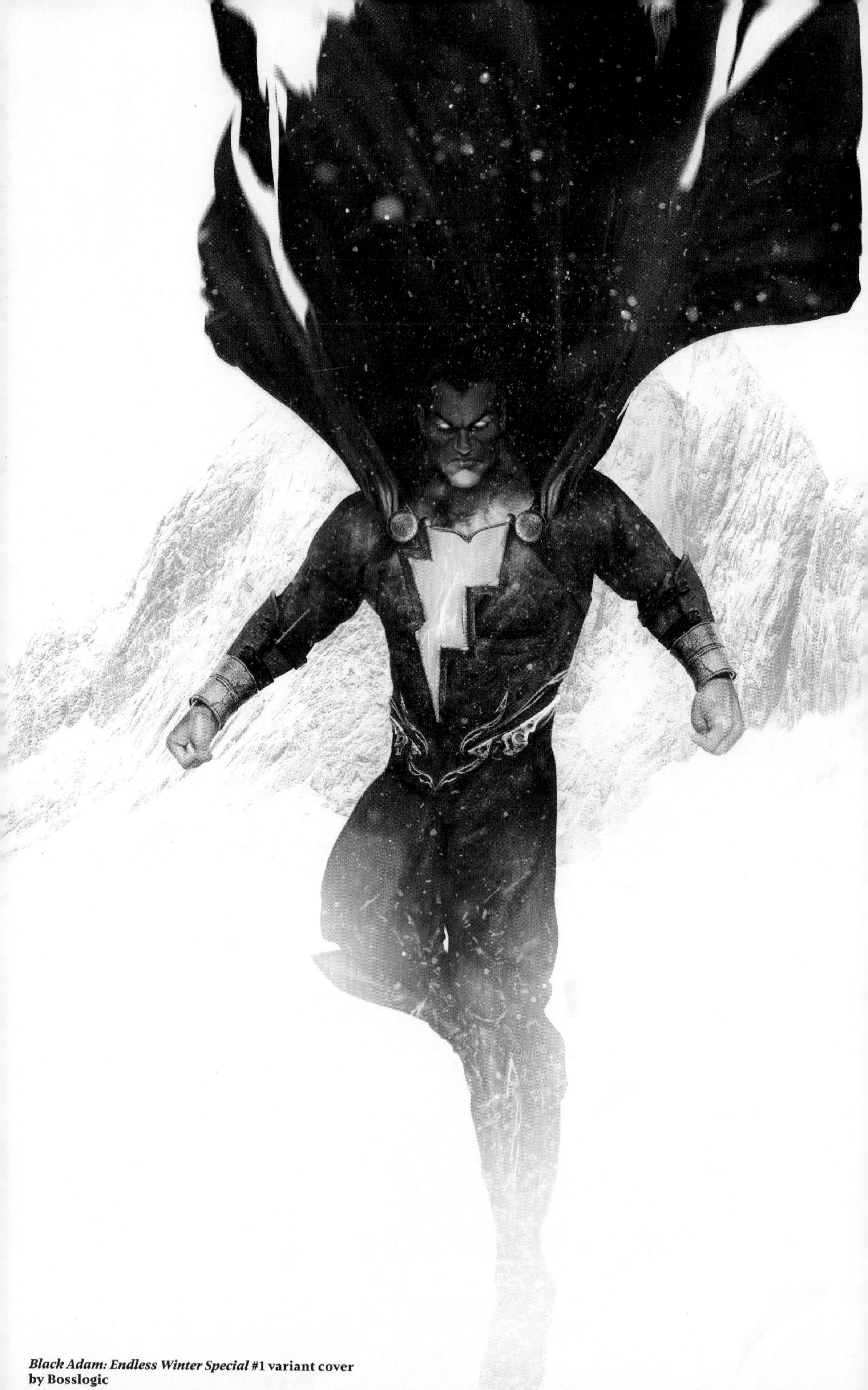

Black Adam: Endless Winter Special **#1 variant cover**
by Bosslogic

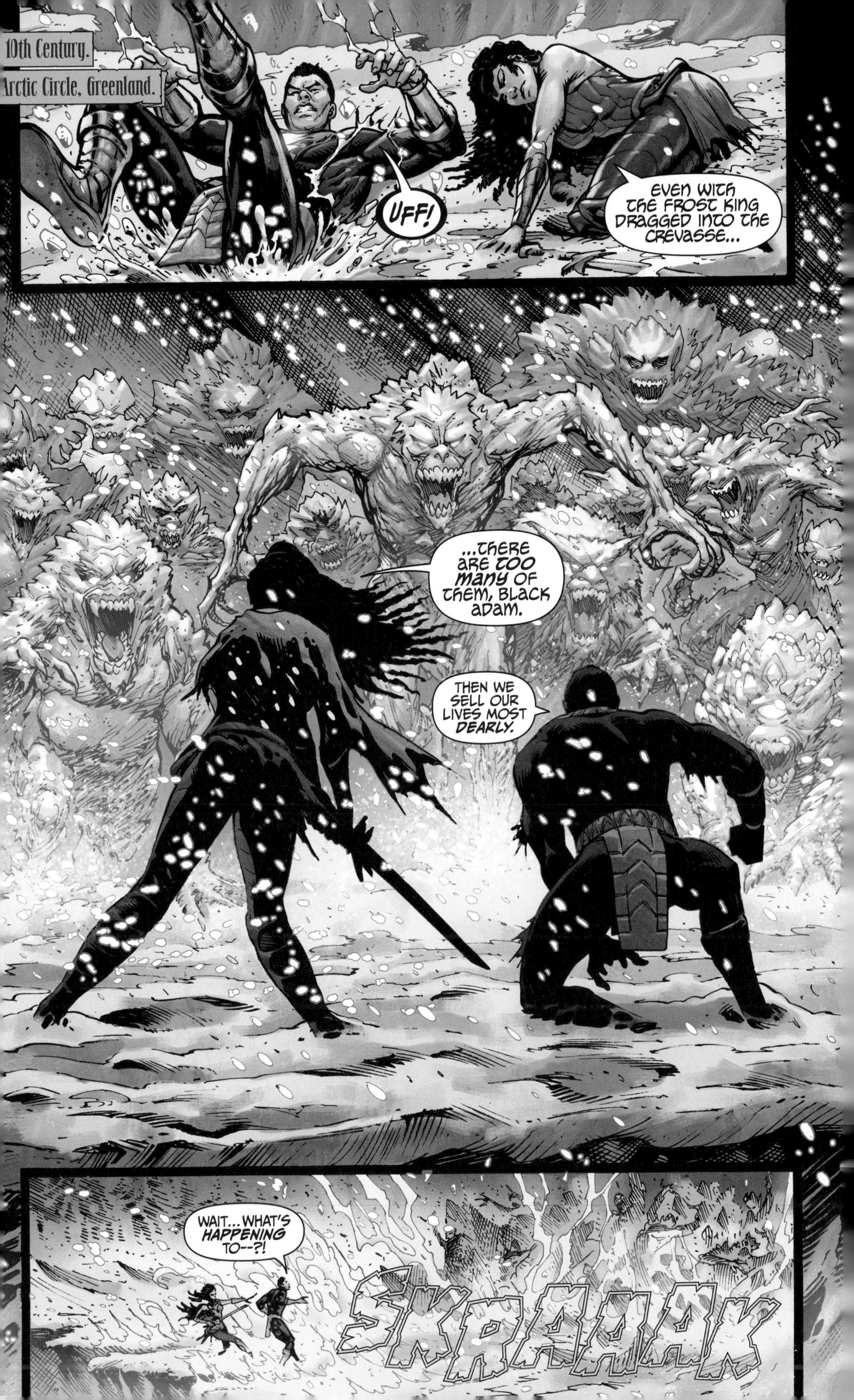
10th Century.
Arctic Circle, Greenland.
UFF!
EVEN WITH THE FROST KING DRAGGED INTO THE CREVASSE...
...THERE ARE TOO MANY OF THEM, BLACK ADAM.
THEN WE SELL OUR LIVES MOST DEARLY.
WAIT...WHAT'S HAPPENING TO--?!

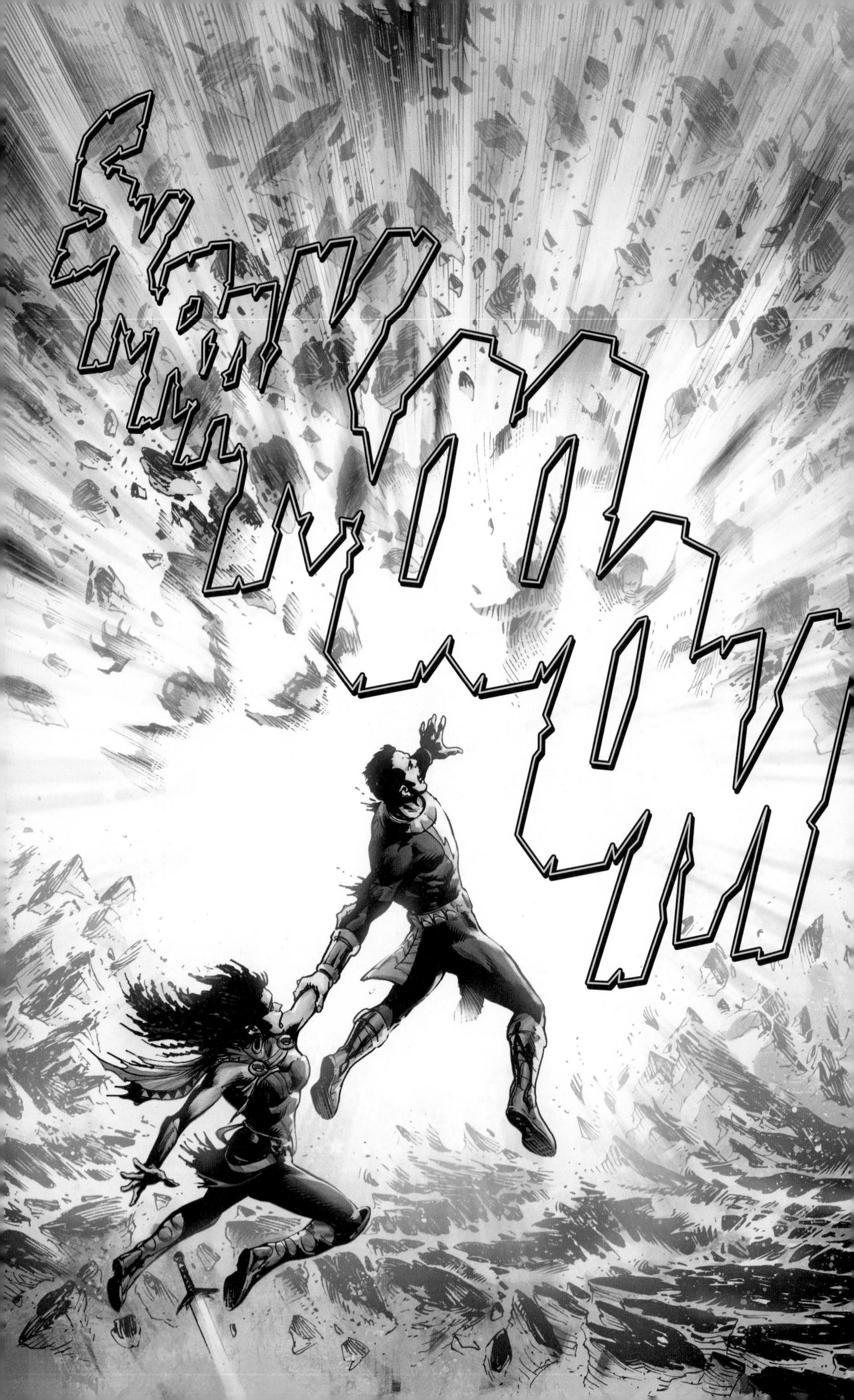

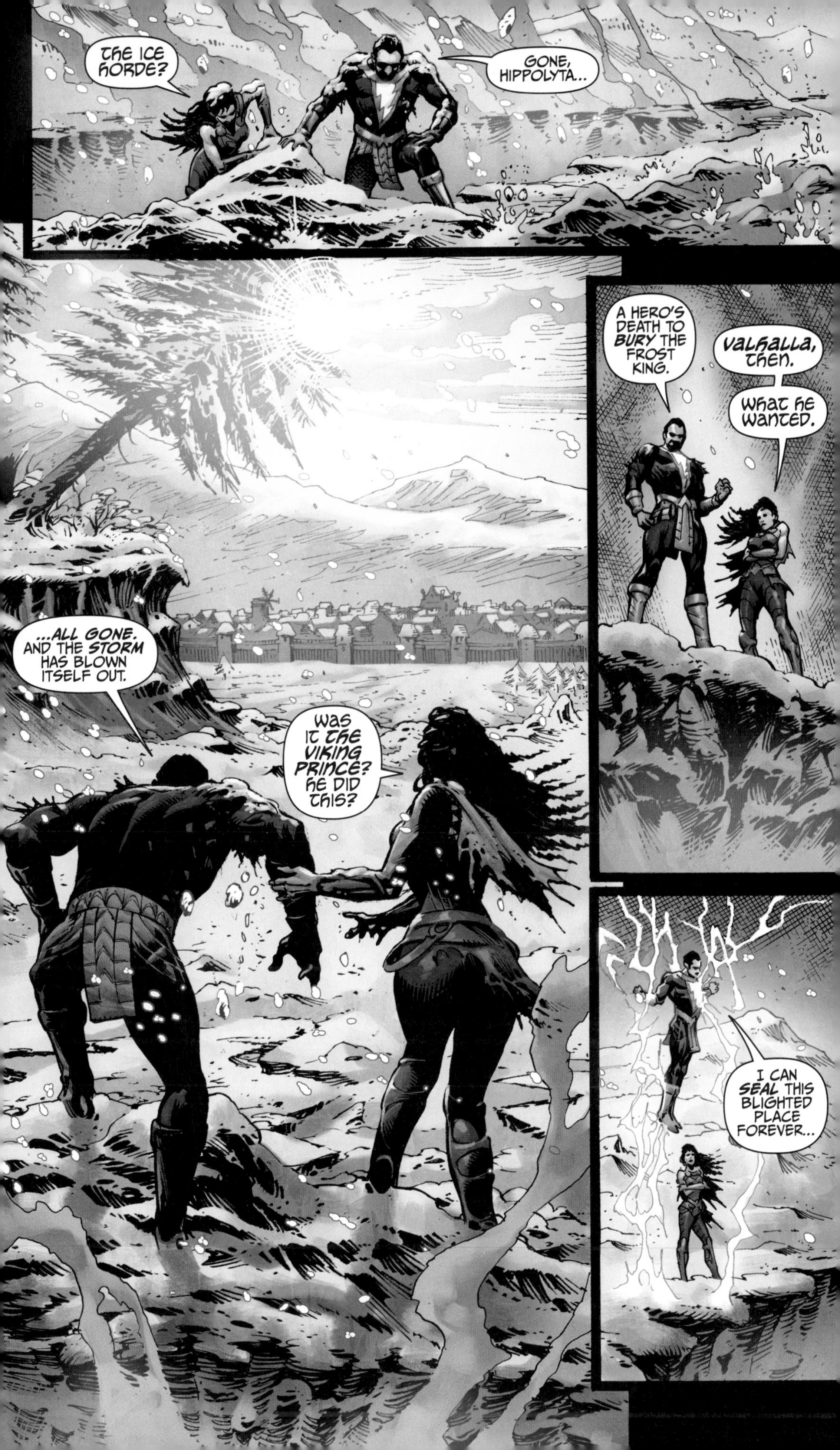

THE ICE HORDE?
GONE, HIPPOLYTA...
...ALL GONE. AND THE STORM HAS BLOWN ITSELF OUT.
WAS IT THE VIKING PRINCE? HE DID THIS?
A HERO'S DEATH TO BURY THE FROST KING.
VALHALLA, THEN.
WHAT HE WANTED.
I CAN SEAL THIS BLIGHTED PLACE FOREVER...

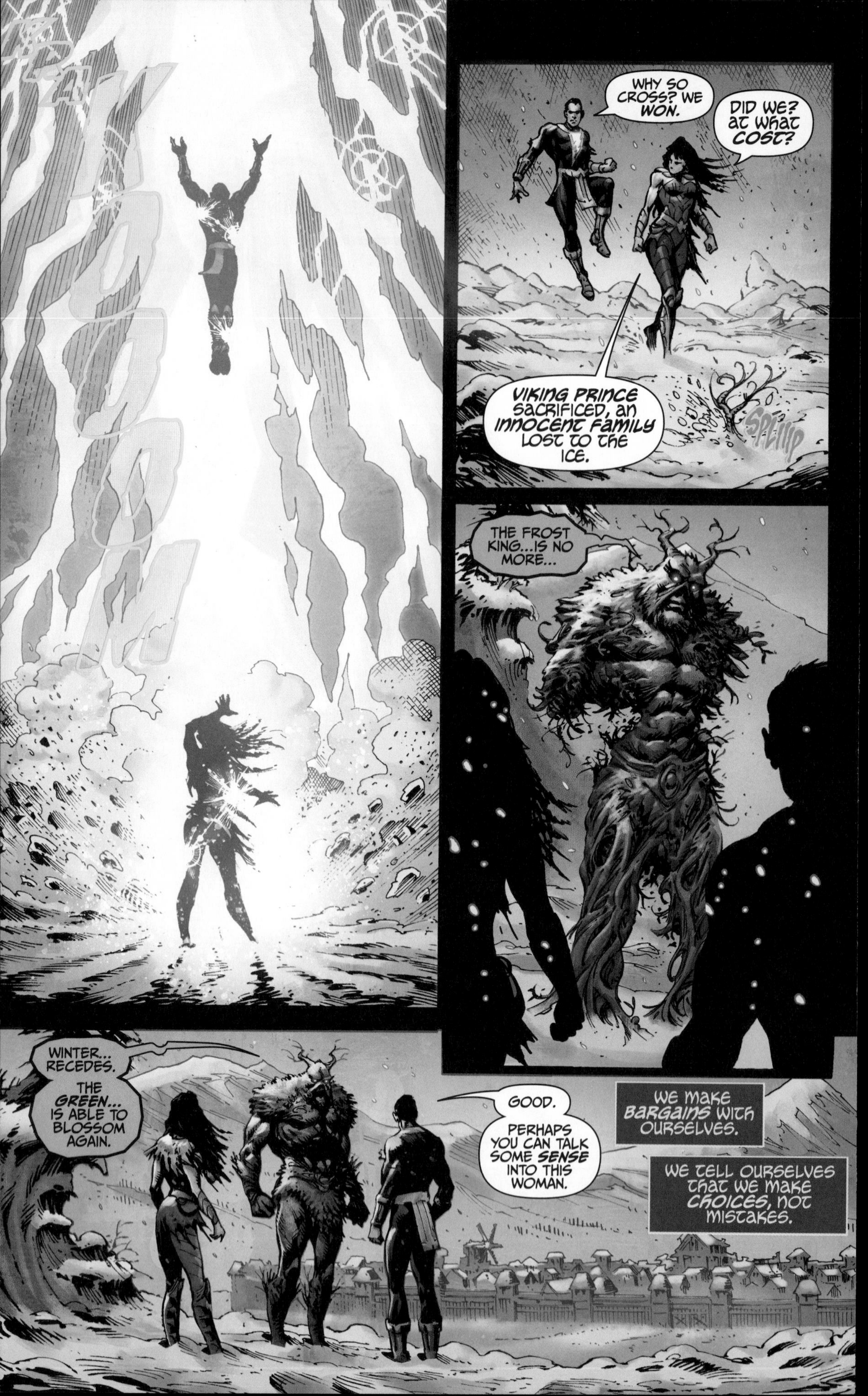

WHY SO CROSS? WE WON.
DID WE? AT WHAT COST?
VIKING PRINCE SACRIFICED, AN INNOCENT FAMILY LOST TO THE ICE.
THE FROST KING...IS NO MORE...
WINTER... RECEDES.
THE GREEN... IS ABLE TO BLOSSOM AGAIN.
GOOD.
PERHAPS YOU CAN TALK SOME SENSE INTO THIS WOMAN.
WE MAKE BARGAINS WITH OURSELVES.
WE TELL OURSELVES THAT WE MAKE CHOICES, NOT MISTAKES.

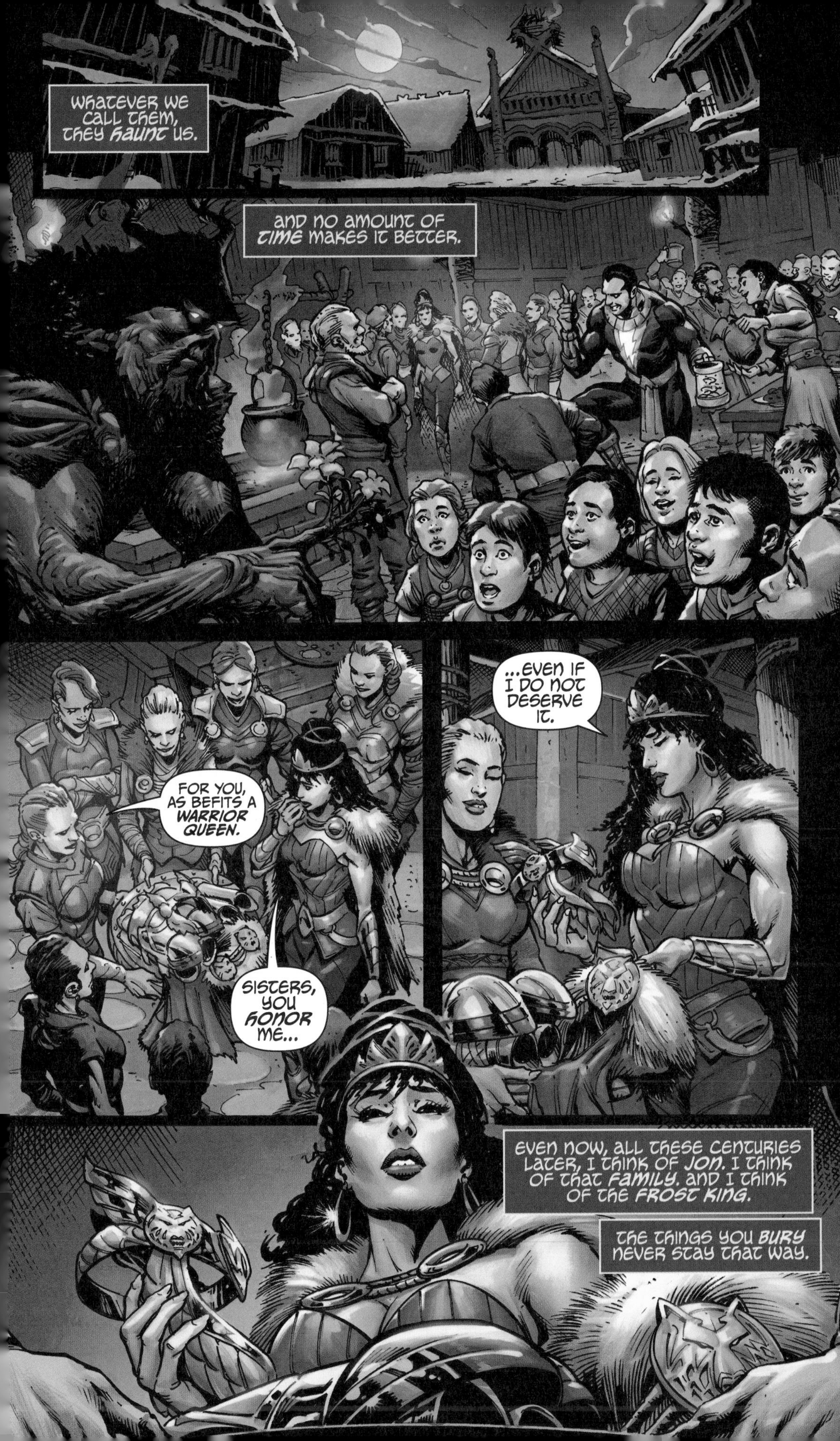
WHATEVER WE CALL THEM, THEY HAUNT US.
AND NO AMOUNT OF TIME MAKES IT BETTER.
FOR YOU, AS BEFITS A WARRIOR QUEEN.
SISTERS, YOU HONOR ME...
...EVEN IF I DO NOT DESERVE IT.
EVEN NOW, ALL THESE CENTURIES LATER, I THINK OF JON. I THINK OF THAT FAMILY. AND I THINK OF THE FROST KING.
THE THINGS YOU BURY NEVER STAY THAT WAY.

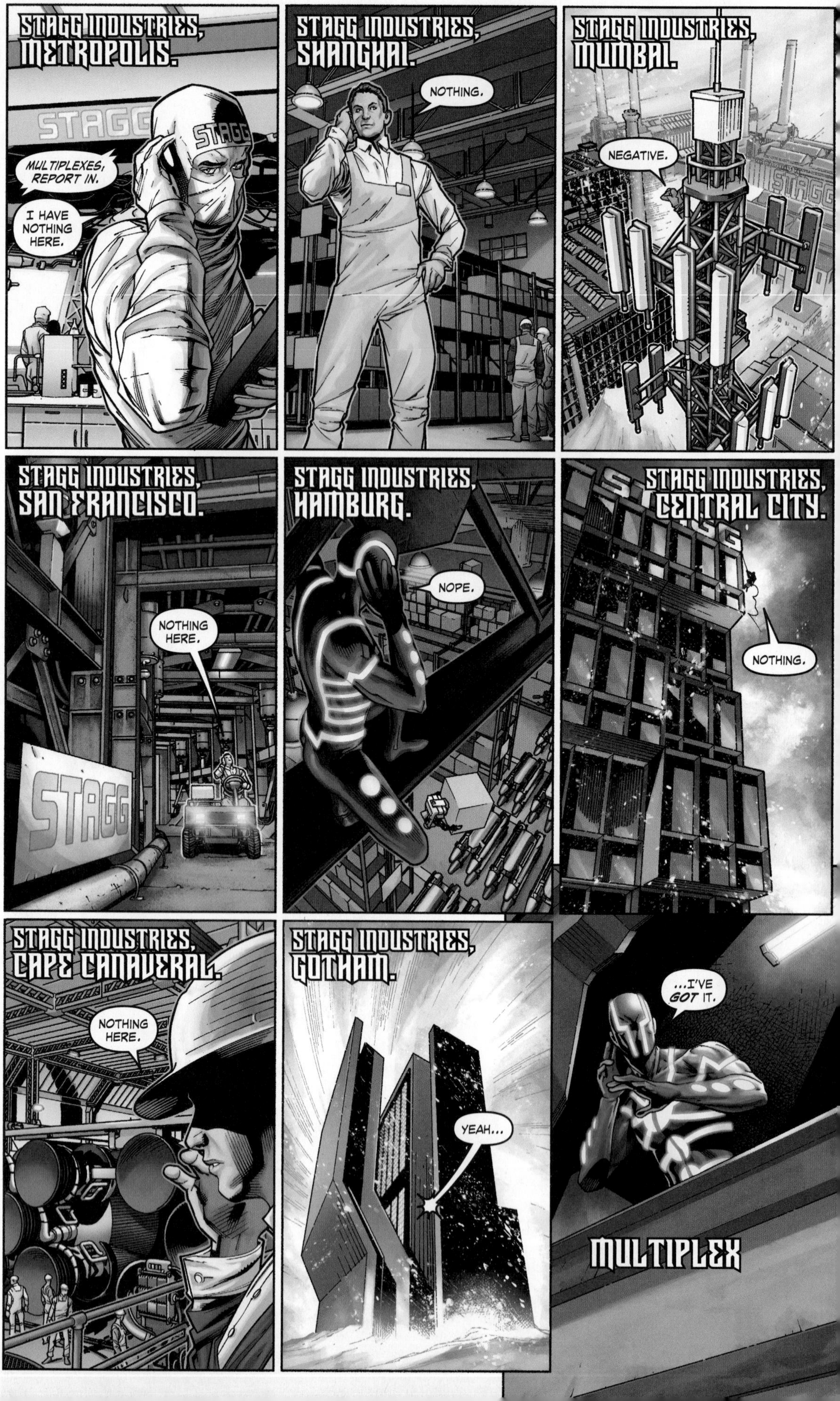
STAGG INDUSTRIES, METROPOLIS.
STAGG
MULTIPLEXES, REPORT IN.
I HAVE NOTHING HERE.
STAGG INDUSTRIES, SHANGHAI.
NOTHING.
STAGG INDUSTRIES, MUMBAI.
NEGATIVE.
STAGG
STAGG INDUSTRIES, SAN FRANCISCO.
NOTHING HERE.
STAGG
STAGG INDUSTRIES, HAMBURG.
NOPE.
STAGG INDUSTRIES, CENTRAL CITY.
NOTHING.
STAGG INDUSTRIES, CAPE CANAVERAL.
NOTHING HERE.
STAGG INDUSTRIES, GOTHAM.
YEAH...
...I'VE *GOT* IT.
MULTIPLEX

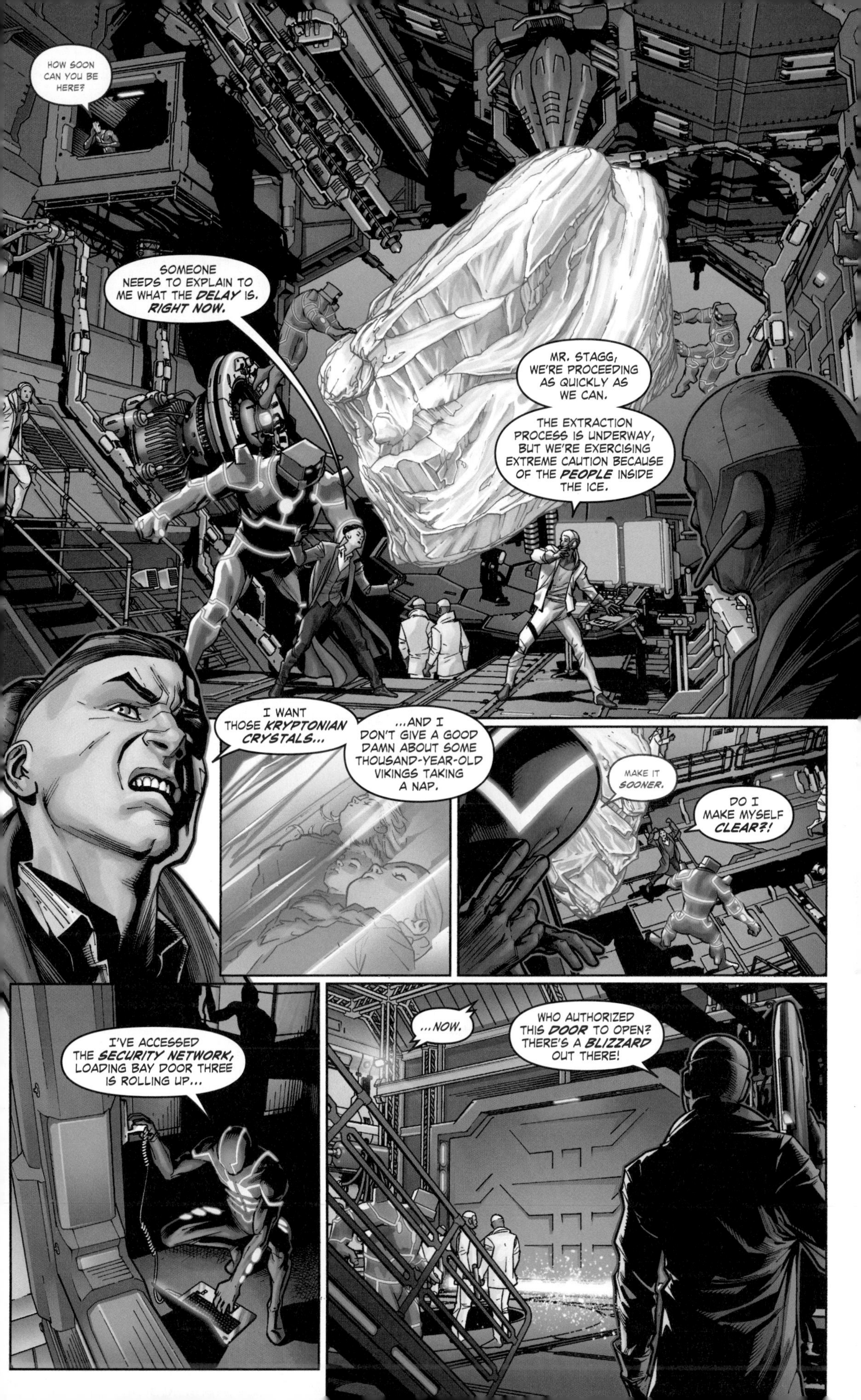
HOW SOON CAN YOU BE HERE?
SOMEONE NEEDS TO EXPLAIN TO ME WHAT THE DELAY IS. RIGHT NOW.
MR. STAGG, WE'RE PROCEEDING AS QUICKLY AS WE CAN.
THE EXTRACTION PROCESS IS UNDERWAY, BUT WE'RE EXERCISING EXTREME CAUTION BECAUSE OF THE PEOPLE INSIDE THE ICE.
I WANT THOSE KRYPTONIAN CRYSTALS...
...AND I DON'T GIVE A GOOD DAMN ABOUT SOME THOUSAND-YEAR-OLD VIKINGS TAKING A NAP.
MAKE IT SOONER.
DO I MAKE MYSELF CLEAR?!
I'VE ACCESSED THE SECURITY NETWORK, LOADING BAY DOOR THREE IS ROLLING UP...
...NOW.
WHO AUTHORIZED THIS DOOR TO OPEN? THERE'S A BLIZZARD OUT THERE!

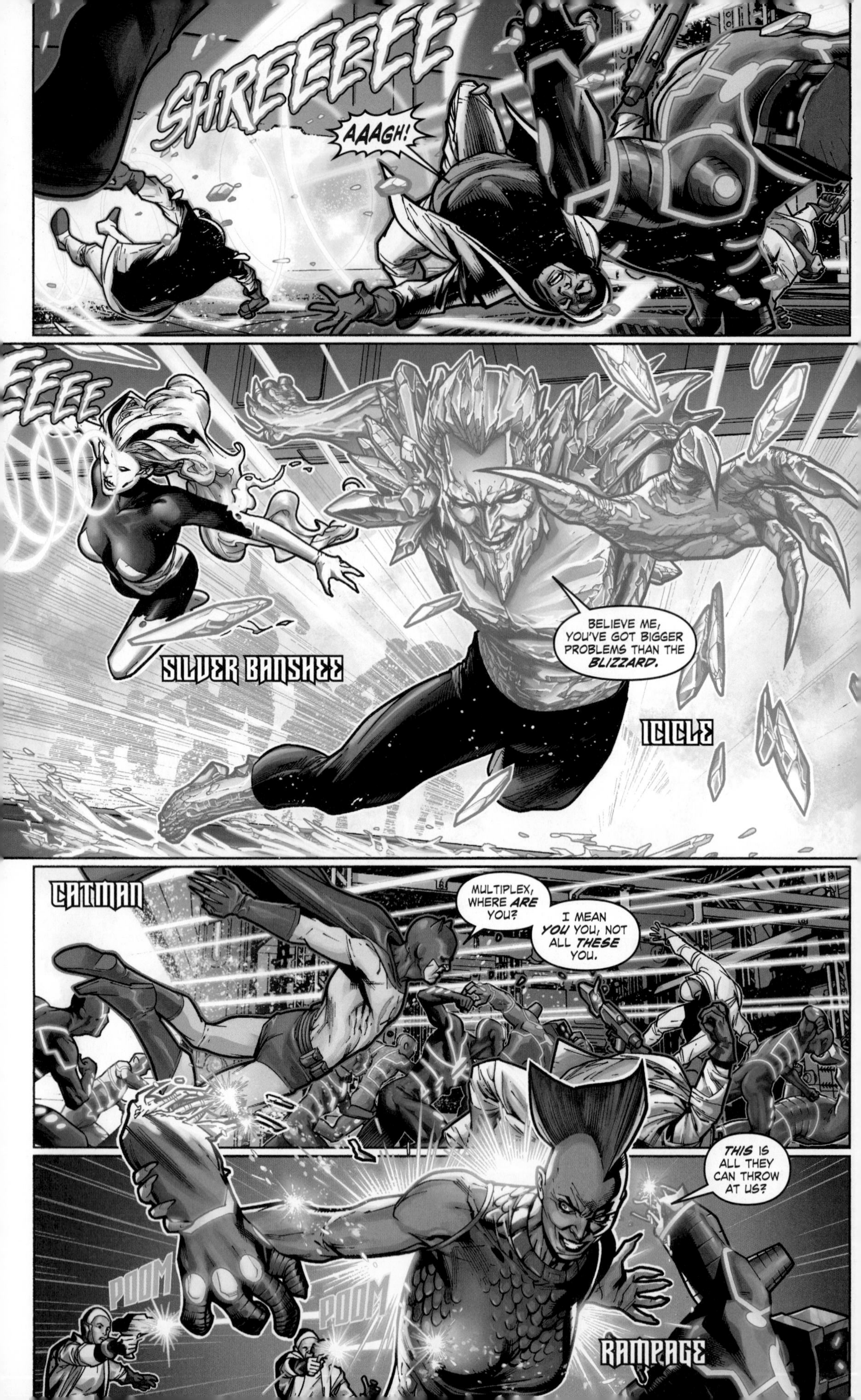
SHREEEEEE
AAAGH!
EEEE
SILVER BANSHEE
BELIEVE ME, YOU'VE GOT BIGGER PROBLEMS THAN THE *BLIZZARD.*
ICICLE
CATMAN
MULTIPLEX, WHERE *ARE* YOU?
I MEAN *YOU* YOU, NOT ALL *THESE* YOU.
THIS IS ALL THEY CAN THROW AT US?
POOM
POOM
RAMPAGE

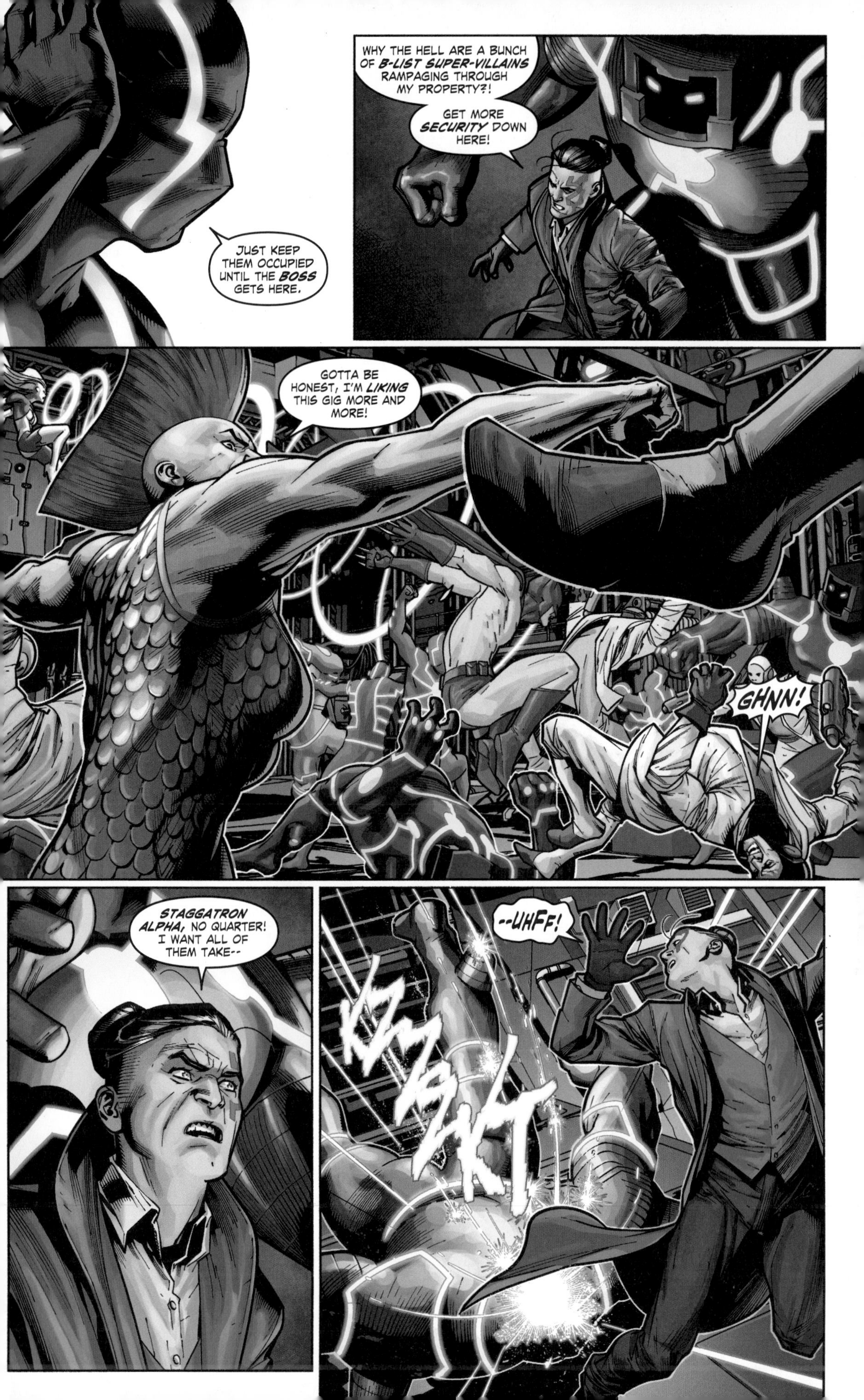
JUST KEEP THEM OCCUPIED UNTIL THE BOSS GETS HERE.
WHY THE HELL ARE A BUNCH OF B-LIST SUPER-VILLAINS RAMPAGING THROUGH MY PROPERTY?!
GET MORE SECURITY DOWN HERE!
GOTTA BE HONEST, I'M LIKING THIS GIG MORE AND MORE!
GHNN!
STAGGATRON ALPHA, NO QUARTER! I WANT ALL OF THEM TAKE--
--UHFF!
KZZZZKT

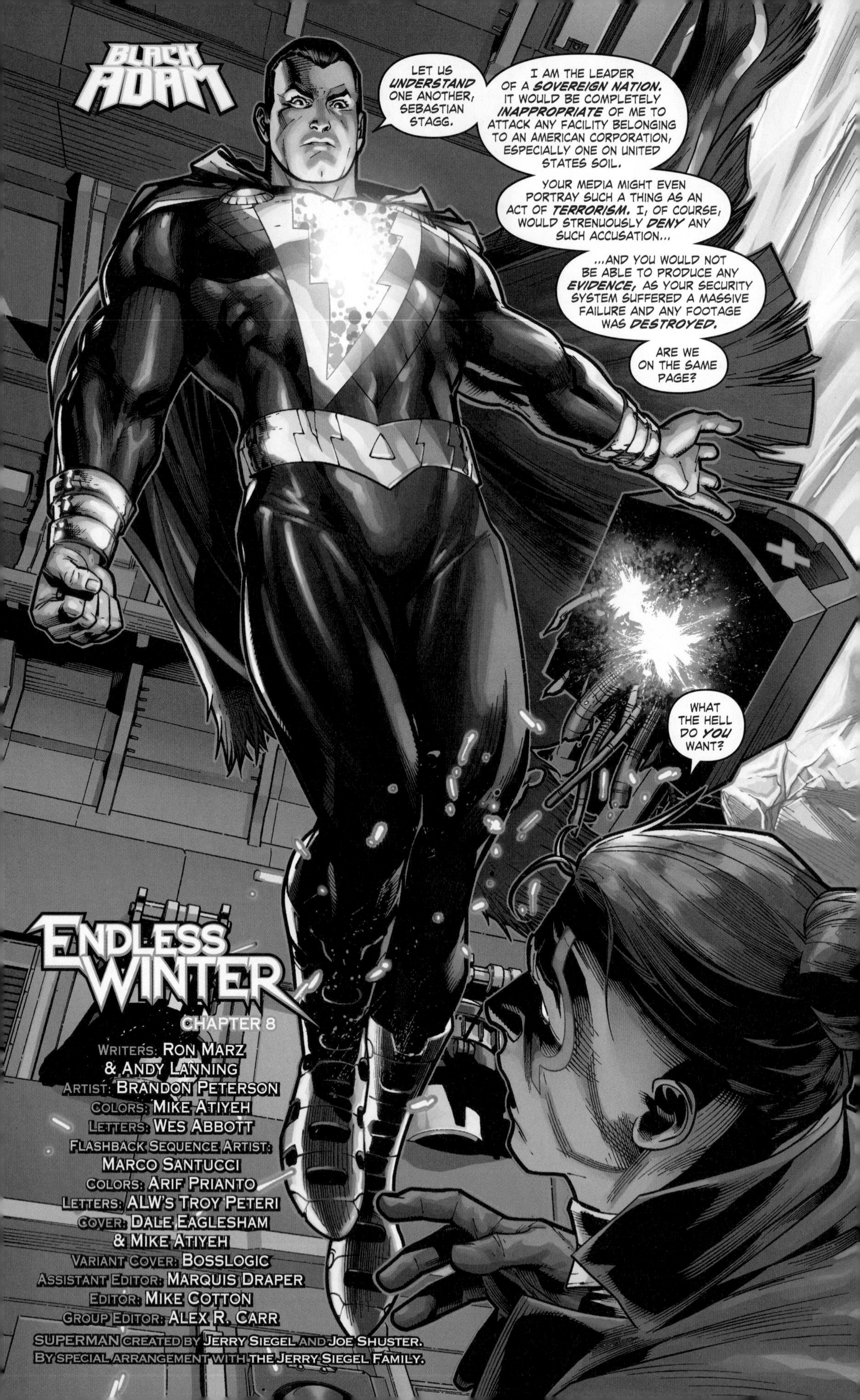

BLACK ADAM
LET US UNDERSTAND ONE ANOTHER, SEBASTIAN STAGG.
I AM THE LEADER OF A SOVEREIGN NATION. IT WOULD BE COMPLETELY INAPPROPRIATE OF ME TO ATTACK ANY FACILITY BELONGING TO AN AMERICAN CORPORATION, ESPECIALLY ONE ON UNITED STATES SOIL.
YOUR MEDIA MIGHT EVEN PORTRAY SUCH A THING AS AN ACT OF TERRORISM. I, OF COURSE, WOULD STRENUOUSLY DENY ANY SUCH ACCUSATION...
...AND YOU WOULD NOT BE ABLE TO PRODUCE ANY EVIDENCE, AS YOUR SECURITY SYSTEM SUFFERED A MASSIVE FAILURE AND ANY FOOTAGE WAS DESTROYED.
ARE WE ON THE SAME PAGE?
WHAT THE HELL DO YOU WANT?
ENDLESS WINTER
CHAPTER 8
WRITERS: RON MARZ & ANDY LANNING
ARTIST: BRANDON PETERSON
COLORS: MIKE ATIYEH
LETTERS: WES ABBOTT
FLASHBACK SEQUENCE ARTIST: MARCO SANTUCCI
COLORS: ARIF PRIANTO
LETTERS: ALW'S TROY PETERI
COVER: DALE EAGLESHAM & MIKE ATIYEH
VARIANT COVER: BOSSLOGIC
ASSISTANT EDITOR: MARQUIS DRAPER
EDITOR: MIKE COTTON
GROUP EDITOR: ALEX R. CARR
SUPERMAN CREATED BY JERRY SIEGEL AND JOE SHUSTER.
BY SPECIAL ARRANGEMENT WITH THE JERRY SIEGEL FAMILY.

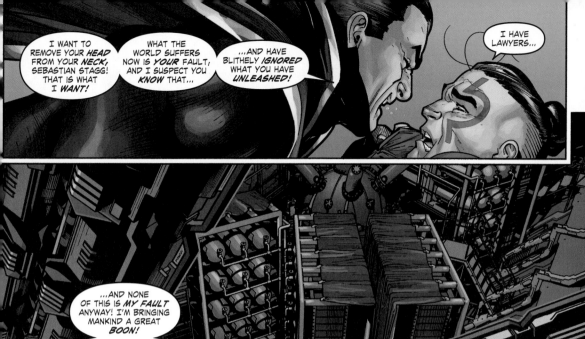

I WANT TO REMOVE YOUR *HEAD* FROM YOUR *NECK*, SEBASTIAN STAGG! THAT IS WHAT I *WANT*!

WHAT THE WORLD SUFFERS NOW IS *YOUR* FAULT, AND I SUSPECT YOU *KNOW* THAT...

...AND HAVE BLITHELY *IGNORED* WHAT YOU HAVE *UNLEASHED*!

I HAVE LAWYERS...

...AND NONE OF THIS IS *MY FAULT* ANYWAY! I'M BRINGING MANKIND A GREAT *BOON*!

WE'RE CREATING *COLD FUSION* FROM TECHNOLOGY THAT *SUPERMAN* JUST LEFT BEHIND IN THE ICE.

IF THIS IS ANYONE'S FAULT, IT'S *HIS*!

THIS IS WHAT YOU BROUGHT BACK FROM THE ARCTIC?

AND THERE ARE...PEOPLE *INSIDE*? *ALIVE*?

THEY'RE IN *STASIS* SOMEHOW. WE WERE DOING ALL WE COULD TO MAKE SURE *NO HARM* COMES TO THEM...

KRRUMBLL

MORE OF YOUR PEOPLE TEARING APART MY BUILDING?

THAT'S NOT *US*...

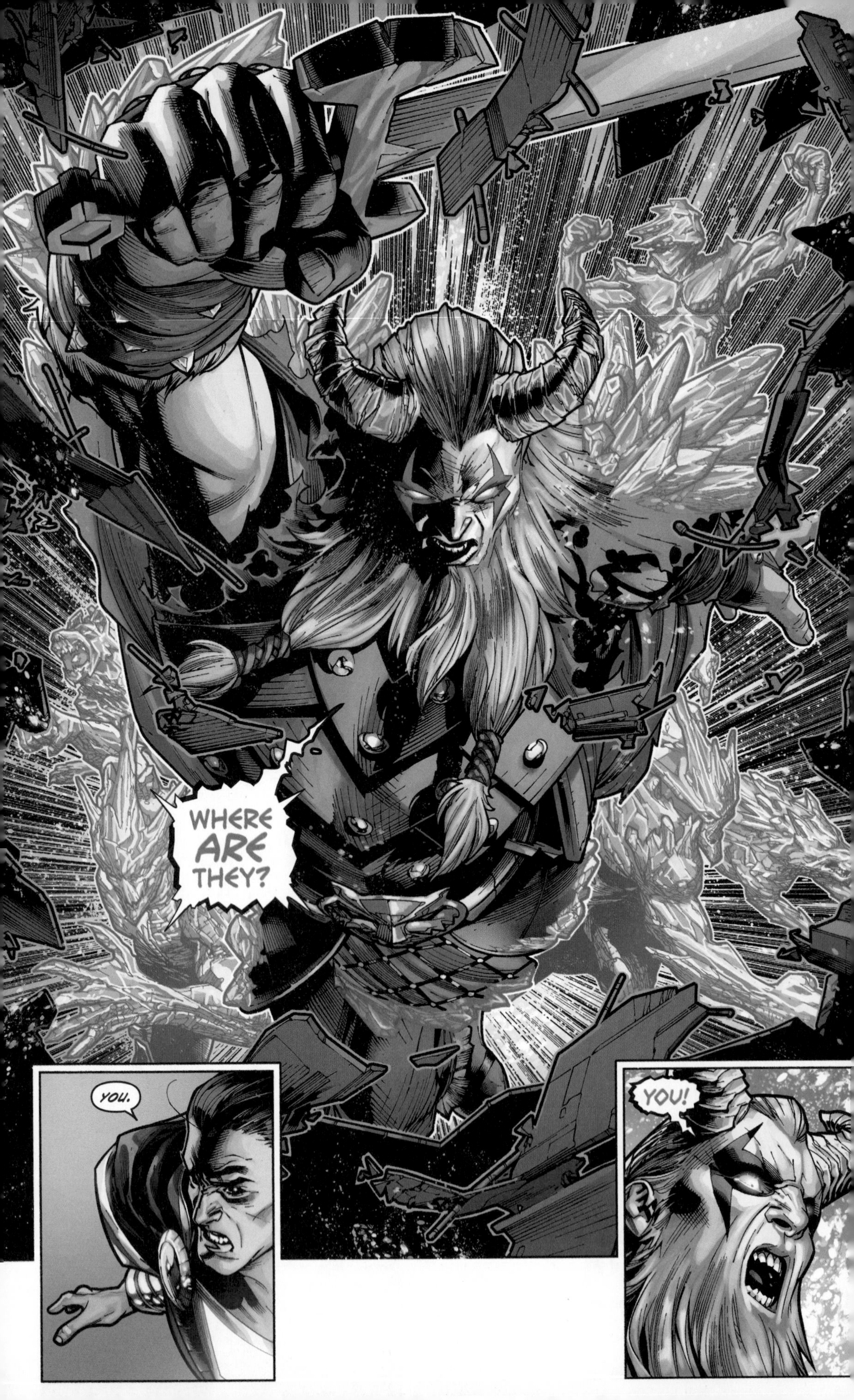
WHERE ARE THEY?
YOU.
YOU!

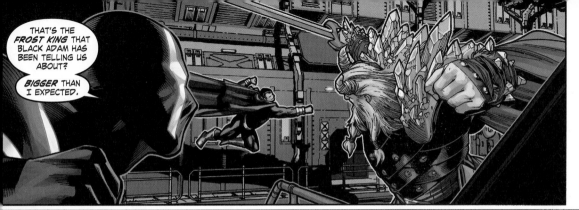

THAT'S THE *FROST KING* THAT BLACK ADAM HAS BEEN TELLING US ABOUT?

BIGGER THAN I EXPECTED.

DOESN'T MATTER IF YOU'RE BIGGER, MORE POWERFUL. I BEAT YOU BEFORE, MONSTER...

...I'LL DO IT *AGAIN.*

THOOM!

FWAKK

MULTIPLEX, *MORE DUPLOIDS!*

MORE OF *ME,* COMING RIGHT UP!

I WANT HIM *OVERWHELMED!*

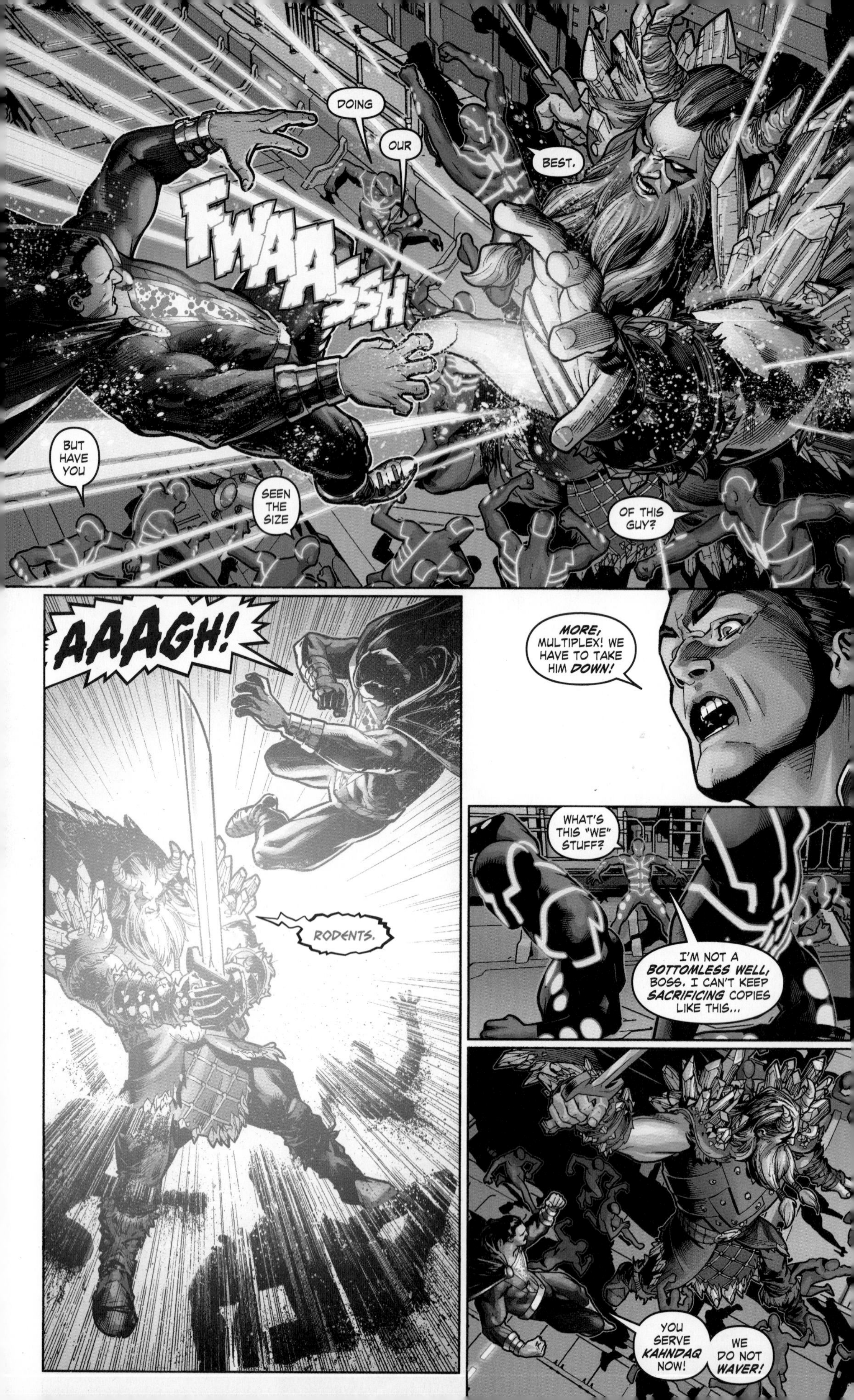
DOING
OUR
BEST.
FWAASSH
BUT HAVE YOU
SEEN THE SIZE
OF THIS GUY?
AAAGH!
MORE, MULTIPLEX! WE HAVE TO TAKE HIM DOWN!
RODENTS.
WHAT'S THIS "WE" STUFF?
I'M NOT A BOTTOMLESS WELL, BOSS. I CAN'T KEEP SACRIFICING COPIES LIKE THIS...
YOU SERVE KAHNDAQ NOW!
WE DO NOT WAVER!

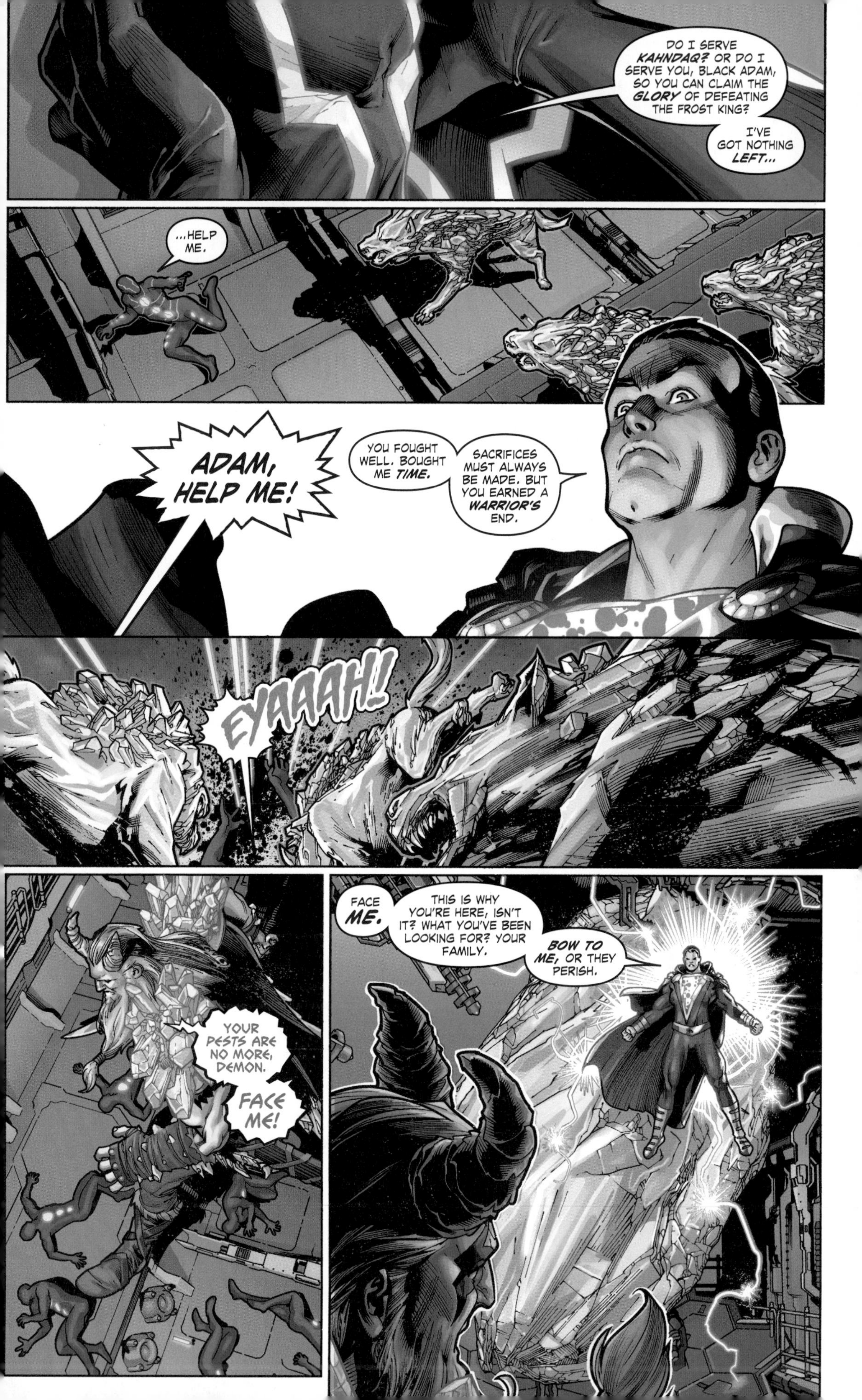
DO I SERVE KAHNDAQ? OR DO I SERVE YOU, BLACK ADAM, SO YOU CAN CLAIM THE GLORY OF DEFEATING THE FROST KING?
I'VE GOT NOTHING LEFT...
...HELP ME.
ADAM, HELP ME!
YOU FOUGHT WELL. BOUGHT ME TIME.
SACRIFICES MUST ALWAYS BE MADE. BUT YOU EARNED A WARRIOR'S END.
EYAAAAH!!
YOUR PESTS ARE NO MORE, DEMON.
FACE ME!
FACE ME.
THIS IS WHY YOU'RE HERE, ISN'T IT? WHAT YOU'VE BEEN LOOKING FOR? YOUR FAMILY.
BOW TO ME, OR THEY PERISH.

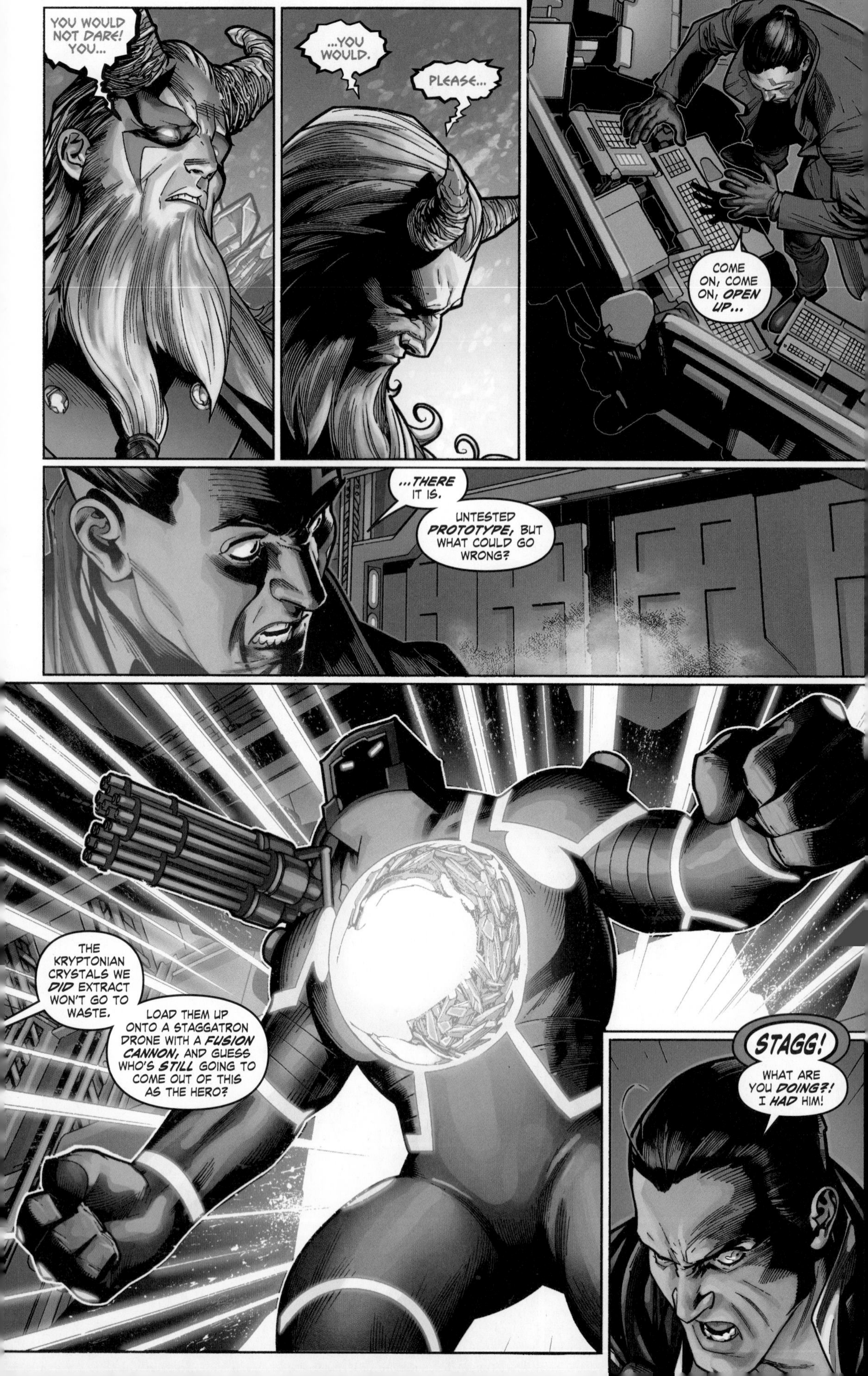
YOU WOULD NOT DARE! YOU...
...YOU WOULD.
PLEASE...
COME ON, COME ON, OPEN UP...
...THERE IT IS.
UNTESTED PROTOTYPE, BUT WHAT COULD GO WRONG?
THE KRYPTONIAN CRYSTALS WE DID EXTRACT WON'T GO TO WASTE.
LOAD THEM UP ONTO A STAGGATRON DRONE WITH A FUSION CANNON, AND GUESS WHO'S STILL GOING TO COME OUT OF THIS AS THE HERO?
STAGG!
WHAT ARE YOU DOING?! I HAD HIM!

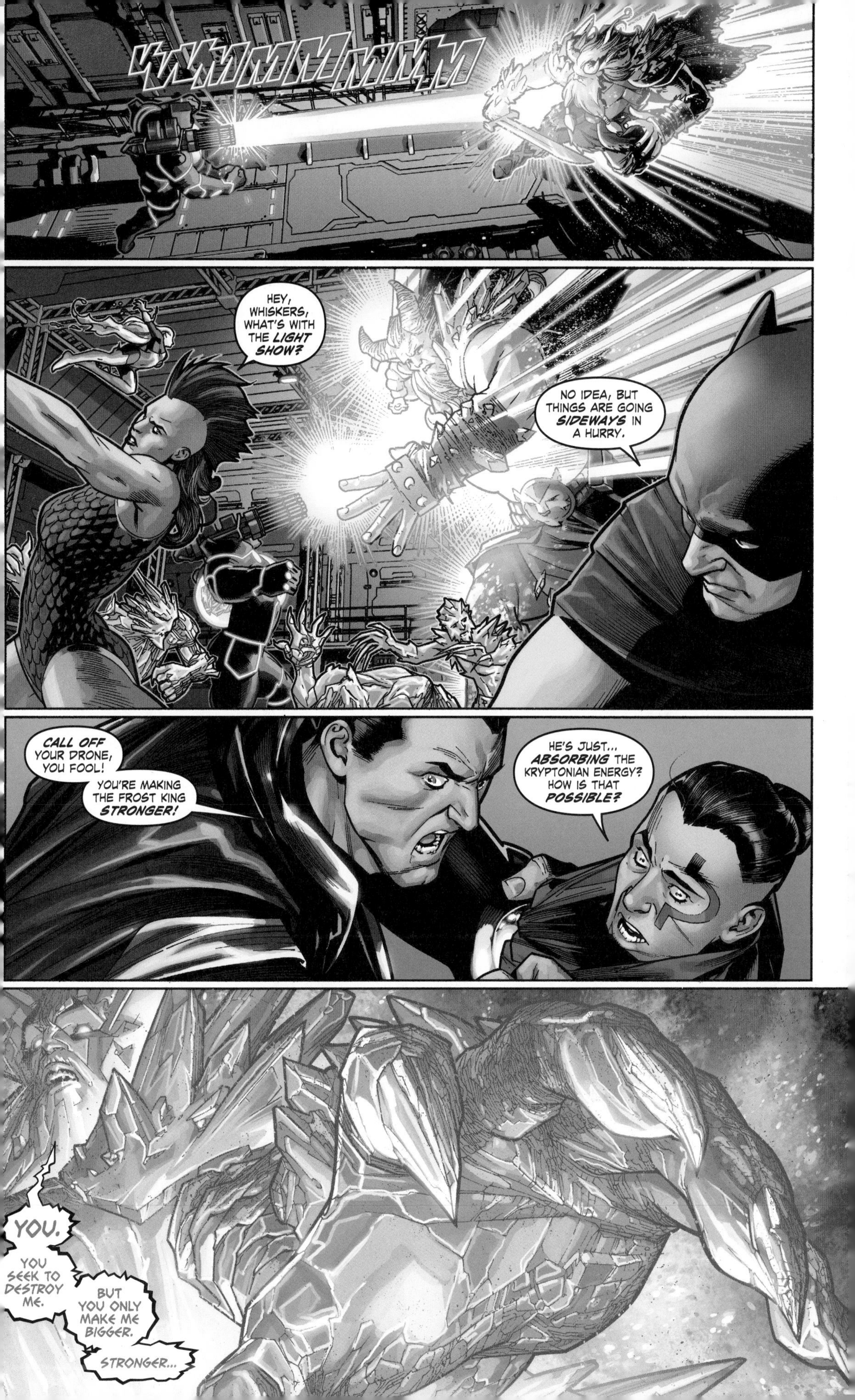
VVVVMMMMMMM
HEY, WHISKERS, WHAT'S WITH THE LIGHT SHOW?
NO IDEA, BUT THINGS ARE GOING SIDEWAYS IN A HURRY.
CALL OFF YOUR DRONE, YOU FOOL!
YOU'RE MAKING THE FROST KING STRONGER!
HE'S JUST... ABSORBING THE KRYPTONIAN ENERGY? HOW IS THAT POSSIBLE?
YOU.
YOU SEEK TO DESTROY ME.
BUT YOU ONLY MAKE ME BIGGER.
STRONGER...

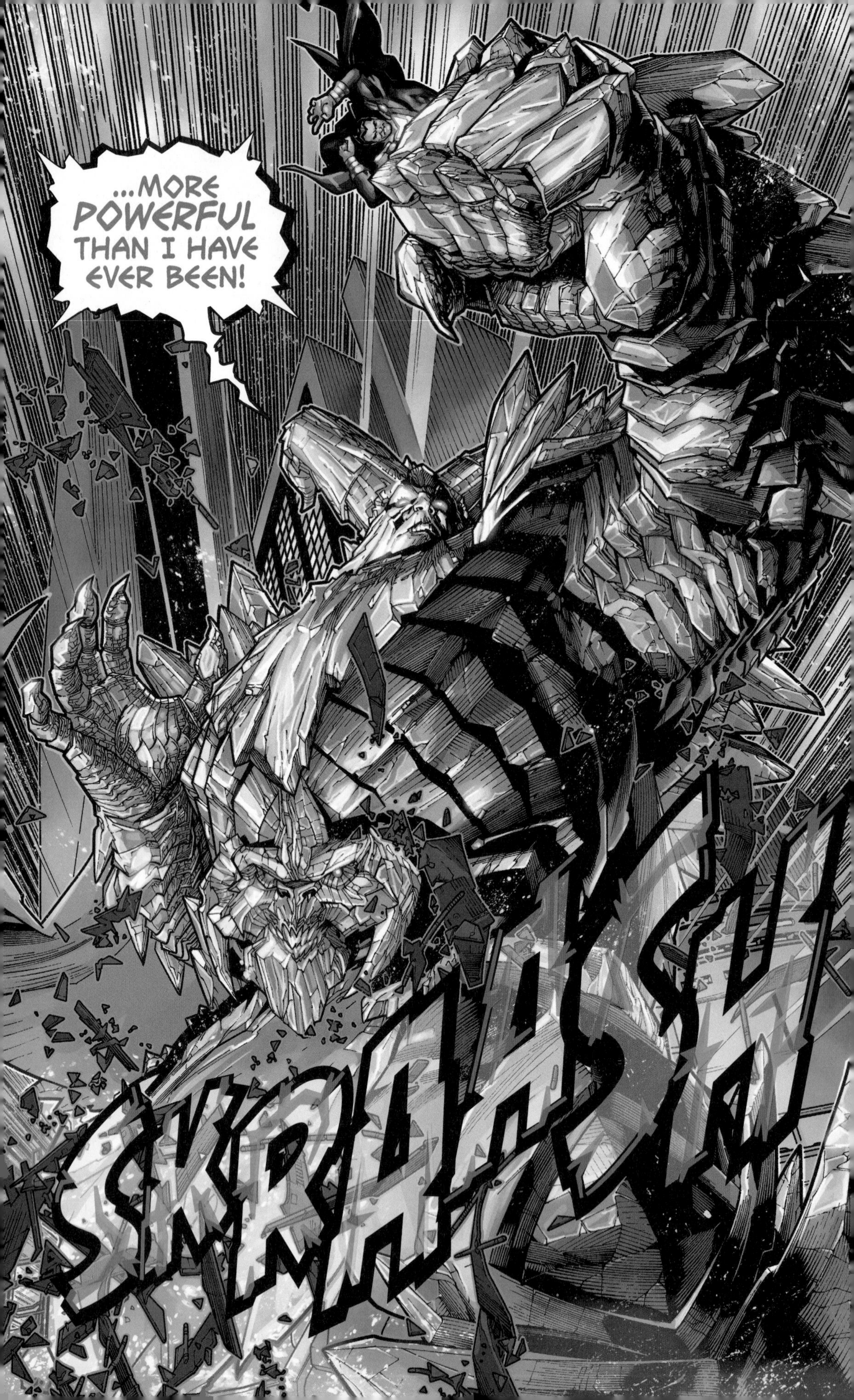
...MORE POWERFUL THAN I HAVE EVER BEEN!

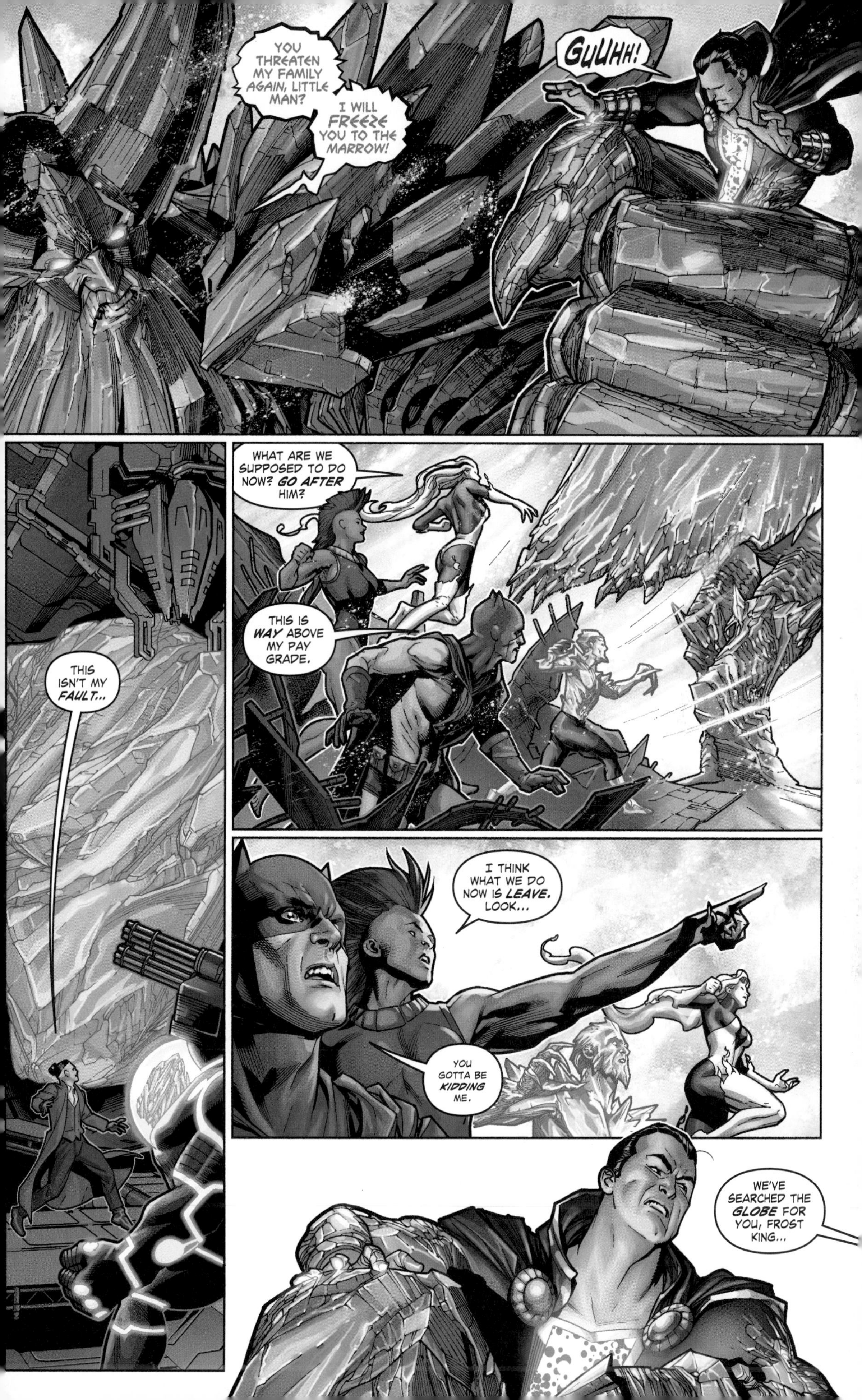
YOU THREATEN MY FAMILY AGAIN, LITTLE MAN?
I WILL FREEZE YOU TO THE MARROW!
GUUHH!
WHAT ARE WE SUPPOSED TO DO NOW? GO AFTER HIM?
THIS IS WAY ABOVE MY PAY GRADE.
THIS ISN'T MY FAULT...
I THINK WHAT WE DO NOW IS LEAVE. LOOK...
YOU GOTTA BE KIDDING ME.
WE'VE SEARCHED THE GLOBE FOR YOU, FROST KING...

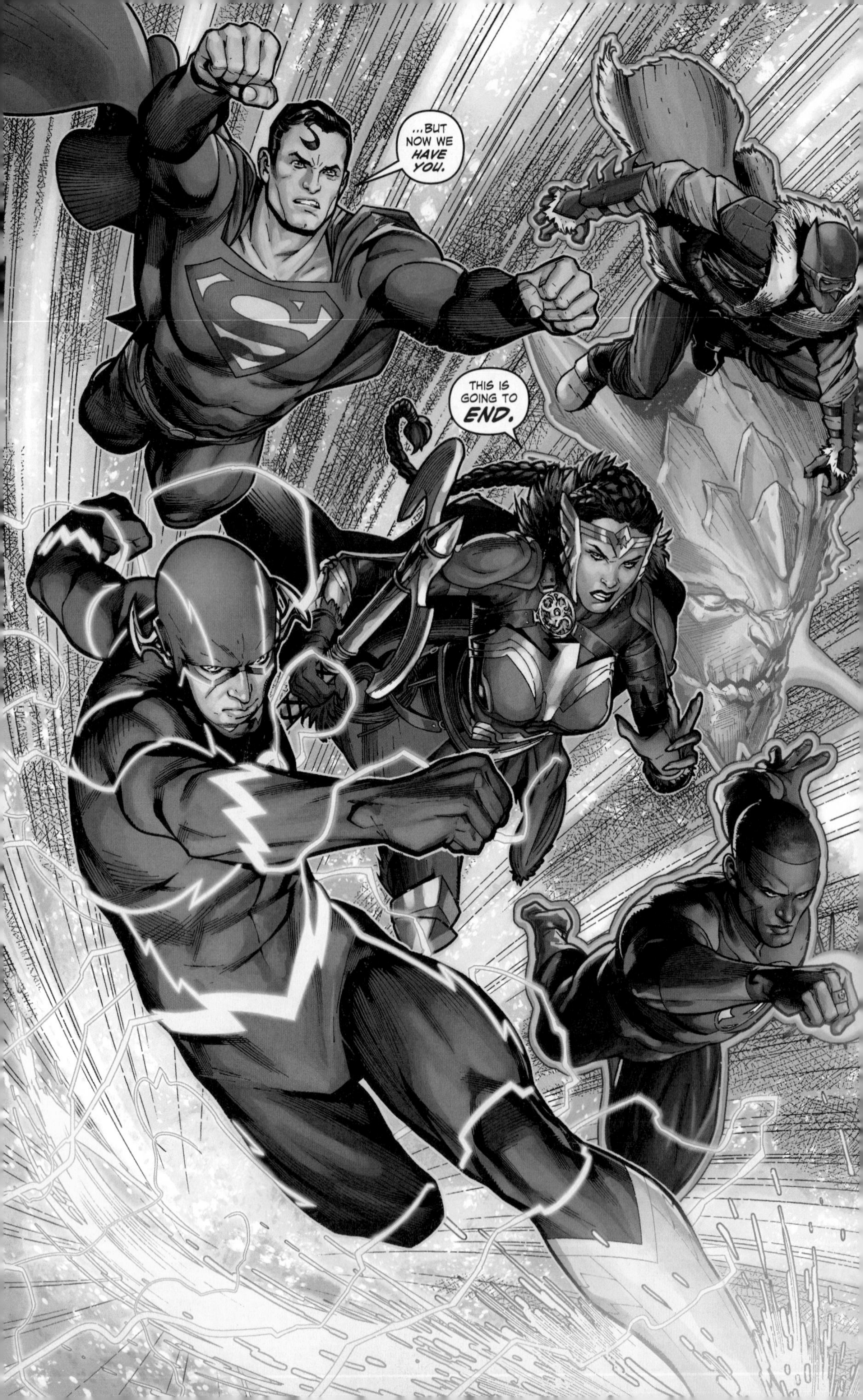
...BUT NOW WE HAVE YOU.
THIS IS GOING TO END.

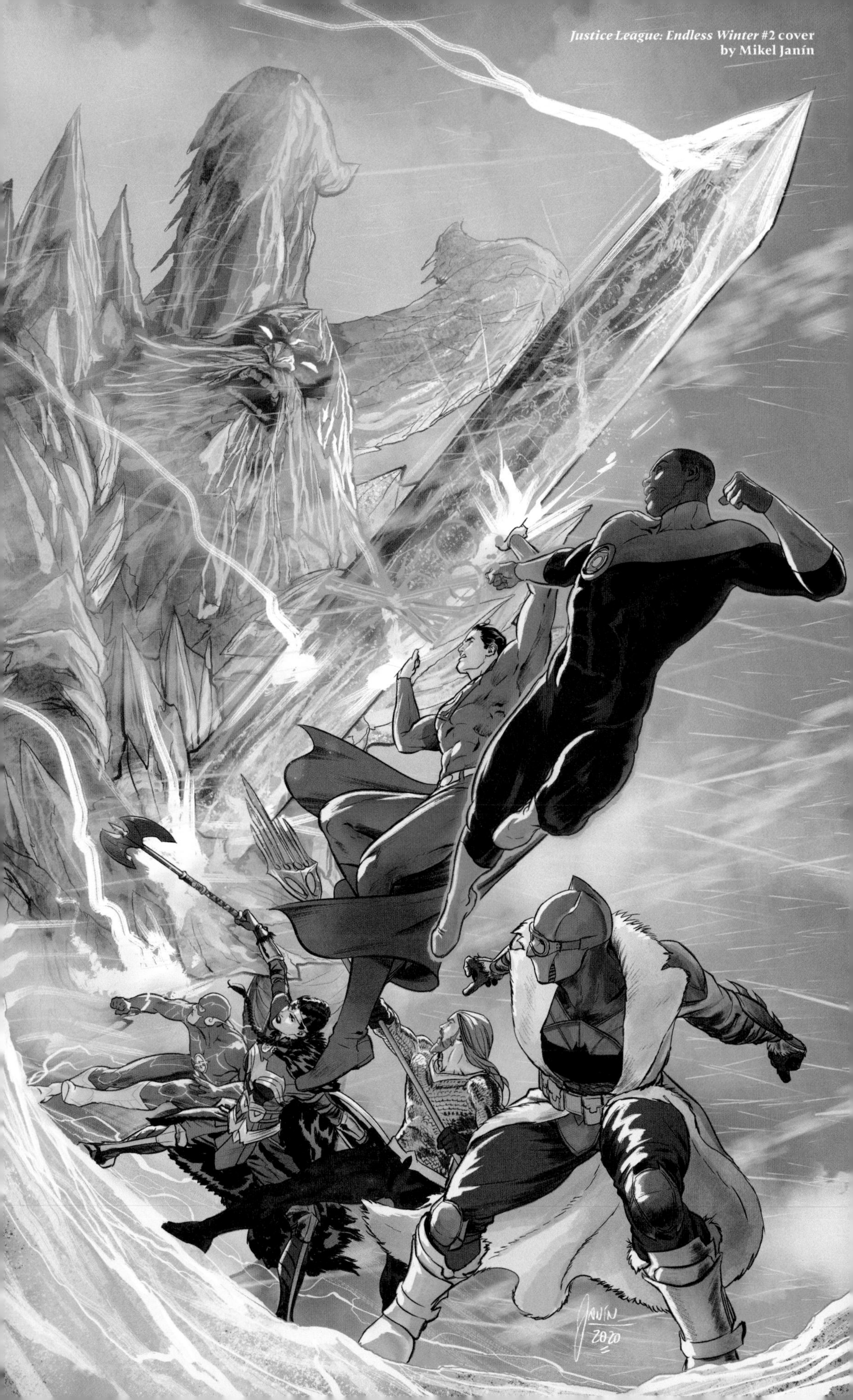

Justice League: Endless Winter #2 cover
by Mikel Janín

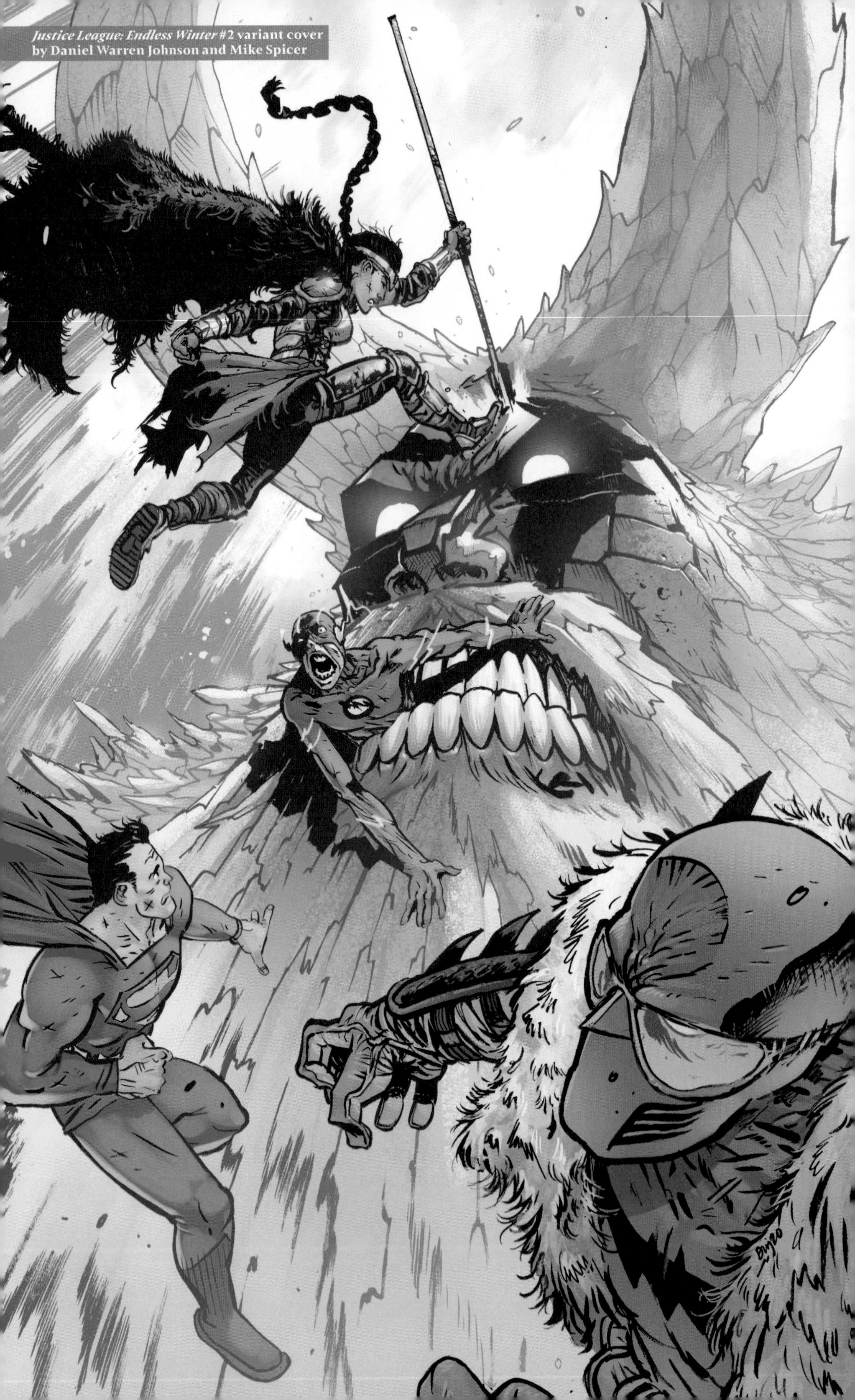

Justice League: Endless Winter #2 variant cover
by Daniel Warren Johnson and Mike Spicer

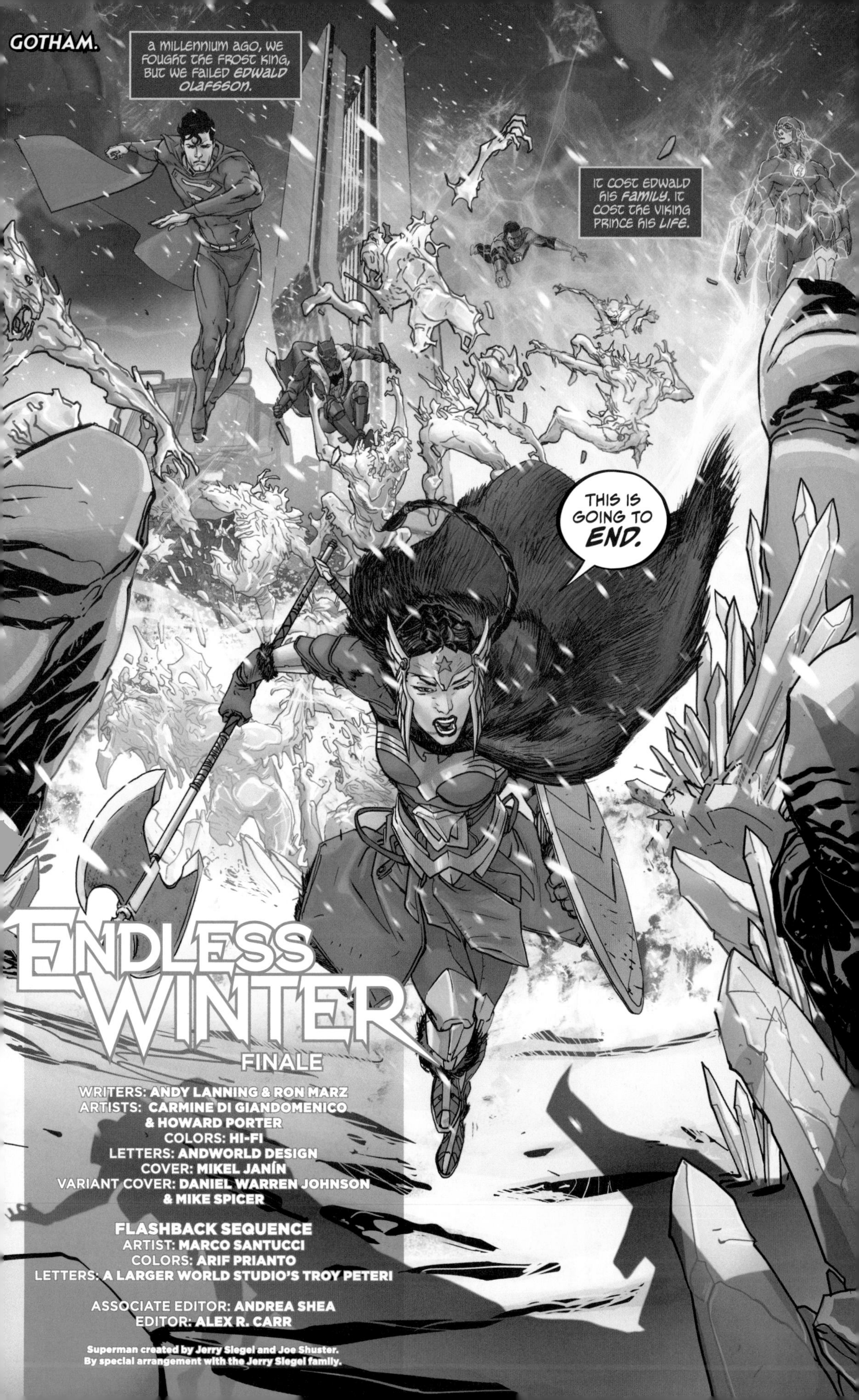
GOTHAM.
A MILLENNIUM AGO, WE FOUGHT THE FROST KING, BUT WE FAILED EDWALD OLAFSSON.
IT COST EDWALD HIS FAMILY. IT COST THE VIKING PRINCE HIS LIFE.
THIS IS GOING TO END.
ENDLESS WINTER
FINALE
WRITERS: ANDY LANNING & RON MARZ
ARTISTS: CARMINE DI GIANDOMENICO & HOWARD PORTER
COLORS: HI-FI
LETTERS: ANDWORLD DESIGN
COVER: MIKEL JANÍN
VARIANT COVER: DANIEL WARREN JOHNSON & MIKE SPICER
FLASHBACK SEQUENCE
ARTIST: MARCO SANTUCCI
COLORS: ARIF PRIANTO
LETTERS: A LARGER WORLD STUDIO'S TROY PETERI
ASSOCIATE EDITOR: ANDREA SHEA
EDITOR: ALEX R. CARR
Superman created by Jerry Siegel and Joe Shuster.
By special arrangement with the Jerry Siegel family.

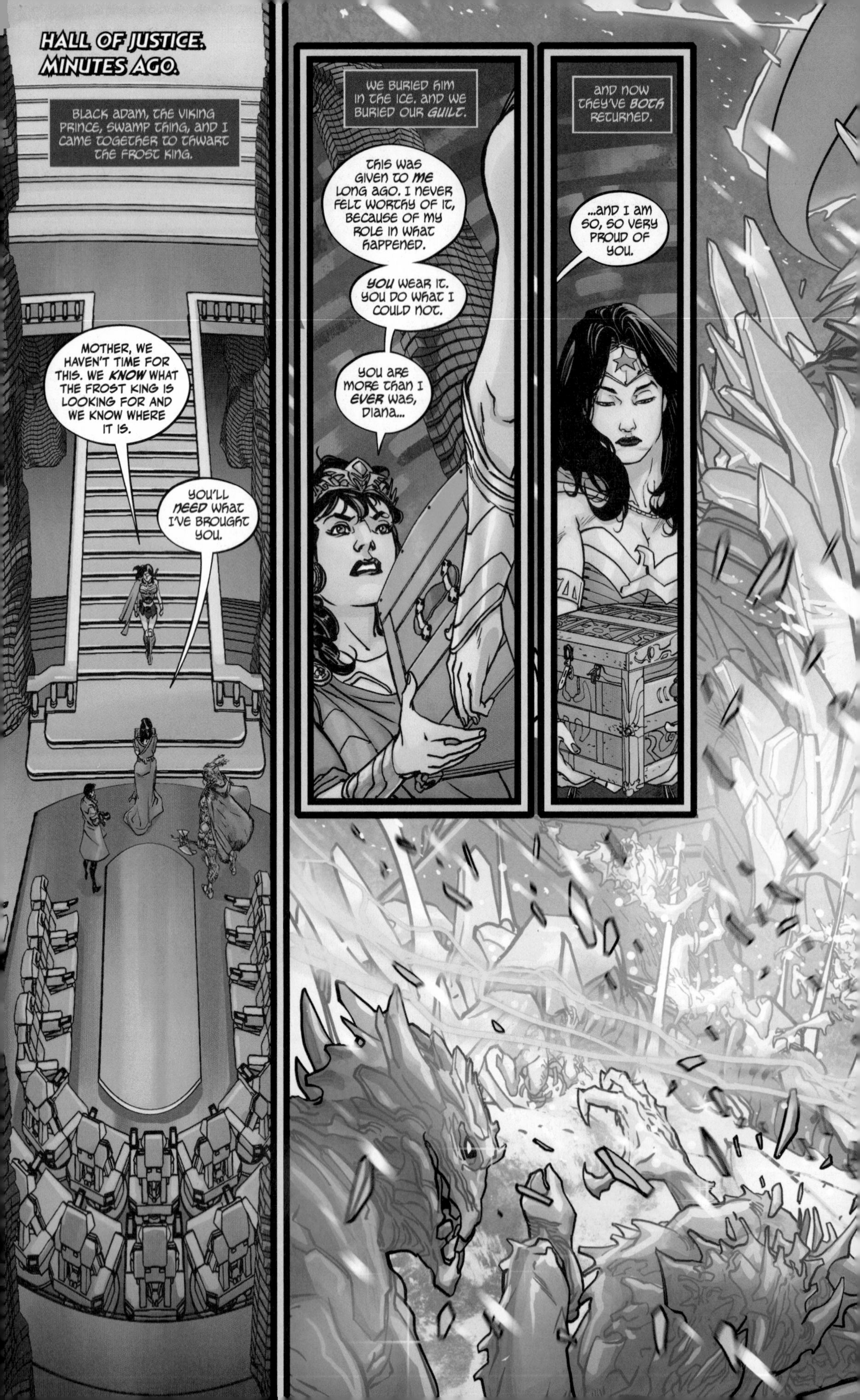
HALL OF JUSTICE. MINUTES AGO.
BLACK ADAM, THE VIKING PRINCE, SWAMP THING, AND I CAME TOGETHER TO THWART THE FROST KING.
MOTHER, WE HAVEN'T TIME FOR THIS. WE *KNOW* WHAT THE FROST KING IS LOOKING FOR AND WE KNOW WHERE IT IS.
YOU'LL *NEED* WHAT I'VE BROUGHT YOU.
WE BURIED HIM IN THE ICE. AND WE BURIED OUR *GUILT*.
THIS WAS GIVEN TO *ME* LONG AGO. I NEVER FELT WORTHY OF IT, BECAUSE OF MY ROLE IN WHAT HAPPENED.
YOU WEAR IT. YOU DO WHAT I COULD NOT.
YOU ARE MORE THAN I *EVER* WAS, DIANA...
AND NOW THEY'VE *BOTH* RETURNED.
...AND I AM SO, SO VERY PROUD OF YOU.

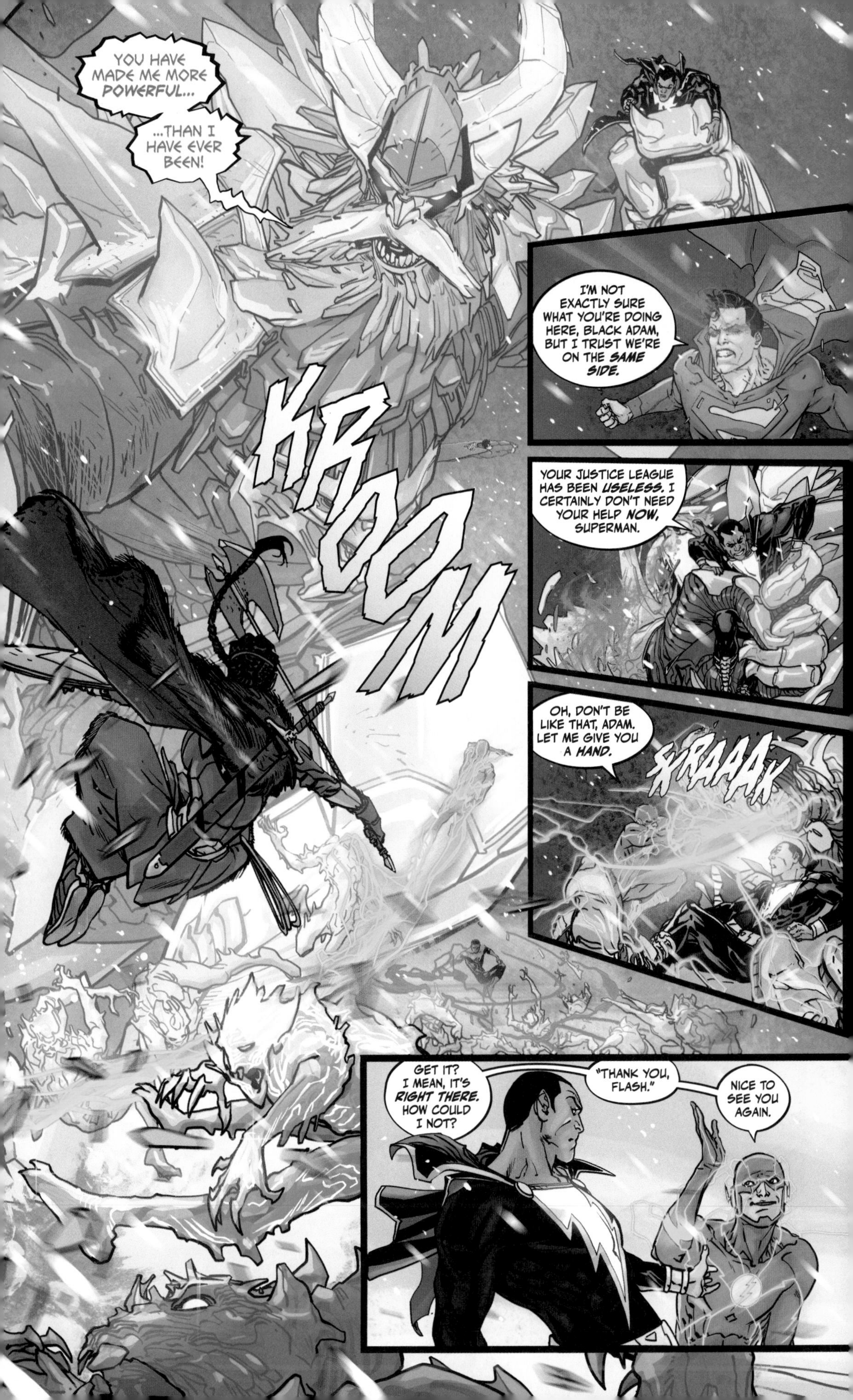

YOU HAVE MADE ME MORE POWERFUL...
...THAN I HAVE EVER BEEN!
KRBOOM
I'M NOT EXACTLY SURE WHAT YOU'RE DOING HERE, BLACK ADAM, BUT I TRUST WE'RE ON THE SAME SIDE.
YOUR JUSTICE LEAGUE HAS BEEN USELESS. I CERTAINLY DON'T NEED YOUR HELP NOW, SUPERMAN.
OH, DON'T BE LIKE THAT, ADAM. LET ME GIVE YOU A HAND.
SKRAAAK
GET IT? I MEAN, IT'S RIGHT THERE. HOW COULD I NOT?
"THANK YOU, FLASH."
NICE TO SEE YOU AGAIN.

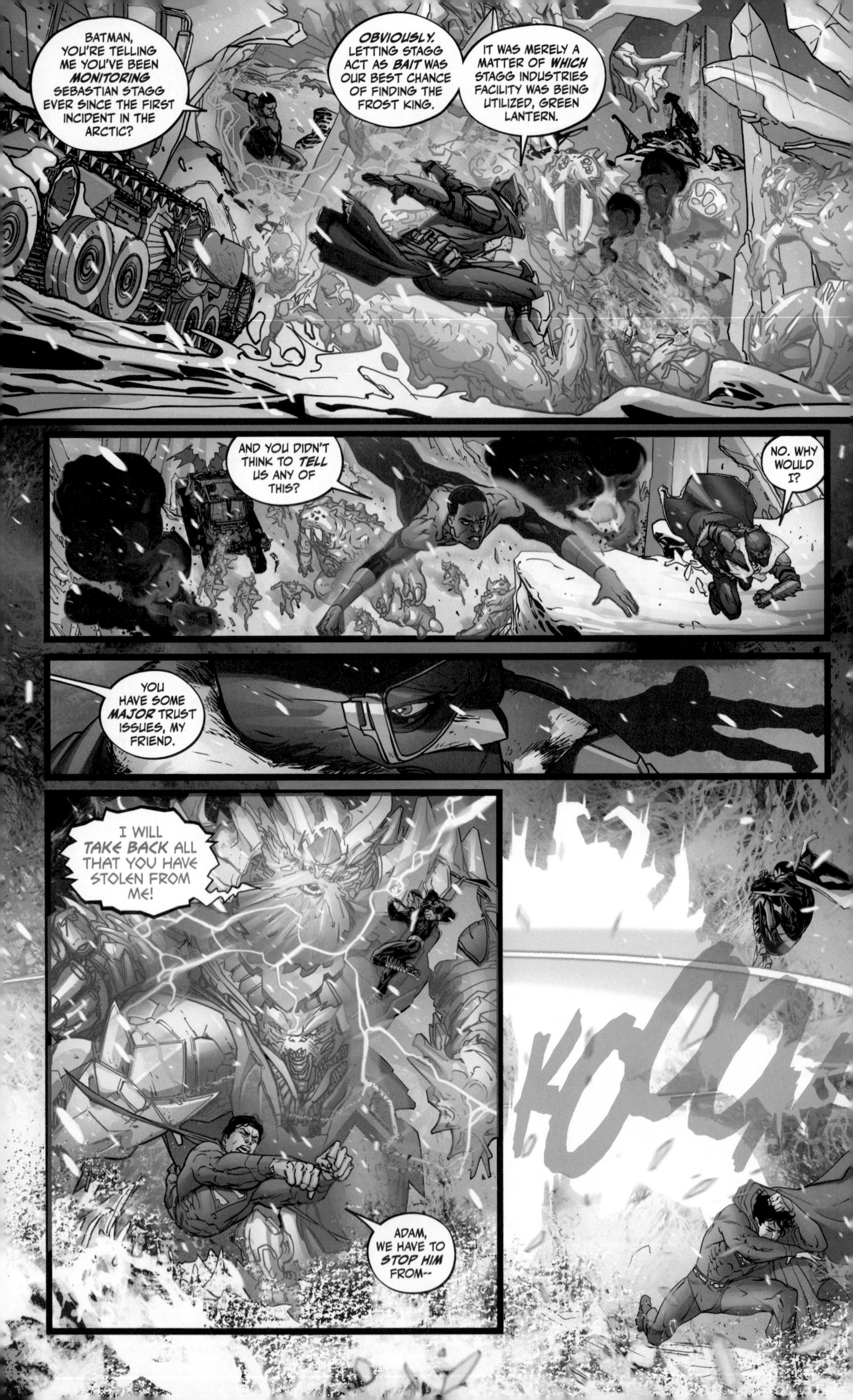
BATMAN, YOU'RE TELLING ME YOU'VE BEEN MONITORING SEBASTIAN STAGG EVER SINCE THE FIRST INCIDENT IN THE ARCTIC?
OBVIOUSLY. LETTING STAGG ACT AS BAIT WAS OUR BEST CHANCE OF FINDING THE FROST KING.
IT WAS MERELY A MATTER OF WHICH STAGG INDUSTRIES FACILITY WAS BEING UTILIZED, GREEN LANTERN.
AND YOU DIDN'T THINK TO TELL US ANY OF THIS?
NO. WHY WOULD I?
YOU HAVE SOME MAJOR TRUST ISSUES, MY FRIEND.
I WILL TAKE BACK ALL THAT YOU HAVE STOLEN FROM ME!
ADAM, WE HAVE TO STOP HIM FROM--
KOOO

GONE AGAIN.

BECAUSE YOU SO-CALLED *HEROES* ARRIVED! I HAD ALL OF IT UNDER CONTROL.

I BEAT HIM *BEFORE*, I'LL DO IT AGAIN!

FLASH? ANYTHING?

NO SIGN OF THE FROST KING *ANYWHERE* ON THE EAST COAST.

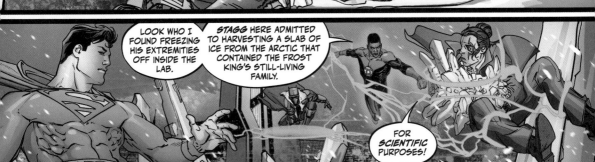

LOOK WHO I FOUND FREEZING HIS EXTREMITIES OFF INSIDE THE LAB.

STAGG HERE ADMITTED TO HARVESTING A SLAB OF ICE FROM THE ARCTIC THAT CONTAINED THE FROST KING'S STILL-LIVING FAMILY.

FOR *SCIENTIFIC* PURPOSES!

NOW THAT SLAB IS *GONE*.

YOU WANTED KRYPTONIAN CRYSTALS SO YOU COULD *EXPLOIT* THEM.

DON'T BLAME *ME* FOR THE MESS YOU LEFT.

STAGG IS RIGHT. THE FAULT HERE IS YOUR *ARROGANCE*.

YOU MIGHT WANT TO RETHINK YOUR *TONE*...

NO TIME FOR THAT.

I PUT A *TRACER* ON THE ICE WHILE WE WERE FIGHTING THE FROST KING. IT'S BACK IN THE ARCTIC...

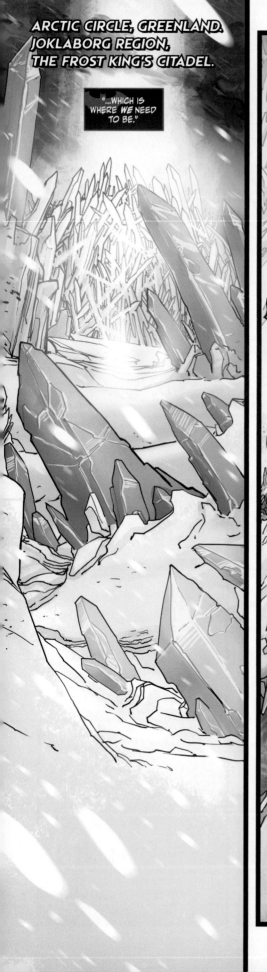

ARCTIC CIRCLE, GREENLAND.
JOKLABORG REGION,
THE FROST KING'S CITADEL.

"...WHICH IS WHERE *WE* NEED TO BE."

WAITING FOR ME, ALL THIS TIME.

MY WIFE, MY SON, MY DAUGHTER...

ONCE I FREE YOU FROM YOUR FRIGID SLUMBER, WE WILL BE REUNITED.

AND THEN I WILL *FINISH* REMAKING THIS WORLD FOR US.

EDWALD OLAFSSON...

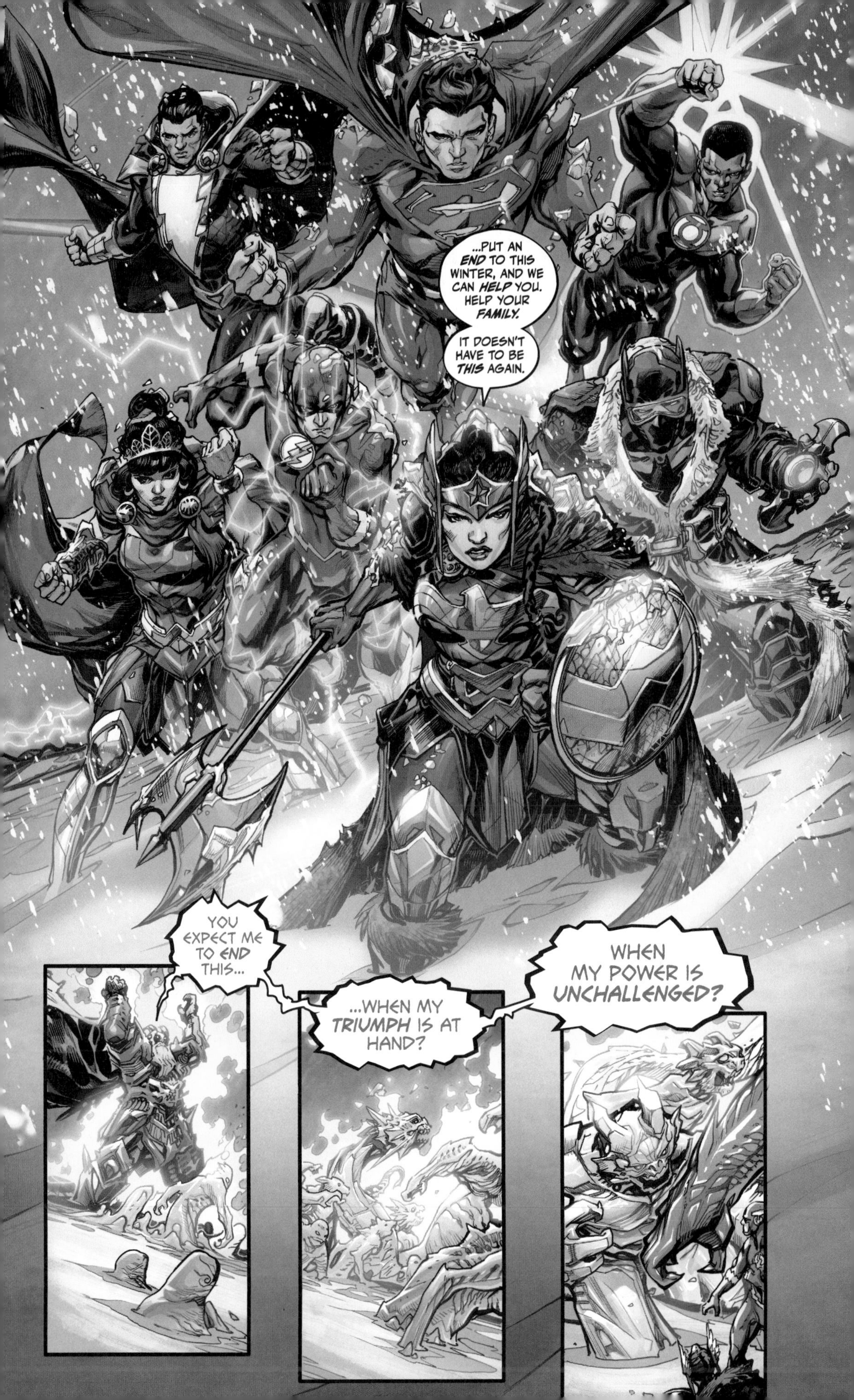
...PUT AN END TO THIS WINTER, AND WE CAN HELP YOU. HELP YOUR FAMILY.
IT DOESN'T HAVE TO BE THIS AGAIN.
YOU EXPECT ME TO END THIS...
...WHEN MY TRIUMPH IS AT HAND?
WHEN MY POWER IS UNCHALLENGED?

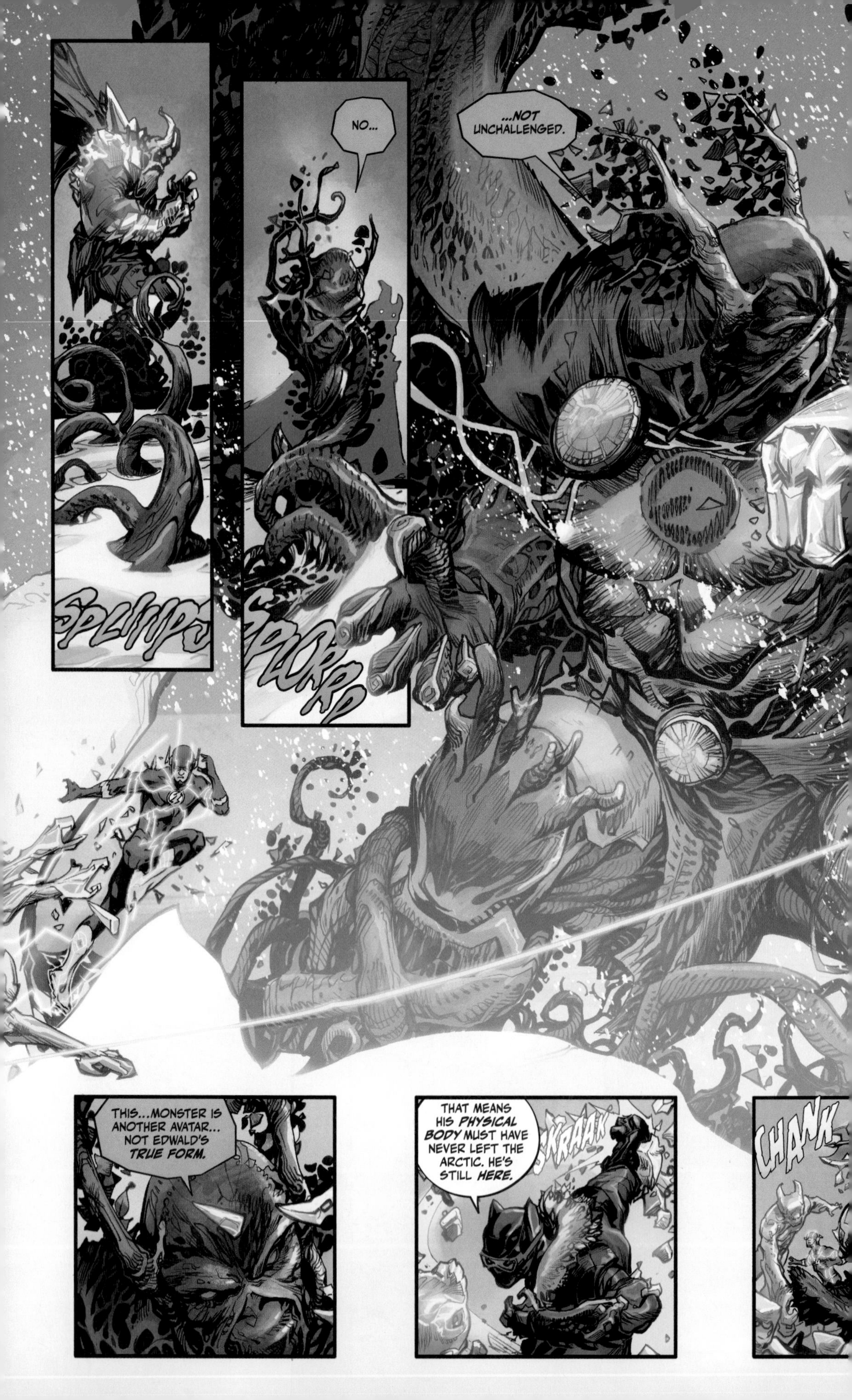

SPLUDSH
NO...
SPLORR
...NOT UNCHALLENGED.
THIS...MONSTER IS ANOTHER AVATAR... NOT EDWALD'S TRUE FORM.
THAT MEANS HIS PHYSICAL BODY MUST HAVE NEVER LEFT THE ARCTIC. HE'S STILL HERE.
SKRAAK
CHANK

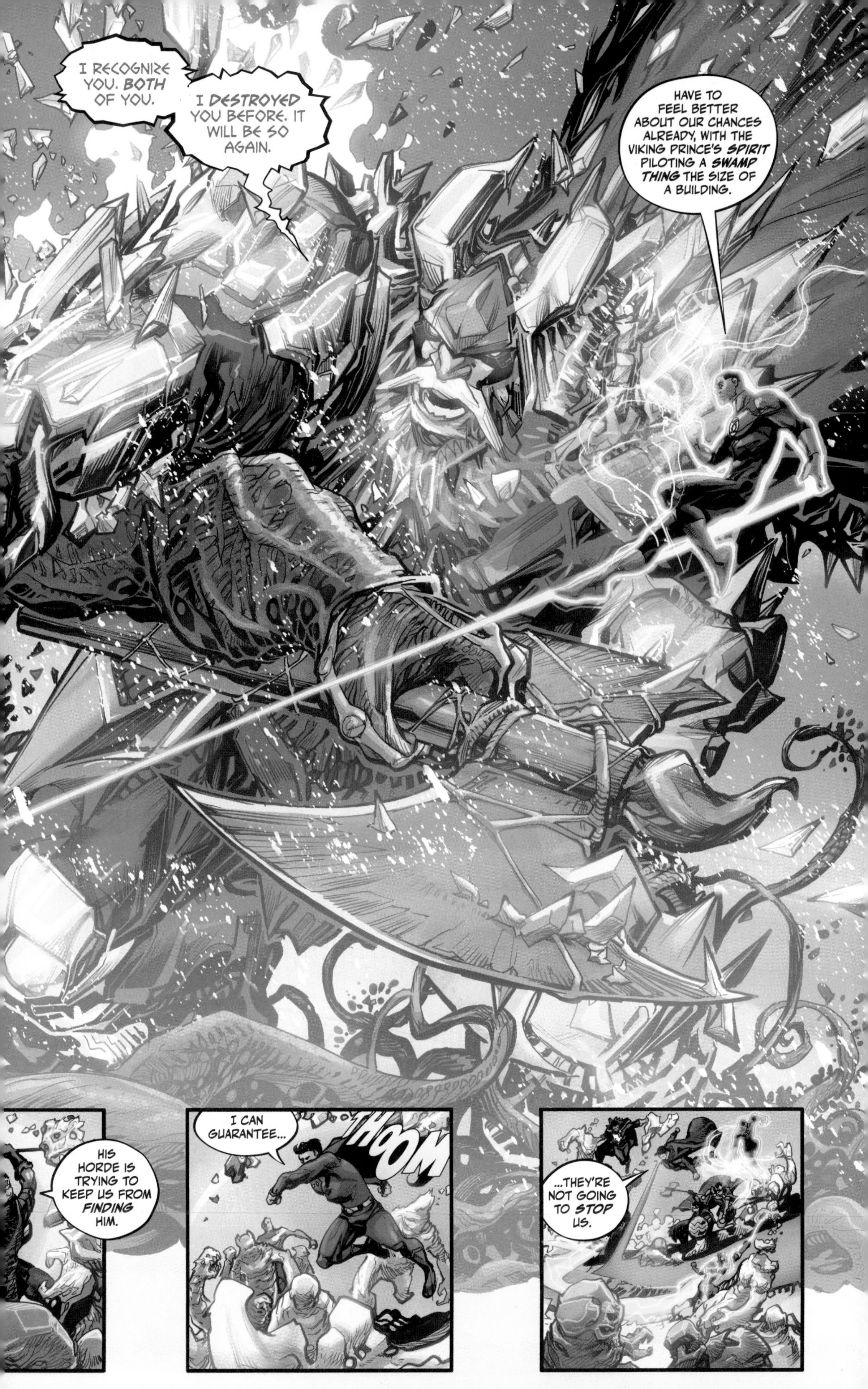
I RECOGNIZE YOU. BOTH OF YOU.
I DESTROYED YOU BEFORE. IT WILL BE SO AGAIN.
HAVE TO FEEL BETTER ABOUT OUR CHANCES ALREADY, WITH THE VIKING PRINCE'S SPIRIT PILOTING A SWAMP THING THE SIZE OF A BUILDING.
HIS HORDE IS TRYING TO KEEP US FROM FINDING HIM.
I CAN GUARANTEE...
THOOM
...THEY'RE NOT GOING TO STOP US.

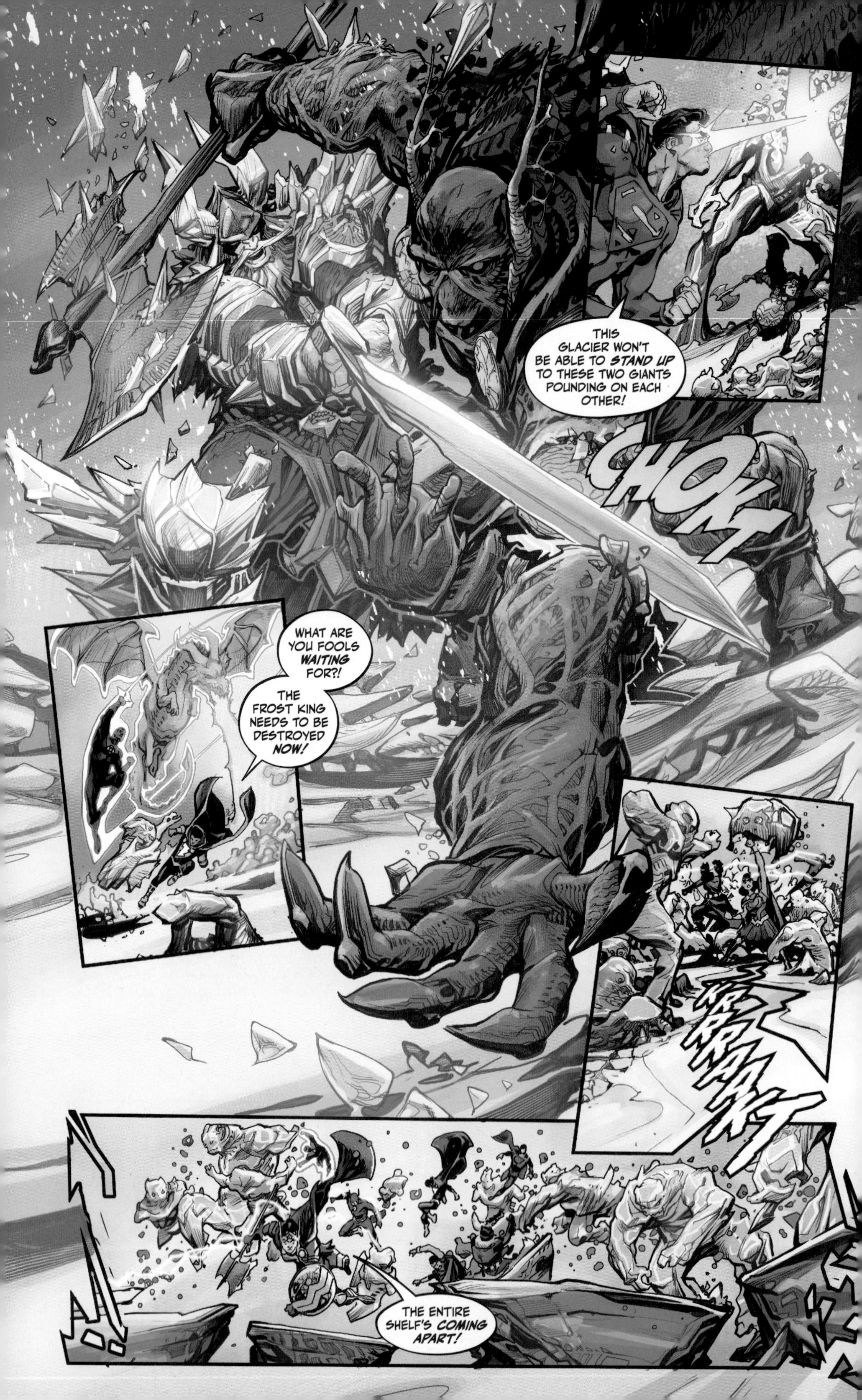
THIS GLACIER WON'T BE ABLE TO *STAND UP* TO THESE TWO GIANTS POUNDING ON EACH OTHER!
CHOKT
WHAT ARE YOU FOOLS *WAITING* FOR?!
THE FROST KING NEEDS TO BE DESTROYED *NOW!*
KRRRAAKT
THE ENTIRE SHELF'S *COMING APART!*

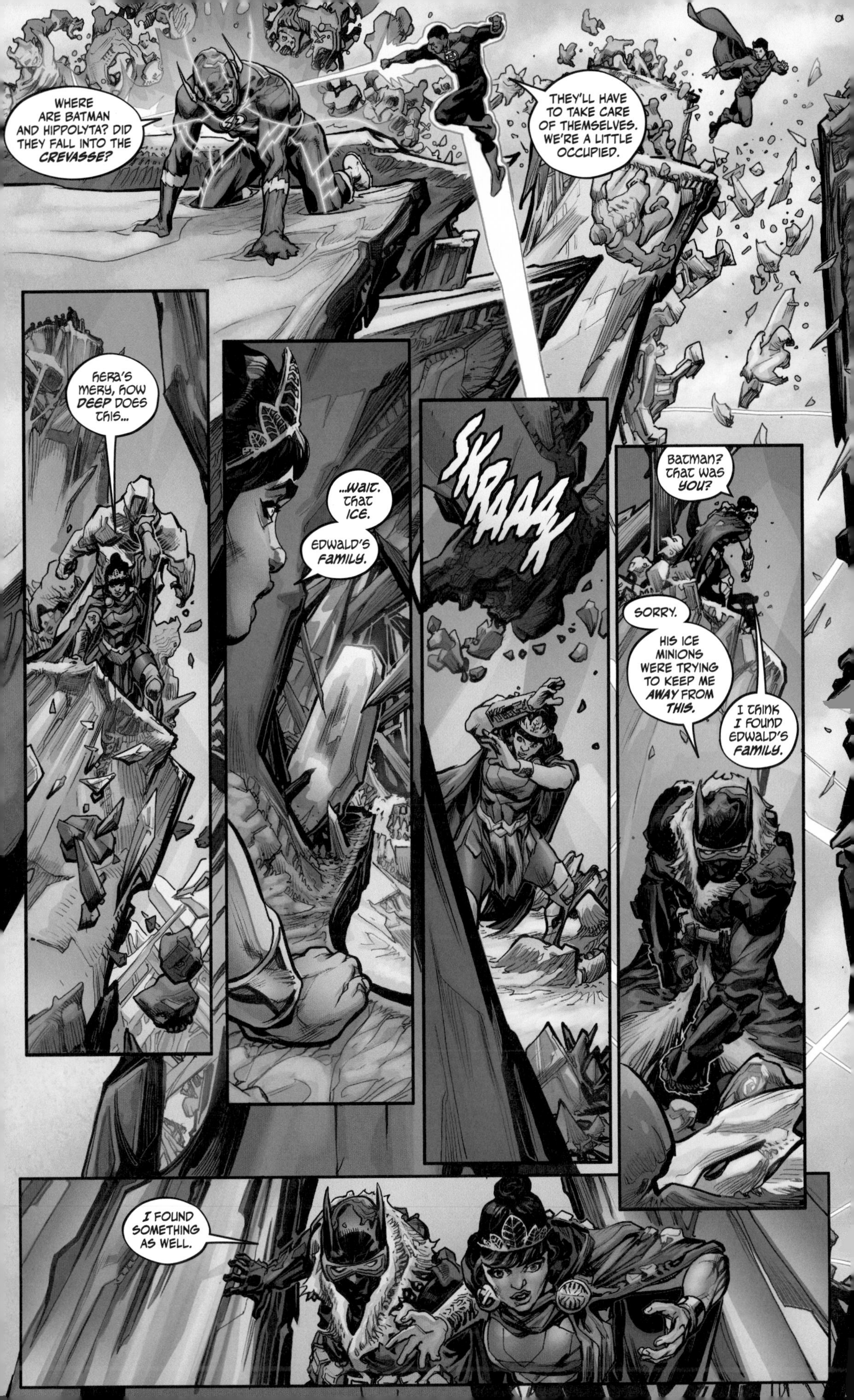
WHERE ARE BATMAN AND HIPPOLYTA? DID THEY FALL INTO THE CREVASSE?
THEY'LL HAVE TO TAKE CARE OF THEMSELVES. WE'RE A LITTLE OCCUPIED.
HERA'S MERY, HOW DEEP DOES THIS...
...WAIT. THAT ICE.
EDWALD'S FAMILY.
SKRAAAK
BATMAN? THAT WAS YOU?
SORRY.
HIS ICE MINIONS WERE TRYING TO KEEP ME AWAY FROM THIS.
I THINK I FOUND EDWALD'S FAMILY.
I FOUND SOMETHING AS WELL.

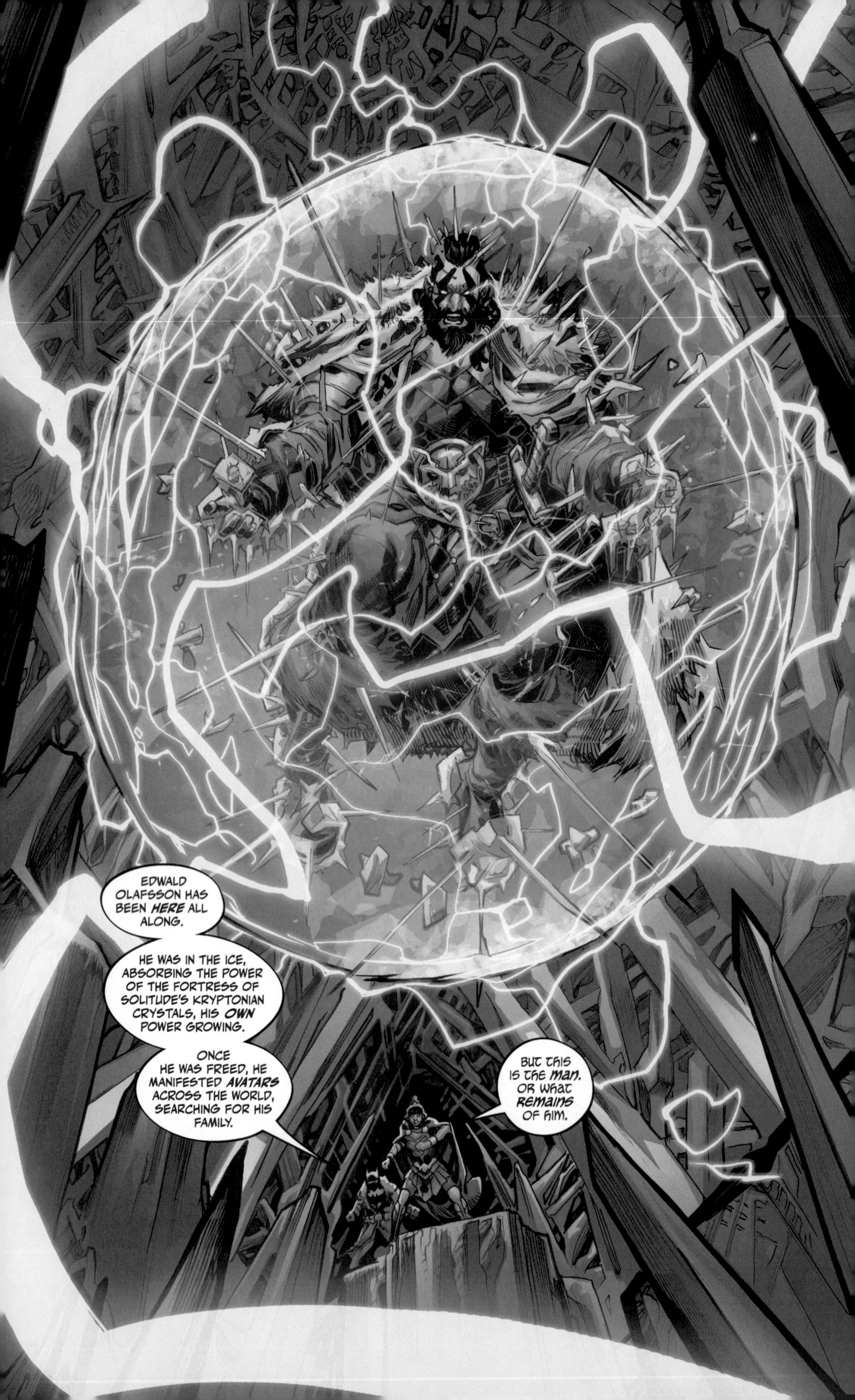
EDWALD OLAFSSON HAS BEEN *HERE* ALL ALONG.
HE WAS IN THE ICE, ABSORBING THE POWER OF THE FORTRESS OF SOLITUDE'S KRYPTONIAN CRYSTALS, HIS *OWN* POWER GROWING.
ONCE HE WAS FREED, HE MANIFESTED *AVATARS* ACROSS THE WORLD, SEARCHING FOR HIS FAMILY.
BUT THIS IS THE *MAN*. OR WHAT *REMAINS* OF HIM.

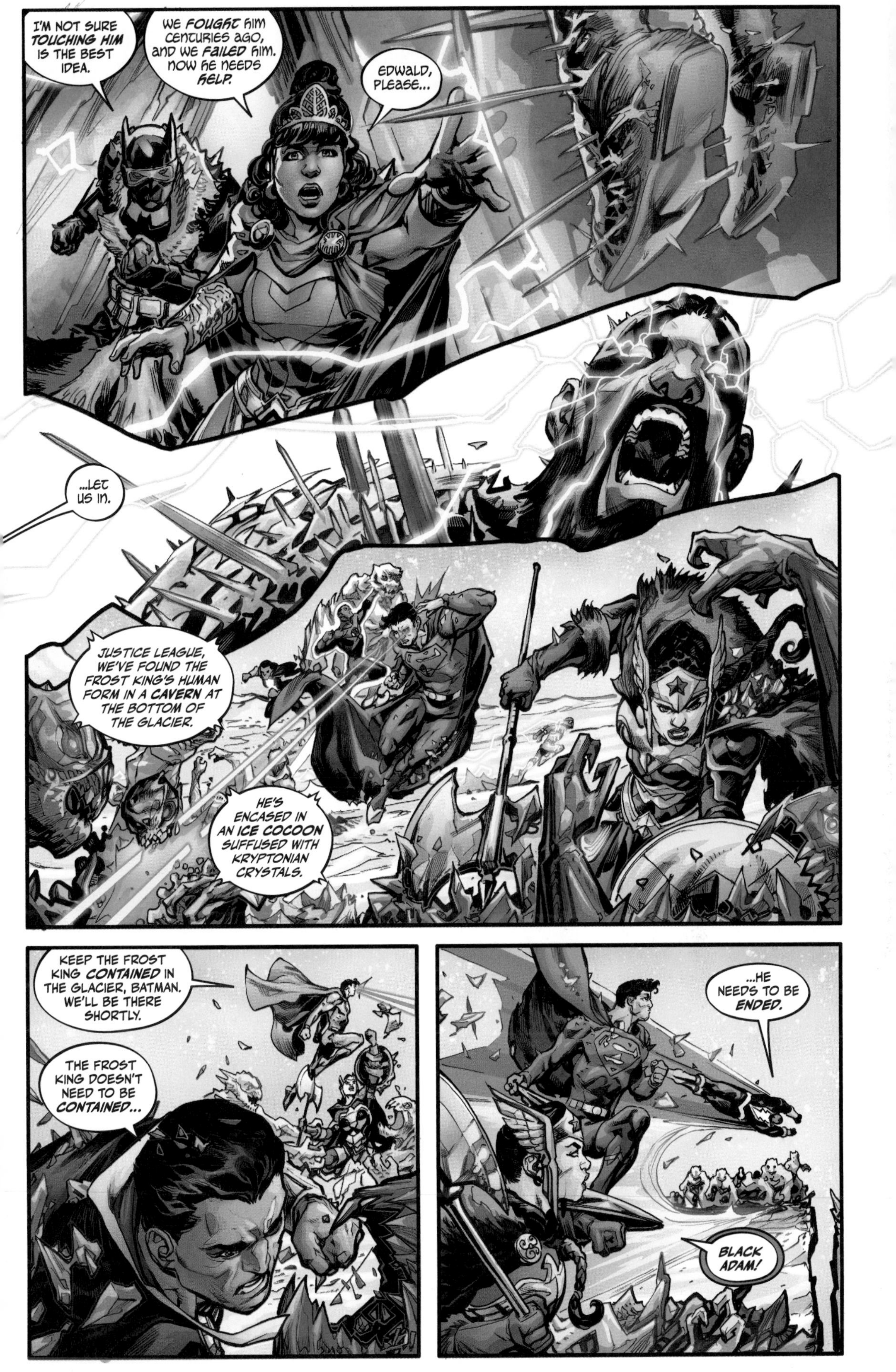
I'M NOT SURE TOUCHING HIM IS THE BEST IDEA.
WE FOUGHT HIM CENTURIES AGO, AND WE FAILED HIM. NOW HE NEEDS HELP.
EDWALD, PLEASE...
...LET US IN.
JUSTICE LEAGUE, WE'VE FOUND THE FROST KING'S HUMAN FORM IN A CAVERN AT THE BOTTOM OF THE GLACIER.
HE'S ENCASED IN AN ICE COCOON SUFFUSED WITH KRYPTONIAN CRYSTALS.
KEEP THE FROST KING CONTAINED IN THE GLACIER, BATMAN. WE'LL BE THERE SHORTLY.
THE FROST KING DOESN'T NEED TO BE CONTAINED...
...HE NEEDS TO BE ENDED.
BLACK ADAM!

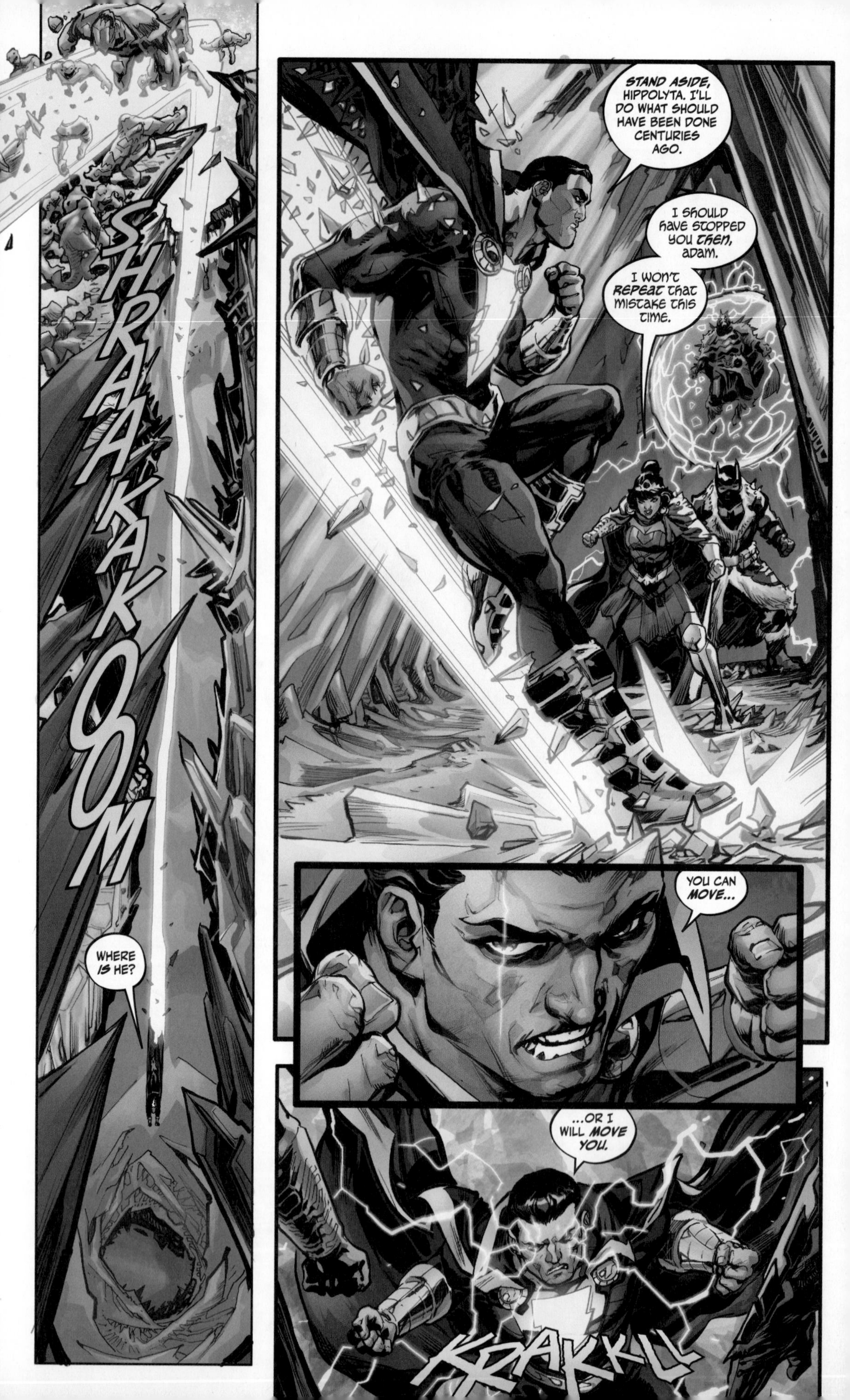
SHRAAKAKOOOM
WHERE IS HE?
STAND ASIDE, HIPPOLYTA. I'LL DO WHAT SHOULD HAVE BEEN DONE CENTURIES AGO.
I SHOULD HAVE STOPPED YOU THEN, ADAM.
I WON'T REPEAT THAT MISTAKE THIS TIME.
YOU CAN MOVE...
...OR I WILL MOVE YOU.
KRAKKL

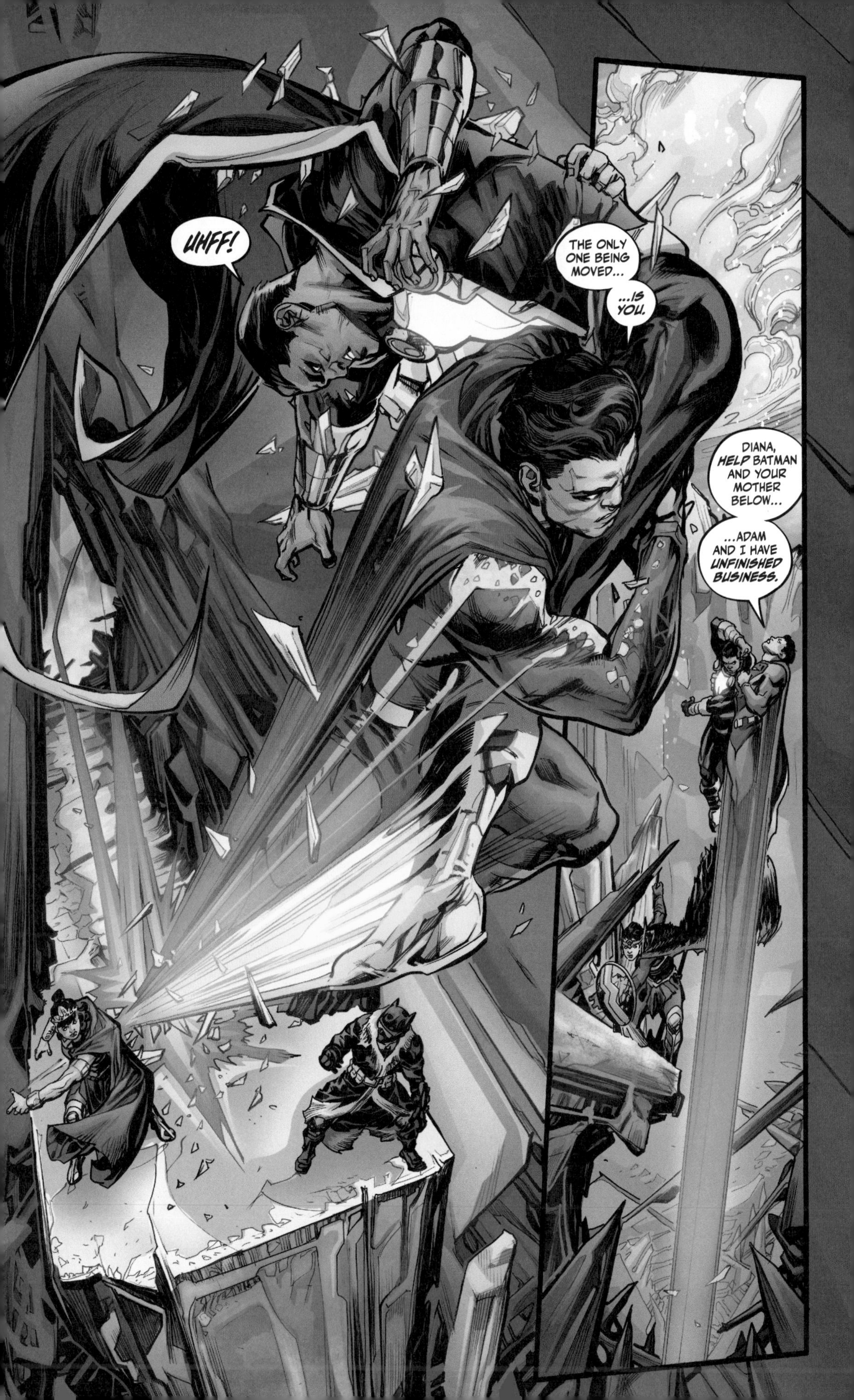
UHFF!
THE ONLY ONE BEING MOVED...
...IS YOU.
DIANA, HELP BATMAN AND YOUR MOTHER BELOW...
...ADAM AND I HAVE UNFINISHED BUSINESS.

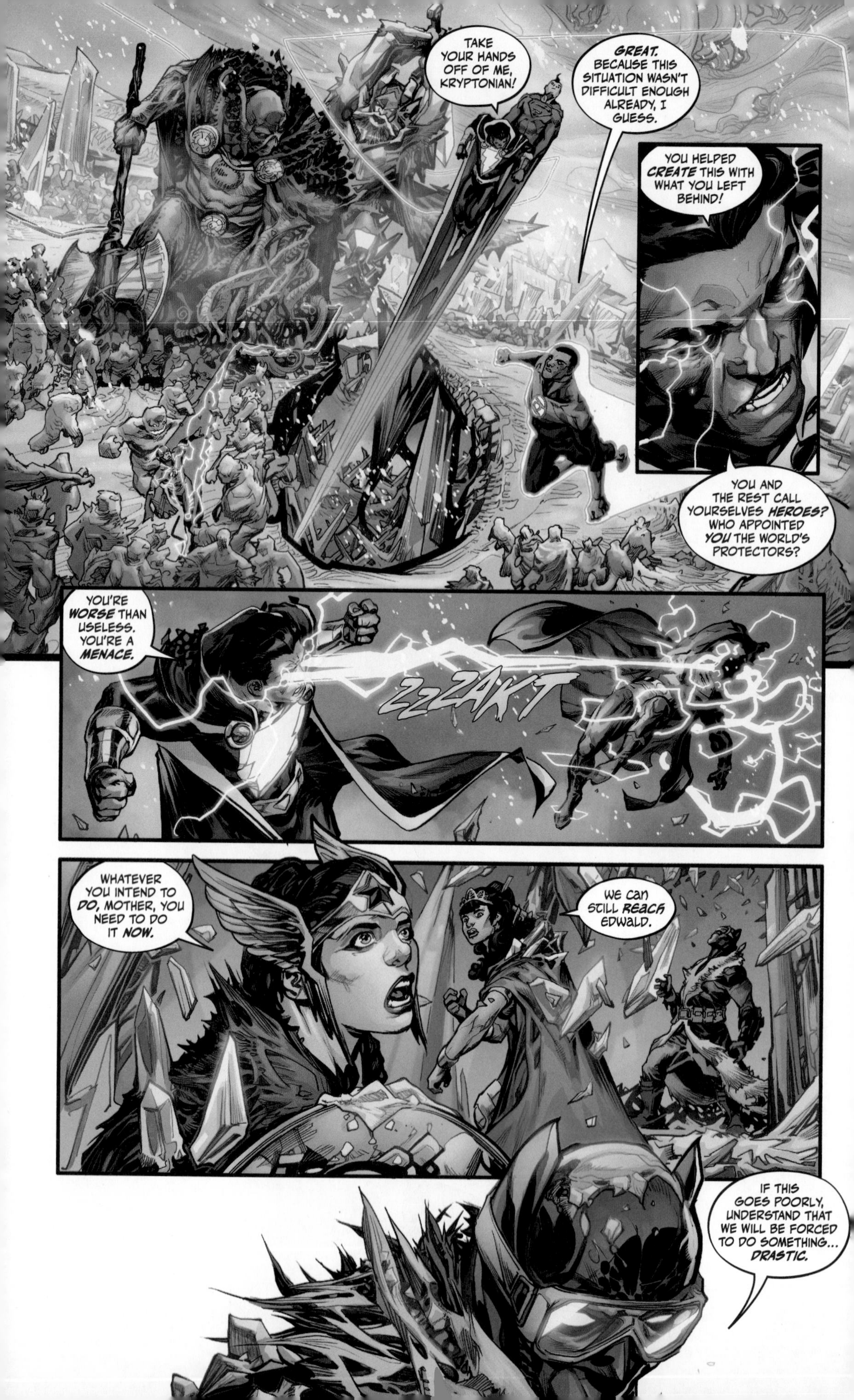
TAKE YOUR HANDS OFF OF ME, KRYPTONIAN!
GREAT. BECAUSE THIS SITUATION WASN'T DIFFICULT ENOUGH ALREADY, I GUESS.
YOU HELPED CREATE THIS WITH WHAT YOU LEFT BEHIND!
YOU AND THE REST CALL YOURSELVES HEROES? WHO APPOINTED YOU THE WORLD'S PROTECTORS?
YOU'RE WORSE THAN USELESS. YOU'RE A MENACE.
ZZZAKT
WHATEVER YOU INTEND TO DO, MOTHER, YOU NEED TO DO IT NOW.
WE CAN STILL REACH EDWALD.
IF THIS GOES POORLY, UNDERSTAND THAT WE WILL BE FORCED TO DO SOMETHING... DRASTIC.

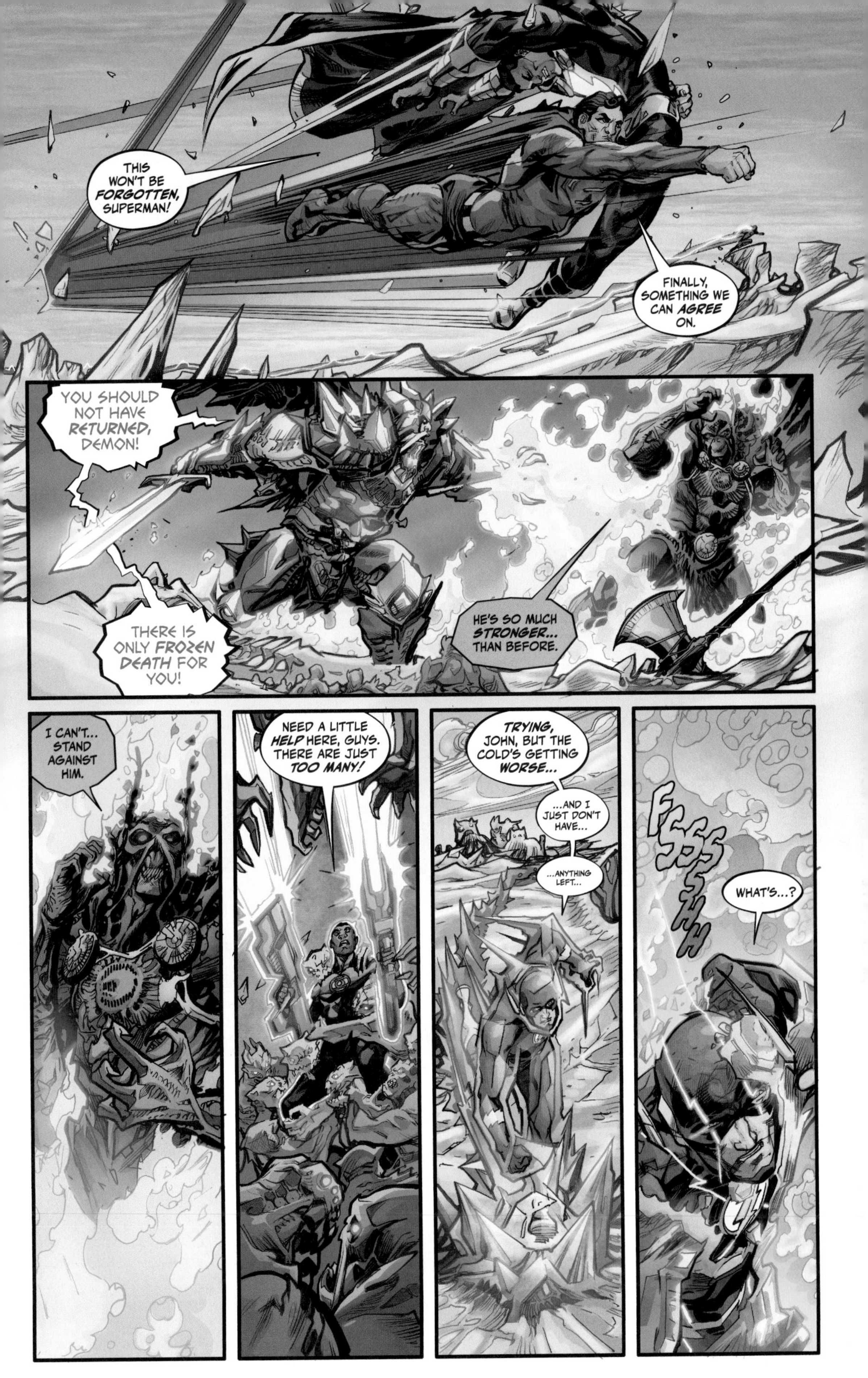
THIS WON'T BE FORGOTTEN, SUPERMAN!
FINALLY, SOMETHING WE CAN AGREE ON.
YOU SHOULD NOT HAVE RETURNED, DEMON!
THERE IS ONLY FROZEN DEATH FOR YOU!
HE'S SO MUCH STRONGER... THAN BEFORE.
I CAN'T... STAND AGAINST HIM.
NEED A LITTLE HELP HERE, GUYS. THERE ARE JUST TOO MANY!
TRYING, JOHN, BUT THE COLD'S GETTING WORSE...
...AND I JUST DON'T HAVE...
...ANYTHING LEFT...
FSSSSHH
WHAT'S...?

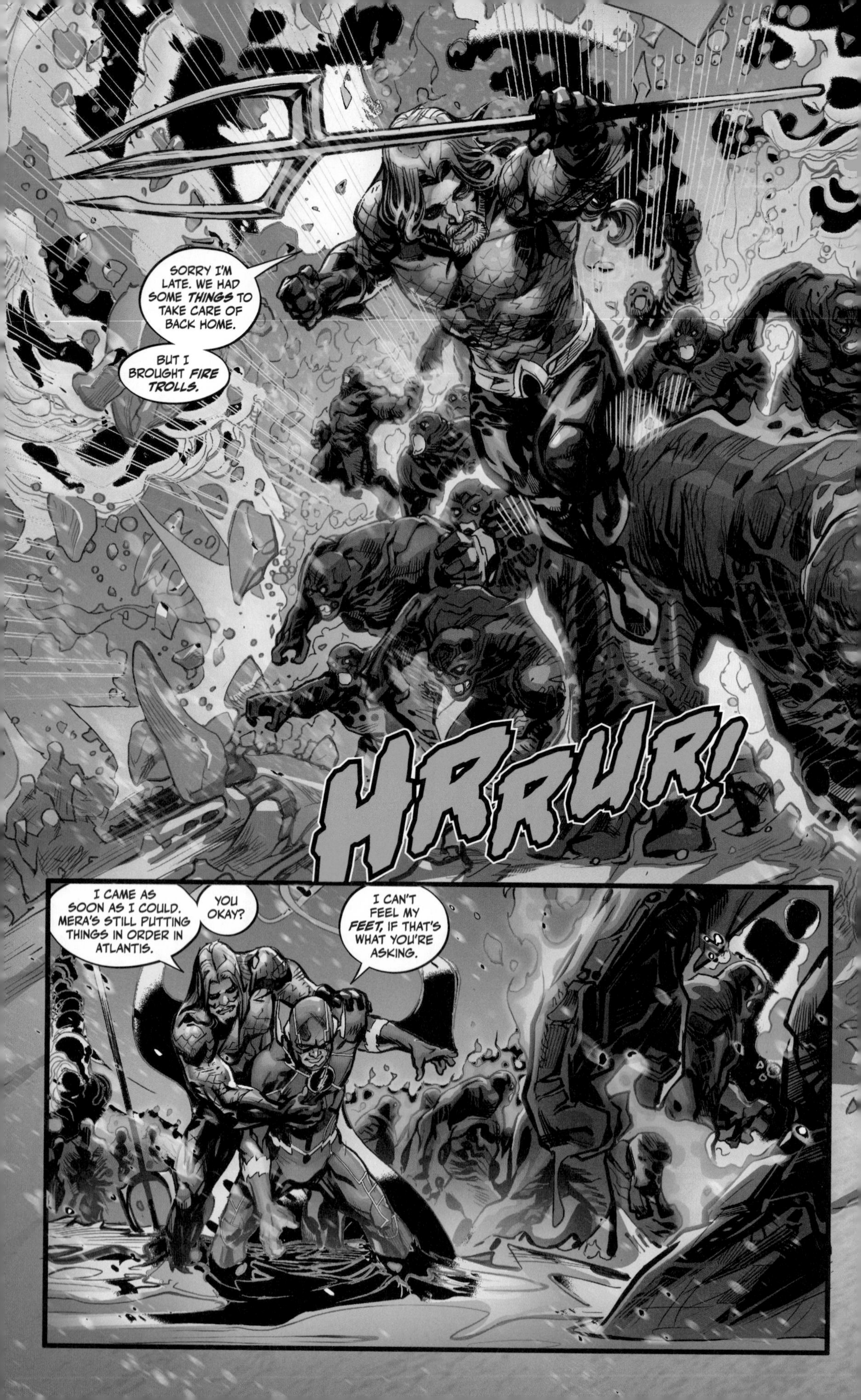
SORRY I'M LATE. WE HAD SOME *THINGS* TO TAKE CARE OF BACK HOME.
BUT I BROUGHT *FIRE TROLLS.*
HRRUR!
I CAME AS SOON AS I COULD. MERA'S STILL PUTTING THINGS IN ORDER IN ATLANTIS.
YOU OKAY?
I CAN'T FEEL MY *FEET,* IF THAT'S WHAT YOU'RE ASKING.

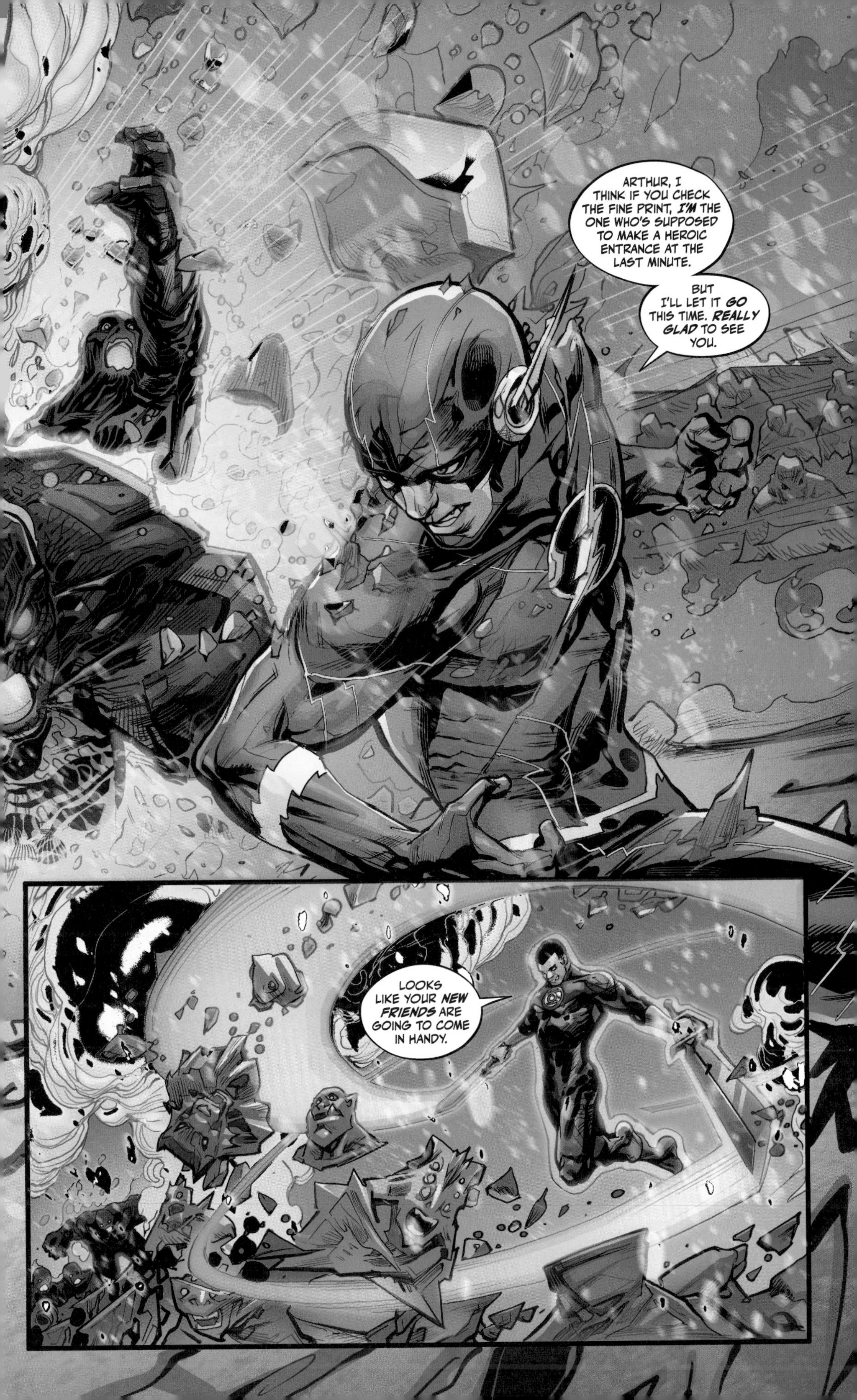
ARTHUR, I THINK IF YOU CHECK THE FINE PRINT, I'M THE ONE WHO'S SUPPOSED TO MAKE A HEROIC ENTRANCE AT THE LAST MINUTE.
BUT I'LL LET IT GO THIS TIME. REALLY GLAD TO SEE YOU.
LOOKS LIKE YOUR NEW FRIENDS ARE GOING TO COME IN HANDY.

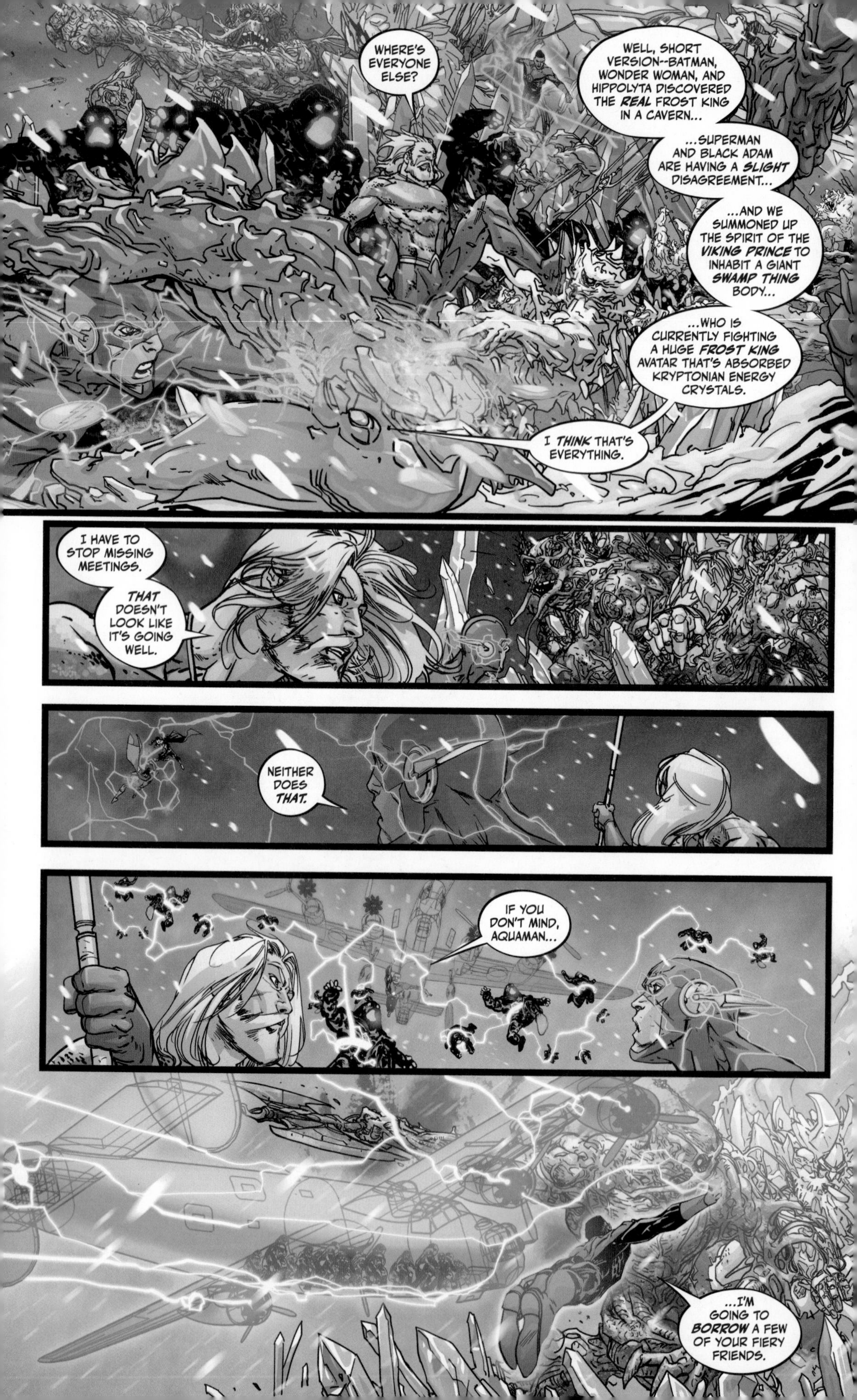
WHERE'S EVERYONE ELSE?
WELL, SHORT VERSION--BATMAN, WONDER WOMAN, AND HIPPOLYTA DISCOVERED THE *REAL* FROST KING IN A CAVERN...
...SUPERMAN AND BLACK ADAM ARE HAVING A *SLIGHT* DISAGREEMENT...
...AND WE SUMMONED UP THE SPIRIT OF THE *VIKING PRINCE* TO INHABIT A GIANT *SWAMP THING* BODY...
...WHO IS CURRENTLY FIGHTING A HUGE *FROST KING* AVATAR THAT'S ABSORBED KRYPTONIAN ENERGY CRYSTALS.
I *THINK* THAT'S EVERYTHING.
I HAVE TO STOP MISSING MEETINGS.
THAT DOESN'T LOOK LIKE IT'S GOING WELL.
NEITHER DOES *THAT.*
IF YOU DON'T MIND, AQUAMAN...
...I'M GOING TO *BORROW* A FEW OF YOUR FIERY FRIENDS.

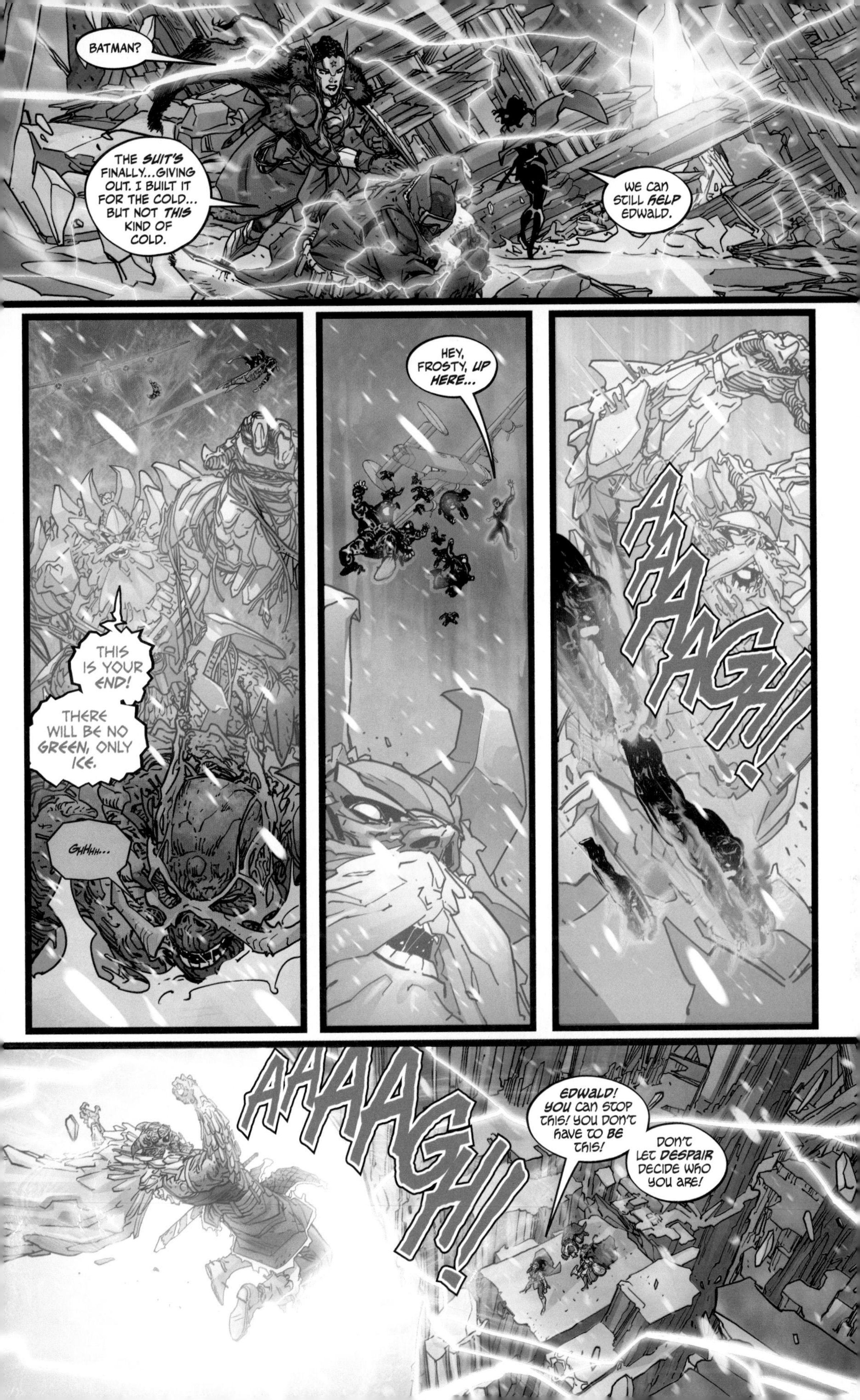
BATMAN?
THE SUIT'S FINALLY...GIVING OUT. I BUILT IT FOR THE COLD... BUT NOT THIS KIND OF COLD.
WE CAN STILL HELP EDWALD.
THIS IS YOUR END!
THERE WILL BE NO GREEN, ONLY ICE.
GHHHH...
HEY, FROSTY, UP HERE...
AAAAAGH!
AAAAAGH!
EDWALD! YOU CAN STOP THIS! YOU DON'T HAVE TO BE THIS!
DON'T LET DESPAIR DECIDE WHO YOU ARE!

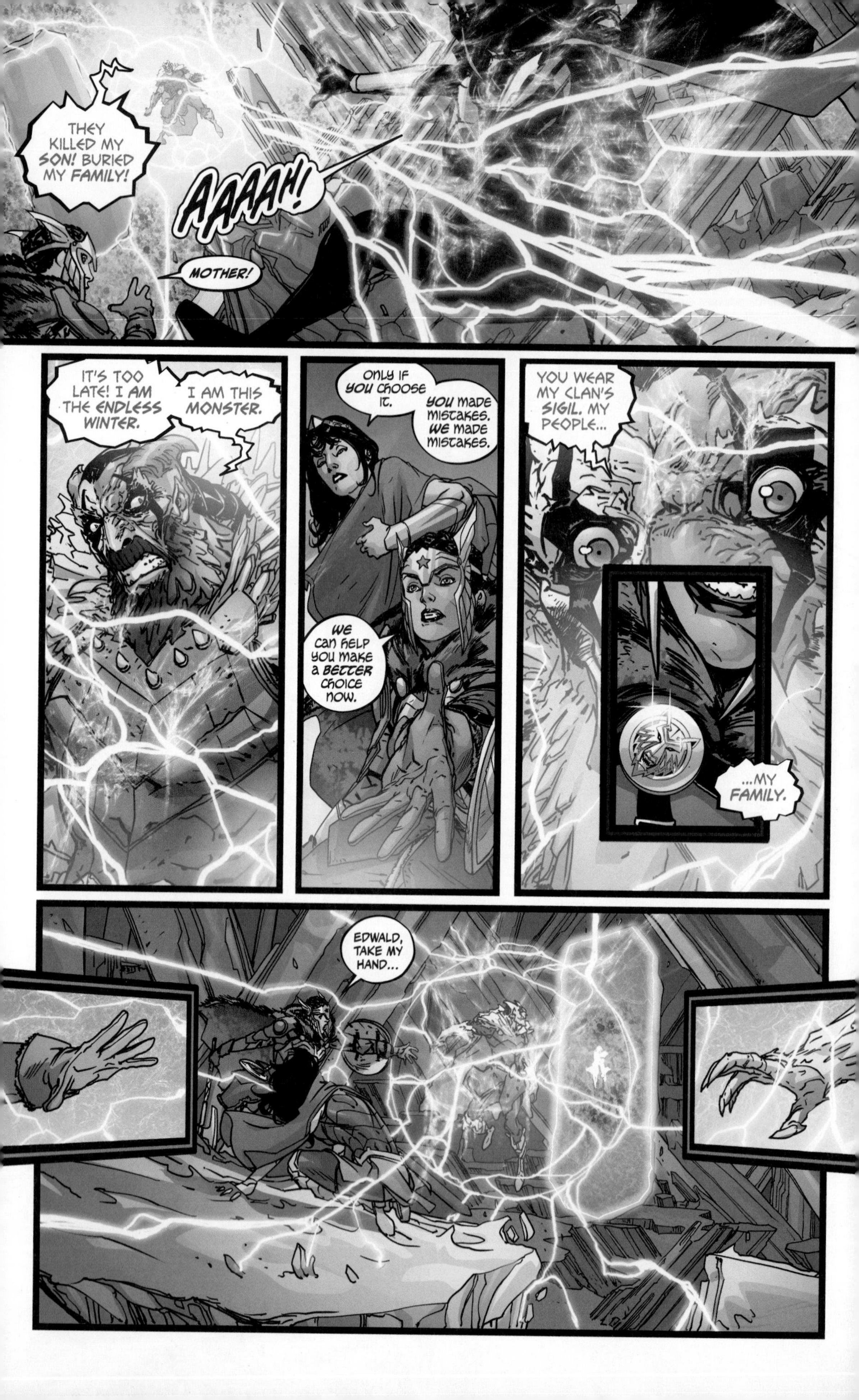
THEY KILLED MY SON! BURIED MY FAMILY!
AAAAH!
MOTHER!
IT'S TOO LATE! I AM THE ENDLESS WINTER.
I AM THIS MONSTER.
ONLY IF YOU CHOOSE IT.
YOU MADE MISTAKES. WE MADE MISTAKES.
WE CAN HELP YOU MAKE A BETTER CHOICE NOW.
YOU WEAR MY CLAN'S SIGIL. MY PEOPLE...
...MY FAMILY.
EDWALD, TAKE MY HAND...

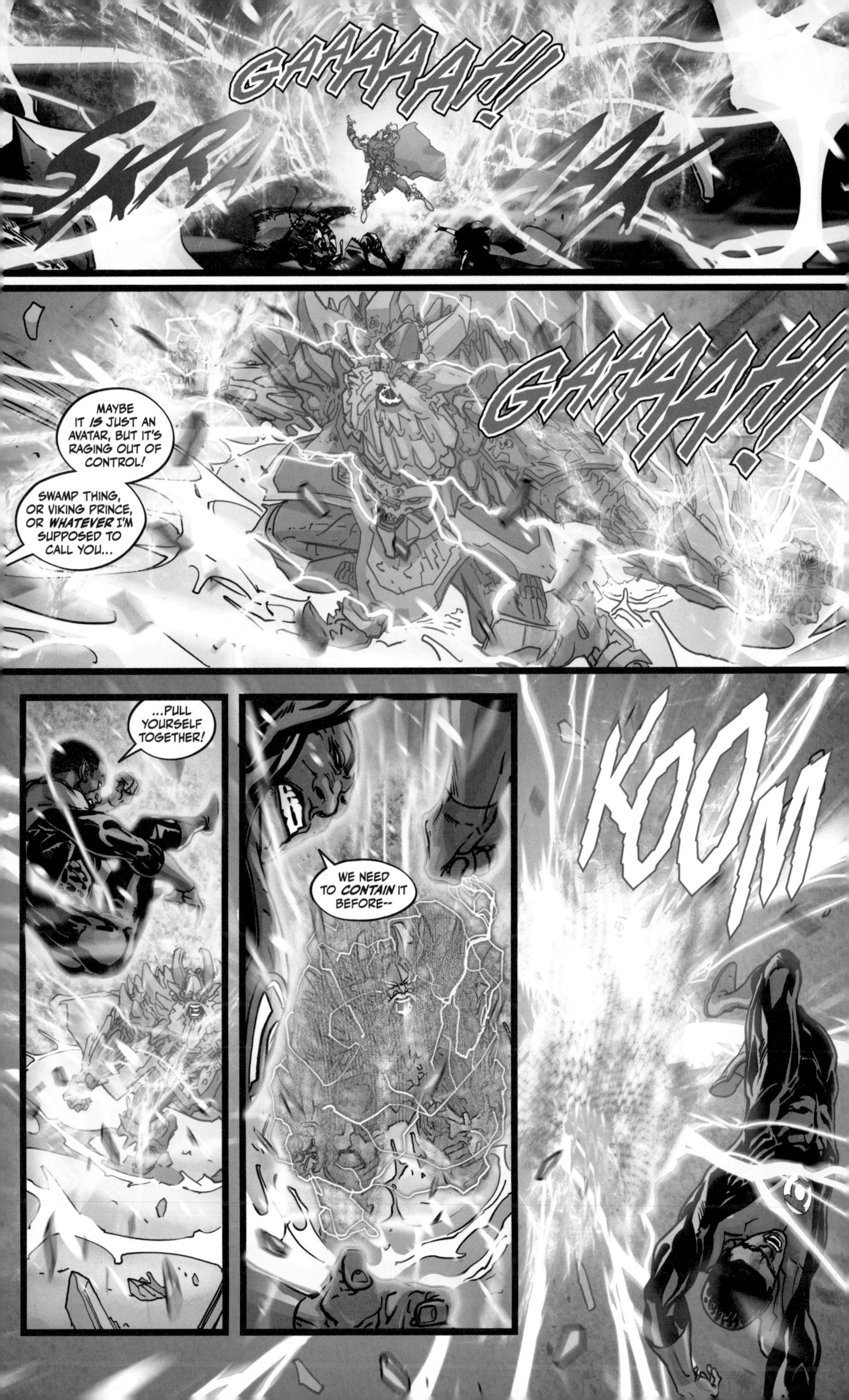

GAAAAAH!!
SHRAAAK
GAAAAAH!!
MAYBE IT *IS* JUST AN AVATAR, BUT IT'S RAGING OUT OF CONTROL!
SWAMP THING, OR VIKING PRINCE, OR *WHATEVER* I'M SUPPOSED TO CALL YOU...
...PULL YOURSELF TOGETHER!
WE NEED TO *CONTAIN* IT BEFORE--
KOOM

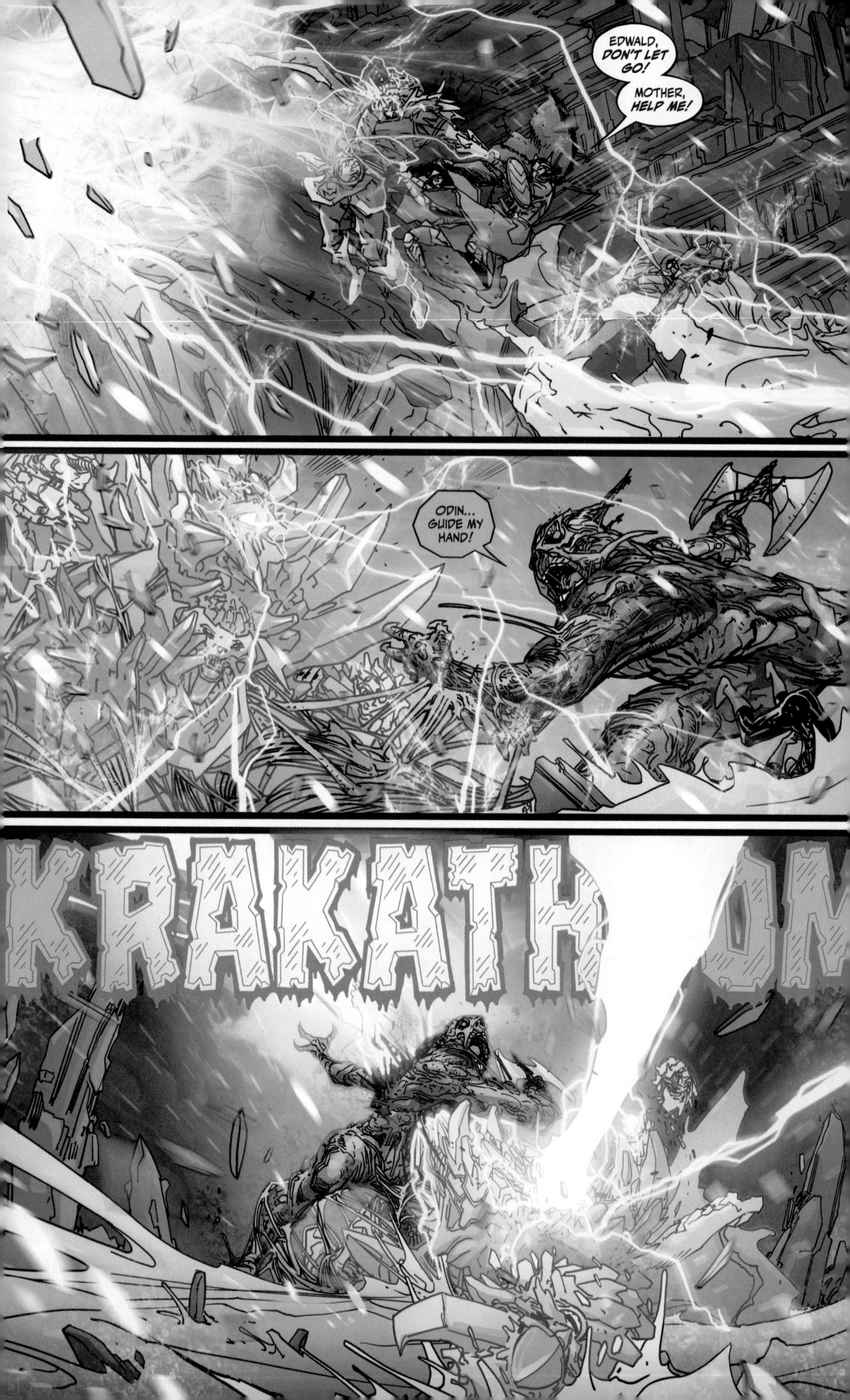

EDWALD, DON'T LET GO!
MOTHER, HELP ME!
ODIN... GUIDE MY HAND!
KRAKATH

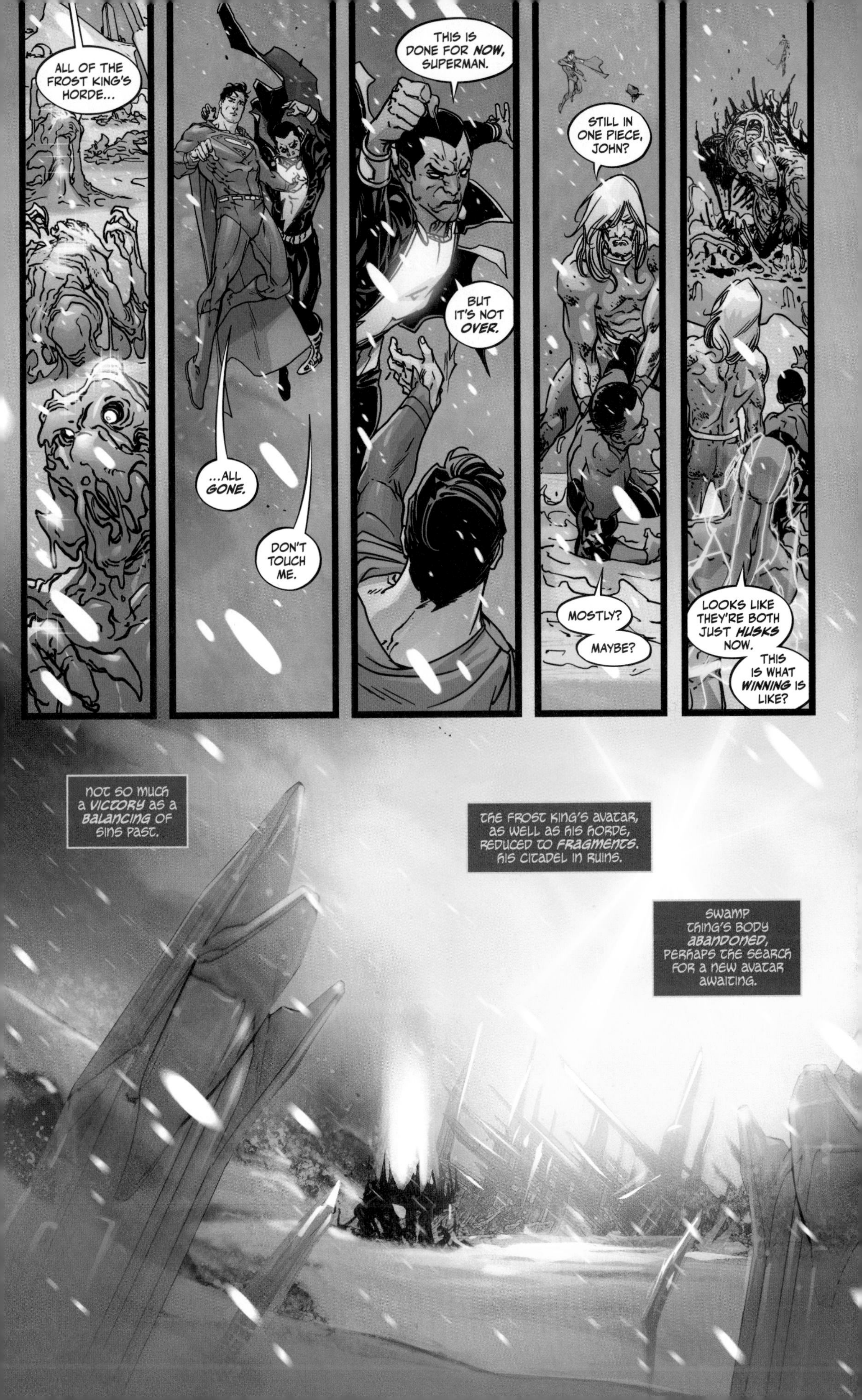
ALL OF THE FROST KING'S HORDE...
...ALL GONE.
DON'T TOUCH ME.
THIS IS DONE FOR NOW, SUPERMAN.
BUT IT'S NOT OVER.
STILL IN ONE PIECE, JOHN?
MOSTLY?
MAYBE?
LOOKS LIKE THEY'RE BOTH JUST HUSKS NOW.
THIS IS WHAT WINNING IS LIKE?
not so much a VICTORY as a BALANCING of sins past.
THE FROST KING'S avatar, as WELL as HIS HORDE, REDUCED TO FRAGMENTS. HIS CITADEL IN RUINS.
SWAMP THING'S BODY ABANDONED, PERHAPS THE SEARCH FOR a NEW avatar awaiting.

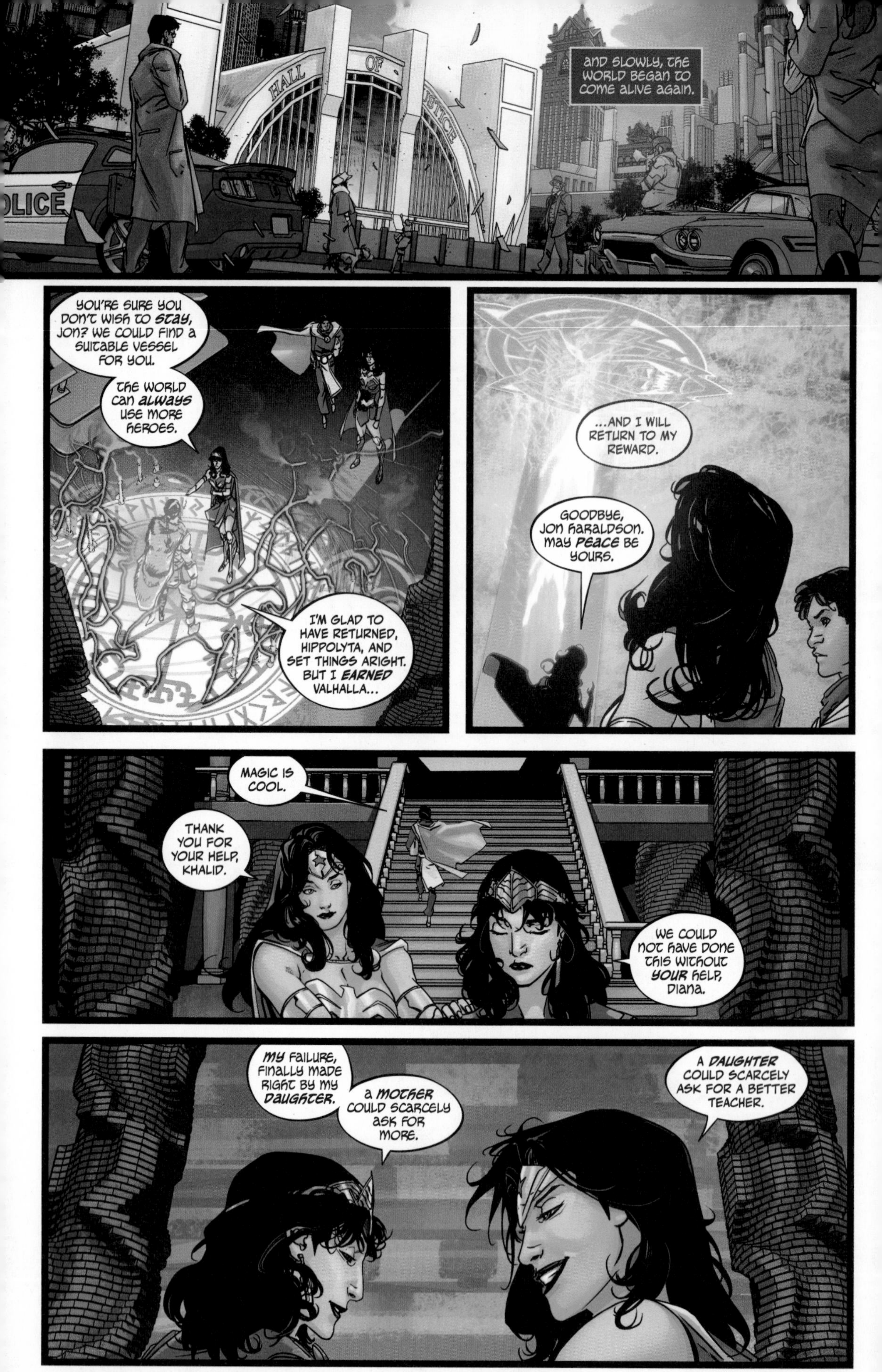

HALL OF JUSTICE
OLICE
AND SLOWLY, THE WORLD BEGAN TO COME ALIVE AGAIN.
YOU'RE SURE YOU DON'T WISH TO STAY, JON? WE COULD FIND A SUITABLE VESSEL FOR YOU.
THE WORLD CAN ALWAYS USE MORE HEROES.
I'M GLAD TO HAVE RETURNED, HIPPOLYTA, AND SET THINGS ARIGHT. BUT I EARNED VALHALLA...
...AND I WILL RETURN TO MY REWARD.
GOODBYE, JON HARALDSON. MAY PEACE BE YOURS.
MAGIC IS COOL.
THANK YOU FOR YOUR HELP, KHALID.
WE COULD NOT HAVE DONE THIS WITHOUT YOUR HELP, DIANA.
MY FAILURE, FINALLY MADE RIGHT BY MY DAUGHTER.
A MOTHER COULD SCARCELY ASK FOR MORE.
A DAUGHTER COULD SCARCELY ASK FOR A BETTER TEACHER.

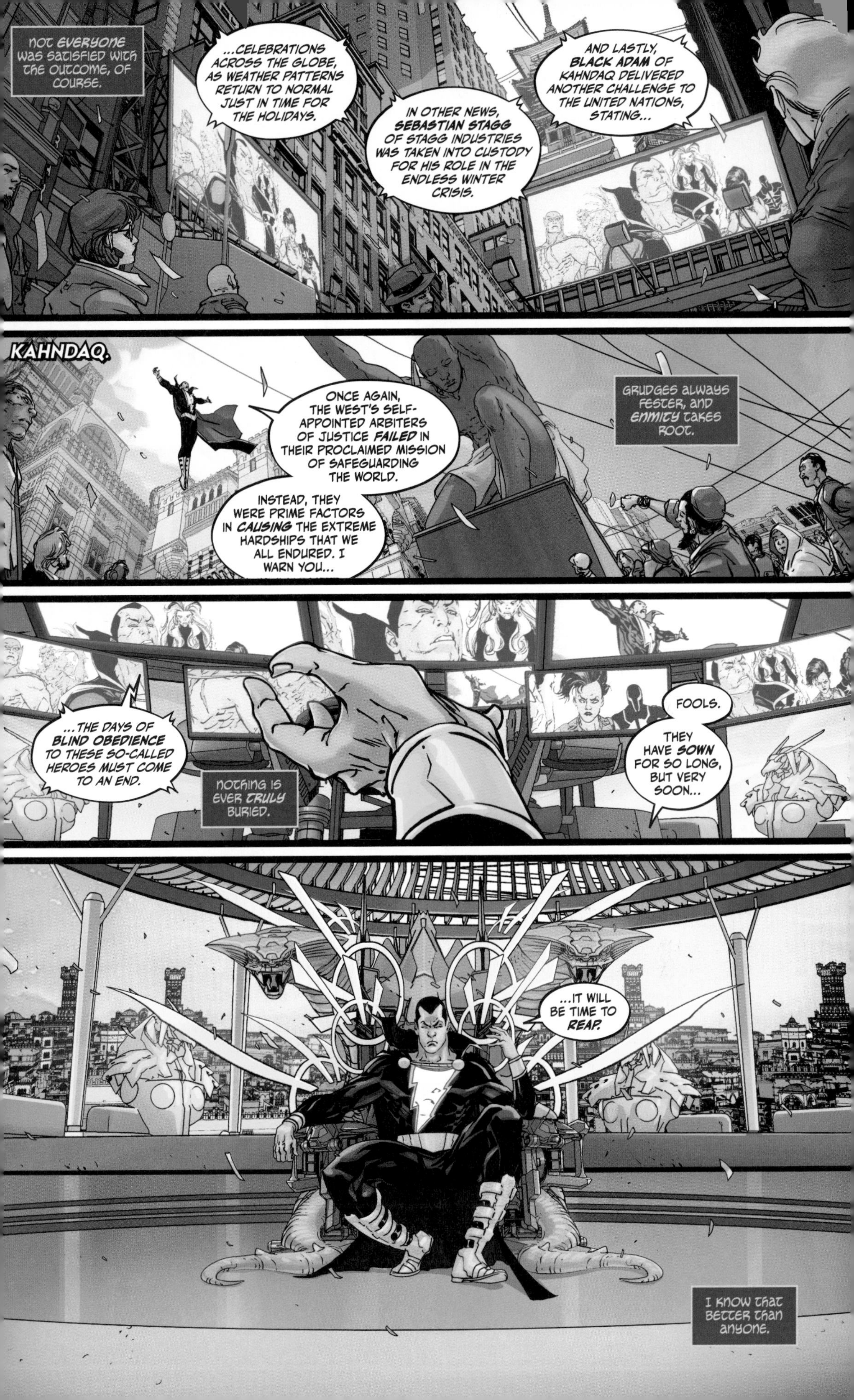
NOT EVERYONE WAS SATISFIED WITH THE OUTCOME, OF COURSE.
...CELEBRATIONS ACROSS THE GLOBE, AS WEATHER PATTERNS RETURN TO NORMAL JUST IN TIME FOR THE HOLIDAYS.
IN OTHER NEWS, SEBASTIAN STAGG OF STAGG INDUSTRIES WAS TAKEN INTO CUSTODY FOR HIS ROLE IN THE ENDLESS WINTER CRISIS.
AND LASTLY, BLACK ADAM OF KAHNDAQ DELIVERED ANOTHER CHALLENGE TO THE UNITED NATIONS, STATING...
KAHNDAQ.
ONCE AGAIN, THE WEST'S SELF-APPOINTED ARBITERS OF JUSTICE FAILED IN THEIR PROCLAIMED MISSION OF SAFEGUARDING THE WORLD.
INSTEAD, THEY WERE PRIME FACTORS IN CAUSING THE EXTREME HARDSHIPS THAT WE ALL ENDURED. I WARN YOU...
GRUDGES ALWAYS FESTER, AND ENMITY TAKES ROOT.
...THE DAYS OF BLIND OBEDIENCE TO THESE SO-CALLED HEROES MUST COME TO AN END.
NOTHING IS EVER TRULY BURIED.
FOOLS.
THEY HAVE SOWN FOR SO LONG, BUT VERY SOON...
...IT WILL BE TIME TO REAP.
I KNOW THAT BETTER THAN ANYONE.

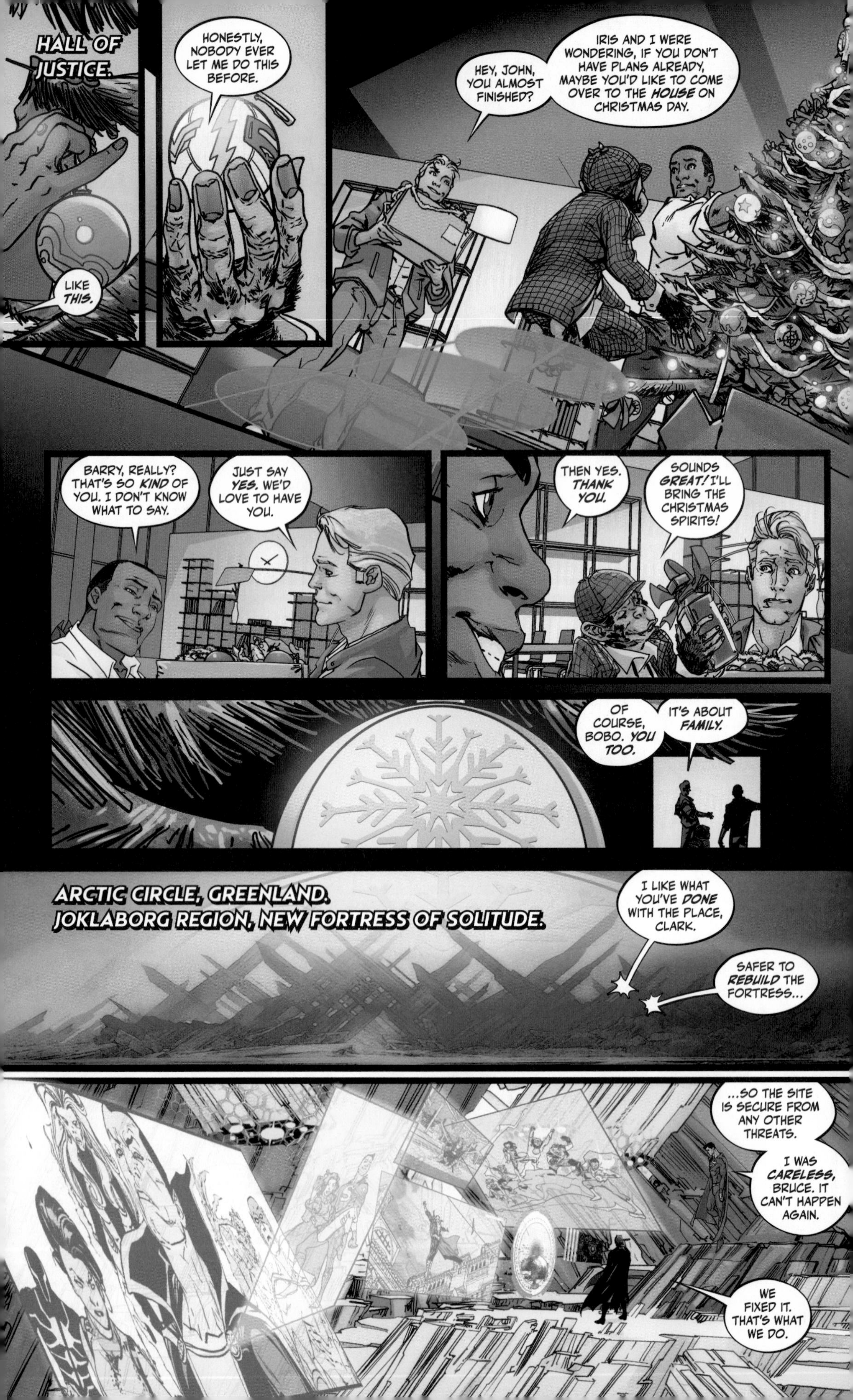
HALL OF JUSTICE.
LIKE THIS.
HONESTLY, NOBODY EVER LET ME DO THIS BEFORE.
HEY, JOHN, YOU ALMOST FINISHED?
IRIS AND I WERE WONDERING, IF YOU DON'T HAVE PLANS ALREADY, MAYBE YOU'D LIKE TO COME OVER TO THE HOUSE ON CHRISTMAS DAY.
BARRY, REALLY? THAT'S SO KIND OF YOU. I DON'T KNOW WHAT TO SAY.
JUST SAY YES. WE'D LOVE TO HAVE YOU.
THEN YES. THANK YOU.
SOUNDS GREAT! I'LL BRING THE CHRISTMAS SPIRITS!
OF COURSE, BOBO. YOU TOO.
IT'S ABOUT FAMILY.
ARCTIC CIRCLE, GREENLAND. JOKLABORG REGION, NEW FORTRESS OF SOLITUDE.
I LIKE WHAT YOU'VE DONE WITH THE PLACE, CLARK.
SAFER TO REBUILD THE FORTRESS...
...SO THE SITE IS SECURE FROM ANY OTHER THREATS.
I WAS CARELESS, BRUCE. IT CAN'T HAPPEN AGAIN.
WE FIXED IT. THAT'S WHAT WE DO.

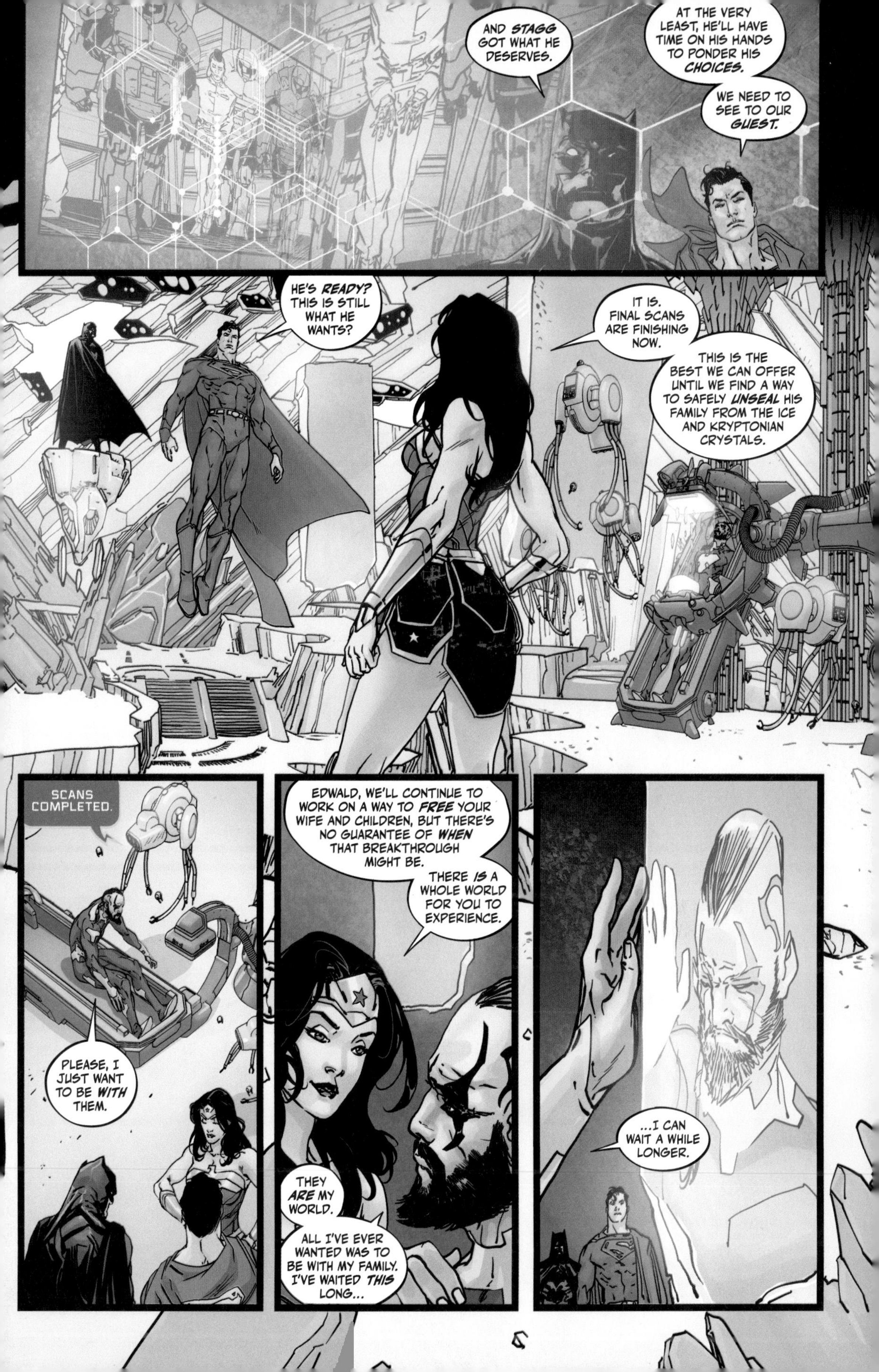
AND STAGG GOT WHAT HE DESERVES.
AT THE VERY LEAST, HE'LL HAVE TIME ON HIS HANDS TO PONDER HIS CHOICES.
WE NEED TO SEE TO OUR GUEST.
HE'S READY? THIS IS STILL WHAT HE WANTS?
IT IS. FINAL SCANS ARE FINISHING NOW.
THIS IS THE BEST WE CAN OFFER UNTIL WE FIND A WAY TO SAFELY UNSEAL HIS FAMILY FROM THE ICE AND KRYPTONIAN CRYSTALS.
SCANS COMPLETED.
PLEASE, I JUST WANT TO BE WITH THEM.
EDWALD, WE'LL CONTINUE TO WORK ON A WAY TO FREE YOUR WIFE AND CHILDREN, BUT THERE'S NO GUARANTEE OF WHEN THAT BREAKTHROUGH MIGHT BE.
THERE IS A WHOLE WORLD FOR YOU TO EXPERIENCE.
THEY ARE MY WORLD.
ALL I'VE EVER WANTED WAS TO BE WITH MY FAMILY. I'VE WAITED THIS LONG...
...I CAN WAIT A WHILE LONGER.

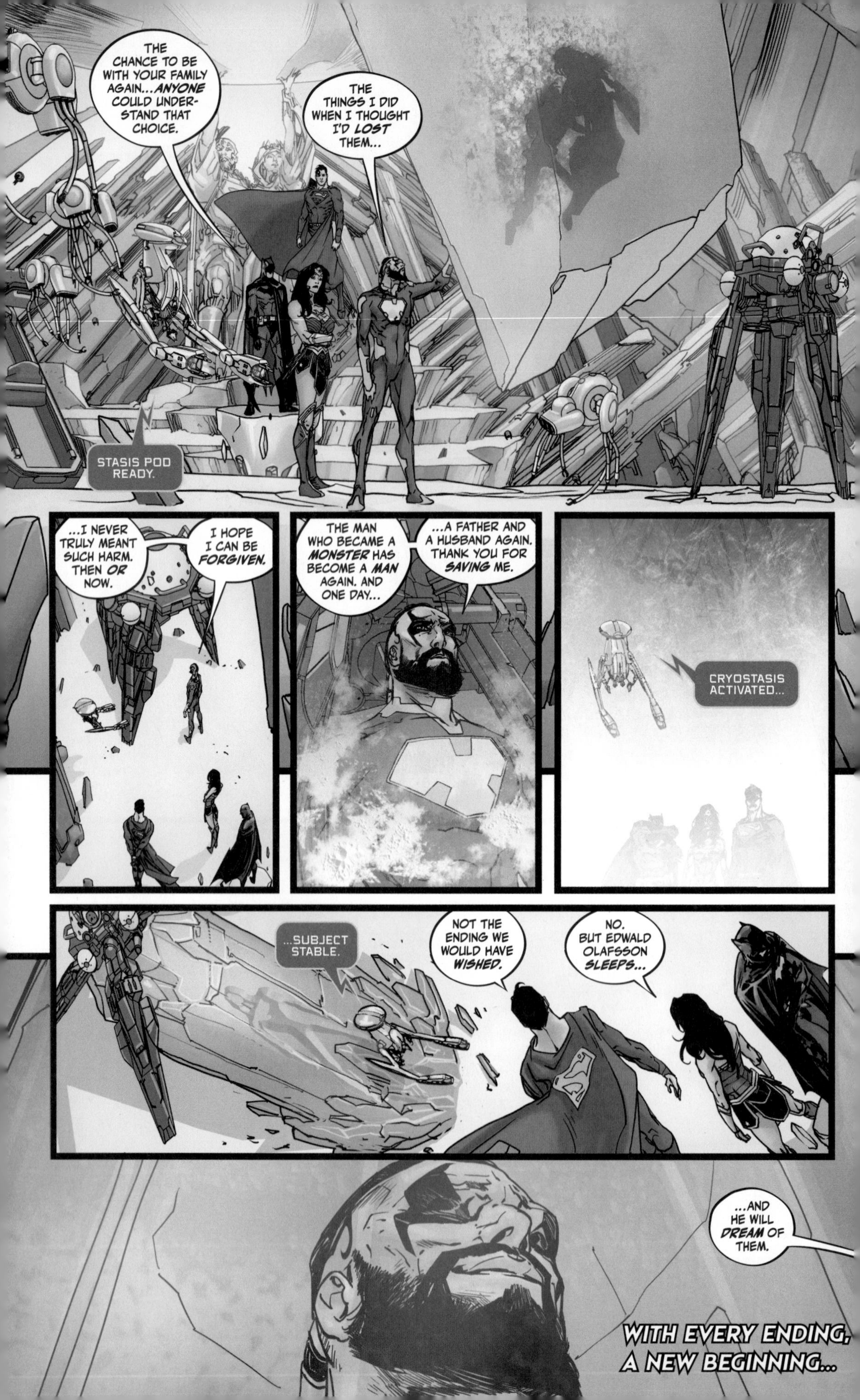
THE CHANCE TO BE WITH YOUR FAMILY AGAIN...ANYONE COULD UNDERSTAND THAT CHOICE.
THE THINGS I DID WHEN I THOUGHT I'D LOST THEM...
STASIS POD READY.
...I NEVER TRULY MEANT SUCH HARM. THEN OR NOW.
I HOPE I CAN BE FORGIVEN.
THE MAN WHO BECAME A MONSTER HAS BECOME A MAN AGAIN. AND ONE DAY...
...A FATHER AND A HUSBAND AGAIN. THANK YOU FOR SAVING ME.
CRYOSTASIS ACTIVATED...
...SUBJECT STABLE.
NOT THE ENDING WE WOULD HAVE WISHED.
NO. BUT EDWALD OLAFSSON SLEEPS...
...AND HE WILL DREAM OF THEM.
WITH EVERY ENDING, A NEW BEGINNING...

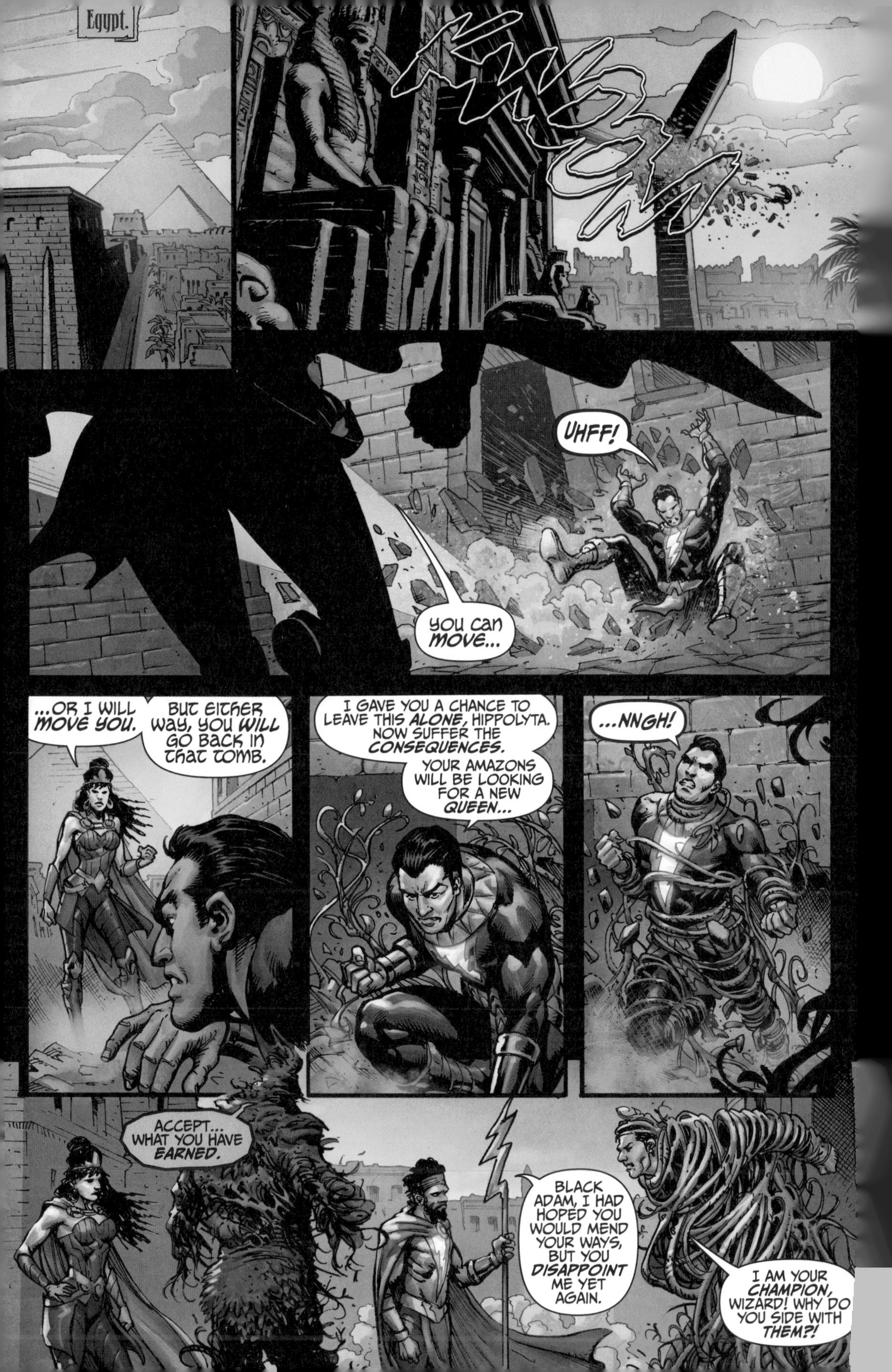
Egypt.
KRAKOOM
UHFF!
YOU CAN MOVE...
...OR I WILL MOVE YOU.
BUT EITHER WAY, YOU WILL GO BACK IN THAT TOMB.
I GAVE YOU A CHANCE TO LEAVE THIS ALONE, HIPPOLYTA. NOW SUFFER THE CONSEQUENCES.
YOUR AMAZONS WILL BE LOOKING FOR A NEW QUEEN...
...NNGH!
ACCEPT... WHAT YOU HAVE EARNED.
BLACK ADAM, I HAD HOPED YOU WOULD MEND YOUR WAYS, BUT YOU DISAPPOINT ME YET AGAIN.
I AM YOUR CHAMPION, WIZARD! WHY DO YOU SIDE WITH THEM?!

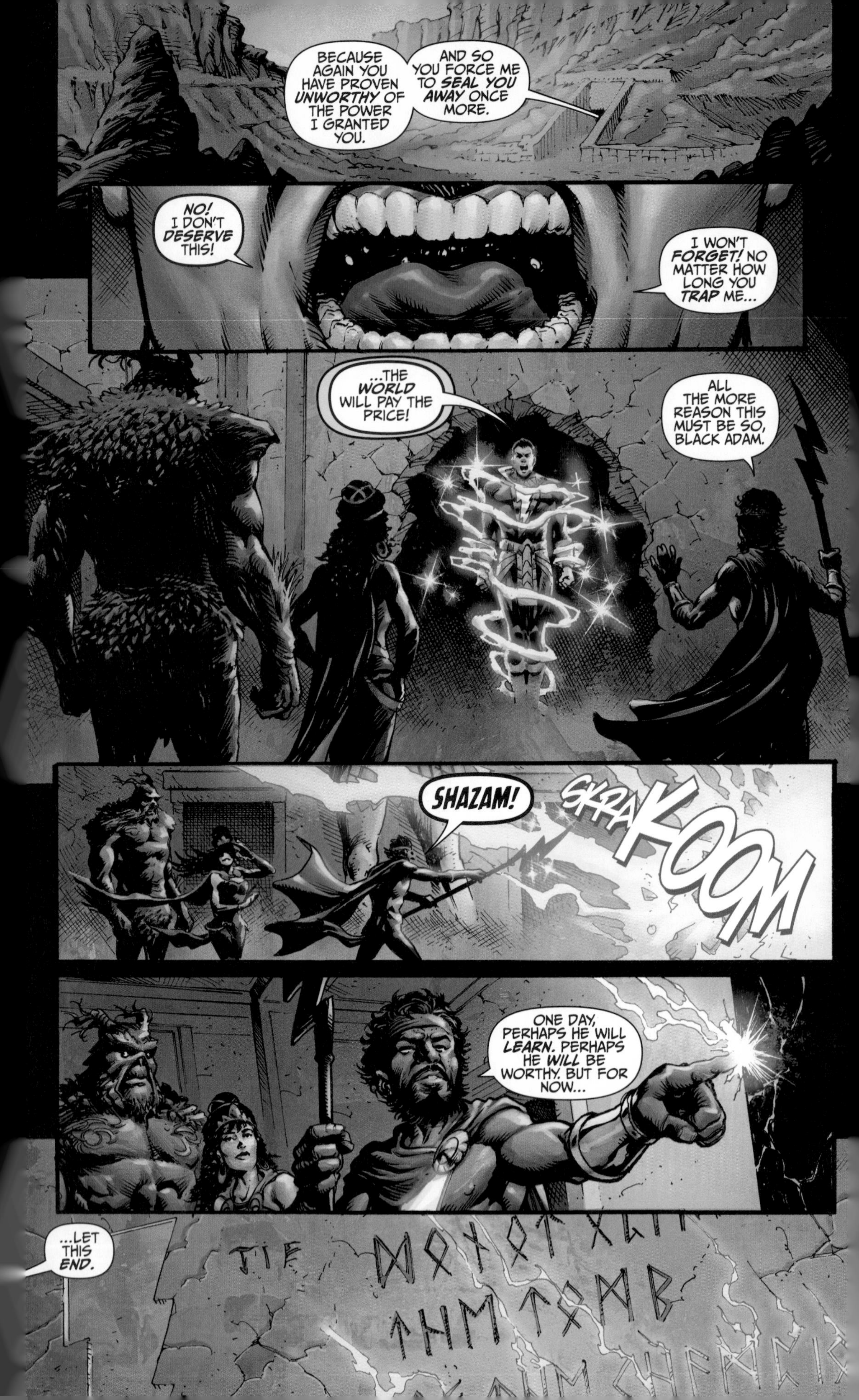

BECAUSE AGAIN YOU HAVE PROVEN UNWORTHY OF THE POWER I GRANTED YOU.
AND SO YOU FORCE ME TO SEAL YOU AWAY ONCE MORE.
NO! I DON'T DESERVE THIS!
I WON'T FORGET! NO MATTER HOW LONG YOU TRAP ME...
...THE WORLD WILL PAY THE PRICE!
ALL THE MORE REASON THIS MUST BE SO, BLACK ADAM.
SHAZAM!
SKRAKOOOM
ONE DAY, PERHAPS HE WILL LEARN. PERHAPS HE WILL BE WORTHY. BUT FOR NOW...
...LET THIS END.

ENDLESS WINTER

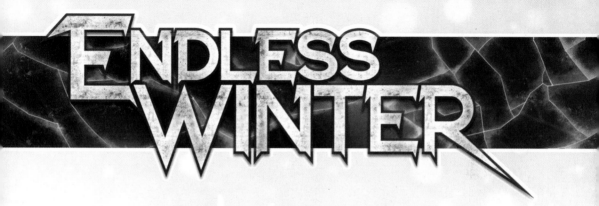

THE DESIGNS

Justice League Viking designs by Marco Santucci

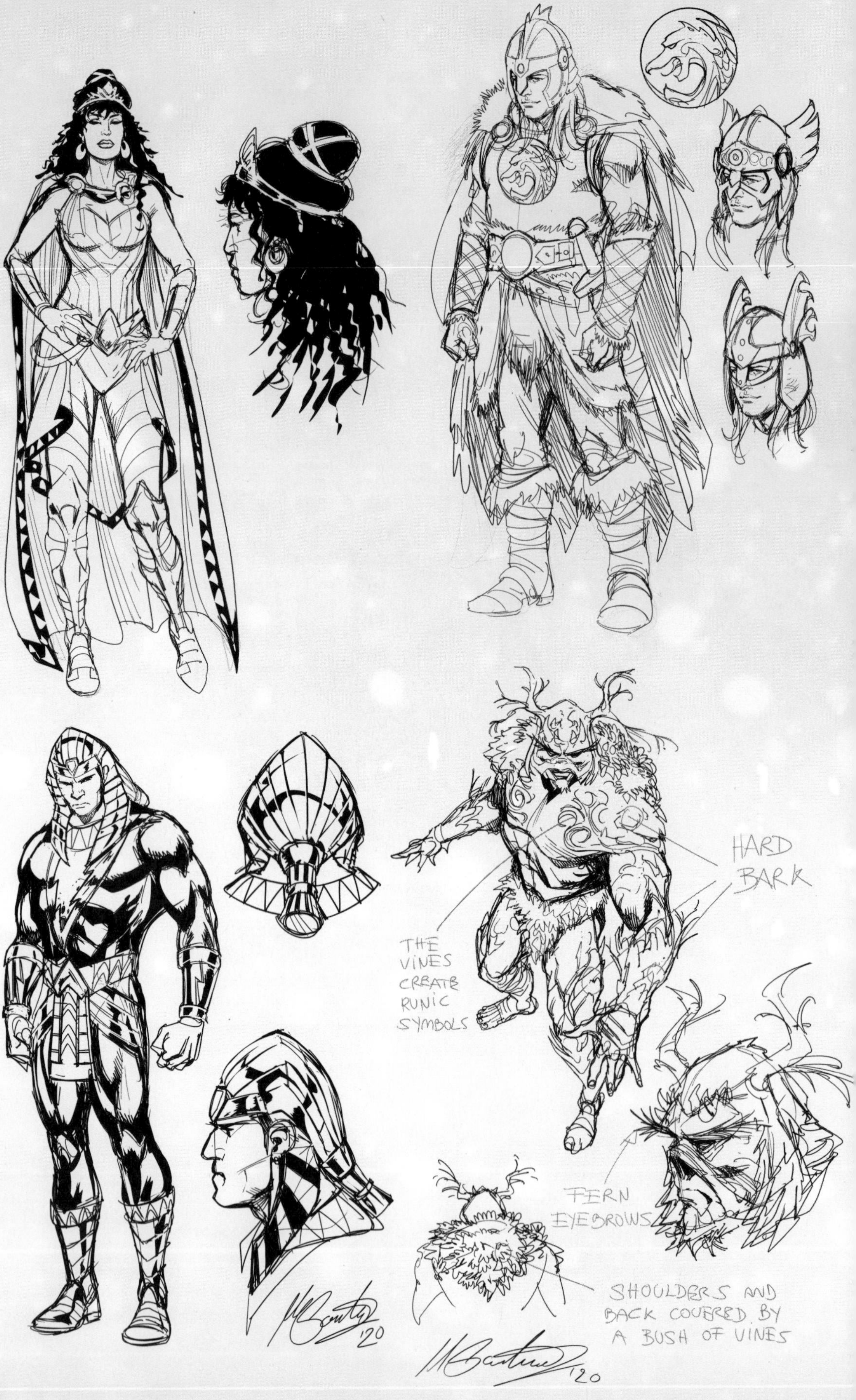
HARD BARK
THE VINES CREATE RUNIC SYMBOLS
FERN EYEBROWS
SHOULDERS AND BACK COVERED BY A BUSH OF VINES

Swamp Viking design by Doug Mahnke

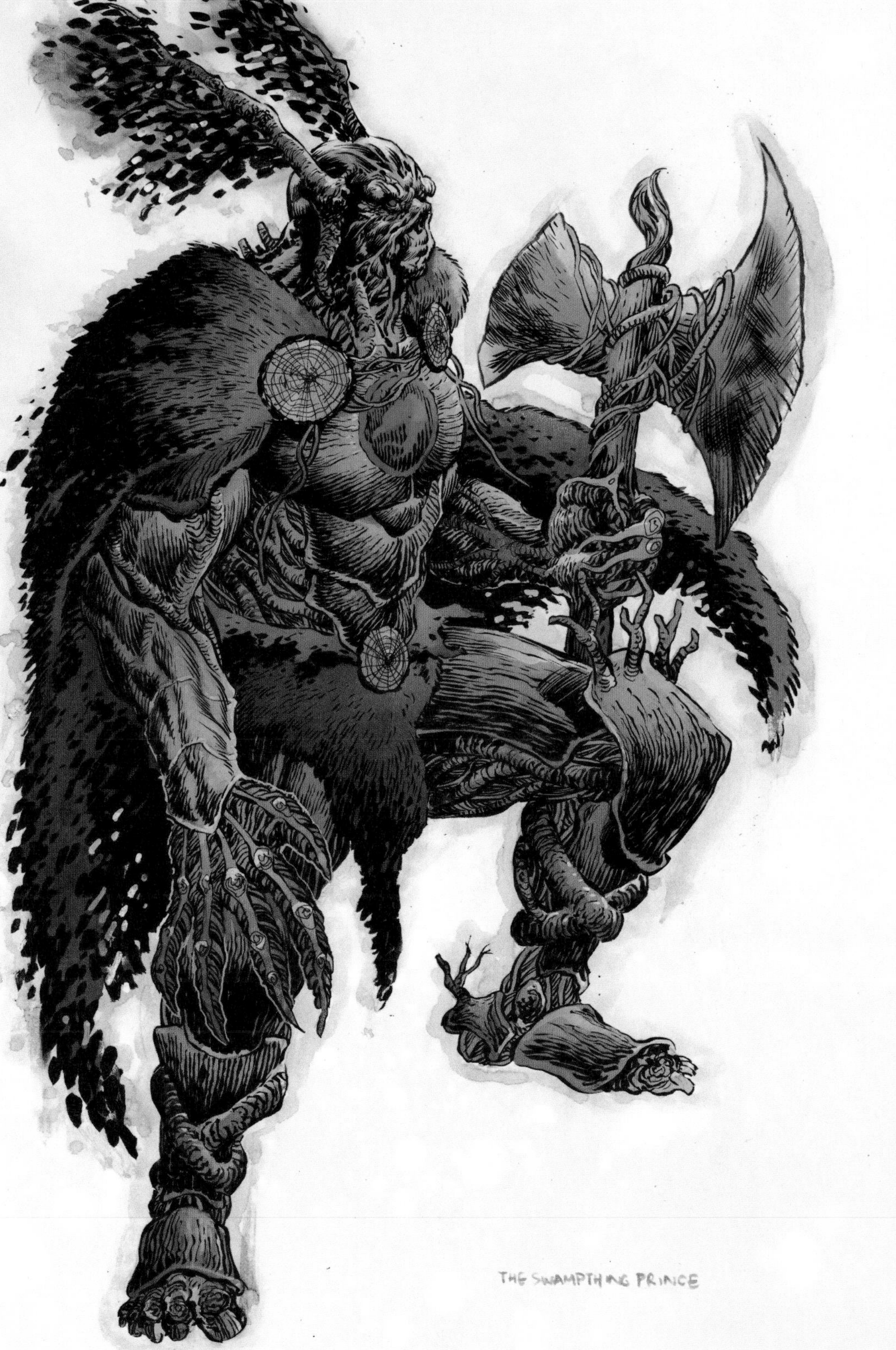
THE SWAMPTHING PRINCE

Past Frost King designs by Marco Santucci

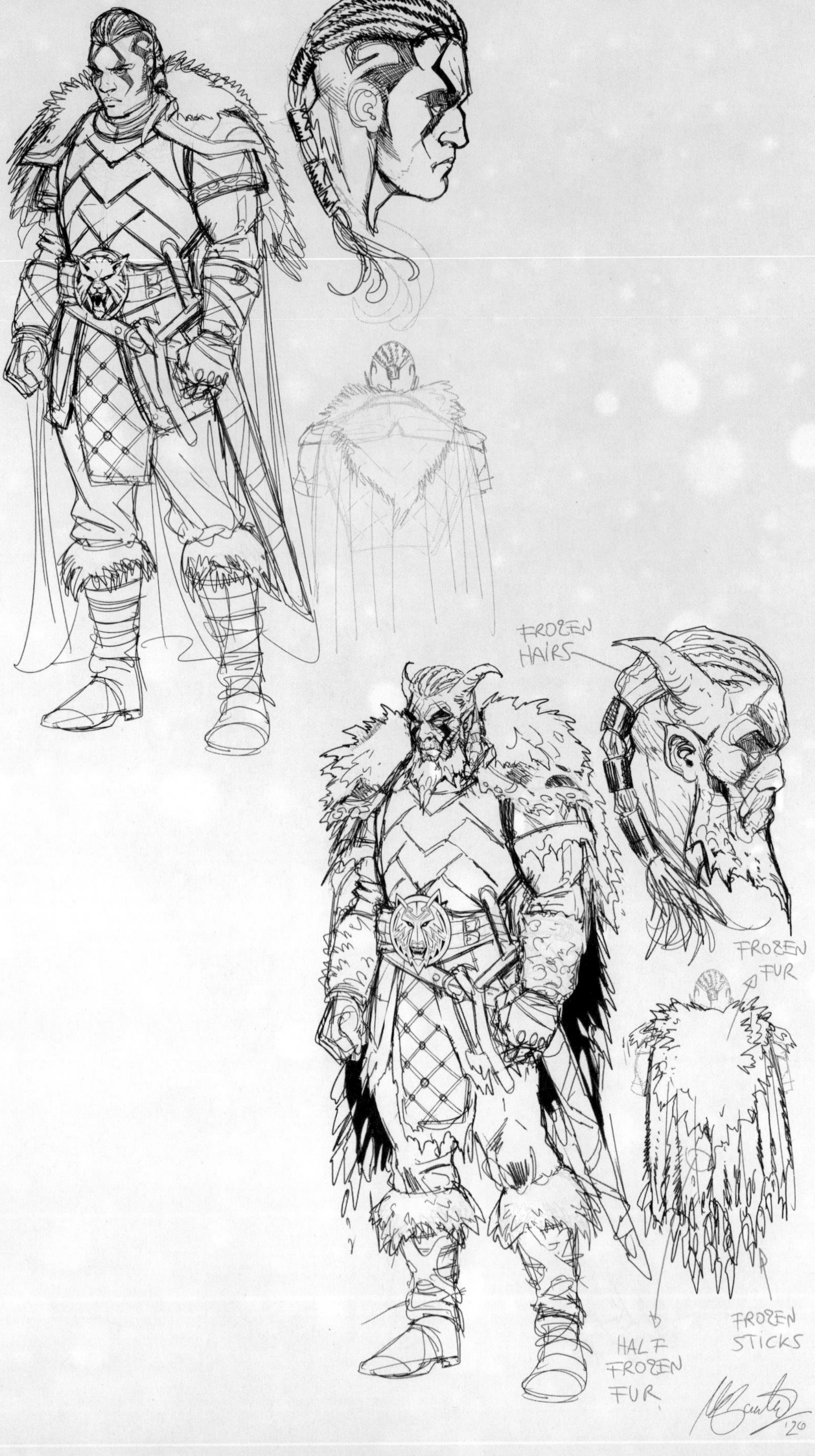
FROZEN HAIRS
FROZEN FUR
HALF FROZEN FUR
FROZEN STICKS
'20

Present Frost King designs by Howard Porter

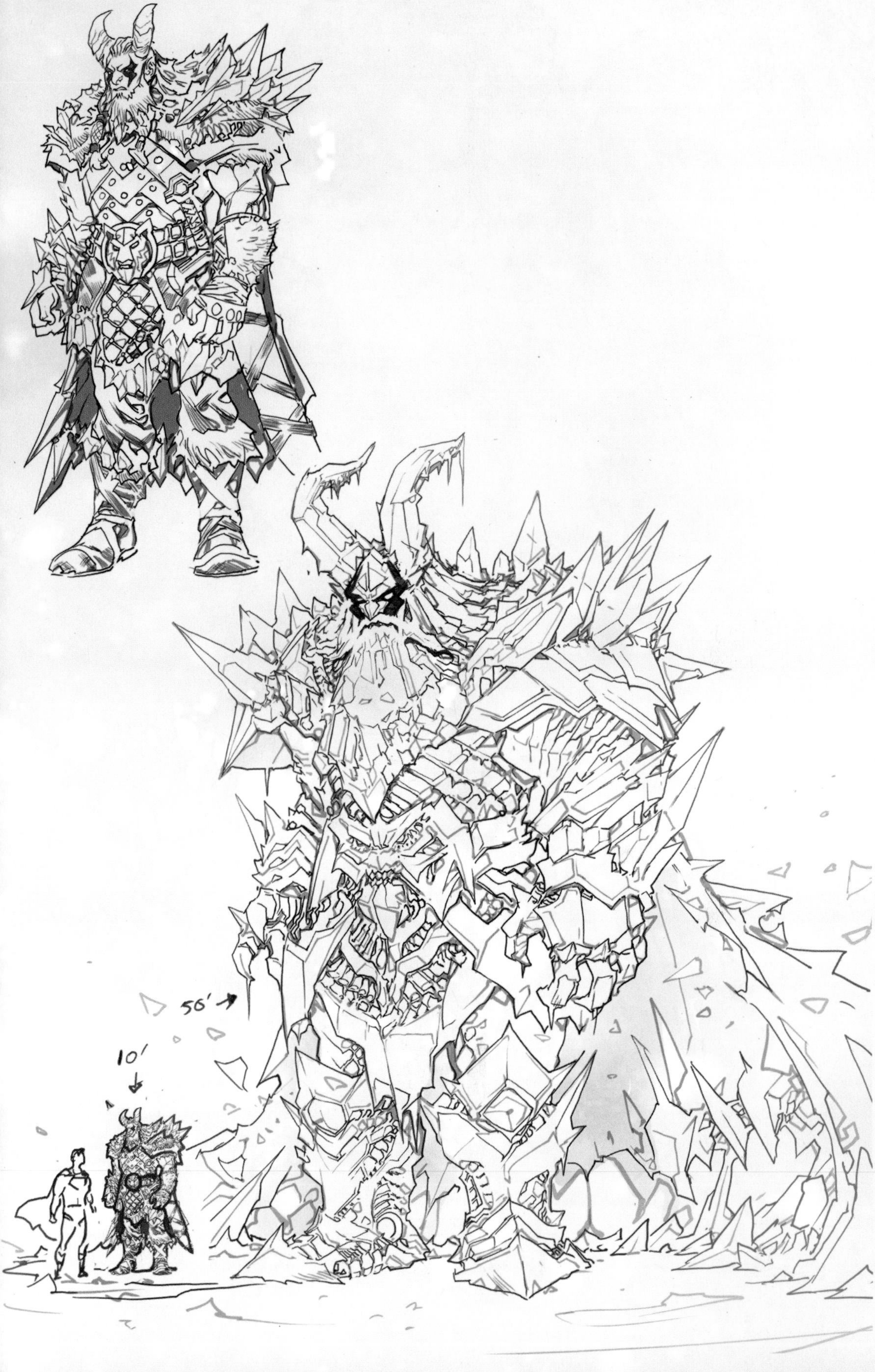

56'
10'

Winter Batman & Wonder Woman designs by Mikel Janín

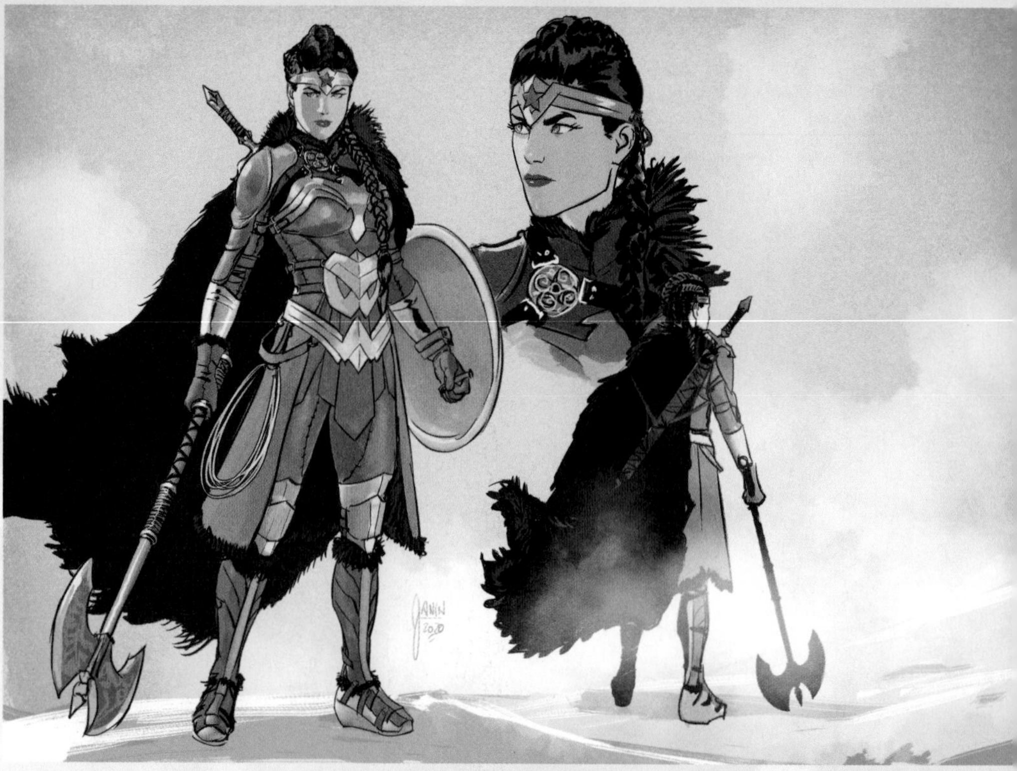

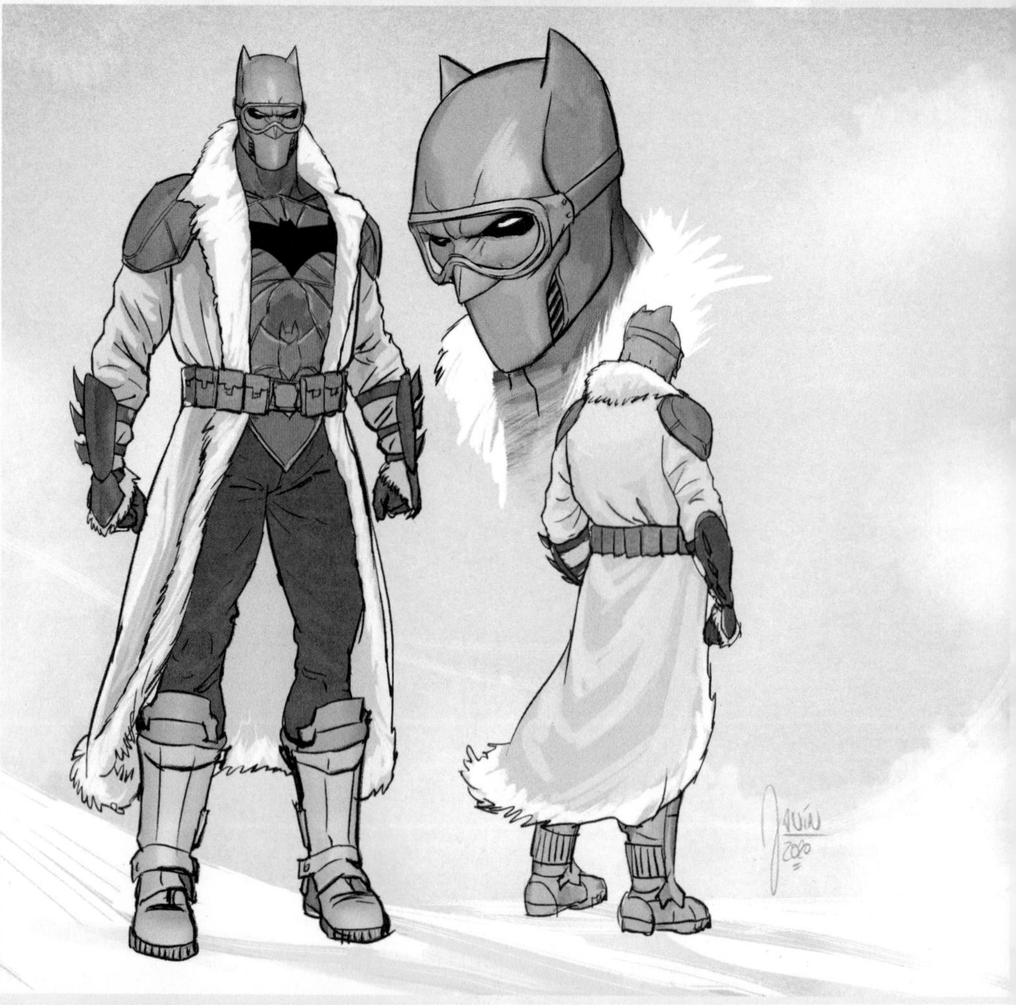